© Nina Subin

KENNETH C. DAVIS is the *New York Times* bestselling author and creator of the Don't Know Much About® series of books, which began in 1990 with the publication of *Don't Know Much About® History*. Davis, who has appeared on hundreds of television and radio shows, has also written the national bestseller *America's Hidden History* and *A Nation Rising*, as well as a series of Don't Know Much About® books for children published by HarperCollins. He has contributed to the *New York Times*, *Smithsonian*, and NPR's *All Things Considered*, among other media outlets, and posts regularly at his own website, dontknowmuch .com. Davis resides with his wife in New York City and is currently at work on *Don't Know Much About® the American Presidents*, for adults.

Merry Christmas

To: **Daddy**   From: **Susan & Angela**

DON'T KNOW
MUCH ABOUT®
HISTORY

ANNIVERSARY EDITION

EVERYTHING
YOU NEED TO KNOW
ABOUT AMERICAN HISTORY
BUT NEVER LEARNED

KENNETH C. DAVIS

HARPER

NEW YORK · LONDON · TORONTO · SYDNEY

HARPER

A hardcover edition of this book was published in 2011 by HarperCollins Publishers.

Don't Know Much About® is a registered trademark of Kenneth C. Davis.

DON'T KNOW MUCH ABOUT® HISTORY, ANNIVERSARY EDITION. Copyright © 2011 by Kenneth C. Davis. All rights reserved. Printed in the United States of America. No part of this book may be used or reproduced in any manner whatsoever without written permission except in the case of brief quotations embodied in critical articles and reviews. For information, address HarperCollins Publishers, 195 Broadway, New York, NY 10007.

HarperCollins books may be purchased for educational, business, or sales promotional use. For information, please e-mail the Special Markets Department at SPsales@harpercollins.com.

First Harper paperback published 2012.

Library of Congress Cataloging-in-Publication Data has been applied for.

ISBN 978-0-06-196054-3 (pbk.)

16   DIX/RRD   10

To my children, Jenny and Colin

CONTENTS

An Era of Broken Trust

When *Don't Know Much About® History* was first published in 1990, it was simply meant to serve as a fresh new take on American history. Busting myths, with a dose of humor and real stories about real people, the book was conceived as an antidote to the dull, dreary textbooks we suffered through in high school or college. A year later, in July 1991, the book began a run of thirty-five consecutive weeks on the *New York Times* best-seller list, proving perhaps that Americans don't hate history—they just hate the dull version they got back in high school.

In 2002, the book was revised and greatly expanded. Now, at the end of 2010, this newly updated edition picks up where that second revision left off—with the bizarre drama of the 2000 presidential election and the immediate aftermath of the September 11, 2001, terror attacks—and brings American history through a churning period of war, calamity, and dramatic upheaval that culminated with the historic 2008 election of Barack Obama and his first year and a half in office.

So what's different about this new revised, updated version? Like the original book and the previous revision, this new edition is organized along chronological lines, moving from America's "discovery" by Europeans to more recent events, including the first Gulf War, the end of the Cold War, the enormous repercussions of September 11, 2001, and the election of the nation's first African American president. But the book's final chapter, which was initially written for the 2002 edition, has been significantly expanded to include a review of the extraordinary events that have taken place since 2001, a brief period that has produced some of the most remarkable changes in America's history.

Much of this new history reflects on the response of the United States to the calamity of 9/11 and how that day has transformed American life and society, from the way we get through airports to fundamental American attitudes about the right to privacy versus a sense of greater security. The new material begins with an overview of 9/11 and what has been learned about that "day of infamy" after nearly a decade. This revision goes on to recap the response of the Bush administration to 9/11, with particular emphasis on the invasions of Afghanistan and Iraq.

In addition, this added material includes discussions of the following events and controversies:

- The emergence of same-sex marriage as a highly divisive, emotional national issue
- The failure of government at every level in responding to Hurricane Katrina, America's worst natural disaster
- The meltdown of the global economy and the "Great Recession" and the historic involvement of the government in rescuing companies, such as General Motors and Citibank, deemed "too big to fail"
- The surprisingly meteoric rise and election of Barack Obama

Besides adding material to cover events that have occurred since this book originally appeared in 1990, I have amplified some of the existing material. This sort of "historical revision" is a necessity because we learn things about the past all the time, often based on new scholarship, scientific advances, and ongoing discoveries that reshape our view of history. For instance, new light has been cast on familiar stories, such as the continuing archaeological dig that is revealing new information about the original fort at Jamestown, Virginia—first discovered in 1996—or the DNA evidence that strongly suggests that Thomas Jefferson had fathered the children of slave Sally Hemings—a nineteenth-century political rumor now treated as near certainty, even at Monticello, Jefferson's home in Virginia.

This revision also reflects the fact that court decisions can greatly alter American life. A bevy of judicial decisions around the nation during the past eight years has forced a major debate on same-sex marriage as well as the Pentagon's "don't ask, don't tell" policy toward homosexuals serving in the military. And in June 2008, the majority on an increasingly conservative Supreme Court struck down a Washington, D.C., ban on handguns in a historic reinterpretation of the Second Amendment and "the right to bear arms" that may impact gun-control laws in most American states.

Finally, history needs to be revised because even "old dog" historians learn new tricks. For instance, in researching and writing two of my recent books, *America's Hidden History* and *A Nation Rising*, I uncovered some surprising "hidden history" in such stories as the fate of the true first Pilgrims—French Huguenots who settled in Florida fifty years before the *Mayflower* sailed and were wiped out by the Spanish in 1565. Or the story of Philadelphia's anti-Catholic, anti-immigrant "Bible Riots" of 1844, another episode missing from most American schoolbooks. This revision now reflects these significant but overlooked events.

When I last revised this book in 2002, I concluded by writing:

> And yet, how much had really changed? Congress still fights over obscure bills. Children still go missing. The stock market's gyrations transfix the nation. But something fundamental seems to have changed. Historians may look back at America in late 2002 as the Era of Broken Trust. In a very short space of time, Americans had lost faith in government agencies, including the FBI and the CIA. The church, in particular the Roman Catholic Church, was devastated by a string of revelations about predatory priests. Corporate bankruptcies and revelations of corruption involving Enron, Tyco, Global Crossing, and WorldCom, among others, shattered America's faith in the financial security of the nation.

As we know, that paragraph has become, if anything, even more salient in 2010. The "Era of Broken Trust" I described at the beginning of the twenty-first century has only worsened as the events of the past decade have further eroded many Americans' belief and confidence in the nation's most basic institutions. The tremendous upheaval in the global economy shook our trust in the financial institutions and the government agencies—many born out of the Great Depression— that were supposed to regulate and police them. The deceptions and mistaken assumptions that led to the invasion and occupation of Iraq continued to weigh the nation down in a costly war. The response to Hurricane Katrina at every level of government was a national disgrace that called into question the ability and commitment of people entrusted with the nation's basic safety. And the woes of the Gulf Coast following Katrina were compounded in 2010 by one of the worst environmental disasters in American history: an oil well nearly a mile beneath the surface of the Gulf of Mexico relentlessly spewed crude oil, befouling beaches, destroying sensitive ecosystems, killing wildlife, and ruining businesses in a catastrophe whose ultimate costs and long-term impact may never be fully known.

Perhaps the best summary of what this period in our history may mean is captured in something President George Bush said on *Good Morning America* on September 1, 2005, during the Katrina catastrophe: "I don't think anyone anticipated the breach of the levees."

Of course, that was not true, as ample evidence has shown. There had been plenty of cautions about the levees from the public officials, engineers, and academics who had warned of the dangers confronting New Orleans as its protective barrier islands were eliminated by development and the levees ringing a city below sea level were deemed insufficient in the face of a major storm. Similarly, many danger signs had been posted about a raft of other protective "levees" that have also been breached—the risks to the financial system, or the concerns about offshore drilling, and the dire warnings about going into Iraq without justification and without proper troop levels.

But just as there is a danger in complacent acceptance of what "they" tell us—whether "they" are corporations, governments, doctors, or churches—there is also a pernicious side effect to the mistrust that has been sown by this record of "official" deceptions. While many people have become disgusted with the "system" or have grown cynical, many others have become all the more susceptible to "alternative" truths.

Americans have always been fascinated and even drawn to "conspiracy theories." In the early nineteenth century, a widely accepted belief among mainstream American Protestants held that Roman Catholics—especially Irish Catholics—were attempting to take over the American government and install the pope in a new Vatican to be built in Cincinnati. At the time, that belief drove anti-immigrant and anti-Catholic rage to violent heights. When Abraham Lincoln was assassinated, rumors of a wide-ranging conspiracy began almost immediately—and they have never fully gone away.

This tendency toward conjuring up a malevolent, elaborate, and often wildly complex web of conspiracy in almost every decision or event in our times has multiplied *virally* in the Internet age. The best example—addressed in the new material added to the final chapter of this book—is the belief that the terrorist strikes of 9/11 and the death and destruction at the twin towers and Pentagon were part of an elaborate conspiracy orchestrated within the American government. While I address that question in the text, I would like to say unequivocally that I consider it a dangerous lie. In rereading the reams of testimony about the terror strikes and in the excellent journalism of such writers as Lawrence Wright in *The Looming Tower* or James Bamford in *Body of Secrets*, even the most skeptical readers will find the truth—if that is what they seek.

Both of these writers, along with many of the other journalists who have done such sterling work during the past decade in relation to 9/11, Al Qaeda, the wars in Afghanistan and Iraq,* or the levees of New Orleans, have asked important questions and relentlessly pursued the answers through the search for evidence and authentication. If there is any overarching lesson to be learned from history—especially from this recent history—is that we all have to ask a lot more questions, especially when it comes to making sure the levees will hold.

Kenneth C. Davis
OCTOBER 2010

*As this book was going to press, President Barack Obama announced late on the night of May 1, 2011, that Osama bin Laden, the mastermind of the Al Qaeda attacks of 9/11, was killed by a team of U.S. Navy SEALs in Pakistan. Declaring, "Justice has been done," President Obama also said, "The death of bin Laden marks the most significant achievement to date in our nation's effort to defeat Al Qaeda." The history of Al Qaeda, those attacks, and the American response are recounted in the final chapter of this revised edition.

INTRODUCTION

Back in the early 1960s, when I was growing up, there was a silly pop song called "What Did Washington Say When He Crossed the Delaware?" Sung to the tarantella beat of an Italian wedding song, the answer went something like "Martha, Martha, there'll be no pizza tonight."

Of course, these lyrics were absurd; everybody knew Washington ate only cherry pie.

On that December night in 1776, George might have told himself that this raid on an enemy camp in Trenton, New Jersey, better work. Or else he might be ordering a last meal before the British strung him up. But as the general rallied his ragged, barefoot troops across the icy Delaware, one of his actual comments was far more amusing than those fanciful lyrics. Stepping into his boat, Washington—the plainspoken frontiersman, not the marbleized demigod—nudged 280-pound General Henry "Ox" Knox with the tip of his boot and said, "Shift that fat ass, Harry. But slowly, or you'll swamp the damned boat."

According to *Patriots*, A. J. Langguth's fascinating history of the Revolution, that is how Knox himself reported the story after the war. I certainly never heard that version of the crossing when I was in school. And that's too bad, because it reveals more of Washington's true, earthy nature than all the hokey tales about cherry trees and nonexistent prayer vigils in Valley Forge. And that's the point of this book: much of what we remember about our history is either mistaken or fabricated. That is, if we remember it at all.

For all too many Americans who dozed through American History 101, the Mayflower Compact might as well be a small car. Reconstruction has something to do with silicone implants. And the Louisiana Purchase means eating out at a Cajun restaurant. When the first edition of this book appeared more than twenty years ago, several writers had just enjoyed remarkable success by lambasting Americans' failure to know our past. Americans were shown to be know-nothings in the books *Cultural Literacy* and *The Closing of the American Mind*.

Well, we're probably not as dumb as those books would have us. But the sad truth is clear: we are no nation of scholars when it comes to history. Just as I was writing the first edition of this book, a highly publicized example of our "historical illiteracy" appeared. It was a 1987 survey of high school juniors that exposed astonishing gaps in what these seventeen-year-olds knew about American history and literature. A third of the students couldn't identify the Declaration of Independence as the document that marked the formal separation of the thirteen colonies from Great Britain. Only 32 percent of the students surveyed could place the American Civil War in the correct half century.

Sadly, I must say that things have not improved much—if at all—in the past twenty years. Every few years, it seems, another survey comes along that blasts the historical ineptness of American students. Part of the problem may be that those juniors who didn't do so well in 1987 may be teachers now!

But why dump on the kids? While there are constant warnings issued about the yawning gaps in the education of American students, another question looms larger. Would most of their parents or older brothers and sisters do any better? Most thirty-seven-year-olds or forty-seven-year-olds might not pass a similar pop quiz. Comedian Jay Leno routinely proves this on *Tonight* with his "Jaywalk" segments in which adults demonstrate that they are incapable of answering the simplest questions about history. When Bill Clinton went to Normandy as president for a D-Day observance, even he had to be tutored on what had happened there. So don't ask for whom the gap yawns. The gap yawns for thee.

The reason for these historical shortcomings is simple. For most of us, history was boring, and a great many Americans were taught by a football coach who got dropped into the history class to give him something to fill out his day. Many of us also learned about the past from textbooks that served up the past as if it were a Hollywood costume drama. In schoolbooks of an earlier era, the warts on our Founding Fathers' noses were neatly retouched. Slavery also got the glossy makeover—it was merely the misguided practice of the rebellious folks down South until the "progressives" of the North showed them the light. American Indians were portrayed in textbooks in the same way they were in Hollywood Westerns. Women were pretty much left out of the picture entirely with the exception of a mythical Betsy Ross or a lovely Dolley Madison rescuing the White House china.

Truth isn't so cosmetically perfect. Our historical sense is frequently skewed, skewered, or plain screwed up by myths and misconceptions. Schools that packaged a tidy set of simplistic historical images are largely responsible for fostering these American myths. There has always been a tendency to hide the less savory moments from our past, the way a mad aunt's photo gets pulled from the family album.

On top of that, the gaping chasms in our historical literacy have been reinforced by images from pop culture. Unfortunately, highly fictionalized films, such as Oliver Stone's *JFK* or Disney's *Pocahontas*, or the 2004 release *Pearl Harbor* make a much greater impression on millions of people than a carefully researched, historically accurate, but numbingly dull documentary. Occasionally there are films like *Glory* or *Saving Private Ryan* or *Charlie Wilson's War* that can stimulate interest in history they way few textbooks or teachers can. Documentary films such as Errol Morris's Oscar-winning *The Fog of War: Eleven Lessons from the Life of Robert S. McNamara* can illuminate controversies in unique ways. But for the most part, mainstream movies and network television have magnified the myths and makeovers. It is important to understand that looking past these myths is revealing. The real picture is far more interesting than the historical tummy tuck. And truth is always more interesting than propaganda.

Somebody will surely read this and say, "So what?"

Why bother with history anyway? What difference does it make if our kids know what the Declaration says—or doesn't say? Why does it matter if most people think Watergate is just old news?

The answer is simple because history is really about the consequences of our actions—large and small. And that has never been more apparent than in the aftermath of the terror attacks of September 11, 2001. If the terror attacks haven't changed anything else, they certainly changed many Americans' appreciation of the past and what it has to do with the present.

History explains how we got where we are. We can use it to connect the dots from past to present. Take the Versailles Treaty. (Please!) I know. The very words sound BORING. I can see your eyes grow heavy as you read the words "Versailles" and "Treaty." But consider what that treaty, which supposedly settled World War I back in 1919, actually did. In one very clear and obvious sense, it laid the groundwork for another world war only twenty years later.

But look past that. You can draw a straight line from the Treaty of Versailles to the modern Middle East, Iran and Iraq, the Balkan countries of Europe, and even Vietnam. All these hot spots of the past few decades were created in the aftermath of Versailles, when the European powers carved up the world into colonies that they thought they could rule as they pleased.

When the CIA overthrew the government of Iran in 1953 during the Eisenhower administration, nobody thought about what it might mean in 25 years. At the time, Americans were worried about Russia and the oil companies. What did it matter what the Iranians thought? Restoring the shah to the Iranian throne in place of a government hostile to America seemed like a good idea. Until the Iranian people thought otherwise in 1979 and began the first wave of Islamic revolutions that have altered recent history.

Another example closer to home is COINTELPRO, a largely forgotten FBI program of illegal wiretaps, dirty tricks, and smears of individuals first aimed at suspected Communists and later at members of the antiwar and civil rights movements. Today, as America debates the future of its intelligence agencies and domestic spying, it is important to remember FBI operations like COINTELPRO and other abuses by America's intelligence agencies in the past. People in the American government, some of them with the absolute best intentions, have trampled rights and destroyed lives in pursuit of short-term goals.

As George Kennan, the American diplomat and architect of America's Cold War "containment" policy, once said, "The worst thing the Communists could do to us and the thing we have most to fear from their activities is that we should become like them." This is the essence of learning from history. But if we all have those enormous gaps in our understanding of the past, how can we possibly learn from it?

This book's intent is to fill those gaps in our historical knowledge with some simple, accessible answers to basic questions about American history. This single volume is obviously not an encyclopedic history of America. For simplicity, I use a question-and-answer approach, and there are literally shelves of books about each of the questions I have included. My intent is to refresh the shaky recollection, remove the old myths, or reshape the misconceptions with some simple answers. Or, in some cases, to point the way to longer answers. I like to consider a *Don't Know Much About* book the first word on the subject rather than the last.

What's different about this version? First, there is an entire new chapter that includes a review of the events that have taken place since I completed the original edition in 1989, including some of the most remarkable events in American history. Like the original, this new edition is organized along chronological lines, moving from America's "discovery" by Europe to more recent events, including the Gulf War, the end of the cold war, and the events leading up to the enormous national tragedy of September 11, 2001. At this writing, we are still trying to uncover the "truth" about the terrorist attacks on September 11, 2001, what the American government knew beforehand, what it did—and didn't do. The answers to those questions are still very much in the air, and as a historian, I find it difficult to assess some of these issues yet. But we can try to figure out how we got to that awful moment in history.

In addition to the new material covering events since the late 1980s, I have included a host of new questions in every chapter. Some of these are stimulated by discoveries made in recent years, such as the archaeological dig that uncovered the original fort at Jamestown, Virginia. In other places, I answer questions that readers have asked me over the past twelve years. Often, when I speak on the radio or in lectures, I get a question that was not in the original edition, and I have included some of these "audience participation" questions. Among them are "Did Columbus's men bring syphilis back to Europe?" Or "Why is there a statue of Benedict Arnold's boot?" And "What was the difference between the Confederate and U.S. constitutions?

The media also create new questions—and mythologies—when a historic revelation gets the attention of news media for a brief time, and the facts are often left a little shaky. Many people, for instance, now accept as proven fact that longtime FBI director J. Edgar Hoover was a secret cross-dresser, because that is how the headlines reported it. However, that account was based on the accusation of a single witness who had been paid for the story. No other source could confirm or substantiate the story, but that subtlety of fact gets missed in the shallow coverage by the general news media. There is plenty that we do know about J. Edgar Hoover and his methods in running the FBI as a personal fiefdom for half a century. And it is far, far more important to understand Hoover's abuse of power than whether he wore strappy high heels or not. Another example of oversimplification is the widespread presumption that Thomas Jefferson had fathered children by a slave, Sally Hemings. The widely reported story that DNA tests had confirmed this as a fact didn't look past the headlines. The DNA testing showed that any of several of the Jefferson males might also have been the father of those children, but those complexities get lost in the eagerness for a snappy tabloid headline. There is plenty of circumstantial evidence, and oral history, to support that idea, and the subject of Jefferson and his slaves is fascinating—and deserves honest but accurate exploration.

Also from the arena of audience questions I have found enormous interest in issues pertaining to religion, gun control, and a number of other hot-button controversies. I have addressed these both in the text—with questions such as "What three-letter word is not in the Constitution?" (Hint: it begins with "G" and ends with "d.")—and in a new appendix that examines constitutional amendments and the role they play in important current political and social debates on such topics as the death penalty, gun control, and school prayer.

In writing the first edition of this book, I attempted to focus on the sort of basic questions that the average person might have, emphasizing names, places, and events that we vaguely recall as being important, but forget exactly why. These are what I call the household names of history. The reader is welcome to read the book straight through as a narrative history, or to use it as a reference book by dipping into a particular question or period. Because wars have been central, shaping events in our history, and because many people lack a sense of what actually happened during these wars, I have included a series of chronologies called "Milestones" that condense the events of the major conflicts in American history. Also scattered throughout the book are "American Voices"—selected quotes, passages from letters, books, speeches, and court decisions that reflect the spirit of the times. While many of these "American Voices" include some of the most famous Americans, others are the voices of Americans whose names you do not know—but should.

Following the seeming ambivalence of the American public toward recent elections and the chaotic events following Election Day 2000, it also seemed appropriate to include an election primer that explains some of the more mysterious elements of the process, from caucuses and delegate counts to the nearly mystical Electoral College. Another appendix presents a quick guide to the American presidents.

One encouraging indication that Americans are really interested in history but just want to learn it in a way that is more appealing than it was in high school is the success of a number of fine works of history that have become major best-sellers in the past few years, whether the World War II works of Stephen Ambrose, Mark Kurlansky's intriguing combination of history and natural science in *Cod*, the reworking of American myths such as Nathaniel Philbrick's *Mayflower*, or masterpieces of biography such as Ron Chernow's *Alexander Hamilton* or David McCullough's *John Adams*—later transformed into an admirable HBO miniseries. I have tried to highlight many of these books with an annotated list of sources for each chapter. The books I cite are either widely accepted standards or recent works that offer fresh insights or update accepted wisdom. I have also tried to single out those critically well received books written for the general reader rather than the specialist, such as James M. McPherson's *Battle Cry of Freedom*, a masterful single-volume history of the Civil War, or Thomas Fleming's *Liberty*, a companion book to a PBS history of the American Revolution, and a gem of regional history like Russell Shorto's history of early

Manhattan, *Island at the Center of the World*. Many of these books are cited in the text as "Must Reads," while the Selected Readings in the back lists books that are valuable resources covering broader periods and themes.

In some cases, these sources take very specific political viewpoints. While I have attempted to present a spectrum of opinions on those issues where there is no broad consensus, I have tried to avoid any particular stance. It is interesting to me that my work was sometimes described as "liberal." What I hoped to do in the first edition, and continue to strive for in this revision and update, is truth and accuracy, about Democrats as well as Republicans, liberals as well as conservatives. If I have a bias, I hope it is for telling the side of the story that the history books and mainstream media often overlook. And if "liberal" means believing in the ideas of America as laid out in the Declaration of Independence and the Constitution—ideas like "All men are created equal," "We, the people," "a more perfect union" (you get the idea)—then I plead guilty to the charge. But I like to think of myself as an equal opportunity basher, eager to reveal the failures on both sides of the political aisle.

Another occasional critic has called this book "anticorporation." Admittedly, the book details the corruption and criminality of big business throughout the country's history. But the Enron scandal is as American as apple pie. So I find myself in complete agreement with the American critic of businessmen who once attacked "men of wealth, who find the purchased politician the most efficient instrument of corruption"; men who were "the most dangerous members of the criminal class—the criminal of great wealth." The man who spoke those words, long before Enron, Global Crossing, WorldCom, and convicted swindler Bernie Madoff existed, was that flaming liberal President Theodore Roosevelt. (By the way, Republican Teddy Roosevelt also attempted to get the words "In God We Trust" off American currency. He not only thought they were unconstitutional, but as a devout Christian, he considered them a sacrilege.)

It is comforting perhaps to pay lip service to a country that is supposedly dedicated to "government of the people, for the people and by the people," but throughout American history, and certainly under our existing corporate-sponsored democracy, a good case can be made that America is and has been a government of, for, and by the special interests. A grassroots backlash to that reality was the motivating force behind the Progressive movement of the late nineteenth century, the New Deal reforms of the 1930s, and the Reform Party movement of Ross Perot in the 1980s. The excesses of corporate America in the era of "too big to fail," and the response of official Washington to those excesses, have helped create the angry mood of America in 2010 as the nation struggles out of the "Great Recession." This conflict was underscored in 2010, when a bitterly divided Supreme Court ruled that the government could not ban contributions by corporations, unions, or other organizations in elections, sweeping aside restrictions on campaign-finance laws.

If there is an underlying theme here, it is that the essence of history is the constant struggle for power. The battle between those holding power—whether it be the power of money, church, land, or votes—and the have-nots—the poor, the weak, the disenfranchised, the rebellious—is one main thread in the fabric of American history. The great disparity in wealth in America, a historical fact, has only increased during the past decade, according to census reports. The "haves" have more and there are more "have-nots." How to correct that great chasm is a matter of constant debate.

With that in mind, it is also important to realize that few social movements or other major developments in American history come from the top down. We like to think of elected officials as leaders, but in fact they often follow where the country is going. Most of the great reform movements in American history, from abolition to temperance, suffrage and the civil rights movement, usually came from the grassroots level, with politicians often dragged reluctantly to catch up with the people as they moved forward. That is a story that is all too often overlooked in our history books. And it is another important reason to study history. Far too many people believe that they have no power, and that is a dangerous idea. The power of one can be a mighty force of change.

A second thread running through this and all Don't Know Much About books is one that our schools and textbooks sadly bury. This is the impact of real people on history. At many turning points, it was the commanding presence of an individual—Washington, Lincoln, Frederick Douglass, the Roosevelts, and Susan B. Anthony, to name a few—that determined events, rather than the force of any idea or movement. Great ideals and noble causes have died for lack of a champion. At other times, the absence of a strong personality has had the reverse effect. For example, if a dominant president had emerged in the years before the Civil War, instead of the string of mediocrities who were elected, Lincoln's emergence might have been stillborn and that deadly war averted.

When I was in the sixth grade, I remember standing in front of the classroom to deliver a current events report about an election in New York City. Although I don't remember much of what I said, I do remember that as soon as I was finished, my teacher humiliated me. I can't recall her exact words, but she dressed me down in front of my classmates. She told me that I had taken an important news story and made it dull and unimportant. I don't know why she picked on me. But I was red-faced and ashamed.

I learned two important lessons that day that I have tried never to forget. The first is that teachers should never humiliate children who stand in front of a classroom. Embarrassment is no way to get kids to learn. And the second lesson? She was probably right. If I was going to talk about an important news story, I had better make it interesting.

And that is what I attempt to do in *Don't Know Much About History*. The only way to make history and politics interesting, I have long believed, is by telling stories of real people doing real things. Over the years, as I have spoken to people around the country on talk radio, in bookstores, and lecture halls and classrooms, the overwhelming response of far too many Americans to history is a single word— "BORING!" For years, we have sent students to school and burdened them with the most tedious textbooks imaginable—deadly dull books written by one set of professors to be read by another set of professors— which completely suck the life out of this most human of subjects.

There is very often an underside, or at least a human side, to the story. Traditionally, we have wanted our heroes to be pure and unsullied. We want to tell a national story that is filled with pride and enthusiasm. But the greatest heroes of the American epic are still people—often flawed people with deep contradictions. The simple view of men like Washington, Lincoln, and Roosevelt as beatified heroes of the American epic doesn't always stand up to scrutiny. The

American story is not that simple. There are moments in our past that can breed feelings of cynicism and disgust. Yet there are other moments that evoke pride and admiration. But to me, it is the humanity of these people, and the fact that they accomplished great things in spite of their flaws and contradictions, that makes them so fascinating.

Generally speaking, Americans have behaved worse than our proudest boosters proclaim. America did not write the book on "ethnic cleansing," but we did contribute some horrific chapters. That is why this history focuses on such moments as the Trail of Tears, Wounded Knee, My Lai, and Iraq's Abu Ghraib prison, among many others. On the other hand, Americans have also shown a capacity to be better than the worst claims of their detractors. America has no monopoly on virtue or villainy. Every country has its share of nightmarish moments it would like to forget or erase. But the job of this historian is to keep these unpleasant memories alive.

A bit more than two hundred years old now, America is still young in the broad sense of history, even though the pace of history has accelerated radically as the twentieth-century techno-revolution has transformed media, travel, and communications. (It boggles my mind to consider that when this book was first written, fax machines, cell phones, and the Internet barely existed for most Americans—including me!) The history of this country is not necessarily a smooth continuum moving toward a perfectly realized republic. More accurately, history has acted like a pendulum with long swings creating a flux in one direction or another. America remains shockingly divided along racial and economic lines. One can look at that rift and feel pessimism. But the optimist points to the distance America has come in a relatively brief time. Of course, that is small consolation to those who have always been on the short end of the stick.

Perhaps what is more important is the commitment to an acknowledgment of the true American dream. Not the one about the house with two cars in the driveway and a barbecue in the backyard. But the dream Jefferson voiced more than two hundred years ago. Even though his vision of "all men created equal" was probably different from our modern understanding, it remains the noblest of dreams and the greatest of aspirations. The struggle to fulfill that dream has been a long, strange trip. And it is never over.

AUTHOR'S NOTE

In the current era of political correctness, Columbus's mistaken identification of the native people he found when he arrived has become suspect. Some prefer "First Americans," "Native Americans," "Amerindians," and even "Aboriginal Americans." This book uses "Indian," following the lead of such eminent historians as Dee Brown, whose seminal work, *Bury My Heart at Wounded Knee*, is subtitled "An Indian History of the American West."

Similarly, the use of "black," which became the preferred term for "Negro," has come under fire, with some writers preferring "African American." Of course, neither "black" nor "African American" is perfectly accurate in describing a group of people who come in many hues and from many diverse backgrounds. Again, this book uses "black" as a widely agreed-upon term of reference. No offense is meant. I hope none is taken.

CHAPTER ONE

BRAVE NEW WORLD

Who really "discovered" America?

If he wasn't interested in the Bahamas, what was Columbus looking for in the first place?

Did Columbus's men bring syphilis back to Europe?

So if Columbus didn't really discover America, who did?

Okay, the Indians really discovered America. Who were they, and how did they get here?

If Columbus was so important, how come we don't live in the United States of Columbus?

What became of Christopher Columbus?

Where were the first European settlements in the New World?

If the Spanish were here first, what was so important about Jamestown?

What was the Northwest Passage?

What was the Lost Colony?

When and how did Jamestown get started?

Did Pocahontas really save John Smith's life?

What was the House of Burgesses?

Who started the slave trade?

Who were the Pilgrims, and what did they want?

What was the Mayflower Compact?

Did the Pilgrims really land at Plymouth Rock?

Highlights in the Development of New England

Who started New York?

Did the Indians really sell Manhattan for $24?

How did New Amsterdam become New York?

When did the French reach the New World?

Why is Pennsylvania the Quaker State?

What were the thirteen original colonies?

ew eras in American history are shrouded in as much myth and mystery as the long period covering America's discovery and settlement. Perhaps this is because there were few objective observers on hand to record so many of these events. There was no "film at eleven" when primitive people crossed the land bridge from Asia into the future Alaska. No correspondents were on board when Columbus's ships reached land. Historians have been forced instead to rely on accounts written by participants in the events, witnesses whose views can politely be called prejudiced. When it comes to the tale of Pocahontas, for instance, much of what was taught and thought for a long time was based on Captain John Smith's colorful autobiography. What is worse, history teachers now have to contend with a generation of prepubescent Americans who have learned a new myth, courtesy of the Disney version of *Pocahontas*, in which a sultry, buxom Indian maiden goes wild for a John Smith who looks like a surfer dude with Mel Gibson's voice. Oh well.

This chapter covers some of the key events during several thousand years of history. However, the spotlight is on the development of what would become the United States, and the chapter ends with the thirteen original colonies in place.

Who really "discovered" America?

"In fourteen hundred and ninety-two, Columbus sailed the ocean blue." We all know that. But did he really discover America? The best answer is, "Not really. But sort of." A national holiday and two centuries of schoolbooks have left the impression of Christopher Columbus as the intrepid sailor and man of God (his given name means "Christbearer") who was the first to reach America, disproving the notion of a flat world while he was at it. Italian Americans who claim the sailor as their own treat Columbus Day as a special holiday, as do Hispanic Americans who celebrate El Día de la Raza as their discovery day.

Love him or hate him—as many do in light of recent revisionist views of Columbus—it is impossible to downplay the importance of Columbus's voyage, or the incredible heroism and tenacity of character his quest demanded. Even the astronauts who flew to the moon had a pretty good idea of what to expect; Columbus was sailing, as *Star Trek* puts it, "where no man has gone before."

However, rude facts do suggest a few different angles to his story.

After trying to sell his plan to the kings of Portugal, England, and France, Columbus doggedly returned to Isabella and Ferdinand of Spain, who had already given Columbus the thumbs-down once. Convinced by one of their ministers that the risks were small and the potential return great, and fueled by an appetite for gold and fear of neighboring Portugal's growing lead in exploration, the Spanish monarchs later agreed. Contrary to myth, Queen Isabella did not have to pawn any of the crown jewels to finance the trip.

Columbus set sail on August 3, 1492, from Palos, Spain, aboard three ships, *Niña*, *Pinta*, and *Santa María*, the last being his flagship. Columbus (christened Cristoforo Colombo) had been promised a 10 percent share of profits, governorship of newfound lands, and an impressive title—Admiral of the Ocean Sea. On October 12 at 2 A.M., just as his crews were threatening to mutiny and force a return to Spain, a lookout named Rodrigo de Triana aboard the *Pinta* sighted moonlight shimmering on some cliffs or sand. Having promised a large reward to the first man to spot land, Columbus claimed that he had seen the light the night before, and kept the reward for himself. Columbus named the landfall—Guanahani to the natives—San Salvador. While it was long held that Columbus's San Salvador was Watling Island in the Bahamas, recent computer-assisted theories point to Samana Cay. Later on that first voyage, Columbus reached Cuba and a large island he called Hispaniola (presently Haiti and the Dominican Republic).

Although he found some naked natives whom he christened *indios* in the mistaken belief that he had reached the so-called Indies or Indonesian Islands, the only gold he found was in the earrings worn by the Indians. As for spices, he did find a local plant called *tobacos*, which was rolled into cigars and smoked by the local Arawak. It was not long before all Europe was savoring pipefuls of the evil weed. Tobacco was brought to Spain for the first time in 1555. Three years later, the

Portuguese introduced Europe to the habit of taking snuff. The economic importance of tobacco to the early history of America cannot be ignored. While we like to think about the importance of documents and decisions, tobacco became the cash crop that kept the English colonies going—where it literally kept the settlers alive. In other words, there is nothing new about powerful tobacco lobbies. They have influenced government practically since the first European settlers arrived.

Still believing that he had reached some island outposts of China, Columbus left some volunteers on Hispaniola in a fort called Natividad, built of timbers from the wrecked *Santa María*, and returned to Spain. While Columbus never reached the mainland of the present United States of America on any of his three subsequent voyages, his arrival in the Caribbean signaled the dawn of an astonishing and unequaled era of discovery, conquest, and colonization in the Americas. Although his bravery, persistence, and seamanship have rightfully earned Columbus a place in history, what the schoolbooks gloss over is that Columbus's arrival also marked the beginning of one of the cruelest episodes in human history.

Driven by an obsessive quest for gold, Columbus quickly enslaved the local population. Under Columbus and other Spanish adventurers, as well as later European colonizers, an era of genocide was opened that ravaged the native American population through warfare, forced labor, draconian punishments, and European diseases to which the Indians had no natural immunities.

AMERICAN VOICES
CHRISTOPHER COLUMBUS, October 12, 1492,
on encountering the Arawak, from his diary
(as quoted by Bartolomé de las Casas):

They must be good servants and very intelligent, because I see that they repeat very quickly what I told them, and it is my conviction that they would easily become Christians, for they seem not to have any sect. If it please our Lord, I will take six of them that they may learn to speak. The people are totally unacquainted with arms, as your Highnesses will see by observing the seven which I have caused

to be taken in. With fifty men all can be kept in subjection,
and made to do whatever you desire.

If he wasn't interested in the Bahamas, what was Columbus looking for in the first place?

The arrival of the three ships at their Caribbean landfall marks what is
probably the biggest and luckiest blooper in the history of the world.
Rather than a new world, Columbus was actually searching for a direct sea route to China and the Indies. Ever since Marco Polo had
journeyed back from the Orient loaded with spices, gold, and fantastic
tales of the strange and mysterious East, Europeans had lusted after the
riches of Polo's Cathay (China). This appetite grew ravenous when
the returning Crusaders opened up overland trade routes between Europe and the Orient. However, when Constantinople fell to the Turks
in 1453, it meant an end to the spice route that served as the economic
lifeline for Mediterranean Europe.

Emerging from the Middle Ages, Europe was quickly shifting from
an agrarian, barter economy to a new age of capitalism in which gold
was the coin of the realm. The medieval Yeppies (Young European
Princes) acquired a taste for the finer things such as gold and precious
jewels, as well as the new taste sensations called spices, and these were
literally worth their weight in gold. After a few centuries of home-
cooked venison, there was an enormous clamor for the new Oriental
takeout spices: cinnamon from Ceylon, pepper from India and Indo-
nesia, nutmeg from Celebes, and cloves from the Moluccas. The new
merchant princes had also acquired a taste for Japanese silks and Indian cottons, dyes, and precious stones.

Led by Prince Henry the Navigator, founder of a great scholarly sea-
port on the coast of Portugal, Portuguese sea captains like Bartholomeu
Dias (who reached the Cape of Good Hope in 1488) and Vasco da
Gama (who sailed all the way to India in 1495) had taken the lead in
exploiting Africa and navigating a sea route to the Indies. Like others
of his day, Columbus believed that a direct westward passage to the
Orient was not only possible, but would be faster and easier. In spite of
what Columbus's public relations people later said, the flat earth idea

was pretty much finished by the time Chris sailed. In fact, an accepted theory of a round earth had been held as far back as the days of the ancient Greeks. In the year Columbus sailed, a Nuremberg geographer constructed the first globe. The physical proof of the Earth's roundness came when eighteen survivors of Magellan's crew of 266 completed a circumnavigation in 1522.

Columbus believed a course due west along latitude twenty-eight degrees north would take him to Marco Polo's fabled Cipangu (Japan). Knowing that no one was crazy enough to sponsor a voyage of more than 3,000 miles, Columbus based his guess of the distance on ancient Greek theories, some highly speculative maps drawn after Marco Polo's return, and some figure fudging of his own. He arrived at the convenient estimate of 2,400 miles.

In fact, the distance Columbus was planning to cover was 10,600 miles by air!

Did Columbus's men bring syphilis back to Europe?

One of the most persistent legends surrounding Columbus probably didn't get into your high school history book. It is an idea that got its start in Europe when the return of Columbus and his men coincided with a massive outbreak of syphilis in Europe. Syphilis in epidemic proportions first appeared during a war being fought in Naples in 1494. The army of the French king, Charles VIII, withdrew from Naples, and the disease was soon spreading throughout Europe. Later, Portuguese sailors during the Age of Discovery carried the malady to Africa, India, and Asia, where it apparently had not been seen before. By around 1539, according to William H. McNeill, "Contemporaries thought it was a new disease against which Eurasian populations had no established immunities. The timing of the first outbreak of syphilis in Europe and the place where it occurred certainly seems to fit what one would expect of the disease had it been imported from America by Columbus's returning sailors. This theory . . . became almost universally accepted . . . until very recently."

Over the centuries, this "urban legend" acquired a sort of mystique as an unintended form of "revenge" unwittingly exacted by the Indians for what Columbus and the arrival of Europeans had done to them. One of the earliest documented signs of syphilis in humans dates to about 2,000 years ago, in remains found in North America.

In fact, other culprits have been blamed for the scourge of syphilis. The word itself was coined in 1530 by Girolamo Fracastoro, an Italian physician and poet. He published a poem called "*Syphilis, sive Morbus Gallicus*," which translates as "Syphilis, or the French Disease." In the poem, a shepherd named Syphilus is supposed to have been the first victim of the disease, which in the fifteenth century was far more deadly and virulent than the form of syphilis commonly known today. Of course, this was also a long time before the advent of antibiotics. The original source of the name Syphilus is uncertain but may have come from the poetry of Ovid. In other words, the Italians blamed the French for syphilis. And in Spain, the disease was blamed on the Jews, who had been forced out of Spain, also in that memorable year of 1492.

According to McNeill, many modern researchers reject the so-called Columbian Exchange version of syphilis. There is simply too much evidence of pre-Columbian syphilis in the Old World. For example, pre-Columbian skeletons recently unearthed in England show distinctive signs of syphilis. So while a definitive answer to the origin of the scourge of Venus remains a mystery, the American Indian as the original source of Europe's plague of syphilis seems far less likely than he once did.

So if Columbus didn't really discover America, who did?

Like the argument about syphilis, the debate over who reached the Americas before Columbus goes back almost as far as Columbus's voyage. Enough books have been written on the subject of earlier "discoverers" to fill a small library. There is plenty of evidence to bolster the claims made on behalf of a number of voyagers who may have reached the Americas, either by accident or design, well before Columbus reached the Bahamas.

Among these, the one best supported by archaeological evidence is the credit given to Norse sailors, led by Norse captain Leif Eriksson, who not only reached North America but established a colony in present-day Newfoundland around A.D. 1000, five hundred years before Columbus. The site of a Norse village has been uncovered at L'Anse Aux Meadows, near present-day St. Anthony, and was named the first World Heritage site by UNESCO, an educational and cultural arm of the United Nations. While archaeology has answered some questions, many others remain about the sojourn of the Norse in the Americas.

Most of what is guessed about the Norse colony in North America is derived from two Icelandic epics called *The Vinland Sagas*. There are three locations—Stoneland, probably the barren coast of Labrador, Woodland, possibly Maine; and Vinland—which the Norse visited. While Leif the Lucky gets the credit in history and the roads and festivals named after him, it was another Norseman, Bjarni Herjolfsson, who was the first European to sight North America, in 985 or 986. But it was Leif who supposedly built some huts and spent one winter in this land where wild grapes—more likely berries, since there are no grapes in any of these places—grew before returning to Greenland. A few years later, another Greenlander named Thorfinn Karlsefni set up housekeeping in Eriksson's spot, passing two years there. Among the problems they faced were unfriendly local tribes, whom the Norsemen called *skrelings* (a contemptuous term translated as "wretch" or "dwarf"). During one attack, a pregnant Norse woman frightened the *skrelings* off by slapping a sword against her bare breast. Terrified at this sight, the *skrelings* fled back to their boats.

In his fascinating book *Cod*, Mark Kurlansky asks, "What did these Norsemen eat on the five expeditions to America between 986 and 1011 that have been recorded in the Icelandic sagas? They were able to travel to all these distant, barren shores because they had learned to preserve codfish by hanging it in the frosty winter air until it lost four-fifths of its weight and became a durable woodlike plank. They could break off pieces and chew them . . ."

There are those who hold out for earlier discoverers. For many years, there were tales of earlier Irish voyagers, led by a mythical St. Brendan, who supposedly reached America in the ninth or tenth century, sailing in small boats called *curraghs*. However, no archaeological or other evidence supports this. Another popular myth, completely unfounded, regards a Welshman named Modoc who established a colony and taught the local Indians to speak Welsh. A more recent theory provides an interesting twist on the "Europeans sailing to Asia" notion. A British navigation expert has studied ancient Chinese maps and believes that a Chinese admiral may have circumnavigated the globe and reached America 100 years before Columbus. Convincing proof of such a voyage would be a stunning revision of history, but to date it is the equivalent of the philosopher's tree falling in the forest: If the Chinese got there first but nobody "heard" it, did they really get there first?

A significant discovery belongs to another of Columbus's countrymen, Giovanni Caboto (John Cabot), who was sailing for the British. In 1496, Cabot (and his son, Sebastian) received a commission from England's King Henry VII to find a new trade route to Asia. Sailing out of Bristol aboard the *Matthew*, Cabot reached a vast rocky coastline near a sea teeming with cod. Cabot reported the vast wealth of this place he called New Found Land, which he claimed for Henry VII, staking a claim that would eventually provide the English with their foothold in the New World. Sailing with five ships on a second voyage in 1498, Cabot ran into bad weather. One of the vessels returned to an Irish port, but Cabot disappeared with the four other ships.

But Cabot and others were not sailing into completely unknown waters. Fishermen in search of cod had been frequenting the waters off North America for many years. Basque fishing boats fished in these waters. Clearly, though, they had decided it was a nice fishing spot but not a place to stay for good. And they were slow to catch on that the coastal land they were fishing near was not Asia. Even in the sixteenth century, according to Mark Kurlansky in *Cod*, Newfoundland was charted as an island off China.

So even though cod fishermen were the Europeans who discovered "America," they—like generations of anglers who keep their best spots to themselves—wanted to keep their fishing grounds secret, and the distinction of being the first European to set foot on what would become United States soil usually goes to Juan Ponce de León, the Spanish adventurer who conquered Puerto Rico. Investigating rumors of a large island north of Cuba that contained a "fountain of youth" whose waters could restore youth and vigor, Ponce de León found and named Florida in 1513 and "discovered" Mexico on that same trip.

Finally, there is the 1524 voyage of still another Italian, Giovanni da Verrazano, who sailed in the employ of the French Crown with the financial backing of silk merchants eager for Asian trade. Verrazano was searching for a strait through the New World that would take him westward to the Orient. He reached land at Cape Fear in present-day North Carolina, sailed up the Atlantic coast until he reached Newfoundland, and then returned to France. Along the way, he failed to stop in either Chesapeake or Delaware Bay. But Verrazano reached New York Bay (where he went only as far as the narrows and the site of the bridge that both bear his name) and Narragansett Bay, as well as an arm-shaped hook of land he named Pallavisino in honor of an Italian general. Still frustrated in the search for a passage to the east, Verrazano returned to France but insisted that the "7000 leagues of coastline" he had found constituted a New World. Seventy years later, Englishman Bartholomew Gosnold was still looking for a route to Asia, which he did not find, of course. However, he did find a great many cod, in shallow waters, and renamed Verrazano's Pallavisino Cape Cod in 1602. But the English sailors who attempted to settle the area—near what is Bristol, Maine—found this new world "over-cold."

But all these European cod fishermen and lost sailors seeking Asia were no more than Johnny-come-latelies in the Americas. In fact, America had been "discovered" long before any of these voyages. The true "discoverers" of America were the people whose culture and societies were well established here while Europe was still in the Dark Ages, the so-called Indians, who, rather ironically, had walked to the New World from Asia.

Must Read: *Cod: A Biography of the Fish That Changed the World* by Mark Kurlansky.

Okay, the Indians really discovered America. Who were they, and how did they get here?

Until fairly recently, it was generally believed that humans first lived in the Americas approximately 12,000 years ago, arriving on foot from Asia. However, new evidence suggests that the people who would eventually come to be called Indians may have arrived in America some 30,000 to 40,000 years ago. Radiocarbon dating of charcoal found in southern Chile and the 1997 discovery of a skeleton in present-day Washington State have not only bolstered the argument that humans lived in America much earlier than had been widely accepted, but also shaken the foundations of who they were and how they got here.

The version of events generally accepted and long supported by archaeological finds and highly accurate carbon testing is that the prehistoric people who populated the Americas were hunters following the great herds of woolly mammoths. During an ice age, when sea levels were substantially lower because so much water was locked up in ice, these early arrivals into the Americas walked from Siberia across a land bridge into modern-day Alaska. While "land bridge" suggests a narrow strip between the seas, the "bridge" was probably a thousand miles across. Once here, they began heading south toward warmer climates, slaughtering the mammoth as they went. Eventually, as the glaciers melted, the oceans rose and covered this land bridge, creating the present-day Bering Strait, separating Alaska from Russia. The earliest known artifacts left by these people were discovered at Clovis, New Mexico, and have been dated to 11,500 years ago.

But a growing body of evidence suggests several more complex and surprising possibilities:

- The Pacific coastal route: According to this theory, people from northern Asia migrated along the western coast of America on foot and by skin-covered boat before the Bering land bridge existed. This theory is based partly on artifacts found in coastal Peru and Chile, dated as far back as 12,500 years ago, that provide early evidence of maritime-based people in the Americas. In Monte Verde, Chile, the artifacts include wooden tools, animal bones, and a human footprint.

  The discovery of the so-called Kennewick man in Washington State further clouded the issue. Dated between 8,000 and 9,300 years old, these remains raised the question of whether this early American was from Asia at all.

- North Atlantic route: The discovery of several sites on the North American east coast have suggested a very different sea route. Artifacts at these sites in present-day Pennsylvania, Virginia, and South Carolina are dated between 10,000 and 16,000 years old, well before the Clovis artifacts. In theory, early Europeans in boats followed the ice surrounding modern Iceland and Greenland down to North America.

- Australian route: Another, more controversial, generally less accepted theory is a modification of the theory propounded by the late Thor Heyerdahl in his book *Kon Tiki*. Heyerdahl contended that the Americas could have been settled by people from southeast Asia who crossed the Pacific to South America. While many scientists consider this farfetched, a skeleton found in Brazil gives some support to the idea, but some scientists think it more likely that the skeleton belonged to some branch of southeast Asian people who moved north along the coast of Asia and then across the Bering Strait.

Of course, it is also possible that any or all of these theories might be correct and more than one group of people migrated into the New World. Some of them might have become extinct, replaced by later groups, or they may have undergone significant physical changes over the many thousands of years since their arrival.

What is far more certain is that, by the time Columbus arrived, there were tens of millions of what might be called First Americans or Amerindians occupying the two continents of the Americas. These were divided into hundreds of tribal societies, the most advanced of which were the Mayas, and later the Aztecs in Mexico and the Incas of Peru, all of whom became fodder for the Spanish under the reign of terror wrought by the conquistadores. Many history books once presented these American Indians as a collection of nearly savage civilizations. A newer romanticized version presents groups of people living in harmony with themselves and nature. Neither view is realistic.

There were, first of all, many cultures spread over the two Americas, from the Eskimo and Inuit of the North down to the advanced Mexican and South American societies. While none of these developed along the lines of the European world, substantial achievements were made in agriculture, architecture, mathematics, and other fields. On the other hand, some important developments were lacking. Few of these societies had devised a written language. Nor were some of these Indians free from savagery, as best witnessed by the Aztec human sacrifice that claimed as many as 1,000 victims a day in Tenochtitlán (near the site of present-day Mexico City) or the practices of the Iroquois, who had raised torture of captured opponents to a sophisticated but ghastly art.

During the past few decades, estimates of the Indian population at the time of Columbus's arrival have undergone a radical revision, especially in the wave of new scholarship that attended the 1992 marking of five hundred years since Columbus's first voyage. Once it was believed that the Indian population ranged from 8 million to 16 million people, spread over two continents. That number has been significantly revised upward to as many as 100 million or higher, spread across the two continents.

Although Hitler's attempt to exterminate the Jews of Europe was a calculated, methodical genocidal plan, the European destruction of the Indians was no less ruthlessly efficient, killing off perhaps 90 percent of the native population it found, all in the name of progress, civilization, and Christianity.

While Europeans were technically more advanced in many respects than the natives they encountered, what really led to the conquest of the Americas was not military might or a superior culture. The largest single factor in the destruction of the native populations in the Americas was the introduction of epidemic diseases to which the natives had no natural immunity.

AMERICAN VOICES

AMERIGO VESPUCCI, in a letter to
Lorenzo Medici, 1504:

In days past, I gave your excellency a full account of my return, and if I remember aright, wrote you a description of all those parts of the New World which I had visited in the vessels of his serene highness the king of Portugal. Carefully considered, they appear truly to form another world, and therefore we have, not without reason, called it the New World. Not one of all the ancients had any knowledge of it, and the things which have been lately ascertained by us transcend all their ideas.

If Columbus was so important, how come we don't live in the United States of Columbus?

The naming of America was one of the cruel tricks of history and about as accurate as calling Indians "Indians." Amerigo Vespucci was another Italian who found his way to Spain and, as a ship chandler, actually helped outfit Columbus's voyages. In 1499, he sailed to South America with Alonso de Hojeda, one of Columbus's captains, reaching the mouth of the Amazon. He made three more voyages along the coast of Brazil. In 1504, letters supposedly written by Vespucci appeared in Italy in which he claimed to be captain of the four voyages and in which the words *Mundus Novus*, or New World, were first used to describe the lands that had been found. Vespucci's travels became more famous in his day than those of Columbus. Some years later, in a new edition of Ptolemy, this new land, still believed to be attached to Asia, was labeled America in Vespucci's honor.

What became of Christopher Columbus?

Following the first voyage, Columbus arrived in Spain in March 1493 after a troubled return trip. He was given a grand reception by Ferdinand and Isabella, even though he had little to show except some trinkets and the Taino Indians who had survived the voyage back to Spain. But the Spanish monarchs decided to press on and appealed to the pope to allow them claim to the lands, ostensibly so they could preach the Christian faith. The pope agreed, but the Portuguese immediately protested, and the two countries began to negotiate a division of the spoils of the New World. They eventually agreed on a line of demarcation that enabled Portugal to claim Brazil—which is why Brazilians speak Portuguese and the rest of South and Central America and Mexico are principally Spanish-speaking countries.

Columbus was then given seventeen ships for a second voyage, with about 1,500 men who had volunteered in the hopes of finding vast riches. When he returned to Hispaniola, Columbus discovered that the men he had left behind at a fort were gone, probably killed by the Taino. Columbus established a second fort, but it was clear that this was not the land of gold and riches that the Spaniards expected. He sailed on to Cuba, still believing that he was on the Asian mainland, and then landed on Jamaica. Returning to Hispaniola, Columbus then began to set the Taino to look for gold—with harsh quotas established and harsher punishments for failing to meet those quotas. The lucky ones lost a hand. The unlucky were crucified in rows of thirteen—one for Jesus and each of the disciples.

Soon the Indians also began to drop from the infectious diseases brought over by Columbus and the Spanish. Reports of the disastrous situation in the colony reached Spain, and Columbus had to return to defend himself. His reputation sank but he was given a third voyage. On May 30, 1498, he left Spain with six ships and fewer enthusiastic recruits. Prisoners were pardoned to fill out the crews. He sailed south and reached the coast of present-day Venezuela.

Following a rebellion on Hispaniola, there were now so many complaints about Columbus that he was brought back to Spain in shackles. Although the king and queen ordered his release, his pardon came with conditions, and Columbus lost most of his titles and governorship of the islands. But he was given one more chance at a voyage, which he called the High Voyage.

In 1502, he left Spain with four ships and his fourteen-year-old son, Ferdinand, who would record events during the trip. Although Columbus reached the Isthmus of Panama and was told that a large body of water (the Pacific Ocean) lay a few days' march away, Columbus failed to pursue the possibility. He abandoned the quest for Asia, exhausted, and suffering from malaria, sailed to Jamaica. Starving and sick, Columbus here supposedly tricked the locals into giving him food by predicting an eclipse of the moon. After being marooned for a year, Columbus left Jamaica, reaching Spain in November 1504. Isabella had died, and Ferdinand tried to convince Columbus to retire. He spent his last days in a modest home in Valladolid, and died on May 20, 1506. He was not impoverished at the time of his death, as legend had it. His remains were moved to Seville and later to Santo Domingo (present-day Dominican Republic). Some believe his bones were then taken to Cuba; others believe his final resting place is on Santo Domingo. (Scientists are attempting to get permission to do DNA tests on the buried bones.)

Where were the first European settlements in the New World?

While we make a great fuss over the Pilgrims and Jamestown, the Spanish had roamed over much of the Americas by the time the English arrived. In fact, if the Spanish Armada launched to assault Queen Elizabeth's England hadn't been blown to bits by storms and the English "sea dogs" in 1588, this might be Los Estados Unidos, and we'd be eating tacos at bullfights.

Following Columbus's bold lead, the Spanish (and, to a lesser extent, the Portuguese) began a century of exploration, colonization, and subjugation, with the primary aim of providing more gold for the Spanish Crown. The Spanish explorers, the conquistadores, amassed enormous wealth for themselves and the Spanish Crown, while also decimating the native populations they encountered. Many of them died as they lived—violently, at the hands of either Indians they battled or their fellow Spaniards eager to amass gold and power. Among the highlights of Spanish exploration:

1499   Amerigo Vespucci and Alonso de Hojeda (or Ojeda) sail for South America and reach the mouth of the Amazon River.

1502   Vespucci, after second voyage, concludes South America is not part of India and names it *Mundus Novus*.

1505   Juan Bermudez discovers the island that bears his name, Bermuda.

1513   After a twenty-five-day trek through the dense rain forests of Central America, Vasco Nuñez de Balboa crosses the Isthmus of Panama and sights the Pacific Ocean for the first time. He names it Mar del Sur (Southern Sea) and believes it to be part of the Indian Ocean. Political rivals later accuse Balboa of treason, and he is beheaded in a public square along with four of his followers. Their remains are thrown to the vultures.

1513   Juan Ponce de León begins searching for a legendary "fountain of youth," a spring with restorative powers. Ponce de León, who had been on Columbus's second voyage and had conquered Boriquén

(Puerto Rico), making a fortune in gold and slaves, reaches and names Florida, claiming it for Spain. (Ponce de León dies after suffering arrow wounds during a fight with Indians.)

1519   Hernán Cortés enters Tenochtitlán (Mexico City). Thought to be the returning Aztec god Quetzalcoatl, Cortés captures Emperor Montezuma, beginning the conquest of the Aztec Empire in Mexico. His triumph leads to 300 years of Spanish domination of Mexico and Central America.

Domenico de Piñeda explores the Gulf of Mexico from Florida to Vera Cruz.

1522   Pascual de Andagoya discovers Peru.

1523   A Spanish base on Jamaica is founded. (Arawak Indians, who were the first people to live in Jamaica, named the island Xaymaca, which means land of wood and water.)

1531   Francisco Pizarro, an illiterate orphan and one of Balboa's lieutenants, invades Peru, kills thousands of natives, and conquers the Incan Empire, the largest, most powerful native empire in South America. The Inca, already devastated by civil war, were decimated by smallpox brought by the Spanish. Pizarro captures and executes the Inca ruler Atahualpa. (In the late 1530s, a dispute between Pizarro and another Spaniard, Almagro, over who was to rule the area around Cuzco led to war. Pizarro's forces won the conflict in 1538 and executed Almagro. In 1541, followers of Almagro's son killed Pizarro.)

1535   Lima (Peru) founded by Pizarro.

1536   Buenos Aires (Argentina) founded by Spanish settlers, but they leave the area five years later because of Indian attacks. A group of settlers from Paraguay, led by a Spanish soldier named Juan de Garay, reestablishes Buenos Aires in 1580.

1538   Bogota (Colombia) founded by Gonzalo Jimenez de Quesada, a Spanish military leader who conquered the area's Chibcha Indians.

1539   Hernando De Soto, a veteran of the war against the Inca in Peru, explores Florida. He is authorized to conquer and colonize the region that is now the southeastern United States.

1539   First printing press in New World set up in Mexico City.

1540   Grand Canyon discovered.

1541   De Soto discovers the Mississippi River; Coronado explores from New Mexico across Texas, Oklahoma, and eastern Kansas. On May 21, 1542, de Soto dies from a fever by the banks of the Mississippi River. The remains of his army, led by Luis de Moscoso, reach New Spain (now Mexico) the next year.

1549   Jesuit missionaries arrive in South America.

1551   Universities founded in Lima and Mexico City.

1565   St. Augustine, the oldest permanent settlement established by Europeans in the United States, is founded by Admiral Pedro Menéndez de Aviles. A colony of French Protestants, or Huguenots, had established a colony in Florida called Fort Caroline. Menéndez attacked the French and wiped them out, and later killed a large number of French sailors who had been shipwrecked in a hurricane.

   The settlement of St. Augustine was razed by English privateer Francis Drake in 1586. Spain ruled St. Augustine until 1763, when the British gained control of it. Spain again ruled the settlement from 1783 until 1821, when Florida became a territory of the United States.

1567   Rio de Janeiro (Brazil) is founded.

1605   (date in dispute; some say 1609) Santa Fe, New Mexico, founded as the capital of the Spanish colony of New Mexico. Santa Fe has been a seat of government longer than any other state capital. (Proud New Mexicans now argue that the first Thanksgiving in America actually took place in Santa Fe.)

If the Spanish were here first, what was so important about Jamestown?

Winners write the history books, so, even though the Spanish dominated the New World for almost a century before the English settlers arrived in Jamestown, the Spanish were eventually supplanted in North America, and the new era of English supremacy began. Just as modern American life is shaped by global happenings, international events had begun to play an increasingly important role at this stage in world history. By the mid-sixteenth century, Spain had grown corrupt and lazy, the Spanish king living off the spoils of the gold mines of the Americas, with a resultant lack of enterprise at home. With gold pouring in, there was little inducement or incentive to push advances in the areas of commerce or invention.

Perhaps even more significant was the revolution that became known as the Protestant Reformation. A zealous Catholic, Spain's King Philip II saw England's Protestant Queen Elizabeth not only as a political and military rival, but as a heretic as well. His desire to defend Roman Catholicism dictated his policies, including his support of the Catholic Mary Queen of Scots against Elizabeth. For her part, Elizabeth saw the religious conflict as the excuse to build English power at Spain's expense. And she turned her notorious "sea dogs," or gentlemen pirates, loose on Spanish treasure ships while also aiding the Dutch in their fight with Spain. The Dutch, meanwhile, were building the largest merchant marine fleet in Europe.

When the English sank the Spanish battleships—the Armada—in 1588, with the help of a violent storm that smashed more Spanish warships than the British did, the proverbial handwriting was on the wall. It was a blow from which Spain never fully recovered, and it marked the beginning of England's rise to global sea power, enabling that tiny island nation to embark more aggressively on a course of colonization and empire-building.

What was the Northwest Passage?

If you answer, "A movie by Alfred Hitchcock," Go Directly to Jail. Do Not Pass Go. (You're thinking of *North by Northwest*, the classic thriller including the famous scene in which Cary Grant is chased by a crop duster.)

Almost a century after Columbus's first voyage, Europeans remained convinced that a faster route to China was waiting to be found and that the New World was just an annoying roadblock—although Spain was proving it to be a profitable one—that could be detoured. Some tried to go around the top of Russia, the "northeast passage." Sebastian Cabot organized an expedition in search of such a passage in 1553. Cabot had also tried going the other way back in 1509, but the voyage failed when his crew mutinied.

In 1576, Sir Humphrey (or Humfrey) Gilbert first used the phrase "North West passage," to describe a sea route around North America, and he continued to search for such a route to China. An Oxford-educated soldier, courtier, and businessman, Gilbert also played a hand in the earliest English attempts at colonization. In 1578, another Englishman, Martin Frobisher, set off for the fabled route and reached the northeast coast of Canada, exploring Baffin Island.

Among the others who searched for the route through the Arctic from Europe to Asia was Henry Hudson, an Englishman sailing for the Dutch, who embarked on his voyage aboard the *Half Moon* to North America in 1609, the voyage on which he discovered the bay and river later named after him. Sailing as far north as present-day Albany, Hudson met Delaware and Mohican Indians along the way and apparently threw a memorable party at which the Indian leaders got quite drunk. But Hudson realized that this was not the route to China.

Like many of the famous explorers, Hudson left a name for himself but his fate was far from happy. In 1610, a group of English merchants formed a company that provided Hudson with a ship called the *Discovery*. When the *Discovery* reached a body of rough water, later named Hudson Strait, that led into Hudson Bay, Hudson thought he had at last come to the Pacific Ocean. Struggling to sail though massive ice, he headed south into what is now James Bay. But lost, frustrated, and cold, Hudson and his crew failed to find an outlet at the south end of this bay. Forced to haul their ship to ground and spend the winter in the sub-Arctic, Hudson and his crew—who had been promised the balmier South Pacific—suffered severely from cold, hunger, and disease. In the spring of 1611, Hudson's crew could take no more. They mutinied and set Hudson adrift in a small boat with his son, John, and seven loyal crewmen. The mutineers sailed back to England, and their report gave continued hope that a passage existed between Hudson Bay and the Pacific. But it didn't prompt Hudson's employers to send a rescue effort. England based its claim to the vast Hudson Bay region on Hudson's last voyage and the Hudson Bay Company soon began the fur trade that would bring the wealth that a route to Asia was supposed to deliver. Hudson and his boat mates were never seen again, although Indian legends tell of white men being found in a boat.

While a northwest passage to the East does exist, it requires sailing through far northern waters that are icebound much of the year, although global warming may be changing that, many scientists fear.

What was the Lost Colony?

In 1578 and again in 1583, Humphrey Gilbert set sail with a group of colonists and Queen Elizabeth's blessings. The first expedition accomplished little, and the second, after landing in Newfoundland, was lost in a storm, and Sir Humphrey with it.

But Gilbert's half brother, Sir Walter Raleigh (or Ralegh, as other historians spell it), the thirty-one-year-old favorite of Queen Elizabeth, inherited Gilbert's royal patent and continued the quest. He dispatched ships to explore North America and named the land there Virginia in honor of Queen Elizabeth, "the virgin queen." In 1585, he was behind a short-lived attempt to form a colony on Roanoke Island on present-day North Carolina's Outer Banks. In 1586, Sir Francis Drake found the colonists hungry and ready to return to England. In the following year, Raleigh sent another group of 107 men, women, and children to Roanoke. It was an ill-planned and ill-fated expedition. The swampy island was inhospitable, and so were the local Indians. Supply ships, delayed by the attack of the Spanish Armada, failed to reach the colony in 1588, and when ships finally did arrive in 1590, the pioneers left by Raleigh had disappeared without a trace.

All that was found was some rusted debris and the word *croatoan*, the Indian name for the nearby island on which Cape Hatteras is located, carved on a tree. Over the years, there has been much speculation about what happened to the so-called Lost Colony, but its exact fate remains a mystery. Starvation and Indian raids probably killed off most of the unlucky colonists, with any survivors being adopted by the Indians, the descendants of whom still claim Raleigh's colonists as their ancestral kin. In his book *Set Fair for Roanoke*, the historian David Beers Quinn produces a more interesting bit of historical detection. Quinn suggests that the Lost Colonists weren't lost at all; instead, they made their way north toward Virginia, settled among peaceable Indians, and were surviving at nearly the time Jamestown was planted but were slaughtered in a massacre by Powhatan, an Indian chief whose name becomes prominent in the annals of Jamestown.

When and how did Jamestown get started?

It took another fifteen years and a new monarch in England to attempt colonization once again. But this time there would be a big difference: private enterprise had entered the picture. The costs of sponsoring a colony were too high for any individual, even royalty, to take on alone. In 1605, two groups of merchants, who had formed joint stock companies that combined the investments of small shareholders, petitioned King James I for the right to colonize Virginia. The first of these, the Virginia Company of London, was given a grant to southern Virginia; the second, the Plymouth Company, was granted northern Virginia. At this time, however, the name Virginia encompassed the entire North American continent from sea to sea. While these charters spoke loftily of spreading Christianity, the real goal remained the quest for treasure, and the charter spoke of the right to "dig, mine, and search for all Manner of Mines of Gold, Silver, and Copper."

On December 20, 1606, colonists — men and boys — left port aboard three ships, *Susan Constant, Goodspeed*, and *Discovery*, under Captain John Newport. During a miserable voyage, they were stranded and their supplies dwindled, and dozens died. They reached Chesapeake Bay in May 1607, and within a month, had constructed a triangle-shaped wooden fort and named it James Fort—only later Jamestown—the first permanent English settlement in the New World. In one of the most significant finds in recent archaeology, the site of James Fort was discovered in 1996.

Jamestown has been long celebrated as the "birthplace of America," an outpost of heroic settlers braving the New World. Here again, rude facts intrude on the neat version of life in Jamestown that the schoolbooks gave us. While the difficulties faced by the first men of Jamestown were real—attacks by Algonquian Indians, rampant disease—many of the problems, including internal political rifts, were self-induced. The choice of location, for instance, was a bad one. Jamestown lay in the midst of a malarial swamp. The settlers had arrived too late to get crops planted. Many in the group were gentlemen unused to work, or their menservants, equally unaccustomed to the hard labor demanded by the harsh task of carving out a viable colony. In a few months, fifty-one of the party were dead; some of the survivors were deserting to the Indians whose land they had invaded. In the "starving time" of 1609–10, the Jamestown settlers were in even worse straits. Only 60 of the 500 colonists survived the period. Disease, famine brought on by drought, and continuing Indian attacks all took their toll. Crazed for food, some of the settlers were reduced to cannibalism, and one contemporary account tells of men "driven through insufferable hunger to eat those things which nature abhorred," raiding both English and Indian graves. In one extreme case, a man killed his wife as she slept and "fed upon her till he had clean devoured all parts saving her head."

AMERICAN VOICES
JOHN SMITH, January 1608
(from Smith's famed memoir in which he writes
of himself in the third person):

Having feasted after their best barbarous manner they could, a long consultation was held, but the conclusion was, two great stones were brought before Powhatan: then as many as could laid hands on him [Smith], dragged him to them, and thereon laid his head, and being ready with their clubs to beat out his brains, Pocahontas, the king's dearest daughter, when no entreaty could prevail, got his head in her arms, and laid her own upon his to save him from death; whereat the emperor was contented he should live. . . . Two days after, Powhatan having disguised himself in the most fearfulest manner he could, caused Captain Smith to be brought forth to a great house in the woods, and there upon a mat by the fire to be left alone. Not long after, from behind a mat that divided the house, was made the most dolefulest noise he ever heard; then Powhatan, more like a devil than man, with some two hundreds more as black as himself, came unto him and told him now they were friends. . . .

Did Pocahontas really save John Smith's life?

A new generation of American children, trotting off to school with Pocahontas lunch boxes, courtesy of Disney, think Pocahontas was an ecologically correct, buxom Indian maiden who fell in love with a hunky John Smith who had a voice just like Mel Gibson's.

If you are a little bit older, this is how you may have learned it in school: Captain John Smith, the fearless leader of the Jamestown colony, was captured by Powhatan's Indians. Powhatan's real name was Wahunsonacock. But he was called Powhatan after his favorite village, which was near present-day Richmond, Virginia. Smith's head was on a stone, ready to be bashed by an Indian war ax, when Pocahontas (a nickname loosely translated as "frisky" — her real name was Matowaka), the eleven-year-old daughter of Chief Powhatan, "took his head in her arms" and begged for Smith's life. The basis for that legend is Smith's own version of events, which he related in the third person in his memoirs, and he was not exactly an impartial witness to history. David Beers Quinn speculates that Smith learned of Powhatan's massacre of the Lost Colonists from the chief himself, but kept this news secret in order to keep the peace with the Indians. This "execution" was actually an initiation ceremony in which Smith was received by the Indians.

One of those larger-than-life characters with mythic stature, Captain John Smith was an English adventurer whose life before Jamestown was an extraordinary one. As a soldier of fortune in the wars between the Holy Roman Empire and the Turks, he rose to captain's rank and had supposedly been held prisoner by the Turkish Pasha and sold as a slave to a young, handsome woman. After escaping, he was rewarded for his services in the war and made a "gentleman." He later became a Mediterranean privateer, returning to London in 1605 to join Bartholomew Gosnold in a new venture into Virginia.

While some large questions exist about Smith's colorful past (documented largely in his own somewhat unreliable writings), there is no doubt that he was instrumental in saving Jamestown from an early extinction. When the Jamestown party fell on hard times, Smith became a virtual military dictator, instituting a brand of martial law that helped save the colony. He became an expert forager and was a successful Indian trader. Without the help of Powhatan's Indians, who shared food with the Englishmen, showed them how to plant local corn and yams, and introduced them to the ways of the forest, the Jamestown colonists would have perished. Yet, in a pattern that would be repeated elsewhere, the settlers eventually turned on the Indians, and fighting between the groups was frequent and fierce. Once respected by the Indians, Smith became feared by them. Smith remained in Jamestown for only two years before setting off on a voyage of exploration that provided valuable maps of the American coast as far north as the "overcold" lands called North Virginia. In 1614, he had sailed north hoping to get rich from whaling or finding gold. Finding neither, he set his crew to catching fish—once again the lowly cod. After exploring the inlets of the Chesapeake Bay, he also charted the coastline from Maine to Cape Cod and gave the land a new name—New England. Smith apparently also made a fortune in the cod he had caught and stored. He had also lured twenty-seven natives on to the ship and took them back to Europe to be sold as slaves in Spain.

But his mark on the colony was indelible. A hero of the American past? Yes, but, like most heroes, not without flaws.

After Smith's departure, his supposed savior, Pocahontas, continued to play a role in the life of the colony. During the sporadic battles between settlers and Indians, Pocahontas, now seventeen years old, was kidnapped and held hostage by the colonists. While a prisoner, she caught the attention of the settler John Rolfe, who married the Indian princess, as one account put it, "for the good of the plantation," cementing a temporary peace with the Indians. In 1615, Rolfe took the Indian princess and their son to London, where she was a sensation, even earning a royal audience. She also encountered John Smith, who had let her think that he was dead. Renamed Lady Rebecca after her baptism, she died of smallpox in England.

Besides this notable marriage, Rolfe's other distinction was his role in the event that truly saved Jamestown and changed the course of American history. In 1612, he crossed native Virginia tobacco with seed from a milder Jamaican leaf, and Virginia had its first viable cash crop. London soon went tobacco mad, and in a very short space of time, tobacco was sown on every available square foot of plantable land in Virginia.

AMERICAN VOICES
POWHATAN to John Smith, 1607:

> Why will you take by force what you may have quietly by love? Why will you destroy us who supply you with food? What can you get by war? . . . In these wars, my men must sit up watching, and if a twig breaks, they all cry out "Here comes Captain Smith!" So I must end my miserable life. Take away your guns and swords, the cause of all our jealousy, or you may all die in the same manner.

What was the House of Burgesses?

Despite the tobacco profits, controlled in London by a monopoly, Jamestown limped along near extinction. Survival remained a day-to-day affair while political intrigues back in London reshaped the colony's destiny. Virginia Company shareholders were angry that their investment was turning out to be a bust, and believed that the "Magazine," a small group of Virginia Company members who exclusively supplied the colony's provisions, were draining off profits. A series of reforms was instituted, the most important of which meant settlers could own their land, rather than just working for the company. And the arbitrary rule of the governor was replaced by English common law.

In 1619, new management was brought to the Virginia Company, and Governor Yeardley of Virginia summoned an elected legislative assembly—the House of Burgesses—which met in Jamestown that year. (A burgess is a person invested with all the privileges of a citizen, and comes from the same root as the French *bourgeois*.) Besides the governor, there were six councilors appointed by the governor, and two elected representatives from each private estate and two from each of the company's four estates or tracts. (Landowning males over seventeen years old were eligible to vote.) Their first meeting was cut short by an onslaught of malaria and July heat. While any decisions they made required approval of the company in London, this was clearly the seed from which American representative government would grow.

The little assembly had a shaky beginning, from its initial malarial summer. In the first place, the House of Burgesses was not an instant solution to the serious problems still faced by the Jamestown settlers. Despite years of immigration to the new colony, Jamestown's rate of attrition during those first years was horrific. Lured by the prospect of owning land, some 6,000 settlers had been transported to Virginia by 1624. However, a census that year showed only 1,277 colonists alive. A Royal Council asked, "What has become of the five thousand missing subjects of His Majesty?"

Many of them had starved. Others had died in fierce Indian fighting, including some 350 colonists who were killed in a 1622 massacre when the Indians, fearful at the disappearance of their lands, nearly pushed the colony back into the Chesapeake Bay. Responding to the troubles at Jamestown and the mismanagement of the colony, the king revoked the Virginia Company's charter in 1624, and Virginia became a royal colony. Under the new royal governor, Thomas Wyatt, however, the House of Burgesses survived on an extralegal basis and would have much influence in the years ahead.

Exactly how representative that house was in those days is another question. Certainly women didn't vote. Before 1619, there were few women in Jamestown, and in that year a shipload of "ninety maidens" arrived to be presented as wives to the settlers. The going price for one of the brides: 120 pounds of tobacco as payment for her transport from England.

Ironically, in the same year that representative government took root in America, an ominous cargo of people arrived in the port of Jamestown. Like the women, these new arrivals couldn't vote, and also like the women, they brought a price. These were the first African slaves to be sold in the American colonies.

Who started the slave trade?

While everyone wants a piece of the claim to the discovery of America, no one wants to be known for having started the slave trade. The unhappy distinction probably belongs to Portugal, where ten black Africans were taken about fifty years before Columbus sailed. But by no means did the Portuguese enjoy a monopoly. The Spanish quickly began to import this cheap human labor to their American lands. In 1562, the English seaman John Hawkins began a direct slave trade between Guinea and the West Indies. By 1600, the Dutch and French were also caught up in the "traffick in men," and by the time those first twenty Africans arrived in Jamestown aboard a Dutch slaver, a million or more black slaves had already been brought to the Spanish and Portuguese colonies in the Caribbean and South America.

Who were the Pilgrims, and what did they want?

The year after the House of Burgesses met for the first time, the Pilgrims of the *Mayflower* founded the second permanent English settlement in America. Their arrival in 1620 has always been presented as another of history's lucky accidents. But was it?

Had Christopher Jones, captain of the *Mayflower*, turned the ship when he was supposed to, the little band would have gone to its intended destination, the mouth of the Hudson, future site of New York, and a settlement within the bounds of the Virginia Company's charter and authority. Instead, the ship kept a westerly route—the result of a bribe to the captain, as London gossip had it—and in November 1620, the band of pioneers found safe harbor in Cape Cod Bay, coming ashore at the site of present-day Provincetown. Of the 102 men, women, and children aboard the small ship, fifty were so-called Pilgrims, who called themselves "Saints" or "First Comers."

Here again, as it had in Queen Elizabeth's time, the Protestant Reformation played a crucial role in events. After the great split from Roman Catholicism that created the Church of England, the question of religious reform continued heatedly in England. Many English remained Catholic. Others felt that the Church of England was too "popish" and wished to push it further away from Rome—to "purify" it—so they were called Puritans. But even among Puritans strong differences existed, and there were those who thought the Church of England too corrupt. They wanted autonomy for their congregations, and wished to separate from the Anglican church. This sect of Separatists—viewed in its day the same way extremist religious cults are thought of in our time—went too far for the taste of the authorities, and they were forced either underground or out of England.

A small band of Separatists, now called Pilgrims, went to Leyden, Holland, where their reformist ideas were accepted. But cut off from their English traditions, the group decided on another course, a fresh start in the English lands in America. With the permission of the Virginia Company and the backing of London merchants who charged handsome interest on the loans they made, the Pilgrims sailed from Plymouth in 1620. Among their number were the Pilgrim families of William Brewster, John Carver, Edward Winslow, and William Bradford. The "strangers," or non-Pilgrim voyagers (men faithful to the Church of England, but who had signed on for the passage in the hope of owning property in the New World), included ship's cooper John Alden and army captain Miles Standish.

What was the Mayflower Compact?

When the rough seas around Nantucket forced the ship back to Cape Cod and the group decided to land outside the bounds of the Virginia Company, the "strangers" declared that they would be free from any commands. Responding quickly to this threat of mutiny, the Pilgrim leaders composed a short statement of self-government, signed by almost all the adult men.

This agreement, the Mayflower Compact, is rightly considered the first written constitution in North America. Cynicism about its creation, or for that matter about the House of Burgesses, is easy in hindsight. Yes, these noble-minded pioneers slaughtered Indians with little remorse, kept servants and slaves, and treated women no differently from cattle. They were imperfect men whose failings must be regarded alongside their astonishing attempt to create in America a place like none in Europe. As the historian Samuel Eliot Morison put it in *The Oxford History of the American People*, "This compact is an almost startling revelation of the capacity of Englishmen in that era for self-government. Moreover, it was a second instance of the Englishmen's determination to live in the colonies under a rule of law."

Despite their flaws, the early colonists taking their toddling steps toward self-rule must be contrasted with other colonies, including English colonies, in various parts of the world where the law was simply the will of the king or the church.

AMERICAN VOICES
From the Mayflower Compact (signed December 1620):

We whose names are under-written . . . doe by these presents solemnly and mutually in the presence of God, and one of another, covenant and combine our selves togeather into a civil body politick, for our better ordering and preservation and furtherance of the ends aforesaid; and by vertue hearof to enacte, constitute, and frame such just and equal lawes, ordinances, acts, constitutions, and offices, from time to time, as shall be thought most meete for the

generall good of the Colonie, unto which we promise all
due submission and obedience. . . .

Did the Pilgrims really land at Plymouth Rock?

After a brief exploration of Cape Cod, the *Mayflower* group sailed
on and found a broad, round harbor that they recognized from Captain John Smith's maps as Plimoth (Plymouth). The Indians called it
Patuxet. On December 16, the *Mayflower*'s passengers reached their
new home. There is no mention in any historical account of Plymouth
Rock, the large stone that can be seen in Plymouth today, into which
the year 1620 is carved. The notion that the Pilgrims landed near the
rock and carved the date is a tradition that was created at least a hundred years later, probably by some smart member of the first Plymouth
Chamber of Commerce.

Like the first arrivals at Jamestown, the Pilgrims and "strangers" had
come to Plymouth at a bad time to start planting a colony. By spring,
pneumonia and the privations of a hard winter had cost the lives of
fifty-two of the 102 immigrants. But in March, salvation came, much
as it had in Virginia, in the form of Indians, including one named
Squanto, who could speak English. Who Squanto was and how he
came to speak English are among history's unsolved mysteries. One
claim is made for an Indian named Tisquantum who had been captured by an English slaver in 1615. A second is made for an Indian
named Tasquantum, brought to England in 1605. Whichever he was,
he moved into the house of William Bradford, governor of the Plymouth colony, and was the means of survival for the Pilgrims until his
death from fever in 1622. Another Indian of great value to the Pilgrim
Fathers was Samoset, a local chief who also spoke English and introduced the settlers to the grand chief of the Wampanoags, Wasamegin,
better known by his title Massasoit. Under the rule of Massasoit, the
Indians became loyal friends to the Pilgrims, and it was Massasoit's
braves who were the invited guests to the October feast at which the
Pilgrims celebrated their first harvest. For three days the colonists and
their Indian allies feasted on turkey and venison, pumpkin and corn.

It was the first Thanksgiving. (Thanksgiving was first officially cele-brated during the presidency of Abraham Lincoln in 1864. It became a national holiday and was moved to its November date by President Franklin D. Roosevelt.)

While life did not magically improve after that first year, the Pil-grims carved out a decent existence and, through trade with the Indi-ans, were able to repay their debts to the London backers and even to buy out the shares that these London merchants held. Their success helped inspire an entire wave of immigration to New England that came to be known as the Great Puritan migration. From 1629 to 1642, between 14,000 and 20,000 settlers left England for the West Indies and New England, and most of these were Anglican Puritans brought over by a new joint stock company called the Massachusetts Bay Com-pany. They came because life in England under King Charles I had grown intolerable for Puritans. Though the newcomers demonstrated a startling capacity for fighting among themselves, usually over church matters, these squabbles led to the settlement and development of early New England.

Must Read: *Mayflower* by Nathaniel Philbrick.

HIGHLIGHTS IN THE DEVELOPMENT OF NEW ENGLAND

1629 Naumkeag, later called Salem, is founded to accept first wave of 1,000 Puritan settlers.

1630 John Winthrop, carrying the Massachusetts Bay Charter, arrives at Naumkeag and later establishes Boston, named after England's great Puritan city. (In 1635, English High and Latin School, the first secondary school in America, is founded. The following year a college for the training of clergymen is founded at Cambridge and named Harvard after a benefactor in 1639.)

1634 Two hundred settlers, half of them Protestant, arrive at Chesa-peake Bay and found St. Mary's, in the new colony of Maryland, granted to Cecil Calvert, Lord Baltimore, who instructs his brother, the colony's leader, to tolerate the Puritans. The so-called Catholic colony, ostensibly named for Charles I's Queen Henrietta Maria, but in fact named to honor the Virgin Mary, will have a Protestant majority from the beginning.

1636 Reverend Thomas Hooker leads a group into Connecticut and founds Hartford; other Connecticut towns are soon founded.

1636 Roger Williams, a religious zealot banished from Boston by Governor Winthrop, founds Providence, Rhode Island, preaching radical notions of separation of church and state and paying Indians for land.

1636–1637 The Pequot War, the first major conflict, is fought between English colonists, joined by their Native American allies (the Mohegan and Narragansett), against the Pequot, a nation that was essentially wiped out in a brief but brutal war.

1638 Anne Hutchinson, banished from Boston for her heretical interpretations of sermons, which drew large, enthusiastic crowds, settles near Providence and starts Portsmouth. (Newport is founded about the same time.) In 1644, Rhode Island receives a royal colonial charter.

1638 New Haven founded.

1643 New England Confederation, a loose union to settle border disputes, is formed by Connecticut, New Haven, Plymouth, and Massachusetts Bay Colony.

AMERICAN VOICES
NATHANIEL MORTON, 1634, witnessing
Roger Williams's demands for freedom of religion
from the Massachusetts Bay Colony:

Whereupon [Williams] never came to the Church Assembly more, professing separation from them as Antichristian, and not only so, but he withdrew all private religious Communion from any that would hold Communion with the Church there, insomuch as he would not pray nor give thanks at meals with his own wife nor any of his family, because they went to the Church Assemblies.

The prudent Magistrates understanding, and seeing things grow more and more towards a general division and disturbance, after all other means used in vain, they passed a sentence of banishment against him out of the Massachusetts Colony, as against a disturber of the peace, both of the Church and Commonwealth. After which Mr. Williams sat down in a place called Providence . . . and was followed by many of the members of the Church of Salem, who did zealously adhere to him, and who cried out of the Persecution that was against him, keeping that one principle, *that every one should have the liberty to worship God according to the light of their own consciences.* [Emphasis added.]

Born in London, Roger Williams (1603?–83), a clergyman, was a strong supporter of religious and political liberty and believed that people had a right to complete religious freedom, rather than mere religious toleration that could be denied at the government's will.

Williams entered Cambridge University, where he received a bachelor's degree in 1627. A religious nonconformist, he disagreed with the principles of England's official church, the Church of England. At the time, King Charles I and William Laud, bishop of London, were persecuting dissenters, and as a result, Williams began to associate with nonconformists who were anxious to settle in New England.

Williams and his wife came to the Massachusetts Bay Colony in 1631. After refusing an invitation to become the minister of the church in Boston because he opposed its ties to the Church of England, he became the minister of the church at nearby Salem. There, many people favored his desire to have a church that was independent of the Church of England and of the colonial government. But Williams gained a reputation as a troublemaker when he argued that the royal charter did not justify taking land that belonged to the Indians, and he declared that people should not be punished for religious differences. When threatened by authorities, he fled into the wilderness in 1636, and Narragansett Indians provided Williams with land beyond the borders of Massachusetts where he founded Providence, later the capital of Rhode Island.

Williams established a government for Providence based on the consent of the settlers and on complete freedom of religion. In 1643, American colonists organized the New England Confederation without including the Providence settlement or other settlements in Rhode Island, because of disagreement with their system of government and of religious freedom.

Williams's most famous work, *The Bloudy Tenent of Persecution* (1644), stated his argument for the separation of church and state. He wrote it as part of a long dispute with John Cotton, the Puritan leader of Massachusetts Bay Colony, and it explained his belief that the church had to be spiritually pure to prepare corrupt and fallen human beings for eternity, and that governments were for earthly purposes only. From 1654 to 1657, Williams was president of the Rhode Island colony. In 1657, he contributed to Rhode Island's decision to provide refuge for Quakers who had been banished from other colonies, even though he disagreed with their religious teachings. Williams earned his living by farming and trading with the Indians. He went on missionary journeys among them and compiled a dictionary of their language. While he had always been a close friend of the Indians, he acted as a captain of the Providence militia and fought against the Indians during King Philip's War (see Chapter 2, p. 49). He died in 1683.

Who started New York?

The Englishmen who were quickly populating the Atlantic seaboard from the Carolinas to New England had no monopoly on the New World. French and Dutch explorers had also been busy, and both nations were carving out separate territories in North America. The Dutch founded New Netherlands in the Hudson Valley of present-day New York State, basing their claims upon the explorations of Henry Hudson in 1609.

An Englishman, Hudson was hired by a Dutch company that wanted to find the Northeast Passage, the sea route to China along the northern rim of Asia. In 1609, Hudson set off instead, aboard the *Half Moon*, for the northwest alternative. Sailing down the Atlantic coast, he entered Chesapeake Bay before making a U-turn and heading back north to explore the Hudson River as far upriver as Albany. Noting the absence of tides, he correctly assumed that this route did not lead to the Pacific. (As noted, the ill-fated Hudson had even worse luck. During another voyage in search of the Northwest Passage, Hudson's crew mutinied in 1611 and put their captain into an open boat in Hudson Bay.)

England was flexing its new muscles in the early 1600s, but it was the Dutch who had become the true world power in maritime matters by building the world's largest merchant marine fleet. There was literally not a place in the known world of that day in which the Dutch did not have a hand in matters. Amsterdam had become the busiest and richest city in the European world. In 1621, the Dutch West India Company was formed with the aim of taking over trade between Europe and the New World, and the Dutch soon took from the Portuguese control of the lucrative slave and sugar trades. Fort Orange, the site of present-day Albany, took hold as a fur trading outpost in 1624. Two years later, the trading village of New Amsterdam, later to be renamed New York, was established at the mouth of the Hudson. The Dutch West India Company did more than trade and set up colonies. In 1628, the Dutch admiral Piet Hein captured a Spanish treasure fleet, pirating away enough silver to provide company shareholders with a 75 percent dividend.

Did the Indians really sell Manhattan for $24?

The first Dutch settlers to arrive on the narrow, twelve-mile-long island of Manhattan didn't bother to pay the Indians for the land they chose for their settlement. But when Peter Minuit arrived in the spring of 1624 and was chosen as leader of the settlement, he quickly met with the local Indian chiefs. Before them he set a sales agreement for all of Manhattan Island and two boxes of trade goods—probably hatchets, cloth, metal pots, and bright beads—worth sixty Dutch guilders. At the time, that equaled 2,400 English cents, which has come down in history as the famous $24 figure.

From its inception, Dutch New Amsterdam was far less pious and more rowdy than Puritan New England. As a trading outpost it attracted a different breed of settler, and unlike Boston, taverns in New

Amsterdam quickly outnumbered churches. As few Dutch settlers were lured to the new colony by the promise of low pay to work on West India Company farms, the company welcomed settlers from any nation, and by 1640, at least eighteen languages were spoken in New York, a polyglot tradition that was to continue throughout the city's history.

Must Read: *The Island at the Center of the World* by Russell Shorto.

How did New Amsterdam become New York?

The Dutch got New York cheap. The English went them one better. They simply took it for nothing. Why pay for what you can steal?

Dutch rule in America was not long-lived, but it was certainly influential in the stamp it put on the future New York. It was the Dutch who erected, as a defense against Indians, the wall in lower Manhattan from which Wall Street takes its name. And what would some Dutch burgher think of finding today's Bowery instead of the tidy *bouweries*, or farms, that had been neatly laid out in accordance with a plan drawn up in Amsterdam? Besides the settlement on Manhattan island, the Dutch had also established villages, such as Breukelen and Haarlem. And early Dutch and Walloon (Belgian Protestant) settlers included the ancestors of the Roosevelt clan.

New Amsterdam developed far differently from the English colonies, which held out the promise of land ownership for at least some of its settlers. Promising to bring over fifty settlers to work the land, a few wealthy Dutch landholders, or *patroons*, were able to secure huge tracts along the Hudson in a system that more closely resembled medieval European feudalism than anything else, a system that continued well after the Revolution and that contributed to New York's reputation as an aristocratic (and, during the Revolution, loyalist) stronghold.

New Amsterdam became New York in one of the only truly bloodless battles in American history. As the two principal competing nations of the early seventeenth century, England and Holland sporadically came to war, and when Charles II reclaimed the throne in 1661 after the period of Oliver Cromwell's Protectorate, he asserted English rights to North America. Charles II granted his brother, the Duke of York, the largest and richest territorial grant ever made by an English monarch. It included all of present New York, the entire region from the Connecticut to the Delaware rivers, Long Island, Nantucket, Martha's Vineyard, and the present state of Maine. In 1664, four English frigates carrying 1,000 soldiers sailed into New York Harbor. The Dutch and other settlers there, unhappy with the administration of the West India Company, gladly accepted English terms despite Peter Stuyvesant's blustery call to resist. Without a shot fired, New Amsterdam became New York.

The Duke of York in turn generously created a new colony when he split off two large tracts of land and gave one each to two friends, Sir George Carteret and Lord John Berkeley, an area that would become New Jersey. Also gained as part of this annexation was a settlement known as New Sweden. Established in 1638 by Peter Minuit (dismissed earlier as governor of New Amsterdam and now in Swedish employ), and centered on the site of Wilmington, Delaware, New Sweden had fallen to the Dutch under Stuyvesant in 1655. (Although this Swedish colony had little lasting impact on American history, the Swedes did make one enormous contribution. They brought with them the log cabin, the construction destined to become the chief form of pioneer housing in the spreading American frontier of the eighteenth century.)

The English exercised a surprisingly tolerant hands-off policy in ruling the former New Amsterdam. Life as it had been under Dutch rule continued for many years.

AMERICAN VOICES
JACQUES CARTIER (1491–1557),
French explorer, on the Hurons:

The tribe has no belief in God that amounts to anything; for they believe in a god they call *Cudouagny*, and maintain that he often holds intercourse with them and tells that what the weather will be like. They also say that when he gets angry with them, he throws dust in their eyes. They believe furthermore that when they die they go to the stars and descend on the horizon like the stars. . . . After they had explained these things to us, we showed them their error and informed them that *Cudouagny* was a wicked spirit who deceived them, and that there is but one God, Who is in Heaven, Who gives everything we need and is the Creator of all things and that in Him alone we should believe. Also that one must receive baptism or perish in hell. . . .

When did the French reach the New World?

French attempts to gain a piece of the riches of the New World began in earnest with Jacques Cartier's voyage of 1534, another expedition in the ongoing search for a China route. Cartier's explorations took him to Newfoundland, discovered by Cabot almost forty years earlier, and up the Gulf of St. Lawrence, sailing as far as the Huron Indian villages of Stadacona (modern Quebec) and Hochelaga (Montreal). In 1541, Cartier's attempt to settle a colony failed and he returned to France. In 1564, during France's religious civil wars, a Huguenot colony was established on the coast of Florida near present-day Jacksonville. The colony, Fort Caroline, was completely destroyed and its inhabitants massacred in 1565 by the Spanish under the command of Admiral Pedro Menéndez, the founder of Saint Augustine, Florida. The slaughter of the French Protestants signaled the end of France's attempts to settle the future United States and they shifted their attention north.

While cod fishermen from France, as well as England and Portugal, continued to make temporary settlements around Newfoundland, the French also began some early fur trading with Indians that would provide France with the real economic impetus for its colonizing efforts. In 1600, Tadoussac, a French trading post on the St. Lawrence, was founded.

The key mover in the French era of exploration was Samuel de Champlain, who founded Quebec in 1608, the year after Jamestown was settled. Champlain made friends with the Algonquian and Huron Indians living nearby and began to trade with them for furs. The two tribes also wanted French help in wars against their main enemy, the powerful Iroquois Indians. In 1609, Champlain and two other French fur traders helped their Indian friends defeat the Iroquois in battle. After this battle, the Iroquois were also enemies of the French. The Huron lived in an area the French called Huronia. Champlain persuaded the Huron to allow Roman Catholic missionaries to work among them and introduce them to Christianity. The missionaries, especially the Jesuit order, explored much of what is now southern Ontario.

Like the Dutch in New Amsterdam, the French explorers who started New France were primarily interested in trading, as opposed to the English settlers of New England and Virginia, who were planting farms and permanent communities.

An inevitable head-to-head confrontation between England and France, already the two great European powers, over sovereignty in the New World existed almost from the beginning of the colonial period. A Scots expedition took a French fort in Acadia, and it was renamed Nova Scotia (New Scotland). Then, in 1629, an English pirate briefly captured Quebec. While New England and the other English colonies were taking in thousands of new settlers during the massive immigration of the mid-seventeenth century, the French were slow to build a colonial presence, and settlers were slow to arrive in New France. Worse for France than the threat of English attack were the Iroquois, the powerful confederacy of five tribes of Indians in New York, and the best organized and strongest tribal grouping in North America at the time. The Iroquois were sworn enemies of France's Indian trading partners, the Huron and Algonquian Indians, and a long series of devastating wars with the Iroquois preoccupied the French during much of their early colonial period.

But if the French failed as colony builders, they excelled as explorers. Led by the *coureurs de bois*, the young French trappers and traders, Frenchmen were expanding their reach into the North American heartland. One of these, Medard Chouart, mapped the Lake Superior–Hudson Bay region and then sold the information to the English, who formed the Hudson Bay Company to exploit the knowledge. An even greater quest came in 1673, when Louis Jolliet and the Jesuit priest Jacques Marquette set out from Lake Michigan and eventually reached the Mississippi, letting the current carry them down into the American South as far as the Arkansas River. Based on these expeditions, the French laid a claim in 1671 to all of western North America in the name of King Louis XIV, the Sun King, a claim reexerted in 1682 by

La Salle, a young French nobleman who named the province Louisiana in honor of his king. From the outset, the English would contest this claim. The stage was set for an epic contest over a very substantial prize—all of North America. La Salle, like Hudson, was another of history's glorious losers. In 1684, at the head of another expedition, La Salle mistook the entrance to Matagorda Bay, in Texas, for the mouth of the Mississippi. He spent two years in a vain search for the great river. Tired of the hardships they were forced to endure, La Salle's men mutinied and murdered him in 1687.

AMERICAN VOICES
FATHER JACQUES MARQUETTE, June 17, 1673,
describing his travels down the Mississippi:

Behold us, then, upon this celebrated river, whose singularities I have attentively studied. The Mississippi takes its rise in several lakes in the North. Its channel is very narrow at the mouth of the Mesconsin [Wisconsin], and runs south until is affected by very high hills. Its current is slow because of its depth. . . . We met from time to time monstrous fish, which struck so violently against our canoes, that at first we took them to be large trees which threatened to upset us. We saw also a hideous monster; his head was like that of a tiger, his nose was sharp, and somewhat resembled a wildcat; his beard was long; his ears stood upright; the color of his head was gray, and his neck black. He looked upon us for some time, but as we came near him our oars frightened him away. . . . We considered that the advantage of our travels would be altogether lost to our nation if we fell into the hands of the Spaniards, from whom we could expect no other treatment than death or slavery.

Jacques Marquette (1637–75) was a French explorer and Roman Catholic missionary in North America. When he and French-Canadian explorer Louis Jolliet went down the Mississippi River, they were probably the first whites to explore the upper Mississippi and parts of Illinois and Wisconsin. The Indians often talked about a great river called the Mississippi, a word that meant "big river" in their language. At that time, little was known about North America, and Marquette thought the river might flow into the Pacific Ocean.

In May 1673, Marquette, Jolliet, and five other men set out in two canoes and eventually reached the Mississippi and realized that it flowed south. They decided that the river probably flowed into the Gulf of Mexico, rather than into the Pacific Ocean. Along the way, they met many friendly Indians. But when the men reached the mouth of the Arkansas River, they encountered hostile Indians. A friendly Indian told Marquette that whites lived farther south on the river. The explorers realized these people must be Spaniards who had settled along the Gulf of Mexico. Marquette and Jolliet feared that the Indians and Spaniards would attack them. Having learned the course of the river, they turned back and traveled up the Mississippi to the Illinois River and from there to the Kankakee River. They journeyed overland from the Kankakee to the Chicago River and on to Lake Michigan. Their journey had taken about five months.

In 1674, Marquette set out from near present-day Green Bay, Wisconsin, to establish a mission among the Kaskaskia Indians near Ottawa, Illinois. But he became ill and died in the spring of 1675.

Why is Pennsylvania the Quaker State?

While the French were making their claims, the English carved out another major colonial territory in 1682, virtually completing the quilt that would become the original thirteen colonies. This was the "holy experiment" of William Penn, one of the most fascinating characters in America's early history. Although the colony, which was named for its founder's father, and its chief city, Philadelphia (City of Brotherly Love), quickly became vibrant centers of commerce and culture, it was primarily founded to allow the Society of Friends, or Quakers, a place to worship, and to permit religious tolerance for all.

A highly individualistic left-wing Protestant sect founded in England by George Fox around 1650, the Friends had an impact on America far greater than their numbers would suggest. But life was never simple for them, in England or the colonies. Fox believed that no ministry or clergy was necessary for worship, and that the word of God was found in the human soul, not necessarily in the Bible, eliminating almost all vestiges of organized religion, including church buildings and formal liturgy. In a Friends meeting, members sat in silent meditation until the "inward light," a direct spiritual communication from God, caused a believer to physically tremble or quake, the source of the group's commonly used name. Fox also took literally the commandment "Thou shalt not kill," beginning a long tradition of Quaker pacifism.

Of course, these notions did not sit well with either the religious or the political authorities, and the Quakers were vigorously persecuted from the beginning. Three thousand English Quakers were imprisoned under Charles II. In America, where freedom to worship had been the ostensible motivating force for many colonists, every colony but Roger Williams's Rhode Island passed strident anti-Quaker laws. The worst of these was in Puritan Massachusetts, where a number of Quakers were hanged when they returned to Boston after having been banished. Back in England, William Penn, the son of a prominent and powerful admiral, became a zealous follower of Fox in 1667, and his devotion, expressed in a tract entitled *The Sandy Foundation Shaken*, earned Penn a stint in the Tower of London. Released through his father's influence, Penn became a trustee of the Quaker community in West Jersey and later, with an inheritance and a proprietary grant from the Duke of York (in payment of debts owed Penn's father), Penn took possession of the territory that would become Pennsylvania.

As with other proprietary grants of colonial territory, Pennsylvania already belonged to somebody, namely the Indians who lived there. But Penn, unlike many other early founders, believed in the rights of the Indians, and on a journey to America in 1682 he negotiated a price for Pennsylvania. Like many colonial chapters, Penn's Indian dealings are obscured by mythology. In a famous painting, Penn is depicted making a treaty under the elm tree at Shackamaxon, a treaty that didn't exist. Part of the deal was known as the Walking Purchase, in which Penn vowed to take only as much land as a man could walk in three days. Penn took a leisurely stroll. (Penn's successors were not as charitable. His son hired three runners to head off at a good pace, and the Indians were forced to relinquish a good bit more of their hunting grounds.)

The new colony faced few of the privations that the first generation of colonists had suffered. In the first place, the territory was already settled by the Swedes who had begun New Sweden, and food was plentiful. Besides the English Quakers, the colony attracted many Dutch and German Quakers and other sects lured by Penn's promise of religious tolerance and the generous terms offered by Penn for buying the new colony's extensive lands. In 1683, for instance, a group of Mennonite families from the Rhineland founded the settlement of Germantown. By 1685, the colony's population numbered nearly 9,000.

Penn's liberal religious views were mirrored in his political beliefs. He developed a plan for a colonial union, and his Frame of Government provided a remarkably progressive constitution for the colony, which included selection of a governor (at first, Penn himself) by ballot. By 1700, Philadelphia trailed only Boston as an American cultural center, possessing the second colonial printing press, the third colonial newspaper, the Penn Charter school, and the colony's best hospital and charitable institutions, all a legacy of Penn's Quaker conscience.

Penn himself fared not nearly as well. He became embroiled in political and financial feuds, even being accused of treason by William and Mary. He lost possession of the colony for a period, but regained it in 1694. Money problems landed him in debtors' prison, and a stroke left him incapacitated. But his legacy of practical idealism marks Penn as one of America's early heroes. And the Quaker traditions of nonviolence and social justice that he established left indelible marks on American history as Quakers stood in the forefront of such movements as Abolitionism, Prohibition, universal suffrage, and pacifism.

What were the thirteen original colonies?

With Pennsylvania quickly established, all but one of the thirteen future states were in place by the end of the seventeenth century. In order of settlement, they were as follows:

1607 Virginia (Jamestown)

1620 Massachusetts (Plymouth and Massachusetts Bay Colony)

1626   New York (originally New Amsterdam; annexed by the English)

1633   Maryland

1636   Rhode Island

1636   Connecticut

1638   Delaware (originally New Sweden; annexed by the Dutch and later the English)

1638   New Hampshire

1653   North Carolina

1663   South Carolina

1664   New Jersey

1682   Pennsylvania

1732   Georgia, last of the original thirteen, was founded by James Oglethorpe, a humanitarian interested in recruiting settlers from English debtors' prisons. The colony, which became another haven for persecuted Protestants, was of special strategic importance, standing as a buffer between South Carolina and possible attacks from Spanish Florida and French Louisiana.

CHAPTER TWO

SAY YOU WANT A REVOLUTION

What was King Philip's War?

What was Nat Bacon's Rebellion?

Who were the witches of Salem?

What was the Great Awakening?

What was John Peter Zenger on trial for?

Who fought the French and Indian War?

What do sugar and stamps have to do with revolutions?

What was the Boston Massacre?

What was the Boston Tea Party about?

What was the First Continental Congress? Who chose its members, who were they, and what did they do?

Somebody dumped some tea into Boston Harbor. Somebody else hung some lights in a church steeple. Paul Revere went riding around the countryside at midnight. Jefferson penned the Declaration. There were a few battles and a rough winter at Valley Forge. But George Washington kicked out the British.

That's the sum of the impression many people keep of the American Revolution. It was not that simple or easy.

This chapter highlights some of the major events in the colonial period leading up to the War of Independence, along with the milestones in the political and military victory over England.

AMERICAN VOICES

An account of the battle against the Pequot Indians,
from GOVERNOR WILLIAM BRADFORD'S
History of the Plymouth Plantation:

> It was a fearful sight to see them thus frying in the fyer, and the streams of blood quenching the same, and horrible was the stincke and sente there of, but the victory seemed a sweet sacrifice, and they gave the prayers thereof to God, who had wrought so wonderfully for them. . . .

What was King Philip's War?

We tend to think of the colonial period after the early "starving time" as a rather calm era in which Yankee resourcefulness and the Puritan work ethic came to the fore, forging a new American character that would burst forth into nationhood in 1776.

Overlooked in this view is the genocidal campaign carried out against the Indians by the Pilgrim fathers and other colonists. The English, French, and Dutch could be as ruthlessly cruel and deadly as the worst of the conquistadores. In 1643, for instance, following the murder of a Dutch farmer, the governor of New Amsterdam ordered the massacre of the Wappinger, a friendly tribe that had come to the Dutch seeking shelter. Eighty Indians were killed in their sleep, decapitated, and their heads displayed on poles in Manhattan. A Dutch lady kicked the heads down the street. One captive was castrated, skinned alive, and forced to eat his own flesh as the Dutch governor looked on and laughed.

In New England, the first of two Indian wars was fought against the Pequot, a powerful Mohican clan treated by the English as a threat. Urged on by Boston preachers and using a trumped-up murder charge as a pretext, the Puritans declared all-out war on the Pequot in 1637.

It was not a war fought by the chivalrous standards of European engagement. The Puritans sacked and burned Indian villages by night. Aided by loyal Narragansett and Mohican forces, the colonial equivalent of a search-and-destroy team entered a stockaded Pequot town near the Mystic River, slaughtered its 600 inhabitants, and burned the village. In the only other confrontation of the war, a group of Pequot was trapped. The men were killed, the boys sold to slavers, and the women and girls kept by the Puritans as slaves. As a tribe, the Pequot were practically exterminated.

The English maintained peace for nearly forty years thanks to their old allies, Massasoit's Wampanoag—saviors of the Pilgrims—and the Narragansett led by Canonicus (who had sheltered Roger Williams after he was banished from Boston). When these two chiefs died, the English were ready to complete the subjugation of the New England Indians. But Massasoit's son Metacom, called King Philip by the English for his adoption of European dress and customs, struck back.

The fighting took place in the summer of 1676, and for the colonists it wasn't as easy as the Pequot battles had been. The combat was the fiercest in New England history, and far bloodier than much of the fighting during the Revolution. Metacom's Indians were equipped with guns and armor acquired through trade, and he was an aggressive leader. The outcome of this war was not assured, particularly in the early going. But the colonists had too much on their side: superior numbers—including 500 Mohican gunmen, blood rivals of the Wampanoag—and devastating battle tactics, including a return to the wholesale massacre of noncombatants.

King Philip was ultimately killed, his head displayed on a pole. His wife and son, the grandson of the chief who had saved the Pilgrims, were sold into slavery in the West Indies, an act of mercy according to the leading Puritan clerics.

What was Nat Bacon's Rebellion?

As the New England colonists learned at great cost from Metacom, the "Indian problem" was not a simple matter. Massed confrontations were risky, so new tactics emerged. The colonists found an effective measure in the "scalp bounty," a Dutch innovation in which a fee was paid for Indian scalps. The common conception is of Indians as scalp takers, but it was the colonists who adopted the tactic as a means of Indian control, and it even became a profitable enterprise. In the Bay Colony in 1703, a scalp brought 12 pounds sterling, a price inflated to 100 pounds by 1722. The most famous American scalp taker of the colonial period was a woman named Hannah Dustin, who was taken captive in 1695 in Haverhill, Massachusetts. She and two other captives killed ten of the twelve Indians holding them. Dustin left but then returned to take their scalps, believing that the Massachusetts Bay Colony would still pay a bounty for the scalps. In her hometown, Dustin was later memorialized with a statue showing her holding a hatchet in one hand and the scalps in the other. It was the first permanent statue built to honor a woman in American history. (The story of Hannah Dustin and relations between colonial settlers and Indians, especially in New England, is recounted in more detail in my recent book *America's Hidden History*.)

In 1676, while New England struggled against King Philip, the Indian issue boiled over into something different in Virginia. This overlooked episode, known as Nat Bacon's Rebellion, can be seen as another in a series of wrongs committed against the Indians. But it was also a demonstration of a new anti-authority sentiment in America, a foreshadowing of the Revolutionary spirit.

A cousin to the scientist and philosopher Sir Francis Bacon, Nathaniel Bacon was a young planter and an up-and-coming member of Virginia's ruling elite. At the time, Virginians were fighting sporadic battles with the Susquehannock, the result of treaties broken by the English. When his plantation overseer was killed, Bacon grew angry at what he thought was the docile Indian policy of Virginia's Governor Berkeley. Without the governor's permission, Bacon raised a militia force of 500 men and vented his rage on the Indians. When his little army attacked the peaceful Occaneechee (instead of the more warlike Susquehannock), Bacon became an immediate local hero, especially among the Indian-hating frontier colonists who favored pushing farther west. In his *Declaration of the People,* written exactly 100 years before another Virginian wrote another declaration, Bacon criticized the Berkeley administration for levying unfair taxes, placing favorites in high positions, and not protecting the western farmers from Indians. Governor Berkeley branded Bacon a traitor, but granted some of the reforms he demanded, and Bacon was later pardoned, having apologized.

When Bacon felt that the governor had reneged on his pledge to pursue the Indians, the fiery rebel focused his anger toward the colonial government. In the first popular rebellion in colonial America, Bacon led troops of lower-class planters, servants, and some free and slave blacks to Jamestown and burned it. Faced with a true rebellion, Governor Berkeley fled. An English naval squadron was sent to capture Bacon, who died of dysentery before they reached him, and the remnants of his backwoods army were rounded up, with two dozen of them ending up on the gallows.

Nat Bacon's Rebellion was the first of almost twenty minor uprisings against colonial governments, including the Paxton uprising in Pennsylvania in 1763, Leisler's Rebellion in New York in 1689, and the Regulator Rebellion in South Carolina in 1771. All of these were revolts against the colonial "haves," those wealthy colonists who owned the bulk of America's land and controlled its prosperity, and the "have-nots," often backwoodsmen or lower-class farmers struggling for survival. By adding these bloody outbreaks of popular resentment against the colonial "establishment" to the numerous riots and slave revolts of the pre-Revolutionary period, the picture of colonial gentility is destroyed. Instead we get a clouded image of unsettled grievances waiting to boil over.

Who were the witches of Salem?

Modern-day Salem does a good business in lightheartedly promoting its Halloween capital image. The town may have more psychics and tarot readers per capita than anywhere else in America. But for the twenty people who died there in 1692, there was little humor in the affair. The hysteria developed, as many New England disputes had, out of religious infighting. New England was a theocracy, a Puritan church state in which church and government were closely connected. And since Puritanism then controlled the politics and economy of most of New England, such a controversy among churchmen was no small matter.

Salem Village was created in 1672 by a group of rural families who wanted their own church instead of going to church in the larger town of nearby Salem, a prosperous trading town. Several years of haggling over ministers followed until Samuel Parris, a former merchant and Harvard dropout, was called and arrived in Salem Village in 1689. No peacemaker, Parris failed to calm his troubled parish, and in two years' time things went haywire. In January 1692, the minister's daughter Betty and his niece Abigail, aged nine and eleven, and twelve-year-old Ann Putnam, daughter of one of the town's most powerful men, began to act strangely. So did five other young girls. A doctor diagnosed them as bewitched and under the influence of an "Evil Hand." Suspicion immediately fell on Tituba, the Parris family's West Indian slave, who had been teaching the girls fortune-telling games.

At first, the slave Tituba and two elderly townswomen, Sarah Good and Sarah Osburn, were arrested on February 29, 1692, accused of witchery, and a general court jailed them on suspicion of witchcraft. But their trial triggered an astonishing wave of accusations, and three of the young girls, basking in their sudden notoriety, ignited a storm of satanic fear throughout the Massachusetts Bay Colony. Governor William Phips convened a special court that formally charged more than 150 people.

The three Salem Village girls were the chief witnesses, and even though they said they had concocted the whole affair for "sport," the trials continued. The charge of witchery soon became a means to settle village feuds. Reason was turned upside-down and the court was right out of *Alice's Adventures in Wonderland*. To escape the hangman's noose, the panic-stricken accused often "confessed" to anything, including broomstick rides and sex with the Devil. Professions of innocence or criticism of the proceedings were tantamount to guilt. Refusal to implicate a neighbor meant a death sentence.

There was nothing peculiarly American about these witch trials. In fact, America was relatively free of the far more murderous rampage of witch hunts that had swept Europe for centuries. Between 1300 and 1700, thousands of people, mostly women, had been executed in Europe. Eventually twenty-eight suspected witches, most of them women, were convicted in Salem. Five of them "confessed" and were spared, two escaped, and a pregnant woman was pardoned. But in the end, nineteen "witches" were hanged, and the husband of one convicted witch was "pressed" to death, or suffocated under a pile of stones for refusing to plead. Three of the executed said they had actually participated in "malefic practices" or black magic. At the belated urging of Increase Mather (1639–1723), the president of Harvard, and other Puritan ministers, Governor Phips called off the trials that were literally ripping the colony apart. He may have been influenced by the fact that his own wife had been accused.

So what caused this extraordinary outbreak? Start with the idea that the girls were actually possessed. The Christian belief in the existence of the Devil is widely accepted in modern America. There have been reports that the pope himself has performed exorcisms. So, for some people, the concept of satanic possession is entirely plausible, if not scientifically verifiable.

Were the girls simply playacting? There is little doubt that they were young girls whose wild stories were used to attract attention, but then got out of hand. It is a plausible explanation, especially when set against the tenor of the times when people were more than willing to accept that the Devil walked in New England, a refrain that they heard every day of their lives, and certainly from the pulpits on the Sabbath.

But that still does not completely explain the strange behavior that was documented and seemed to go beyond playacting. Perhaps the girls had inadvertently discovered what we might call "magic mushrooms"? An intriguing scientific answer to the behavior of the Salem girls was put forth by behavioral psychologist Linda Caporeal, who likened their actions to those of LSD users. While there was no LSD in colonial Massachusetts, there was ergot, a fungus that affects rye grain and the natural substance from which LSD is derived. Toxicologists know that ergot-contaminated foods can lead to convulsions, delusions, hallucinations, and many other symptoms that are present in the records of the Salem trials. At the time, rye was a staple grain in Salem, and the "witches" lived in a region of swampy meadows that would have bred the fungus. Caporeal's theory is based on circumstantial evidence and is unprovable, but is quite intriguing nonetheless.

Natural highs aside, there is another medical explanation. Were the girls mentally ill? Did they suffer from a neurotic condition that doctors like Freud later called *hysteria*? As Frances Hill writes, "There can be no doubt that what beset the Goodwin children, Elizabeth Knapp, and all the others . . . was clinical hysteria. The extraordinary body postures, inexplicable pains, deafness, dumbness, and blindness, meaningless babbling, refusal to eat, destructive and self-destructive behavior . . . are just the same in all three accounts. So are the exhibitionism, the self-control even in apparent abandonment and the complete power over parents . . ." According to Hill, clinical hysteria is understood differently today, and one of its most frequent forms of expression is anorexia, the eating disorder that primarily affects adolescent girls. She also notes that hysteria often occurs among ill-educated, rural populations.

Whatever the real cause, the incident at Salem had no real lasting impact on the course of American history. However, it certainly demonstrated a strain of intolerance and stiff-necked sanctimoniousness of the New England Puritan spirit. The incident also demonstrates the danger of a church state, an institution vigorously avoided by the Framers of the Constitution. The failure of an entire community to prevent the madness was a sad tribute to moral cowardice, a trait not limited in American history to either New England or the colonial period. (Another "witch hunt" with eerie parallels to the Salem affair but far more damaging was carried out by Senator Joseph McCarthy against alleged Communists in government in the 1950s, and is covered in Chapter 7. Arthur Miller's play *The Crucible*, written in 1953 in response to the McCarthy Red Scare, and filmed in 1997 with Winona

Ryder and Daniel Day-Lewis, is a compelling dramatic treatment of the Salem incident.)

Finally, and perhaps most significantly, the Salem incident underscores the importance of the protections for the accused that the Framers would solidify in the Constitution and, to a greater extent, in the Bill of Rights about one hundred years after the Salem trials. The rule of law—presumption of innocence, jury trials, right to counsel, and other protections that were codified as the birthright of Americans and the foundation of the American legal system—were all lacking in 1691. They might well have saved innocent lives. That is an important lesson to keep in mind whenever panic threatens to overcome the restraints that governments and people are often too willing to abandon in the name of security.

Must Read: A *Delusion of Satan: The Full Story of the Salem Witch Trials* by Frances Hill.

AMERICAN VOICES

Puritan leader COTTON MATHER, writing in 1705 to Rev. John Williams, held captive by the French, after a French-Indian raid on the settlement of Deerfield, Massachusetts, in 1704:

My Dear Brother,

You are carried into the Land of the Canadiens for your good. God has called you to glorify Him in that land. Your patience, your constancy, your Resignation under your vast Affliction, bring more glory to Him, than ye best Activity in any other Serviceableness. You visit Heaven with prayers, and are visited of Heaven with comfort, Our prayers unite with yours. You are continually and affectionately remembered in ye prayers of New England. The faithful, throughout ye country, remember you, publickly, privately, Secretly.

Williams was a minister in the colonial village of Deerfield in western Massachusetts. During a February 1704 raid by the French and their Indian allies, some forty-eight men, women, and children were massacred. The raid's purpose was to take Williams hostage and exchange him for a French prisoner then being held in Boston by the British. Williams was eventually "redeemed" after negotiations. But his seven-year-old daughter, Eunice, remained with her Indian captors. To the great horror of her Puritan family, Eunice joined the Indians, embraced the Catholicism they had learned from the French Jesuits, and took a Mohawk husband.

Must Read: *The Unredeemed Captive: A Family Story from Early America* by John Demos.

What was the Great Awakening?

Another, more benevolent outpouring of religious fervor swept the middle colonies, New England, and the rest of the colonies in the 1740s. A wave of fundamental, orthodox Protestantism that touched every colony, the Great Awakening was largely created by two powerful, charismatic evangelists who—without benefit of television crusades and religious theme parks—would have put the likes of such modern "televangelists" as Pat Robertson, Jimmy Swaggart, Jim and Tammy Bakker, and Oral Roberts to shame.

American-born Jonathan Edwards, pastor of a church in Northampton, Massachusetts, became famous for his fire-and-brimstone, pit-of-hell sermons, which provoked near hysteria in his listeners. Edwards was responding to a softening of religious attitudes that had been occurring throughout the colonies. As the colonies prospered, attention had turned from observing the Sabbath to such earthly pursuits as real estate, slave trading, the rum business, and other profitable worldly enterprises. In the most famous of his sermons, "Sinners in the Hands of an Angry God," Edwards likened his sinning listeners to a spider hung over a flame. When his popularity and influence later waned, Edwards became a missionary to the Indians and was later appointed president of the College of New Jersey (later Princeton), but died before taking office.

(Edwards's grandson, Aaron Burr, would later attend the school that had been cofounded by Aaron Burr Sr. Among Burr's classmates was a young Virginian, James Madison.)

George Whitefield, an Oxford-trained Anglican minister, was one of those influenced by Edwards. An orator of legendary ability, Whitefield attracted thousands to his outdoor meetings. His emotionally charged sermons chastised his listeners and then brought the promise of salvation. Even Benjamin Franklin, no model of piety, was moved by Whitefield and commented on how he transformed all who heard him. But Edwards and Whitefield's influence went beyond religion. Their ardent followers tended to be lower or middle class, with little education or influence. The wealthy, powerful elite of America, its new ruling class, preferred traditional worship, and the differences between these factions threatened to turn radical.

Although the Awakening eventually ran its course, it did have a considerable long-term impact on America. In a practical sense, the split among the various factions encouraged the founding of several new colleges, including Princeton, Brown, Rutgers, and Dartmouth. In political terms, the divisions the Awakening had created contributed to a new spirit of toleration and secularism. The old-guard Puritans no longer held complete control over church and political matters. New religious forces forced the loosening of ties between church and state throughout the colonies, a new secular spirit that would become embedded in the Constitution.

AMERICAN VOICES
ANDREW HAMILTON,
in defense of Zenger, August 1735:

It is an old and wise caution, that when our neighbor's house is on fire, we ought to take care of our own. For tho', blessed be God, I live in a government where liberty is well understood, and freely enjoy'd; yet experience has shown us all that bad precedent in one government is soon set up for an authority in another; and therefore I cannot but think it mine, and every honest man's duty that . . . we ought at the same time to be upon our guard against power, wherever we apprehend that it may affect ourselves or our fellow-subjects. . . .

I should think it my duty, if required, to go to the

utmost part of the land, where my service could be of any use in assisting to quench the flame of prosecutions upon informations, set on foot by the government, to deprive a people of their right to remonstrating (and complaining too) of the arbitrary attempts of men in power.

What was John Peter Zenger on trial for?

In 1732, a wealthy landowner, Lewis Morris, founded the *New York Weekly Journal*. Like others before and since, the *Journal* contributed to a grand American newspaper tradition, not by reporting the news, but by axgrinding and mudslinging at a political opponent. In this case the target was New York governor William Cosby and his allies, among them the prominent merchant James DeLancey.

A German-born printer, John Peter Zenger, was hired to edit and produce the paper, but editorial policy was in the hands of a Morris ally, attorney James Alexander. The *Journal's* front page usually offered a polemic on the right of the people to be critical of rulers. But what Governor Cosby found intolerable were the back-page "advertisements," thinly veiled attacks in which the governor was likened to a monkey and his supporters to spaniels. Cosby shut down the paper, charged Zenger with seditious libel, and had him jailed for ten months.

In the trial that followed, Zenger's attorney, the Philadelphia lawyer Andrew Hamilton (no relation to the more famous Alexander Hamilton), contended that the articles in question were truthful and therefore not libelous. Although the judges ruled Hamilton's argument out of order, the jury was swayed. Hamilton's defense carried the day and Zenger was acquitted. Of the jury, Hamilton later said, "You have laid a noble foundation for securing to ourselves that to which Nature and the Laws of our country have given us a Right—The Liberty—both of exposing and opposing arbitrary Power by speaking and writing Truth."

For a royal colony still forty years away from independence, that was pretty heady stuff. Though subjects of the English Crown, an American jury had demonstrated a stiff resolve that they did not feel duty-bound by English civil law. Just as important, Zenger's trial and acquittal marked the first landmark in the tradition of a free press, a somewhat radical notion that became the law of the land as the First Amendment in the Bill of Rights. There was a practical effect as well. In the immediate years ahead, that freedom would become an important weapon in the war of words that preceded the War for Independence.

AMERICAN VOICES

GEORGE WASHINGTON, describing his first night in the Wilderness in March 1748
(from *The Diaries of George Washington*):

We got our Supper and was lighted into a Room and not being so good a Woodsman as ye rest of my Company stripped myself very orderly and went into ye bed as they called it when to my Surprize I found it to be nothing but a Little Straw-Matted together without Sheets or anything else but only one thread Bear blanket with double its weight of Vermin such as Lice, Fleas &c. I was glad to get up (as soon as ye Light was carried from us) I put on my Cloths and lay as my Companions. Had we not been very tired I am sure we should not have slep'd much that night I made a Promise not to Sleep so from that time forward, chusing rather to sleep in ye open Air before a fire.

When they said, "Don't let the bedbugs bite" in colonial America, they meant it, as seventeen-year-old George Washington discovered during his first foray into what was then the "wilderness" of colonial Virginia's Blue Ridge Mountains and Shenandoah Valley. Besides showing what life was like in the "West" for young George, this passage also demonstrates that he, like many Americans of his day, was not well schooled in spelling and grammar, which often had tremendous local variations.

Who fought the French and Indian War?

No. It was not the French against the Indians.

At the end of the seventeenth century, North America was an

extremely valuable piece of real estate, teeming with the beavers so prized by the hatmakers of Europe and claimed in part by the Dutch, the French, and the Spanish, as well as by the king of England. The people in Canada and America were pawns in a larger chess game. Between 1689 and the War for Independence, the major European powers engaged in a series of wars, usually fought under the guise of disputes over royal succession. In fact, they were wars of colonial expansion, fought for territory, raw materials, and new markets for exports.

EUROPEAN WARS FOUGHT IN THE COLONIES

Date	European Name	Colonial Name
1689–97	War of the League of Augsburg	King William's War
1702–13	War of the Spanish Succession	Queen Anne's War
1740–48	War of the Austrian Succession	King George's War
1756–63	Seven Years War	French and Indian War

In the first three of these, the colonists played supporting roles. Most of the fighting was limited to sporadic surprise attacks by one side or another, usually joined by their respective Indian allies. Colonial losses, especially in New England and Canada, were still heavy, and the costs of these wars created a serious inflation problem, particularly in Massachusetts, where paper money was printed for the first time to finance the fighting. By the time the first three wars had been played out, England and France were left standing as the two major contenders, and England had acquired a good portion of Canada from France. In the last of the four wars, however, these two rivals fought for absolute dominion over North America. And it was the French and Indian War that most shaped America's destiny.

The conflict started inauspiciously enough for the Anglo-American cause when a young Virginian was dispatched by Virginia's Governor Dinwiddie to the Pennsylvania backwoods in 1753 to tell the French that they were trespassing on Virginia's territory. During an evening in which the French drank some brandy and the young Virginian did not, he learned that the French had no intentions of leaving the territory. With this important intelligence, the young Virginian spent a few difficult weeks returning to Virginia where he delivered his report. He wrote a small book, *The Journal of Major George Washington*, describing his adventure. All London soon agreed that the young author was a man of courage and intelligence.

Soon after, this inexperienced twenty-two-year-old son of a planter was made an officer and sent back with a militia force of 150 men and orders to build a fort. To his dismay, the new lieutenant colonel found the French already occupying a fort they called Duquesne (on the site of Pittsburgh). Though outnumbered, the young commander, along with some Indian allies, attacked a French party, took no prisoners, and hastily constructed a fort that was aptly named Necessity. Surrounded by French forces, he surrendered, and the French sent him packing back to Virginia, where he was still hailed a hero for taking on the sworn enemies of England. Without realizing, George Washington had ordered the shots that began the French and Indian War.

It was during that skirmish with the French that Washington had his first taste of battle and famously wrote his brother, Jack, "I can assure you. I heard Bullets whistling and believe me there was something charming in the sound." When King George II heard this tale, he remarked, "He would not say so had he been used to hear many."

How differently world history might have turned out had the French decided to do away with this green soldier when they had cause and opportunity! Instead, twenty-two years later, the French would again come to the aid of George Washington in his war of revolution against England.

Bad went to worse for the English and their colonial allies in the war's early years. The 90,000 French in America, vastly outnumbered by 1.5 million English colonials, were better organized, were more experienced fighters, and had the most Indian allies. To the Indians, the French were the lesser of two evils; there were fewer French than English, and they seemed more interested in trading for beaver pelts than did the English, who were pushing the Indians off their lands.

For many Indians, the war also provided an opportunity to repay years of English treachery. The Indians' rage exploded in the viciousness of their attacks, which were met with equal savagery by the British. Scalp taking was a popular British tactic, and the British commander, General Edward Braddock, offered his Indian allies five pounds sterling for the scalp of a French soldier, one hundred pounds for that of a Jesuit missionary, and a grand prize of two hundred pounds for the hair of the powerful Delaware chieftain Shinngass.

For the English side, the great disaster of this war came in 1755, when 1,400 redcoats, under General Braddock, marched on Fort Duquesne in a poorly planned mission. A much smaller force of French slaughtered the English, leaving George Washington, Braddock's aide-de-camp, to straggle home with 500 survivors. The English suffered similar defeats in New York.

This colonial war became linked to a global clash that commenced in 1756, the first true world war. Things went badly everywhere for the English until there was a change of leadership in London, with William Pitt taking over the war effort in 1758. His strategy emphasized naval warfare and the conquest of North America, which Pitt viewed as the key to overall victory. He poured in troops and found talented new commanders in James Wolfe and Jeffrey Amherst. One of Amherst's novel tactics, when negotiating with some attacking Indians, was to give them blankets from the smallpox hospital. A string of victories between 1758 and 1760 gave the English control over the American colonies and, with the fall of Montreal in 1760, all of Canada.

In 1763, the Treaty of Paris brought peace and, with it, a complete British triumph. The English now owned all of Canada, America east of the Mississippi Valley, Florida, and a number of Caribbean islands. France lost its American colonies, except for a few islands in the French West Indies, and France's overseas trade had been crippled by the British navy.

Colonial Americans, now fully blooded in a major armed conflict, took pride and rejoiced at the victory they had helped win for their new king, George III, who had taken the throne in 1760. George Washington, who played no small part in the fighting, rode back to Williamsburg, Virginia, to resign his command. A career as a professional soldier no longer interested him.

What do sugar and stamps have to do with revolutions?

In the short space of thirteen years, how did the colonies go from being loyal subjects of King George III, flush in their victory over the French, to becoming rebels capable of overthrowing the most powerful nation on earth?

Obviously, no single factor changes the course of history. And different historians point to different reasons for the Revolution. The established traditionalist view is that the American Revolution was fought for liberties that Americans believed they already possessed as British citizens. The more radical political and economic viewpoint holds that the Revolution was simply a transfer of power from a distant British elite to a homegrown American power class that wanted to consolidate its hold over the wealth of the continent.

History is a boat big enough to carry both views comfortably, and a mingling of these perspectives brings an approximation of truth. It is safe to say that British bungling, economic realities, a profound philosophical revolution called the Enlightenment, and historical inevitability all played roles in the birth of the American nation.

As for the British bungling: In the immediate aftermath of the Seven Years War, England had an enormous wartime debt to pay. In London, it was naturally assumed that the colonies should chip in for some of the costs of the defense of America as well as the yearly cost of administering the colonies. To do this, Parliament enacted what it thought an entirely reasonable tax, the so-called Sugar Act of 1764, which placed tariffs on sugar, coffee, wines, and other products imported into America in substantial quantities. A postwar colonial depression—economic doldrums typically following the free spending that accompanies wartime—sharpened the act's pain for American merchants and consumers. Almost immediately, negative reaction to the tax set in, an economic dissent that was summed up in a new political slogan, "No taxation without representation." James Otis, one of the most vocal and radical leaders in Massachusetts, wrote that everyone should be "free from all taxes but what he consents to in person or by his representative."

In real terms, the representation issue was a smokescreen—a useful slogan for galvanizing popular protest, but not really what the new breed of colonial leaders wanted. They had the wisdom to see that getting a handful of seats in Parliament for the colonies would be politically meaningless. Growing numbers of American politicians saw a wedge being driven between the colonies and Mother England, and they had their eyes on a larger prize.

Resistance to the sugar tax, in the form of drafted protests from colonial legislatures and halfhearted boycotts, failed to materialize. Until, that is, Parliament tightened the screws with a second tax. The Stamp Act of 1765 set stiff tariffs on virtually every kind of printed matter, from newspapers and legal documents to playing cards. One member of Parliament, protesting the new tax plan, used the phrase "Sons of Liberty" to describe the colonists, and it was quickly adopted by men in every colony. While the Sugar Act reflected Parliament's power to tax trade, the Stamp Act was different. It was a direct tax, and the protests from America grew louder, stronger, and more violent. Riots broke out, the most violent of which were in Boston, where the house of Governor Thomas Hutchinson was destroyed by an angry mob. In New York, the home of the officer in charge of the stamps was also ransacked. A boycott of the stamps, widely joined throughout the colonies, was followed by a general boycott of English goods. Hit hard by the economic warfare, London's merchants screamed, and the law was repealed in 1766.

But it was a case of closing the barn door after the horses had scattered. In America, forces were gathering that most London politicos, ignorant of American ways, were too smug to acknowledge.

What was the Boston Massacre?

Having been kicked once by the colonial mule, Parliament failed to grasp the message of the Stamp Act boycott, and in 1767 thought up a new set of incendiary taxes called the Townshend Acts, once again placing itself directly behind the mule's hind legs. Once again, an American boycott cut imports from England in half. The British answer to the Americans' protest was a typical superpower response — they sent in troops.

Soon there were 4,000 British redcoats in Boston, a city of 16,000 and a hotbed of colonial protest. These troops, however, did not just idly stand guard over the populace. In a town already hard-pressed for jobs, the British soldiers competed for work with the laborers of Boston's waterfront. Early in March 1770, a group of ropemakers fought with a detachment of soldiers who were taking their jobs, and all around Boston, angry encounters between soldiers and citizens became more frequent. Tensions mounted until March 5, when a mob, many of them hard-drinking waterfront workers, confronted a detachment of nine British soldiers. The scene turned ugly as snow and ice, mixed with stones, began to fly in the direction of the soldiers. Confronted by a taunting mob calling for their blood, the soldiers grew understandably nervous. It took only the word "fire," most likely yelled by one of the crowd, to ignite the situation. The soldiers shot, and five bodies fell. The first to die was Crispus Attucks, the son of an African father and a Massachusetts Natick Indian mother, a former slave who had gone to sea for twenty years to escape slavery.

It did not take long for the propagandists, Samuel Adams chief among them, to seize the moment. Within days the incident had become the Boston Massacre, and the dead were martyred. An engraving of the shootings made by Henry Pelham, a half-brother of the painter John Copley, was "borrowed" by silversmith Paul Revere, whose own engraving of the incident got to the printer first and soon became a patriotic icon. As many as 10,000 marched at the funeral procession (out of Boston's population of 16,000).

In the wake of the killings, British troops were withdrawn from the city. With the Townshend Acts repealed (coincidentally on the day of the Massacre), a period of relative calm followed the Massacre and the trial of the soldiers—defended by John Adams, who wanted to ensure fairness—most were acquitted and two were branded and discharged—but it was an uneasy truce at best.

What was the Boston Tea Party about?

In the thick of the 1988 presidential election campaign, candidate George Bush made Boston Harbor an issue that badly hurt his opponent, Michael Dukakis. Bush made political hay out of the fact that the harbor was an ecological disaster zone, and placed the blame squarely in the lap of Dukakis, the Massachusetts governor. Once before, the mess in that harbor played a role in history, and back then the results were quite extraordinary. If George Bush thought Boston Harbor was a mess in 1988, he should have seen it in 1773.

The post-Massacre peace and the end of the nonimportation boycott brought renewed prosperity to the colonies and with it a respite from the bickering with London. Fearing this calm would soften resistance, Samuel Adams and his allies tried to fan the embers over such local issues as moving the Massachusetts assembly out of Boston and who should pay the governor's salary. These were important legal questions, but not the sort of outrages that inspire violent overthrow of the government. Things heated up considerably when a party of patriots in Rhode Island boarded and burned the *Gaspee*, a grounded Royal Navy boat intensely disliked for its antismuggling patrols.

While the *Gaspee* arsonists avoided arrest, the British Crown threatened to bring the guilty to England for trial, rebuffing the English tradition of right to trial by a community jury. It was the bit of tinder that Samuel Adams needed to stoke the flames a little higher. In Virginia, the House of Burgesses appointed Patrick Henry, Thomas Jefferson, and Richard Henry Lee as a Committee of Correspondence, and by 1774, twelve of the colonies had such committees to maintain a flow of information among like-minded colonists.

But a burning—or boiling—issue was still lacking until Samuel Adams found one in tea. In 1773, Parliament had granted a legal monopoly on tea shipment to America to the nearly bankrupt East India Company. The injury was made worse by the insult of funneling the tea business through selected loyalist merchants, including the sons of Governor Hutchinson of Massachusetts. The East India Company could now undercut American merchants, even those using smugglers, on the sale of tea. Tea first, thought the colonists, what will be next?

In November 1773, three tea-laden cargo ships reached Boston. Led by Samuel Adams and a powerful ally, John Hancock, one of the richest men in America and one of those most threatened by the possibility of London-granted trade monopolies, the patriots vowed that the tea would not be landed. Governor Hutchinson, whose sons stood to profit by its landing, put his back up. After two months of haggling, the Boston patriots made up their minds to turn Boston Harbor into a teapot.

On the night of December 16, 1773, about 150 men from all layers of Boston's economy, masters and apprentices side by side, blackened their faces with burnt cork, dressed as Mohawk Indians, and boarded the three ships. Once aboard, they requested and received the keys to the ships' holds, as their target was the tea alone and not the ships or any other cargo aboard. Watched by a large crowd, as well as the Royal Navy, the men worked for nearly three hours, hatcheting open the cases of tea and dumping it into the harbor. So much was dumped that the tea soon piled up in the waters and spilled back onto the decks, where it was shoveled back into the water.

The Boston Tea Party, as it was quickly anointed, was soon followed by similar tea parties in other colonies and served to harden lines, both in America and England. Patriots became more daring; loyalist Tories became more loyal; Parliament stiffened its back. The Sons of Liberty had slapped London's face with a kid glove. The king responded with an iron fist. "The die is now cast," King George told his prime minister, Lord North. "The colonies must either submit or triumph."

What was the First Continental Congress? Who chose its members, who were they, and what did they do?

From the moment the tea was dumped, the road to revolution was a short one. In a post–Tea Party fervor, Parliament passed a series of bills, called the Coercive Acts, the first of which was the Port Bill, aimed at closing down Boston until the dumped tea was paid for. It was followed by the Administration of Justice Act, the Massachusetts Regulating Act (which virtually nullified the colony's charter), and the Quebec Act, establishing a centralized system of government in Canada and extending the borders of Canada south to the Ohio River. Parliament backed up these acts by sending General Thomas Gage to Boston as the new governor, along with 4,000 troops. In addition, it reinforced provisions of the Quartering Act, which gave the army the right to demand food and shelter from colonists.

In response to these Intolerable Acts, as the colonists called them, the colonial assemblies agreed to an intercolonial meeting, and each assembly selected a group of delegates. Gathering in Philadelphia from September 5 to October 26, 1774, the First Continental Congress was made up of fifty-six delegates from every colony but Georgia. They represented the full spectrum of thought in the colonies, from moderates and conservatives like New York's John Jay or Pennsylvania's Joseph Galloway, who were searching for a compromise that would maintain ties with England, to fiery rebels like Samuel Adams and Patrick Henry of Virginia (Thomas Jefferson was not selected to make the trip). As they gathered, John Adams privately worried, "We have not men fit for the times. We are deficient in genius, in education, in travel, in fortune—in everything."

But his opinion would soon change as the debate began, and Adams became aware that he was indeed in remarkable company. The first Congress moved cautiously, but ultimately adopted a resolution that opposed the Coercive Acts, created an association to boycott British goods, and passed ten resolutions enumerating the rights of the colonists and their assemblies.

Taxes and representation were only part of the issue, as Theodore Draper writes in *A Struggle for Power*. "The struggle to deprive Parliament of its power over taxation struck at the heart of British power in the Colonies and spilled over everything else."

Before adjourning, they provided for a second session to meet if their grievances had not been corrected by the British. While they had not yet declared for independence, the First Congress had taken a more or less unalterable step in that direction. In a very real sense, the Revolution had begun. It needed only for the shooting to start.

Must Read: *A Struggle for Power: The American Revolution* by Theodore Draper.

What was "the shot heard 'round the world"?

Now governor of Massachusetts, General Gage wanted to cut off the rebellion before it got started. His first move was to try to capture hidden stores of patriot guns and powder and arrest John Hancock and Sam Adams, the patriot ringleaders in British eyes. The Sons of Liberty had been expecting this move, and across Massachusetts the patriot farmers and townspeople had begun to drill with muskets, ready to pick up their guns on a minute's notice, giving them their name, Minutemen.

In an increasingly deserted Boston, Paul Revere, silversmith and maker of false teeth, waited and watched the British movements. To sound an early warning to Concord, Revere set up a system of signals with a sexton at Christ Church in Boston. One lantern in the belfry meant Gage's troops were coming by land; two lanterns meant they were crossing the Charles River in boats. Late on the night of April 18, 1775, as expected, it was two lanterns. Revere and another rider, Billy Dawes, started off to Lexington to warn Hancock and Adams and alert the Lexington Minutemen that the British regulars were coming. Continuing on to Concord, Revere and Dawes were joined by Samuel Prescott, a young patriot doctor. A few minutes later a British patrol stopped the three men. Revere and Dawes were arrested and held briefly, while Prescott was able to escape and warn Concord of the British advance.

Meanwhile, in Lexington, the group of seventy-seven Minutemen gathered on the green to confront the British army. The British tried to simply march past the ragtag band when an unordered shot rang out. Chaos ensued, and the British soldiers broke ranks and returned fire. When the volleying stopped, eight Minutemen lay dead.

Warned by Prescott, the Concord militia was ready. Farmers from the nearby countryside responded to the church bells and streamed toward Concord. The resistance became more organized, and the Concord Minutemen attacked a troop of British holding a bridge leading into Concord, and later took up positions behind barns, houses, stone walls, and trees, pouring fire down on the British ranks. Unused to such unfair tactics as men firing from hiding, the British remained in their standard formations until they reached Lexington again and were met by reinforcements.

By the day's end, the British tallied 73 dead and 174 wounded.

The Second Continental Congress, meeting in Philadelphia on May 10, 1775, had come to the crisis point. The bloodshed at Lexington meant war. With swift action, the patriots could bottle up the whole of the British army in Boston. To John Adams, all that needed to be done was to solidify the ranks of Congress by winning the delegates of the South. The solution came in naming a Southerner as commander of the new Continental Army. On June 15, 1775, George Washington, a delegate from Virginia who had hinted at his ambitions by wearing his old military uniform to the Philadelphia meetings, received that appointment.

MILESTONES IN THE AMERICAN REVOLUTION

1775

April 18–19 Seven hundred British troops march on Concord, Massachusetts, to secure a rebel arsenal. They are met on the Lexington village green by a small force of colonial Minutemen, and an unordered shot—the "shot heard 'round the world"—leads to the killing of eight Americans. During a pitched battle at Concord and on their return to Boston, the British are harassed constantly by colonial snipers and suffer heavy losses.

May 10 Under Ethan Allen and Benedict Arnold, a colonial militia force takes the British arsenal at Fort Ticonderoga, New York, capturing cannon and other supplies; in a separate attack, the British garrison at Crown Point on Lake Champlain is seized.

June 15 The Second Continental Congress decides to raise an army and appoints George Washington to lead it.

June 17 In the Battle of Bunker Hill (actually fought on Breed's Hill), the British sustain heavy losses, with more than 1,100 killed or wounded, before forcing a rebel retreat. Nathanael Greene, an American commander, comments, "I wish we could sell them another hill at the same price." In the wake of this costly victory, General Gage is replaced by Howe as the British commander in America.

1776

January   Tom Paine publishes the pamphlet *Common Sense*, a persuasive and widely read argument for independence.

March 4–17   Rebel forces capture Dorchester Heights, overlooking Boston Harbor. Cannon captured by the Americans at Ticonderoga are brought in, forcing a British evacuation of Boston.

May   King Louis XVI of France authorizes secret arms and munitions assistance for the Americans.

June 11   Congress appoints a committee to compose a declaration of independence.

June 28   Under General Charles Lee, American forces in Charleston, South Carolina, fend off a British attack, damaging the British fleet. The British suspend operations in the South for another two years.

July 2   British General Sir William Howe lands an army at Staten Island, New York, eventually amassing 32,000 troops, including 9,000 German mercenaries.

July 4   The Declaration of Independence is formally adopted by Congress.

August 27–29   Battle of Long Island. Howe forces withdrawal of Washington's army from Brooklyn Heights to Manhattan. Before Howe can finish off the rebel army, a miraculous retreat saves Washington and the army. In September, Washington evacuates New York.

September 22   Nathan Hale, captured by the British in Long Island, is hanged, without trial, as a spy. He goes to his death bravely and is reported to have said, "I only regret that I have but one life to give for my country."

October–November   Crushing American defeats at the battles of White Plains (New York) and Fort Lee (New Jersey) force Washington to move westward through New Jersey and into Pennsylvania.

Again, Howe fails to pursue Washington vigorously, and the army is saved.

December 25 In a surprise Christmas Day attack, Washington leads troops across the Delaware River for a successful attack on British forces at Trenton, New Jersey. Although a small victory, it boosts American morale. It is followed by a second victory, at Princeton.

Must Read: *The Winter Soldiers* by Richard M. Ketchum.

1777

April 27 Benedict Arnold defeats the British at Ridgefield, Connecticut.

June The American seaman John Paul Jones is given command of the *Ranger* and begins raiding English shipping.

July 6 The British retake Fort Ticonderoga.

July 27 The Marquis de Lafayette, a twenty-year-old French nobleman, arrives in America to volunteer his services to the Revolution.

August 16 Battle of Bennington (Vermont). Americans wipe out a column of General Burgoyne's men.

September 9–11 Battle of Brandywine (Pennsylvania). Howe drives Washington's army toward Philadelphia; Congress is forced to flee.

September 19 First Battle of Saratoga. An American victory.

September 26 General Howe occupies Philadelphia.

October 4–5 Battle of Germantown (Pennsylvania). A costly American defeat, the battle is inconclusive as Howe fails again to finish Washington.

October 7–17 Second Battle of Saratoga. British are routed and 5,700 surrender. A major turning point for the American cause as Europe is encouraged to aid the revolution, including formal French recognition of American independence.

December 17   Washington's Continental Army enters winter quarters at Valley Forge, Pennsylvania, remaining there until June 1778. The horrors of that winter cannot be told in simple statistics, but an estimated 2,500 soldiers out of 10,000 died during these six months, but it was most often due to American mismanagement, graft, speculation, and indifference. Pennsylvania farmers sold their produce to the British in Philadelphia, and the same was true elsewhere in New England and New York, where farmers sought hard cash for their crops.

1778

February   Franco-American treaties of alliance and commerce are signed.

February 23   The Prussian Baron von Steuben arrives and assists Washington in drilling and training the army at Valley Forge. By the end of the difficult winter, the Continental Army is a cohesive, disciplined fighting force.

May 8   Howe is replaced by Henry Clinton as the British commander in America.

July 8   Continental Army headquarters are established at West Point.

July 9   The Articles of Confederation are signed by Congress.

July 10   A French fleet arrives; France declares war against Britain.

December 29   The British capture Savannah, Georgia, from American General Robert Howe.

1779

January 10   The French give a dilapidated ship to John Paul Jones. It is refitted and renamed *Bonhomme Richard* in honor of Ben Franklin, internationally renowned as Poor Richard of *Almanac* fame.

January 29   British forces capture Augusta, Georgia.

February 25 Americans under George Rogers Clark defeat the British at Vincennes, Indiana.

May 10 Portsmouth and Norfolk, Virginia, captured and burned by the British.

June 16 Spain declares war on England, but makes no American alliances.

July 15 American general Anthony Wayne recaptures Stony Point, New York, and takes some 700 prisoners while suffering 15 casualties.

August 19 American general Henry Lee drives the British from Paulus Hook, New Jersey.

August 29 American generals John Sullivan and James Clinton defeat combined loyalist and Indian forces at Newton (Elmira, New York).

September 3–October 28 An attempt to recapture Savannah results in a disastrous loss for the American-French combined forces.

September 23 In a naval battle off the coast of England, John Paul Jones captures the British warship *Serapis*, although he loses the *Bonhomme Richard*. A French vessel takes another British ship.

September 27 Congress appoints John Adams to negotiate peace with England.

October 17 The Continental Army returns to winter quarters at Morristown, New Jersey, where it will suffer a winter even worse than the year before at Valley Forge. Desertions and mutiny are commonplace. Record-breaking cold creates an ordeal of unbelievable suffering.

1780

January 28 A fort is established on the Cumberland River to defend North Carolina from Indian attack. It is later named Nashville.

February 1 A British fleet carrying 8,000 men from New York and Newport, Rhode Island, reaches Charleston, South Carolina.

May 6   Fort Moultrie falls to the British, and with it Charleston. In the heaviest single American defeat of the war, 5,400 Americans are captured along with ships, munitions, and food supplies.

May 25   A major mutiny in Morristown is put down by Pennsylvania troops, and two leaders of the mutiny are hanged.

June 22   Reinforcements sent by Washington join General Horatio Gates in North Carolina, as the focus of the war shifts to the South.

July 11   Five thousand French troops under Rochambeau arrive at Newport, Rhode Island, but are trapped by a British blockade.

August 3   Benedict Arnold is appointed commander of West Point. He has been secretly communicating Washington's movements to the British commander Henry Clinton.

August 16   At Camden, South Carolina, American forces under General Gates are overwhelmingly defeated by General Charles Cornwallis; Gates is relieved of command.

September 23   Carrying the plans for Benedict Arnold's surrender of West Point, British Major John André is captured and later hanged as a spy. Arnold flees to a British ship and is made a brigadier general in the British army.

October 7   A frontier militia force captures a loyalist force of 1,100 at Kings Mountain, North Carolina, forcing General Cornwallis to abandon plans for an invasion of North Carolina.

October 14   General Nathanael Greene replaces General Gates as commander of the southern army. Greene begins a guerrilla war of harassment against the British.

1781

January 17   The Battle of Cowpens (South Carolina). American forces under General Daniel Morgan win a decisive victory.

March 15   Despite a victory at the Battle of Guilford Courthouse (North Carolina), Cornwallis suffers heavy losses, abandons plans to control the Carolinas, and retreats to await reinforcements.

June 10   American forces under Lafayette are reinforced by General Anthony Wayne in Virginia to combat Cornwallis.

August 14   Washington receives news that French admiral de Grasse is sailing a fleet carrying 3,000 men to Chesapeake Bay. Washington secretly abandons plans to attack Clinton in New York and moves south instead.

August 31   French troops, under de Grasse, land at Yorktown, Virginia, and join American forces under Lafayette, blocking off a retreat by Cornwallis.

September 5–8   In a naval battle off Yorktown, the French fleet is victorious and additional French troops arrive from Newport, Rhode Island.

September 14–24   American troops under Washington are transported to Williamsburg, Virginia, by de Grasse's ships.

September 28   A combined force of 9,000 Americans and 7,000 French begin the siege of Yorktown.

October 19   Cornwallis, with 8,000 troops, surrenders at Yorktown, effectively ending British hopes of victory in America. Aware of Cornwallis's predicament, Clinton fails to send British reinforcements in time. They sail back to New York.

1782

January 1   Loyalists in America, fearing confiscation and reprisals, begin to leave for Nova Scotia and New Brunswick.

February 27   The House of Commons votes against waging further war in America; the English Crown is empowered to seek peace negotiations. In March, Lord North resigns as prime minister and is replaced by Lord Rockingham, who seeks immediate negotiations with America.

April 19   The Netherlands recognizes the independence of the United States.

August 27 A skirmish in South Carolina is the last wartime engagement on the eastern seaboard.

November 30 A preliminary peace treaty is signed in Paris.

1783

January 20 Preliminary peace treaties are signed between England and France and England and Spain.

February 4 Great Britain officially declares an end to hostilities in America.

April 11 Congress declares a formal end to the Revolutionary War.

June 13 The main part of the Continental Army disbands.

September 3 The Treaty of Paris is signed, formally ending the war. The treaty is ratified by Congress in January 1784.

THE PATRIOTS

John Adams (1735–1826) Born in Braintree (Quincy), Massachusetts, a Harvard-educated lawyer, he was the cousin of Samuel Adams. A thorough but cautious patriot, Adams safely crossed a political high wire in defending the British soldiers accused in the Boston Massacre. A prominent member of the Continental Congresses, Adams was among those named to draft the Declaration of Independence, which he later signed. As America's wartime envoy to France and Holland, he was instrumental in obtaining the foreign aid of both of those countries, and then joined in negotiating the Peace of Paris ending the war.

After the war he served as first U.S. minister to Great Britain and then returned home to serve as Washington's vice president for two terms. Adams succeeded Washington as the second president in 1796, but was defeated by Thomas Jefferson in 1800. Both Adams and Jefferson died on July 4, 1826, the fiftieth anniversary of the Declaration of Independence.

Must Read: *John Adams* by David McCullough.

Samuel Adams (1722–1803) After squandering an inheritance, ruining his father's brewery business, and failing as a tax collector, this most fiery of Adamses found his calling as a rabble-rouser. Always a step ahead of arrest or debtors' prison, he was one of the most radical of the patriots, far better at brewing dissent than beer. Samuel Adams was the chief political architect behind the machinations that led to the Boston Tea Party, as well as tutor to his younger cousin, John Adams. A signer of the Declaration, he all but faded from the national picture after the war was over, holding a variety of state offices and leaving his more illustrious cousin to take a leading role.

Dr. Benjamin Church (1734–78?) Although not as notorious as Benedict Arnold, Church earned the unpleasant distinction of being the first American caught spying for the British. A physician from Boston, Church had established powerful credentials as a patriot zealot, being the first on hand to treat the wounded after the Boston Massacre. But in 1775, coded documents he was transmitting to the British were intercepted and he was tried as a spy. Found guilty, he was spared the hanging that George Washington requested.

Benjamin Franklin (1706–90) Of all the figures in the Revolutionary pantheon, perhaps only Washington has inspired more myths than Franklin. Printer. Writer. Philosopher. Scientist. Politician. Diplomat. All the labels fit, but none defines the man who was, during his life, one of the most famous men in the world.

Born in Boston, he was the fifteenth of a candlemaker's seventeen children. His brief formal schooling ended when he was apprenticed to his older half-brother James, printer of the *New England Courant* and a member of the young radicals of Boston. Failing to get along with James, Ben moved to Philadelphia and found work as a printer, quickly gaining the confidence of the most powerful men in that cosmopolitan city. A trip to London followed in 1724, although financial support promised to Franklin by Pennsylvania's governor fell through and he was forced to find work as a printer.

Returning to Philadelphia in 1726, he began a rise that was professionally and financially astonishing. By 1748, he was able to retire, having started a newspaper; begun a tradesmen's club called the Junto; founded the first American subscription library; become clerk to the Pennsylvania legislature; established the first fire company; become postmaster of Philadelphia; established the American Philosophical Society; and launched *Poor Richard's Almanac*, the collection of wit, wisdom, and financial advice he produced for twenty-five years.

Franklin turned his attention to science and politics. He performed his electrical experiments—most famously the silken kite experiment, which proved that lightning and electricity were the same force of nature—and he invented the lightning rod. He added to his list of inventions with bifocal eyeglasses and the efficient Franklin stove. A key mover in the Pennsylvania legislature, he was sent to England as the colony's agent in 1764, emerging as the leading spokesman against the Stamp Act. (His illegitimate son William, who had assisted at the famous kite experiment, became the colonial governor of New Jersey and remained a loyalist. In 1776, William Franklin was arrested and declared a "virulent enemy to this country." Exchanged with a patriot prisoner, William lived out his life in London, while Franklin raised William's son Temple. The deep fracture of this relationship was never repaired.)

With war looming, Franklin returned to America a month before the battles at Lexington and Concord. During the war, he sat in the Second Continental Congress, was a member of the committee that was formed to draft the Declaration, and soon afterward was sent to Paris to negotiate an alliance with the French, staying in Europe to make the terms of peace.

Must Read: *The First American: The Life and Times of Benjamin Franklin* by H. W. Brands; *Benjamin Franklin: An American Life* by Walter Isaacson.

Nathan Hale (1755–76) A Connecticut schoolteacher, Hale joined Washington's army but saw no action. When Washington called for volunteers to gather information on British troops, Hale stepped forward. Recognized and reported by a Tory relative, he was arrested by the British, in civilian clothing with maps showing troop positions. After confessing, Hale was hanged. While his dignity and bravery were widely admired and he became an early martyr to the rebel cause, his famous last words of regret are most likely an invention that has become part of the Revolution's mythology. The words have never been documented.

John Hancock (1736–93) The richest man in New England before the war, Hancock, an ally of the Adamses, was a merchant who had inherited his wealth from an uncle who had acquired it through smuggling. Hancock's purse assured him a prominent place among the patriots, and he bankrolled the rebel cause. Hancock attended the Continental Congresses and served as president of the Congress. Despite a total lack of military experience, Hancock hoped to command the Continental Army and was annoyed when Washington was named. He was the first and most visible signer of the Declaration, but his wartime service was undistinguished, and after the war he was elected governor of Massachusetts.

Patrick Henry (1736–99) Far from being a member of the Virginia aristocracy, Henry was the son of a frontier farmer whose first attempts to earn a living met with failure. Through influential friends, he was licensed to practice law and made a name for himself, eventually winning a seat in the House of Burgesses. An early radical and an ambitious self-promoter, Henry represented frontier interests against the landed establishment and was known throughout the colonies for his fiery orations. He went to both Continental Congresses, and following the first, he returned to Virginia to make the March 20, 1755, speech for which he is most famous.

He was elected first governor of Virginia, and sent George Rogers Clark to expel the British. After the war he opposed the Constitution, but later reversed himself. His poor health kept him from taking a position offered in Washington's administration.

AMERICAN VOICES
PATRICK HENRY to the House of Burgesses:

Is life so dear or peace so sweet as to be purchased at the price of chains and slavery? . . . I know not what course others may take, but as for me, give me liberty or give me death!

Thomas Jefferson (1743–1826) Born into a well-off farming family in Virginia's Albemarle County, the Declaration's author distinguished himself early as a scholar, and gained admission to the Virginia bar in 1767. Although no great admirer of Patrick Henry's bombastic style, Jefferson was drawn to the patriot circle around Henry after Jefferson was elected to the House of Burgesses, having provided voters with rum punch, a colonial tradition for candidates. His literary prowess, demonstrated in political pamphlets, prompted John Adams to put Jefferson forward as the man to write the Declaration, a task he accepted with reluctance.

Most of his war years were spent in Virginia as a legislator and later as governor. After his wife's death, in 1783, he joined the Continental Congress and served as ambassador to France, where he could observe firsthand the French Revolution that he had helped inspire. Returning to America in 1789, Jefferson became Washington's secretary of state and began to oppose what he saw as a too-powerful central government under the new Constitution, bringing him into a direct confrontation with his old colleague John Adams and, more dramatically, with the chief Federalist, Alexander Hamilton.

Running second to Adams in 1796, he became vice president, chafing at the largely ceremonial role. In 1800, Jefferson and fellow Democratic Republican Aaron Burr tied in the Electoral College vote, and Jefferson took the presidency in a House vote. After two terms, he returned to his Monticello home to complete his final endeavor, the University of Virginia, his architectural masterpiece. As he lay dying, Jefferson would ask what the date was, holding out, like John Adams, until July 4, 1826, the fiftieth anniversary of the Declaration.

Richard Henry Lee (1732–94) A member of Virginia's most prominent family and the House of Burgesses, Lee was a valuable ally of Patrick Henry and Samuel Adams. Sent to the Continental Congress in 1776, he proposed the resolution on independence and was one of the signers of the Declaration.

James Otis (1725–83) A descent into madness kept this Boston lawyer, a writer and speaker on a par with the greats of the era, from earning a greater place in Revolutionary history. Samuel Adams's first ally, Otis became one of the most fiery of the Boston radicals, his pamphlets declaring the rights of the colonists and introducing the phrase "no taxation without representation." Although he attended the 1765 Stamp Act Congress, by 1771 his behavior was increasingly erratic. Walking the streets of Boston, he fired pistols and broke windows until his family bound him and carted him off to a country farm. In and out of asylums, he died when his farmhouse was struck by lightning.

Thomas Paine (1737–1809) One of the Revolution's pure idealists, the English-born Paine lived up to his name in the eyes of those he attacked. Unsuccessful in London, where his radical notions got him into trouble, he came to America with the aid of Benjamin Franklin. At Franklin's urging, he wrote *Common Sense* and helped push the colonies toward independence.

With the Continental Army in retreat, he later wrote a series of pamphlets at Washington's request that became *The Crisis*. In 1781, he went to France and helped secure a large gold shipment for the rebel cause. After the war he returned to England and wrote *The Rights of Man*, which earned him a conviction on charges of treason. He took refuge in France, where his antimonarchist ideas were welcomed as France went through the throes of its great Revolution. But as that revolution began to eat its own, Paine was imprisoned and wrote *The Age of Reason* while awaiting the guillotine. Spared execution, he returned to America. The eternal gadfly, Paine alienated the new American powers-that-be with his *Letter to Washington*, and died a poor outcast.

AMERICAN VOICES
From *The Crisis* by THOMAS PAINE:

These are the times that try men's souls. The summer soldier and the sunshine patriot will shrink from the service of his country. . . . Tyranny, like Hell, is not easily conquered.

Paul Revere (1735–1818) "Listen my children and you shall hear . . ."
It is perhaps the best-known bit of doggerel in American literature.
But like most epic poems, Longfellow's tribute to the Boston silversmith fudges the facts. Boston born, Revere was the son of a Huguenot, the French Protestants who had been driven from France. In
America, he changed his name from Apollos Rivoire. A silversmith
like his father, Paul Revere also went into the false-teeth business.
A veteran of the French and Indian War, he was in the Samuel
Adams circle of rebels, serving as a messenger. He took an active
part in all the events leading up to the war, and his famous engraving of the Massacre, which had been lifted from the work of another
artist, became an icon in every patriot home.

But it was the ride to Lexington that brought him immortality of
sorts. In fact, he made two rides. The first was to warn the patriots to
hide their ammunition in Concord, and the second was the famous
"midnight ride." After receiving the signal from the South Church,
Revere and two other riders set off. Although he was able to reach
Lexington and warn John Hancock, Samuel Adams, and the Minutemen of the British approach, Revere was soon captured.

His wartime record was also slightly tarnished. Despite his services as a trusted courier, he had not received a commission from
Congress and served out the war in a militia unit. In one of his few
actions, Revere was ordered to lead troops against the British at Pe-
nobscot. Instead he marched his men back to Boston when American ships failed to engage the British. Because he was relieved of
command and accused of cowardice, Revere's honor was smudged
until a court acquittal in 1782.

Joseph Warren (1741–75) A Boston physician, Warren became one
of Sam Adams's most devoted protégés. An active participant in the
major prewar event in Boston, Warren became an instant hero when
he charged into enemy fire at Lexington to treat the wounded. His
fame was short-lived as he became one of the first patriot martyrs.
Commissioned a general despite a lack of experience, he joined the
ranks on Breed's Hill and was killed in the fighting there.

Mercy Otis Warren (1728–1814) Sister of the patriot leader James
Otis, Mercy Warren surmounted the heavy odds placed before

women in eighteenth-century America to become a writer of considerable influence. A dramatist, she was unable to see her plays performed because Puritan Boston did not permit theatrical works. An outspoken critic of the Constitution, she wrote widely to defeat its ratification. In 1805, she published the first history of the Revolution, the three-volume *Rise, Progress and Termination of the American Revolution*. While rich in anecdotal material and period detail, the book was colored by Warren's fierce anti-Federalist bias, and was written in the full fervor of postwar patriotic sentiment.

THE SOLDIERS

Ethan Allen (1738–89) A flamboyant veteran of the French and Indian War and a giant of a man, Allen raised a private army in Vermont called the Green Mountain Boys during an ongoing border dispute with Vermont's sister colony, New York. After Lexington, Allen and his men, joined by Benedict Arnold, captured the undermanned Fort Ticonderoga in upstate New York from the British, but he was voted out of command of the Green Mountain Boys. Captured during an assault on Montreal in 1775, Allen was thrown in irons and returned to England to stand trial. He was held prisoner for two years. Later he attempted to negotiate a separate peace treaty with the British. And in May 1778, he joined Washington at Valley Forge, was given a commission, and returned to Vermont, where he pressed the cause of Vermont's independence from New York and New Hampshire. There is a suggestion that he was negotiating with the British to make Vermont a province of Canada. He died of apoplexy before Vermont was admitted as the 14th state.

George Rogers Clark (1752–1818) A surveyor and frontiersman, Clark led the successful military operations against the British and their Indian allies on the western frontier in what would later become Kentucky.

Horatio Gates (c. 1728–1806) A British-born soldier, he was badly wounded in his first action during the French and Indian War. Gates took up the patriot cause and led the American forces that won the key battle at Saratoga in 1777. But later that year he took part in an abortive attempt to wrest control of the army from George Washington. In 1780, he was given command of the army in the South, but was badly defeated at Camden, South Carolina, and lost his command. After the war, Gates was reinstated as the army's second ranking officer.

Nathanael Greene (1724–86) A Rhode Island Quaker with no military experience, Greene became a self-taught student of military history and emerged as one of the war's most successful tacticians, rising to the rank of general. At the war's outset, he commanded Rhode Island's three regiments but was picked by Washington for rapid advancement. With Washington at the defeats in Long Island and Manhattan as well as the victory at Trenton, he made his greatest contribution as a commander in the South. Using a guerrilla strategy, he harassed Cornwallis from the Carolinas, forcing him back toward Virginia and the Yorktown showdown. At the end of the war, his reputation was second only to that of Washington. After the war he fell into financial difficulty because he had pledged much of his personal fortune to an associate who went bankrupt. In 1785, he settled on the confiscated estate of a loyalist near Savannah, Georgia, but died there the following year from sunstroke.

Alexander Hamilton (1757–1804) Born in the West Indies, Hamilton was proof that low birth need not be an impediment in early America. The illegitimate son of a shopkeeper mother whose father deserted them, Hamilton caught the attention of wealthy benefactors who sent him to King's College (now Columbia University) in New York. He became an ardent patriot and, at age nineteen, was leading a company of New York artillery.

At Trenton he caught Washington's eye and became a favorite, rising to the position of Washington's aide and private secretary, and later commanding in the field. A convenient marriage to the daughter of Philip Schuyler, a powerful New Yorker, gave him entrée to society and additional clout.

His career was even more significant after the war, when he established a law practice in New York and became a key figure in the constitutional convention of 1787. Hamilton was one of the chief essayists behind *The Federalist Papers* arguing for the Constitution's ratification (see Chapter 3). He became Washington's secretary of the treasury, and was a crucial figure in the first two administrations, establishing the nation's economic policies. But he became involved in political and amorous intrigues that crippled his career.

He returned to private practice, remaining a central figure in the Federalist Party, and his views were the source of the feud that led to his fatal duel with Aaron Burr.

John Paul Jones (1747–92) Essentially an adventurer who followed the action, America's first naval hero was born John Paul in Scotland and began his career on a slave ship. He came to America under a dark cloud following the death of one of his crewmen, and added Jones to his name. When the Congress commissioned a small navy, Jones volunteered and was given the *Providence*, with which he raided English ships. With the *Ranger*, he sailed to France and continued his raids off the English coast. The French later gave him a refitted ship called the *Bonhomme Richard*, and with it he engaged the larger British ship *Serapis* in a battle he won at the loss of *Bonhomme Richard*. A hero to the French, Jones was later sent to France as an emissary, and received a congressional medal in 1787. He finished his sea career with the Russian navy of the Empress Catherine before his death in Paris. (In 1905, his supposed remains were returned to the U.S. and reburied at Annapolis, Maryland.)

AMERICAN VOICES

JOHN PAUL JONES during the battle against *Serapis*:

I have not yet begun to fight.

Henry Knox (1750–1806) A Boston bookseller and a witness to the Boston Massacre, Knox rose to become the general in charge of Washington's artillery and one of the commander-in-chief's most trusted aides. His nickname, Ox, came from both his substantial girth—he stood six feet, three inches and weighed some 280 pounds—and for the exploit in which, during the dead of winter in 1775, he transported the British cannons captured at Fort Ticonderoga by oxcart back to Boston. In Washington's first engagement as commander, these guns were placed on Dorchester Heights, forcing General Howe's army to evacuate the city without a shot being fired.

At Yorktown, Knox commanded the artillery bombardment of General Cornwallis's forces and after the war, he served in Congress. War secretary under the Articles of Confederation, Knox was a trusted aide to Washington and became the first war secretary following Washington's election. He also founded the Society of the Cincinnati, an organization formed (1783) by former officers of the Continental Army. Initially nonpolitical, the society became a conservative Federalist power and was criticized as an aristocratic military nobility. To counter the Society, Tammany societies were formed by working-class veterans in cities like New York and Philadelphia, which soon evolved into an anti-Federalist power. (Both Knoxville and Fort Knox are named for him.)

Marquis de Lafayette (1757–1834) One of the Revolution's idealists, this young Frenchman came to America at age nineteen, wealthy enough to pay for his own ship to make the journey. Like other young European aristocrats for whom war was a matter of personal honor and social standing, Lafayette came in search of glory and adventure. In exchange for a major general's rank, he offered to serve without pay, and quickly earned Washington's affection. They developed an almost father-son relationship. Given a minor command, Lafayette proved to be an able and loyal commander.

During a trip back to France, he was instrumental in securing the French military assistance that was the key to the American victory at Yorktown. At the surrender, Lafayette's personal band proudly piped "Yankee Doodle Dandy," once a song mockingly sung by the British to taunt the Americans. After the war, Lafayette returned to France with enough American soil in which to be buried.

Charles Lee (1731–82) A British-born soldier who rose to general in the patriot army, Lee had fought in the French and Indian War with Braddock, and had seen combat in Europe as well. A professional soldier, he was far more experienced than most of the American commanders, including Washington, whom he grew to disdain. Commissioned a major general, he justified the rank with his defense of Charleston early in the war. He was later captured and held by the British for fifteen months. Allegedly, he offered his captors a plan for defeating the Americans. At the Battle of Monmouth, Lee ordered a confused and costly retreat, for which he was court-martialed and broken of command. He returned to Virginia, where he died in a tavern before the peace treaty was signed.

Francis Marion (1732?–95) Best known as the Swamp Fox, Marion led a successful guerrilla war against British and vicious Tory troops under General Cornwallis in the Carolinas. It was the efforts of Marion and other guerrillas, including Charles Sumter, in the southern colonies that frustrated the British strategy to control the South. One British officer complained that he "would not fight like a Christian."

Daniel Morgan (1735–89) A veteran of Braddock's French and Indian disaster, Morgan had driven supply trains, earning his nickname Old Wagoner. During the French and Indian War, Morgan had received 500 lashes over a fight with a British officer and he held a grudge. Another of Washington's most valuable commanders, he led a troop of buckskinned frontier riflemen who played a crucial role in the victory at Saratoga. Elevated to general, he commanded half the southern army and led the key victory at Cowpens and was also instrumental in the bloody Battle of Guilford Court, where General Cornwallis's losses were so heavy that the British commander had to abandon his plans to hold the Carolinas and retreat to Virginia.

Molly Pitcher (1754–1832) During the exhausting summer heat of the Battle of Monmouth (1778), Mary McCauley Hays, the wife of Private John Hays, fetched water for her husband and his gun crew, earning her the sobriquet Molly Pitcher. When her husband was wounded in the battle, she knew his job well enough to help the gun crew continue firing. An apocryphal story they perhaps didn't tell you in grade school was that a cannonball passed through Molly's legs and tore away her petticoats. Molly is said to have told the men that it was a good thing it hadn't been higher, or it would have carried away something else! After the war, Mary Hays became a scrubwoman and the Pennsylvania Assembly later granted her a yearly pension of $40.

Israel Putnam (1718–90) A colonel in the Connecticut militia, Old Put left his plow, in the great tradition of civilian soldiers, and headed for Boston when the shooting started at Lexington. One of those in command on Breed's Hill, he achieved immortality of sorts with his order, "Don't fire until you see the whites of their eyes," a well-known piece of military advice of the day.

When the rebel troops started to break ranks after inflicting heavy losses on the British, Putnam unsuccessfully tried to keep his troops in place. But his failure to reinforce an American position was one reason the patriot army left off the battle when a victory might have been won, and Putnam was nearly court-martialed. Instead, Congress made him a general out of regional political considerations. Though never a great strategist or commander, he remained a loyal aide to Washington throughout the war.

Comte de Rochambeau (1725–1807) Commander of the 7,000 French troops sent to aid the rebels, Rochambeau had far more experience than Washington. Coordinating his movements with the French war fleet under Admiral de Grasse, Rochambeau deserves much of the credit for forcing the showdown at Yorktown at a time when Washington seemed to prefer an assault on New York.

Deborah Sampson (1760–1827) Assuming the name Robert Shurtleff, this former indentured servant enlisted in the Continental Army in 1782 and became the only woman to serve formally in the Revolution. Fighting with the Fourth Massachusetts, she managed to maintain her disguise, although her fellow soldiers nicknamed her Molly because of her hairless face. A fever finally uncovered her true identity, and Sampson was discharged in 1783. She married the next year and received a small military pension. In 1802, she began a lecture tour, one of the first American women to do so, recounting her experiences as a soldier, a performance capped by her donning a soldier's uniform. Congress granted her heirs a full military pension in 1838.

George Washington (1732–99) As for the cherry tree story, it was one of many fabrications created by Washington's "biographer," Parson Weems, who also fashioned the "fact" that he was rector of a nonexistent parish at Mount Vernon. The coin tossed across the Rappahannock—not the Potomac—was another of Weems's inventions. The legends began there, leaving "the father of our country" enshrouded in more layers of myth than any other figure in American history. Most of those myths came from the pen of Mason Locke Weems, whose *Life and Memorable Actions of Washington* was published in 1800. Many of his tales were invented to underscore Washington's heroic qualities.

Washington was born into a modestly prosperous Virginia family. The death of his father, a tobacco planter, reduced his fortune, but with the help of relatives he did well, eventually inheriting the family estate at Mount Vernon. He was given a modest amount of "grammar school," but never went to college. A plan to send him to the Royal Navy was squelched by his mother, who assumed— probably correctly—that a young American would never go far in the rigidly aristocratic British navy. Washington's mother was tough and smoked a corn-cob pipe and, while he was respectful of her, they clearly did not have a warm relationship. He eagerly took the chance to live with an older half-brother.

An excellent horseman, with a natural affinity for math—as a boy, he counted the number of windowpanes and the stairs in staircases—Washington eventually combined his love for the outdoors with his mathematical ability by becoming a surveyor. Eventually he began to acquire some of the land he had been mapping. His early military career was mostly remarkable for the fact that he survived it. Yet when the French and Indian War was over, Washington was something of a homegrown American military hero.

His wealth came from his marriage to Martha Dandridge Custis, the young widow of one of Virginia's wealthiest men. By the time of the Revolution, Washington was among the richest men in America, although his holdings were in land and slaves rather than cash. As expected of men of his station, he ran for the House of Burgesses and was sent to the two Continental Congresses. After volunteering to serve without pay, he was unanimously chosen commander of the Continental Army when it became apparent that for political reasons a southerner had to fill the job.

There are conflicting views about his military leadership. Traditionalists say that he held together a ragged, ill-equipped army by sheer force of will, chose his commanders well, and had to spend too much time dickering with Congress for enough money to arm his men. This view also holds that he was a master of the strategic retreat, and tricked the British into believing his point of attack would be New York when it was actually Yorktown.

The revisionist view holds that Washington was an unduly harsh leader who maintained brutal discipline in the ranks, nearly lost the war several times, to be saved only by greater incompetence on the part of the British, was better at politicking than commanding, and had to be dragged against his will by the French to attack Yorktown. Several historians argue that Charles Lee or Horatio Gates would have been more daring commanders who might have ended the war sooner. It is an intriguing speculation that will remain unanswered, although Lee's actions in battle and assistance to the British while a captive do little to arouse confidence in his abilities.

Clearly, Washington was no tactical genius on the order of Caesar or Napoleon. He fought nine battles during the war and won three of them. But that does not mean he was not a great leader. A story reported during the early days of the war is telling: in Boston, bands of American rebel fighters had gotten into a near riot. Washington raced to the scene on horseback and landed in the midst of a brawl. Physically imposing, Washington grabbed two of the men fighting, lifted each off the ground, and shouted commands at the rest. A witness to this scene, Major General John Sullivan of New Hampshire, later said, "From the moment I saw Washington leap the bars at Cambridge, I never faltered in the faith that we had the right man to lead the cause of American liberty."

The fact remains that Washington, dealt a weak hand, surmounted the odds of poorly outfitted troops, political intrigues, numerous betrayals, and a vastly better equipped opposition to sweep up the jackpot. If nothing else, he was a consummate survivor, and that may have been what America required at the time. That he was universally loved by his soldiers seems unlikely; there were frequent mutinies for the suppression of which Washington kept a well-fed and -trained group of militia. He did inspire fierce loyalty among his officer corps, perhaps the true strength of a commander. For the American people, he was the first larger-than-life national hero, something a new nation arguably needs to survive.

In London after the war, King George III met with American painter Benjamin West and asked what Washington would do after the war. When West said that the general would resign and return to private life, the amazed king reportedly said, "If he does that, sir, he will be the greatest man in the world." After his emotional farewell at Fraunces Tavern in New York, Washington did just that. He retired to Mount Vernon, until he was called back to serve as president at a time when probably no other man in America could have united the country behind the new government.

What was *Common Sense*?

When the Continental Congress met for the second time, in May 1775, it was a very different group. The first Congress had been cautious and even conciliatory, with conservative and moderate voices holding sway. But the pendulum was swinging to the radical position, and there were new faces among the delegates, Benjamin Franklin — once cautious, now rebellious — and Thomas Jefferson among them.

Events were also moving swiftly. The battles at Lexington and Concord, the easy victory at Fort Ticonderoga, the devastating casualties inflicted on the British army by the rebels at Breed's Hill, and the evacuation of British troops from Boston in March 1776 had all given hope to the Whig (patriot) cause. But the final break — independence — still seemed too extreme to some. It's important to remember that the vast majority of Americans at the time were first and second generation. Their family ties and their sense of culture and national identity were essentially English. Many Americans had friends and family in England. And the commercial ties between the two were obviously also powerful.

The forces pushing toward independence needed momentum, and they got it in several ways. The first factor was another round of heavy-handed British miscalculations. First the king issued a proclamation cutting off the colonies from trade. Then, unable to conscript sufficient troops, the British command decided to supplement its regulars with mercenaries, soldiers from the German principalities sold into King George's service by their princes. Most came from Hesse-Cassel, so the name Hessian became generic for all of these hired soldiers.

The Hessians accounted for as much as a third of the English forces fighting in the colonies. Their reputation as fierce fighters was linked to a frightening image—reinforced, no doubt, by the British command—as plundering rapists. (Ironically, many of them stayed on in America. Benjamin Franklin gave George Washington printed promises of free land to lure mercenaries away from English ranks.) When word of the coming of 12,000 Hessian troops reached America, it was a shock, and further narrowed chances for reconciliation. In response, a convention in Virginia instructed its delegates to Congress to declare the United Colonies free and independent.

The second factor was a literary one. In January 1776, an anonymous pamphlet entitled *Common Sense* came off the presses of a patriot printer. Its author, Thomas Paine, had simply, eloquently, and admittedly with some melodramatic prose, stated the reasons for independence. He reduced the hereditary succession of kings to an absurdity, slashed down all arguments for reconciliation with England, argued the economic benefits of independence, and even presented a cost analysis for creating an American navy.

With the assistance of Ben Franklin, Thomas Paine came to America from London and found work with a Philadelphia bookseller. In the colonies for only a few months, Paine wrote, at Franklin's suggestion, a brief history of the upheaval against England. It is almost impossible to exaggerate the impact and importance of *Common Sense*. Paine's polemic was read by everyone in Congress, including General Washington, who commented on its effects on his men. Equally important, it was read by people everywhere. The pamphlet quickly sold 150,000 copies, going through numerous printings until it had reached half a million. (Approximating the American population at the time, including slaves, at 3 million, a current equivalent pamphlet would have to sell more than 35 million copies!) For the first time, mass public opinion had swung toward the cause of independence.

AMERICAN VOICES
From a letter written by ABIGAIL ADAMS to
her husband, John, who was attending
the Continental Congress, March 31, 1776:

In the new Code of Laws which I suppose it will be necessary for you to make I desire you would Remember the
Ladies, and be more generous and favourable to them
than your ancestors. Do not put such unlimited powers
into the hands of the Husbands. Remember all men would
be tyrants if they could. If particular care and attention is
not paid to the Ladies, we are determined to foment a Rebellion, and will not hold ourselves bound by any laws in
which we have no voice, or Representation.

Upon receipt of this directive from home, a bemused John Adams
replied, in part, "Depend upon it. We know better than to repeal our
Masculine systems."

What exactly does the Declaration of Independence say? What did Congress leave out?

On June 7, 1776, Richard Henry Lee, a delegate from Virginia and a
member of one of that colony's leading families, rose in Philadelphia
to propose a three-part resolution: (1) to declare the colonies independent; (2) to form foreign alliances; (3) to prepare a plan of confederation.
After days of debate, Congress compromised. In that time-honored
congressional tradition of putting off important decisions, this Congress decided to form committees, one for each of these points.

The committee selected to draw up some document declaring that
America was free of England naturally included John Adams and Ben
Franklin, already an internationally known writer. Robert Livingston,
a conservative from New York, was named along with Roger Sherman
of Connecticut. A southerner was needed for political balance, and
John Adams lobbied hard for the fifth member. His choice, Virginian

Thomas Jefferson, was seen as a compromise. Jefferson had a reputation as a writer, and had already contributed one pamphlet to Congress, *A Summary View of the Rights of British America*. Although a bitter political rival in later years, Adams now deferred to Jefferson because, as he admitted, Jefferson could write ten times better than he.

Distracted by his wife's health and a preference to work on the new constitution of Virginia that was being written while he was in Philadelphia, Jefferson was a reluctant author. But closeting himself away, he set to work quickly, writing on a portable desk he had designed. He presented his draft to the committee, which recommended changes and forwarded it to Congress for debate.

Of course the delegates demanded changes, all of which Jefferson considered deplorable. The most debated was Jefferson's charge that the king was responsible for the slave trade. The southern delegates, joined by northerners who were known to have profited from, in Jefferson's own phrase, "this execrable commerce," deleted this section.

With the advantage of hindsight, cynicism about this Congress and Thomas Jefferson in particular is easy. But the baffling question remains: How could a man who embodied the Enlightenment—who wrote so eloquently that "all Men are created equal" and are endowed by the Creator with the right of liberty—how could such a man keep black slaves, of which Jefferson (like Washington and many others in Congress) possessed many? There is no truly satisfying answer. Earlier in his life, as a lawyer and member of the Burgesses, he had unsuccessfully argued against aspects of slavery. At worst, Jefferson may not have thought of slaves as men, not an unusual notion in his time. And he was a man of his times. Like other men, great and small, he was not perfect.

On July 2, Lee's resolution of independence was passed by Congress. On the evening of July 4, the Declaration of Independence, which explained the act of independence, was adopted. At the signing, John Hancock reportedly urged unanimity. "There must be no pulling different ways. We must hang together," he said.

"Yes," said the inimitable Ben Franklin. "We must indeed all hang together, or most assuredly we shall all hang separately." (Whether the story is true, most biographers agree that it certainly suits Franklin wit and wisdom.)

Although Jefferson suffered doubts because of the changes forced upon him, many of which many historians agree were for the better, the finished document was cheered throughout the colonies. Jefferson had voiced all the pent-up anguish that the American rebels had been feeling for years.

Must Read: *American Scripture: Making the Declaration of Independence* by Pauline Maier.

Why is there a statue of Benedict Arnold's boot?

Once trusted and admired, Benedict Arnold (1741–1801) became the most famous traitor in United States history, his name synonymous with treachery. Yet in Saratoga, New York, one of the most unusual memorials in America is a statue of a boot that stands in his honor.

Born in Norwich, Connecticut, Arnold learned the apothecary trade and, in 1762, established a book and drug store in New Haven, while also carrying on trade with the West Indies. By 1774, he was one of the wealthiest men in New Haven and became a captain in the Connecticut militia. Soon after the war began, he was commissioned as a colonel in the patriot forces. Along with Vermont's Ethan Allen, Arnold led the capture of Fort Ticonderoga, in New York, on May 10, 1775, one of the most significant early victories for the American rebel army.

Later that year, Arnold led 1,100 soldiers, including three companies of Colonel Daniel Morgan's well-trained western riflemen, into Canada. It was a disastrously unsuccessful assault on Quebec in an attempt to get Canadians to join the other colonies in the struggle for liberty. Severely wounded in the assault, Arnold gained a growing reputation for courage and audaciousness and won promotion to brigadier general, despite criticism that he was recklessly bold.

But then he began to suffer a series of bitter disappointments. Passed over for promotion in February 1777, when Congress appointed five new major generals, Arnold, who had more seniority than any of the men promoted, nearly left the army. He was convinced to remain by General Washington, and in May 1777 Congress promoted Arnold to major general as a reward for his bravery in helping drive a British raiding party out of Connecticut. But it did not restore his seniority and Arnold seethed, again coaxed by Washington to stay in the army.

Later that year, Arnold served under General Horatio Gates against the British general John Burgoyne. During two days of crucial fighting near Saratoga in upstate New York in October 1777, Arnold showed gallant courage against Burgoyne and suffered a serious wound to the same leg that he had wounded in the fighting at Quebec. These engagements, won by the patriots, led to Burgoyne's surrender at Saratoga several days later. General Gates received credit for the victory, but Congress voted Arnold the country's thanks and instructed Washington to restore Arnold's rank. The Saratoga statue of Arnold's boot, among the most curious of America's historical statues, honors Arnold's heroic role in a battle that surely changed the course of the war and perhaps all of American history. Had Arnold died from his wounds that day, he would have probably gone down as one of the Revolution's most significant martyrs. Another tall obelisk monument at the Saratoga National Historic Park honors General Philip Schuyler, General Horatio Gates, and Colonel Daniel Morgan. A niche for Arnold stands empty–stark testimony to what most people think of when they hear Arnold's name: the greatest traitor in American history.

In 1778, Arnold took command of the Philadelphia area and married Margaret (Peggy) Shippen, a young woman from a prominent family. They lived extravagantly and began to incur debts. Arnold also argued with local authorities. When the executive council of Pennsylvania accused Arnold of using soldiers to do personal favors, a court-martial cleared Arnold, but it ordered General Washington to rebuke him, which Washington did reluctantly. To Arnold, his service had been met with ingratitude and injustice, and he began corresponding with the British commander Sir Henry Clinton, an acquaintance of Arnold's father-in-law, a wealthy Pennsylvania judge with Tory (pro-British) leanings.

Given command of West Point, then a crucial strongpoint overlooking and controlling the Hudson River (and the future home of the United States Military Academy), Arnold worked out a plan to surrender that important military base to the British commander. But Clinton's director of intelligence, Major John André, was captured in

1780 by American militiamen, and papers pertaining to the plot were found in his boot. Arnold escaped to New York City, while André was to be hanged as a spy. André appealed to Washington, asking to be shot instead of hanged but Washington declined. "All that I request of you gentlemen," André is said to have told his captors, "is that you will bear witness to the world that I die like a brave man."

Although Washington made several plans to kidnap Arnold after he deserted, they all failed, and Arnold became a brigadier general in the British army. He demanded 20,000 pounds from the British for the losses he incurred in joining them, but he received only 6,315 pounds. As a British officer, he led expeditions that burned Richmond, Virginia, and New London, Connecticut. He also advised Henry Clinton, the overall British commander in America, to support the British army at Yorktown. Clinton ignored that advice with disastrous results for the British.

Arnold was received warmly by King George III when he went to England in 1782, but others there scorned him. In 1797, the British government granted him 13,400 acres (5,423 hectares) in Canada, but the land was of little use to him. He spent most of his remaining years as a merchant in the West Indies trade. In his last days, Arnold was burdened with debt, became discouraged, and was generally distrusted before his death in London in 1801.

Must Read: *Saratoga: Turning Point of America's Revolutionary War* by Richard M. Ketchum.

What were the Articles of Confederation?

Congress had invented a wonderful new machine, with a flag and an army, but they didn't quite know how to work it. Ben Franklin, who knew a thing or two about inventing, had been tinkering with the idea of a colonial confederation as far back as 1754, but his attempts to create one had been in vain. Local colonial power brokers wanted to see that power stayed that way—local and in their hands, not in the hands of the rabble. But now, with independence declared, British warships floating off the coast, and the threat of the hangman's noose if they failed, a little machinery of government seemed a sensible idea.

In August, the Congress began to debate what would become the Articles of Confederation, the first loosely organized federal government. Disagreement hinged on questions of representation and voting: Should votes be apportioned on population, or should each state receive a single vote in Congress? Obviously, big states wanted population to determine votes; small states wanted one vote per state. The war diverted their attention to other matters—such as saving their own necks. It was 1777 before the Articles were submitted to the states for ratification, and 1781 before they were ratified. As foundations for national governments go, this was a rather shaky one. Under the Articles, the presidency was a powerless office, and Congress lacked the power to tax. Owing to uncertainties about what kind of power the government should have, the Articles provided almost none. But Congress was able to sputter through the war until it could build itself a better mousetrap.

Betsy Ross: Did she or didn't she?

On January 1, 1776, George Washington raised a new flag over his rebel lines in Boston. But it wasn't the stars and stripes. The first American flag was a banner with thirteen alternating red and white stripes with the crosses of St. George and St. Andrew set into the upper left corner. These were symbols of the British throne and captured the hope that there might still be a political resolution that would maintain some connection between Americans and the throne of England. Many Americans of that time—John Adams thought as many as a third—were still loyalists. Many others still considered themselves Englishmen, and this flag—the flag of the Grand Union—symbolized that connection.

By June 1777, it was clear that such a reconciliation was not possible and Congress resolved that the flag of the U.S. should be "13 stripes alternate red and white and the union be 13 stars in a blue field, representing a new constellation."

The record doesn't show who made the decisions or was responsible for the design.

It is definite that it was *not* Betsy Ross.

Elizabeth Griscom Ross was a Philadelphia seamstress, married to John Ross, an upholsterer who was killed in an explosion in 1776. She kept the upholstery shop going and lived on Arch Street, not too far from the State House on Chestnut, where the Continental Congress was in sessions. According to popular legend, George Washington was a frequent visitor to the Ross home before receiving command of the army, and Betsy Ross embroidered his shirt ruffles. Later, as the general of the Continental Army, George Washington supposedly appeared on Mrs. Ross's doorstep with two representatives of Congress. They asked that she make a flag according to a rough drawing they carried with them. Mrs. Ross suggested that Washington redraw the flag design to employ stars of five points instead of six. (This account of the creation of the stars and stripes was first brought to light in 1870 by one of her grandsons, William J. Canby. After Canby's death, a book called *The Evolution of the American Flag*, published in 1909, presented the claims for Betsy Ross made by William Canby in 1870.)

In the many years since the story was told, no one has been able to verify Canby's claims. It is known that Betsy Ross made "ships colors" for Pennsylvania state ships for which she was paid. Beyond that, the Betsy Ross story is simply family myth.

After the war, Francis Hopkinson, a Philadelphia poet, took credit for the flag's design, but he was not taken seriously. So the men who deserve full credit for the design of the American flag remain a faceless, anonymous congressional committee.

How did the colonies win the war?

Does this sound familiar? The world's most powerful nation is caught up in a war against a small guerrilla army. This superpower must resupply its troops from thousands of miles away, a costly endeavor, and support for the war at home is tentative, dividing the nation's people and leadership. The rebels also receive financial and military support from the superpower's chief military and political antagonist. As the war drags on and casualties mount, generals are disgraced and the rebels gain momentum, even in defeat.

The United States in Vietnam? It could be. But it is also the story of the British loss of the American colonies. There are numerous parallels between the two conflicts. For the United States, substitute England under George III, the dominant world power of the day, but caught up in a draining colonial conflict that stretches its resources. For the Vietcong, substitute the colonial army under Washington, a ragtag collection if ever there was one, who used such unheard-of tactics as disguising themselves in British uniforms and attacking from the rear. British generals, accustomed to precisely drawn battle formations, were completely taken aback, just as American commanders schooled in the tank warfare of World War II were unprepared for the jungles of Vietnam. For foreign support, substitute England's chief European adversary, France (as well as Spain and the Netherlands) for the Soviet (and Red Chinese) supplying of the Vietcong.

There can be no question that without France's armies, money, and supplies (as much as 90 percent of the American gunpowder used in the war came from France), the American forces could not have won. Why did the French do it? Certainly King Louis XVI and his charming wife, Marie Antoinette, had no particular sympathy for antimonarchist, democratic rabble. Their motive, actually the strategy of a pro-American minister, the Comte de Vergennes, was simple: to bloody England's nose in any way they could and perhaps even win back some of the territory lost after the Seven Years War. Had the monarchy and aristocracy of France known that their own subjects would be greatly inspired by the American Revolution a few years later, the French royalty might have thought the matter over a bit longer. An American loss might have saved their necks. *C'est la vie!*

Equally important to America's victory was the consistent bungling of the British high command, which treated the war as an intolerable inconvenience. At any number of points in the fighting, particularly in the early years, before France was fully committed, aggressive generalship from various British commanders might have turned the tide.

If Washington's army had been destroyed after Long Island or Germantown . . .

If Congress had been captured and shipped off to England for trial—and most likely the noose . . .

And what if England had "won"? Could it possibly have maintained sovereignty over a large, prosperous, diverse, and expanding America, a vast territory far richer in resources than England? It is unlikely. Independence was a historical inevitability, in one form or another. It was simply an idea whose time had come, and America was not alone, as the revolutions that followed in Europe would prove.

The British had to weigh the costs of maintaining their dominance against its returns. They would have seen, as America did in Vietnam, and as the Soviets did more recently in Afghanistan, that the costs of such wars of colonial domination are usually more than a nation is willing or able to bear.

It's a pity that America's military and political leaders never learned a lesson from our own past, a fact that speaks volumes about the arrogance of power.

What did America win?

The Peace of Paris, negotiated for the United States by Benjamin Franklin, John Adams, and John Jay, was formally signed on February 3, 1783. At the same time, England signed treaties with America's allies, France, Spain, and the Netherlands. The most important thing the treaty did was to recognize the independence of the United States of America. Beyond that, it marked the boundaries of the new nation.

The United States now meant everything from the Atlantic west to the Mississippi River, save New Orleans and the Floridas. This area was ceded by England back to Spain as part of New Spain, the massive empire that now stretched from South America north, well into coastal California, and included much of the American Southwest, east to the Florida peninsula. The northern border was set at the Great Lakes and along the provincial frontiers of Quebec and Nova Scotia.

During the eight years of the American Revolution, there had been more than 1,300 land and sea battles. American losses have been calculated conservatively at 25,324. Of these, only 6,284 were killed in action. More than 10,000 died of diseases such as smallpox and dysentery, and another 8,500 died while captives of the British.

The victory also left America with a considerable foreign debt. In a report to Congress several years later, Alexander Hamilton would place this debt at $11,710,379 (in addition to domestic and state debts totaling more than $65 million). This enormous debt was just one of the problems that would threaten the new nation in its first years of independence. Behaving like thirteen independent countries, the states churned out worthless paper money. New York began to place taxes on every farmer's boat that crossed the Hudson River from New Jersey.

Must Read: *Liberty!: The American Revolution* by Thomas Fleming; *Patriots: The Men Who Started the American Revolution* by A. J. Langguth; *The Creation of America: Through Revolution to Empire* by Francis Jennings for a very different view of the Revolution as the work of a privileged elite, dreaming of empire.

AMERICAN VOICES
GEORGE WASHINGTON,
in a 1786 letter to Robert Morris:

There is a not a man living who wishes more sincerely than I do to see a plan adopted for the gradual abolition of [slavery].

DR. HARRIS, a black veteran of the Revolution, speaking to the Congregational and Anti-Slavery Society of Francestown, New Hampshire:

I served in the Revolution, in General Washington's army. . . . I have stood in battle, where balls, like hail, were flying all around me. The man standing next to me was shot by my side—his blood spotted upon my clothes, which I wore for weeks. My nearest blood, except that which run in my veins, was shed for liberty. My only brother was shot dead instantly in the Revolution. Liberty is dear to my heart—I cannot endure the thought, that my countrymen should be slaves.

Some 5,000 blacks served in the Revolution. (Perhaps another 1,000, mostly runaways who had been promised freedom, fought for the British.) When George Washington had taken command, he told recruiters not to enlist any more Africans. Fearful of a slave insurrection, southerners in Congress balked at the idea of arming and training blacks. But when the army's numbers started to thin, Washington reversed himself and asked Congress to resolve the issue. The Congress voted to allow any black to reenlist if he had already served. But as Thomas Fleming noted in his history of the Revolution, "The break in the color line would eventually make the Continental army more integrated than any American force except the armies that fought in the Vietnam and Gulf wars."

CHAPTER THREE

GROWTH OF A NATION

From the Creation of the Constitution to Manifest Destiny

What was Shays's Rebellion?

What was the Constitutional Convention?

What are checks and balances?

Basic powers and checks

What three-letter word is not in the Constitution?

What does *e pluribus unum* mean?

Who were the Federalists, and what were the Federalist Papers?

Who elected George Washington the first president?

What was the Bill of Rights?

Guarantees in the Bill of Rights

The 1790 Census

Why didn't Jefferson like Hamilton?

Was George Washington killed by his doctors?

What was the Revolution of 1800?

After the shooting stopped, the United States of America was recognized by the world's major powers as independent. But this gangling new child was an ugly duckling among nations, a loose collection of states under the Articles of Confederation, not yet a completely sovereign nation. The big question was "Now what?" Following eight years of fighting, this new entity had to face the realities of governing. As might be expected, different people from different states had a lot of different ideas about how that should be done.

But during the next seventy-odd years, powered by dynamic forces, America would expand swiftly and aggressively. However, in that expansion, and in the way in which the new nation formed itself, the seeds of the next great American crisis were being sown. This chapter highlights the milestones in a developing America between the end of the Revolution and the prelude to the Civil War.

What was Shays's Rebellion?

Rebellion, as the Founding Fathers would quickly discover, could be a catchy tune.

Besides independence, the end of the war had brought economic chaos to America. As with most wars, the Revolution had been good for business. Everybody works, soldiers spend money, factories turn out ships and guns, armies buy supplies. That's the good news. The bad news is that after war comes inflation and depression. The years immediately following the Revolution were no different. America went through bad economic times. Established trading patterns were in disarray. Under the Articles of Confederation, Congress had no power to tax. In the thirteen states, where power was centered, the separate currencies had created an economic shambles.

While the situation was bad almost everywhere, in Massachusetts, the home of the Adamses and birthplace of the patriot cause, the economic dislocation boiled over into bloodshed between Americans. Like the prewar Bacon's Rebellion, the Regulator Movement in the

Carolinas, and the Paxton Boys of Pennsylvania, this "little rebellion," as Thomas Jefferson would call it, was a sign of serious class conflict, a symptom of the economic tension that had always existed in America between, on one side, the working-class frontier farmers, inner-city laborers, the servant class, smaller merchants, and free blacks, and on the other side the "haves," the landed, slaveholding gentry, and the international merchants of the larger cities.

Massachusetts passed a state constitution in 1780 that found few friends among the poor and middle class, many of them veterans of the Continental Army still waiting for promised bonuses. When they learned that they were now barred from voting and holding office, they must have wondered what they had been fighting for. As the economy worsened, many farms were seized to pay off debts. When the local sheriffs looked to the militia to defend the debt courts against angry crowds, the militia sided with the farmers.

In the summer of 1786, an army veteran named Daniel Shays emerged on the scene. With 700 farmers and working-class people, Shays marched on Springfield and paraded around town. Onetime radical Sam Adams, now part of the Boston establishment, drew up a Riot Act, allowing the authorities to jail anyone without a trial. Revolt against a monarch was one thing, said Adams, but against a republic it was a crime punishable by death.

Shays soon had a thousand men under arms and was marching on Boston, the seat of wealth and power. Then General Benjamin Lincoln, one of Washington's war commanders, brought out an army paid for by Boston's merchants. There was an exchange of artillery fire, leaving some casualties on both sides, and Shays's army scattered. Lincoln's army pursued the rebels, but refrained from attacking when the rout was assured. A harsh winter took its toll, and Shays's amateur army disintegrated. Some of the rebels were caught, tried, and hanged. Others were pardoned. Shays, on the run in Vermont, was pardoned, but died in poverty in 1788.

Writing from the safe distance of Paris, Thomas Jefferson said of the uprising, "A little rebellion now and then is a good thing. . . . God forbid that we should ever be twenty years without such a rebellion. . . . The tree of liberty must be refreshed from time to time with the blood of patriots and tyrants."

Lacking cohesion and stronger leadership, the Shaysites disintegrated. However, several of the reforms they had demanded were made, including the end of the state's direct taxation, reduced court costs, and the exemption of workmen's tools and household necessities from the debt process.

AMERICAN VOICES

GEORGE MASON, delegate from Virginia, writing on the eve of the Constitutional Convention in May 1787:

> I have reason to hope there will be greater unanimity and less opposition, except for the little States, than was at first apprehended. The most prevalent idea in the principal States seems to be a total alteration of the present federal system, and substituting a great national council or parliament, consisting of two branches of the legislature, founded upon the principles of equal proportionate representation, with full legislative powers upon all subjects of the Union; and an executive: and to make the latter a power of a negative upon all such laws as they shall judge contrary to the interest of the federal Union. It is easy to foresee that there will be much difficulty in organizing a government upon this great scale, and at the same time reserving to the State legislatures a sufficient portion of power for promoting and securing the prosperity and happiness of their respective citizens; yet with the proper degree of coolness, liberality and candor (very rare commodities by the by), I doubt not but it may be effected.

A Virginia statesman who wrote the first American bill of rights—the Virginia Declaration of Rights of 1776—George Mason (1725–92) is not usually mentioned in the same breath with the more familiar Founding Fathers. Though he held few public offices, he was one of the most significant and influential men of the day.

Before the Revolution, his most important contribution was the Virginia Declaration of Rights, from which Jefferson borrowed to craft the Declaration of Independence. Mason played an active role in creating the Constitution, but disagreed with parts of it and refused to sign the final draft of the United States Constitution.

Chief among his complaints was the lack of a bill of rights to protect personal liberties. Another of those slaveholding delegates who were uncomfortable with slavery, Mason also found fault with some of the compromises that would be made over slavery. Dissatisfied when these concerns were not addressed, he was one of the few delegates who refused to sign the Constitution. When the Constitution was submitted to the states for ratification, he opposed it, and made the absence of a bill of rights his main objection.

What was the Constitutional Convention?

While the Massachusetts uprising was a relatively minor affair that did not spread armed insurrection throughout the states, it sufficiently shook up America's new ruling class. Something stronger than the Articles of Confederation was needed; the states had little ability to control local rebellion, let alone a foreign attack—a genuine threat as Spain and England both maintained troops in America. Equally pressing was the substantial danger posed by Indians on the western frontier who outnumbered the state militias. Nor could the states adequately handle the other two related crises facing America: the disruption of overseas trade and the postwar financial and currency collapse.

On May 25, 1787, after a delay of ten days because too few delegates had arrived, the convention to draw up a new plan of government gathered in Philadelphia. Every state but Rhode Island sent delegates, and George Washington was unanimously selected to preside over the convention. In the course of the next four months, they would create the Constitution. (While Washington presided at the convention and is recognized as the first president, there were actually several earlier presidents. Under the Articles of Confederation, John Hanson of Maryland had been elected "President of the United States in Congress Assembled.")

At various times during the four months, fifty-five delegates were present at what is now called Independence Hall in Philadelphia, but rarely were they all there at the same time. Forty-five of them had served in Congress; thirty had served in the war. To delegates like Patrick Henry, it consisted of "the greatest, the best, and most enlightened of our citizens." John Adams was not there. Nor was Thomas Jefferson, who from Paris called the convention "an assembly of demigods." In his book *The Vineyard of Liberty*, James McGregor Burns neatly encapsulated this group as "the well-bred, the well-fed, the well-read, and the well-wed," and it applied to most of them, America's new aristocracy. They included the likes of Pennsylvania's Robert Morris, one of America's wealthiest men, who had funded the Revolution. To other modern historians, they represented not the broad masses, but the wealthy merchants of the North and the wealthy, slaveholding plantation owners of the South.

Of them, the oldest was also perhaps the most famous, eighty-one-year-old Benjamin Franklin; Jonathan Dayton of New Jersey was youngest at twenty-seven. Their median age was forty-three. A little more than half (thirty-one) were college-educated, the same number as were lawyers. Seventeen of the delegates who were present to "establish justice . . . and secure the blessings of liberty to ourselves and our posterity" (in the words of the preamble) owned several thousand black slaves; John Rutledge (South Carolina), George Mason (Virginia), and George Washington (Virginia) were among the largest slaveholders in the country.

After two hundred years of rule under the Constitution, we have come to think of it as a perfect ideological and idealistic document created by a gathering of legislative geniuses. It has often been said that no new nation before or since has enjoyed a more politically experienced group than the men who wrote the Constitution. It might be useful to think of them as a collection of, in a modern phrase, special interest groups and regionally minded legislators, almost all of them admittedly brilliant politicians. And in politics, then as now, the art of compromise is the secret of success.

The Constitution was no different; it was a political creation, hammered together in a series of artfully negotiated compromises, balancing political idealism with political expediency. There were conflicts everywhere: between small states and large states, North and South, slave states and abolitionist states.

While there was near unanimity that a federal government was necessary, there was less agreement about the structure of such a government.

The first broad scheme for the Constitution came from the Virginians, young James Madison chief among them, and came to be known as the Virginia Plan. Its key points were a bicameral (two-chamber) legislature, an executive chosen by the legislature, and a judiciary also named by the legislature. An alternative, known as the New Jersey Plan, was favored by smaller states. Through the heat of summer, debate dragged on, the convention facing a deadlock essentially over two key questions.

The first was representation. Should representation in Congress be based on population, with larger states getting proportionately more votes, or should each state receive equal representation?

The second question was that of slavery. The southern states wanted to have their cake and eat it, too. Faced with growing abolitionist sentiments, the southern delegates would not bend on questions affecting slavery, nor would they grant freed blacks the vote. On the other hand, they wanted slaves counted for the purpose of determining representation in Congress. In other words, it was "Now you see 'em, now you don't."

With an impasse near, Roger Sherman proposed what is called the Connecticut Compromise, or Great Compromise. Seen in retrospect, it seems an obvious solution to the representation issue, providing for equal representation in the upper house of Congress (the Senate) and proportional representation in the lower house (the House of Representatives).

Two more compromises "solved" the issue of slavery and slaves, words that appear nowhere in the Constitution. Instead, flowery euphemisms like "no person held in service," and "all other persons" were coined in accordance with the Constitution's flowing legal prose. Under these bargains, Congress was prohibited from taking any action to control slavery for a period of twenty years (until 1808), although the gentlemen did agree that the slave trade could be taxed. (Apparently the antislave forces thought, "We may not like it, but at least let's make some money out of it.") And for the purposes of determining representation, slaves ("all other persons") would be counted as three-fifths of their total population. In hindsight, it was a small step forward for blacks. At least they had gone from being ignored to being three-fifths human. If they could hold out for another seventy years, they would be free! In turn, the southern states agreed to allow a maximum of three new future states that would ban slavery.

One of the last of the central debates regarded the executive and the role of the president. The delegates were men who feared too much power in the hands of a single man—they had just fought a long war to do away with one monarch. The Virginia Plan called for a chief executive to be elected by Congress. Virginia's George Mason proposed three presidents. Elbridge Gerry, a leading opponent of a strong federal government, wanted the president elected by the state governors. Alexander Hamilton, a proponent of a strong federal government, wanted the president to serve for life. Another proposal was to bar anyone from the presidency who was not worth at least $100,000 (the equivalent of a multimillionaire). The solution came from New York's Gouverneur Morris, who at the time was living in the same house as George Washington. Morris proposed an executive elected by the people. Morris also proposed that he be commander-in-chief of the armed forces as well. As Thomas Fleming points out in *Liberty*, "One suspects that when Gouverneur Morris spoke, they were hearing advice from George Washington. Also, as Pierce Butler of South Carolina pointed out, there sat Washington, the man who was certain to be the first President. There was no need to fear that he would become a tyrant."

And in the ultimate exercise of compromise, the men who put the Constitution together recognized that it might have to be changed, so they built in an acceptable form of amending their work. Change would not be easy, but it was possible.

As is true of other moments in American history, cynicism born of perfect hindsight is easy. On the other hand, credit should be given where it is due. The Framers were intelligent, even brilliant men; they knew their history and their law. The Constitution they forged was then the pinnacle of thousands of years of political development. They were familiar with, and could draw on, such sources and models as the Greek philosophers, the Roman republic, and the evolution of the English democratic tradition running from the Magna Carta through Parliament and the English Bill of Rights of 1689. Above all, in the Constitution—and earlier, in the Declaration—they embodied the triumph of the Enlightenment, that glorious flowering of ideas in the seventeenth and eighteenth centuries that elevated the powers of human reason and strove for new forms of government, free of tyranny. The philosophies they were striving to fulfill had been expressed by such giants of the age as Hume, Locke, Rousseau, Voltaire, and Kant. They were all familiar to the Framers, and these ideas contributed to the heady debate, a debate that centered on the ongoing struggle between liberty and democracy, two ideas that often clash.

As for debate, there was plenty. Even with the broad outlines agreed upon, major differences cropped up at every turn. It took nearly six hundred separate votes to settle them all. These were not small matters of detail, either, but large questions that might have altered the course of the nation. For instance, New York's Alexander Hamilton, one of the staunchest advocates of powerful central government and the chief representative of northern commercial interests—he was one of the founders of the Bank of New York—wanted the president and the Senate appointed for life. He also argued for giving the "first class," the wealthy men of America, among whom he could certainly be counted, "a distinct permanent share of the government."

Hamilton's suggestion was turned down, but the Constitution did not provide for direct elections, except for the House of Representatives, where it was still left to the states to determine who voted. Property ownership was the key qualification in almost every state. And of course, women, Indians, and blacks—free or slave—had no vote. It is simple to dismiss even that basic decision as the result of sexism and racism. But, again, the temper of the times must be considered. In a period in which class differences were so clearly delineated, though less so in America than in Europe, it may have been inconceivable for these men to consider allowing just anyone to vote. They took as an article of faith that to participate responsibly in a democracy required education and the measure of property that would allow one the leisure to read and think. That said, however, they also did everything they could to make sure that women, Indians, blacks, and the white poor would be excluded from obtaining such education and property.

The final form of the Constitution, prepared by New York's Gouverneur Morris, was put to a vote on September 17, 1787. Thirty-nine of the delegates present voted in favor; three were opposed. Another thirteen of the principals were absent, but seven of these were believed to favor the Constitution. It was sent on to Congress, which decided to submit the document to the states for ratification, with the approval of nine states needed for passage.

AMERICAN VOICES
Preamble to the Constitution of
the United States of America:

We the People of the United States, in Order to form a more perfect union, establish Justice, insure domestic Tranquility, provide for the common defence, promote the general Welfare, and secure the Blessings of Liberty to ourselves and our Posterity, do ordain and establish this CONSTITUTION for the United States of America.

For any and all of the Constitution's flaws—as well as those of the men who wrote it—this document was, and remains, a remarkable achievement. As Leonard W. Levy argues in *Original Intent and the Framers' Constitution*, "The Constitution lacks the eloquence and passion of the Declaration of Independence, although the opening of the Preamble, 'We the People,' summons forth the still radically democratic idea that the government of the United States exists to serve the people, not the people to serve the government. That is fundamental to the Framers' original intent, as is the related idea that government in the United States cannot tell us what to think or believe about politics, religion, art, science, literature or anything else; American citizens have the duty as well as the right to keep the government from falling into error, not the other way around."

What are checks and balances?

This has nothing to do with monthly bank statements. Whether out of wisdom or fear, the Constitution's architects created a fundamental principle underlying the strength and tension of the federal government. The fear was obvious; no one wanted anyone else to become too powerful. So for almost every power they granted to one branch of government, they created an equal power of control for the other two. The legislature could "check" the power of the president, the Supreme Court could "check" the power of Congress, and so on, maintaining a careful symmetry, or "balance," among the three branches.

BASIC POWERS AND CHECKS

EXECUTIVE POWERS (PRESIDENT)

- Approves or vetoes federal bills.
- Carries out federal laws.
- Appoints judges and other high officials.
- Makes foreign treaties.
- Can grant pardons and reprieves to federal offenders.
- Acts as commander-in-chief of armed forces.

CHECKS ON EXECUTIVE POWERS

- Congress can override vetoes by two-thirds vote.
- Senate can refuse to confirm appointments or ratify treaties.
- Congress can impeach and remove the president.
- Congress can declare war.
- Supreme Court can declare executive acts unconstitutional.

LEGISLATIVE POWERS (CONGRESS)

- Passes federal laws.
- Establishes lower federal courts and the number of federal judges.
- Can override the president's veto with two-thirds vote.

CHECKS ON LEGISLATIVE POWERS

- Presidential veto of federal bills.
- Supreme Court can rule laws unconstitutional.
- Both houses of Congress must vote to pass laws, checking power within the legislature.

JUDICIAL POWERS

- Interprets and applies the law by trying federal cases.
- Can declare laws passed by Congress and executive actions unconstitutional.

Checks on Judicial Powers

- Congress can propose constitutional amendments to overturn judicial decisions. (These require two-thirds majority in both houses, and ratification by three-quarters of states.)
- Congress can impeach and remove federal judges.
- The president appoints judges (who must be confirmed by the Senate).

What three-letter word is not in the Constitution?

There is an American political drama that has been played out in recent years during the Democratic convention. Someone, usually a conservative Republican with ties to the Christian right, blasts away at the Democratic Party's platform because it doesn't mention God. Then, if all goes according to form, a Democratic Party spokesperson will fire back that the United States Constitution doesn't mention God, either. In this case, the Democrats have it right.

Unlike the Declaration of Independence, which tiptoed around the question of a deity with euphemisms like "Nature's God," "Creator," "Supreme Judge of the World," and "Divine Providence," the Constitution makes no such nods to divine intervention. Instead, the Constitution calls the nation the creation of the will of the people. In a country in which the role of religion is constantly debated and politicians routinely point to America's "Judeo-Christian heritage" and "the faith of our fathers," the question of the missing deity in the Constitution raises a larger point: What did the Founding Fathers believe? Few questions have generated as many myths or misconceptions.

In fact, eighteenth-century America was predominantly Christian — and overwhelmingly Protestant. But that was a big tent, covering a large crowd whose faith was far from monolithic. New England was dominated by Congregationalism, derived from the Pilgrim and Puritan tradition, and Congregational churches received government support in some states. But the Protestants of the South leaned toward the Episcopal, aligned with the very Church of England from which the Puritans had separated themselves. In Virginia, the Anglican, or Episcopal, church also received state money. In Maryland, founded as a refuge for Catholics, the Roman Catholic presence was larger than in other states, but many Americans regarded Roman Catholics, or "Papists," with suspicion—or worse. Nonetheless, Charles Carroll, a signer of the Declaration and the richest man in Maryland and quite possibly the whole nation, was a devout Roman Catholic. His faith was one of the reasons that Carroll would later have such disdain for Thomas Jefferson, who, by 1800, was being denounced as an atheist. There was also a whole slew of other Protestant sects and denominations, including the Methodists, Presbyterians, and Quakers, each group finding fertile ground in the new American landscape.

This was, after all, the Age of Enlightenment when science and reason were elevated above both church and king. The work of scientists like Newton in upsetting the status quo of belief had spilled over into politics. By proving that the universe was governed by mathematically proven laws of nature in the late 1600s, Sir Isaac Newton helped Enlightenment thinkers like John Locke (1632–1704) shake political thought free from the past. Locke wrote, "A government is not free to do as it pleases. The law of nature, as revealed by Newton, stands as an eternal rule to all men." Locke's ideas, in turn, profoundly influenced Jefferson.

During this period of extraordinary intellectual, political, and religious ferment, many of the Founding Fathers—most of them educated, wealthy, and aristocratic—rejected the orthodoxy of religion, just as they had rejected the divinity of the English throne. What many of the Founding Fathers believed in was deism, which had replaced the highly personal God of Judeo-Christian biblical tradition with "Providence," an amorphous force that George Washington once referred to as "it." A survey of a handful of the most influential Founding Fathers is useful in assessing what these men did believe:

- Benjamin Franklin: During the colonial religious revival known as the Great Awakening (see Chapter 2), Franklin befriended George Whitefield, one of the most prominent leaders of the Awakening. Though Franklin supported Whitefield's good works, he "drew the line short of his own conversion," as Franklin biographer H. W. Brands put it in *The First American*.

Along with Jefferson probably the best example of the American Enlightenment Man, Franklin was skeptical of organized religion. Describing Franklin's spiritual thought, Brands writes, "As the deists did, Franklin measured the immensity of the universe against the minisculity of the earth and the inhabitants thereof and concluded from this that it was 'great vanity in me to suppose that the Supremely Perfect does in the least regard such an inconsiderable nothing as man.' Moreover, this Supremely Perfect had absolutely no need to be worshipped by humans; He was infinitely above such sentiments or actions."

Proponents of America as a "Christian nation" and those who favor public prayer often cite Franklin's entreaty that the constitutional convention open its meetings with a prayer. What they conveniently leave out is what actually happened following that suggestion. Alexander Hamilton first argued that if the people knew that the convention was resorting to prayer at such a late date, it might be viewed as an act of desperation. Nonetheless, Franklin's motion was seconded. But then Hugh Williamson of North Carolina pointed out that the convention lacked funds to pay a chaplain, and then the proposition died. Franklin later noted, "The convention, except three or four persons, *thought prayers unnecessary*" (emphasis added).

Late in his life, Franklin wrote what could almost pass for a modern New Age statement of faith:

"Here is my creed. I believe in one God, creator of the universe. That he governs it by his Providence. . . . That the soul of man is immortal, and will be treated with justice in another life respecting its conduct in this. . . . As to Jesus of Nazareth. I think the system of morals and his religion . . . the best the world ever saw or is likely to see; but I apprehend it has received various corrupting changes, and I have . . . some doubts as to his divinity." He added, "I have ever let others enjoy their religious sentiments. . . . I hope to go out of the world in peace with all of them."

• George Washington: The image of Washington on his knees at prayer in Valley Forge is an American icon. And like many Washington images, it is largely mythical. While Washington prayed regularly and fervently, he was never seen doing it in the snows of Pennsylvania.

Clearly a believer who often resorted to calls to "Providence," the father of the country regularly attended the Episcopal church, whether at home in Virginia, at the Philadelphia conventions, or in New York as president. But as Thomas Fleming notes in *Duel*, "Washington usually left before the communion service, pointedly if silently stating his disbelief in this central ceremony of the Christian faith."

But Washington was certainly a Christian and in his 1796 Farewell Address expressed his belief that religion and morality were "pillars of human happiness," then adding, "Let us with caution indulge the supposition that morality can be maintained without religion."

Perhaps more significantly, the nominally Episcopalian Washington was also a Freemason, along with numerous other Founders, including John Hancock, Paul Revere, and Franklin. (While he was in France, Franklin met the philosopher Voltaire, also a Freemason.) When Washington laid the cornerstone of the Capitol in 1793, the local Masonic lodge organized the ceremony, and Washington wore a Masonic apron made for him by the wife of the Marquis de Lafayette, who belonged to the Masons as well. Washington took his oath of office as president with a Masonic Bible.

One of the oldest and largest fraternal organizations in the world, Freemasonry was invented in London in 1717, a semisecret society that has inspired substantial mythology ever since. It was formed by a group of intellectuals who took over a craft guild and fostered what they called "enlightened uplift," dedicated to the ideals of charity, equality, morality, and service to God, whom the Masons describe as the Great Architect of the Universe. The order spread quickly through Enlightenment Europe and included men as diverse as Voltaire, King Frederick II of Prussia, and the Austrian composer Wolfgang Amadeus Mozart. (First performed in Vienna, Austria, in 1791, Mozart's opera *The Magic Flute* deals symbolically with Masonic beliefs and rituals.)

As it developed, Freemasonry was viewed as anticlerical and was later thought to be antireligious by conservative Congregationalists in the United States. An anti-Mason movement took hold in the nineteenth century, and the Antimasonic Party became the first significant third party in American politics. (In 1831, the Antimasonic Party became the first party to hold a nominating convention to choose candidates for president and vice president. Its candidate, William Wirt, won a respectable seven electoral votes in 1832.) The controversy grew when a disgruntled ex-Mason announced he would publish the group's secret rituals. He was abducted and disappeared. Twenty-six Masons were indicted on murder and six came to trial, with four of them convicted on lesser charges. But the fact is that Masonry was a voluntary fraternal order—a kind of eighteenth-century spiritual Rotary Club—and not a sinister cult intent on world domination as it has often been portrayed, including more recently by Reverend Pat Robertson, leader of the Christian right.

Some people believed—and many still do—that this powerful Masonic influence can be seen in symbols on the American dollar bill, and that they were put there by the "Masonic president," Franklin Delano Roosevelt, to show that the country had been taken over by Masons. The objects in question on the dollar bill are actually the two sides of the Great Seal of the United States, which dates from the late 1700s (see page 126). It is Mason Benjamin Franklin who is often credited—or blamed—for them. But even that may be a myth. The symbols in question are the representation of an eye and an unfinished pyramid. The All-Seeing Eye of Deity is mentioned in Freemasonry, but the concept behind the image dates back to the Bible. An unfinished pyramid symbolizes that the work of nation building is not completed, but the pyramid is not a particularly Masonic symbol. The eye in the pyramid, still featured on America's money, was a common symbol of an omniscient Deity that dated to Renaissance art. In other words, the Masons may have adopted the design as a symbol later on and not the other way around.

As a footnote to Masonry in America, it should be pointed out that the Enlightenment spirit went only so far. In spite of its idealism, American Masonry was neither color-blind nor sexually enlightened. Just as blacks and women were kept out of the Constitution, they were barred from Masonry's chummy club as well. In

1765, Prince Hall, a free black Methodist minister who settled in the Boston area, founded a Masons for blacks. (They would later be called Prince Hall Masons.) In 1775, a British army lodge admitted Hall and fourteen other free blacks who formed African Lodge 1, but white American Masons refused to grant the lodge a charter. The group finally received its charter from the Grand Lodge of England in 1787, as African Lodge 459. Prince Hall and other early black Masons protested slavery and sought to improve the status of free blacks. Later Prince Hall members included W. E. B. DuBois, the historian, writer, and one of the founders of the NAACP, and Thurgood Marshall, the first black justice of the U.S. Supreme Court.

- Thomas Jefferson: More radical in his beliefs than either Franklin or Washington was Thomas Jefferson, who inveighed against "every form of tyranny over the mind of man," by which he meant organized Christianity. In 1782, Jefferson's Statute for Religious Freedom was approved by the Virginia legislature. This landmark legislation guaranteed every citizen the freedom to worship in the church of his or her choice and ended state support for the Episcopal church in Virginia. The statute passed thanks to the efforts of James Madison.

    Jefferson had also once produced an edited version of the Gospels (still available in book form as *The Jefferson Bible*) in which he highlighted the moral and ethical teachings of Jesus while editing out any reference to his divinity or miracles. The reference to Providence at the close of the Declaration was an addition made by the Continental Congress while the document was debated.

- Aaron Burr: The libertinish Burr, usually regarded as one of the scoundrels in America's past, is not usually discussed in the same breath with American religious tradition. But he was the grandson of Jonathan Edwards, the greatest name in New England church history and another leader of the Great Awakening (see Chapter 2). Burr had spent a year studying for the ministry before deciding that he lacked sufficient faith. According to historian Thomas Fleming's *Duel*, Burr's decision was "typical of a general decline in theological fervor throughout America. The French Revolution's assault on religion as the bulwark of the ruling class accelerated this trend. In the Yale class of 1796, a poll revealed that only one graduate believed in God—a glimpse of why the Federalists' attacks on Thomas Jefferson's supposed atheism went nowhere."

Ultimately, what is far more important than what any of the so-called Founding Fathers personally believed is the larger concept that most of them embraced passionately: the freedom to practice religion, as well as not to. And certainly, to a man, they emphatically opposed the idea of a government-sponsored religion. Franklin shuddered at the intrusion of religion into politics. Washington denounced spiritual tyranny and felt that religion was a private matter with which government had no business meddling. To him, government existed to protect people's rights, not save their souls.

In a famous letter to members of the Newport Hebrew Congregation, the oldest synagogue in America, Washington wrote in 1790: "It is now no more that toleration is spoken of, as if it was by the indulgence of one class of people, that another enjoyed the exercise of their inherent natural rights. For happily *the government of the United States, which gives to bigotry no sanction — to persecution no assistance, requires only that they who live under its protection should demean themselves as good citizens*" (emphasis added).

As for Jefferson, he famously wrote that it made no difference to him whether his neighbor affirmed one god or twenty, since "it neither picks my pocket nor breaks my leg." It was this concept—that the government should neither enforce, encourage, nor otherwise intrude on religion—that would find its way into the Constitution in the form of the First Amendment.

AMERICAN VOICES
"A Bill for Establishing Religious Freedom," enacted by
the Virginia General Assembly in 1786:

We the General Assembly of Virginia do enact that no man shall be compelled to frequent or support any religious worship, place or ministry whatsoever, nor shall be enforced, restrained, molested, or burthened in his body

or goods, nor shall otherwise suffer, on account of his religious opinions or belief; but that all men shall be free
to profess, and by argument to maintain, their opinions
in matters of religion, and that the same shall in no wise
diminish, enlarge, or affect their civil capacities.

Jefferson introduced this bill in 1779, and passage was secured
while he was in Paris with the collaboration of James Madison. Along
with his authorship of the Declaration of Independence and his establishment of the University of Virginia, Jefferson had his authorship of
this bill included on his tombstone.

What does *e pluribus unum* mean?

E pluribus unum is the Latin motto on the face of the Great Seal of
the United States and the phrase means "out of many, one." It can be
traced back to Horace's *Epistles*. It refers to the creation of one nation,
the United States, out of thirteen colonies. Benjamin Franklin, John
Adams, and Thomas Jefferson, members of the first committee for the
selection of the seal, suggested the motto in 1776. Since 1873, the law
requires that this motto appear on one side of every United States coin
that is minted.

The Great Seal of the United States is the symbol of the sovereignty
of the United States, adopted on June 20, 1782. European countries
had long used seals, and the new nation signified its equal rank by
adopting its own seal. William Barton, a specialist in heraldry, advised
the committee responsible for creating the seal, and designed most of
the seal's reverse side. Charles Thomson, secretary of the Congress,
prepared the images used on the face, which is used on official documents. The American eagle, with an escutcheon, or shield, on its
breast, symbolizes self-reliance. The shield's thirteen vertical stripes
came from the flag of 1777, but seven are white, while in the 1777 flag
seven are red. The eagle holds an olive branch of thirteen leaves and
thirteen olives in its right talon, and thirteen arrows in its left, symbol-
izing the desire for peace but the ability to wage war. In its beak is a
scroll inscribed *e pluribus unum*. Above its head is the thirteen-star

"new constellation" of the 1777 flag, enclosed in golden radiance, breaking through a cloud.

The reverse side of the seal is familiar from the back of the one-dollar bill, but it has never been used as a seal. A pyramid of thirteen courses of stone, representing the Union, is watched over by the Eye of Providence enclosed in a traditional triangle. The upper motto, *Annuit coeptis*, means "He [God] has favored our undertakings." The lower motto, *Novus ordo seclorum*, means "the new order of the ages" that began in 1776, the date on the base of the pyramid.

Who were the Federalists, and what were the Federalist Papers?

Two hundred years of miseducation have left an image of the Constitution as a sort of American Ten Commandments, divinely inspired and carved in stone. So it is hard to imagine that its ratification was not assured. Like an unsuccessful organ transplant, it was nearly rejected by the body politic. When the Constitution left Philadelphia, the country was almost evenly split between those favoring the strong central government it promised, who came to be known as Federalists, and those for a weaker central government with stronger states' rights, a.k.a. the anti-Federalists.

Loyal Americans and staunch patriots—many of them were Revolutionary leaders and veterans—the anti-Federalists feared a new brand of elected monarchy at the expense of individual liberties. They were led by such major contemporary figures as Virginia's governor, Patrick Henry; Boston's Samuel Adams of Revolution fame; and New York's longtime governor, George Clinton. Their disdain for the Constitution might best be summed up in the words of Thomas Paine: "Government, even in its best state, is but a necessary evil." The anti-Federalists believed that men like Alexander Hamilton were trying to reintroduce an American form of monarchy.

But no small part of their resistance was personal; many anti-Federalists simply didn't *like* their opposites among the Federalists. No better examples of this could be found than in Virginia, where Patrick Henry kept James Madison, the chief architect of the Constitution, from being elected to the Senate, and New York. where the anti-Federalists were led by New York's governor, George Clinton. Alexander Hamilton and Clinton were philosophical rivals, but their mutual disdain went far beyond policy into personality and rivalries. Clinton and his allies were more or less credited with creating the spoils system—in which patronage jobs were doled out to friends, family, and financial supporters. In 1792, Clinton had stolen the governor's race in New York from Hamilton's handpicked candidate, John Jay, simply by declaring the votes of three counties invalid and declaring himself the winner. (From "The More Things Change, the More They Stay the Same" Department comes this wisdom from William "Boss" Tweed, the notorious nineteenth-century "fixer" of all things political in New York City, who said on Election Day in 1871, "As long as I count the votes, what are you going to do about it?")

Championing the Federalist cause, Hamilton, Madison, and John Jay—then serving as the head of the Confederation's state department—attempted to influence the ratification debate with a series of pseudonymous newspaper letters signed "Publius" and later collected as the Federalist Papers. Eighty-five of these essays were published, and while they are considered among the most significant political documents in American history, after the Declaration of Independence and the Constitution, their direct impact on the debate of the day is dubious. Probably most of the people who counted had already made up their minds.

Of far greater consequence than the papers was the proratification stance of America's two most prominent men, Franklin and Washington, the latter of whom everyone assumed would become the first president under the new Constitution. Of Washington's impact on Virginia's ratification vote, James Monroe wrote to Jefferson, "Be assured his influence carried this government." One by one, the state conventions voting on the question came to ratification—some unanimously; others, like Massachusetts, by the narrowest of margins. The oldest kind of "smoke-filled room" politicking was often required, and several states agreed only with the proviso that a bill of rights be added to the Constitution. Delaware, a small state happy with the representation it would receive, was the first to ratify and was joined in succession by Pennsylvania, New Jersey, Georgia, Connecticut, Massachusetts, Maryland, South Carolina, and New Hampshire, the ninth ratifying state.

But even with the required nine states, there was uncertainty.

Virginia and New York had not spoken, and rejection by either or both of these powerful, wealthy states might have rendered the Constitution meaningless. With the Bill of Rights compromise that had worked elsewhere, Virginia voted in favor. In New York, aggressive speechmaking and buttonholing by Alexander Hamilton, combined with John Jay's gentler persuasion, carried the day for ratification.

AMERICAN VOICES

JAMES MADISON, reporting on the signing
of the Constitution in September 1787:

Whilst the last members were signing, Dr. Franklin looking towards the president's chair, at the back of which a rising sun happened to be painted, observed to a few members near him, that painters had found it difficult to distinguish in their art, a rising from a setting sun. "I have," said he, "often and often, in the course of the session, and the vicissitudes of my hopes and fears as to its issue, looked at that behind the president, without being able to tell whether it was rising or setting; but now, at length, I have the happiness to know that it is a rising, and not a setting sun."

Who elected George Washington the first president?

In their wisdom and foresight, not to mention their fear of the rabble, the Framers of the Constitution had created a remarkably curious beast when it came to selecting the president. The Electoral College was the Constitution's last-ditch defense against an overdose of democracy.

In the Framers' scheme, each state would choose electors equal to its representation in Congress (House seats plus Senate seats). How the electors were chosen was a decision left to the separate states. The electors would then meet in their states and vote for two persons for president. The winner was the man with a majority. The Framers figured nobody—besides George Washington, that is—could win a clear majority, in which case the election would be decided in the House of Representatives, where each state got one vote.

Political parties were not only absent at this time, but were considered contemptible. Ideally in a debate, men would line up on one side or the other and then fall back into nonalignment, awaiting the next issue. The men who made the Constitution did not foresee the rise of the two-party system as we know it, although its beginnings were apparent in the debate over ratification. The Federalists, led by Alexander Hamilton and John Adams, would be the first political party formed in America.

Although February 4, 1789, has come down as the traditional first presidential election date, that was actually the day on which the first electors cast their ballots. It was preceded by a crazy quilt of elections taking place in late 1788 and the first months of 1789, with each state setting its own rules as to who could vote for what. Some states allowed the electors to be chosen directly by voters; in other states, electors were chosen by the state legislature. While being a male freeholder (property owner) was generally the key to a vote, some states had very ambiguous voting rules. In New Jersey, for instance, women indeed did vote for president in the first election. In Pennsylvania, any taxpayer was eligible.

But the result was the same. On March 4, the first Congress was supposed to convene in New York, but a quorum wasn't reached until April 1. Finally, on April 6, the Senate counted the electoral ballots and declared the inevitable. Washington was elected unanimously. John Adams had been named on enough ballots to qualify as vice president. Officially informed of his election on April 14, Washington left Mount Vernon two days later for an eight-day triumphal journey past adoring crowds along the way, and on April 30, 1789, he took the oath of office at Federal Hall in New York, which would be the seat of government for the next year and a half.

Washington earned a salary of $25,000 a year, a rather handsome sum at the time; however, he had to pay his own expenses. After moving to 39–41 Broadway, he hired fourteen white servants and brought seven slaves from Mount Vernon.

AMERICAN VOICES
GEORGE WASHINGTON, taking the oath of office
(Article II of the Constitution directs the president-elect
to take the following oath or affirmation to be
inaugurated as president):

I do solemnly swear [affirm] that I will faithfully execute
the office of President of the United States, and will to the
best of my ability, preserve, protect, and defend the Constitution of the United States.

Custom, not constitutional directive, dictates that the president-
elect place his left hand on a Bible and keep his right hand slightly
raised for the duration of the oath. When George Washington took the
oath in 1789, he ad libbed a bit and added the words, "So help me
God" at the end of the oath, according to legend. This report is disputed. Since then, every president has customarily said the same words.

AMERICAN VOICES
MARTHA WASHINGTON on life as first lady in
New York City:

I live a dull life here. I never go to any public place.
Indeed, I am more like a state prisoner than anything
else . . . and I cannot do as I like, I am obstinate and stay
home a great deal.

What was the Bill of Rights?

For the new government, no order of business was more pressing than
delivering on a promised set of amendments to the Constitution. These
were demanded during ratification by those who feared the states would
be destroyed by the new central government. Madison took the lead in
preparing the amendments, and on September 25, 1789, a list of twelve
was submitted by the Congress, meeting in New York City, for ratification by the states. Ten of the twelve amendments were finally ratified

and in force on December 15, 1791, and became known as the Bill of Rights. (See Appendix 1 for a complete text and discussion of the Bill of Rights, along with other constitutional amendments.)

Although England had a Bill of Rights, it was narrower and could be repealed by Parliament. The American version was broader, and repeal could be made only through the states. The intention of the amendments was to guarantee freedoms not specifically named in the original Constitution. While legal scholars argue that such guarantees may have been logically unnecessary, they have become an integral part of the American legal system and remain at the core of many of the major controversies in American history, including those confronting contemporary America.

GUARANTEES IN THE BILL OF RIGHTS

First Amendment. Guarantees separation of church and state and freedom to worship, freedom of speech and the press, the right to assemble and petition for changes.

Second Amendment. The right to keep and bear arms. (The key to gun control debate. Those who favor gun controls point to the Bill's specification of "a well-regulated Militia." Advocates of gun ownership cite this amendment in its most literal sense.)

Third Amendment. Soldiers cannot be housed in a private home without the consent of the owner. (A reaction to the British Quartering Act, one of the intolerable acts leading to the Revolution.)

Fourth Amendment. The right to be free from "unreasonable search and seizure." (Another hot issue, criminal rights versus law enforcement, hinges on the interpretation of this amendment.)

Fifth Amendment. Provisions concerning prosecution and due process of law, including the requirement of a grand jury indictment, double jeopardy restriction—a person cannot be tried for the same crime twice—and the protection from testifying against oneself. (See "Who was Miranda?" in Chapter 8.)

Sixth Amendment. Guarantees the right to a speedy, public trial in the district where the crime has been committed, as well as other protections for the accused.

Seventh Amendment. Guarantees trial by jury.

Eighth Amendment. Prohibits excessive bails or fines and "cruel and unusual punishment," the amendment at the heart of the capital punishment debate.

Ninth Amendment. Based on the idea that all human beings have certain fundamental rights, this amendment covers basic rights not specifically set forth in the Constitution.

Tenth Amendment. Guarantees that any powers not specifically delegated to the federal government or denied to the states in the Constitution rest with the states or the people.

(Two proposed amendments dealing with the apportionment of members and congressional compensation were not ratified at that time, although versions of each article have since been ratified.)

Amended by the Bill of Rights, the Constitution was still a political document, not an act of God. Like most works of men, it was flawed and imperfect in many ways — its flagrant denial of the rights of blacks, women, and Indians chief among its flaws. Many modern commentators argue that the Constitution was the perfectly realized means of assuring the control of the wealthy over the weak, with enough table scraps for the working and middle classes to assure popular support. From the beginning, critics have said the Constitution and Bill of Rights were selectively enforced and often ignored, as in the case of the Alien and Sedition Acts of the Adams administration (1798), which clearly trampled the guarantees of the First Amendment.

On the other hand, what was the alternative? If the northern delegates had taken the moral high ground and not compromised on the issue of slavery, the constitutional convention would have disintegrated. Under the Articles of Confederation, the states would have remained economically weak and ripe for invasion by awaiting foreign forces.

The 1790 Census

To determine how many delegates each state would have in the House of Representatives, the Census Act was passed in 1790. The first census was completed in August 1790. Some highlights:

- Total U.S. population: 3,929,625.
- Black population: 697,624 slaves; 59,557 free blacks. (Massachusetts reported no slaves.)
- Philadelphia is the largest city, with 42,000; New York is second, with 33,000.
- Virginia is the most populous state, with more than 820,000 people.
- Nearly half of the population (48.5 percent) lives in the southern states, with the rest divided between New England and the middle states.
- America is youthful: 490 of every 1,000 whites are under the age of sixteen.

American Voices

Virginian ROBERT CARTER III, one of the wealthiest men and largest slaveholders in America (1791):

Whereas I Robert Carter of Nomini Hall in the county of Westmoreland & Commonwealth of Virginia [own] . . . many negroes & mulatto slaves . . . and Whereas I have for some time past been convinced that to retain them in Slavery is contrary to the true principles of Religion and justice . . . I do hereby declare that such . . . shall be emancipated.

Unlike other Founding Fathers who bemoaned slavery and kept slaves, Robert Carter III put his money where his mouth was. The grandson of Robert "King" Carter, the wealthiest of all Virginians, Robert Carter III had begun something akin to a spiritual quest. His grandfather built Christ Church on Virginia's Northern Neck peninsula, one of the most beautiful old churches in America. And to ensure that no one missed the point, churchgoers were expected to wait until the Carter coach arrived before entering the church. Leaving the Anglican church of his youth and family, Robert Carter III became a deist, then a Baptist, but continued listening to other preachers, including Methodists. He became one of the most influential supporters of Virginia's Statute for Religious Freedom, which allowed Virginians to choose their religion and ended taxpayer support for the Episcopal church. Then in 1791, Carter shocked his neighbors by announcing he would emancipate his slaves. Not all of the neighbors were pleased by the news.

Why didn't Jefferson like Hamilton?

Under Washington and the new Congress, the government moved rapidly toward organization. Drawing from a rich array of political talent, Washington selected appointees to the key posts in his administration, often turning to old friends and war veterans, such as Henry Knox, who became secretary of war. A 1,000-man army was established, principally to confront the Indians on the western frontier. The Supreme Court was created, and John Jay was chosen first chief justice. But the two giants of this administration, and the men who would personify the great debate and division within the country in the years ahead, were Thomas Jefferson and Alexander Hamilton. Dumas Malone, Jefferson's most prominent biographer, has stated their difference simply. "No other statesman has personified national power and the rule of the favored few so well as Hamilton, and no other has glorified self-government and the freedom of the individual to such a degree as Jefferson."

America's envoy in Paris as the Bastille was stormed in 1789, beginning the French Revolution, Jefferson returned to New York to lead the State Department. Although a member of the aristocratic, slaveholding class, Jefferson despised the monarchy and saw Hamilton and his allies as a "British party," trying to restore a form of elected monarchy to the new nation. He had only disdain for what he called "money men." In theory, he wanted a weak government and envisioned America as a democracy of farmers and workers.

An illegitimate child born in the West Indies, Hamilton had risen during the Revolution to become Washington's confidential secretary. He had become an attorney in New York, founder of the Bank of New York, and one of that state's and the nation's most powerful men, first helping to frame, then selling the Constitution. Hamilton was no "man of the people," though. The masses, he said, were a "great beast." He wanted a government controlled by the merchant and banking class, and the government under Hamilton would always put this elite class first. He would fill the critical role of Washington's chief adviser in money matters.

Hamilton's work was cut out for him. The nation's finances were chaotic. America owed money to foreign nations, principally France and the Netherlands, and there was massive domestic debt. Even worse, there was no money to pay the debts off. The government needed money, and a series of excise taxes were passed, not without a little argument from congressmen, who wanted either local products free from taxes, or overseas products protected by tariffs. Many of them were the same items that had been taxed by the English a few years earlier, prompting the first rebellious actions in the colonies.

There were two key components of Hamilton's master plan for the financial salvation of America. The first came in his *Report on Public Credit*, which provoked a firestorm of controversy by recommending that all creditors of the government be given securities at par with old, depreciated securities. Since most of these older securities were in the hands of speculators (mostly northern) who had bought them from original holders (mostly southern farmers and many of them veterans of the War for Independence) for a fraction of their worth, Hamilton was attacked viciously for selling out to the "eastern" speculators. When he added the suggestion that the federal government assume the debts of the states, he was also pilloried by the southern states because most of them had already paid their debts, and Hamilton's plan would be a boon to the "eastern" states.

A real estate deal solved this problem. Opposed to Hamilton's plan, Jefferson and James Madison, the latter a leader in the House of Representatives, swung the South to support it in exchange for an agreement establishing the site for a new federal city in the South. The nation's future capital would be located on the banks of the Potomac. (Until the new city was ready, Philadelphia would become the nation's capital.) But this compromise did not patch up the differences between Hamilton and Jefferson. Their political differences over almost every issue confronting the new government eventually grew to personal enmity.

The second major component of Hamilton's master plan was the establishment of a national bank to store federal funds safely; to collect, move, and dispense tax money; and to issue notes. The bank would be partly owned by the government, but 80 percent of the stock would be sold to private investors. Again, Jefferson balked. It was unconstitutional, he argued; the government had no such power. Hamilton responded by arguing that the bank was legal under the congressional power to tax and regulate trade. This time there was no compromise, and President Washington went along with Hamilton.

It was a dazzling move in terms of the new nation's finances. According to Thomas Fleming, "Hamilton had taken a country floundering in a morass of $80 million in state and federal war debts . . . and in a series of brilliant state papers, persuaded Congress to transform this demoralizing legacy of the Revolution into a national asset. . . . To stabilize the new system and prime the national financial pump, Hamilton persuaded Congress to create the semipublic Bank of the United States. In five years, the United States had the highest credit rating in the world and a reliable money supply was fueling prosperity from Boston to Savannah" (*Duel*, p. 5).

The differences between Jefferson and Hamilton extended to foreign affairs. With England and France again at war and the French Revolution under way, Hamilton openly favored the English. Jefferson admired the French and their Revolution, which America had certainly helped inspire, even if he detested the rushing rivers of blood that the guillotine was creating. The lines were similarly drawn over Jay's Treaty, a settlement made with the British in the midst of another English-French war that threatened to involve the United States. Under its terms, British soldiers withdrew from their last outposts in the United States, but other portions of the treaty were viewed as excessively pro-British, and it was attacked by Jefferson's supporters. (The treaty was ratified by the Senate in 1795.)

As part of their ongoing feud, both men supported rival newspapers whose editors received plums from the federal pie. Jefferson's platform was the *National Gazette*, and Hamilton's was the *Gazette of the United States*, both of which took potshots at the opposition. These were not mild pleasantries, either, but mudslinging that escalated into character assassination. More important, the feud gave birth to a new and unexpected development, the growth of political parties, or factions, as they were then called.

To this point, organized parties were viewed as sinister. There was no scheme for a two-party system consisting of a government party and a loyal opposition. Instead this system evolved piecemeal, and the seeds were sown in the Jefferson-Hamilton rivalry. Jefferson and James Madison, a Federalist during the ratification debate but now swung to Jefferson's views, began to organize factions to support their growing opposition to Washington's Federalist administration. Their supporters eventually adopted the name Democratic Republicans in 1796. (Now stay with this: The name was shortened to Republicans, but during Andrew Jackson's presidency, they became Democrats.) These first Republicans generally favored a democratic, agrarian society in which individual freedoms were elevated over strong, centralized government. Hamilton and his supporters coalesced in 1792 as the Federalist Party, favoring a strong central government, promoting commercial and industrial interests, and supported by the elite and powerful of the nation. Under Washington, who openly disdained any "factions," the Federalists held most of the power in Washington for several years to come, dominating Congress during the two Washington administrations and the Adams presidency.

To call these two groups the forerunners of the modern Democrats and Republicans is a bit of an oversimplification. The process leading to the present two-party system was a long, slow one, with several interruptions along the way. If he were alive today, would Jefferson be a Democrat or a Republican? His notions of less federal government would sit well with those Republicans who want to dismantle the federal bureaucracy. His preoccupation with civil liberties would seem more at home with the Democrats. And Hamilton? Certainly his commercial and banking instincts would place him in the old guard eastern establishment Republican mainstream. But his insistence on a powerful federal government pulling the economic strings would be heresy to more conservative, laissez-faire, small government Republicans.

The personal in these politics would soon explode. Married to the daughter of one of New York's most powerful men, General Philip Schuyler, Hamilton was at the peak of his power as both Treasury secretary and a New York state power broker. But he was about to be brought down in a scandal over, what else, money and sex.

In 1791, Hamilton had become involved with a Philadelphia woman named Maria Reynolds. (He was also rumored to have had an ongoing affair with his sister-in-law, Angelica Schuyler Church. But times were different for eighteenth-century men, whose illicit dalliances, if not expected, were at least tolerated.) James Reynolds, the husband of Maria, had begun charging Hamilton for access to his wife—call it blackmail or pimping. Reynolds then began to boast that Hamilton was giving him tips—"insider information," in modern terms—that allowed him to speculate in government bonds. Accused of corruption, Hamilton actually turned over love letters from Maria Reynolds to his political enemies to prove that he might have cheated on his wife, but he wasn't cheating the government. But in 1797, the letters surfaced publicly through a pamphlet by James Thomson Callender (who may have gotten the letters from Virginia's James Monroe, a Jefferson ally). He accused Hamilton of immense speculation on Treasury policies. Hamilton confessed the affair publicly, and his career seemed over. But Hamilton had powerful, loyal friends. Most of all, he had the support of the "first friend." With George Washington's public show of loyalty, Hamilton survived, the eighteenth century's version of the comeback kid.

AMERICAN VOICES
GEORGE WASHINGTON, from the Farewell Address:

I have already intimated to you the danger of Parties in the State, with particular reference to the founding of them on Geographical discriminations. Let me now take a more comprehensive view, and warn you in the most solemn manner against the baneful effects of the Spirit of Party, generally.

This spirit, unfortunately, is inseparable from our nature, having its root in the strongest passions of the human

Mind. It exists under different shapes in all Governments, more or less stifled, controuled [sic], or repressed; but, in those of the popular form it is seen in its greatest rankness and is truly their worst enemy.

The alternate domination of one faction over another, sharpened by the spirit of revenge natural to party dissention [sic], which in different ages and countries has perpetrated the most horrid enormities, is itself frightful despotism. . . . [T]he common and continual mischiefs of the spirit of Party are sufficient to make it in the interest and the duty of a wise People to discourage and restrain it.

Was George Washington killed by his doctors?

With a last hurrah, Washington led troops once more in 1794 to suppress the so-called Whiskey Rebellion in the frontier of western Pennsylvania. Like Shays's Rebellion, it was a revolt of backwoods farmers against the establishment, this time over a stiff excise tax placed on whiskey. With 13,000 troops—more men than he had led during the war—Washington rode out in uniform, with Treasury secretary Alexander Hamilton by his side, to put down the uprising with ease.

In September 1796, setting aside requests that he take a third term, Washington made the last of his many retirement speeches in his Farewell Address, warning against political parties and "passionate attachments" to foreign nations. He was basically ignored on both counts.

Washington's retirement to Mount Vernon was interrupted by the near outbreak of a war with France, which was basically kidnapping American sailors to man its ships in its wars against England. In 1798, Congress asked him to lead the army once more, and Washington agreed. He asked Alexander Hamilton to be his second-in-command, but the disagreement with France was settled, and Washington returned to Mount Vernon.

After a winter ride in December 1799, Washington fell ill with a throat infection, then called "quinsy" (most likely what is now called strep throat). With his throat badly swollen, Washington had difficulty breathing. Following standard medical practice of the day, Washington was first given a mixture of tea and vinegar. This was followed by cal-omel, a commonly used laxative also called "blue mass," which was intended to flush out sickness. Finally, he was bled by his doctors, a total of four times, taking over half the blood in his body. While the bleeding did not kill him, it certainly didn't help Washington's cause. "I die hard," he said on his deathbed, "but I am not afraid to go." Washington died on December 14, 1799, two months before his sixty-eighth birthday.

Prior to his death, Washington had told a British visitor to Mount Vernon, "I can clearly foresee that nothing but the rooting out of slavery can [save] our Union." While he had done little to bring that end about in his lifetime other than fret about it, his will included specific conditions for the problem that he had publicly and privately wrestled with—his slaves. From 1775, Washington had stopped selling slaves, a profitable enterprise, and the plantation's slave population actually doubled. All were to be freed after his wife Martha's death. (She released her husband's slaves before she died in 1800, and the estate supported some as pensioners until 1833.)

What was the Revolution of 1800?

With Washington's retirement came the first true presidential campaign, which got under way in 1796. Gathering in a "caucus," the Federalist congressmen selected John Adams, the vice president, as their standard-bearer, with Thomas Pinckney of South Carolina as a second candidate. The other Federalist leader, Alexander Hamilton, was deemed too strong-willed and monarchist for even the staunchest of Federalists. Jefferson was the obvious choice of the Democratic Republicans, with their second on the ticket being Aaron Burr, an ambitious New Yorker who brought control of Tammany Hall, the first "political machine," to the ticket.

Shrewd and ambitious, Hamilton thought he could pull a power play by getting Pinckney elected and becoming the man pulling the strings, but this stratagem backfired when New England Federalists caught on to Hamilton's plan and voted for Jefferson instead. Adams squeaked into the presidency, and Jefferson, although of the opposing party, won the second most electoral votes and became vice president. Obviously, it would be back to the drawing board for presidential elections.

Adams's years in office were distinguished mostly by the animosity that had been unleashed between the two competing parties. Although the Federalists had held sway through Washington's administrations and into that of Adams, their power was beginning to decline. Neither the Jay Treaty nor Adams was broadly popular, and Adams endured much abuse from the Republican press. His greatest accomplishment was managing to avoid a wider war with France when it seemed likely; his low point came with passage of a series of repressive measures called the Alien and Sedition Acts, which expressed the fear of foreigners in the young nation while attempting to suppress all criticism of the Federalist administration.

Yet the next election, in 1800, would be a close one, in more than one way. Adams once again led the Federalist ticket, with Charles C. Pinckney (the brother of Thomas Pinckney) as his party's number two choice. Jefferson and Burr were again the Republican nominees. The campaign produced a torrent of slurs and abuses from both sides. And newspapers loyal to either party were filled with crude rumors of sexual philandering by both Adams and Jefferson. To the Federalists, Jefferson was an atheist who would allow the excesses of the French Revolution to come to America.

When the ballots were counted, however, the Republicans held the day. But the problem was, which Republican? There was no separate election of president and vice president, and Jefferson and Burr had collected seventy-three votes each. Under the Constitution, the tie meant the House of Representatives, still under Federalist control, would decide the question.

Faced with a choice between these two, Alexander Hamilton lobbied for Jefferson. He hated Jefferson but he detested fellow New Yorker Burr, in his opinion a "most unfit and dangerous man." Burr played his hand cautiously, not campaigning for himself, but not withdrawing, either. The votes of nine of the House's state delegations were needed to win, and Jefferson failed to gain them through thirty-five ballots. The crisis was real, and some historians believe that civil war over this election was not only possible but likely. Some Republican leaders were threatening to call out their state militias to enforce the popular will. Finally, with Jefferson privately assuring the Federalists that he would maintain much of the status quo, the House elected him on February 17, 1801. He was inaugurated on March 4, 1801, in the new federal capital of Washington. (The difficulties of selecting the president in 1800 resulted in passage of the Twelfth Amendment in 1804, which provides for separate balloting for the vice president and president. See Appendix 1 for more on this amendment.)

This electoral crisis marked a triumph of level heads in both parties, who put the orderly succession and continuity of government first. This Revolution of 1800, as Jefferson called it, was a bloodless one, but its impact was real. The Federalist Party was all but guillotined; it lost both the presidency and Congress, but John Adams had made certain that its influence did not die with his defeat.

Must Read: *John Adams* by David McCullough.

What was *Marbury v. Madison?*

In his last weeks before leaving the presidency, John Adams did what Franklin D. Roosevelt, Ronald Reagan, and other presidents have only dreamed of accomplishing. Working with a "lame duck" Federalist Congress that would soon be out of power, Adams created dozens of new judgeships. He signed appointments until late into the night before Jefferson was inaugurated, and these "midnight judges" of staunch Federalist beliefs throughout the federal courts resulted in the most successful "court-packing" operation in American judicial history. In doing so, Adams influenced the course of events long after his rather inconsequential four years in office were over.

Most prominent among Adams's appointments was that of John Marshall, who had served as Adams's secretary of state, to be chief justice of the United States in 1801. Although he had studied law only briefly and had no judicial experience, Marshall held that post until his death in 1835. He placed a stamp on the Court and the young nation that is still felt today. Of his many decisions, one of the most important came in the 1803 case of *Marbury v. Madison.*

The case grew out of the ongoing political fight to the death between the Federalists and the Jeffersonian Democratic Republicans. In the last-minute rush to appoint judges who would uphold the Federalist principle of a strong central government, William Marbury, one of the "midnight judges," was named to a lower federal court. But Marshall, as secretary of state, had failed to present Marbury with his commission, and James Madison, the secretary of state for the incoming Jefferson administration, refused to grant Marbury's commission. Marbury sued and appealed to the Supreme Court—now with Marshall presiding—to order Madison to grant the commission.

But Marshall refused Marbury's request, saying that although Marbury was theoretically entitled to the post, a section of the Judiciary Act of 1789, which had established the federal court system, was unconstitutional and void. For the first time the Supreme Court had overturned an act of Congress. Although Marshall's decision in this case affected only the right of the court to interpret its own powers, the concept of judicial review, a key principle in the constitutional system of checks and balances, got its first test.

AMERICAN VOICES
From CHIEF JUSTICE MARSHALL'S decision
in *Marbury v. Madison*:

It is emphatically the province and duty of the judicial department to say what the law is. . . . Thus the particular phraseology of the constitution of the United States confirms and strengthens the principle, supposed to be essential to all written constitutions, that a law repugnant to the constitution is void. . . .

How did America purchase Louisiana?

While America enjoyed its bloodless Revolution of 1800, France was still in the throes of its more violent contortions. In 1799, Napoleon Bonaparte engineered the coup that overturned the Revolutionary Directory, eventually making himself ruler of France. While most of Napoleon's grandiose plans focused on Europe, America had a place in the Little Corporal's heart. His first step was to force a weak Spain to return the Louisiana Territory to France, which it did in 1800. The second step was to regain control of the Caribbean island of St. Domingue. In 1793, at the time of the French Revolution, the island had come under control of a self-taught genius, General Toussaint L'Ouverture, who had led a successful slave revolt. To launch any offensive in North America, Napoleon needed the island as a base, and he sent 20,000 troops to retake it.

All this French scurrying around in America's backyard alarmed President Jefferson, who knew that French control of New Orleans and the western territories would create an overwhelming threat to America. Jefferson had an option play ready. Although he preferred neutrality between the warring European nations, Jefferson dropped hints to the British about an alliance against the French, and found them receptive. At the same time, he directed Robert Livingston and James Monroe to offer to buy New Orleans and Florida from France. Such a sale seemed unlikely until the French army sent to St. Domingue was practically wiped out by yellow fever after regaining control of the island. (The French withdrew to the eastern half of St. Domingue, and the western half was renamed Haiti, the original Arawak name for the island, with Toussaint's successor, Dessalines, proclaiming himself emperor. The island, Columbus's Hispaniola, remains split today between Haiti and the Dominican Republic.)

Without the safe base on the island, a French adventure into Louisiana was out of the question. Preparing to open a new European campaign, Napoleon wrote off the New World. He needed troops and cash. Almost on a whim, he ordered his foreign minister, Talleyrand, to offer not only New Orleans and Florida but the whole of the Louisiana Territory to America. Livingston and Monroe dickered with the French over price, but in May 1803, a treaty turning over all of Louisiana was signed. Nobody knew exactly what Napoleon sold, but under the treaty's terms, the United States would double in size for about $15 million, or approximately four cents an acre. Left unclear were the rights to Texas, western Florida, and the West Coast above the Spanish settlements in California. Spain had its own ideas about these territories. Ironically, the purchase was made with U.S. bonds, the result of Hamilton's U.S. Bank initiative, which Jefferson had resisted as unconstitutional.

about five Oclock this evening one of the wives of Char-
bon was delivered of a fine boy. it is worthy of remark that
this was the first child which this woman had boarn, and
as is common in such cases, labour was tedious and the
pain violent; Mr. Jessome informed me that he had frequently administered a small portion of the rattle of the
rattle-snake, which he assured me had never failed to produce the desired effect, that of hastening the birth of the
child; having the rattle of a snake by me I gave it to him
and he administered two rings of it to the woman broken
in small pieces with the fingers and added to a small quantity of water. Whether this medicine was truly the cause or
not I shall not undertake to determine, but I was informed
that she had not taken it more than ten minutes before she
brought forth perhaps this remedy may be worthy of future
experiments, but I must confess that I want faith as to its
efficacy.

Who were Lewis and Clark?

Months before the purchase was made, Jefferson had the foresight to
ask Congress for $2,500 to outfit an expedition into the West. Osten-
sibly its purpose was to "extend the external commerce" of the United
States, but Jefferson had several other motives: to get America into the
fur trade; to feel out the political and military uses of the West; and,
reflecting his philosophy as a true Enlightenment man, to collect scientific information about this vast, uncharted land.

With the purchase complete, the little expedition now became a
major adventure to find out what exactly America now owned. For this
job, Jefferson selected thirty-year-old Meriwether Lewis (1774–1809),
his private secretary, an army veteran, and a fellow Virginian. Lewis
selected another Virginia soldier, thirty-four-year-old William Clark
(1770–1838), a veteran of the Indian wars and brother of Revolutionary

War hero George Rogers Clark, as his co-commander. With some forty soldiers and civilians, including Clark's slave York, they set out from St. Louis in the winter of 1803–4 aboard three boats, a fifty-five-foot keelboat with twenty-two oars and two *pirogues*, or dugout canoes, each large enough to hold seven men. They carried twenty one bales of gifts to trade with Indians. Working their way upstream was arduous, and strict martial discipline was maintained with regular floggings, but the company reached what is now North Dakota in the fall of 1804, built Fort Mandan (near present-day Bismarck), and wintered there.

In the spring of 1805, they set out again for the West, now joined by Charbonneau, a French-Canadian trapper, and one of his Indian wives, a pregnant teenager named Sacagawea, who acted as guides and interpreters. Crossing the Rockies in present-day Montana, they built boats to take them down the Clearwater and Columbia rivers, reaching the Pacific coast in November, where they built Fort Clatsop (near the site of Astoria, Oregon). Hearing the Indians speak some "sailor's" English, presumably learned from traders, the expedition believed a ship might pass and they decided to winter there. When no ship appeared, they set off for an overland return, splitting the expedition in two after crossing the Rockies to explore alternative routes. The parties reunited at the site of Fort Union, and arrived together in St. Louis on September 23, 1806.

After twenty-eight months of incredible hardships met in traveling over difficult, uncharted terrain, in skirmishes with Indians, and in encounters with dangerous animals from rattlesnakes to grizzly bears, the Lewis and Clark expedition had suffered only a single casualty: one man had succumbed to an attack of appendicitis.

The journals they kept, the specimens they brought or sent back, the detailed accounts of Indians they had encountered and with whom they had traded were of inestimable value, priming an America that was eager to press westward.

While William Clark lived long and was influential in Indian affairs, Lewis suffered from melancholy and committed suicide. Although some historians later claimed Lewis was murdered, there is scant evidence to support that notion. Suffering from what was then described as "hypochondria," which is how later Lincoln described his own depression, the modern term would more likely have been manic depression, or bipolar syndrome. There is also some suggestion that Lewis suffered from the effects of syphilis. Contrary to common myth that she survived to her nineties, Sacagawea actually died in her twenty-eighth year. Her son, born on the trip and nicknamed Pomp, was later raised by Clark and traveled in Europe before returning to America, where he became a trapper and guide.

Must Read: *Undaunted Courage: Meriwether Lewis, Thomas Jefferson, and the Opening of the American West* by Stephen Ambrose.

Why did Aaron Burr shoot Alexander Hamilton?

Thomas Jefferson did not sit around idly while waiting for his two adventurers to return. The deal with France was the centerpiece of Jefferson's first administration, and while the few remaining Federalists in Congress tried to undermine it on constitutional grounds, the acquisition and the president were so popular that resistance was futile.

Jefferson had earlier made the historically popular move of cutting taxes, including repeal of the Whiskey Tax that Washington had led an army to enforce. He won more admirers when he balked at the widely accepted practice of paying tribute to pirates based in North Africa—the "Barbary pirates." A brief naval war followed, which did not end the tribute payments, but did give America some new naval heroes (Stephen Decatur chief among them), inspired the line in "The Marines' Hymn" about "the shores of Tripoli," and earned America a new measure of international respect. (It also provided members of the Marine Corps with their distinctive nickname. To ward off sword blows, the marines wore a protective piece of leather around their necks—hence "leathernecks.")

By election time in 1804, Jefferson's popularity was so great that the opposition Federalist Party was all but dead.

But a group of Federalists known as the Essex Junto did attempt a bizarre break from the Union. Their conspiracy would have been historically laughable had it not ended in tragedy. Part of their plan was to support Aaron Burr for governor of New York. No friend of Jefferson's, Burr had been frozen out of power in the Jefferson administration, and then unceremoniously dumped by his party as candidate for vice president (and replaced by George Clinton, the aging governor of New York). The long-standing hatred between Burr and Alexander Hamilton resurfaced as Hamilton used all his influence to defeat Burr in the governor's race. To Hamilton, Burr was a "dangerous man, and one who ought not to be trusted with the reins of government." That was the polite attack; others were aimed at Burr's notorious sexual exploits. An admitted adulterer, Hamilton was no paragon of marital fidelity, either, and Burr pulled no punches in his counterassaults.

Hamilton's political destruction of Burr was successful, but with awful results. A few months after the election, Burr challenged Hamilton to a duel, and they met on the morning of Wednesday, July 11, 1804, on the cliffs above the Hudson in Weehawken, New Jersey. Hamilton's son had died in a duel, and he opposed the idea of dueling, but personal honor and that of the fading Federalist Party forced his hand. The widely accepted version of events is that Hamilton fired his pistol but deliberately missed, an intention he had supposedly stated before the duel. Others dispute that, and say Hamilton just missed. Burr did not. (As Gore Vidal's fictional Aaron Burr put it in the novel *Burr*, "at the crucial moment his hand shook and mine never does.") Hamilton was mortally wounded, and suffered for an excruciating thirty hours before dying. Aaron Burr, who had nearly been president a few years before, was now a fugitive.

But Burr was hardly finished as a factor in American politics, or as a thorn in Thomas Jefferson's side. Perhaps inspired by Napoleon, an ambitious colonel who had become an emperor, Burr envisioned securing a western empire he intended to rule. With James Wilkinson, one of Washington's wartime generals who was appointed by Jefferson to govern Louisiana, but who was secretly on the Spanish payroll, Burr organized a small force in 1806 to invade Mexico and create a new nation in the West. For some reason, Wilkinson betrayed Burr, and the conspiracy was foiled. Burr was captured and placed on trial for treason, with Chief Justice John Marshall presiding. Jefferson's hatred for Burr was unleashed as he did everything in his power to convict his former vice president. But the crafty old Federalist Marshall saw the trial as another way to undermine Jefferson, and his charge to the jury all but acquitted Burr. Following a second treason charge, Burr jumped bail and fled to Europe, where he remained for five years, attempting to persuade Napoleon to organize an Anglo-French invasion of America. He did return to New York in 1812, where he continued a colorful and lusty life until his death in 1836.

Must Read: *Duel: Alexander Hamilton, Aaron Burr, and the Future of America* by Thomas Fleming.

AMERICAN VOICES
From the *Richmond Recorder*, published by
James Thomson Callender (1802):

**A Song Supposed to have been written by
the SAGE OF MONTICELLO**

When pressed by loads of state affairs
I seek to sport and dally
The sweetest solace of my cares
Is in the lap of Sally,
She's black you tell me—grant she be—
Must colour always tally?
Black is love's proper hue for me
And white's the hue for Sally

Callender, the muckraking journalist who had revealed Hamilton's affair a few years earlier, was disappointed when he failed to get a patronage job from Jefferson in 1800. He turned the tables and began to attack Thomas Jefferson with the charges that Jefferson kept a slave as his lover.

Thomas Jefferson and Sally Hemings: Did he or didn't he?

The DNA evidence is in. Or is it?

While Jefferson won the election of 1804 in a landslide, the campaign was notable for the one juicy bit of mudslinging gossip it had produced. A popular Federalist claim of the day was that Jefferson had carried on an affair with a young slave named Sally Hemings while he was envoy in Paris, and that she had given birth to Jefferson's illegitimate children. What makes the Hemings story all the more re-markable is that fact that "dusky Sally," as the newspaper called her, was the half-sister of Jefferson's wife, Martha Wayles Skelton Jefferson. Sally's mother had become the mistress of Martha Jefferson's father, John Wayles, after the death of Martha's mother, and as a result Sally was Martha's slave half-sister. Martha Jefferson died in 1782, when Sally was nine, and Jefferson, then thirty-nine years old, was grief-stricken, apparently to the point of suicide. But while Jefferson was in Paris, in 1787, his daughter Maria was brought to France during an epidemic in Virginia. She was accompanied by Sally, now almost sixteen. Some believe that at this time, Sally Hemings became Thomas Jefferson's mistress and eventually bore him children during a thirty-eight-year relationship. (This relationship is also lovingly but fictionally depicted in the Merchant-Ivory film *Jefferson in Paris*.)

Jefferson remained silent on Callender's charges, and while the public was certainly aware of them, they had little impact on the election in 1804. What the incident shows is that there is nothing new about "negative campaigns" and mudslinging during presidential races.

The controversy was mostly forgotten over the years, as Jefferson was lionized for his role in the founding of the country, placed on Mt. Rushmore, and celebrated in a Broadway musical called *1776*. But the story gained new life with the publication of two books, *Jefferson: An Intimate History* (1974), Fawn Brodie's "psychobiography," and Barbara Chase Riboud's novel *Sally Hemings* (1979), both of which became best-sellers by claiming the relationship was real. Defenders of Jefferson countered that while Jefferson certainly had a love affair while in Paris, it was with Maria Cosway, the wife of an English painter, and whether it was consummated is a matter of conjecture. Others, including Virginius Dabney, author of *The Jefferson Scandals* (1981), a refutation of the Sally Hemings rumor, point to two of Jefferson's nephews as Sally's lovers and the possible fathers of her children.

Then came another book, a scholarly work called *Thomas Jefferson and Sally Hemings: An American Controversy*, by Annette Gordon-Reed, followed by DNA tests on descendants of Jefferson and Hemings in 1998. The national news media widely reported that these tests confirmed the Jefferson-Hemings relationship, and that Eston Hemings, who was freed in Jefferson's will, was Jefferson's son. In fact, they do not do so conclusively. Out of seven tests, the DNA match found one match identical to twenty-five Jefferson males then living in Virginia. Six of these Jefferson males were between fourteen and twenty-seven and could have been responsible for impregnating Sally Hemings. The controversy spilled into very public view when the descendants of Hemings sought to be admitted into the Monticello Association, an organization of descendants of Jefferson, which would entitle them to be buried in the Jefferson cemetery. The Jefferson group declined to accept the Hemings group because the scientific evidence was deemed inconclusive, but they did offer a separate burial area for descendants of Jefferson's slaves.

In 2008, Gordon-Reed published a new book, *The Hemingses of Monticello*, winner of the 2009 Pulitzer Prize in History, in which she essentially concluded that Thomas Jefferson had fathered Sally's children, an opinion that has become more widely accepted. At Jefferson's home, Monticello, this long-rumored relationship is now acknowledged.

Does it matter whether it was really Jefferson, or one of his younger relatives? What is the real historical import of the question? What takes this story out of the context of a *People* magazine article or a daytime television talk show? Ultimately, the story of Jefferson and his slaves is about the great American contradiction, particularly as it is embodied by Jefferson—the contradiction between "all men are created equal" and the "peculiar institution" on which Jefferson's life and fortune were built. It is that great contradiction that led Samuel Johnson to rise in Parliament during the Revolution and ask, "How is it that we hear the loudest yelps for liberty from the drivers of Negroes?"

Harvard professor Orlando Patterson, who has written several histories of slavery, once attempted to resolve this contradiction when he wrote in the *New York Times*, "Jefferson was no saint, but his reflections on African-Americans must be understood in the context of his times and his relationship with an African-American woman. Nearly all Caucasians of his day, including most abolitionists, simply assumed that African-Americans were racially inferior. Jefferson was unusual in the degree to which he agonized over the subject. He was overtly inclined to what we would consider today to be racist views, but he also held out the possibility that he might be wrong. In this regard, he was ahead of his times."

What was impressment?

Following Washington's example, Jefferson declined an opportunity to run again. (There was no constitutional limitation on the number of presidential terms of office a single individual might serve until after Franklin Delano Roosevelt's unique election to a fourth term in 1944. The Twenty-second Amendment, ratified in 1947, limits a president to two terms or to a single elected term for a president who has served more than two years of his predecessor's term. When Ronald Reagan left office in 1989, he stated his opposition to this limitation on principle, expressing the belief that the people should be entitled to vote for the candidate of their choice. For more on this amendment, see Appendix 1.) Although Jefferson had been reelected at the peak of his popularity, he left under less happy circumstances, primarily because of his unpopular Embargo Act.

Passed in 1807, the act was the result of America's international weakness at a time when Napoleon had turned the world into a battleground with England and its allies. Jefferson wanted to keep America—a weak, third-rate nation with no real army and a skeleton navy—neutral in the wars that had left Napoleon in control of Europe and had made the British masters of the seas. America had actually flourished economically during the fighting, as the warring nations eagerly bought American goods and ships. But American neutrality did not protect her merchant ships from being stopped by British vessels, which could take any British subject off the ship and "impress" him into Royal Navy service. On board the ships, legal distinctions such as "naturalized citizenship" were meaningless, and Americans were being seized along with British subjects.

The Embargo Act, which prohibited all exports into America as economic retaliation for the British impressment policy and as a means to keep America out of war, was one of the most unpopular and unsuccessful acts in American history. In his last week in office, Jefferson had it abolished, replaced by the Nonintercourse Act, which prohibited trade only with England and which provoked only more impressment attacks.

Jefferson's handpicked successor was his secretary of state, fellow Virginian and longtime ally James "Jemmy" Madison, who was elected in 1808 for the first of two terms. When Madison took office, war with England and perhaps with France seemed inevitable.

Who were Tecumseh and the Prophet?

The coming war got some provocation from one of the most remarkable Indian leaders of American history. A young Shawnee chief from the Ohio valley, Tecumseh envisioned a vast Indian confederacy strong enough to keep the Ohio River as a border between Indians and whites, preventing further westward expansion. He and his brother, Tenskwatawa, the Prophet, an Indian mystic who called for a revival of Indian ways and a rejection of white culture, traveled extensively among tribes from Wisconsin to Florida. With Tecumseh's organizing brilliance and the Prophet's religious fervor, younger warriors began to fall in line, and a large army of braves, a confederacy of midwestern and southern tribes, gathered at the junction of the Tippecanoe and Wabash rivers.

General William Henry Harrison, governor of the Indiana Territory (and a future president and grandfather of a president), was given the task of confronting Tecumseh, whom he met twice. After one of those meetings, Harrison wrote, "The implicit obedience and respect which the followers of Tecumseh pay to him, is really astonishing, and more than any other circumstance bespeaks him one of those uncommon geniuses which spring up occasionally to produce revolutions and overturn the established order of things."

Harrison took 1,000 men out to camp near the Indians. Tecumseh, then on one of his organizing and recruiting trips, was absent when his brother, the Prophet, ordered a badly calculated assault on Harrison's troops in November 1811. The Indians inflicted heavy losses, but were eventually driven back and scattered. Harrison and his troops destroyed their food stores, their village, and the Prophet's claim of invincible magic, shattering Indian confidence and ending hopes for Tecumseh's confederation.

To western Americans, the Indian confederation was a convenient excuse to fan anti-British sentiment in Congress. Calling Tecumseh's confederation a British scheme, land-hungry westerners heightened the war fever, clamoring for the expulsion of the British from North America, even if it meant invading Canada to do it.

AMERICAN VOICES
TECUMSEH of the Shawnees:

Where today are the Pequot? Where are the Narragansett, the Mohican, the Pokanoket, and many other powerful tribes of our people? They have vanished before the avarice and the oppression of the White Man, as snow before a summer sun.

Will we let ourselves be destroyed in our turn without a struggle, to give up our homes, our country bequeathed to us by the Great Spirit, the graves of our dead and everything that is dear and sacred to us? I know you will cry with me, "Never! Never!"

Tecumseh died during the War of 1812, fighting alongside the British on the Thames River in Ontario. Tecumseh was shot and killed in October 1813. His body was reportedly skinned and mutilated by Kentucky militiamen, and he was buried in a mass grave near the battlefield, according to R. David Edmunds in the *Encyclopedia of North American Indians.*

What was the War of 1812 about?

With the British encouraging the Indians and the continuing controversy over English impressment of sailors taken from American ships, there was a powerful cry for war among the land-crazed "war hawks" of the West. Led by the bellicose but powerful young House speaker, Henry Clay of Kentucky, Madison was pushed to what Jefferson had tried to avoid, a war with England. The War of 1812 finally got under way in June, in the midst of the presidential campaign.

It was not a war that America was ready to fight. A regular army of 12,000 was scattered and led by political appointees rather than by experienced commanders. There was a small navy, hardly equal in numbers or experience to England's.

Neither side apparently prosecuted this war with much enthusiasm. The results showed in a meandering war effort that went on for the next two and a half years, ending early in 1815. After its humbling experience in the Revolution, and preoccupied with Napoleon's armies on the continent, England fought a reluctant war. English commercial interests saw America as an important market and supplier, so their support for war was halfhearted. America didn't lose this war. Nor did it really win. And the greatest single American victory in the war, at the Battle of New Orleans, came after peace had already been signed.

MILESTONES IN THE WAR OF 1812

1812

July   Aiming to conquer Canada, American troops under General William Hull launch an assault. British-Canadian troops, augmented by 1,000 of Tecumseh's braves, send Hull's army reeling. Hull is later court-martialed and sentenced to death for cowardice, but is pardoned by Madison.

August–December   A series of surprising American sea victories by the *Constitution* (Old Ironsides) and the *United States* commanded by Stephen Decatur are morale boosters, but have no influence on the war's outcome.

December   Madison is reelected president, beginning an American political tradition: no president has been turned out of office in wartime. Madison's new vice president is Elbridge Gerry, a signer of the Declaration, who wins a place in posterity for creating another political tradition. Gerry carved Massachusetts into election districts that favored his party. These districts, say his opponents, were shaped like wriggling salamanders, giving the American political dictionary a new word, "gerrymander."

The British begin a naval blockade of Chesapeake and Delaware bays.

1813

March   Commodore Isaac Chauncey, with the assistance of young Captain Oliver Perry, begins to build warships on Lake Erie to control the Great Lakes.

April   American forces capture York (Toronto) and burn government buildings there.

May   American forces under Winfield Scott take Fort George, forcing British withdrawal from Lake Erie.

June   The American frigate *Chesapeake* is captured by the British. Before dying, the American captain, James Lawrence, orders his men, "Don't give up the ship." They listened, prevailed, and the words soon become the American navy's rallying cry.

September   The American fleet on Lake Erie, led by Oliver Hazard Perry, defeats a British counterpart, giving the United States control of this strategic waterway. Perry's message to a happy President Madison: "We have met the enemy and they are ours."

October   The Battle of the Thames. Americans under William Henry Harrison defeat retreating British and Indian forces. Harrison's Indian adversary, Tecumseh, is killed in the battle, depriving the Indians of the strong leader who might have united them.

November   American forces under James Wilkinson are defeated at Montreal. A disgraced Wilkinson is later court-martialed for cowardice, but is acquitted.

The British navy extends its blockade north to Long Island. Only ports in New England remain open to commerce, and merchants in New York and New England continue to supply the British.

1814

March   While the war against the British goes on, General Andrew Jackson of the Tennessee militia has been fighting the Creek Indian War. Jackson achieves a decisive victory in this war at the Battle of Horseshoe Bend in Alabama, ending the Creek War.

April   Napoleon Bonaparte is overthrown, freeing some 14,000 British troops to concentrate on the war in America.

The British blockade is extended to New England. The Americans retaliate by privateering, and capture 825 British vessels by the summer.

July   Battle of Chippewea. Outnumbered American forces under Winfield Scott defeat British forces.

August   Peace negotiations begin in Ghent.

After routing an American army at Bladensburg in a battle watched by President Madison, British troops march unopposed into Washington, D.C. In retaliation for the earlier American burning of York, the British set fire to the Capitol, the president's mansion, and other government buildings. The British withdraw from the capital for an attack on Baltimore, and Madison returns to Washington at the end of August.

AMERICAN VOICES
FIRST LADY DOLLEY MADISON, in a letter to
her sister (August 23–24, 1814):

Will you believe it, my sister? We have had a battle, or skirmish, near Bladensburg, and here I am still, within sound of the cannon! Mr. Madison comes not. May God protect us! . . . At this late hour a wagon has been procured, and I have filled it with plate and the most valuable portable articles, belonging to the house. . . . I insist on waiting until the large picture of General Washington is secured and it requires to be unscrewed from the wall. This process was found too tedious for these perilous moments; I have

ordered the frame to be broken, and the canvas taken out. It is done!

After the war, the president's mansion was painted white to cover the scorch marks left by the British. That is when everyone started to call it the White House.

September An American victory on Lake Champlain forces the British to abort a planned offensive south from Canada.

The siege of Baltimore. A successful defense of the city and Fort McHenry is witnessed by Francis Scott Key, an American civilian held on board a British ship, who is inspired to write "The Star-Spangled Banner." Two elements of the British strategy, one assault from Canada and another into the middle states, have now been thwarted, leaving a third British army aimed at the Gulf Coast.

December Andrew Jackson arrives in New Orleans, unaware that a large British invasion fleet is sailing there from Jamaica. When he learns of the attacking force, he begins preparing a defense of New Orleans, and an elaborate system of fortifications is completed just before Christmas.

December 24 The Treaty of Ghent is signed, ending the war. The treaty leaves unresolved most of the issues that led to the fighting, including impressment, now a moot point because the end of the Napoleonic wars ends the British need for more sailors. Clear boundaries between Canada and the United States are set, and a later agreement demilitarizes the Great Lakes. The Oregon Territory in the Pacific Northwest is placed under joint British-American control for a period of ten years.

1815

January The Battle of New Orleans. Unaware that peace was made two weeks earlier, the British attack. The American defenders, under General Andrew Jackson, are aided by the French privateer Jean Lafitte, who has been courted by the British as well. Heavily outnumbered by British troops fresh from the victory over

Napoleon's armies, the Americans use artillery and sharpshooting riflemen to repulse numerous British charges against their defensive position, inflicting massive losses. The British suffer more than 20,000 dead; U.S. casualties are 8 dead and a small number wounded. Although the war's outcome is unaffected by this rout, Jackson becomes an instant national hero. The news of the Treaty of Ghent finally reaches America in February.

What was the Monroe Doctrine?

America suffered one notable casualty in the War of 1812. The Federalist Party, which had opposed the war, was mortally wounded. Peace had delivered a large political bonus for Madison and his party. In 1816, the Federalists barely mounted opposition to Madison's chosen successor, James Monroe, next in the "Virginian dynasty" that started with Washington, was delayed by Adams, and continued through Jefferson and Madison.

Elected at age fifty-eight, Monroe had seen much in his life. A veteran of the War of Independence, he had fought at Trenton, was twice governor of Virginia and then a senator from that state. As a diplomat he helped engineer the Louisiana Purchase. Like Jefferson and Madison before him, he had served as secretary of state, giving that post and not the vice presidency the luster of heir apparent's office.

With the great foreign disputes settled and the nation comfortably accepting one-party rule, Monroe's years were later dubbed the Era of Good Feelings. It was a period of rapid economic expansion, especially in the Northeast, as manufacturing began to replace shipbuilding as the leading industry. These calm years saw the beginnings of the machine age, as men like Eli Whitney, Seth Thomas of mechanical clock fame, and Francis Cabot Lowell were bringing America into the first stages of the Industrial Revolution. A series of postwar treaties with the British solidified the nation's boundaries and eliminated the threat of another war with England.

But the most notable historical milestone in this administration came in an address given to Congress in 1823. The speech was as much the work of Monroe's secretary of state, John Quincy Adams, son of the second president, but some decades later it came to be called the Monroe Doctrine.

In this speech, Monroe essentially declared that the United States would not tolerate intervention in the Americas by European nations. Monroe also promised that the United States wouldn't interfere with already established colonies or with governments in Europe. In one sense, this declaration was an act of isolationism, with America withdrawing from the political tempests of Europe. But it was also a recognition of a changing world order. Part of this new reality was the crumbling of the old Spanish Empire in the New World, and rebellions swept South America, creating republics under such leaders as Simon Bolívar, José de San Martín, and—the most unlikely name in South American history—Bernardo O'Higgins, the son of an Irish army officer and leader of the new republic of Chile. By 1822, America recognized the independent republics of Mexico, Brazil, Chile, Argentina, and La Plata (comprising present-day Colombia, Ecuador, Venezuela, and Panama).

On the positive side, the doctrine marked what might be called the last step in America's march to independence, which had begun in the Revolution and moved through post-independence foreign treaties, the Louisiana Purchase, the War of 1812, and the postwar agreements. But from another historical perspective, the Doctrine became the basis for a good deal of high-handed interference in South American affairs as the United States embarked on a path of meddling in Central and South America. As demonstrated by the "revolution" that created Panama with Teddy Roosevelt's help (see p. 293) and, more recently, the long war against Fidel Castro and the illegal support of the contra rebels in Nicaragua during the 1980s, that hemispheric interference has continued for centuries.

What was the Missouri Compromise?

As proof of the "good feelings," Monroe was almost unanimously re-elected in 1820, winning 231 of the 232 electoral votes cast that year. Popular legend has it that one elector withheld his vote to preserve Washington's record as the only unanimously elected president. But the facts show that the one elector who voted for Secretary of State John Quincy Adams did not know how everyone else would vote, and simply cast his ballot for Adams because he admired him.

While it may have been the Era of Good Feelings, not everyone felt so good. Certainly the Indians who were being decimated and pushed into shrinking territories by the rapacious westward push didn't feel so good. Nor did the slaves of the South, who now had to harvest a new crop in cotton, which had replaced tobacco as king. And it was the question of slavery that led to the other noteworthy milestone in the Monroe years—one about which Monroe had little to say—the Missouri Compromise of 1820.

From the day when Jefferson drafted the Declaration, through the debates at the Philadelphia convention, slavery was clearly an issue that America would be forced to confront. The earlier compromises of the Declaration and Constitution were beginning to show their age. Even though the slave trade had been outlawed in 1808 under a provision of the constitutional compromise, an illicit trade in slaves continued. The chief argument of the day was not about importing new slaves, however, but about the admission of new states to the Union, and whether they would be free or slave states.

It is important to realize that while strong abolitionist movements were beginning to gather force in America, the slavery debate was essentially about politics and economics rather than morality. The "three-fifths" compromise written into the Constitution, allowing slaves to be counted as part of the total population for the purpose of allocating congressional representation, gave slave states a political advantage over free states. Every new state meant two more Senate votes and a proportional number of House votes. Slave states wanted those votes to maintain their political power. Of course, there was an economic dimension to this issue. Wage-paying northerners were forced to compete against slave labor in the South. For southerners, wealth was land. With Eli Whitney's cotton gin (the word "gin" is short for "engine") allowing huge increases of efficiency in production, and the new factories of Lowell in New England to make cloth, the market for cotton was booming. Slaveholding southerners needed more land to grow more cotton to sell to the textile mills of the Northeast and England, and slaves were needed to work that land. If gaining new land to plant meant creating new states, slaveholders wanted them to be slave states.

By adding massive real estate to the equation under the Louisiana Purchase, the United States brought the free state/slave state issue to a head, particularly in the case of Missouri, which petitioned for statehood in 1817. With Henry Clay taking the lead, Congress agreed on another compromise. Under Clay's bill, Missouri would be admitted as a slave state, but slavery would not be allowed anywhere else north of Missouri's southern border. But every politician in America, including an aging Thomas Jefferson, could see the strict sectional lines that were being drawn, and few believed that this Missouri Compromise would solve the problem forever. Of course, the issue would soon explode.

THE UNION IN 1821

This is an alphabetical list of the twenty-four states in the Union following the Missouri Compromise, divided into free and slave states. The dates given denote the date of entry into the Union or ratification of the Constitution for the original thirteen states; the number following the date denotes order of entry.

Free States	Slave States
Connecticut (1788; 5)	Alabama (1819; 22)
Illinois (1818; 21)	Delaware (1787; 1)
Indiana (1816; 19)	Georgia (1788; 4)
Maine (1820; 23)	Kentucky (1792; 15)
Massachusetts (1788; 6)	Louisiana (1812; 18)
New Hampshire (1788; 9)	Maryland (1788; 7)
New Jersey (1787; 3)	Mississippi (1817; 20)
New York (1788; 11)	Missouri (1821; 24)
Ohio (1803; 17)	North Carolina (1789; 12)
Pennsylvania (1787; 2)	South Carolina (1788; 8)
Rhode Island (1790; 13)	Tennessee (1796; 16)
Vermont (1791; 14)	Virginia (1788; 10)

The possessions of the United States at this time also included the Florida Territory, ceded by Spain in 1819; the Arkansas Territory, which extended west to the existing border with Mexico (farther north than the modern border); the Michigan and Missouri Territories, comprising the Midwest to the Rockies; and the Oregon Country, then under joint British-American rule.

According to the census of 1820, the U.S. population was 9,638,453. New York had become the most populous state with 1.3 million people, followed by Pennsylvania with a little over a million. The population in the northern free states and territories was 5,152,635; the total for the southern states was 4,485,818.

What was the "corrupt bargain"?

There is a good deal of talk today about the problem of negative advertising in presidential campaigns. We like to look back fondly to the genteel days of the past, when high-minded gentlemen debated the great issues in the politest terms. Take 1824, for example. Candidate Adams was a slovenly monarchist who had an English wife. Candidate Clay was a drunkard and a gambler. And candidate Jackson was a murderer.

If America needed any evidence that Monroe's Era of Good Feelings was over, it came with the election of 1824. For a second time, the choice of a president would be sent to the House of Representatives after a ruthlessly bitter campaign demonstrated how clearly sectionalism, or the division of the country into geographic areas with their own agendas, had replaced party loyalties. The leading candidates for president in 1824 were all ostensibly of the same party, the Democratic Republicans of Jefferson, Madison, and Monroe. Even John Quincy Adams, son of the last Federalist president, was now a member of this party and, as Monroe's secretary of state, a leading contender for the presidency. The other chief candidates, all from the South or West, were General Andrew Jackson, senator from Tennessee; House Speaker Henry Clay of Kentucky; William H. Crawford, Monroe's Treasury secretary, from Georgia; and Secretary of War John C. Calhoun of South Carolina. After considerable infighting, Calhoun dropped from the race and opted for the vice presidency, with an eye on a future presidential bid.

Crawford was the choice of the congressional power brokers who nominated him in caucus. But given the growing popular resentment against the caucus system, that designation did more harm than good. When Crawford suffered a stroke during the campaign, his candidacy was left crippled. Issues became negligible in the campaign; personalities were the only subject of debate, and slanderous charges were thrown about by all. Adams and Jackson took the lead as popular favorites, but the election was inconclusive, with neither winning a majority of electoral votes, and the choice was given to the House, as it had been in 1800. Jackson, with 43.1 percent of the popular vote and ninety-nine electoral votes, had a legitimate claim to the office. But Clay, also a powerful westerner, wanted to keep his rival Jackson from the office. It is likely that Clay legitimately believed Adams was the more experienced candidate, but he also knew that an Adams election would clearly benefit Clay's political future at the expense of Jackson's. Clay threw his considerable influence in the House behind Adams, who won on the first ballot. Adams then named Clay to be his secretary of state. Jackson supporters screamed that "a corrupt bargain" had been made between the two. In Jackson's words, Clay was the "Judas of the West."

Whether a deal was made in advance or not didn't matter. The damage was done. In the public eye, the people's choice had been circumvented by a congressional cabal. Brilliant in many ways and well intentioned, Adams was an inept politician. His administration was crippled from the start by the political furor over the "corrupt bargain," and Adams never recovered from the controversy. The Tennessee legislature immediately designated Jackson its choice for the next election, and the campaign of 1828 actually began in 1825.

What were Jacksonian democracy and the spoils system?

Jackson got his revenge in 1828, after a campaign that was even more vicious than the one of four years earlier. The label of murderer was reattached to Jackson, an outgrowth of the general's numerous dueling encounters and his penchant for strict martial law, which had led to hangings of soldiers under his command. One Adamsite newspaper claimed that Jackson's mother was a prostitute brought to America by British soldiers, and that she had married a mulatto. Jackson's own marriage became an issue as well. He had married Rachel Robards in 1791, after she had presumably been divorced from her first husband. But the first husband had not legally divorced her until after her marriage to Jackson. Jackson remarried Rachel following the official divorce, but Adams supporters asked, "Ought an adultress and her paramour husband be placed in the highest offices?" One popular campaign ditty went:

> *Oh Andy! Oh Andy!*
> *How many men have you hanged in your life?*
> *How many weddings make a wife?*

(The attacks on his wife particularly enraged Jackson, as Rachel was sick and died soon after the election.)

John Quincy Adams was not safe from character assault, either. For purchasing a chess set and a billiard table, he was accused of installing "gaming furniture" in the White House at public expense. In another campaign charge, Adams was charged with having procured a young American girl for the pleasure of Czar Alexander I when he had served as minister to Russia in 1809–11, under Madison.

Jackson won a substantial victory in the popular vote, and took 178 electoral votes to Adams's 83. For the first time in America's brief history, the country had a president who was neither a Virginian nor an Adams. (John Quincy Adams left the White House and returned to Congress as a representative from Massachusetts, the only former president ever to serve in the House of Representatives. He served there with considerable dignity and distinction, leading the antislavery forces in Congress until his death in 1848.) That a new American era was born became apparent with Jackson's victory and inaugural. A large crowd of Old Hickory's supporters, mostly rough-hewn western frontiersmen with little regard for niceties, crowded into Washington, flush with the excitement of defeating what they saw as the aristocratic power brokers of the Northeast. When Jackson finished his inaugural address, hundreds of well-wishers stormed into the White House, where tables had been laid with cakes, ice cream, and punch. Jackson was hustled out of the mansion for his own protection, and the muddy-booted mob overturned chairs and left a chaotic mess. All of the Adamsite fears of rule by "King Mob" seemed to be coming true.

This was the beginning of so-called Jacksonian democracy. Part of this new order came with reformed voting rules in the western states, where property ownership was no longer a qualification to vote. Unlike the earlier Jeffersonian democracy, which was a carefully articulated political agenda voiced by Jefferson himself, this new democracy was, in modern political language, a grassroots movement. Jackson was no political theorist and hardly a spokesman for the changing order, but he was its symbol. Orphan, frontiersman, horse-racing man, Indian fighter, war hero, and land speculator, Andrew Jackson embodied the new American spirit and became the idol of the ambitious, jingoistic younger men who now called themselves Democrats. At its best, Jacksonian democracy meant an opening of the political process to more people (although blacks, women, and Indians still remained political nonentities). The flip side was that it represented a new level of militant, land-frenzied, slavery-condoning, Indian-killing greed.

A large number of the unruly crowd that upset the ice cream in the White House had come to Washington looking for jobs. It was expected that Jackson would sweep out holdovers from the hated Adams administration. They had won the war and were looking for the "spoils" of that war in the form of patronage jobs in the Jackson White House. There was nothing new about this "spoils system"; it had been practiced by every administration from the beginning of the republic. But the widespread and vocal calls for patronage that followed Jackson's election have linked the spoils system to Jackson. Ironically, only a few new patronage jobs were created during his years in office, with most posts going to previous jobholders, all established Washington insiders—proof once again that the more things change, the more they stay the same.

MARGARET BAYARD SMITH, witness to the
inauguration of Andrew Jackson (March 11, 1829):

But what a scene did we witness! The majesty of the people
had disappeared, and a rabble, a mob, of boys, Negroes,
women, children, scrambling, fighting, romping. What a
pity, what a pity! No arrangements had been made, no police officers placed on duty, and the whole house had been
inundated by the rabble mob. We came too late. The president, after having been literally nearly pressed to death and
almost suffocated and torn to pieces by the people in their
eagerness to shake hands with Old Hickory, had retreated
through the back way or south front and had escaped to his
lodgings at Gadsby's.

What was the Trail of Tears?

From the moment Columbus stepped onto the sands of San Salvador,
the history of European relations with the natives they encountered
could be written in blood. It was a story of endless betrayals, butchery,
and broken promises, from Columbus and the conquistadores through
John Smith, the Bay Colony, the French and Indian War, right up to
the War of 1812. From the outset, superior weapons, force of numbers,
and treachery had been the Euro-American strategy for dealing with
the Indians in manufacturing a genocidal tragedy that surely ranks as
one of the cruelest episodes in man's history.

Hollywood has left the impression that the great Indian wars came
in the Old West during the late 1800s, a period that many think of
simplistically as the "cowboy and Indian" days. But in fact that was a
mopping-up effort. By that time the Indians were nearly finished, their
subjugation complete, their numbers decimated. The killing, enslave-
ment, and land theft had begun with the arrival of the Europeans. But
it may have reached its nadir when it became federal policy under
President Jackson.

During the Creek War of 1814 that first brought him notice, Jackson earned a reputation as an Indian fighter, and a particularly ruthless

one. To the Indians, Jackson became Sharp Knife. Confronted by a tenacious Creek Nation in the South as commander of the Tennessee militia, Jackson had used Cherokee, who had been promised governmental friendship, to attack the Creek from the rear. As treaty commissioner, Jackson managed to take away half the Creek lands, which he and his friends then bought on attractive terms.

In 1819 he embarked on an illegal war against the Seminole of Florida. Claiming that Florida, still in Spanish hands, was a sanctuary for escaped slaves and marauding Indians, Jackson invaded the territory, unleashing a bloody campaign that left Indian villages and Spanish forts smoldering. Jackson's incursion set off a diplomatic crisis, eventually forcing the Spanish to sell Florida to the United States in 1819 on terms highly favorable to the Americans. Again, Jackson became governor of the newly conquered territory. As a land speculator, Jackson knew that he and his friends would profit handsomely by moving the Indians off the land.

But the harsh treatment of the Indians by Jackson as a general, as well as throughout earlier American history, was later transformed. It went from popular anti-Indian sentiment and sporadic regional battles to official federal policy initiated under Jackson and continued by his successor, Martin Van Buren. The tidy word given this policy was "removal," suggesting a sanitary resolution of a messy problem, an early-nineteenth-century equivalent of the Third Reich's "final solution." The Indians called it the Trail of Tears.

Some historians ascribe humane motives to Jackson's call for the wholesale forced migration of Indians from the southeastern states to unsettled lands across the Mississippi. Better to move them, argued Jackson, than to slaughter them, which was already happening. In 1831, for instance, Sac tribes under Black Hawk balked at leaving their ancestral lands in Illinois. But when a group of some 1,000 Indians attempted to surrender to the militia and the regular army, they were cut off by the Mississippi River and cut down by bayonets and rifle fire, with about 150 surviving the slaughter.

The removals were concentrated on the so-called Five Civilized Tribes of the Southeast. Contrary to popular sentiment of the day and history's continuing misrepresentation, the Choctaw, Chickasaw, Creek, Cherokee, and Seminole tribes had developed societies that were not only compatible with white culture, but even emulated European styles in some respects. The problem was that their tribal lands happened to be valuable cotton-growing territory. Between 1831 and 1833 the first of the "removals" forced some 4,000 Choctaw from Mississippi into the territory west of Arkansas. During the winter migration, there was scarce food and poor shelter. Pneumonia took its toll, and with the summer came cholera, killing the Choctaw by the hundreds. The Choctaw were followed by the Chickasaw and then the Creek, or Muskogee, who did not go as peacefully. The tribe refused to leave, and the Creek war of 1836–37 followed. Winfield Scott, the American commander of the operation, eventually captured 14,500 Creek—2,500 of them in chains—and marched them to Oklahoma.

The final removal began in 1835, when the Cherokee, centered in Georgia, became the target. Like the other tribes that had been forced out, the Cherokee were among the "civilized" tribes who clearly provided proof that the "savages" could coexist with white, Euro-American culture. The Cherokee, at the time of their removal, were not nomadic savages. In fact, they had assimilated many European-style customs, including the wearing of gowns by Cherokee women. They built roads, schools, and churches, had a system of representational government, and were becoming farmers and cattle ranchers. A written Cherokee language had also been perfected by a warrior named Sequoya. The Cherokee even attempted to fight removal legally by challenging the removal laws in the Supreme Court and by establishing an independent Cherokee Nation.

But they were fighting an irresistible tide of history. In 1838, after Andrew "Sharp Knife" Jackson left office, the United States government forced out the 15,000 to 17,000 Cherokee of Georgia. About 4,000 of them died along the route, which took them through Tennessee and Kentucky, across the Ohio and Missouri rivers, and into what would later become Oklahoma (the result of another broken treaty). This route and this journey were the Trail of Tears.

The strongest resistance to removal came from the Seminole of Florida, where the Indians were able to carry out another costly war, in which 1,500 U.S. soldiers died and some $20 million was spent. The leader of the Seminoles was a young warrior named Osceola, and he was captured only when lured out of his camp by a flag of truce.

He died in a prison camp three months later. With Osceola gone, the Seminole resistance withered and many Seminole were eventually removed to the Indian Territory. But several bands remained in the Everglades, continuing their struggle against the federals.

Who was Tocqueville, and why did he say all those things about America?

One of the most eloquent witnesses to the cruelties against the Indians was a young French magistrate studying America's penal system. Observing a Choctaw tribe — the old, the sick, the wounded, and newborns among them — forced to cross an ice-choked Mississippi River during the harsh winter, he wrote, "In the whole scene, there was an air of destruction, something which betrayed a final and irrevocable adieu; one couldn't watch without feeling one's heart wrung." The Indians, he added, "have no longer a country, and soon will not be a people."

The author of those words was a young aristocrat named Alexis Charles Henri Clerel de Tocqueville (1805–59), who arrived in America in May 1831 with his friend Gustave de Beaumont. As young men who had grown up in the aftermath of the French Revolution and the Napoleonic Empire, they came to examine American democracy with an eye to understanding how the American experience could help form the developing democratic spirit in France and the rest of Europe. The two spent nine months traveling the nation, gathering facts and opinions, interviewing Americans from President Jackson to frontiersmen and Indians. On their return to France, Tocqueville reported on the U.S. prison system, and Beaumont wrote a novel exploring the race problem in America.

But it is for an inspired work combining reportage, personal observation, and philosophical explorations, and titled *Democracy in America*, that Tocqueville's name became a permanent part of the American sociopolitical vocabulary. The book appeared in two volumes, the first in 1835, the second in 1840. More than 150 years after its appearance, *Democracy in America* remains a basic text in American history and political theory. With his keen insight into the

American character and his extraordinary prescience, Tocqueville is still regarded as a valuable commentator on American politics and democracy in general.

While he admired the republican system, Tocqueville found what he considered a great many shortcomings. Perhaps his aristocratic background left Tocqueville unprepared for the "general equality of condition among the people" he found. There were clearly class differences in America, but Tocqueville found that the lines were not as sharply or as permanently drawn as they were in Europe, with its centuries of aristocratic tradition. Admittedly, he also spent most of his time with the upper and middle classes, overlooking much of the rank poverty that existed in America among the working poor. Most of the latter were gathered in the sprawling urban centers of New York, Philadelphia, and other northern cities, where waves of poor European immigrants were drawn by the millions and consigned to the spreading inner-city slums and tenements. In this "equality of condition," Tocqueville saw a social leveling that would result, in his opinion, in a reign of mediocrity, conformity, and what he called the "tyranny of the majority."

Although many of his commentaries and observations were remarkably astute, and seem to apply as neatly to modern America as they did to the United States he found in 1831, Tocqueville did not always bat a thousand. Perhaps one of his greatest oversights was his assessment of the presidency as a weak office. In fact, he wrote at a time when Andrew Jackson was shaping the office as preeminent among the three branches, establishing the mold of a strong presidency that would be repeated in such chief executives as Lincoln and the Roosevelts. Critical of slavery (as well as the treatment of the Indians), the Frenchman could see civil strife ahead. However, his prediction that the Union would fall in the face of such a regional conflict was wide of the mark.

In many more matters, however, he was right on target and remains eerily correct about the American addiction to practical rather than philosophical matters and the relentless and practically single-minded pursuit of wealth. As he observed, "I know of no country, indeed, where the love of money has taken a stronger hold on the affections of men."

Perhaps his most astute forecast was the prediction of the future competition that would arise between the United States and Russia.

What made the South fear a slave named Nat Turner?

Nothing struck deeper fear into the hearts of southerners, whether they held slaves or not, than the idea of a slave revolt. Contrary to the popular image of docile slaves working in peaceful servitude, there had been numerous small rebellions and uprisings of slaves, often in union with Indians or disaffected whites, as far back as slavery in the New World under the Spanish. These were not limited to the South, as murderous uprisings took place in colonial Connecticut, Massachusetts, and New York. One of the bloodiest of these uprisings occurred in South Carolina in 1739, when slaves killed some twenty-five whites under the leadership of a slave named Jemmy.

But the greatest horror for young America came from the Caribbean, where Toussaint L'Ouverture, a former carriage driver and a natural military genius, led the slaves of St. Domingue (Haiti and the Dominican Republic) in a successful rebellion during the 1790s. Inspired by the revolutions in America and France, Toussaint's rebellion resulted in some 60,000 deaths and a republic of freed slaves on the island. Yet Toussaint was a remarkable administrator as well, and successfully integrated the white minority into the island's government. In 1800, Napoleon sent troops to retake the island with little success until Toussaint was lured to the French headquarters under a truce flag, arrested, and jailed in the Alps, where he died in a jail cell.

Slaveholders tried for years to keep the news of Toussaint and his rebellion from their slaves. But as Lerone Bennet writes in *Before the Mayflower*, "Wherever slaves chafed under chains, this man's name was whispered." In 1831, a new name came to the fore as the most fearful threat to white control, that of Nat Turner (1800–31). Nat Turner's rebellion followed two earlier unsuccessful rebellions by slaves. The first was of some thousand slaves led by Gabriel Prosser in an aborted assault on Richmond, Virginia, in 1800. The second, in Charleston in 1822, was led by another charismatic slave, Denmark Vesey, and failed because of betrayals.

Although Turner's rebellion also ultimately failed, it changed the South. Born in 1800, Turner was a mystic and preacher who used his visions and biblical authority to build a devoted following. In August 1831, Turner and about seventy followers started their rampage. Beginning with his own masters, Turner embarked on a death march that spared no one. The whites around Southampton, Virginia, were thrown into utter panic, many of them fleeing the state. Turner's small army, lacking discipline, halted its march, allowing a group of whites to attack. Turner counterattacked, but was soon vastly outnumbered and went into hiding. Thousands of soldiers were pressing the search for this one man who had thrown the country into hysterical terror. A massacre of any slaves even suspected of complicity followed. Turner eluded capture for some two months, during which he became a sort of bogeyman to the people of the South. To whites and slaves alike, he had acquired some mystical qualities that made him larger than life, and even after his hanging, slave owners feared his influence. Stringent new slave laws were passed, strict censorship laws aimed at abolitionist material were passed with Andrew Jackson's blessing, and, perhaps most important, the militant defense of slavery took on a whole new meaning.

AMERICAN VOICES

WILLIAM LLOYD GARRISON (1805–79), in the first issue of the abolitionist journal *The Liberator* (1831):

On this subject I do not wish to think, or speak, or write, with moderation. No! no! Tell a man whose house is on fire, to give a moderate alarm; tell him to moderately rescue his wife from the hands of the ravisher; tell the mother to gradually extricate her babe from the fire into which it has fallen; but urge me not to use moderation in a cause like the present. I am in earnest—I will not equivocate—I will not excuse—I will not retreat a single inch—AND I WILL BE HEARD.

Who were the Whigs?

Andrew Jackson's Democratic Party was largely an outgrowth of Jackson's personality and individual opinions rather than of the strict orthodoxy associated with modern party politics. And Jackson's popularity was undeniable, resulting in his handy 1832 reelection (55 percent of the popular vote; 77 percent of the electoral vote), which also brought in New York politico Martin Van Buren (1782–1862) as the new vice president.

Jackson's personal platform was fairly simple: suspicion of the upper classes and big business, typified by the Bank of the United States, which Jackson vetoed in 1832; freedom of economic opportunity, including elimination of Indians to open up their lands for white expansion; increased voting rights (for white men, at least); and a general opening of the political process to the middle and lower classes, which had been closed out by the earlier, gentry-based administrations. On the growing question of the Union versus states' rights, Jackson tiptoed a cautious path, proclaiming a strong Unionist position but tending to limit the powers the federal government held over the states, the ostensible reason behind his opposition to the Bank of the United States.

Jackson's general popularity almost completely stifled opposition, but not entirely. Out of the ashes of the old Federalists came heirs of Hamilton who believed in a national approach to economic problems, coupled with the more extremist states' rights advocates and those who simply disliked Jackson and feared his unchecked power. From this loose coalition a new party started to take life with two congressional giants, Daniel Webster (1782–1852) and Henry Clay (1777–1852), its most prominent leaders. In 1834, they took the name Whigs, recalling the pre-Revolution days when patriots adopted that name to contrast themselves with Tories loyal to the British Crown. For this new generation of Whigs, the tyrant was not a foreign monarch but King Andrew, as Jackson was called by friend and foe alike.

The Whigs mounted their first presidential campaign in 1836, but failed to coalesce behind a single nominee, sending out three favorite sons instead. William Henry Harrison, a former general, did best, with Hugh White and Daniel Webster finishing far out of the running. Easily outdistancing them was Martin Van Buren, Jackson's vice president and handpicked successor, who also carried the distinction of being the first president born an American citizen. An adept tactician, Van Buren had begun to master the new politics of group voting, or "machine politics," and was responsible for delivering New York's electoral votes to Jackson. But he utterly lacked Jackson's ability to win popular support. A severe economic depression during his term—the Panic of 1837—ruined Van Buren's chances for a second term, but he was really undone by a new Whig strategy that turned the tables on Andrew Jackson's earlier campaign against John Quincy Adams, which had cast Adams as a remote aristocrat.

In the "log cabin" campaign of 1840, the Whigs cast Van Buren, nicknamed Martin Van Ruin, as a bloated aristocrat. They presented themselves as the people's party and General Harrison (1773–1841), their candidate, as a common man living in a log cabin. In fact, he was from a distinguished family, the son of one of the Declaration's signers. He was also presented as a war hero in Jackson's image for his battles against Tecumseh at Tippecanoe. With Virginia's John Tyler (1790–1862) as his running mate, their campaign slogan was the memorable "Tippecanoe and Tyler too!" The campaign of 1840 was a raucous affair, with huge rallies, an impressive voter turnout, and plenty of hard cider spilled. One linguistic legacy of the campaign: a distiller named E. C. Booz bottled whiskey in log cabin–shaped containers. Although the word "booze" was derived from the Dutch word *bowse*, Booz reinforced the use of the word, and soon it became a permanent part of the language.

One month after he was inaugurated, Harrison fell ill with pneumonia and died. John Tyler, his vice president, a Virginian and an ardent states' righter, became the first "accidental president."

AMERICAN VOICES
JOSÉ MARÍA SÁNCHEZ, a Mexican surveyor, sent on an expedition to the border of Mexico, which then included Texas and Louisiana (April 27, 1828):

This village has been settled by Mr. Stephen Austin, a native of the United States of the North. It consists, at present, of forty or fifty wooden houses on the western bank of

the large river known as Rio de los Brazos de Dios. . . . Its
population is nearly two hundred persons, of which only
ten are Mexicans, for the balance are all Americans from
the North with an occasional European. Two wretched
little stores supply the inhabitants of the colony: one sells
only whiskey, rum, sugar, and coffee; the other rice, flour,
lard, and cheap cloth. . . . The Americans . . . eat only
salted meat, bread made by themselves out of corn meal,
coffee, and home-made cheese. To these the greater part
of those who live in the village add strong liquor, for they
are in general, in my opinion, lazy people of vicious character. Some of them cultivate their small farms by planting
corn; but this task they usually entrust to their negro slaves,
whom they treat with considerable harshness. . . . In my
opinion the spark that will start the conflagration that will
deprive us of Texas will start from this colony.

Who fought at the Alamo?

When Jackson left office, there were clearly unanswered questions
about the nation's future. Southern politicians were already setting
forth the argument that because states had freely joined the Union,
they could just as freely leave. And while there was much talk of tariffs
and banks, the real issue was slavery. The slave question pervaded the
national debate on almost every question before Congress, including
the momentous one regarding the fate of Texas, then a part of Mexico.

Led by Stephen F. Austin (1793–1836), Americans settled the area
at the invitation of Mexican authorities. President Jackson, and Adams
before him, offered to buy Texas from Mexico, but were turned down.
By 1830, more than 20,000 white Americans had been drawn to the
fertile, cotton-growing plains, bringing with them some 2,000 slaves.
They soon outnumbered the Mexicans in the territory, and in 1834,
Austin asked the authorities in Mexico City to allow Texas to separate
from Mexico as a prelude to statehood. Besides the obvious reason that
these Americans wanted to remain American, an overriding cause for
their request was Mexico's prohibition of slavery. Austin was arrested

and jailed. By 1836, President Santa Anna of Mexico announced a unified constitution for all Mexican territories, including Texas.

The Americans in Texas decided to secede. With an army of 6,000
men, Santa Anna marched against what he viewed as the treasonous
Texans. With a force of 3,000, Santa Anna approached San Antonio,
held by 187 men under the command of Colonel William B. Travis.
The defenders took a defensive stand behind the walls of a mission
called the Alamo. For ten days, in a now-legendary stand, the small
group fended off Santa Anna's massed troops, inflicting tremendous
casualties on the Mexicans. But the numbers were insurmountably in
the Mexicans' favor. As the Mexican bands played the "Degüello," literally "throat-cutting," artillery breached the walls of the Alamo, and
Travis's band was overrun. The American defenders who survived the
final onslaught were then apparently executed. All of the Americans'
corpses were soaked in oil and then set on fire. Among the dead was
Jim Bowie, a Louisiana slave trader who became best known for the
infamous long knife he carried on his belt, and Davy Crockett (1786–
1836), the professional backwoodsman, congressman, and veteran of
Andrew Jackson's Creek War. Only three Americans came out of the
Alamo alive: a soldier's wife named Susanna Dickenson, her fifteen-
month-old baby, and Travis's slave Joe. They were freed by Santa Anna
and went by foot to warn Sam Houston (1793–1863), commander of
the Texas army, of the fate that awaited them if they continued to resist.

A second slaughter, in which hundreds of Texans were slain by
Santa Anna's troops at the town of Goliad, stoked the flames higher.
Santa Anna pressed the small Texan army that remained under Houston until the forces met at San Jacinto in April 1836. With "Remember the Alamo!" as their rallying cry, the vastly outnumbered Texans
swept into the lines of the Mexicans, who had been granted a siesta by
the self-assured Santa Anna. The battle was over in eighteen minutes.
With the loss of nine men, the Texans killed hundreds of Mexicans,
captured hundreds more, including Santa Anna, and sent the bulk of
the Mexican army into a confused retreat across the Rio Grande.

The Texans immediately ratified their constitution, and Houston,
who nearly died from gangrene after the San Jacinto battle, was made
president of the new republic. They then petitioned for annexation
into the United States. Jackson did nothing until his last day in office,

when he recognized Texan independence. Van Buren also hesitated. Both men feared war with Mexico, but more seriously, the admission of Texas added fuel to the burning slave debate. The southern states wanted another slave territory. The North saw the annexation of Texas as breaching the balance that had been reached in the Missouri Compromise (under which slave state Arkansas and free state Michigan had been admitted as the twenty-fifth and twenty-sixth states). For the next nine years, the Texas question simmered, further dividing North and South over slavery, and pushing relations with Mexico to the brink of war.

Must Read: *Three Roads to the Alamo: The Lives and Fortunes of David Crockett, James Bowie, and William Barret Travis* by William C. Davis.

What was Manifest Destiny?

The annexing of Texas was a symptom of a larger frenzy that was sweeping through America like a nineteenth-century version of Lotto fever. In 1845, this fervor was christened. In an expansionist magazine, the *United States Magazine and Democratic Review*, journalist John L. O'Sullivan wrote of "the fulfillment of our manifest destiny to overspread the continent allotted by Providence for the free development of our yearly multiplying millions."

O'Sullivan's phrase, quickly adopted by other publications and politicians, neatly expressed a vision that sounded almost like a religious mission. Behind this vision was some ideological saber rattling, but the greatest motivator was greed, the obsessive desire for Americans to control the entire continent from the Atlantic to the Pacific. As each successive generation of Americans had pressed the fringes of civilization a little farther, this idea took on the passion of a sacred quest. The rapid westward movement of large groups of settlers was spurred by the development of the famous trails to the West. The Santa Fe Trail linked Independence, Missouri, with the Old Spanish Trail to Los Angeles. The Oregon Trail, mapped by trappers and missionaries, went northwest to the Oregon Territory. The Mormon Trail, first traveled in 1847, initially took the religious group and then other settlers from

Illinois to Salt Lake City. And in the Southwest, the Oxbow Route, from Missouri west to California, carried mail under a federal contract.

The fact that California, with its great ports, was still part of Mexico, and that England still laid claim to Oregon, only heightened the aggressiveness of the American desire to control all of it.

Why did the Mormons move west?

While the majority of nineteenth-century Americans believed that God's plan was to send them west, others in America were finding other religious paths. The early part of the century saw an extraordinary period of spiritual reawakening that produced such groups as the Shakers, founded in New York in 1774 by an Englishwoman called Mother Ann Lee. They flourished for some years, but eventually died out when their policy of celibacy became self-induced extinction. Other "spiritual" movements of this period included the utopian communities of Oneida, where, in contrast to the Shakers, promiscuity was encouraged, and Brook Farm, the retreat of the New England Transcendentalists.

But the most historically significant and prominent new religious group to emerge in this period was the Church of Jesus Christ of Latter-Day Saints, also called the Mormons. The group was founded in western New York in 1823 by Joseph Smith, a visionary who claimed that he had been given, by an angel named Moroni, an ancient text, the Book of Mormon, written in hieroglyphics on golden plates, which Smith translated and claimed was divinely inspired. Smith and a small band of followers moved to Ohio, where their communal efficiency attracted converts, but their claim to divine revelations attracted the ridicule and enmity of more traditional Protestant Americans, setting off a pattern of antagonism that would send the Mormons on an odyssey in search of a home in the wilderness.

With his church growing in numbers of converts, Smith was gaining political clout as well, but resentment exploded into persecution when another of Smith's visions called for polygamy in 1843. In Missouri, their antislavery views brought the Mormons into conflict with local people. So did their polygamy and religious views. By 1838, the governor of Missouri, Lilburn Boggs, had ordered that all Mormons be expelled from his state. In what is known as the "Extermination Order," Boggs wrote, "The Mormons must be treated as enemies, and must be exterminated, or driven from the state." Provoked by the governor's order, an anti-Mormon mob slaughtered at least eighteen church members, including children, in the Haun's Mill Massacre of October 30, 1838. And in 1844, Joseph Smith and his brother, Hyrum, were murdered while jailed in Carthage, Illinois, by members of another militia mob. No one was ever convicted of the crime.

The group was held together under the autocratic hand of Brigham Young, who saw the church's future in the Far West, away from further persecution. In 1847, Young and a small band of Mormons pushed to the basin of the Great Salt Lake, the new Promised Land. They began a community that became so entrenched as a Mormon power base that Young was able to dictate federal judgeships. As waves of Mormons pressed along the trail to Utah, it became a major route to the West, and the Mormons profited handsomely from the thousands heading for California and gold.

The Mormons were not the only religion facing persecution in an overwhelmingly Protestant America. Many Americans had despised Catholics, especially Irish Catholics, for centuries, going back to the days of the Puritans. The animosity was not only sectarian but national; Italian and Irish Catholics were especially hated, and there was a widely held belief that Roman Catholics were coming to America in large numbers to take over the United States and hand it over to the pope, with a new Vatican to be built in Cincinnati. That sectarian hatred led to numerous acts of violence, including the burning of a convent in Charlestown, Massachusetts, in 1834 and the deadly "Bible Riots" fought between Catholics and Protestants in 1844. In two waves of rioting, hundreds of houses were burned, two Catholic churches were destroyed, and more than twenty people died in the street fighting between "Nativist" Protestants and Irish Catholics who had come to Philadelphia to work on the railroads and canals that became the "Main Line."

Must Reads: *Under the Banner of Heaven: A Story of Violent Faith* by Jon Krakauer; *A Nation Rising* by Kenneth C. Davis.

From "The Raven" by EDGAR ALLAN POE (1845):

And the Raven, never flitting, still is sitting,
*   still is sitting*
On the pallid bust of Pallas just above my
*   chamber door;*
And his eyes have all the seeming of a demon's
*   that is dreaming,*
And that lamp-light o'er him streaming throws
*   his shadow on the floor;*
And my soul from out that shadow that lies
*   floating on the floor*
Shall be lifted—nevermore!

Drug addict. Alcoholic. Cradle robber. Necrophiliac. These are
some of the epithets associated with Poe (1809–49). Most of them
were the creations of a vindictive literary executor who spread the
lies following the poet's death. Later research proved many of those
charges to be unfounded slanders. But there was still plenty about Poe
that was strange, and his work certainly seemed to justify those bizarre
stories.

Born in Boston, Poe was raised by an uncle after the death of his
parents when he was three. He first attended the University of Virginia,
but dropped out, then later went to West Point, but managed to get
dismissed from that institution also. He turned to newspaper editing
and writing, and published a few poems and short stories. He also married his thirteen-year-old cousin—an act considered less outrageous in
those days than it seems now. In 1845, *The Raven and Other Poems* appeared, winning Poe instant recognition. He continued as a successful
magazine editor, at the same time writing the short stories of mystery,
horror, and the supernatural—"The Murders in the Rue Morgue,"
"The Gold Bug," "The Fall of the House of Usher"—for which he is
most famed. After the death of his wife, he suffered a nervous breakdown. Two years later, while on a train taking him to a planned second
marriage, he died of unexplained causes.

Poe was a member of America's first generation of noteworthy authors, including Hawthorne, Melville, Emerson, and Thoreau, who began to flourish in this period. They represented, as Poe did, the Romantic spirit in writing that flowered in the early nineteenth century, as well as a burst of American cultural maturity that reflected a nation moving out of adolescence.

CHAPTER FOUR

APOCALYPSE THEN

To Civil War and Reconstruction

Why was there a war with Mexico?

Milestones in the Mexican War

What did America gain from the Mexican War?

How did Frederick Douglass become the most influential black man of his time?

Where did the Underground Railroad run?

What was the Compromise of 1850?

Why was *Uncle Tom's Cabin* the most important and controversial novel of its time?

What forced the Republicans to start a new political party?

Why was Kansas "bloody"?

What was the difference between a man named Dred Scott and a mule?

What did Lincoln and Douglas debate?

Why did John Brown attack a federal arsenal?

Why did the southern states secede from the United States?

The 1860 Census

What was the difference between the Confederate and U.S. constitutions?

Milestones in the Civil War

What did the Civil War cost America?

Was Abe really honest?

Why did the Union win the war?

Who killed Lincoln?

What was Reconstruction?

Who celebrates Decoration Day and Juneteenth?

Why was President Johnson impeached?

Who were the carpetbaggers?

The space of time separating George Washington's first inauguration in April 1789 from Lincoln's first in March 1861 was only seventy-two years, a finger snap in the long stream of history. But that slice of history contained extraordinary events. From a third-rate republic, a sliver of sparsely populated seaboard extending inland for a few hundred miles from the Atlantic, threatened by foreign powers and dangerous Indian tribes, America had become a pulsing, burgeoning world economic power whose lands stretched across an entire continent.

It was a nation in the midst of powerful growth. Canals were spreading across the country, connecting the inland regions to the busy Atlantic ports. The first generation of steamships was beginning to make use of those canals and to carry prospectors around Cape Horn to California. The first railroads were being built, linking the great, growing cities across the widening landscape of America. A new generation of invention was alive, with Americans turning their attention, as Tocqueville noted, to practical pursuits. In 1834, Cyrus McCormick patented his horsedrawn reaper that would begin a revolution in American agriculture. Borrowing from an earlier invention, Eli Whitney improved on a machine that made cotton king in the South—the famous cotton "gin," short for "engine"—and then set up a factory in the North using the idea of interchangeable parts to ease mass production—an idea that helped produce the guns that would help the Union defeat the Confederacy. In 1843, Congress voted funds to construct a telegraph line from Baltimore to Washington, and Samuel Morse (1791–1872) perfected the design of the telegraph and devised a code to use it. By 1851, America's mass-produced innovations—clocks and locks, Colt revolvers and sewing machines, reapers and railroads—were the talk of Europe.

Writing from Paris in the throes of France's bloody revolution, Jefferson had once almost giddily expressed the notion that "a little rebellion" was good for the republic. Had Jefferson known how devastating the ultimate rebellion would be, he might have acted more forcefully to forestall it during his years of power and influence. History is an unending stream of such speculations and backward glances.

Why was there a Civil War? Could it have been avoided? Why didn't the North just let the South go? (A popular sentiment in 1860.) These questions have troubled and fascinated Americans ever since the war took place. No period in American history has been written about more, and with more sentiment and emotion—and even romance. Each year, dozens of new volumes appear in the vast library of books about Lincoln, slavery, the South, the war and its aftermath. It is hardly surprising that one of America's most popular novels—and the equally adored film it inspired—is set during the Civil War era. Without arguing its historical or literary values, there is no question that Margaret Mitchell's *Gone with the Wind* typifies—and is partly responsible for—the American passion about and romance with the Civil War era.

But as other historians and novelists have made much clearer, there was very little that was truly romantic about the Civil War. It was four years of vicious, devastating warfare that cost hundreds of thousands of lives, murderously divided families and friends, and left much of southern territory smoldering. Political and military bungling occurred on both sides. There were war atrocities of the worst sort. Even today the issues behind the Civil War and the wounds it left continue to underscore the political and social debate in America.

To comprehend the Civil War's roots, it might be useful to think of America in the first half of the nineteenth century not as one large country but as two separate nations. The America of the North was rushing toward modernity as it underwent its urban and industrial revolutions. While agriculture was still important in the North's economic structure, it was the enormous commercial enterprises—railroads, canals, and steamship lines; banks and booming factories—that were shaping the northern economy. Its population was mushrooming as massive influxes of European immigrants escaping the famines and political turmoil of Europe came to its cities, lured by the growing myth of America's unlimited wealth and opportunity.

Starting in 1845, the first year of the potato blight and famine in Ireland, some 1.5 million Irish came to America over the course of the next several years. By 1860, one-eighth of America's 32 million people were foreign-born, and most of them had settled in the North, drawn to the mill towns of Rhode Island, Massachusetts, Connecticut, New Jersey, and Pennsylvania. It was these foreign workers who would feed the ravenous appetite of the new industrial machine and be pressed into the sprawling slums and tenements of the cities, where they were held captive by companies that were far from enlightened. They dutifully joined the political machines that claimed to represent them, and ultimately provided cannon fodder under the Civil War's conscription laws.

The southern states, on the other hand, had largely remained the agrarian, slave-based economy they were in Jefferson's time, when the gentlemen planters of Virginia had helped create the nation. The basis of their wealth was now cotton—produced only to be shipped to the textile factories of Great Britain and New England—and the slaves who produced that cotton, as well as the tobacco, rice, and corn that were staples in the southern states. Although importation of slaves had been outlawed in 1807, the slave population continued to grow at an astonishing rate. And though overseas slave trade was prohibited, trading slaves between states was an enormous business. This contradiction of logic—no foreign slave trade, but a lively domestic one—was one of the laws that many southerners felt were unfairly forced upon them by the North.

But even without African trade, the slave numbers were incredible. The nearly 700,000 slaves counted in the census of 1790 had swollen to 3.5 million in 1860. At the same time, the general population of the South grew far more slowly, absorbing few of the immigrants flocking to American shores. It was room to grow more cotton, and slaves to plant, pick, and produce it, that underscored all debate about America's expansion, prompting at least one foreign war and southern talk of the conquest of Cuba and other lands to the south.

The United States was now two countries, two cultures, two ideologies destined for a collision. The simplest explanation for the war might be that southerners, in a very basic expression of human nature, did not want to be told how to live their lives—with respect to slavery, politics, or any number of other questions. This basic resistance to being ruled by someone else had been ingrained into the American character before the Revolution, became part of the national debate from the time Jefferson drafted the Declaration, and was written into the compromises that created the Constitution. But it was a powder keg with a long-burning fuse, an emotional question of ideology that simmered for those decades between Washington and Lincoln, factoring into every question facing the nation and every presidential election of that time, until it ultimately exploded with such horrifying results.

[Note: This chapter is meant to briefly summarize the events leading up to the Civil War, the conduct of the war itself, and the immediate aftermath. Since this book was first written, I decided that the Civil War was the central—and often most misunderstood—event in the American drama and felt it needed to be addressed in a separate book. *Don't Know Much About the Civil War* was published in 1996.]

Why was there a war with Mexico?

For the first time in America's short history, the nation didn't go to war with a foreign power over independence, foreign provocation, or global politics. The war with Mexico was a war fought unapologetically for territorial expansion. One young officer who fought in Mexico later called this war "one of the most unjust ever waged by a stronger against a weaker nation." He was Lieutenant Ulysses S. Grant.

The war with Mexico was the centerpiece of the administration of James K. Polk, the most adept of the presidents between Jackson and Lincoln. Continuing the line of Jacksonian Democrats in the White House after Tyler's abbreviated Whig administration, Polk (1795–1849) was even dubbed Young Hickory. A slaveholding states' rights advocate from North Carolina, Polk slipped by Van Buren in the Democratic convention and was narrowly elected president in 1844. His victory was possible only because the splinter antislavery Liberty Party drew votes away from Whig candidate Henry Clay. A swing of a few thousand votes, especially in New York State, which Polk barely carried, would have given the White House to Clay, a moderate who might have been one president capable of forestalling the breakup of the Union and the war.

It was a Manifest Destiny election. The issues were the future of the Oregon Territory, which Polk wanted to "reoccupy," and the annexation of Texas, or, in Polk's words, "reannexation," implying that Texas was part of the original Louisiana Purchase. (It wasn't.) Even before Polk's inauguration, Congress adopted a joint resolution on his proposal to annex Texas. The move made a war with Mexico certain, which suited Polk and other expansionists. When Mexico heard of this action in March 1845, it severed diplomatic relations with the United States.

Treating Texas as U.S. property, Polk sent General Zachary Taylor into the territory with about 1,500 troops in May 1845, to guard the undefined "border" against a Mexican "invasion." After months of negotiating to buy Texas, Polk ordered Taylor to move to the bank of the Rio Grande. This so-called army of observation numbered some 3,500 men by January 1846, about half the entire U.S. army. Escalating the provocations, Polk next had Taylor cross the Rio Grande. When a U.S. soldier was found dead and some Mexicans attacked an American patrol on April 25, President Polk had all the pretext he needed to announce to Congress, "War exists." An agreeable Democratic majority in the House and Senate quickly voted—with little dissent from the Whig opposition—to expand the army by an additional 50,000 men. America's most naked war of territorial aggression was under way.

MILESTONES IN THE MEXICAN WAR

1846

May 3 An indication of the war's course comes in the first battle. At Palo Alto, 2,300 American soldiers scatter a Mexican force twice their size. In the ensuing Battle of Resaca de la Palma, 1,700 Americans rout 7,500 Mexicans. Accompanied by a group of Whig newspapermen, General Taylor is made an immediate national hero and is touted as the next Whig president. President Polk orders a blockade of Mexican ports on the Pacific and the Gulf of Mexico.

June 6 In the related conflict with the British over the jointly controlled Oregon Territory, Polk submits a treaty with England setting a boundary between Canada and the United States at forty-nine degrees north latitude. Eliminating the threat of war with Great Britain, Polk can concentrate on the Mexican invasion.

June 14 American settlers in California, also a Mexican possession, proclaim the independent Republic of California. On July 7, Commodore John Sloat lands at Monterey and claims California for the United States. In August, California is annexed by the United States, and Commodore David Stockton establishes himself as governor.

August 15   Colonel Stephen Watts Kearney arrives in Las Vegas and announces the annexation of New Mexico, also a Mexican territory, by the United States. Kearney occupies Santa Fe without firing a shot, and sets up a provisional government there.

September 20–24   General Taylor captures the city of Monterey, Mexico, but he agrees to an armistice allowing the Mexican army to evacuate the city, earning President Polk's great displeasure.

November 16   General Taylor captures Saltillo, the capital of Mexico's Coahuilla province. The successful military exploits of General Taylor, a Whig, are increasing his heroic stature at home, to the annoyance of both President Polk and General Winfield Scott, the commanding general in Washington and also a Whig. The three men know well the political dividends brought by battlefield success, having cut their political teeth in the age of Andrew Jackson. Facing political pressure, Democrat Polk places General Winfield Scott in command of an expeditionary force that sails for the Mexican fortress city of Vera Cruz.

1847

January 3   General Scott orders a force of 9,000 of General Taylor's men to assault Vera Cruz by land.

February 22–23   The Battle of Buena Vista. Ignoring Scott's orders, Taylor marches west to Buena Vista and, after refusing to surrender to a superior Mexican force commanded by Santa Anna, Taylor's 4,800 men, mostly raw recruits, defeat a Mexican army of 15,000 largely untrained peasants. One of the heroes on the American side is Jefferson Davis, who leads a Mississippi infantry regiment in a counterattack using eighteen-inch Bowie knives. With loyal Whig newspapers trumpeting another triumph for Taylor, his run for the next presidency seems assured.

February 28   Marching south from El Paso, Colonel Alexander Doniphan wins a battle against massed Mexican forces at Sacramento Creek, Mexico, and occupies the city of Chihuahua the next day.

March 9–29   The Battle of Vera Cruz. Scott's forces land near Vera Cruz, the most heavily fortified city in the Western Hemisphere. Scott lays siege to the city. After a long bombardment with high civilian casualties, the city falls three weeks later. Scott's losses are minimal.

April   Pressing his offensive, Scott begins a march toward Mexico City. By mid-May he takes the cities of Cerro Gordo, capturing 3,000 prisoners, and Puebla, only eighty miles from Mexico City.

June 6   Through a British intermediary, Nicholas P. Trist, chief clerk of the U.S. State Department, begins peace negotiations with Mexico.

August 20   As Scott nears Mexico City, Santa Anna asks for an armistice. Peace negotiations fail, and the armistice ends on September 7.

September 8   Scott takes Molino del Rey. In another hard-fought battle, although heavily outnumbered, Scott takes the heights of Chapultepec, overlooking Mexico City. Formal peace is still several months away, but the actual fighting concludes with the triumphal entry of Scott's army into the Mexican capital.

November 22   Nicholas Trist leaves Washington to negotiate a peace treaty with Mexico.

December 22   A somewhat obscure freshman congressman from Illinois rises to speak against the Mexican War. It is Abraham Lincoln's first speech as a member of the House of Representatives.

1848

February–March   The Treaty of Guadalupe Hidalgo, ending the war with Mexico, is signed and then ratified by the Senate. Under its terms, the United States receives more than 500,000 square miles of Mexican territory, including the future states of California, Nevada, Utah, most of New Mexico and Arizona, and parts of Wyoming and Colorado, as well as Texas. The border with Mexico is set at the Rio Grande. In return, Mexico is paid $15 million and the United States takes on claims against Mexico by Americans, totaling another $3.25 million. One Whig newspaper announces, "We take nothing by conquest. . . . Thank God."

What did America gain from the Mexican War?

Won quickly and at relatively little expense, the Mexican War completed the dream of Manifest Destiny. Then came what seemed a heavenly confirmation of the popular notion that God had ordained America to go from coast to coast. On the morning of January 24, 1848, James Marshall, a New Jersey mechanic building a sawmill for Johann Sutter on the American River, east of San Francisco, spotted some flecks of yellow in the water. These proved to be gold, sparking the mad California gold rush of 1849, which sent a hundred thousand people or more racing west that year. During the next few years, some $200 million worth of gold would be extracted from the hills of California.

Apart from the profitable return on investment brought about by the gold rush, the aftermath of the Mexican War and the Oregon Treaty brought other, less happy dividends. The addition of these enormous parcels of new territory just made the future of slavery a bigger question; there was now that much more land to fight about. From the outset of the fighting, opposition to the war was heard from abolitionists like the zealous William Lloyd Garrison (1805–79) of the American Anti-Slavery Society, who said the war was waged "solely for the detestable and horrible purpose of extending and perpetuating American slavery." Garrison was joined in his views by antislavery pacifist Horace Greeley (1811–72), who protested the war from its beginning in his *New York Tribune*. Another ornery gadfly went to jail in Massachusetts for his refusal to pay poll taxes that supported a war he feared would spread slavery. Henry David Thoreau (1817–62) spent only a single night in jail—an aunt paid his fine—but his lecture "Resistance to Civil Government" (later titled "Civil Disobedience") was published in 1849 in the book *A Week on the Concord and Merrimack Rivers*.

The most ironically horrible aftermath of the war with Mexico was the practical battle experience it provided for a corps of young American officers who fought as comrades in Mexico, only to face one another in battle fifteen years later, when North met South in the Civil War. Among the many young West Pointers who fought in Mexico were two lieutenants named P. T. Beauregard and George McClellan, who served on General Scott's staff. Beauregard would lead the attack on Fort Sumter that would begin the Civil War. McClellan later commanded the armies of the North. Two other comrades at the Battle of Churubusco, Lieutenants James Longstreet and Winfield Scott Hancock, would face each other at Gettysburg. A young captain named Robert E. Lee demonstrated his considerable military abilities as one of Scott's engineers. A few years later, Scott urged Lincoln to give Lee command of the Union armies, but Lee would remain loyal to his Virginia home. When Lee and Grant met years later at Appomattox Court House, Grant would remind Lee that they had once encountered each other as comrades in Mexico.

AMERICAN VOICES
From "Civil Disobedience" by
HENRY DAVID THOREAU (1849):

Unjust laws exist: shall we be content to obey them, or shall we endeavor to amend them, and obey them until we have succeeded, or shall we transgress them at once? Men generally under such a government as this, think that they ought to wait until they have persuaded the majority to alter them. They think that, if they should resist, the remedy would be worse than the evil. But it is the fault of the government itself that the remedy is worse than the evil. It makes it worse. Why is it not more apt to anticipate and provide for reform? Why does it not cherish its wise minority? Why does it cry and resist before it is hurt? . . . Why does it always crucify Christ, and excommunicate Copernicus and Luther, and pronounce Washington and Franklin rebels?

The American ideals of individual freedom and the democratic spirit found an extreme expression in the literature of the New England writers known as the Transcendentalists. Chief among them was Ralph Waldo Emerson (1803–82), who urged Americans to stop imitating Europe and "go beyond the world of the senses." Emphasizing individuality and an intuitive spirituality, he balked at the emerging industrial society around him.

A student and friend of Emerson's, Henry David Thoreau took Emerson's ideas a step further, removing himself from society to the cabin on Walden Pond, near Concord, Massachusetts, which provided the experience for his masterpiece *Walden* (1854). Thoreau's writings deeply influenced Mahatma Gandhi, who adopted Thoreau's notion of "civil disobedience" as the means to overthrow British rule in India; and Gandhi, in turn, influenced Martin Luther King's philosophy of nonviolent resistance.

Also part of this "flowering of New England," as it was called by the critic Van Wyck Brooks, was Nathaniel Hawthorne (1804–64). But the author of the American classics *The Scarlet Letter* (1850) and *The House of the Seven Gables* (1851) rejected the Transcendentalists and Emerson, whom he called "a seeker for he knows not what." The Transcendentalist utopian community Brook Farm was the model for Hawthorne's *Blithedale Romance*. Depicting the New England obsession with sin and guilt, Hawthorne expressed a rejection of the grim Puritanism that dominated the era.

How did Frederick Douglass become the most influential black man of his time?

Among the most outspoken critics of the Mexican War was a man who called the war "disgraceful, cruel and iniquitous." Writing from Rochester, New York, in his newspaper, the *North Star*, Frederick Douglass criticized other opponents of the war for their weak response. "The determination of our slaveholding President to prosecute the war, and the probability of his success in wringing from the people men and money to carry it on, is made evident, rather than doubtful, by the puny opposition arrayed against him. . . . None seem willing to take their stand for peace at all risks."

For anyone to write so defiantly against a generally popular war was remarkable. That the author was an escaped slave writing in his own newspaper was extraordinary.

Frederick Douglass (1817–95) was born to a slave mother and most likely sired by his first owner. He was taught to read by the wife of one of his masters—although she had been told that it was illegal and unsafe to teach a slave to read—and taught himself to write in the shipyards of Baltimore. In 1838, he escaped, disguising himself as a sailor to reach New York and then Massachusetts, finding work as a laborer in bustling New Bedford, the shipbuilding and whaling center. After making an extemporaneous speech to an antislavery convention in Nantucket, Douglass began a life devoted to the cause of freedom, for women as well as blacks. In the process, he became one of the most famous men in America, black or white. A speaker of extraordinary power, Douglass was first employed by William Lloyd Garrison's Anti-Slavery Society. His lectures were grand performances that would leave his audiences in turns laughing and tearful. He braved hecklers, taunts, eggs, and death threats, and with each lecture his fame and influence grew. In 1845 the Society printed his autobiography, *Narrative of the Life of Frederick Douglass.*

It remains one of the most chilling accounts of life as a Maryland slave, containing the power to provoke utter revulsion at the "peculiar institution." The book's appearance and Douglass's growing celebrity as a speaker forced him to move to England out of fear that he would be seized as a fugitive. He returned to America in 1847 and began publication of the *North Star* in Rochester, putting him in the front lines of the abolitionist forces. Douglass and Garrison later fell out over tactics, but his stature continued to grow. In one of his most famous speeches, given in 1857, Douglass said, "Those who profess to favor freedom and yet deprecate agitation, are men who want crops without plowing up the ground, they want rain without thunder and lightning. They want the ocean without the roar of its many waters."

During the Civil War, he became an adviser to Lincoln, recruiting black soldiers for the Union cause and lobbying for their equal pay, which was reluctantly granted. After the war he accepted a number of government appointments, and was later made ambassador to Haiti. (It is worth noting, however, that many of his friends and supporters of both races were unhappy when late in life Douglass married a white woman after the death of his first wife, Anna. In 1884, he married Helen Pitts, a college-educated suffragist twenty years younger than Douglass. She was disowned by her family, and the white press accused her of marrying for fame and money. It was also reported that the marriage proved that the black man's highest aspiration was to have a white wife. The couple remained active in social causes until his sudden death of a heart attack in 1895.)

AMERICAN VOICES

FREDERICK DOUGLASS, from a letter to his former master, published in the *North Star* (September 8, 1848), ten years after his escape:

The grim horrors of slavery rise in all their ghastly terror before me; the wails of millions pierce my heart and chill my blood. I remember the chain, the gag, the bloody whip; the death-like gloom overshadowing the broken spirit of the fettered bondman; the appalling liability of his being torn away from wife and children, and sold like a beast in the market. . . .

Your mind must have become darkened, your heart hardened, your conscience seared and petrified, or you would have long since thrown off the accursed load, and sought relief at the hands of a sin-forgiving God. How, let me ask you, would you look upon me, were I, some dark night, in company with a band of hardened villains, to enter the precincts of your elegant dwelling, and seize the person of your own lovely daughter, Amanda, and carry her off from your family, friends, and all the loved ones of her youth—make her my slave—compel her to work, and I take her wages—place her name on my ledger as property—disregard her personal rights—fetter the powers of her immortal soul by denying her the right and privilege of learning to read and write—feed her coarsely—clothe her scantily, and whip her on the naked back occasionally; more, and still more horrible, leave her unprotected—a degraded victim to the brutal lust of fiendish overseers, who would pollute, blight, and blast her fair soul. . . . I ask, how would you regard me, if such were my conduct?

. . . I intend to make use of you as a weapon with which to assail the system of slavery. . . . I shall make use of you as a means of exposing the character of the American church and clergy—and as a means of bringing this guilty nation, with yourself, to repentance. . . .

I am your fellow-man but not your slave.
Frederick Douglass

Where did the Underground Railroad run?

Douglass had used his wits and unusual abilities to escape slavery. The *Narrative* was deliberately vague about the assistance he received along the way. Douglass did not want to endanger those who aided him, or make it easier for slave-chasers to figure out his route, thereby making escape difficult for other slaves. But he was helped by some brave individuals along the road.

For thousands of other blacks who refused submission between 1840 and 1861, the mostly anonymous people who led the way to freedom became known as the Underground Railroad. A loose network of individuals who believed that every single freed slave represented a victory against slavery, the Underground Railroad ran from the South northward through Philadelphia and New York, its two key stations, to freedom in Canada or the Northeast. While claims for the numbers of slaves it moved to freedom were vastly inflated in later years, the railroad existed and performed a dangerous and noble service.

From "station" to "station," as each safe spot along the treacherous route was known, the slaves slipped in the dark of night, led by the "conductors." While many of these were white abolitionists, often Quakers, the ranks of "conductors" were also joined by escaped slaves who risked far more by returning to help other slaves out. Of these, the most famous was Harriet Tubman (1820?–1913). Born a Maryland slave, like Douglass, Tubman made her way northward to freedom in 1849 and immediately returned to the South to aid other slave escapes. She made at least nineteen trips herself, and was personally responsible for bringing out at least 300 slaves, sometimes "encouraging" them to leave at gunpoint. She even succeeded in freeing her parents in 1857. Her success did not go unnoticed in the South; at one point there was a reward of $40,000 for her capture.

Although illiterate, she was a natural leader and a brilliant planner. Her life was undoubtedly saved when illness kept her from joining abolitionist John Brown's suicidal raid on the arsenal at Harpers Ferry. But during the Civil War she continued her militant defiance, serving with Union troops as a cook and as a spy behind Confederate lines. On another occasion she reportedly led 750 slaves to freedom, with the help of Union troops.

AMERICAN VOICES
SENATOR JOHN C. CALHOUN of South Carolina, from a March 4, 1850, speech read to the Senate for the ailing Calhoun before his death:

I have, Senators, believed from the first that the agitation on the subject of slavery would, if not prevented by some timely and effective measure, end in disunion. Entertaining this opinion, I have on all proper occasions, endeavored to call the attention of both the two great parties which divide the country to adopt some measure to prevent so great a disaster, but without success. The agitation has been permitted to proceed with almost no attempt to resist it, until it has reached a point when it can no longer be disguised or denied that the Union is in danger. You have thus had forced upon you the greatest and gravest question that can ever come under your consideration—How can the Union be preserved?

. . . What has endangered the Union?

To this question there can be but one answer,—the immediate cause is the almost universal discontent which pervades all the States composing the Southern section of the Union. [The discontent] commenced with the agitation of the slavery question and has been increasing ever since. . . .

One of the causes is, undoubtedly, to be traced to long-continued agitation of the slave question on the part of the North, and the many aggressions which they have made on the rights of the South during the time.

What was the Compromise of 1850?

The election of 1848 was really about the future of slavery and the Union. But you wouldn't know it from the chief candidates. The hero of the Mexican War, General Zachary Taylor, got the Whig nod without expressing or even possessing any opinions about the chief question of the day: the future of slavery in the new territories. The Democratic nominee, Lewis Cass, sidestepped the issue with a call for "popular sovereignty," or leaving the decision up to territorial governments. The only clear stand on slavery was taken by an aging Martin Van Buren, who had given up equivocating and was now running on the Free Soil ticket, a splinter group of antislavery Democrats. Taylor's image as the conquering hero won the popular imagination, and with Van Buren's third party draining Democratic votes from Cass, Taylor was elected.

As president, Taylor had no policy or plan to cope with the new territories, including the impact of the gold rush on the American economy. But when California petitioned for admission as a free state in 1849, the issue was placed squarely once more before Congress, with the fate of the Union hanging in the balance. Southerners, who accepted the Oregon Territory as free, didn't want slaves kept out of another state, especially one of California's size and wealth.

Only another compromise saved the Union for the moment, this one as distasteful to abolitionists as all the others in history had been. A package of bills, mostly the work of the aging Henry Clay, was introduced and heatedly debated in the Senate, chiefly by the other two congressional giants of the age, Daniel Webster—who was willing to accept limited slavery in preservation of the Union—and South

Carolina's John Calhoun (1782–1850), the preeminent spokesman for the slave-plantation system. Because Calhoun was too ill to speak, his views were presented by Senator James Murray Mason of Virginia. Vowing secession, Calhoun died before the compromise was signed into law. New faces on the congressional stage also joined the fray. William Seward of New York weighed in with an impassioned antislavery speech. The new senator from Illinois, Stephen Douglas, finally ramrodded the compromise through by dividing it into five separate bills and pulling together sufficient support for each of these.

It was only Zachary Taylor's death in office in 1850 that finally allowed passage of the Compromise of 1850. Taylor's successor, Millard Fillmore (1800–74), signed the five bills that made up the Compromise of 1850. Under these bills:

- California was admitted as a free state;
- New Mexico and Utah were organized without restrictions on slavery;
- Texas, also unrestricted as to slavery, had its boundaries set and received $10 million for the land that would become New Mexico;
- The slave trade (but not slavery itself) was abolished in the District of Columbia;
- A new Fugitive Slave Act provided federal jurisdiction to assist slave owners in the recovery of escaped slaves.

It was the last of these bills that provoked the most controversy, since it gave slave owners enormous powers to call on federal help in recovering escaped slaves. Under the law, no black person was safe. Only an affidavit was needed to prove ownership. Commissioners were granted great powers—thoroughly unconstitutional in modern light—to make arrests. Even the expenses of capturing and returning a fugitive slave were to be borne by the federal government. Although the burden of proof was on the accused fugitives, they were not entitled to a jury trial and couldn't defend themselves. And citizens who concealed, aided, or rescued fugitives were subject to harsh fines and imprisonment.

Suddenly free blacks, many of whom thought they had been safely established for years in northern towns, were subject to seizure and transport back to the South. Angry mobs in several cities bolted at the law with violent protests. In Boston, seat of abolitionist activity, William and Ellen Craft, who gained fame when they escaped through a ruse that involved Ellen posing as the male owner of William, were defended and hidden from slave catchers. When federal marshals snatched a fugitive named Shadrach, a mob of angry blacks overwhelmed the marshals and sent Shadrach to Montreal. Outraged by this defiance of federal law, President Fillmore sent troops to Boston to remove a seventeen-year-old captured slave named Thomas Sims.

Resistance grew elsewhere. In Syracuse, New York, a large group of mixed race broke into a jail and grabbed William McHenry, known as Jerry, from his captors, spiriting him off to Canada. And in Christiana, Pennsylvania, a Quaker town that openly welcomed fugitives, troops again were called out after some escaped slaves shot and killed an owner and then escaped to Canada. President Fillmore sent marines after these slaves, but Canada refused to extradite them. In the South, these were viewed as affronts to what was considered their owners' property and honor. New anger was spilling over into renewed threats of the Union's dissolution.

Why was *Uncle Tom's Cabin* the most important and controversial American novel of its time?

The number of blacks actually captured and sent south under the Fugitive Slave Act was relatively small, perhaps three hundred. But the law did produce another, unintended effect. Calling the law a "nightmare abomination," a young woman decided to write a novel that shook the conscience of America and the world.

Harriet Beecher Stowe's *Uncle Tom's Cabin* is certainly not the great American novel. It is far from the best-selling American novel. But for a long time it was surely the most significant American novel.

Harriet Beecher Stowe was the daughter, sister, and wife of Protestant clergymen. Her father, the Reverend Lyman Beecher, was a Calvinist minister who took the family to Cincinnati, where he headed a new seminary. There Harriet Beecher met and married Calvin Stowe, a professor of biblical literature. The seminary was a center of abolitionist sentiment, and a trip to nearby Kentucky provided the young woman with her only firsthand glimpse of slavery. In 1850, her husband took a teaching job at Bowdoin College in Maine, and there, after putting her children to bed at night, Stowe followed her family's urgings to write about the evils of slavery.

Uncle Tom's Cabin, or Life Among the Lowly first appeared in serial form in the *National Era*, an abolitionist journal. In 1852 a Boston publisher brought out the book in its complete form. Simplistic and overly melodramatic, the novel was also deeply affecting. The plot attempted to depict the lives of slaves and slaveholders through three primary characters: Eliza, a slave who wants to keep her child who is about to be sold off, and sets off in search of the Underground Railroad; Eva, the angelic but sickly daughter of a New Orleans plantation owner; and Uncle Tom, the noble slave sold to a series of owners, but who retains his dignity through all the degradations he suffers in hopes of being reunited with his family. That family, living together in Tom's idealized cabin on a Kentucky farm, represented the humanity of slaves, depicting them as husbands and wives, parents and children, in stark counterpoint to the common image of slaves as mere drudges.

Many of the book's characters were simply caricatures calculated to jolt tears from even the most heartless. But the book contained unforgettable images and scenes, perhaps the most famous of which was the picture of the barefoot Eliza, her child in her arms, leaping from one ice floe to another across the frozen Ohio River to escape a ruthless slave trader. There was the cherubic child Eva, trying to bring out the good in everyone in a weepy death scene; the vicious plantation owner, Simon Legree—pointedly written as a transplanted Yankee—vainly trying to break the will and spirit of Tom; and Uncle Tom himself, resilient and saintly, the novel's Christlike central character, beaten by Legree but refusing to submit to overseeing the other slaves.

The reaction of the public—North, South, and worldwide—was astonishing. Sales reached 300,000 copies within a year. Foreign translations were published throughout Europe, and sales soon afterward exceeded 1.5 million copies worldwide, a staggering number of books for the mid-nineteenth century, when there were no paperbacks or big bookstore chains. A dramatic version played on stages around the world, making Stowe one of the most famous women in the world, although not necessarily wealthy; pirated editions were commonplace. The theatrical presentation also spawned a brand of popular minstrel entertainments called Tom Shows, which provided the basis for the use of Uncle Tom as a derisive epithet for a black man viewed by other blacks as a shuffling lackey to whites.

In a time when slavery was discussed with dry legalisms and code words like "states' rights" and "popular sovereignty," this book personalized the question of slavery as no amount of abolitionist literature or congressional debate had. For the first time, thousands of whites got some taste of slavery's human suffering. In the South, there was outraged indignation. Yet even there the book sold out. Stowe was criticized as naive or a liar. In one infamous incident, she received an anonymous parcel containing the ear of a disobedient slave. Faced with the charge that the book was deceitful, Stowe answered with *A Key to Uncle Tom's Cabin*, which provided documentation that every incident in the novel had actually happened.

In 1862, Lincoln met Harriet Beecher Stowe and reportedly said, "So you're the little woman that wrote the book that made this great war." The copies sold can be counted, but the emotional impact can't be calculated so easily. It is safe to say that no other literary work since 1776, when Tom Paine's *Common Sense* incited a wave of pro-independence fervor, had the political impact of *Uncle Tom's Cabin*.

What forced the Republicans to start a new political party?

After Polk left the White House, America was cursed by a string of presidents who were at best mediocre and at worst ineffectual or incompetent. Polk's successor in the White House, Zachary Taylor, had enormous battlefield experience but was ill prepared for the political wars of his administration. Before he had a chance to grow in office, he died of cholera in 1850 and was succeeded by Vice President Millard Fillmore (1800–74). Overshadowed by the congressional giants of his time—Webster, Clay, and Calhoun—Fillmore made little impact in his abbreviated administration other than by winning passage of the Compromise of 1850 and dispatching Commodore Matthew C. Perry to open trade and diplomatic relations with Japan, a further extension of the Manifest Destiny mood that had spilled past the California coast to overseas expansionism.

The campaign of 1852 brought another ineffectual leader to the White House in Franklin Pierce (1804–69), and his election was symptomatic of the country's problems. The two major parties, Whig and Democrat, were fracturing over slavery and other sectional conflicts. Having once been a significant third-party factor, the Free Soil Party, which had opposed the Compromise of 1850, was leaderless. Looking for the battle-hero charm to work once more, the Whigs put up General Winfield Scott, the commander during the Mexican War. But this time the charm had worn out. A northern Democrat taking a southern stand, Pierce outpolled Scott easily, but in his attempts to appease southern Democrats, he lost northern support and any hope of holding the middle ground against the two ends.

The election results meant political chaos. The Whigs were in a tailspin, no longer led by Clay and Webster, the two congressional masters who once gave the party its strength. Northern Democrats, rapidly outnumbered by the growing ranks of southerners in their party, were being pushed out. Out of the chaos came a new alliance. A series of meetings, the first occurring in Ripon, Wisconsin, in 1854, resulted in the birth of a new party known as the Republicans. A group of thirty congressmen adopted this party label on May 9, 1854. Although the Republicans made antislavery claims that attracted former Free Soilers and other antislavery groups, the party's opposition to extending slavery beyond its existing boundaries came from economic and political reasoning rather than from moral outrage. Essentially, the party appealed to the free, white workingman. Its basic tenet was that the American West must be open to free, white labor. Not only were the Republicans opposed to slaves in the West; they wanted all blacks kept out. This was hardly the ringing message of morality that we tend to associate with the antislavery movement, but it was a message that appealed to many in the North. In 1854 the Republicans won 100 seats in Congress. Just six years after the party was born, it would put its first president into the White House.

Why was Kansas "bloody"?

In 1854, Dorothy and Toto wouldn't have recognized Kansas. The next battlefield in the free-slave conflict, the Kansas Territory was where the debate moved from harsh rhetoric to bloodshed in what might be called the first fighting of the Civil War. At the heart of the hostilities was the long-debated question of whether slavery should be extended into new territory. Convinced that the North was trying to overwhelm them economically and politically, southerners believed the answer to the question was new slave territory. Behind that question, however, were old-fashioned greed and political ambition.

In 1854, Stephen Douglas (1813–61), the Democratic senator from Illinois who had pushed through the Compromise of 1850, wanted to organize new territory in the West that would become Kansas and Nebraska. His motive was simple: he was a director of the Illinois Central Railroad and a land speculator. The new territory would open the way for railroad development, with Chicago as its terminus. But Kansas would lie above the line marking slavery's boundary under the Missouri Compromise and would have to be free. To win approval for the new territory, Douglas bargained with southern Democrats who would not vote for a new free territory. Looking to a presidential run in 1856, for which he would need southern support, Douglas offered a solution. To win over southerners, he agreed to support repeal of the Missouri Compromise, which had governed new territories for thirty-four years. With Douglas and his southern Democratic allies, the Kansas-Nebraska Act did just that in May 1854.

The betrayal of the Missouri Compromise just about killed the Democratic Party in the North. With opposition to the Kansas-Nebraska Act as their cornerstone, the Republican Party mushroomed. Another new party also profited from Douglas's bargain with the South. Born of fierce opposition to the waves of immigrants entering America, they were called Nativists, and an ugly racist streak lay beneath their dislike of foreigners and Catholics. Initially a secret society that preached the twin virtues of white Protestantism and defensive nationalism, they were called the Know-Nothings because they always answered, "I don't know" when asked about their party. Their message struck home in the mid-1850s, and they became a powerful splinter party force, capturing a substantial number of Congressional seats and state legislatures.

With the Kansas-Nebraska Act calling for "popular sovereignty" in the territories, Kansas was flooded with groups from both sides of the slavery issue. Northerners opposed to slavery's expansion attempted to transport antislavery settlers to Kansas to ensure that the territory would eventually vote against slavery. Enraged by this interference from the New England "foreigners," thousands of Missourians called Border Ruffians poured across the line into Kansas to tip the balance in favor of slavery in the territory. In an illegal and rigged election, the pro-slave Ruffians won, but antislavery forces refused to concede defeat and set up a provisional free state government in Topeka.

President Pierce denounced this government, giving the pro-slave forces justification for an offensive. And the first blow in the Civil War was struck in May 1856 when the town of Lawrence, established as an antislavery center, was sacked by pro-slave forces. Three days later in retaliation, a fanatical abolitionist named John Brown attacked a pro-slavery town on Pottawatomie Creek, slaughtering five settlers in the night. These attacks brought Kansas to a state of chaos. By October 1856, some 200 people had died in the fighting in Bloody Kansas and President Pierce's mishandling of the Kansas fighting left him without support.

The political disarray produced another weak president in James Buchanan (1791–1868). Ignoring the ineffectual Pierce, the Democrats turned to Pennsylvania's James Buchanan, a Democratic Party loyalist whose chief political asset seemed to be that he was minister to England during the Kansas furor, and couldn't be blamed for it. In fact, he said little during the campaign, prompting one Republican senator to say that there was no such person as Buchanan—that "he was dead of lockjaw."

Gaining popular strength as blood was spilled in Kansas, the Republicans took a page from the old Whig playbook and chose the Pathfinder, John C. Frémont, the celebrated western explorer and high priest of Manifest Destiny who had led the way to California, as its 1856 standard-bearer. Like the Whig generals before him, Frémont was a military man with no political experience, although his father-in-law, Senator Thomas Hart Benton, was one of the most powerful men in Congress. The Pathfinder's campaign slogan was simple: "Free Soil, Free Speech, Free Men, Frémont."

The Know-Nothings or American Nativists, also bolstered by the Kansas debacle, sent up former president Millard Fillmore. Pledging secession if the Republican Frémont was elected, southern Democrats forced preservation of the Union to the forefront of the election. Their threat carried some weight. With only 45 percent of the popular vote, Buchanan was elected as Frémont (33 percent) and Fillmore (22 percent) split the rest of the vote. The last of the Democratic heirs to Andrew Jackson, Buchanan was perhaps the weakest, most ineffectual of all the prewar presidents. Inaugurated in 1857, James Buchanan was the last president born in the eighteenth century, the oldest president at his inauguration (until Ronald Reagan in 1981), and the nation's only bachelor president. (That distinction has inspired a century and a half of speculation. Massachusetts Congressman Barney Frank, who is openly gay, once described Buchanan as the nation's only homosexual president. Buchanan's orphaned niece, Harriet Lane, then in her twenties, served as his official hostess and there were also whispers of a relationship between them, as well as speculation about Buchanan's frequent visits to a well-known widow, Mrs. Rose Greenhow, who lived across the street from the White House and was arrested during the Civil War as a Confederate spy. But no evidence of Buchanan's sexual preferences has ever been offered.) Though Buchanan pledged noninterference and popular sovereignty, it was too late for these empty slogans.

AMERICAN VOICES
ROBERT E. LEE, in a letter to his wife
Mary Custis Lee (December 1856):

In this enlightened age there are few, I believe, but will acknowledge that slavery as an institution is a moral and political evil in any country. It is useless to expatiate on its disadvantages. I think it, however, a greater evil to the white man than to the black race, and while my feelings are strongly interested in behalf of the latter, my sympathies are stronger for the former. The blacks are immeasurably better off here than in Africa, morally, socially, and physically. *The painful discipline they are undergoing is necessary for their instruction as a race, and I hope, will prepare and lead them to better things.* [Emphasis added.]

This letter was written some four years before Robert E. Lee (1807–70) was appointed to lead the Confederate Army of Northern Virginia in April 1861. Lee had just completed three years as superintendent of the U.S. Military Academy at West Point and was serving in Texas. He was the son of Henry "Light-Horse Harry" Lee, a famed Revolutionary War hero. His mother, Ann Carter Lee, came from the most prominent family in Virginia, and his wife, Mary Custis Lee, was a descendant of Martha Custis Washington. They were part of the Virginia slaveholding aristocracy, and during the war, their home and property in Arlington, Virginia, would be confiscated by the federal government and eventually provide the land for Arlington National Cemetery.

What was the difference between a man named Dred Scott and a mule?

Buchanan hoped the Supreme Court could settle the burning questions of slavery in the territories and reconciliation between North and South. He publicly expressed his hope that the Court would remove the burden of a solution from Congress and himself in his inaugural address on March 4, 1857. The slavery question, he said, "belongs to the Supreme Court of the United States, before whom it is now pending, and will, it is understood, be speedily and finally settled." But Buchanan was suffering from a terminal case of wishful thinking—or he was seriously deluded. Two days later, the Supreme Court altered the future of the debate and of the nation.

Instead of solving the problem, the court's ruling threw gasoline on a smoldering fire. Any hopes of judicial or legislative settlement to the questions were lost in the Dred Scott decision.

The ruling came in a case brought on behalf of Dred Scott; the case was a legal odyssey that began 1834 when Dr. John Emerson joined the army as a surgeon. Emerson spent several years at a number of posts, including Illinois, Wisconsin Territory, and his home state of Missouri.

During all of these moves, Dr. Emerson had been accompanied by his personal servant, Dred Scott, a slave. Emerson died in 1846, and with the help of a sympathetic lawyer, Scott sued for his freedom, claiming that because he had lived in territories where slavery was illegal (Illinois barred slavery under the Northwest Ordinance; Wisconsin under the Missouri Compromise), he was legally free. A St. Louis county court accepted Scott's position, but the Missouri supreme court overruled this decision and remanded Scott, his wife, and their child to slavery. On appeal, the case finally went to the U.S. Supreme Court, where the chief justice was Roger Taney, an eighty-year-old former slave owner and states' rights advocate who had been appointed by President Andrew Jackson after serving as Jackson's attorney general. He had taken the seat of John Marshall.

The Court split along regional and party lines, although Justice Robert Grier of Pennsylvania joined the majority. Letters later revealed that he had done so at the request of President Buchanan, who interfered to prevent a purely sectional decision. While each justice wrote an opinion, it was Taney's ruling that stood as the majority decision. False in some parts, in others illogical, Taney's ruling contained three principal points, all of them death blows to antislavery hopes. Free or slave, said Taney, blacks were not citizens; therefore, Scott had no standing before the court. Negroes, he wrote, "are so inferior that they had no rights which a white man was bound to respect."

Taney could have stopped there, but he went much further. Scott had never ceased to be a slave and therefore was not a citizen, but property of his owner, no different from a mule or a horse. This led to his final and most damaging conclusion. Because slaves were property, and property was protected by the Fifth Amendment in the Bill of Rights, Taney argued that Congress had no right to deprive citizens of their property—including slaves—anywhere within the United States. In his judgment, only a state could prohibit slavery within its boundaries. With one sweeping decision, Taney had obliterated the entire legislative history of compromises that restricted slavery, from the Northwest Ordinance of 1787 to the Missouri Compromise of 1820 and the Compromise of 1850.

Southerners, overjoyed by the ruling, wanted to go another step. Armed with the force of Taney's decision, southerners were poised to question the constitutionality of the 1807 law prohibiting the slave trade itself and any laws that proscribed slavery. Conciliatory northerners thought that the Court had given its approval to the notion of popular sovereignty, allowing the states to set their own slavery policy.

But instead of giving slavery a new lease on life and destroying the Republican Party, the decision produced two unexpected results. It further split the Democrats between North and South, and it strengthened the Republicans, politically and morally. Rather than accepting Taney's decision as a defeat for their position opposing slavery's spread, Republicans grew more defiant. In the North and in border states, many people who had been fence-sitters on the slavery question were driven into the Republican camp. The situation got uglier when prominent Republicans charged that President Buchanan knew in advance of the Court's ruling and had conspired with Taney to extend slavery by this decision, a conspiracy theory that won popular approval in the North and advanced the Republican cause and which later evidence would show to be completely true.

AMERICAN VOICES
CHIEF JUSTICE ROGER B. TANEY, from
Dred Scott v. Sandford (March 6, 1857):

> The right of property in a slave is distinctly and expressly affirmed in the Constitution. The right to traffic in it, like an ordinary article of merchandise and property, was guaranteed to the citizens of the United States, in every State that might desire it, for twenty years. And the Government in express terms is pledged to protect it in all future time, if the slave escapes from his owner. . . . And no word can be found in the Constitution which gives Congress a greater power over slave property, or which entitles property of that kind to less protection than property of any other description. The only power conferred is the power coupled with the duty of guarding and protecting the owner in his rights.

What did Lincoln and Douglas debate?

A year after the decision in *Dred Scott v. Sandford,* two men stood on a platform with Taney's ruling hanging over their heads like a black cloud. One of them was the dapper, short, but powerfully robust Little Giant, Stephen Douglas. As he stood in the Illinois summer sun, Douglas must have known that he was one of the most powerful and well-known men in America, but that he was fighting for his political life and perhaps the future of the nation. Unable to win the Democratic nomination for president in 1852 and 1856, Douglas kept alive his hopes of making a run in 1860, believing that he could hold the Union together by a conciliatory approach to the South that would accept a moderate form of slavery through "popular sovereignty." But before he could run for president in 1860, Douglas had to hold on to his Senate seat.

His Republican opponent seemed unimpressive. A former one-term representative, at six feet, four inches in height, Abraham Lincoln may have towered over Douglas, but he lacked the senator's stature and clout. But Douglas was not fooled. As he commented to a friend, "He is the strong man of the party—full of wit, facts, dates—and the best stump speaker, with his droll ways and dry jokes, in the West. He is as honest as he is shrewd."

Born in 1809 in Kentucky, Lincoln was the son of an illiterate pioneer farmer. At age seven, Lincoln moved with his family to Indiana, and in 1830, the Lincolns settled in southern Illinois. Upon leaving his family home, Lincoln went to New Orleans and returned to Illinois to manage a general store in New Salem. He led a detachment of Illinois militia in the Black Hawk War, but as he liked to say, fought nothing but mosquitoes. At twenty-five, Lincoln won a seat in the Illinois legislature while studying for the bar, and he became a lawyer in 1836. A Whig, Lincoln graduated to Congress in 1846 for a single term marked by his partisan opposition to "Polk's war" in Mexico. Although he lost his seat and returned to Springfield to build his legal practice, he joined the Republican Party in 1856 and was prominent enough to win 110 votes for a vice presidential nomination at the first Republican national convention. In 1858, after delivering his "House Divided" speech to a state Republican convention in Springfield, he was the unanimous choice of the Illinois Republicans to oppose Douglas.

Feeling that his chances would be improved by head-to-head confrontation, Lincoln challenged Douglas to a series of debates at various spots around the state. With much to lose, Douglas agreed to seven such meetings. Even though the nation had plunged into a depression in 1857 after a panic in the stock market, and there were other questions of national importance, it was clear that Lincoln and Douglas would battle over one question: their views on slavery.

Each man had a simple plan of attack. Douglas would make Lincoln look like a raving abolitionist; Lincoln would depict Douglas as pro-slavery and a defender of the Dred Scott decision. In fact, Lincoln and Douglas were not far apart in their views, but their ambitions exaggerated their differences and their attacks on each other forced them into dangerous corners. Douglas was not afraid of race baiting to paint Lincoln as a radical who favored racial mixing.

This attack forced Lincoln more than once into adopting conservative language that seemed to contradict some of the opinions he had stated earlier. He opposed slavery, but wouldn't force the states where it existed to surrender their rights. Lincoln stated that slavery would die gradually, but, when pressed, guessed it would take one hundred years to happen. And while he argued, in the words of the Constitution, that "all men are created equal," he balked at the notion of allowing blacks the vote, jury duty, intermarriage, or even citizenship. Lincoln said, "I am not nor ever have been in favor of bringing about in any way the social and political equality of the white and black races . . . I am not nor ever have been in favor of making voters or jurors of negroes, nor of qualifying them to hold office, nor to intermarry with white people; and I will say in addition to this that there is a physical difference between the races which I believe will for ever forbid the two races living together on terms of social and political equality."

These debates paired off two men of great intellect, presence, wit, speaking ability, and political instincts. A crucial moment came when Lincoln asked Douglas if the people of a territory could exclude slavery before the territory became a state. This sprang a costly trap on Douglas. He answered that the people had the power to introduce or exclude slavery, no matter what the Supreme Court said. This was a roundabout denunciation of the Dred Scott ruling and it probably gave Douglas a temporary victory. Douglas retained his Senate seat when the Democrats maintained control of the Illinois legislature, which then selected the state's senator. But in the long run, he had shot himself in the foot. Southern Democrats would never support a man for president who equivocated about Dred Scott.

Lincoln lost the election, but it did him no harm. In fact, it increased his national visibility tremendously. With the Democrats further fracturing along North-South lines, the Republicans were beginning to feel confident about their chances in the presidential campaign of 1860. And Abraham Lincoln had the look of a candidate who might be able to win the White House for them.

AMERICAN VOICES
LINCOLN'S "House Divided" speech at
Springfield, Illinois (June 17, 1858):

"A house divided against itself cannot stand."

I believe this government cannot endure, permanently half slave and half free.

I do not expect the Union to be dissolved; I do not expect the house to fall; but I do expect it will cease to be divided. It will become all one thing, or all the other. Either the opponents of slavery will arrest the further spread of it, and place it where the public mind shall rest in the belief that it is in course of ultimate extinction; or its advocates will push it forward, till it shall become alike lawful in all the States, old as well as new—North as well as South.

Why did John Brown attack a federal arsenal?

Debates, antislavery novels, abolitionist conventions, Congress, and the Supreme Court had all failed. Some said action was needed. And the man shouting loudest for action was John Brown (1800–59). Viewed through history as a lunatic, psychotic, fanatic, visionary, and martyr, Brown came from a New England abolitionist family, several of whom were quite insane. A failure in most of his undertakings, he had gone to Kansas with some of his twenty-two children to fight for the antislavery cause, and gained notoriety for an attack that left five pro-slavery settlers hacked to pieces.

After the massacre at Pottawatomie, Brown went into hiding, but he had cultivated wealthy New England friends who believed in his violent rhetoric. A group known as the Secret Six formed to fund Brown's audacious plan to march south, arm the slaves who would flock to his crusade, and establish a black republic in the Appalachians to wage war against the slaveholding South. Brown may have been crazy, but he was not without a sense of humor. When President Buchanan put a price of $250 on his head, Brown responded with a bounty of $20.50 on Buchanan's.

Among the people Brown confided in was Frederick Douglass; Brown saw Douglass as the man slaves would flock to, a "hive for the bees." But the country's most famous abolitionist attempted to dissuade Brown, not because he disagreed with violence but because he thought Brown's chosen target was suicidal. Few volunteers answered Brown's call to arms, although Harriet Tubman signed on with Brown's little band. She fell sick, however, and was unable to join the raid.

On October 16, 1859, Brown, with three of his sons and fifteen followers, white and black, attacked the federal arsenal at Harpers Ferry, Virginia, on the Potomac River not far from Washington, D.C. Taking several hostages, including one descendant of George Washington, Brown's brigade occupied the arsenal. But no slaves came forward to join them. The local militia was able to bottle Brown up inside the building until federal marines under Colonel Robert E. Lee and J. E. B. Stuart arrived and captured Brown and the eight men who had survived the assault.

Within six weeks Brown was indicted, tried, convicted, and hanged by the state of Virginia, with the full approval of President Buchanan. But during the period of his captivity and trial, this wild-eyed fanatic underwent a transformation of sorts, becoming a forceful and eloquent spokesman for the cause of abolition.

While disavowing violence and condemning Brown, many in the North came to the conclusion that he was a martyr in a just cause. Even peaceable abolitionists who eschewed violence, such as Henry

David Thoreau and Ralph Waldo Emerson, overlooked Brown's homicidal tendencies and glorified him. Thoreau likened Brown to Christ; Emerson wrote that Brown's hanging would "make the gallows as glorious as the cross."

The view in the South, of course, was far different. Fear of slave insurrection still ran deep, and the memory of Nat Turner (see Chapter 3) remained fresh. To southern minds, John Brown represented Yankee interference in their way of life taken to its extreme. Even conciliatory voices in the South turned furious in the face of the seeming beatification of Brown. When northerners began to glorify Brown while disavowing his tactics, it was one more blow forcing the wedge deeper and deeper between North and South.

AMERICAN VOICES

JOHN BROWN at his execution:

I am quite certain that the crimes of this guilty land will never be purged away but with blood.

Why did the southern states secede from the United States?

Within days of Lincoln's election in 1860, the South Carolina legislature voted to secede from the Union. In his final message to Congress, lame-duck president Buchanan stressed that states had no right to secede, but having always favored the southern cause, Buchanan did nothing to stop such an action. In South Carolina, local militia began to seize the federal forts in Charleston's harbor. Buchanan attempted weakly to reinforce Fort Sumter, the last Charleston fort in federal hands, but the supply ship turned back. (On leaving the White House, Buchanan is supposed to have told Lincoln, "My dear sir, if you are as happy in entering the White House as I shall feel on returning to Wheatland [his Pennsylvania home], you are a happy man indeed."

Before Lincoln was inaugurated, five more states seceded, and in February 1861, these seven states, all from what is called the "lower South" (Alabama, Florida, Georgia, Louisiana, Mississippi, South Carolina, and Texas), formed the Confederate States of America. Jefferson

Davis (1808–89), U.S. senator from Mississippi, was elected president. By the time the war began, the first seven states of the Confederacy would be joined by four more: Virginia, Arkansas, North Carolina, and Tennessee.

On March 4, 1861, after secretly slipping into Washington to foil an assassination plot that had been uncovered, Lincoln was inaugurated. In one of history's great ironies, the oath of office was administered by Chief Justice Roger Taney, author of the Dred Scott decision, which had greatly contributed to Lincoln's election.

For years, secession had been held out as a blustering threat that both sides believed would never be used. Why did it finally happen? There were many factors: the widespread southern feeling that the South was being overpowered by northern political, industrial, banking, and manufacturing strength; the fear that the southern way of life was threatened by northern control of Congress; race-baiting hysteria that southern editorialists and politicians fanned with talk of black control of the South and widespread intermarriage and rape of southern white womanhood. Typical of the rhetoric at the time were these comments: "Do you love your mother, your wife, your sister, your daughter? In ten years or less our children will be the slaves of negroes." A South Carolina Baptist preacher said, "If you are tame enough to submit, abolition preachers will be at hand to consummate the marriage of your daughters to black husbands." And, "Submit to have our wives and daughters choose between death and gratifying the hellish lust of the negro!! . . . Better ten thousand deaths than submission."

All these disparate emotions and political views coalesced in the slavery issue. In the southern view, secession was the last resort to block emancipation. Faced with a legislative confrontation in which its political power was diminishing, the South resorted to the one power it possessed to control its destiny: leaving the Union.

What cannot be overlooked in any discussion of political, social, and economic reasons for the South's breaking away are human nature and historical inevitability. History has repeatedly shown that a more powerful force—in this case the North—will attempt to overwhelm a weaker one for its own interests. For those white southerners who held no slaves—and they were a majority—there was the common denominator of fear. Fear that Lincoln, the Republicans, and the abolitionist

Yankees who owned the banks and the factories that set the prices for their crops would make them the slaves of free blacks. Human nature dictates that people who are pushed to the wall either break or push back. To ask why cooler heads did not prevail and settle these questions amicably overlooks the character of the South—proud, independent, individualistic, loyal to the land, and even chivalrous. For such people, a stubborn refusal to submit was the answer. As the new president of the Confederacy, Jefferson Davis, put it, "Will you be slaves or be independent? Will you consent to be robbed of your property?" To Davis, submission meant the loss of liberty, property, and honor itself.

Given the social, economic, historical, social, and psychological reasons behind secession, there is another issue that is often overlooked: the two sides were not made up of two monolithic points of view—pro-slavery, anti-Union secessionists in the South, and abolitionist, pro-Union forces in the North. That they were is a myth and a vast oversimplification. After the first seven states sceded, there were still eight slave states left, and attempts were being made in Washington to craft some compromise to keep the Union intact. Did all southerners want to leave the Union? Hardly. While the lower South states where slavery was more deeply entrenched were solidly secessionist, according to James McPherson's *Battle Cry of Freedom*, the voters in Virginia, Arkansas, and Missouri had elected a majority of pro-Unionists to state conventions that would decide the question. In North Carolina and Tennessee, the voters had rejected secession conventions entirely. Conventions in Missouri and Arkansas rejected secession. Even in Texas, Governor Sam Houston, the greatest hero of Texas independence, opposed secession. The Texas secession deposed him as governor. (It may be stating the obvious, but blacks and women did not figure into these votes.) That is one reason it is more appropriate to call the two sides Union and Confederacy, instead of North and South.

Why didn't the North allow the South to go its own way? Some people, including such prominent abolitionist voices as New York newspaperman Horace Greeley, argued that the North should do just that, although he may have believed that the southern states would not actually go through with it. Hardcore abolitionists were glad that the slaveholders had broken the "covenant with death," as some of them, like Garrison, called the Constitution. But if the seceding states were permitted to go, it would mean the end of the United States of America as it was created in the Declaration and the Constitution. The result would be anarchy. The practical result would be economic dislocation and international weakness that could only result in the collapse of the nation's institutions.

There were certainly deep philosophical and patriotic reasons that many people had for wanting to preserve the Union. But to most northerners, the issue was more practical: simple economics. In his prize-winning book *The Metaphysical Club*, Louis Menand sums up the prewar attitudes of a great many Americans in the North: "We think of the Civil War as a war to save the Union and to abolish slavery, but before the fighting began most people regarded these as incompatible ideals. Northerners who wanted to preserve the union did not wish to see slavery extended into the territories; some of them hoped it would wither away in the states where it persisted. But many Northern businessmen believed that losing the South would mean economic catastrophe, and many of their employees believed that freeing the slaves would mean lower wages. They feared secession far more than they disliked slavery, and they were unwilling to risk the former by trying to pressure the South into giving up the latter."

AMERICAN VOICES
From LINCOLN'S first inaugural address
(March 4, 1861):

In your hands, my dissatisfied fellow countrymen, and not in mine, is the momentous question of civil war. The Government will not assail you. You can have no conflict without being yourselves the aggressors. You have no oath registered in heaven to destroy the Government, while I shall have the most solemn one to "preserve, protect, and defend it."

I am loath to close. We are not enemies, but friends. We must not be enemies. Though passion may have strained, it must not break our bonds of affection. The mystic chords of memory, stretching from every battlefield and patriot grave to every living heart and hearthstone all over this broad land, will yet swell the chorus of the Union when again touched, as surely they will be, by the better angels of our nature.

The 1860 Census

History doesn't show whether London's touts laid odds on the war's outcome. On paper, as they say in sports, this contest looked like a mismatch. About the only thing the South seemed to have going for it was a home-field advantage. Looking at numbers alone, the South's decision and fortunes seemed doomed from the outset. But as the history of warfare has consistently proven, Davids often defeat Goliaths—or, at the least, make them pay dearly for their victories. The South needed no better example than the patriots who had defeated England in the Revolution.

UNION

- Twenty-three states, including California, Oregon, and the four slaveholding "border states" of Missouri, Kentucky, Delaware, and Maryland, and seven territories. (West Virginia would join the Union in 1863.)
- Population: 22 million (4 million men of combat age).
- Economy: 100,000 factories.
    1.1 million workers.
    20,000 miles of railroad (70 percent of U.S. total; 96 percent of all railroad equipment).
    $189 million in bank deposits (81 percent of U.S. total bank deposits).
    $56 million in gold specie.

CONFEDERACY

- Eleven states.
- Population: 9 million (3.5 million slaves; only 1.2 million men of combat age).
- Economy: 20,000 factories.

101,000 workers.
9,000 miles of railroad.
$47 million in bank deposits.
$27 million in gold specie.

In addition, the North vastly outproduced the South in agricultural products and livestock holdings (except asses and mules). The only commodity that the South produced in greater quantities than the North was cotton, raised by slave labor. The North had the means to increase its wartime supplies and ship them efficiently by rail. The South would have to purchase weapons, ships, and arms from foreign sources, exposing itself to a Union naval blockade.

On the South's side of the balance sheet were several small but significant factors. The U.S. Army was largely comprised of and led by southerners who immediately defected to the South's cause. The armies of the North were largely going to be made up of conscripts from urban areas, many of them immigrants who spoke little or no English, were less familiar with arms and tactics, and would be fighting on "foreign" turf for the dubious goals, in their minds, of "preserving the Union" and stopping the spread of slavery. All of this gave the southern armies an immediate advantage in trained soldiers and command leadership. In addition, the war would be fought primarily in the South. All the advantages of fighting at home—familiarity with terrain, popular partisan support, the motivation of defending the homeland—which had contributed to the American defeat of the British in the Revolution, were on the side of the Confederacy.

What was the difference between the Confederate and U.S. constitutions?

One week after Lincoln's inaugural address, on March 11, the Confederacy adopted a constitution. Given the long-held arguments that the crisis was over such issues as federal power and states' rights, and not slavery, it might be assumed that the new Confederate nation adopted some very different form of government, perhaps more like the Articles of Confederation, under which the states operated before the Constitution was adopted.

In fact, the Constitution of the Confederate States of America was based almost verbatim on the U.S. Constitution. There were, however, several significant but relatively minor differences, as well as one big difference:

- The preamble added the words, "each State acting in its sovereign and independent character," and instead of forming "a more perfect Union," it was forming "a permanent federal government." It also added an invocation to "Almighty God" absent from the original (see Chapter 3: "What three-letter word is not in the Constitution?").

- It permitted a tariff for revenue but not for protection of domestic industries, though the distinction between the two was unclear.

- It altered the executive branch by creating a presidency with a single six-year term, instead of (then) unlimited four-year terms. However, the presidency was strengthened with a line item veto with which certain parts of a budget can be removed by the president. (Many U.S. presidents of both parties have argued for the line item veto as a means to control congressional spending. A line item veto was finally passed in 1996 and used first by President Bill Clinton. However, in 1998 the U.S. Supreme Court ruled that the line item veto was unconstitutional.)

- The major difference between the two constitutions regarded slavery. First, the Confederate version didn't bother with neat euphemisms ("persons held in service") but simply and honestly called it slavery. While it upheld the ban on the importation of slaves from abroad, the Confederate constitution removed any restrictions on slavery. Slavery was going to be protected and extended into any new territory the Confederacy might acquire.

In other words, while "states' rights" is a powerful abstraction, and the back-and-forth between federal power and the power of the states has been a theme throughout American history, there was really only one right that the southern states cared about. Examining the speeches by southern leaders (see Calhoun above) and the Confederate constitution itself underscores the fact that the only right in question was the right to continue slavery without restriction, both where it already existed and in the new territories being opened up in the West.

MILESTONES IN THE CIVIL WAR

1861

April 12   The war officially begins when South Carolina militia forces commanded by General Pierre G. T. Beauregard (1818–93), second in the West Point class of 1838, bombard Fort Sumter, the federal garrison in the harbor at Charleston, South Carolina. Lacking sufficient supplies, the fort's commander surrenders.

April 15   Declaring a state of "insurrection," Lincoln calls for 75,000 volunteers for three months' service. Lincoln rejects the suggestion that black volunteers be accepted.

April 17   Virginia secedes, the eighth and most influential state to do so. Poorly defended, Washington, D.C., lies but a hundred miles from Richmond, seat of the Confederacy. From the White House, Lincoln can see Confederate flags flying over Arlington, Virginia.

April 19   In Baltimore, crowds sympathetic to the Confederacy stone Union troops marching to reinforce the capital; four soldiers are killed, the first casualties of the war. President Lincoln orders a naval blockade of southern ports. The blockade will prevent cotton, the South's principal cash crop, from being shipped to Europe and limit imports of munitions and other supplies crucial to the South's war effort. The Union navy is small at the time, and many of its commanders and sailors are southerners who defect, but the American merchant marine is powerful, and merchant ships are pressed into service. Coupled with a major shipbuilding effort, the navy soon has hundreds of ships—including the first generation of ironclad warships—available to enforce the blockade, making this strategy a significant element of the Union's eventual victory.

At the suggestion of General Winfield Scott, the seventy-five-year-old, arthritic, and overweight commander of the U.S. Army, Lincoln asks Robert E. Lee (1807–70) to take field command of the Union forces. Instead, Lee resigns his U.S. Army commission on April 20 and assumes a commission in the Confederate army. Torn over the oath he took upon entering the United States Army, Lee decides he cannot take up arms against his home state of Virginia.

Lee is not alone. Many of the battle-tested commanders in the U.S. Army are southerners who join the Confederate forces. In the war's early period, the Union armies will be led by generals who are political appointees. This disparity in leadership quality is a major factor in keeping the Confederacy's military hopes alive and prolonging the war.

May 6 Arkansas and Tennessee secede, the ninth and tenth states to join the Confederacy, although the eastern parts of Tennessee remain loyal to the Union and contribute troops to Union armies.

May 13 British queen Victoria announces Great Britain's neutrality in the conflict. Although the Confederacy is not recognized diplomatically, it is given "belligerent status," meaning British merchants could trade with the Confederate States.

May 20 North Carolina secedes, the eleventh and final Confederate state. It will suffer the heaviest death toll of any Confederate state.

May 24 Union troops move into Alexandria, Virginia, across the Potomac River from Washington, D.C. Elmer Ellsworth, a close friend of Lincoln's, becomes the first combat fatality of the war. He is shot while removing a Confederate flag from a hotel roof. The hotel keeper who shot him, James T. Jackson, is killed by Union troops. Both men become martyrs to their respective sides.

July 2 Lincoln authorizes the suspension of the constitutional right of habeas corpus.

July 21 The First Battle of Bull Run (or First Manassas). In Virginia, Confederate armies under Generals Joseph E. Johnston (1807–91) and Beauregard rout Union troops. Poor Union generalship is largely to blame, a problem that bedevils the Union war effort as Lincoln searches for effective commanders. During the fighting, Confederate General Thomas J. Jackson (1824–63), West Point class of 1846 and a professor of military tactics and natural philosophy at Virginia Military Institute, is given the nickname Stonewall for his leadership of the stand made by his troops that turned the tide of battle.

August 5   After the crushing defeat at Bull Run, the Union realizes that this is not going to be a ninety-day war. To pay for the war, Congress passes the first income tax law, and enlistment periods are increased from three months to two years.

August 10–30   In the West, Union forces are defeated at Wilson's Creek, Missouri, and one of the Union's most experienced commanders, General Frémont, the Pathfinder, withdraws, surrendering much of Missouri, a border state that had not joined the Confederacy. To reverse his military losses, Frémont declares martial law and announces that the slaves of secessionists are free. Lincoln requests that this order be withdrawn, but Frémont refuses, and Lincoln removes him from command.

October 21   Battle of Ball's Bluff (Virginia). Another rout of Union forces, with some 1,900 Union troops killed.

November 1   Lincoln forces aging General Winfield Scott to retire, and replaces him with George B. McClellan (1826–85) as general-in-chief.

1862

January 11   Edwin Stanton replaces Simon Cameron as war secretary. Cameron's War Department had been riddled by corruption and mismanagement.

January 27   Lincoln issues General War Order Number 1, calling for a Union offensive; McClellan ignores the order.

January 30   The Union ironclad ship *Monitor* is launched.

February 6 Opening a Union offensive in the West, General Ulysses S. Grant (1822–85) initiates a campaign in the Mississippi Valley, capturing Fort Henry on the Tennessee River. Ten days later, Grant takes Fort Donelson, near Nashville.

February 25 Nashville, Tennessee, surrenders to Union troops, and the city remains in Union control for the rest of the war.

March 9 In the first battle between two ironclad ships, the Union *Monitor* engages the Confederate *Virginia* (formerly the USS *Merrimac*) off Hampton Roads, Virginia. The battle is inconclusive, but the *Virginia* is scuttled to prevent her capture.

March 11 Annoyed at McClellan's inaction, Lincoln removes him as general-in-chief, replacing him with General Henry W. Halleck, but makes him head of the Army of the Potomac.

April 4 The Union Army of the Potomac begins the Peninsular Campaign aimed at Richmond, capital of the Confederacy. Stonewall Jackson will successfully tie up these Union troops for two months.

April 6–7 Battle of Shiloh (Pittsburg Landing, Tennessee). Confederate forces under General Albert S. Johnston (1803–62) attack Grant's army. Union forces are nearly defeated, but reinforcements arrive and drive off the Confederate army. Losses are staggering: 20,000 Union and Confederate soldiers are killed or wounded in the two days of fighting; the combined losses are more than the total American casualties in the Revolution, the War of 1812, and the Mexican War put together.

April 16 President Jefferson Davis signs the Confederate Conscription Act, the first military draft in American history.

April 25 The important port city of New Orleans, Louisiana, surrenders to Union Flag Officer David Farragut. Pushing north on the Mississippi River, Farragut captures Natchez, Mississippi, on May 12.

May 4–14 In Virginia, McClellan's army takes Yorktown, Williamsburg, and the White House, only twenty miles from Richmond. But in spite of his numerical superiority, the overcautious McClellan halts to await reinforcements instead of pressing the offensive.

June 2   Robert E. Lee takes command of the Confederate Armies of Northern Virginia.

June 6   Memphis, Tennessee, falls to Union forces.

June 25–July 2   The Seven Days' Battles. Lee attacks McClellan and eventually drives him away from Richmond. The Peninsular Campaign, which might have captured Richmond and ended the war, is over.

July   Congress passes a second Confiscation Act that frees the slaves of all rebels. It also authorizes the acceptance of black recruits.

August 9   Battle of Cedar Mountain (Virginia). Confederate forces under Stonewall Jackson defeat Union troops.

August 30   Second Battle of Bull Run (Second Manassas). Confederate generals Lee, Jackson, and James Longstreet (1821–1904) defeat Union forces under General John Pope (1822–92), forcing Union troops to evacuate all the way back to Washington. In less than a month, Lee has pushed two Union armies twice the size of his from the gates of Richmond all the way back to the Union capital. Pope is sacked and McClellan is reinstated. Pope is sent west to Minnesota to quell an Indian uprising there.

September 17   Battle of Antietam (Sharpsburg, Maryland). With Pope's retreat, Lee takes the offensive, but in one of those small moments that alter history, a copy of his orders falls into Union hands, allowing McClellan to anticipate Lee's strategy. In the single bloodiest day of the war, McClellan's Union forces meet Lee's advancing army. The dead and wounded exceed 10,000 for both sides. Lee pulls back, his invasion blunted, but McClellan fails to pursue the retreating Confederate army. The battle is a critical turning point. With Lee's offensive stalled, the likelihood of European recognition of the Confederacy is sharply reduced.

September 22   With the Union success at Antietam, Lincoln feels he can issue the Emancipation Proclamation from a position of strength. The proclamation is published in northern newspapers the following day.

By itself, the Emancipation Proclamation doesn't free a single slave, but does change the character and course of the war. Lincoln's contemporary critics and cynical modern historians point to the fact that Lincoln freed only the slaves of the Confederacy, not those in border states or territories retaken by Union forces; as one newspaper of the day comments, "The principle is not that a human being cannot justly own another, but that he cannot own him unless he is loyal to the United States."

Lincoln's position is that under his war powers he can legally free only those slaves in rebel-held territory; it is up to Congress or the states to address the question of universal emancipation. But abolitionist voices, such as Frederick Douglass and William Lloyd Garrison, welcome Lincoln's decision.

In the Confederacy, of course, the proclamation simply seems to confirm what secessionists have always believed: that Lincoln plans to force them to surrender slavery, a right they believe to be theirs, constitutionally granted and protected. They also see the proclamation as an incitement to slave rebellion, and stiffen their resolve to defend the South against Yankee encroachment.

The proclamation produces two other immediate results. First, because of it, France and England end a tense diplomatic dance, finally resolving not to recognize the Confederacy. To do so would endorse slavery, which is illegal and politically unpopular in both countries. Second, in the North, the proclamation has the effect of making the war considerably less popular. White workers, who were volunteering freely when the cause was the Union's preservation, are less interested in freeing slaves who they think will overrun the North, taking jobs and creating social havoc. The serious decline in enlistments forces passage of the Conscription Act in March 1863, which applies to all men between twenty and forty-five—unless they are wealthy enough to pay a substitute—and later leads to violent anticonscription reaction.

November 5 Annoyed that McClellan did not follow Lee after Antietam, Lincoln relieves him as the head of the Army of the

Potomac and he is replaced by Ambrose Burnside, with disastrous results. General Burnside (1824–81) had enjoyed early successes in devising an amphibious assault on the North Carolina coastline, but when it comes to command of the entire army, even Burnside feels he is out of his depth. He will soon be proved correct. McClellan returns to New Jersey and does not command again, but he will run against Lincoln in 1864.

December 13   Battle of Fredericksburg (Virginia). Despite an overwhelming numerical advantage, General Burnside's Union troops are routed by Lee with severe casualties, losing 12,000 to the Confederates' 5,000.

"IN GOD WE TRUST"

The motto was added to money in 1862 under the Legal Tender Act by Salmon Chase. Lincoln's secretary of the treasury, Chase was a devout Epsicopalian and abolitionist who sang hymns as he bathed. These "greenbacks" were the first federal paper money. (Previously states had issued paper currency.) Although no politician would dare to contest these words today, one popular American president later wanted to do away with the words. Theodore Roosevelt, as religiously moral and Christian-minded as any president America has ever seen, wanted to remove the slogan for seemingly opposite viewpoints. As a constitutional conservative, he believed that the words were unconstitutional in that they established a religion in opposition to the First Amendment. As a very devout Christian, Teddy Roosevelt also believed putting God on the money was a sacrilege.

1863

January 1   The Emancipation Proclamation is formally issued. The proclamation frees only those slaves in rebel states with the exception of some counties and parishes already under Union control. In England, the news is greeted by mass rallies that celebrate emancipation.

January 3 Battle of Murfreesboro (or Stone River, Tennessee). The Union advance toward Chattanooga, a southern rail center, is checked after a costly draw.

January 4 Grant is ordered by Lincoln to repeal his General Order Number 11, which had expelled Jews from his area of operations. Grant had issued the order because he thought that most of the merchants following his army and charging excessive prices were Jewish. (He was incorrect.)

January 25 The hapless General Burnside is replaced as head of the Army of the Potomac by General Joseph Hooker (1814–79). Despite his failure as a military leader, Burnside earns historical notoriety for his bushy "muttonchop" facial hair, which will come to be called, in a reversal of his name, "sideburns."

January 26 The secretary of war authorizes the governor of Massachusetts to recruit black troops. While blacks fought in every previous American war, a 1792 law barred them from the army. The 54th Massachusetts Volunteers is the first black regiment recruited in the Union. Eventually, 185,000 black soldiers in the Union army will be organized into 166 all-black regiments. Nearly 70,000 black soldiers come from the states of Louisiana, Kentucky, and Tennessee. While most are pressed into support units forced into the most unpleasant tasks, and are paid less than their white counterparts, black troops are involved in numerous major engagements, and sixteen black soldiers will receive the Medal of Honor. Their impact is even greater in the navy, where one in four sailors is black; four of these will win Medals of Honor.

March 3 Lincoln signs the first Conscription Act. Enrollment is demanded of males between the ages of twenty and forty-five; substitutes can be hired or payments of $300 can be used for an exemption.

May 2–4 Battle of Chancellorsville (Virginia). In another devastating battle, losses for both sides exceed 10,000 men. Lee's army defeats Hooker's Army of the Potomac. During the fighting, Stonewall Jackson leads a daring rear-end attack, forcing the Union withdrawal. But as he returns to Confederate lines, he is mistakenly shot by a Confederate soldier and dies of pneumonia on May 10, costing the Confederates one of their most effective field generals.

May 14   Battle of Jackson (Mississippi). Union general William Tecumseh Sherman (1820–91), named at birth for the notorious Indian chief and adding the William later, defeats the Confederates under General J. E. Johnston.

May 22   General Grant, in concert with Sherman, begins the long siege of the Confederate citadel at Vicksburg, Mississippi, the key to control of the Mississippi River.

The U.S. War Department establishes the Bureau of Colored Troops to supervise recruitment and enlistment of black soldiers.

June 22   Pro-Union West Virginia, severed from Virginia, is admitted as the thirty-fifth state, with a state constitution calling for gradual emancipation.

June 24   Planning an invasion of Pennsylvania that signals a shift in southern strategy, Lee's army crosses the Potomac and heads toward Gettysburg, Pennsylvania, with the idea that a victory there will give Lee a clear road to Washington.

June 25   General George Meade (1815–72) is put in charge of the Army of the Potomac after General Hooker is removed by Lincoln for his failure to be more aggressive. Meade begins organizing his army for the coming confrontation with Lee, who has begun an invasion of the North.

July 1–3   The Battle of Gettysburg. Confederate troops in search of shoes meet up with a detachment of Union cavalry. Reinforcements are poured in. In three days of ferocious fighting that mark the final turning point in the war, the Union army takes a strong defensive position and turns back repeated Confederate assaults. Confederate losses reach 28,000 killed, wounded, or missing, a third of the army's effective strength, to the Union's 23,000. Now severely undermanned, Lee retreats to Virginia, unable to press his drive against the North. His army in tatters, Lee seems ripe for picking, and Lincoln wants the remnants of the Confederate army destroyed, ending the war. But Meade, licking his own wounds, fails to press Lee, allowing him to cross the Potomac and escape safely into Virginia.

July 4 General U. S. Grant's long siege of Vicksburg ends in victory as he demands an unconditional surrender, giving new popular meaning to his initials. More than 29,000 Confederate troops lay down their arms, and the Union now possesses complete control of the Mississippi River, effectively splitting the Confederacy in two, east from west.

July 13–16 New York's draft riots. In New York City, resentment against the Conscription Act turns into deadly rioting in which blacks are lynched. Federal troops sent from the Gettysburg battlefield eventually quell the rioting. Similar riots occur in several major northern cities, including Boston, Rutland, Vermont, and Troy, New York. The crowd's anger has two sources: the idea of fighting to free the slaves, and the unfairness of allowing the wealthy to avoid conscription by paying a substitute. In some northern counties, taxes are raised to pay for large numbers of substitutes so that residents of those counties will not have to fight. Many working-class men raise the slogan, "It's a rich man's war but a poor man's fight."

July 18 In the charge made famous by the film *Glory*, the 54th Massachusetts Volunteers assault Fort Wagner. Protecting the harbor of Charleston, South Carolina, the fort is considered nearly impregnable.

AMERICAN VOICES
LEWIS DOUGLASS, serving the 54th, writing to his
fiancée before the second charge on Fort Wagner,
describes the previous day's action:

This regiment has established its reputation as a fighting regiment, not a man flinched, though it was a trying time. Men fell all around me. A shell would explode and clear a space twenty feet. Our men would close up again, but it

> was no use—we had to retreat, which was a very hazardous undertaking. . . . My Dear girl I hope again to see you. I must bid you farewell should I be killed. Remember if I die in a good cause, I wish we had a hundred thousand colored troops—we would put an end to this war.

Lewis Douglass was one of Frederick Douglass's two sons serving in the 54th, which lost half its men in the assault. Despite the loss, the bravery of the regiment amazed many whites and encouraged more black regiments. Both of Douglass's sons survived.

August 21   While most of the war is fought between organized armies, in the western states of Kansas, Missouri, and Arkansas a cruel form of partisan war takes place, with its roots in the Bloody Kansas wars. Of these partisan guerrillas, the most vicious is William C. Quantrill, whose "raiders" include the psychopathic "Bloody Bill" Anderson, who carries his victims' scalps on his saddle, and the future outlaws Jesse James and Cole Younger. With 450 men, Quantrill raids Lawrence, Kansas, and slaughters more than 150 civilians. The following October, he commits another such raid of terror in Baxter Springs, Kansas. In 1865, Quantrill will head east, intending to assassinate Lincoln, but will be killed in Kentucky by Union soldiers in May after the war's official end.

September 19–20   The Battle of Chickamauga (Georgia). The Union armies led by Generals William Rosecrans (1819–98) and George H. Thomas (1816–70) are defeated by Confederates under General Braxton Bragg (1817–76). Once again, losses for both sides are extremely high: 16,000 Union casualties to 18,000 Confederate. The Union army retreats to Chattanooga.

October 16   Grant is given command of Union forces in the West; Grant replaces Rosecrans in Chattanooga with General George Thomas, nicknamed the Rock of Chickamauga for his heroic stand in that battle.

November 19   Dedicating a military cemetery on the notorious Pennsylvania battlefield, Lincoln delivers the Gettysburg Address, one of the immortal speeches in history. (Written in snatches over several days and completed the morning he delivered it, the speech was not written on the back of a letter, as myth has it.)

November 23–25   In a stunning assault, Grant sweeps up over mountains to drive General Bragg's Confederate forces away from Chattanooga. Tennessee is again brought under Union control. Grant's Union forces, having split the South east from west by controlling the Mississippi, can now split it horizontally with a march through Georgia to the sea that will be led by General Sherman.

December 8   Looking toward the end of the war, Lincoln offers a Proclamation of Amnesty and Reconstruction that will pardon Confederates who take an oath of loyalty.

1864

January 14   General Sherman begins his march across the South by occupying Sheridan, Mississippi. His strategy is simple—total war. Sherman either destroys or takes anything that might be used by the enemy to continue fighting. He demonstrates his planned tactics for the march ahead by burning and destroying railroads, buildings, and supplies.

March 10   His star rising after Vicksburg and Chattanooga, Grant is named commander of the Union armies, replacing General Halleck.

April 17   Grant suspends prisoner-of-war exchanges with the Confederates. His intention is to further weaken the Confederate forces. While it is effective, this strategy leads to the deaths of many Union soldiers held prisoner in overcrowded camps where food supplies are meager.

May 4   Grant begins an assault on Virginia with an army of 100,000 aimed at Lee's Virginia army.

May 5–6   Battle of the Wilderness (Virginia). During two days of inconclusive but bloody fighting, many of the wounded on both sides die when caught by brushfires ignited by gunfire in the dense woods of the battleground.

May 8–12   Battle of Spotsylvania (Virginia). Another five days of in-conclusive fighting make Grant's plan clear: a war of attrition that will wear down Lee's outnumbered, poorly fed, and ill-clothed forces.

May 13–15   In Georgia, with an army of 110,000, Sherman defeats General Johnston, but Johnston preserves his smaller army with a skillful retreat.

June 3   Battle of Cold Harbor (Virginia). Ignoring horrible losses, Grant continues to assault Lee's impregnable defenses, a ghastly mistake that Grant later admits. To date, in this campaign, Grant has suffered more than 60,000 casualties, a number equal to Lee's entire army. One southern general comments, "This is not war, this is murder." But Grant's costly strategy is accomplishing its purpose of wearing out Lee's army.

June 15–18   Grant begins the long siege of Petersburg, Virginia, recalling the tactics he used earlier against Vicksburg.

June 27   Johnston's Confederate forces turn back Sherman at Kenesaw Mountain, Georgia.

July 2–13   A year after Gettysburg, Confederate forces under General Jubal Early (1816–94) raid Maryland, heading toward Washington, D.C. With a small force, Early continues to harry Union troops in Virginia.

July 14   General Early is slowed down by Union General Lew Wallace (1827–1905). The lightly defended city of Washington is reinforced, although Early reaches the District of Columbia but then withdraws. (Later governor of New Mexico and minister to Turkey, General Wallace gains his greatest fame as the author of the novel *Ben Hur*.)

July 17   Despite his success at preserving his forces against Sherman's assault, Johnston is replaced by General John B. Hood (1831–79), who attempts to take the offensive against Sherman.

July 22   General Hood's first attack on Sherman outside Atlanta is turned back, as is a second assault six days later.

July 30 At Petersburg, General Burnside oversees the mining of Confederate fortifications. In a disastrously miscalculated explosion, his own force suffers nearly 4,000 casualties. Burnside is relieved of any command.

August 5 In a Union naval attack on the key southern port of Mobile, Alabama, Admiral David Farragut (1801–70) orders his fleet to continue to attack after mines in the harbor sink one of his ships. From the rigging of his flagship, Farragut shouts, "Damn the torpedoes. Full speed ahead!" He successfully closes the port, cutting off the South from vital supplies being smuggled in by blockade runners. Farragut is given the new rank of vice admiral, created especially for him, and ecstatic wealthy New Yorkers give him a purse of $50,000.

AMERICAN VOICES
GENERAL WILLIAM T. SHERMAN, in a letter to the
mayor and councilmen of Atlanta (September 1864):

You cannot qualify war in harsher terms than I will. War is cruelty, and you cannot refine it; and those who brought this war into our country deserve all the curses and maledictions a people can pour out. I know I had no hand in making this war, and I know I will make more sacrifices today than any of you to secure peace. But you cannot have peace and a division of our country. . . . You might as well appeal against the thunder-storm as against these terrible hardships of war. . . . The only way the people of Atlanta can hope once more to live in peace and quiet at home, is to stop the war, which can only be done by admitting that it began in error and is perpetuated in pride.

After capturing the city, Sherman gave orders for it to be evacuated and burned.

September 2 Sherman takes Atlanta after Hood's withdrawal. Much of the city is set on fire. With Atlanta and Mobile in Union hands, northern morale is lifted, providing Lincoln a much-needed boost in the coming election, in which Lincoln's chances do not look good.

September 19 and October 19   Union forces under General Philip Sheridan (1831–88) twice defeat Jubal Early's Confederates while taking heavy losses. The Confederates are driven from the Shenandoah Valley, one of their remaining supply sources.

November 8   Lincoln has been campaigning against two generals he has sacked, John C. Frémont and George McClellan. Although Frémont withdraws from the race, Lincoln wins reelection by less than a half-million popular votes, but his margin in the electoral vote is sweeping.

November 16   Sherman begins his notorious march from Atlanta to the sea at Savannah, destroying everything in his path by cutting a forty-mile-wide swath through the heart of the South, earning him the title Attila of the West in the southern press. A Confederate attempt to cut Sherman's supply lines is crushed, effectively destroying General Hood's army. Three days before Christmas, Sherman marches into Savannah unopposed, completing the horizontal bisection of the South. He sends Lincoln a telegram offering Savannah as a Christmas present. Of his march, Sherman comments, "We have devoured the land. . . . To realize what war is, one should follow our tracks."

January 15   Fort Fisher, North Carolina, falls to Union land and sea forces, closing off another southern port of supply.

January 16   Sherman's army wheels north through the Carolinas on a march as destructive as his Georgia campaign.

February 4   Robert E. Lee is named commander-in-chief of the Confederate army, accepting the post despite the seeming hopelessness of the cause.

February 17   Columbia, South Carolina, is burned; General Sherman and retreating Confederate forces are both blamed for setting the fires. A day later, Sherman occupies Charleston.

February 22   Wilmington, North Carolina, the last open southern port, falls to Union forces.

March 4   Lincoln is inaugurated for a second term.

With malice toward none, with charity for all, with firmness in the right, as God gives us to see the right, let us strive on to finish the work we are in, to bind up the nation's wounds, to care for him who shall have borne the battle and for his widow, and his orphan—to do all which may achieve and cherish a just and lasting peace among ourselves and with all nations.

April 1 The Battle of Five Forks (Virginia). In the last major battle of the war, General Sheridan throws back a Confederate assault.

April 2 Lee withdraws from Petersburg, ending the six-month siege. He advises President Jefferson Davis to leave Richmond. A day later, Union troops enter Petersburg and Richmond. Two days after that, Lincoln tours Richmond and sits in President Davis's chair.

April 8 Surrounded and facing starvation, Lee surrenders to Grant at Appomattox Court House in Virginia. At Lincoln's request, the terms of surrender are generous, and Confederate officers and men are free to go home with their horses; officers may retain their sidearms, although all other equipment must be surrendered.

April 11 In his last public address, Lincoln urges a spirit of generous conciliation during the reconstruction.

April 14 While watching a comedy at Ford's Theatre, Lincoln is shot and mortally wounded by the actor John Wilkes Booth, a Confederate sympathizer. The first president to be assassinated, Lincoln dies the following day, and Andrew Johnson, the vice president, takes the oath of office.

April 26 Booth is cornered and shot dead near Bowling Green, Virginia.

April 18 Confederate general Johnston surrenders to Sherman in North Carolina. Scattered resistance continues throughout the South for several weeks, ending in May, when Confederate general

Richard Taylor surrenders to Union general Edward R. S. Canby, and General Kirby Smith surrenders western Confederate forces.

May 10   Captured in Georgia, Jefferson Davis, presumed (incorrectly) to be a conspirator in the Lincoln assassination plot, is jailed awaiting trial. Later released on bail, he is never tried. The only southern officer executed for war crimes was Major Henry Wirz, commander of the infamous Confederate prison at Andersonville, Georgia, despite evidence showing he had tried to ease the suffering of his prisoners. In 1868, as one of his final acts in office, President Johnson grants amnesty to all southerners, including Davis, who declines to accept it.

What did the Civil War cost America?

The federal army began force reductions on April 13, 1865. According to Senate figures at the time, the Union had enlisted 2,324,516 soldiers, approximately 360,000 of whom were killed. The Confederate army peaked at about one million soldiers, with losses of some 260,000. The war cost the Union side more than $6 million and the Confederate states about half that much.

The number of war dead was equal to nearly 2 percent of the population at the time. Civilian casualties are difficult to measure, but James McPherson, the prominent Civil War historian, puts the number at more than 50,000, mostly in the South. (Using 2000 census figures of a population of some 280 million Americans, an equivalent loss today would be well more than 5.5 million dead.) Thousands more were critically wounded or disabled. A wave of syphilis, fostered by the thousands of young men who had frequented the many brothels that sprouted up in most cities during the war, was spread to many women.

But it is impossible to measure the cost in lives and dollars alone. A generation of America's "best and brightest"—the young, well-educated, and motivated Americans on both sides—died. It is impossible to calculate the loss of their intelligence, invention, and productive potential. The deep animosity—regional and racial—that had been created in the wake of the bitter war would continue to bedevil American society and politics for most of the next 150 years.

Was Abe really honest?

After George Washington, no American president—or any American historical figure—has been draped in more mythic splendor than Abraham Lincoln. The Railsplitter. The Great Emancipator. Honest Abe. Assailed in office, nearly denied the nomination to a second term, vilified by the South, and martyred in death, Lincoln eventually came to be considered this country's finest president. Was he?

Unlike other "log cabin" presidents of an earlier era, Lincoln was truly from pioneer family stock. His father was illiterate, his family dirt poor. After his mother's death, his stepmother encouraged his bookishness and introduced him to the Bible. That was important. Without self-righteousness or false piety, Lincoln was a deeply spiritual man, and he needed every ounce of spiritual reserve for the trials he faced.

Lincoln was that quintessential American hero, the self-made man—reading law on his own, winning local election, gaining the Illinois bar and election to the House in 1847. He was unquestionably tall, at six feet four. And he could tell a good story around the general store—no small asset in American politics, as another, more recent president has shown. He was also honest, generally a political liability. Newsman John G. Scripps once remarked that Lincoln was "a scrupulous teller of the truth, too exact in his notions to suit the atmosphere of Washington as it now is."

By modern American standards, Lincoln was a racist. By the standards of his day he was liberal, or, in the less polite phrase of the time, a "nigger lover." Like other presidents who have achieved greatness, Lincoln grew in office. His grudging acceptance of slavery in the states where it existed was gradually replaced by the sentiment voiced in the Gettysburg Address, a recommitment to the Jeffersonian ideal that "all men are created equal."

A melancholy man who suffered greatly, for both public and private reasons, Lincoln was faced with problems graver than those faced by any other president, and in his ability to bend the presidency to the exigencies of the day, he did things that modern presidents never could have done. While Congress was out of session, he created an army out of state militias, called up volunteers, blocked ports, and, most controversially of all, suspended the writ of habeas corpus in order to detain thousands without firm charges and due process of law. A breach of basic constitutional rights, this suspension was provided for, argued Lincoln, "in cases of rebellion or invasion."

During the war, he faced opposition from one side by so-called Radical Republicans and abolitionists for his moderation toward slavery. More dangerous opposition came from the Peace Democrats, the remnants of the northern Democratic Party who were given the name Copperheads by a newspaper because they were so poisonous. Sympathetic to the South, the Copperheads wanted to stop the war and considered Lincoln a dictator for his suspension of the writ of habeas corpus, the draft acts, and even the Emancipation Proclamation.

Lincoln surmounted these challenges, winning the reelection that cost him his life. By the time of his assassination, Lincoln had moved from resolute commander-in-chief, prosecuting the war at horrendous costs, to healing unifier. While some called him a dictator, there is little doubt that a weaker president might have failed in the most basic test of Lincoln's presidency—preserving the Union from dissolution.

Why did the Union win the war?

The simplest answer is that the Confederacy was fighting history, not just the Union. In many respects, the Confederate states fielded an eighteenth-century army to fight a nineteenth-century war against a twentieth-century power. And while the South fought ferociously, the numbers were finally too great for it.

Outmanned two to one, the Confederate armies were worn away by Grant's woeful tactics of attrition. The successful blockade of southern ports reduced supplies of munitions, food, and other necessities to the point of bringing the South to starvation. The ultimate failure of the Confederacy to gain foreign recognition further weakened its prospects. The oft-cited superiority of southern military leadership overlooks two factors: the number of these commanders, like Stonewall Jackson, who died early in the conflict; and the rise of Grant and Sherman in the western war against the less brilliant Confederate commanders there. When Grant gained command of the army and Sherman began his march, their willingness to wage total war, matched with the manufacturing strength, wealth, and great population advantage of the North, simply proved too much for the South.

In retrospect, it was a war that also turned on a number of small moments, the speculative "ifs" that make history so fascinating. At a number of turning points, small things, as well as larger strategic decisions, might have changed the course of the war.

If McClellan hadn't been given Lee's battle plans at Antietam . . .

If Lee had listened to Longstreet at Gettysburg and attempted to outflank the Union troops . . .

If the 20th Maine hadn't pushed back a rebel assault at Gettysburg with a bayonet charge . . .

The speculation is interesting but ultimately useless, because it didn't happen that way, and any of those changes might simply have prolonged the inevitable.

Who killed Lincoln?

On Friday, April 14, 1865—Good Friday—Lincoln met with his cabinet and then lifted the blockade of the South. His mood was high in those days, and he was preaching moderation and reconciliation to all around him, preparing a moderate plan of reconstruction that would bring the rebellious states back into the Union fold with a minimum of recriminations and punishment. That evening he took his wife and a young couple they knew to see a play called *Our American Cousin* at Ford's Theatre in downtown Washington. The Washington policeman guarding the president left his post, either for a drink or to get a better view of the play. There was a pistol shot. Lincoln slumped over. A man jumped from the president's box to the stage, in the process catching his spur on the bunting that draped the box and breaking his shin. He brandished his gun and shouted either "*Sic semper tyrannis!*" ("Thus be it ever to tyrants.") or "The South shall live." Then he escaped through a back exit to a waiting horse.

A second assassin had assaulted Secretary of State William Seward at home with a knife. Attacks on General Grant and vice president Johnson were planned but never carried out. Lincoln was taken to a lodging house across the street from the theater, where he died the next morning, throwing the shocked nation into a profound grief of a kind it had never experienced before. Hated and derided during the war years by the Copperheads, Radical Republicans who thought him too moderate, and a host of other groups who found fault with him for one reason or another, Abraham Lincoln had become, in death, a hero of the entire nation. Even leaders of the Confederacy spoke of his death with regret.

Secretary of War Stanton took charge, and martial law was announced in Washington. The assassin, it was soon discovered, was John Wilkes Booth, an actor like his more famous father, Junius Brutus Booth, and his brother Edwin Booth. A fanatical supporter of the South—though he never joined the Confederate army—Booth first plotted with a small group of conspirators in a Washington boardinghouse to kidnap Lincoln. Then he planned instead to assassinate the president along with other key government figures.

An intensive, unprecedented manhunt followed in which a $50,000 reward was placed on Booth's head and hundreds of people with any connection to the actor were arrested. Booth was finally trapped in a Bowling Green, Virginia, tobacco-drying barn on April 26 after the Union army was tipped off to his whereabouts. After Booth refused to surrender, the barn was set afire by a Union officer. Limping from his broken leg, Booth moved toward the barn door and was shot. He lived another two and a half hours; it was his twenty-seventh birthday.

A military tribunal sentenced four other captured conspirators, including boardinghouse owner Mary Surratt, to be hanged. Although conspiracy theories involving Jefferson Davis and most other prominent leaders of the Confederacy abounded in the press, they were all dismissed and disproven. Davis was captured and held for two years without trial, but eventually released to go home to write his version of events in the war. (Another more farfetched conspiracy theory had Secretary of War Stanton plotting Lincoln's death, but it is completely unsupported by evidence.)

Must Read: *April 1865: The Month That Saved America* by Jay Winik.

AMERICAN VOICES
"O Captain! My Captain!" by WALT WHITMAN
(from *Memories of President Lincoln*):

*O Captain! my Captain! our fearful trip is
 done,*
*The ship has weather'd every rack, the prize we
 sought is won,*
*The port is near, the bells I hear, the people all
 exulting,*
*While follow eyes the steady keel, the vessel
 grim and daring;*
But O heart! heart! heart!
O the bleeding drops of red,
Where on the deck my Captain lies,
Fallen cold and dead.

Born on Long Island, New York, Walt Whitman (1819–92) was a self-educated son of a house builder. He learned the printing trade and edited newspapers in New York and Brooklyn between 1838 and 1855, the year in which produced the 12-poem first edition of *Leaves of Grass*. (By the time of his death, it included more than 350 poems.) Now considered a classic of original American literature, it was not thought so in antebellum America. Reviewers were shocked by his references to anatomy and "body electric."

During the Civil War, he served as a "wound dresser," or nurse, to soldiers in Union hospitals and camps, and his prose reports of the carnage he witnessed are extraordinary accounts of the suffering. In addition to "O Captain," which the public liked but critics did not, Whitman wrote "When Lilacs Last in the Dooryard Bloom'd," and two other elegies to the dead Lincoln.

"I have not gained acceptance in my own times," he said himself before his death following a series of crippling strokes. But he would eventually be recognized as one of the greatest and most original of America's poetic voices.

What was Reconstruction?

In the aftermath of the war, the southern states were devastated—physically, economically, even spiritually. The postwar South, it has been said, was worse off than Europe after either of the twentieth-century world wars. Provisional military governors were established in the rebellious states, but Lincoln's plans for restoring the secession states to full membership in the Union were moderate and reconciliatory. Southerners could become citizens once more by taking a simple loyalty oath. When 10 percent of the citizens of a state had taken the oath, the state could set up a government. Radical Republicans, led by Thaddeus Stevens of Pennsylvania, Ben Wade of Ohio, and Charles Sumner of Massachusetts, wanted stricter terms, and the situation was at a standstill when Lincoln died and was succeeded by Andrew Johnson (1808–75).

Johnson's life was an incredible American success story. Born in Raleigh, North Carolina, perhaps even poorer than Lincoln, Johnson was the son of a hotel porter who died when the boy was three. He never attended school, and the impoverished Johnson family indentured him to a tailor, at nine years old. He ran away six years later and set up his own tailor shop in Greenville, Tennessee, at age seventeen. At eighteen, he married his sixteen-year-old wife, Eliza, and she later taught him to read, write, and do mathematics more effectively. He entered politics on a local level and devoted his energy to the free laboring class. Although he held slaves, he had no love for the South's planter elite. A Jackson Democrat, he served as a U.S. representative, Tennessee's governor, and senator from Tennessee, where he was one of the architects of the Homestead Act, which granted free public land to settlers. He campaigned for the Democratic presidential nomination in 1860, but he stayed loyal to the Union after Lincoln's election, the only senator from a seceding state to remain in Congress, proclaiming in 1861, "Show me the man who makes war on the government, and fires on its vessels, and I will show you a traitor." In 1862, he was appointed military governor of Tennessee, and in 1864, Lincoln saw Johnson as a "war Democrat," a loyal southerner who would help win votes in the border states. The choice was not widely applauded by northern Republicans. "To think that one frail life stands between this insolent, clownish creature and the presidency! May God bless and spare Abraham Lincoln," said the *New York World* in 1865. Johnson did not help his cause when, because of an extreme case of the nerves, he had a few too many whiskeys before he was sworn in as Lincoln's vice president, resulting in a rambling, drunken speech. One of the co-conspirators in the Lincoln assassination, George Atzerodt, had been assigned to target Johnson, and he stalked the vice president, but his courage failed at the last minute.

As president after Lincoln's assassination, Johnson favored Lincoln's moderate approach to what he called "restoration," which would readmit states after they had ratified the Thirteenth Amendment, abolishing slavery, which had been passed in December 1865. But Johnson would butt heads with the Radical Republicans, who not only wanted retribution but wanted to maintain the control of Congress they had enjoyed during the war years, when Democrats, mostly southerners, were missing from Congress.

As the southern states gradually returned to the fold, they antagonized northerners by returning to Congress the leadership of the Confederacy, and by passing so-called Black Codes, meant to control former slaves. Obviously designed to circumvent the Thirteenth Amendment, the codes outraged the Republicans, who formed a Committee of Reconstruction that soon heard tales of violence and cruelty toward freed slaves. Congress established a Freedmen's Bureau aimed at helping the approximately four million freed slaves, and then passed the Civil Rights Act of 1866, which declared blacks citizens and denied states the power to restrict their rights. Johnson vetoed the bill, but the Republicans had the votes to override the veto, for the first time in American history. Johnson was left weaker than ever. This override was a symbol of strength, giving Congress the upper hand in the power struggle that followed the war and leading to passage of a series of Reconstruction Acts.

The first of these acts divided the South into military regions under the control of generals. Unlike Lincoln's proposed plan, statehood could only be attained by adopting a state constitution allowing blacks to vote, and by accepting the Fourteenth Amendment, which extended citizenship to blacks and provided for punishment of any state that denied the vote to any of its adult male citizens. (This still fell shy of barring race as a voting qualification, and women and Indians were still left on the outside looking in.)

Who celebrates Decoration Day and Juneteenth?

On May 1, 1865, a northern abolitionist named James Redpath, who had come to Charleston, South Carolina, to organize schools for freed slaves, led black children to a cemetery for Union soldiers killed in the fighting nearby to scatter flowers on their graves. According to legend, southern women had begun to do the same thing to the graves of fallen Confederate soldiers. This was the beginning of the tradition of Decoration Day, as it was known, a ceremony to honor the fallen of the war. Several towns wanted to lay claim to what would become known as Memorial Day, and Waterloo, New York, was granted the official distinction by Congress for its ceremony on May 5, 1866.

In 1866, Congress created national military cemeteries, foremost of them in Arlington, on the land confiscated from the family of Robert E. Lee. In 1866, the tradition gained new importance when General John Logan founded the Grand Army of the Republic, a powerful veterans' organization. Logan ordered all GAR posts to decorate graves on May 30. By 1873, New York had made Memorial Day a legal holiday, and every northern state soon followed suit.

But the bitterness of the war carried over even into these solemn ceremonies. In the early days of these ceremonies, the division between North and South remained stark. In the South, women formed Ladies Memorial Associations with the purpose of disinterring soldiers in distant graves and reburying them nearer their homes. Their efforts led to Confederate Memorial Days, which varied in date from April to late May throughout the South. By the 1890s, the United Daughters of the Confederacy had taken over the task. In Arlington Cemetery in 1869, guards were placed around a handful of Confederate graves to prevent them from being decorated. Southern states kept separate memorial days, considering May 30 a "Yankee" holiday. And in 1876, a bill making the date a national holiday was defeated. (By the early twentieth century, as most veterans of the Civil War were dead, the tradition was fading. But following the two world wars, veterans' groups successfully lobbied for a national holiday on May 30 to honor the dead in all America's wars. In 1968, Memorial Day was made one of five "Monday" holidays, and many people simply think of it as the first official weekend of the summer vacation season now.)

At around the same time that Decoration Day ceremonies were flowering with much official support, another more grassroots tradition was taking hold. But it has yet to achieve national recognition. On June 19, 1865, Union general Gordon Granger informed slaves in the area from the Gulf of Mexico to Galveston, Texas, that they were free. Lincoln had officially issued the Emancipation Proclamation on January 1, 1863, but it had taken two more years of Union victories to end the war and for this news to reach slaves in remote sections of the country. According to folk traditions, many of the newly freed slaves celebrated the news with ecstasy. Many of them began to travel to other states in search of family members who had been separated from them by slave sales.

That spontaneous celebration—commonly called Juneteenth—has become an unofficial holiday celebrating emancipation in many parts of the United States.

Why was President Johnson impeached?

As the first president to take office after an assassination, Johnson encountered his next unfortunate first when he became the first president to be impeached. Under Article II, Section 4 of the Constitution, "the President, Vice-President, and all civil officers of the United States, shall be removed from office on impeachment for, and conviction of, treason, bribery, or other high crimes and misdemeanors."

What were Johnson's "high crimes and misdemeanors"? Ostensibly the issue was a law that Congress called the Tenure of Office Act, which prohibited the president from dismissing any official who had been appointed with Senate consent without first obtaining Senate approval. Challenging the law's constitutionality, Johnson tried to dismiss War Secretary Edwin M. Stanton, an ally of the Radical Republicans. The House promptly impeached him.

The equivalent of a grand jury indictment, Johnson's impeachment meant he would be tried before the Republican-controlled Senate, with Chief Justice Salmon P. Chase presiding. Under the guise of constitutional law, this was a blatant partisan attempt by Congress to fundamentally alter the system of checks and balances. And it came remarkably close to success. On May 16, 1868, the Senate voted 35–19 in favor of conviction, but that fell one vote short of the two-thirds needed for removal of the president.

Four days later, Ulysses S. Grant was nominated by the Republicans to run for the presidency. To face the hero of the war, the Democrats chose Horatio Seymour of New York instead of the incumbent Johnson. For the remainder of his administration, Johnson was politically crippled, and the Republican Congress pressed forward with its more aggressive Reconstruction plan strengthened.

After unsuccessful tries for the Senate and House, Johnson returned to the Senate in 1875, the only former president to serve in the Senate. He survived a cholera epidemic but was never completely well again. He suffered a series of strokes and died in office a few months later. A champion of religious freedom who resented the practice of selling church pews to the wealthy, he had a Masonic funeral and was buried wrapped in an American flag with a copy of the Constitution beneath his head.

Who were the carpetbaggers?

The era of Reconstruction would prove to be a very mixed bag. Northern philanthropists opened or revitalized what would become the leading colleges of the South. More significantly, Reconstruction produced the first—albeit limited—black political power in the nation's history. Indeed, Ulysses Grant's margin in the popular ballot was based on the large black vote that turned out in his favor. Republican legislators who saw the full impact of the black vote rushed to provide for black suffrage with the Fifteenth Amendment, which would bar race as a condition for voting. The simple idea that blacks had any political power just a few years after they were released from slavery and declared citizens was an extraordinary achievement, if not a revolutionary one.

The underside of this achievement was the corruption of power the period produced, and the backlash it created among whites. Largely uneducated and illiterate, the newly freed blacks were ill prepared for the intricacies of constitutional government. They were ripe for exploitation by whites, some of whom came from the North and were called carpetbaggers because they traveled with all their possessions carried in a carpetbag, a type of soft luggage made of carpet material.

The traditional view has been that these carpetbaggers were charlatans who wanted to acquire power by using black votes to gain office. One such northerner was George Spencer, who made money with contraband cotton and later served in the Senate. Yet the historian Eric Foner dismisses the myth of the carpetbagger in his massive study of the period, *Reconstruction*. Rather than low-class manipulators, Foner demonstrates that many of those northerners who moved to the South were middle-class professionals who saw the South as a means for personal advancement and opportunity, just as others went west after the war. Of the so-called carpetbaggers, argues Foner, quite a few were idealists who had moved south before blacks got the vote.

Another maligned class was the "scalawag," the southern-born white Republican, even more hated than carpetbaggers by southern Democrats, because they were seen as traitors to both race and region. Again, Foner says, the traditional view of the scalawags as corrupt profiteers exploiting illiterate blacks reflects more postwar antagonism than political reality.

Reconstruction, in the strict political sense of the word, had little to do with the physical rebuilding of the South. Emancipation had undone slavery, which had been the keystone of the southern economy. Now that four million slaves were free, what exactly were they free to do? Senator Thad Stevens, one of the Radical Republicans, proposed breaking up the largest plantations in the South and providing slaves with "forty acres and a mule." But even the most progressive thinkers of the day still believed property was sacred, and the plan went nowhere. Confusion reigned as many freedmen moved to the towns, looking for work that didn't exist. The Southern Homestead Act of 1867, which was supposed to open up public lands in the South to blacks and whites loyal to the Union, failed because the poor didn't have even the small amount needed to buy the land. Instead, most of the land went to big speculators, lumber companies, and large plantation owners.

A gap between intent and reality quickly arose, and the sharecropping system was developed to fill that gap. It was essentially slavery under a new face. Now free blacks worked the land as tenant farmers, splitting the crop with the owner, who also provided the seed and supplies at a price he set, payable in crops. Somehow the sharecroppers never seemed to earn enough to pay off their debts to the landowners.

Another problem was capital. With the end of the war, the West again beckoned to expansionists, and northern banks were sending money west to be spent on building railroads. Without hard cash to finance rebuilding, it was difficult for the South to sustain the growth it needed. Some manufacturing centers slowly came to life, especially around the coal-rich region of Birmingham, Alabama, where steel mills grew, but their development was insignificant compared with the outburst of industrial and railroad growth in the North and West. The fact that Republicans controlled the politics and the banks created a deep distrust and hatred of Republicanism that sent white southerners scrambling for the Democratic Party. By 1877, most southern governments were back in conservative, white, Democratic hands. Those hands kept the South Democratic until Richard Nixon and Ronald Reagan were able to tap the region's underlying conservatism in the 1970s and 1980s.

An even more fearful outgrowth of the white backlash to Reconstruction came about as antagonized whites of the South, bitter over their losses, looked for new means of acquiring power. To a large class of white southerners, the idea of blacks in politics, and even controlling southern state legislatures, was simply unacceptable. The need to combat black political power gave rise to secret paramilitary societies dedicated to maintaining white supremacy. Some had names like the Knights of the White Camellia and the Pale Faces, but the most notorious, powerful, and ultimately long-lived was the Ku Klux Klan, which first met in Nashville's Maxwell House in April 1867.

Organized by former commanders, soldiers, and leaders of the Confederacy as well as southern churchmen, and using a combination of mystical talk, claims of being ghosts of dead Confederate soldiers—hence the white sheets—and outright terror tactics, the Klan gained enormous power in the postwar South. Through lynchings, beatings, burnings, and other forms of political terrorism, it successfully intimidated both blacks and "liberal" white Republicans. As Lerone Bennet eloquently puts it in *Before the Mayflower,* "The plan: reduce blacks to political impotence. How? By the boldest and most ruthless political operation in American history. By stealth and murder, by economic intimidation and political assassinations, by the political use of terror, by the braining of the baby in its mother's arms, the slaying of the husband at his wife's feet, the raping of the wife before the husband's eyes. By fear."

Northern outrage over these injustices quickly faded as the nation busied itself with other concerns, like the spread westward. The reforms of the Reconstruction Acts, whether truly well intentioned or powered purely by political ambition, faded as the nation turned its attention to building an empire in the West and coping with a depression, so often the aftermath of wartime economies, that followed another stock market panic in 1873.

On balance, the era of Reconstruction created some opportunities, but fell far short of the lofty goals of true freedom for blacks in the South, as the near future would so oppressively prove.

AMERICAN VOICES

CHIEF JUSTICE SALMON P. CHASE, writing for the majority in the case of *Texas v. White* (1869):

> The Constitution, in all its provisions, looks to an indestructible union, composed of indestructible States. . . . Considered therefore as transactions under the Constitution, the Ordinance of Secession, adopted by the convention and ratified by a majority of the citizens of Texas, and all the Acts of her Legislature intended to give effect to that ordinance were absolutely null. They were utterly without operation on law. . . . Our conclusion therefore is that Texas continued to be a State, a State of the Union, notwithstanding the transactions to which we have referred.

This postwar decision, involving the payment of U.S. Treasury bonds, made it clear that secession was unconstitutional.

CHAPTER FIVE

WHEN MONOPOLY WASN'T A GAME

The Growing Empire from the Wild West to World War I

What happened at Custer's Last Stand?

What happened at Wounded Knee?

Who were the cowboys?

Who were the robber barons?

Of what was William Tweed boss?

What happened at Haymarket Square?

Who were the Populists?

What was the Cross of Gold?

What did "separate but equal" mean?

Who was Jim Crow?

Who fought in the Spanish-American War?

In thirty-five years, from the Civil War's end to the twentieth century, America moved with astonishing speed from a war-torn nation of farmers to an industrial empire holding far-flung possessions. By the end of the First World War in 1918, the United States stood among the first rank of global powers.

Powering this dynamic growth was a lightning bolt of industrial development that spread railroads, built steel mills, and opened oil fields. This industrial surge was joined to a simultaneous explosion of practical invention, best exemplified by names that are now familiar parts of the American vocabulary: Edison, Bell, Westinghouse, Wright, and Pullman.

But progress carries a price tag. It was, as Mark Twain and Charles Dudley Warner titled their collaborative novel about this era, *The Gilded Age*: beautiful on the surface, but cheap, base, and tarnished underneath. For every mile of railroad laid, every ton of coal or iron ore mined, thousands of workers died. Many of them were immigrants or war veterans, miserably underpaid, working in unsafe and unsanitary conditions, with little or no political voice. The new fortunes being made opened up an era of astonishing corruption. The outlaws of the Wild West were small-time hoodlums compared with the politicians of New York and Washington, who brazenly bilked millions, and to the millionaire industrialists who kept these politicians in their pockets.

Since the Revolution, the American political process had opened up through agonizingly slow reforms, but power remained in the tight grip of the few. That was what the Founders had envisioned: a nation ruled by an enlightened aristocracy comprising gentlemen with the leisure and education to debate issues and rule judiciously. But in this period of a growing empire, more than ever before, the keys to government were pocketed by the powerful and wealthy, the great industrial and banking magnates who literally owned the government and turned it to their personal enrichment. It was what Alexander Hamilton might have had in mind when the Constitution was being debated, and it was light-years away from the agrarian republic that Jefferson envisioned.

The new industrialists were America's Medici, and they dictated

American policies as surely as those Italian bankers had owned popes and principalities. Viewed beside Morgan, Gould, Rockefeller, and Carnegie, the postwar presidents in office were either weak, inept, or corrupt. Not until the rise of Theodore Roosevelt—himself the scion of a wealthy family and certainly no liberal in the modern sense of the word—would the White House be powerful enough to challenge these merchant princes.

Pitted against them were the powerless. Immigrant laborers dying in the deserts and mountains as the railroad inched across the West. The urban poor working the factories and only slowly acquiring power through the unions that were fought with the deadly force of state militias and federal troops. Homesteaders who lost out to the railroad czars and cattle barons in incredible land grabs. Women filling the sweatshops of the swelling cities, yet still invisible on Election Day. And the Indians, last remnants of the millions in America when Columbus arrived. It was the subjugation of the few unconquered tribes that opened this era, but they did not go gently to their deaths.

AMERICAN VOICES
GENERAL WILLIAM TECUMSEH SHERMAN, 1867:

The more Indians we can kill this year, the less will have to be killed the next war, for the more I see of these Indians, the more convinced I am that they all have to be killed or be maintained as a species of paupers.

CHIEF GALL, a leader of the Hunkpapa Sioux warriors at Little Bighorn:

If you had a country which was very valuable, which had always belonged to your people . . . and men of another race came to take it away by force, what would your people do? Would they fight?

What happened at Custer's Last Stand?

The most famous Indian battle in American history was a final flourish to the Indians' hopelessly valiant war dance. The battle itself was simply the result of the actions of one vain, headstrong—some have suggested mad—soldier, George Armstrong Custer. The Indian victory at the Little Bighorn merely hastened the inevitable: the brutal end of Indian resistance and extinction for their singular way of life.

While the white men wearing blue and gray uniforms fought one another to the death, there were about 300,000 American Indians left in the West. They had been pushed and pressed inward from both coasts by the War of 1812, Manifest Destiny, the Mexican War, the California and Colorado gold rushes, and all the other reasons that whites had for stripping the Indians of their hunting lands. The "permanent Indian frontier" pledged by Andrew Jackson during the removals earlier in the century had long been breached by private and public enterprises, as had every treaty in the sad history of the Indians. When the Civil War ended, the politicians, prospectors, farmers, railroad builders, and cattlemen were ready to take up where they had left off when the war interrupted.

The most powerful and numerous of the surviving tribes were the Sioux, divided into several smaller groupings: the Santee Sioux of western Minnesota, who had tried to accept white ways; the Teton Sioux, those extraordinary horse warriors of the Great Plains, led by the Oglala chief Red Cloud; the Hunkpapa, who would produce Sitting Bull and Crazy Horse; and the Tetons' allies, the Cheyenne of Wyoming and Colorado. Farther south were other tribes: the Arapaho of Colorado; the Comanche of Texas; the Apache, Navajo, and Pueblo of New Mexico.

For twenty-five years, from 1866 to 1891, the United States army fought a continuous war against these Indian tribes at considerable cost in lives and money. The final thrust began when the Sioux balked at the opening of the Bozeman Trail, a route to the gold fields of California that passed through Indian territory in Montana. Under Red Cloud, the Sioux attacked, destroying the forts that the army was trying to build along the trail. A treaty in 1867 ended this phase of the fighting, but it would get worse. Herded onto small reservations overseen by the scandalously corrupt Bureau of Indian Affairs, the Indians attempted to live under the white man's rules.

Gold again proved the undoing of any hope for peace. Trespassers on the Indian reservations in South Dakota's Black Hills, led by Custer himself, found gold, and there was soon a rush into the territory. The Indians were ordered off the land, but decided to go on the warpath instead. Joined by the Cheyenne, the Sioux concentrated their strength in the Bighorn River region of southern Montana. In the summer of 1876, setting out against specific orders to refrain from attacking, Custer led his 250 men in a direct frontal assault, ignoring warnings that from 2,000 to 4,000 Indians awaited his attack. Sitting Bull, the spiritual leader of the Sioux, had dreamed of a victory over the soldiers, but had performed a "Sun Dance" just before the battle and was too weak to fight. Led by Crazy Horse and another chief, Gall, the Indians destroyed Custer's force to the last soldier, allowing only a half-Indian scout to escape from the Battle of the Little Bighorn on June 25, 1876.

Of course, it didn't read that way in the newspapers back East. In the midst of the nation's Centennial celebrations, an outraged nation read only of a massacre of brave soldiers by bloodthirsty Indians. The romanticized reports of "Custer's Last Stand," and a famous painting of the scene, provoked a furious popular and political reaction, demanding total warfare on the Sioux. The army's response was savage, and half of the United States army was sent to exact revenge. The remnants of the Sioux tribe were hunted down, their camps wiped out, forcing them onto reservations. In May 1877, Crazy Horse led some of the last free Sioux into the Red Cloud reservation to surrender. Sitting Bull took the Hunkpapa into Canada, where a government agent allowed them to live and hunt freely. In September 1877, thirty-five-year-old Crazy Horse was arrested under the guise of a meeting with General Crook of the U.S. Army. Seeing that he was about to be taken captive, the war chief resisted, was bayoneted by a soldier, and died.

After the Sioux wars came the great mopping-up battles in the Northwest, against Chief Joseph of the Nez Perce, and in the Southwest, against Geronimo and his Apache. Captured in 1886, the ferocious chieftain Geronimo was displayed at the St. Louis World's Fair, where he sold his picture postcard for a quarter.

From the last words of CRAZY HORSE (1877):

We had buffalo for food, and their hides for clothing and for our teepees. We preferred hunting to a life of idleness on the reservation, where we were driven against our will. At times we did not get enough to eat, and we were not allowed to leave the reservation to hunt.

We preferred our own way of living. We were no expense to the government. All we wanted was peace and to be left alone. Soldiers were sent out in the winter, who destroyed our villages.

Then "Long Hair" [Custer] came in the same way. They say we massacred him, but he would have done the same thing to us had we not defended ourselves and fought to the last. Our first impulse was to escape with our squaws and papooses, but we were so hemmed in that we had to fight.

What happened at Wounded Knee?

The Little Bighorn had proved a costly victory for the Indians, only hastening the inevitable. Their subsequent battles against federal troops were all disastrous, as one Indian leader after another was captured or killed, and surviving bands were forced onto reservations. But in spite of the odds, some Indians refused to submit, leading to the last resistance movement of the nineteenth century and a notorious massacre that truly marked the end of the era of the Indian wars.

In 1888, a Paiute Indian named Wovoka spawned a religious movement called the Ghost Dance. Ghost Dancers believed that the world would soon end and that the Indians, including the dead of the past, would inherit the earth. Wovoka preached harmony among Indians and rejection of all things white, especially alcohol. The religion took its name from a ritual in which the frenzied dancers would glimpse this future Indian paradise.

The religion quickly took hold and was widely adopted by Indians throughout the Plains, the Southwest, and the Far West. But it took on new importance when two Sioux medicine men claimed that "ghost shirts" worn by the dancers could stop white men's bullets, leading to a new militant fervor among some Indians.

Alarmed by the Ghost Dancers, the army attempted to arrest a number of Indian leaders, including the great chief Sitting Bull, who had not joined the Ghost Dancers but was then living on a reservation after touring with Buffalo Bill's Wild West show. Fearful of Sitting Bull's influence, Indian police in the hire of the government went to arrest Sitting Bull. On December 15, 1890, during a scuffle, he was killed by the Indian police sent to capture him.

Another chief named Big Foot, also sought by the army, was dying from pneumonia and wanted peace. But three days after Christmas Day in 1890, his band of some 350 women, children, and men was intercepted by an army patrol and taken to an encampment at Wounded Knee, South Dakota, on the Pine Ridge Reservation. There on the morning of December 29, 1890, as the Indians were surrendering their weapons to the soldiers, the gun of a deaf Indian named Black Coyote discharged. Whether it was accidental or deliberate is uncertain. But the soldiers immediately panicked, and turned their guns and artillery pieces on the disarmed Indians. At least 150 Indians, and probably as many as 300, died in the barrage. Wounded Knee was the Indians' "last stand."

The following twenty years would be the nadir of American Indian history, as the total Indian population between 1890 and 1910 fell to fewer than 250,000. (It was not until 1917 that Indian births exceeded deaths for the first time in more than fifty years.) But nearly facing extinction, the American Indian proved resilient if nothing else. With agonizingly slow progress, Indians gradually gained legal rights. In 1924, all native-born United States Indians were granted American citizenship. The ruling was in large measure a reaction of gratitude to the large number of Indians who fought for America during World War I, yet paternalism, discrimination, and exploitation were still commonplace.

By the time of the Great Depression (see Chapter 6), the plight of the Indians on reservations was, in the words of one government report, "deplorable." During Franklin Roosevelt's tenure, a cultural anthropologist named John Collier was appointed commissioner of Indians and proposed sweeping reforms that would recognize the right of Indian tribes to remain distinct and autonomous, with rights beyond those of other Americans. This was the so-called New Deal for Indians but it was a short-lived period of reform, replaced by the subsequent policy of "termination" under which the government sought to end the special status of Indians. As late as 1954, some states still kept Indians from voting. Yet, by the time of the 1980 census, there were some 1.5 million American Indians (including Aleuts and Eskimos), among the fastest-growing minority groups in America. As a group, however, they remain among the poorest and most unemployed Americans.

Must Read: *Bury My Heart at Wounded Knee: An American Indian History of the American West* by Dee Brown; *500 Nations: An Illustrated History of North American Indians* by Alvin M. Josephy Jr.

AMERICAN VOICES
BLACK ELK, an Oglala holy man who was present at Pine Ridge in 1890 (from *Black Elk Speaks*, as told through John G. Neihart):

I did not know then how much was ended. When I look back now from this high hill of my old age, I can still see the butchered women and children lying heaped and scattered all along the crooked gulch as plain as when I saw them with eyes still young. And I can see that something else died there in the bloody mud, and was buried in the blizzard. A people's dream died there. . . .

The nation's hoop is broken and scattered, there is no center any longer, and the sacred tree is dead.

AMERICAN VOICES
I pledge allegiance to the flag of the United States of America and to the Republic for which it stands, one Nation, indivisible, with liberty and justice for all.

Public school children first recited the pledge as they saluted the flag during the National School Celebration held in 1892 to mark the 400th anniversary of the discovery of America. The original pledge was probably written by Francis Bellamy (1855–1931), a minister and Socialist. Some scholars believe James B. Upham (1845–1905) wrote the pledge. Both men were from Boston and worked for *The Youth's Companion*. The National Flag Conferences of the American Legion expanded the original wording in 1923 and 1924.

In 1942, Congress made the pledge part of its code for the use of the flag. In 1954, during the anti-Communist fervor of the times, it added the words "under God." Bellamy, a Socialist, would never have intended those words to be used.

Who were the cowboys?

This nation, turning 100 years old, had no *Odyssey*, no St. George slaying the dragon, no Prometheus. The emerging American genius for making a lot of money was a poor substitute for King Arthur and his knights (although the Horatio Alger myth of rags to riches was good for a lot of mileage). Without a mythology and set of ancient heroes to call its own, America had to manufacture its heroes. So the mythmaking machinery of nineteenth-century American media created a suitably heroic archetype in the cowboys of the Wild West. The image was of the undaunted cattle drivers living a life of reckless individualism, braving the elements, staving off brutal Indian attacks. Or of heroic lawmen dueling with six-guns in the streets at high noon. This artificial Wild West became America's *Iliad*.

It was an image so powerful, appearing first in the newspapers and reinforced in dime novels and later through countless Hollywood movies, television series, and cigarette commercials, that it entered the American political mentality. This code of the cowboy shaped policy and presidents, perhaps most notably Teddy Roosevelt, Lyndon Johnson, and Ronald Reagan.

The heyday of the cowboy lasted approximately twenty years, from 1867 to 1887. The life wasn't as glamorous or as romantically dangerous as it has been portrayed. The modern politicians' comparison of drug-ravaged urban streets to the Wild West does a disservice to the West. The famed cow and mining towns of Tombstone, Abilene, Dodge City, and Deadwood had fewer shootouts and killings in their combined history than modern Washington, D.C., has in a few months.

The soul of the cowboy myth was the cattle drive, and it began with the famous trails out of Texas, where Spanish cattle introduced by the conquistadores later mixed with the English cattle of American settlers to produce a genetic marvel, the Texas longhorn steer. Moving north from Texas along trails like the Chisholm, charted out in 1867 by a half-Cherokee named Jesse Chisholm, the drives ended at the newly opened railheads in Kansas City and Sedalia in Missouri, Cheyenne in Wyoming, and Dodge City and Abilene in Kansas. The rowdiest of the Wild West towns, Abilene was founded by an Illinois cattleman as a railhead to meet the cattle drovers from Texas. It soon sported a boisterous barroom and brothel business that grew to meet the demand of the drovers who had just traveled from Texas over rugged terrain for several months, accompanied only by cattle who fattened themselves on the open range. The situation demanded "peacekeepers," men whose histories were often more violent than those of the people they were supposed to police. The most famous was James Butler "Wild Bill" Hickok, who shot only two people while presiding over Abilene; one of them was another policeman. But Hickok, and other western legends like Jesse James, were being brought back to easterners in newspaper reports and dime novels that made the West seem romantic and adventurous.

By the 1890s, the Wild West had already begun to fade. Cattlemen learned that the hearty steer could survive on the northern plains, killing off the need for the long drives. The advent of barbed wire in 1874 meant they were able to enclose huge areas of land (which they often didn't own, or claimed under very questionable authority). The freebooting days of the postwar period were gradually replaced by cattle raising as big business, and the era of the cowboys and Wild West outlaws ended, their place taken by a much more sinister and ornery character, the American businessman.

AMERICAN VOICES
MATTHEW JOSEPHSON, describing the Gilded Age,
in his 1934 book, *The Robber Barons*:

At Delmonico's the Silver, Gold and Diamond dinners of
the socially prominent succeeded each other unfailingly. At
one, each lady present, opening her napkin, found a gold
bracelet with the monogram of the host. At another, cigarettes rolled in hundred-dollar bills were passed around after coffee and consumed with an authentic thrill. . . . One
man gave dinner to his dog, and presented him with a diamond collar worth $15,000.

Who were the robber barons?

Wall Street's insider trading scandals and the New York City corruption high jinks of the 1980s are polite misdemeanors when viewed
against the wholesale corruption of American business and politics
during the late nineteenth century. This was the era when political
genius took a backseat to a genius expressed in accumulating and holding more private wealth and power than had been possessed in history.
One illustration of this power was the financier John P. Morgan Sr.'s
refusal to make loans to the U.S. government because it lacked collateral. In 1895, Morgan bailed out a nearly bankrupt federal government
by exchanging gold for U.S. bonds, which he promptly resold at an
enormous profit.

The accumulation of American wealth in the hands of a few was
nothing new; since colonial times a minority had held the vast majority of the nation's wealth. But the late nineteenth century brought this
concentration of wealth to unprecedented heights.

After the war, the lands of the West were opened up, cleared of Indians, and ready for the great surge. To reach these rich lands—to bring
the cattle and wheat to eastern markets to feed the factory workers who
made the tools and machinery to mine the gold, silver, and copper—
called for cheap, fast transportation. Building more railroads required
four basic components: land, labor, steel, and capital. The federal
government provided the land; immigrants on both coasts supplied

cheap labor; Andrew Carnegie provided the steel. And J. P. Morgan Sr. and Jr., the bankers' bankers, provided the cash.

With unlimited vistas of western wealth, the plan to link East and West by railroad provided equally unlimited schemes to bilk the Treasury. Corruption came to the fore with the exposure of the Crédit Mobilier scandal in 1872. Massachusetts congressman Oakes Ames was a shovel maker and one of the directors of the Union Pacific Railroad, the company taking the line westward from Nebraska. Ames and the Union Pacific created a company called Crédit Mobilier of America, which was awarded all construction contracts. The company was paid $94 million by Congress for work actually worth $44 million. Ames had smoothed the way for this deal in Washington by spreading around plenty of Crédit Mobilier shares, selling them at half their value on the New York Stock Exchange. Among those enjoying this "insider trading" were congressional leaders, including future president James A. Garfield, and President Grant's first- and second-term vice presidents, Schuyler Colfax and Henry Wilson, giving the "vice" in the title a whole new dimension.

The Central Pacific, owned by Leland Stanford, built eastward from California and did the same things, winning land grants, contracts, and enormous overpayments to Stanford's railroad-owned construction company. Stanford got away with it and eventually built a university; Ames and Representative James Brooks of New York were censured by Congress, but neither of them got a university out of the deal. Other legislators were exonerated.

Besides the enormous costs in graft, the linking of East and West by rail, completed on May 10, 1869, at Promontory Point, Utah, cost thousands of workers' lives as the lines snaked their way over mountains, across deserts, or through Indian territory, decimating the buffalo as they went to feed the workers. Workers' lives and sound construction principles were cast aside, sublimated to greed and the rush to lay track to win bonuses. Bribes were paid by towns that wanted the railroad lines to run through them, and millions of acres of land were given away to the railroads as plums.

Grant's two terms were boom times for the corruptible. Besides the Crédit Mobilier scandal, which reached into the White House, there was the Whiskey Ring scandal, which defrauded the government of millions in taxes with the assistance of the Treasury Department and Grant's personal secretary, Orville Babcock, a man with his proverbial finger in every pie. In the Bureau of Indian Affairs, corruption was equally widespread, with millions in kickbacks paid to administration officials all the way down the line, ending up with Indians on the reservation getting rotten food, when they were fed at all.

The millions made in these scandals were still small change when compared against the fortunes being made by the so-called robber barons, a phrase coined by historian Charles Francis Adams in his 1878 book, *Railroads: Their Origins and Problems.* But they raised their form of thievery to sound business organizations and called them "trusts."

For many of these men, such as Gould and Vanderbilt, the railroad was the ticket to enormous wealth. "Commodore" Cornelius Vanderbilt (1794–1877) started by building a Staten Island ferry business into a steamship empire, expanding into railroads after the war. Through graft and bribery, Vanderbilt built the New York Central into the largest single railroad line in America, passing down a vast amount of wealth to his family, who then gave new definition to "conspicuous consumption" with lavish parties at which guests dug in a trough for jewels.

Jay Gould (1836–92), one of Vanderbilt's fiercest competitors, started with the Erie railroad line in New York, but was forced out after revelations of stock watering so blatant that officials in this "anything goes" era had to step in. Gould built a large empire with small lines in the Southwest, integrating them into a regional monopoly. In 1869, Gould and James Fisk, who had made millions selling shoddy blankets to the Union through Tammany Hall (see p. 273), attempted to manipulate the gold market, which was then governed by the traders in the Gold Room of the New York Stock Exchange rather than by the U.S. government, using an unwitting President Grant for their purposes. Slow to catch on to the scheme, President Grant stopped gold sales for a time, forcing up gold prices until he realized what was going on and released $4 million in gold, driving gold prices down on "Black Friday" (September 24, 1869), causing a stock market panic that set off a depression lasting several years. (Gould was later shot dead by a former business partner in a quarrel over a shared mistress.)

With corruption and monopoly at the core of the railroad systems, and the depression unleashed by the "Black Friday" panic, the railroads were ripe for disaster. By the 1890s, many of the lines were nearly bankrupt from intense competition and poor economic conditions. In stepped John Pierpont Morgan Sr. (1837–1913). (J. P. Morgan Sr. and Jr. are often confused, because of their names, appearance, and power.)

The son of an American banker who was based in London, Pierpont Morgan had not only avoided fighting in the Civil War, but had profited handsomely from it. Pierpont financed the purchase of some obsolete carbine rifles for $3.50 apiece. Then he refinanced the purchase of the same rifles to a second man who paid $11.50 each. The weapons were updated and resold for $22 each. In a three-month period, the government had repurchased its old, altered rifles at six times the original price, and Morgan had financed the whole deal. As Ron Chernow writes in his book *The House of Morgan*, "The unarguable point is that he saw the Civil War as an occasion for profit, not service. . . . Like other well-to-do young men, Pierpont paid a stand-in $300 to take his place when he was drafted after Gettysburg—a common, if inequitable practice that contributed to draft riots in July 1863." Later during the war, when the gold market responded to war news with sharp ups and downs, Morgan tried to rig the market by shipping gold out of America.

By the turn of the century, Morgan had his hand in almost every major financial undertaking in America. His banking house was a millionaires' club that loaned money to other banks. Through Morgan, a small group of men was able to take control of the railroads of America, and by 1900, Morgan owned half of America's track mileage. His friends owned most of the rest, enabling them to set the railroad rates across the country.

In 1900 also, Morgan and steel king Andrew Carnegie (1835–1919) met at a party. Carnegie scribbled a figure, Morgan agreed, and U.S. Steel was born, the first billion-dollar corporation. Unlike Morgan, Carnegie embodied at least a portion of the rags-to-riches myth. Born in Scotland, he immigrated to the United States with his family in 1848, and first worked in a cotton factory. His rise to power was mythic, going from telegraph clerk to secretary to the head of the Pennsylvania Railroad, and later becoming a Wall Street broker selling railroad commissions. When oil was found on a property he owned, Carnegie moved into the oil industry and later into iron and steel. Using an improved steel production technique called the Bessemer method, which he had seen in England, Carnegie revolutionized steel production in the United States, and with ruthless efficiency, he set out to control the American steel market.

Carnegie and one of his managers, Henry Clay Frick, were violently anti-union. In 1892, while Carnegie was in Scotland, Frick provoked a bloody strike when he demanded a pay cut and an end to the union at his Homestead plant in Pennsylvania. When the workers refused to accept Frick's demands, he fired the entire workforce, surrounded the plant with barbed wire, and hired Pinkerton guards to protect the strikebreakers he brought in. Two barges carrying the Pinkerton guards were met by thousands of strikers and their friends and families, who kept the guards from landing, in a battle that left twenty strikers dead. Stiffening his back, Frick called on the state governor to send in 7,000 militiamen to protect the replacement workers. During the four-month confrontation, a young anarchist named Alexander Berkman—the lover of "Red Emma" Goldman (1869–1940), the most notorious anarchist leader of the day—shot Frick in the stomach, but only wounded him, and he was back in his office that day.

After the militia arrived, strike leaders were charged with murder, but all were acquitted. The plant kept producing steel with workers shipped in by railroad, and other Carnegie plants failed to join the Homestead strike, a union defeat that kept labor unorganized in Carnegie plants for years to come.

Another of the era's "giants" was John D. Rockefeller (1839–1937), a bookkeeper by training who was once hired to investigate the investment promise of oil. Rockefeller told his employers it had "no future" and then invested in it himself, buying his first refinery in 1862. With a group of partners he formed the South Improvement Company, a company so corrupt it was forced out of business. Rockefeller responded by forming Standard Oil of Cleveland in 1870. Standard bought off whole legislatures, made secret deals with railroads to obtain favorable rates, and weakened rivals through bribery and sabotage until Rockefeller could buy them out with Standard Oil stock. By 1879, Standard controlled anywhere from 90 to 98 percent of the nation's refining capacity at precisely the moment when oil's value to an industrial society was becoming apparent.

Twenty years later, Standard Oil had been transformed into a "holding company" with diversified interests, including the Chase Manhattan Bank. The key to this diversification had been the invention of the "trust" by one of Rockefeller's attorneys, Samuel C. T. Dodd, who was looking for ways around state laws governing corporations. Standard Oil, for instance, was an Ohio corporation prohibited from owning plants in other states or holding stock in out-of-state corporations. Dodd's solution was to set up a nine-man board of trustees. Instead of a corporation issuing stock, Standard Oil became a "trust" issuing "trust certificates." Through this new device, Rockefeller gobbled up the entire industry without worrying about breaking corporate antimonopoly laws. The idea was soon copied in other industries, and by the early 1890s, more than 5,000 separate companies had been organized into 300 trusts. Morgan's railroad trust, for instance, owned all but 40,000 miles of track in America.

The trusts and the enormous monopolies kept prices artificially high, prevented competition, and set wages scandalously low. They were obviously not popular among working Americans. Standard Oil became the most hated company in America. Many of these monopolies had been built through graft and government subsidies, on the backs of poorly paid workers whose attempts to organize were met with deadly force. If any vague hope for reform rested in the presidency, it was a false hope.

For a generation, beginning with Andrew Johnson's abbreviated term and the Grant years, the president almost seemed superfluous. In 1876, Rutherford B. Hayes (1822–93) became president because of a fraudulent election that stole the presidency from Democrat Samuel J. Tilden, resulting in a compromise with Southern Democrats that killed congressional Reconstruction and any hope for civil rights in the South. When Grover Cleveland (1837–1908) was elected in 1884, he named William Whitney his secretary of the navy. Whitney had married into the Standard Oil fortune and set out to build a "steel navy" by buying Carnegie steel at inflated prices.

Attempts at "reform" were mostly dogs without much bark or bite, intended to mollify a public sick of corruption. The Interstate Commerce Commission, established during Cleveland's administration to regulate railroads, was a charade for public consumption. Cleveland's successor, Benjamin Harrison (1833–1901), was a former railroad attorney who had broken railroad strikes as a soldier. During his tenure, as a reaction to public sentiment, Congress passed the Sherman Anti-Trust Act of 1890, named for Senator John Sherman, brother of General William Tecumseh Sherman, for the purpose of protecting trade against "unlawful restraints."

It was a weak law made even more puny when the Supreme Court ruled in 1895 that a company owning 98 percent of the nation's sugar-refining capacity was a manufacturing monopoly, not one of commerce, and was therefore immune to the law. During an extremely conservative, pro-business period, the high court also ruled that anti-trust laws could be used against railway strikers who were "restraining trade." This Alice in Wonderland Court took its perverse interpretations another step when it ruled that the Fourteenth Amendment, passed to guarantee the rights of freed slaves, was a protection for corporations, which the court said were "persons deserving the law's due process."

Were any honest fortunes made? Of course. As the nation spread west—at the expense largely of the vanishing Indian—incredible opportunity opened up for Americans—many of them newly arrived immigrants or their children—to prosper. But in the broad historical sweep, it is safe to say that the era—and the nation—belonged to a small group of wealthy men, in other words, a plutocracy. As conservative historian Kevin Phillips recently wrote in *Wealth and Democracy*, "The measure of the Gilded Age, beginning in the 1870s, was that by the 1890s the goliaths of U.S. business, railroading, and finance had gained de facto control over many state legislatures, the federal judiciary, and the U.S. Senate."

AMERICAN VOICES
From ANDREW CARNEGIE's article "Wealth"
(published in the *North American Review*, 1890):

The Socialist or Anarchist who seeks to overturn present conditions is to be regarded as attacking the foundation upon which civilization itself rests, for civilization took its start from the day when the capable, industrious workman said to his incompetent and lazy fellow, "If thou dost not sow, thou shalt not reap," and thus ended primitive Communism by separating the drones from the bees. One who studies this subject will soon be brought face to face with the conclusion that upon the sacredness of property civilization itself depends—the right of the laborer to his hundred dollars in the savings bank, and equally the legal right of the millionaire to his millions. . . . Not evil, but good, has come to the race from the accumulation of wealth by those who have had the ability and energy to produce it.

Of what was William Tweed boss?

In New York, quite a bit of energy and ambition were directed toward acquiring wealth. But much of it was being acquired through systematic corruption on a grand scale. The epidemic of greed didn't begin or end with Washington and the great captains of industry. It extended to the local level, perhaps most notoriously in New York, the seat of power of William Marcy Tweed (1823–78), the infamous "boss" of Tammany Hall. The word Tammany was a corruption of the name Tamanend, who was a Delaware Indian chief of the early colonial period said to be "endowed with wisdom, virtue, prudence, charity." These were qualities in conspicuously short supply in the club named for the chief.

Tammany began as one of many fraternal societies that adopted Indian names in post-Revolution days. Unlike the Society of Cincinnatus, which was reserved for Washington's officers, groups like Tammany were for the common soldier, and their political value soon became apparent to clever power brokers like Aaron Burr and Martin Van Buren. By the time of the Civil War, the clubs not only had political pull, but had become quite corrupt, serving as a conduit for government contracts to crooked suppliers who sold the Union shoddy blankets and maggot-ridden meat.

A mechanic by trade, Tweed rose to his greatest heights of power ostensibly as chief of the Department of Public Works in New York City. But that small title gave no sense of the grip he possessed on almost every facet of city life. As the leader of Tammany Hall, the New York City Democratic clubhouse, he built a simple but effective means of control. In exchange for the votes of the waves of immigrants, factory workers, disenchanted homesteaders returning to the city, and even their dead relatives, Tweed and his ring arranged small "favors"—a job, an insurance settlement. With these votes, Tweed could maneuver favorable bills through the New York legislature at will. Rich in electoral votes, New York also wielded immense political clout in presidential politics, and Tweed used this power as well. Fraudulent contracts, patronage in the highest offices, kickbacks, false vouchers—all the usual tools of corruption were raised to an art form by Tweed's Tammany Club.

Tweed's most notable opponent was the cartoonist Thomas Nast, who once received an offer of $500,000 from Tweed not to run a particular cartoon. Tweed could well afford the bribe; conservative estimates of his rape of New York's treasury ran upwards of $30 million, derived from every deal in New York, from the building of the Brooklyn Bridge to the sale of the land for Central Park.

It was only when a Tweed associate felt shortchanged that Tweed got into trouble. In 1872, Samuel Tilden (1814–80), a reform Democrat and future governor of New York who later lost the White House in an election scandal that stripped him of the electoral votes he rightfully deserved, finally won a conviction of Tweed. Sentenced to twelve years in jail, the boss escaped to Cuba and then to Spain, only to be returned by Spanish authorities despite the lack of an extradition treaty between the two countries. While in jail, Tweed made a full and damning confession, expecting immunity. But he died in prison, the only member of the ring to be convicted.

Tammany's shenanigans did not end with the breakup of the Tweed ring. Powerful "sachems" continued their hold on New York's legislature into the twentieth century. When Theodore Roosevelt entered the New York State legislature in the 1880s, Tammany's influence was still prevalent in state politics, and the club held the key votes that controlled almost all legislation.

One of the most colorful of Tammany's sachems was George Washington Plunkitt, who once instructed a newspaper reporter on the distinction between "honest" and "dishonest" graft. "There's an honest graft," said Plunkitt, "and I'm an example of how it works. I might sum up the whole thing by sayin': 'I seen my opportunities and

I took 'em.' . . . I'm tipped off, say, that they are going to lay out a new park at a certain place. . . . I go to that place and I buy up all the land I can and then there is a rush to get my land. Ain't it perfectly honest to charge a good price and make a profit on my investment and foresight? Of course, it is. Well, that's honest graft."

AMERICAN VOICES
HAMILTON S. WICKS, witness to the Great Oklahoma Land Rush (April 22, 1889):

On the morning of April 23, a city of 10,000 people, 500 houses, and innumerable tents existed where twelve hours before was nothing but a broad expanse of prairie. The new city changed its appearance every twenty-four hours, as day by day the work of construction went on. The tents were rapidly superseded by small frame structures, until at the end of a month there were scarcely any tents to be seen. The small frame structures in turn gave place to larger ones, and a number of fine two-story frame buildings were erected on the principal thoroughfares before the end of sixty days.

Wicks described the birth of the city of Guthrie, Oklahoma. Enid and Oklahoma City were also begun that day. The land rush was the result of the federal government opening up lands under the Homestead Act. Fifty thousand prospective settlers waited until noon of April 22 when the rush began and they could stake a claim to a homestead. Many other people had already jumped the gun—they would be called Sooners. The land had been opened up by confiscating territory from the Five Civilized Tribes (Cherokee, Chickasaw, Choctaw, Creek, and Seminole) who had been relocated there during the removals earlier in the nineteenth century (see Chapter 3, "What Was the Trail of Tears?"). These Indians had made the unfortunate decision to side with the Confederacy during the Civil War.

What happened at Haymarket Square?

While the wealth piled higher in the houses of Morgan and Rocke-feller, the working men and women of America fell deeper and deeper into poverty, victimized by the periodic depressions of the late nine-teenth century. The forces of labor were slow to organize, confronted by the combined power of the businessmen and banks working in league with state and federal governments. Unions also had to contend with the natural difficulties of organizing workers who did not all speak the same language and were suspicious of one another. The Irish hated the Italians. The Germans hated the Irish. They all hated the Chinese. And, of course, blacks were beyond the pale to most white workers. The idea of integrated unions was unspeakable to white workingmen, most of whom were preoccupied with fighting for jobs rather than with obtaining decent wages and safer conditions.

But small gains had been made. In 1860, shoe workers in Lynn, Massachusetts, organized a strike on Washington's Birthday. At their peak, the strikers numbered 10,000 workers marching through the city. While refusing to recognize the union, the factory owners conceded on wages, and it counted as the first real victory in American labor history.

It would be a long time before labor could claim another one. The post–Civil War period was littered with the bodies of strikers who were killed by strikebreakers, hired guards, or soldiers. Among those worst off were coal miners, who faced nightmarish dangers for pennies. In 1875, in Pennsylvania, a group of Irish coal miners organized as the Molly Maguires, taking their name from an Irish revolutionary organi-zation. Infiltrated by an informer, the Molly Maguires were accused of violence, leading to the execution of nineteen members of the group.

Two years later, in 1877, there were massive railroad strikes spread-ing across the country, brought on by wage cuts imposed on workers al-ready laboring twelve hours a day for low pay. By the time this wave of strikes was over, more than a hundred people had died and a thousand strikers were jailed. But the idea of organized labor had begun to take root, and the first generation of powerful national unions was emerg-ing. The first was the Noble Order of the Knights of Labor, begun in 1869, which quickly acquired a large measure of political and negoti-ating power. In 1884, robber baron Jay Gould suffered the indignity of bargaining at the same table with the Knights, whose membership blossomed to more than 700,000. But the history of the Knights would end in smoking disaster.

In Chicago, in 1886, the Knights of Labor were involved in a strike to force an eight-hour workday. On May 3, 1886, strikebreakers at the McCormick Reaper Company were attacked by striking workers, and police fired on the crowd, killing six and wounding dozens more. The next day, several thousand people gathered at Haymarket Square to protest the police action. As the police arrived to break up the rally, a bomb was thrown into their midst, killing seven officers.

Although there was no real evidence, blame fell on anarchist labor leaders. Anarchists were those who believed in the replacement of government with free cooperation among individuals. Fears of anarchist cells in America's cities incited a wave of panic across the country. Within months, several anarchist labor leaders were tried and quickly convicted. Some of them were hanged, and others received life sentences. (In 1893, three surviving anarchists still in prison were pardoned by German-born governor John Altgeld, who was convinced of their innocence but committed political suicide with the pardon.) Tarred with the anarchist brush after the Haymarket Square riot, the Knights of Labor were badly discredited. By 1890, their membership had fallen to 100,000.

Their place would be filled by two more powerful leaders, Eugene V. Debs (1855–1926) and Samuel Gompers (1850–1924). Debs's labor career began with work as a locomotive fireman—a dirty, dangerous job, as was almost all railroad work of the period. Thousands of workers were killed or maimed each year in accidents and boiler explosions. In the midst of another severe economic depression in 1893, Debs organized the militant American Railway Union, which absorbed remnants of the Knights of Labor and called for a strike in 1894 against the Pullman Car Company. Since Pullman cars were to be found on almost every train in the country, the strike soon became national in scope. The strike peaked when 60,000 railworkers went out, and the federal government, at the railways' behest, stepped in. Attorney General Richard Olney, a former railroad lawyer, declared that the strike interfered with federal mails; the Supreme Court agreed, and President Grover Cleveland called out troops to suppress the strike. After a pitched battle in Chicago, in which strikers were killed, Debs was arrested and jailed for contempt of court. He later joined the Socialist Party and ran for president five times.

Cigarmaker Samuel Gompers played it far more safely. Making the sweatshops of the Lower East Side of New York his base, Gompers wasn't interested in utopian dreams of improving society. Rather than organizing for political ends, Gompers stuck to "bread and butter" issues such as hours, wages, and safety, organizing the American Federation of Labor (AFL) as a collection of skilled craft unions. Presiding over the AFL almost continuously from 1886 to 1924, Gompers used the strike fiercely and effectively, winning eight-hour days, five- and six-day work weeks, employer liability, mine safety reforms, and, above all, maintaining the right of collective bargaining, a term that is accepted entirely today, but that reeked of Communism when it was introduced. The AFL's effectiveness in working for laborers' specific interests rather than for the broad social changes sought by anarchists or Socialists showed in its growth. With about 150,000 members in 1886, the union passed the million-member mark in 1901.

They were impressive gains, but they might have been larger. The federation had a great shortcoming, however, that hurt it morally and probably reduced its effectiveness in the long run. The AFL had hung out a sign that read "No Colored Need Apply."

AMERICAN VOICES
SAMUEL GOMPERS (1894):

Year by year man's liberties are trampled underfoot at the bidding of corporations and trusts, rights are invaded and law perverted. In all ages wherever a tyrant has shown himself he has always found some willing judge to clothe that tyranny in the robes of legality, and modern capitalism has proven no exception to the rule.

You may not know that the labor movement as represented by the trades unions, stands for right, stands for justice, for liberty. You may not imagine that the issuance of an injunction depriving men of a legal as well as a natural right to protect themselves, their wives, their little ones, must fail of its purpose. Repression or oppression never yet succeeded in crushing the truth or redressing a wrong.

Who were the Populists?

While organized labor inched painfully toward acceptance, the other people who suffered most from the economic upheavals of the period were the farmers. The millions of small farmers, principally in America's West and South, were at the mercy of many forces besides the weather that they were unable to control: eastern banks controlled credit; manufacturing monopolies controlled the price of machinery; eastern railroad trusts set freight prices; depression wiped out land values and sent crop prices spiraling downward. With the population booming and mechanization increasing farm efficiency, it should have been a time of plenty. Instead, farmers were being squeezed tighter and tighter, forced to sell their lands at panic prices and move to factory jobs in the cities.

But a backlash set in, producing a wave of farm belt radicalism that swept the country. Locally it produced farmers' organizations called Granges that gained sufficient political clout to press for reforms, although many of these, like the Interstate Commerce Commission, proved to be unloaded guns in the war against monopolies. In the South, for the first time since the end of the Civil War, poor blacks and working-class white farmers began to see that they shared common problems and interests, and the beginnings of an alliance of black and white farmers emerged. The farmers also reached out to join with city workers to form a powerful new alliance that could transform American politics.

Meeting in St. Louis in 1892, the Grangers and remnants of the Knights of Labor organized the People's, or Populist, Party. In a national convention later that year, the Populists put together a platform calling for national ownership of railroads and telegraph and telephone systems, a system of keeping nonperishable crops off the market, and a graduated income tax. Their platform was an eloquent indictment of the times: "We meet in the midst of a nation brought to the verge of moral, political, and material ruin. Corruption dominates the ballot-box, the Legislatures, the Congress, and touches even the ermine of the bench. The people are demoralized. . . . The newspapers are largely subsidized or muzzled, public opinion silenced. . . . The fruits of the toil of millions are boldly stolen to build up colossal fortunes for a few. . . . From the same prolific womb of governmental injustice we breed the two great classes—tramps and millionaires."

These weren't the rantings of wild-eyed college kids who had just read Karl Marx. The Populists were working-class, backbone-of-America types who had been pushed too far by the excesses of business in league with government. The men in power did not watch idly. In the South, Democrats undermined the Populist organizing effort by heightening racial fears. The mass of urban workers were never drawn to Populism, preferring to deal with the Democratic machines that they thought were defending their interests. In the election of 1892, in which Democrat Grover Cleveland recaptured the White House he'd lost four years earlier to Benjamin Harrison, the Populists finished a distant third. But the Populists still made strides as a third party, especially in the farm belt states, where they captured state legislatures, a governorship, and a substantial number of congressional seats in 1894. The two major parties realized that these farmers were a force to be reckoned with.

AMERICAN VOICES
Populist organizer MARY ELIZABETH LEASE (1890):

What you farmers need to do is raise less corn and more Hell!

What was the Cross of Gold?

During the next few years the real issues raised by the Populist Party were drowned in an obscure argument over currency. By 1895, the conflict over gold versus silver coins had absorbed all political debate in the country. "Free silver" became the new Populist rallying cry, a demand to return America to a standard using both silver and gold coins. To many Populists, this simplistic response to the depression brought about by a panic in 1893 seemed to be a cure-all. But it was a diversion that camouflaged the serious economic problems confronting the country, and it sapped much of the Populist Party's energy.

President Cleveland was a staunch supporter of the gold standard. But when federal gold reserves fell to near-bankruptcy levels in 1896 and Cleveland had to turn to J. P. Morgan for a bailout, his political life was finished. Morgan and his associates turned around and sold off at an enormous profit the government bonds they had received, and Cleveland was seen as a Morgan puppet, which, in the public eye, was no different from being in league with the devil.

With Cleveland politically dead, some Democrats saw the Populist manifesto as a way to hold on to the White House. A young delegate-at-large from Nebraska, William Jennings Bryan (1860–1925) spotted the political gold to be found in the "free silver" cry, and he seized the moment.

Addressing the Democrats' 1896 nominating convention, the silver-tongued Bryan captured the audience of 20,000 with a speech regarded as the most thrilling and effective in party convention history. Raising the banner of silver against gold, western farmers against eastern business, Bryan said, "Burn down your cities and leave our farms and your cities will spring up again as if by magic; but destroy our farms and the grass will grow in the streets of every city in the country."

With a great theatrical flourish, he concluded, "You shall not press down upon the brow of labor this crown of thorns," and extending his arms like Christ crucified, Bryan said, "You shall not crucify mankind on a Cross of Gold."

The speech was met with wild acclaim, and the following day, Bryan—who was being subsidized by western silver and copper interests—was named the Democrats' choice—at age thirty-six the youngest presidential nominee ever. With the Democrats chanting "Cross of Gold," the Populist platform had been co-opted and the Populists were forced to throw their support behind Bryan. Populism was Jonah in the belly of the mainstream Democratic whale.

In the meantime, the guiding hand and pocketbook of the wealthy Ohio industrialist "kingmaker" Mark Hanna literally bought the Republican nomination for Ohio's governor William McKinley (1843–1901). In a campaign thoroughly modern in its "packaging" of a candidate, the Hanna-led Republicans outspent the Democrats by $7 million to $300,000. McKinley's election marked the triumph of eastern industrial interests over western farm interests. One of McKinley's first acts in office was to kick Senator John Sherman up to the State Department, allowing Hanna to take Sherman's Senate seat. Populism as an effective political third party was just about finished, joining the long list of American third parties that had burst into prominence, only to flicker and fade after a brief flash of brilliance.

What did "separate but equal" mean?

Homer Plessy was seven-eighths Caucasian and one-eighth black. But when he tried to sit in a railroad coach reserved for whites, that one-eighth was all that counted. Plessy was arrested, in accordance with an 1890 Louisiana law separating railroad coaches by race. Plessy fought his arrest all the way to the Supreme Court in 1896. Unfortunately, this was the same Supreme Court that had protected corporations as "persons" under the Fourteenth Amendment, ruled that companies controlling 98 percent of the sugar business weren't monopolies, and jailed striking workers who were "restraining trade."

In Plessy's case, the arch-conservative, business-minded Court showed it was also racist in a decision that was every bit as indecent and unfair as the *Dred Scott* decision before the Civil War. The majority decision in the case of *Plessy v. Ferguson* established a new judicial idea in America—the concept of "separate but equal," meaning states could legally segregate races in public accommodations, such as railroad cars and public schools. In his majority opinion, Justice Henry Brown wrote, "We consider the underlying fallacy of the plaintiff's argument to consist in the assumption that the enforced separation of the two races stamps the colored race with a badge of inferiority. If this be so, it is not by reason of anything found in the act, but solely because the colored race chooses to put that construction upon it."

The problem with this fine notion, of course, was that every facet of life in the South was increasingly separate—schools, dining areas, trains and later buses, drinking fountains, and lunch counters—but they were never equal.

The lone dissenter in this case, as in so many others during this period, was John Marshall Harlan (1833–1911) of Kentucky. In his eloquent dissent, Harlan wrote, "The arbitrary separation of citizens, on the basis of race, while they are on a public highway, is a badge of servitude wholly inconsistent with the civil freedom and the equality before the law established by the Constitution. It cannot be justified upon any legal grounds.

". . . We boast of the freedom enjoyed by our people above all other peoples. But it is difficult to reconcile that boast with a state of the law which, practically, puts the brand of servitude and degradation upon a large class of our fellow-citizens, our equals before the law."

In practical terms, the Supreme Court of this period had turned congressional Reconstruction upside down. Its perversion of the Fourteenth Amendment had been used to protect corporations instead of blacks. *Plessy v. Ferguson* had given the Court's institutional stamp of approval to segregation. It would be another sixty years before another Supreme Court decision overturned the "separate but equal" doctrine.

Who was Jim Crow?

With the blessing of the Supreme Court, the floodgates opened. In the years following the *Plessy* decision, almost every former Confederate state enacted "separate but equal" laws that merely gave the force of law to what had become a fact of life—slavery under a new name. And to blacks and whites alike, the name was Jim Crow.

Like Uncle Tom of the minstrel shows that followed in the wake of Stowe's momentous novel, the name Jim Crow came from a white man in blackface. According to historian Lerone Bennet Jr., a white entertainer named Thomas Dartmouth Rice wrote a song-and-dance tune that became an international hit in the 1830s.

> *Weel a-bout and turn a-bout*
> *And do just so*
> *Every time I weel about*
> *I jump Jim Crow.*

"By 1838," writes Bennett, "Jim Crow was wedged into the language as a synonym for Negro." And the image it conveyed was of a comic, jumping, stupid rag doll of a man.

Jim Crow railroad cars came first, creating the situation addressed in *Plessy*. Afterward came separate waiting rooms, factory entrances, and even factory windows. Eventually Jim Crow said that white nurses couldn't tend black patients and vice versa. Black barbers couldn't cut the hair of white women and children. Perhaps most damaging was the separation of education into white and black schools, a system in which white schools regularly received ten times the funding of black schools, and teaching was as segregated as the classrooms. Some states failed to provide blacks with high schools, a fact that carried over well into the twentieth century. In fact, there was no facet of life that was untouched by Jim Crow, even criminal life: in New Orleans, prostitution was segregated.

At the roots of Jim Crow were two fears. One was sexual—the fear, either primal or institutionalized, of black men having sexual contact with white women. In the words of one notable southern politician of the time, "Whenever the Constitution comes between me and the virtue of the white women of the South, I say to hell with the Constitution."

The other fear combined politics and economics. When the Populist movement threatened to unite poor blacks and whites, the old elite white regimes in the South drove poor whites back into line with fear of black economic power. Voting fell back along strict racial lines. Ultimately, Jim Crow meant the end of black voting power in the South, as restrictive registration laws kept blacks away from the ballot boxes through poll taxes, literacy requirements, and a dozen other technical tricks.

Where laws failed to keep blacks in their place, another technique proved even more effective: the terror of lynching. Blacks were strung up throughout the South with impunity through much of the late nineteenth and early twentieth centuries, often but not always on the pretext of the rape of a white woman. Lynchings of blacks became so commonplace that they were advertised in newspapers, providing a sort of spectator sport.

Out of this period stretching from the late nineteenth century to the recent past, the major black voice in America was one of accommodation. Booker T. Washington (1859–1915) was born a slave but was able to receive an education under congressional Reconstruction. Working as a janitor to pay his way through Hampton Normal and Agricultural School, he became a schoolteacher. He was clearly an impressive figure who could mesmerize a crowd, as Frederick Douglass had done a generation earlier. Almost single-handedly he built Alabama's Tuskegee Institute from a shack beside a church into the major vocational training school for blacks in the country. In a sense, Washington was trying to adopt the rags-to-riches American dream for southern blacks, preaching the virtues of hard work and economic survival through education and advancement into the professions. Critics of Washington, both in his day and later, complained that his accommodation to and acceptance of the status quo was weak, even cowardly. Others have defended Washington as one man who was doing his best in a time of very limited options. After all, he lived in a time when a lynch mob needed no more excuse to hang a man than that he was "uppity."

AMERICAN VOICES
BOOKER T. WASHINGTON,
"The Atlantic Compromise" (1895):

> To those of my race who depend on bettering their condition in a foreign land or who underestimate the importance of cultivating friendly relations with the Southern white man, who is their next-door neighbor, I would say: "Cast down your bucket where you are. . . ."
>
> The wisest among my race understand that the agitation of questions of social equality is the extremest of folly.

Who fought in the Spanish-American War?

The racism expressed in Jim Crow didn't end at southern, or even American, borders. The vigorous rise of a belief in white, Anglo-Saxon superiority extended overseas. One popular writer of 1885 was the clergyman Josiah Strong, who argued that the United States was the true center of Anglo-Saxon virtue and was destined to spread it over the world. "This powerful race," wrote Strong in the best-selling book *Our Country*, "will move down upon Mexico, down upon Central and South America, out upon the islands of the sea, over upon Africa and beyond." Then, borrowing from Charles Darwin, whose ideas were being floated around, Strong concluded, "Can any one doubt that the result of this competition of races will be the 'survival of the fittest'?" Strong left no doubt as to who he thought the "fittest" was.

Strong's message found a receptive audience in the corridors of American power, and a few years later the message went out in a war with Spain. This was America's muscle-flexing war, a war that a young and cocky nation fought to shake off the cobwebs, pull itself out of the economic doldrums, and prove itself to a haughty Europe.

Watching England, Germany, France, and Belgium spread their global empires in Asia and Africa, America fought this war to expand and protect its trade markets overseas, capture valuable mineral deposits, and acquire land that was good for growing fruit, tobacco, and sugar. It was a war wanted by banks and brokers, steelmakers and oilmen, manufacturers and missionaries. It was a war that President McKinley didn't seem to want, and a war that Spain certainly didn't want. But there were a lot of powerful people who did want it. And, perhaps above all, it was a war the newspapers wanted. War, after all, was good for circulation.

The ostensible reason for going to war with Spain was to "liberate" Cuba, a Spanish colony. A fading world power, Spain was trying to maintain control over a native population that demanded its freedom, as America had demanded and won its independence a century earlier. When Spain sent a military governor to throw rebels into concentration camps, America acted the part of the outraged sympathizer. It was a convenient excuse. But an element of fear also played into the game. There was already one black republic in the Western Hemisphere, in Haiti. The United States didn't want another one in Cuba.

Forces outside the government were matched by powerful men inside it who wanted war. Chief among them were Henry Cabot Lodge (1850–1924), the influential senator from Massachusetts; Theodore Roosevelt, then assistant secretary of the Navy, and Captain Alfred Mahan, author of a book called *The Influence of Sea Power Upon*

History, 1660–1783, an influential work calling for expansion of American naval power to bases around the world, especially in the Pacific. Roosevelt, the great admirer of the cowboy spirit, once told a friend, "I should welcome almost any war, for I think this country needs one."

Lodge was an even more outspoken booster of American imperialism. When President Cleveland failed to annex Hawaii in 1893, Lodge lashed out angrily and spoke about his aims for America: "In the interests of our commerce and our fullest development, we should build the Nicaraguan canal, and for the protection of that canal and for the sake of our commercial supremacy in the Pacific we should control the Hawaiian Islands and maintain our influence in Samoa. . . . Commerce follows the flag, and we should build up a navy strong enough to give protection to Americans in every quarter of the globe."

Pressing the war cries from the outside were the two most powerful newspaper czars in American history, William Randolph Hearst (1863–1951) and Joseph Pulitzer (1847–1911). Both men had learned from the Civil War that war headlines sold newspapers. Tabloid headlines depicting Spanish atrocities against Cubans became commonplace, and the influential papers of both men were outdoing each other in the sensationalized screaming for war. The expansionist doctrine that had grown out of Manifest Destiny also sold newspapers, so the papers of both men were soon hawking war. When the artist Frederic Remington (1861–1909) went to Cuba to send back pictures for Hearst's papers, he cabled his boss he couldn't find a war. "You furnish the pictures," Hearst supposedly responded in a fury. "I'll furnish the war." Whether apocryphal or not, the story is an accurate indication of how both Hearst and Pulitzer viewed the war—as a circulation boon—and they were not afraid of sensationalizing any accounts of Spanish atrocities to heighten the war fever.

Against the urgings of party and press, and of businessmen and missionaries calling for bringing Anglo-Saxon Christianity to the world, McKinley tried to avert war. But finally he found it easier to go with the flow. Through a series of diplomatic ultimatums, McKinley pushed Spain into a corner of a room and then closed the only window that would have provided escape. What Secretary of State John Hay would call a "splendid little war" lasted a few months. But like all wars, it carried a price in lives and perhaps in virtue.

MILESTONES IN THE SPANISH-AMERICAN WAR
1898

January 25   The U.S. battleship *Maine* arrives in Havana Harbor. Its stated purpose is to protect the interests of Americans who are being brutalized by the Spanish governor, according to reports in the tabloids.

February 9   A private letter by Spain's ambassador to the United States is published in Hearst's *New York Journal* in which President McKinley is characterized as feebleminded, provoking a wave of indignation, fanned by the Hearst and Pulitzer newspapers.

February 15   The battleship *Maine* mysteriously explodes while anchored in Havana Harbor, resulting in the deaths of 260 crew members. The newspapers and war hawks soon trumpet, "Remember the *Maine*! To hell with Spain!" as a battle cry. The source of the blast is said to be an external explosion. While the Americans claim the blast was caused by a mine in the harbor, Spanish authorities assert it was an internal explosion, perhaps in the heavily loaded ship's magazine.

March 9   By unanimous vote, Congress appropriates $50 million "for national defense," and the country moves toward a war footing.

March 27   President McKinley offers Spain several conditions to avert a war that is widely desired by the banking and military interests of the country. The conditions include negotiations with Cuban rebels, revocation of concentration camps, and U.S. arbitration to settle the rebel question in Cuba. While Spain seems to express willingness to negotiate and accept McKinley's conditions, war hawks continue to apply pressure.

April 11   McKinley delivers a "war message." Fearing peace will split his party, he ignores Spanish peace overtures as the call for war is pressed by the Hearst and Pulitzer papers, Henry Cabot Lodge in Congress, and Assistant Secretary of the Navy Theodore Roosevelt.

April 19 Congress adopts a war resolution calling for Cuban independence from Spain and evacuation of Spanish forces from the island. The measure asserts that the United States is uninterested in exerting control over the island, and the coming war is depicted as a war of "liberation" of a western colony from a European power, which will allegedly permit the Cubans to "determine their fate."

April 20 To prevent the use of diplomatic channels to avoid a war, the Spanish ambassador's passport is returned before he can deliver the U.S. ultimatum. A day later, Spain breaks off diplomatic relations with the United States.

April 22 Congress passes the Volunteer Army Act, which calls for organization of a First Volunteer Cavalry—a "cowboy cavalry" that the press will christen Rough Riders. Resigning his post as assistant secretary of the navy and chief instigator of war within the McKinley administration, Theodore Roosevelt takes a commission as lieutenant colonel of the brigade, which is commanded by Leonard Wood. Hundreds of applications for the Rough Riders come from all over the country, and Roosevelt will draw on Ivy Leaguers as well as cowboys. The U.S. Navy begins a blockade of Cuban ports, and a Spanish ship is captured in the first actual encounter of the war.

April 23 McKinley issues a call for 125,000 recruits.

April 24 Spain declares war on the United States.

April 25 The United States declares that a state of war exists as of April 21, the day Spain broke off diplomatic relations.

May 1 While Cuba is the focus of hostilities, the United States launches a surprise naval attack on the Philippines. Commodore (later Rear Admiral) Dewey's Asiatic Squadron has been preparing for this attack for some time, at the secret order of Theodore Roosevelt. In a seven-hour battle outside Manila Bay, where the outdated and outgunned Spanish ships have maneuvered to avoid civilian casualties, the United States sinks all the Spanish ships, killing more than 300 Spanish, at a loss of no American ships and incurring only a few wounded. With a quick and easy victory under its belt, America's hawkishness quickly explodes into outright war fever.

May 12   The United States bombards San Juan, Puerto Rico.

May 19   With American assistance, the Philippine guerrilla leader Aguinaldo arrives in Manila. At the same time, back in Cuba, the Spanish fleet moves into Santiago Harbor.

May 25   The first American troopships leave for Manila. McKinley calls for another 75,000 volunteers.

May 29   The American fleet blockades the Spanish fleet in Santiago Harbor.

June 10   A force of 647 marines lands at Guantanamo Bay, beginning the invasion of Cuba.

June 22   Nearly 20,000 American troops arrive at the fishing village of Daiquiri, eighteen miles east of Santiago.

June 24   Led by Joseph Wheeler, formerly of the Confederate cavalry—who occasionally lapses in battle and calls the Spanish Yankees—and Leonard Wood, 1,000 regular army and Rough Riders, accompanied by several war correspondents, win the first land battle of the war at Las Guasimas, Cuba. In his first action, Roosevelt is accompanied by two major war correspondents and is already being marked as a war hero.

July 1   The battles of El Caney and San Juan Hill. Against much smaller Spanish forces, Americans take heavy casualties in the major pitched battle of the war. An American balloon sent aloft to observe Spanish troop placements simply gives the Spanish gunners a perfect indication of American positions. More than 6,000 U.S. soldiers suffer 400 casualties at El Caney against a Spanish force of only 600. At San Juan Heights, confusion and delayed orders result in severe U.S. casualties as Spanish guns rake the waiting troops. Colonel Theodore Roosevelt finally takes the initiative, leading an assault first on Kettle Hill and a second charge on San Juan Heights. After successfully taking San Juan Heights, the American forces have command of Santiago below. But the American position is very weak. They are short of supplies, and casualties are heavy. Yellow fever and malaria have already begun to take their toll, as the Spanish defenders had expected. Roosevelt himself writes to Henry Cabot Lodge, "We are within measurable distance of a terrible military disaster." After the Battle of San Juan Heights, 1,572 Americans are dead or wounded, but Roosevelt achieves instant war-hero status.

July 3 Against his own belief that he is risking certain defeat, Spanish admiral Cervera is ordered to break through the American blockade of Santiago Harbor. After the battle, the Spanish fleet is utterly destroyed. There is one American dead, another wounded.

July 4 In the Pacific, American troops take the deserted Wake Island.

July 8 Admiral Dewey takes Isla Grande near Manila.

July 10 With the destruction of the Spanish fleet guarding Santiago, U.S. troops launch a final attack on the city. By agreement with the Spanish command, there will be no resistance.

July 17 Santiago surrenders to American forces, and the U.S. flag is raised over the government building.

July 25 The town of Guánica in Puerto Rico is taken by U.S. troops.

July 26 Through the French ambassador, Spain requests peace terms. The "splendid little war" ends after three months of fighting. McKinley announces the following terms: independence is granted to Cuba; the United States takes control of Puerto Rico; the United States will occupy Manila until further negotiations.

August 9 McKinley's terms are accepted by Spain, and a protocol of peace is signed.

What did America gain from the Spanish–American War?

There were 5,462 American deaths in the war, only 379 of which were battle casualties. Yellow fever, malaria, and other diseases were primarily responsible for most of them. Tainted meat sold to the army by the Armour Company may have led to some others. When Roosevelt and his men had opened tinned meat on the way to Cuba, they promptly tossed the putrid contents overboard.

In the aftermath of the war, several unexpected developments arose. America found itself not only in possession of Cuba and Puerto Rico as the island bases Henry Cabot Lodge hoped for, but in control of Wake Island, Guam, and the Philippines as well. President McKinley was somewhat uncertain about what should be done with them. His choices were to give them back to Spain, or to give them to France or Germany, which seemed foolish; to leave them alone seemed equally foolish. The best remedy was to keep them for America. With the annexation of Hawaii in 1898, America had in place its "stepping-stones" to a new Pacific empire.

The people in the Philippines had other ideas about whom they needed protection from. Emiliano Aguinaldo, the rebel leader brought back to the Philippines by Admiral Dewey, was no more interested in American rule than he had been in Spanish rule. What followed was a war more bloody than the one with Spain: the Philippine incursion. It carried with it all the earmarks of a modern imperial war: massive strikes against civilians, war atrocities, and a brutality that had been missing from American wars with Europeans. Fighting against the "brown" Filipinos removed all excuses for civility. The Philippines would be an unhappy "protectorate" in the American Pacific for years to come. Five thousand Americans died fighting the Filipinos.

The other development that came home from Cuba was a real, live war hero in Teddy Roosevelt. Unashamedly, he rode his Rough Rider fame into the statehouse of New York in 1898, where his reform-minded ideas unsettled fellow Republicans and the industries they represented. A number of Republicans felt it would be an eminently prudent idea to stash Teddy away in the vice president's office, where he couldn't do any harm. Senator Mark Hanna did not join in this thinking. The chairman of the Republican Party, Hanna commented, "Don't any of you realize there's only one life between this madman and the presidency?"

Roosevelt initially balked at the post, believing that the office was a political dead end. The bullet fired by anarchist Leon Czolgosz, which struck President McKinley in Buffalo in September 1901, changed all that. At age forty-two, Theodore Roosevelt became the youngest president in American history. In one of his first acts in office, he invited Booker T. Washington to the White House. It was an act that the South would never forgive or forget.

Who built the Panama Canal?

While America prepared for war in Cuba, the American battleship *Oregon*, stationed off the coast of California, was ordered to Cuba. Steaming around South America, the *Oregon* was followed in the press like the Kentucky Derby. The voyage took two months, and while the Oregon arrived in time to take part in the Battle of Santiago Harbor, it was clear that America needed a faster way to move its warships from ocean to ocean.

This wasn't a new idea. The dream of connecting the Atlantic and the Pacific had been held almost since Balboa stood on the cliffs of Darien in modern Panama. President Grant sent a survey team to look for the best route to dig a canal across Central America, and an American company later built a small railroad line to take steamship passengers across the isthmus, drastically cutting travel time from coast to coast.

Plenty of other people saw the commercial as well as strategic advantages of this undertaking. In 1880, a French group led by Ferdinand de Lesseps, chief architect of the Suez Canal, put together a company with the capital of thousands of investors to build a canal across the Isthmus of Panama, then still a part of Colombia. In the growing macho mood of America's leaders, President Hayes announced that no European country would control such a canal, saying, "The policy of the country is a canal under American control."

Corruption on a grand scale, miserable engineering plans, the harsh realities of the Central American jungle with its rainy-season floods, earthquakes, yellow fever, and malaria doomed the de Lesseps effort. After some preliminary excavations and thousands of deaths by accident and disease, the French company abandoned its canal cut amid a national scandal and left everything behind, the rusted machinery looking like some mechanical dinosaurs fossilized in the dense jungle.

After the war in Cuba and the *Oregon* incident, the American appetite for a canal was reawakened. President McKinley authorized a commission to investigate the best route for the canal. When Roosevelt, the great apostle of American sea power, took the White House, the enthusiasm became that of a raging bull. Initially, Roosevelt tilted toward a Nicaraguan canal, a longer route but thought to be an easier dig. A Nicaraguan canal also offered the advantage of being closer to American ports on the Gulf of Mexico. An angry Senate debate followed, with Senator Mark Hanna leading the way for Panama. When the French company dropped the asking price for its assets from $109 million to $40 million, the Panama route became more attractive. Only one problem remained. The "dagos" in Colombia, in Roosevelt's phrase, who still owned the territory, were asking too much.

The solution presented to Roosevelt was simple. If Colombia stood in the way, just make a new country that would be more agreeable. Led by a former director of the French canal company with U.S. Army assistance, Panamanians revolted against Colombia in November 1903. The American battleship *Nashville* steamed south and pointed its guns in Colombia's direction, and Panama was born with the U.S. Navy for a midwife.

Recognized faster than any new government had ever been, Panama's regime received $10 million, a yearly fee of $250,000, and guarantees of "independence." In return the United States got rights to a ten-mile swath across the country—the Canal Zone—"in perpetuity." Since the zone comprised most of Panama and would be guarded by American troops, the United States effectively controlled the country. Years afterward, Roosevelt would proudly say, "I took the Canal and let Congress debate."

A few months later, Americans took over the remnants of the French project, and in 1904 the first Americans were in Panama. From day one, the work was plagued by the same problems the French met: tropical heat, the jungle, and the mosquitoes. One of the few positive results of America's Cuban experience was the discovery that mosquitoes spread yellow fever, and the disease had been eliminated from Havana during the American occupation. But there were still plenty of people who thought the idea that mosquitoes carried disease was nonsense, and they kept U.S. Army doctor William Gorgas, the health officer in Panama, from carrying out a plan of effective mosquito control.

When railroad builder John Stevens came to Panama in 1905 as head of the project, to give the dig the organization it needed, he also gave Dr. Gorgas a free hand to eliminate malaria and yellow fever, a task accomplished with remarkable efficiency, given the circumstances of the environment and lack of scientific appreciation. Unfortunately, Jim Crow also came to Panama. Most of the laborers were blacks from the Caribbean. They were housed and fed separately, and paid in silver, while whites were paid in gold. According to David McCullough's epic account of the creation of the canal, *The Path Between the Seas*, the death rate by accident and disease for blacks was about five times that of whites in Panama.

Without explanation, Stevens left the dig, replaced by army engineer George W. Goethals. Roosevelt put an army man in charge so he couldn't quit as previous administrators had done in the face of the project's overwhelming difficulties. Taking over in 1907 and building on the plan and reorganization left behind by Stevens, Goethals completed the canal ahead of schedule and under budget, despite the challenges the canal posed and the enormous changes the original plan had undergone as work proceeded. More remarkably, according to McCullough, it was completed without suspicion of corruption, graft, kickbacks, or bribery.

First planned under McKinley, aggressively begun by Roosevelt, and carried out by his successor, Taft, the Panama Canal was completed in 1914, under Woodrow Wilson. Ironically, the grand plans for a gala opening were canceled. War in Europe was looming, and news of the canal's completion was lost in preparations for the coming hostilities.

Must Read: *The Path Between the Seas: The Creation of the Panama Canal* by David McCullough.

ORVILLE WRIGHT, describing the first flight at Kitty Hawk, North Carolina (December 17, 1903):

The machine lifted from the truck just as it was entering on the fourth rail. Mr. Daniels took a picture just as it left the tracks. I found the control of front rudder quite difficult on account of its being balanced too near the center and thus had a tendency to turn itself when started so that the rudder was turned too far on one side and then too far on the other. As a result the machine would rise suddenly to about 10 ft. and then as suddenly, on turning the rudder, dart for the ground. A sudden dart when about 100 feet from the end of the tracks ended the flight. Time about 12 seconds (not known exactly as watch was not promptly stopped).

What happened at Kitty Hawk?

On December 17, 1903, two self-taught engineer-inventors named Wilbur and Orville Wright did something that other people had only dreamed of for centuries. In a 750-pound plane powered by a twelve-horsepower motor and launched from a railroad track laid in the sand dunes of Kitty Hawk, North Carolina, they flew the first heavier-than-air craft. Surprisingly, their initial success didn't cause much of a stir. Many people, including the members of the press, initially did not believe them. Even the U.S. Army was dubious and refused to offer the Wrights a contract for more than three years.

But their first flights launched a revolutionary era of aviation heroics. It is astonishing to think that those brief flights would lead to a moon landing only sixty-six years later, while also creating a huge industry in wheeled luggage and small bags of roasted nuts.

In September 1908, Orville Wright took the first passengers on a flight. One passenger, Thomas Selfridge, holds an unfortunate distinction. He was the first man to die in a plane crash from injuries suffered on September 17, 1908.

What was the "big stick"?

That he would start a revolution to suit his needs came as no surprise to anyone who knew Theodore Roosevelt. His record to that point—as cattle rancher, New York State legislator, civil service commissioner, New York City police commissioner, Navy secretary, soldier, governor of New York, and then president—had been to act forcefully and leave questions of law, propriety, and good sense for others. His favorite saying, used often in public and private, was an old African proverb: "Speak softly, and carry a big stick; you will go far."

Although he rarely spoke softly himself, he was always ready to use a big stick, abroad and at home. His first chance to use the big stick came when 140,000 mine workers went on strike in May 1902. Underpaid, forced to buy overpriced supplies in company stores and to live in company-owned houses, the miners were kept in perpetual debt and had organized as the United Mine Workers (UMW) under John Mitchell. The mine companies, owned almost exclusively by the railroads (meaning, for the most part, J. P. Morgan), refused to recognize the union or to negotiate. As the work stoppage threatened to cripple an economy largely run on coal power, Roosevelt stepped in and threatened to use troops. But unlike in the past, when they had been used as deadly strikebreakers to force workers back into the mines, these troops would operate the mines in the "public interest." With this "big stick" over their heads, the mine owners agreed to accept the ruling of an Arbitration Commission, which ruled favorably for the miners. The victory was more Roosevelt's than the union's, but it allowed the cowboy president to carve another notch on his six-shooter.

Using the strengthened Sherman law, Roosevelt went after other selected targets, subjectively labeled "bad trusts," such as the "beef trust" (*Swift & Co. v. United States*, 1905) and the American Tobacco Company. Roosevelt was hardly a radical; he believed that monopoly was fine as long as it could be regulated, and that there were benevolent trusts, such as International Harvester. But his tenure produced reforms that were significant and long-lasting, such as the strengthening of the Interstate Commerce Commission, the creation of a cabinet-level Department of Labor and Commerce (later separated into two departments), and the passage of the Pure Food and Drug Act, a law inspired by a bunch of "muckrakers" (see below).

In foreign affairs, Roosevelt was even more willing to wield his big stick, especially in the Caribbean and the Philippines. In 1904, he sent troops into the Dominican Republic, which had reneged on debts to Great Britain. Roosevelt put Americans in charge of Dominican revenues until the debt problem was solved. This was an example of what was called the Roosevelt Corollary, which added to the Monroe Doctrine and said the United States had "international police power" to correct wrongs within its "sphere of influence." Though effective, Roosevelt's overbearing treatment of nations he viewed as racially inferior won America no friends in Latin America, which had been reduced to a collection of vassal states.

Ironically, in the wake of policing the Caribbean and overseeing the subjugation of the Philippines, Roosevelt won the Nobel Peace Prize by mediating an end to the Russo-Japanese War in 1905 at Portsmouth, New Hampshire. Divvying up substantial chunks of Asia, the treaty may have created more trouble than it solved. Japan got Korea and guaranteed that it would leave its hands off the Philippines, now in the American "sphere of influence." But the high-handedness of Roosevelt's dealings left a bitter taste in Japanese mouths.

To prove to the Japanese that he meant business, Roosevelt sent forth the big stick in the form of the Great White Fleet. The result of a modernization and overhaul of the navy, this armada of sixteen ships cruised around the world in 1907, an impressive display of American naval power that also pointed up to the Navy its shortcomings in being too dependent on foreign supplies at sea.

Must Read: *Mornings on Horseback* by David McCullough; *The Rise of Theodore Roosevelt* by Edmund Morris; *Theodore Rex* by Edmund Morris.

Who were the muckrakers?

"Big stick" was only one of Roosevelt's frequent expressions that became enshrined in the language. Among presidents, he had a singular ear for a turn of phrase. A voracious reader with an astonishing sense of recall, he could quote at will from a wide range of sources, from African proverbs to obscure military dissertations or, in another famous case, John Bunyan's allegory *Pilgrim's Progress*. In 1907, exasperated by the work of a growing number of journalists who concentrated on exposing graft and corruption, Roosevelt compared them to Bunyan's "man with the Muck-Rake," a character so preoccupied with the filth at his feet that he fails to grasp for the "celestial crown."

The appellation "muckraker" stuck and was happily accepted by a new breed of American journalist best represented by Ida M. Tarbell, Lincoln Steffens, and Upton Sinclair. In newspapers, magazines such as *McClure's* and *Atlantic Monthly*, and books—both nonfiction and fiction—a generation of writers had begun to attack the widespread abuses that abounded in American business and politics. In a sense, the trend began with Twain and Warner in *The Gilded Age*. But muckraking reached its heights in the early twentieth century. In 1903, *McClure's* began to serialize the articles written by Ida M. Tarbell (1857–1944) about Standard Oil. The result was her landmark investigation of the company, *History of Standard Oil Company*. At the same time, *McClure's* was running a series by Lincoln Steffens (1866–1936) about urban corruption, collected in the book *The Shame of the Cities* (1904). *McClure's* also ran early portions of social reformer Jane Addams's book *Twenty Years at Hull-House* (1910). Addams founded Hull-House with Ellen Gates Starr as a settlement house to assist immigrants in adjusting to American life, and more than four hundred of these sprang up in cities around America, inspired by Addams's example. At first culturally high-minded, the settlement houses eventually provided basic educational and health care that could not be found elsewhere for hundreds of thousands of immigrants in the sprawling tenements of the inner cities. But Addams and her colleagues were fighting an impossible battle in an era when government assistance to the poor was considered blasphemous and communistic.

In New York, the plight of immigrants also emerged through the reports and photographs of Jacob Riis, himself an immigrant. In his 1890 book, *How the Other Half Lives*, Riis exposed the crime, disease, and squalor of the urban slums.

A new generation of novelists was adapting these journalistic techniques to fiction as well: Stephen Crane in *Maggie, a Girl of the Streets*; William Dean Howells in *The Rise of Silas Lapham*; Frank Norris in *The Octopus*. Perhaps most famous of all was Upton Sinclair's *The Jungle*, a novel that blisteringly exposed the disgusting conditions in the meatpacking industry in Chicago. (Read the book even today, and you may swear off sausage!) Publication of *The Jungle* in 1906 cut American meat sales overnight and immediately forced the industry to accept federal meat inspection as well as passage of the Pure Food and Drug Act. These were the first toddling steps in modern consumerism, and the muckrakers were the ancestors of consumer advocates such as Ralph Nader, unsparing critics of fraud, abuse, and industrial and political corruption.

AMERICAN VOICES
JANE ADDAMS, from *Twenty Years at Hull-House*:

Our very first Christmas at Hull-House, when we as yet knew nothing of child labor, a number of little girls refused the candy which was offered them as part of the Christmas good cheer, saying simply that they "worked in a candy factory and could not bear the sight of it." We discovered that for six weeks they had worked from seven in the morning until nine at night, and they were exhausted as well as satiated. . . .

During the same winter three boys from a Hull-House club were injured at one machine in a neighboring factory for lack of a guard which would have cost but a few dollars. When the injury of one of these boys resulted in his death, we felt quite sure that the owners of the factory would share our horror and remorse. . . . To our surprise, they did nothing whatever, and I made my first acquaintance then with those pathetic documents signed by the parents of working children, that they will make no claim for damages resulting from "carelessness."

Who were the Wobblies?

The Jungle was more than a muckraking novel. It was the most prominent example of a Socialist novel. Besides being a scathing exposé of meatpacking practices, the book was a call to workers to unite, ending with a utopian vision of a workers' society. In fact, it had first been published in a Socialist newspaper, *Appeal to Reason*. Years of being associated with Soviet and Chinese Communism have permanently tarred socialism in the American mind as dangerous. But for a period in the early twentieth century it was a growing political force, especially among the working class, who saw it as a way to distribute wealth through government control rather than through private enterprise. Since few workers in America were getting any wealth distributed by the Morgans and Rockefellers, they decided to give socialism a try.

While the conservative, mainstream AFL stayed away from Socialist ideas, not wanting to be associated with the Bolshevism that was taking over Russia (where 10,000 American troops were involved in a secret war to prevent the Bolshevik revolution during World War I), another union sprang up and proudly unfurled the Socialist banner. It was the Industrial Workers of the World (IWW), and its members became better known, for reasons historically unclear, as the Wobblies. Unlike the AFL, which was open only to white, skilled craftsmen, the Wobblies were organized to accept all workers into "one big union." At their first meeting, in 1905, were "Big Bill" Haywood (1869–1928), a miner; Eugene V. Debs, leader of the Socialist Party; and Mary Harris "Mother" Jones (1830–1930), a seventy-five-year-old organizer for the United Mine Workers.

The Wobblies' cause flared for about ten years, met with the full force of anti-union violence as its leaders were jailed, beaten, and, in the case of the legendary Joe Hill (1872?–1915), framed and executed, although he gained a sort of immortality in the song "I Dreamed I Saw Joe Hill Last Night."

Under Debs, the Socialist Party attracted notable personalities, including Helen Keller, and managed to win as much as 6 percent of the presidential vote until the war intervened and in its wake the first powerful wave of anti-Communism swept the country, all but eradicating socialism as a force in American politics and life.

Who was W. E. B. DuBois?

One man who briefly joined the Socialists emerged from this period as the most eloquent and forceful voice for blacks since Frederick Douglass. In stark counterpoint to the accommodating spirit of Booker T. Washington (see p. 285), W. E. B. DuBois (1868–1963) became the trumpeter of a new spirit of "manly agitation." The great civil rights upheaval in America was still half a century away, but DuBois was its John the Baptist, the voice in the wilderness. Born in Massachusetts, he was the first black to receive a Ph.D. from Harvard, in 1895. He taught, lectured, and wrote, his most notable work being the classic *The Souls of Black Folk* (1903). Rejecting Washington's conservative restraint, DuBois joined in founding the National Association for the Advancement of Colored People (NAACP) in 1909, at that time a white-dominated organization, and became editor of its journal, *The Crisis*, where he served for a quarter-century.

DuBois left the NAACP in 1934, when he promoted a more radical strategy and returned to teaching. Ten years later he rejoined the NAACP, and in 1945 was one of the Americans in attendance at the founding of the United Nations. DuBois later joined the Communist Party, left America, and renounced his citizenship, moving to Ghana, where he died.

Must Read: *W. E. B. DuBois: A Biography of a Race, 1868–1919* by David Levering Lewis.

AMERICAN VOICES
W. E. B. DuBois,
from *The Souls of Black Folk* (1903):

So far as Mr. [Booker T.] Washington preaches thrift, patience, and industrial training for the masses, we must hold up his hands and strive with him, rejoicing in his honors and glorying in the strength of this Joshua called of God and of man to lead the headless host. But so far as Mr. Washington apologizes for injustices, North or South, does not rightly value the privileges and duty of voting, belittles the emasculating effects of caste distinctions, and opposes the higher training and ambition of our brighter minds — so far as he, the South, or the nation, does this — we must unceasingly and firmly oppose them.

What was the Bull Moose Party?

Though he could have run for another term and probably would have won handily, given his popularity, Teddy Roosevelt accepted the unwritten rule observed since Washington (and unbroken until Teddy's cousin Franklin D. came along). Having served out most of McKinley's unfinished term and his own full term, Roosevelt left a handpicked successor in the White House in William Howard Taft (1857–1930). In 1908, with Roosevelt's blessing and running on the Roosevelt record, Taft easily defeated the unsinkable William Jennings Bryan, who made his third unsuccessful bid for the White House. At the time, a common joke said the name Taft stood for "Take Advice From Teddy."

Roosevelt decided that he would head off for an African safari to stay out of Taft's way. But a year of bagging big game didn't quench Teddy's political hunting instincts. When he came back, he set about to recapture the Republican nomination from Taft, whose star could never shine as brilliantly as Roosevelt's had. Pegged a conservative, Taft had actually brought more antitrust suits than Roosevelt had, including the one that broke up Standard Oil in 1911, and Teddy's backers included a former Morgan banker. But this was to be an election fought to see who appeared most progressive. And it was Roosevelt who projected himself as the champion reformer. After a bloody battle in which Taft recaptured the Republican nomination, Roosevelt led a group of dissatisfied liberal Republicans out of the fold and into the Progressive Party. Claiming at one point that he was "as strong as a bull moose," Roosevelt gave the party its popular name.

The Democrats struggled through forty-six ballots before turning to Woodrow Wilson (1856–1924), then governor of New Jersey, a surprise choice, and, for his times at least, rather liberal. The Democratic Party solidified behind Wilson, especially in the South, where

Roosevelt was never forgiven for welcoming Booker T. Washington to the White House. Taft essentially threw in the towel and stayed out of the campaign—later to head the Supreme Court, the job he really always wanted. In spite of an unsuccessful assassination attempt that seemed to confirm his invincibility, Roosevelt campaigned hard, and Wilson's popular vote was less than the combined Taft-Roosevelt vote. (Socialist candidate Eugene V. Debs polled 6 percent of the vote—nearly a million votes, and an indication that the political winds had clearly shifted to the left.) But Wilson's electoral victory was sweeping. Taft won only two states and Roosevelt six. The rest of the country was solidly Democratic behind Wilson. And once again, a third-party candidacy had changed the course of American politics.

Like his opponents, Wilson ran on a progressive reform platform he called the New Freedom. During his first administration, his legislative success was quite remarkable. Duties on foreign goods, the almost sacred weapon held by big business to keep out foreign competition, were reduced for the first time since the Civil War. The Sixteenth Amendment, imposing an income tax, was ratified. The Seventeenth Amendment, providing for election of U.S. senators by popular direct vote, was ratified. (Previously, U.S. senators had been chosen by state legislatures.) And a Federal Reserve Act gave the country its first central bank since Andrew Jackson's time. In other key reforms, the Federal Trade Commission was created and the Clayton Antitrust Act was passed; both were intended to control unfair and restrictive trade practices, exempting unions and farm groups.

The shame of Wilson's "progressive" administration was his abysmal record on civil rights. Under Wilson, Jim Crow became the policy of the U.S. government, with segregated federal offices, and blacks losing some of the few government jobs they held. Virginia-born, Wilson was a product of the post–Civil War South, and he reflected that mentality to a remarkable extent for a man who seemed so forward-thinking in other respects. But his treatment of blacks was of little concern to a nation that was warily watching the approach of a European war.

Who was Pancho Villa?

Under Woodrow Wilson, America went from "big stick" to Big Brother when it came to Latin America. With the nearly completed Panama Canal to defend, Wilson was going to ensure that American power in the hemisphere would not be threatened. Local unrest in the Caribbean left American troops controlling Nicaragua, Haiti, and the Dominican Republic. All were pushovers for American military might. Less simple to deal with was the instability in Mexico that produced Pancho Villa.

Mexico had undergone a series of coups and dictatorships in the early twentieth century, leaving General Victoriano Huerta installed as president in 1911 with the help of the American ambassador and the blessings of foreign investors who wanted only the stability that allowed them to exploit Mexico. But President Wilson refused to recognize Huerta's government, throwing Mexico into more turbulence. Using as a pretext the arrest of some American sailors, Wilson sent the U.S. Navy to invade Vera Cruz in 1914, and Huerta soon abdicated. The door was opened for another general, Venustiano Carranza, and two of his "generals," Emiliano Zapata and Pancho Villa. An illiterate Indian, Zapata made some claims for social reform by giving land to the poor. Villa was simply a bandit who eventually rose against Carranza and seized Mexico City.

In an attempt to undermine Carranza, Villa began to attack the United States. He killed a dozen American passengers aboard a train in northern Mexico, and then began to make raids across the border into New Mexico, murdering a group of American mining engineers. An outraged Wilson sent General John J. Pershing (1860–1948) into Mexico in pursuit of Villa. But chasing the wily outlaw general was like trying to catch the wind. Villa led the American troops deeper into Mexican territory on a nine-month fox hunt that only served to alarm Carranza, raising tensions between America and Mexico.

With involvement in Europe's war growing more likely, Wilson relented and recalled Pershing from Mexico in 1917. Within a few years, Villa, Zapata, and Carranza were all dead by assassination in the turbulent world of Mexican politics, a world that was being drawn in by the powerful pull of European war.

How did a dead archduke in Sarajevo start a world war?

On June 28, 1914, Archduke Francis Ferdinand, heir to the Austrian throne, was in the city of Sarajevo (in modern Yugoslavia), then part of the Austro-Hungarian Empire. A group of young student nationalists who wanted to join independent Serbia to Austria's south plotted to kill the archduke. One of them, Gavrilo Princip, shot the archduke in his automobile. Within days, the Austrian Empire declared war on Serbia, Austria's tiny neighbor to the south, claiming it was responsible for the assassination. Allied to Serbia, Russia mobilized its troops. Austria's ally Germany responded by declaring war on Russia and its ally, France. Also bound by defense treaties, Great Britain declared war on Germany as German troops began an invasion of Belgium on their way to France.

Ferdinand's death was merely the spark that ignited a short fuse that exploded into what was then called the Great War, and only later, at the time of the Second World War, became known as World War I. Another way to put it is that the assassination was a final piece in a Rube Goldberg contraption, a crazy scheme of interlocking parts that finally sent Europe reeling into a war that covered most of the globe.

On the eve of war, Europe was more in the nineteenth century than the twentieth. The German Empire had been consolidated into the continent's leading power during the late nineteenth century by the Iron Chancellor Bismarck, and was linked to the Austrian Empire through aristocratic bloodlines and military alliance. Together they constituted the Central Powers in Europe and were also allied to the Ottoman Empire, which controlled much of the modern Middle East. The German Empire had been partly built at French expense after Germany won a war in 1870 that humiliated France and gave Germany the rich territories of Alsace and Lorraine. Resentment over this loss and surrender of French territory had never subsided between the two nations, and France, in the wake of its disastrous defeat at Germany's hands, had rearmed heavily, reorganized its armies, and become an intensely militarized nation with plans to eventually retake the steel-producing region it considered its property.

Thrown into this simmering stew of alliances was the coming revolution in Russia. Czarist Russia was tied to England and France through mutual defense treaties and bloodlines (the king of England and the czar were relatives). The threat of a Socialist revolution pledged to destroy the monarchy on its eastern borders pressed on Kaiser Wilhelm, Germany's autocratic young leader who had dismissed Bismarck as chancellor.

As tensions heightened, all these nations had armed heavily, producing a state of military readiness that did wonders for the armament industry, and the huge munitions makers of Europe happily kept the cauldron bubbling. International tension was good for profits. But whenever countries feel so well armed, they believe themselves invincible—and that was the case in the major European capitals. The urge to use such might acquires a life of its own. Fierce nationalism, visions of invincibility, complicated alliances, and antagonism from an earlier century were combining to suck Europe into a violent maelstrom. Again, as throughout history, personalities determined the course of events as much as did economics or border disputes. Cooler heads and gentlemanly diplomacy were lost to nineteenth-century ideals of honor and country in a new century in which people didn't know how powerful their destructive powers had become. Perhaps the men raised in the nineteenth century on chivalrous, aristocratic ideals and wars still fought on horseback had no idea what havoc their twentieth-century arsenals could wreak. The world of sabers and cavalry charges was giving way to such inventions as mustard gas, U-boats, and the flamethrower (perfected by Germany), the tank (developed by the British), and a new generation of hand grenades and water-cooled machine guns. When these modern tools failed, the ancient bayonet would be the weapon of last resort. The carnage was unbelievable in battles that have become legend. Marne. Ypres. Gallipoli. Verdun. Argonne Forest. Soon these fields and plains sprouted forests of crosses.

The scenes of battle were played out for the most part in Europe, especially on the flat plains in Belgium and France, where the inhuman trench warfare would eat bodies as a flame consumes dry wood. But the real prize was elsewhere. The bottom line was that the nations of Europe were fighting over the course of empire. The spoils of victory in this Great War were Africa, Asia, and the Middle East. Whatever the professed reasons for going to war, it was the material wealth—the gold and diamonds of South Africa, the metals and rubber of Africa, the rubber of Malaysia, the oil of the Mideast—that was at the heart of the conflict.

By the time the archduke lay dead in Sarajevo, the competition had long since commenced. Germany was a well-established power in Africa, as was Belgium. France's empire extended into Indochina. England's empire covered much of Asia, Africa, and the Far East. British armies had already been bloodied in the Boer War for control of South Africa and in the Crimean War for control of the Middle East, where England had also taken over the Suez Canal. Supreme on the oceans, England was now threatened by a German navy that was being built with only one conceivable purpose—to challenge that British supremacy for eventual control of the wealth of the empire. The leaders of Europe knew their own national resources were exhaustible. Power, even survival, in the new age of industry and mechanization would come from control of these resources in the colonial worlds. The dead might pile up at Verdun, Ypres, the Marne, and a dozen other storied battlefields, but to the victor would go the riches of other continents.

Who sank the *Lusitania*, and what difference did it make?

For generations of American schoolchildren, the reason America finally decided to enter the war in Europe was to protect the open seas from German raiders in their U-boats who were killing innocent Americans aboard passenger ships. The most notorious example of this practice was supposedly the sinking of the passenger ship *Lusitania*. The problem with this explanation is that it has little to do with the facts.

Secure in its control of two continents and holding on to sufficient bits of an empire in Asia and the Pacific, America was wary of involving itself in Europe's war. Avoiding "entangling alliances" had been the underpinning of American foreign policy since the days of Washington and Jefferson. Neutralism and isolationism were powerful forces in America, where a good deal of the population was descended from the countries now at one another's throats in the mud of France. Eight million German Americans had no desire to see America at war with Germany. Another 4.5 million Irish Americans held no love for Great

Britain, then in the midst of tightening its grip on Ireland as the Irish Republican movement was reaching its peak.

Early in May 1915, the German embassy in Washington published advertisements in American papers warning Americans to avoid sailing on British ships in the Atlantic. On May 7, 1915, the Cunard liner *Lusitania* was torpedoed by a German U-boat off the coast of Ireland. In only eighteen minutes, the huge ship went down, taking with it almost 1,200 of its 1,959 passengers and crew. Among the dead were 128 Americans.

President Wilson resisted the indignant clamor for war that followed the sinking, and dealt with the Germans through a series of diplomatic notes demanding reparations and German disavowal of passenger ship attacks. William Jennings Bryan, the American secretary of state, thought even these notes were too severe a response, and resigned. Although the German government agreed to make reparations, it held to its claim that the *Lusitania* was carrying armaments and thus was a war vessel. The British denied this, but it was later revealed that the *Lusitania* carried 4,200 cases of ammunition and 1,250 shrapnel cases, which exploded when the torpedo struck, speeding the *Lusitania*'s demise.

While the sinking definitely increased tension between America and Germany, the incident had little to do with drawing America into the war. President Wilson continued to press his policies of neutrality while seeking to negotiate a settlement. He campaigned for reelection in 1916 under the Democratic slogan "He Kept Us Out of War." It would be April 1917, almost two years after the sinking, before America entered the war, already in its closing stages. In February 1917, the Germans began unlimited submarine warfare against all merchant shipping, including American ships, and Wilson broke off diplomatic relations with Germany. The crucial change came with the revelation of the Zimmermann Telegram, which uncovered a German plot to start a war between Mexico and the United States. British agents turned over this information to America, and when German submarines began to attack U.S. ships without warning in March, enraged Americans demanded war.

The stated reasons for America's involvement were freedom of the seas and the preservation of democracy. But neither side in this war had a monopoly on illegal naval warfare. Nor was the democratic ideology so powerful among America's allies that Wilson thought he should fight to maintain it as far back as 1914.

In his favor, Wilson tried admirably to restrain both sides and mediate a peace. But as in almost every other war America has fought, powerful forces in industry, banking, and commerce cynically thought that war was healthy. And if the world was going to be divvied up after the fighting was over, America might as well get its fair share of the spoils.

MILESTONES IN WORLD WAR I

1914

June 28   The crown prince of Austria, Archduke Francis Ferdinand, is murdered in the city of Sarajevo by Gavrilo Princip. Using the assassination as a pretext, the Austro-Hungarian government declares war on Serbia, its tiny southern neighbor, five days later. Russia begins to mobilize its troops in defense of Serbia.

August 1   Allied to Austria, Germany declares war on Russia. Two days later, Germany declares war on France.

August 4   Bound by mutual defense treaties, Great Britain declares war on Germany as German troops invade Belgium on the way to France.

August 5   The United States formally declares its neutrality and offers to mediate the growing conflict. In America, opinions are divided two ways: pro-Allies press for aid for England, France, and Belgium, who are depicted as victims of barbarous German aggression and atrocities; neutralists and pro-Germans—mostly German Americans—both want the United States to avoid taking sides. Pro-Allies form the Lafayette Escadrille to join the French air force, while other Americans join the British army and the French Foreign Legion or, like Ernest Hemingway, become ambulance drivers. Irish Americans denounce any assistance to Great Britain.

August 6   Germany's Central Powers ally, Austria-Hungary, declares war on Russia.

August 23 Japan declares war on Germany.

September 5 The Battle of the Marne. In the first horrific battle of the war, with each side taking casualties of 500,000, a French-English repulse of the German invasion stalls Germany's plan to quickly subdue continental Europe before Allied forces can fully mobilize. Instead, German forces fall back, beginning three years of devastating, stalemated trench warfare. The defeat also forces Germany to step up its U-boat (*Unterseeboot*) warfare to counter British naval superiority, which threatens to cut Germany off from essential war supplies. Although the German U-boats initially concentrate their attacks on warships, the submarines eventually turn to commercial and passenger shipping, a strategy that will ultimately give the United States its justification to join the Allied side.

1915

January 28 The *William P. Frye*, an American merchant ship carrying wheat to England, is torpedoed by a U-boat, the first such attack against American commercial shipping.

January 30 Colonel Edward M. House (1858–1938), a Texan who was responsible for Wilson's nomination and is now the president's most powerful adviser, sails to Europe to attempt to mediate a peace agreement. Each side feels that a quick victory is possible, and all parties decline to negotiate.

February 4 Germany declares the waters around the British Isles a war zone, threatening all shipping that approaches England.

May 1 The American tanker *Gulflight* is sunk by a German U-boat. Germany apologizes, but the ocean war is escalating as the British call for a blockade of all German ports, despite President Wilson's protest.

May 7 The British ocean liner *Lusitania* is sunk by a U-boat. Germany claims—reliably, it turns out—that the liner carried munitions; the British deny this. Nearly 1,200 of the 1,959 passengers aboard die; 128 of them are Americans who had disregarded the warnings published by Germany in American newspapers to avoid passage on vessels carrying wartime cargoes. A diplomatic crisis follows, as Germany refuses to pay reparations or disavow the attack. Secretary of State William Jennings Bryan, a pacifist, resigns in protest over what he deems a tilt toward England in Wilson's reaction to the *Lusitania*'s sinking. In a series of notes to Germany, Wilson warns against infringement of American rights. Although the sinking of the *Lusitania* has come down in history as one of the reasons the U.S. joined the war, the actual impact of the sinking was slight, and it would be almost two full years before America committed itself to war.

July 2   A German professor at Cornell University explodes a bomb in the U.S. Senate and shoots J. P. Morgan the next day. The captured professor commits suicide. A few days later, the head of German propaganda in the United States leaves on a New York subway train a suitcase filled with information about the existence of a German spy ring. It is found by the Secret Service and released to the press, further arousing anti-German sentiment.

July 25   The American merchant ship *Leelanaw*, carrying flax, is sunk off the coast of Scotland by a U-boat.

August 10   General Leonard Wood of Rough Riders fame establishes the first of several private military camps that will train 16,000 "unofficial" soldiers by 1916.

November 7   Twenty-seven Americans die in an Austrian submarine attack on the Italian liner *Ancona*.

December 7   President Wilson requests a standing army of 142,000 and reserves of 400,000.

1916

January 7   Responding to American pressure, Germany pledges to abide by international rules of naval warfare.

February 2   A congressional resolution warns Americans to avoid travel on ships owned by the warring nations. In response, President Wilson declares that American rights must be protected.

March 15 The Army Reorganization Act is passed by Congress. Under this measure, the army will be brought to a strength of 175,000 and the National Guard to 450,000 by the end of June.

March 24 Three more Americans die when a French ship is torpedoed in the English Channel, and public sympathies turn increasingly in favor of the Allied cause and against Germany.

April 20 The Easter Uprising begins. Organized with German assistance, the Irish rebellion is supposed to create a diversionary revolution in Ireland to distract Great Britain from the war in Europe. On Good Friday, April 21, both a German ship delivering arms to Ireland and a German U-boat carrying Sir Roger Casement to lead the uprising are captured by the British, who have discovered the plan through their intelligence reports. On Easter Monday, April 24, the Citizens' Army strikes in Dublin without Casement's leadership or the expected weapons, and takes over several buildings. A few days later, British troops recapture Dublin and put down the rebellion. Casement is quickly tried and hanged, as are fifteen of the rebels from Dublin. Seen as harsh "tyranny," the executions are a severe blow to British prestige in America, while the German complicity is overlooked. American sentiment for England falls to its wartime low.

June 16 Wilson is renominated by the Democrats under the slogan "He Kept Us Out of War," all the while preparing the nation for entrance into the war on the Allied side. Running on a platform of "Peace and Preparedness," he is nearly defeated by Charles Evans Hughes, a Supreme Court justice and former governor of New York who has the bellicose Teddy Roosevelt's still-influential support. It takes a week after Election Day to confirm that Wilson has carried California, where Hughes inadvertently snubbed the popular Republican governor, who then failed to campaign for him; this gaffe may have cost Hughes the state and the White House. By a thin popular and electoral margin, Wilson wins a second term. The East is solidly Republican, but the Democrat Wilson keeps the South and West. As a referendum on war policy, the election makes it clear that Americans want to stay out of the conflict. A few weeks after the election, Wilson asks the warring powers for their conditions for peace.

1917

January 22 In a speech to Congress, Wilson calls for a league of peace, an organization to promote the resolution of conflicts. But neither side is willing to agree to negotiations while holding on to the prospect of victory.

January 31 Having rapidly built its submarine fleet to over one hundred boats, Germany resumes unrestricted submarine warfare, believing it can starve the Allies into submission in six months.

February 3 Citing the German decision, Wilson breaks diplomatic relations with Germany.

February 24 In what will become known as the Zimmermann Telegram incident, the British Secret Service intercepted a telegram from German Foreign Minister Arthur Zimmermann to the German ambassador in Mexico, attempting to incite Mexico to join Germany's side in the event of war with the United States. In return, Germany promises to help Mexico recover Texas, New Mexico, and Arizona. The British have held the note until an appropriate moment when its revelations will presumably push Wilson over the brink of his wavering neutrality and into war. After the telegram is released, there is an angry public outcry over what is considered German treachery.

February 26 After asking Congress for permission to arm merchant ships, Wilson is told by his attorney general that he has that power. He issues the directive on March 9.

March 15 The Czar of Russia is forced to abdicate after the Russian Revolution. The U.S. government recognizes the new government formed by Aleksandr Kerensky.

March 12–21 Five more American ships are sunk, all without warning.

April 2 Wilson asks Congress to declare war on Germany.

It is a fearful thing to lead this great peaceful people into
war, into the most terrible and disastrous of all wars, civilization itself seeming to be in the balance. But the right is
more precious than peace, and we shall fight for the things
which we have carried nearest our hearts—for democracy,
for the right of those who submit to authority to have a
voice in their own Governments, for the rights and liberties
of small nations, for a universal dominion of right by such
a concert of free people as shall bring peace and safety to
all nations and make the world itself at least free.

Wilson's speech was met with wild applause, and Congress
overwhelmingly approved war a few days later. After delivering the
speech, Wilson told an aide, "My message today was a message of
death for our young men. How strange it seems to applaud that."

One of the only dissenting voices in Congress is that of Nebraska
Senator George W. Norris, who speaks against the declaration of war,
voicing the view of the war's opponents that it is a fight for profits
rather than for principles. Quoting from a letter written by a member
of the New York Stock Exchange favoring the war and the bull market it would produce, Norris denounces the Wall Street view:

Here we have the man representing the class of people who
will be made prosperous should we become entangled in
the present war, who have already made millions of dollars,
and who will make many hundreds of millions more if we
get into the war. Here we have the cold-blooded proposition that war brings prosperity. . . . Wall Street . . . see[s]
only dollars coming to them through the handling of
stocks and bonds that will be necessary in case of war.

Their object in having war and in preparing for war is
to make money. Human suffering and sacrifice of human
life are necessary, but Wall Street considers only the dollars
and the cents. . . . The stock brokers would not, of course,

go to war. . . . They will be concealed in their palatial offices on Wall Street, sitting behind mahogany desks.

May 18 The Selective Service Act is passed, authorizing the registration and drafting of males between the ages of twenty-one and thirty. (The Supreme Court upholds the government's right of conscription in January 1918 under the constitutional power to declare war and raise and support armies.) General John J. Pershing will lead the first contingent of Americans, the American Expeditionary Force, to France on June 24. The Rainbow Division, under Colonel Douglas MacArthur, will reach Europe on November 30.

June The Espionage Act is passed by Congress, ostensibly to prevent spying. However, it is used chiefly to silence American critics of the war. A year after its passage, Eugene Debs, the Socialist leader and presidential candidate, is arrested and sentenced to ten years in prison for making a speech that "obstructed recruiting." Debs actually ran for president again in 1920 from prison, and was eventually pardoned by President Harding after serving thirty-two months.

July 4 The first military training field for airmen opens. At the outset of war the army has fifty-five planes; by war's end there were nearly 17,000 planes in service.

November 6 The Kerensky government is overthrown by the Bolsheviks, who make peace with Germany in March 1918. The United States denies recognition of the new government.

December 7 The United States declares war on Austria-Hungary.

1918

January 8 Wilson's Fourteen Points for Peace speech. The speech outlines a generous and liberal attempt to settle the war. The last of the points states, "A general association of nations must be formed under specific covenants for the purpose of affording mutual guarantees of political independence and territorial integrity to great and small states alike." (This point will form the nucleus of the League of Nations.) Allied reaction is tepid. French prime minister Clemenceau says the Fourteen Points "bore him," and adds, "Even Almighty God has only ten."

March 21   Attempting a final concentrated assault before U.S. forces are fully involved, German troops mass for an offensive on the western front. Their eastern front is safe after the November treaty with the Bolsheviks and the collapse of the Italian forces. After an initial thrust, the Germans force the Allied lines back forty miles.

April 14   Named commander of Allied forces, French General Ferdinand Foch pleads for more troops, and 313,000 soldiers arrive by July.

June 25   After two weeks of fighting, a U.S. Marine brigade captures Belleau Wood. Casualties are nearly 9,500, more than half the brigade's entire strength.

July 17   The Allies halt the German drive in the second Battle of the Marne. A German offensive is repulsed, and an Allied counteroffensive at Soissons turns the tide.

August   Ten thousand American troops join in a Japanese invasion of Russian territory, occupying Vladivostok and some of Siberia. American troops become involved in the internal fighting as they join "White Russians" in the fighting against the Bolsheviks, and more than 500 Americans die fighting in Russia.

August 10   General Pershing establishes an independent American army with Allied permission. Colonel George C. Marshall is made operations officer.

September 14   American forces under Pershing take the salient at Saint-Mihiel.

September 26   More than 1 million Allied troops, including 896,000 Americans, join for an offensive in the last major battle of the war. Casualties reach 120,000. At the same time, British forces farther north crack the German line of defense, the Hindenburg Line.

October 3   Germany forms a parliamentary government as the army collapses and the navy revolts. The kaiser abdicates, and Germany begins peace overtures based on Wilson's Fourteen Points.

October 30   Austria asks Italy for an armistice and surrenders on November 4.

November 11   Germany signs an armistice treaty at 5 A.M., and six hours later, at the "eleventh hour of the eleventh day of the eleventh month," fighting ends. (For years, the day would be honored in America as Armistice Day, but in 1954 it was changed to Veterans Day, a federal holiday honoring all Americans who have fought or served in defense of the United States.)

1919

June 28   The Treaty of Versailles is signed, under which Germany is required to admit guilt, return the rich Alsace-Lorraine region to France, surrender its overseas colonies, and pay reparations that total $32 billion—reparations that won't be collected. (Germany spent more than $100 billion to finance the war.) Under the treaty, German rearmament is strictly limited, and the Allies take temporary control of the German economy. The League of Nations is accepted by all signatories, but a Republican-controlled U.S. Senate, left out of the treaty negotiations by Wilson, refuses to ratify the treaty. Without American participation, the League of Nations is doomed to pointlessness.

September 25   On a cross-country tour to promote popular support for the Treaty of Versailles and the League of Nations, President Wilson suffers a stroke in Colorado. Only a few insiders are allowed to see him, including Wilson's wife, Edith (who literally makes presidential decisions during his recovery), his doctor, his secretary, and Bernard Baruch. Wilson should have turned over the reins of government to his vice president, but doesn't. By November 1, he is sufficiently recovered to appear in control once more. During his absence, the Senate has hardened against the treaty and refuses to ratify it.

What was the cost of World War I?

The cost of the "war to end all wars" was nightmarish. Some 10 million died on the battlefields of Europe. Almost an entire generation of young men was decimated in Russia and France. The Russian combat death toll was 1,700,000; 1,357,000 French soldiers died, and 908,000 British. On the Central Powers side, German dead numbered 1,800,000; Austrians 1,200,000; and 325,000 Turks died in combat. Those were the dead fighters—another 20 million people died of disease, hunger, and other war-related causes. Six million more were left crippled. American losses for its short-term involvement in the war were 130,174 dead and missing and more than 200,000 wounded. The American wartime bill totaled around $32 billion.

Given these losses, the Allies were not in a forgiving mood, and the Versailles Treaty showed that they expected Germany to pay for the war that everyone had helped to start. But far more dangerous than the impossible economic terms demanded of Germany, Austria, and Turkey under the postwar settlements was the reshaping of the world map. Hungary, once part of a huge empire, lost two-thirds of its lands and was reduced to fewer than 8 million people. The independent states of Yugoslavia, Czechoslovakia, and Poland, with a corridor to the Baltic, were arbitrarily carved out of former Austro-Hungarian and German territory. Almost 3 million Austro-Germans were incorporated into Czechoslovakia. They were known as Sudeten Germans, and that name would loom large a few years later when a rebuilt Germany decided to annex the Sudetenland. The other half of the former empire became tiny Austria. And in 1939, it, too, would become part of the rationale for Germany's aggression.

The lands of the Middle East that had been the Ottoman Empire (Turkey) were split among the winners, leaving Turkey a small, impoverished state. The Balkan peninsula, part of the Ottoman Empire, was divided into a handful of new states, including Czechoslovakia and Yugoslavia. The British took Palestine, Jordan, and oil-rich Mesopotamia (modern Iraq). France won Lebanon and Syria. A young Vietnamese who had been living and studying in Paris attempted to get independent status for his country. When the French balked, Ho Chi Minh, as he was later known, went to Moscow to study the revolutionary techniques that he would later use to wrest Vietnam away from the French and American armies. The German possessions in Africa were similarly divided among the victors under a League of Nations "mandate" that simply transferred control of these African lands to new colonial powers.

In all these postwar dealings, the seeds were being sown for the next war in Europe as well as generations of deadly division in the Middle East, Africa, Eastern Europe, and Indochina.

AMERICAN VOICES

HELEN KELLER, in a letter to Eugene V. Debs, whom she addressed as "Dear Comrade" (March 11, 1919):

I write because I want you to know that I should be proud if the Supreme Court convicted me of abhorring war, and doing all in my power to oppose it. When I think of the millions who have suffered in all the wicked wars of the past, I am shaken with the anguish of a great impatience. I want to fling myself against all brute powers that destroy the life, and break the spirit of man.

What most people know of Helen Keller (1880–1968) comes from the play and film *The Miracle Worker*, which tell the remarkable story of the relationship between Helen Keller, who became blind and deaf at the age of two, and her teacher Anne Sullivan. That story stops with Keller's triumph in learning to sign. With Sullivan as her companion, Keller went on to Radcliffe, then Harvard's female counterpart, from which she graduated in 1904 with honors. Born into a conservative Alabama family, Keller eventually became both an outspoken feminist and a pacifist. In 1909, she joined the Socialist Party and became friends with party leader Eugene V. Debs, who was imprisoned for expressing his antiwar views at the time Keller's letter was written.

CHAPTER SIX

BOOM TO BUST TO BIG BOOM

From the Jazz Age and the Great Depression to Hiroshima

What happened in Tulsa and Rosewood?

Why were Sacco and Vanzetti executed?

Why was Prohibition one of the greatest social and political disasters in American history?

Who were the suffragists?

What was the scandal over Teapot Dome?

Did Henry Ford invent the automobile?

What was so lucky about Lucky Lindy?

Why did investors panic in 1929, leading to the Great Crash?

What was so "great" about the Great Depression?

What was the Bonus Army?

The Great War was over. Disillusioned and shocked by its frightful toll, Americans wanted to retreat to the safe shell of prewar isolationism. The country wanted to get back to business. That meant putting Republicans back in the White House. Starting in 1921, a Republican held the presidency for the next twelve years. First was Warren G. Harding (1865–1923), who campaigned on the promise of a "return to normalcy." (Although now commonly used, "normalcy" was not grammatically correct when Harding said it; the correct word is "normality.") After he was elected in 1920, the highlights of his weak administration were the loud whispers of presidential philandering and the infamous Teapot Dome scandal of 1922.

In the midst of that scandal, Harding died and was replaced by Calvin Coolidge (1872–1933), best remembered for his pronouncement that "the business of America is business." Known as Silent Cal, he also said, "The man who builds a factory builds a temple. And the man who works there worships there."

Under Coolidge, America seemed to prosper during the Roaring Twenties, a period in which the booming stock market was the centerpiece of a roaring economy. This was the exuberant era in which convention and old-fashioned morality were tossed aside—in spite of Prohibition—in favor of the freewheeling spirit of the Jazz Age, the days of wild new dances like the Charleston, of hip flasks and of women shucking Victorian undergarments and donning short skirts. It was the period that provided the inspiration for the fiction of F. Scott Fitzgerald, including the great representative character of the era, Jay Gatsby. The disillusionment with war and society also brought forth angry new literary voices like those of John Dos Passos (1896–1970), author of the World War I novel *Three Soldiers* (1921), and Ernest Hemingway (1899–1961), whose first novel was *The Sun Also Rises* (1926). Also bucking the conventions of the day were the acerbic journalist H. L. Mencken (1880–1956), whose writings skewered what he called the "booboisie," the complacent middle-class puritanical Americans who were also the target of Sinclair Lewis (1885–1951) in such books as *Main Street* (1920), *Babbitt* (1922), *Arrowsmith* (1925), and his great novel of religious hypocrisy, *Elmer Gantry* (1927), a body of work that brought Lewis the 1930 Nobel Prize, a first for an American author.

But the self-satisfied America targeted by these writers was very happy with the ways things were, thank you. A new industry in a far-off patch of California called Hollywood was producing a diversion that took America's mind off its troubles, which seemed to be few in the twenties. By 1927, a Jewish singer in blackface named Al Jolson told the country, "You ain't seen nothing yet," in the first "talkie," *The Jazz Singer*, and Hollywood was soon mounting multimillion-dollar productions to meet an insatiable demand for movies.

Seemingly contented with its wealth and diversions, America stayed the course in 1928 by electing Calvin Coolidge's commerce secretary, Herbert Hoover (1874–1964), an international hero as the World War I food administrator praised for keeping Europe from starving. But Hoover's reputation as a brilliant manager faded fast. He was cursed with overseeing the greatest economic collapse in history.

In the midst of the worldwide economic collapse, Hoover was dropped in 1932 in favor of the governor of New York, Franklin D. Roosevelt (1882–1945), already crippled by polio but elected overwhelmingly by a nation that desperately wanted a new direction. The economic crisis was met in America by Roosevelt's progressivism and the "New Deal." Overseas, there were different responses. As the answer to their woes, Germany turned to Hitler and Italy to Mussolini. By the middle of the depressed thirties, the war that was not supposed to be was on the horizon.

AMERICAN VOICES
"Returning Soldiers" by W. E. B. DuBois
(May 1919):

We return.
We return from fighting.
We return fighting.

What happened in Tulsa and Rosewood?

If hundreds of Americans were taken out and shot, burned alive, or tied to cars and dragged to death by a foreign army or bands of terrorists, it would certainly make front-page news and probably would have wound up in your history books. If six Americans were chased from their homes and murdered, and the homes of hundreds of others torched by an invading army, that also would have been worth a mention in the history books. But when Americans did these things to other Americans, it didn't merit much attention because the victims were black Americans in what was then a very different America.

These two massacres of large groups of innocent American citizens—or "race riots," as they were characterized—took place in Tulsa, Oklahoma, and Rosewood, Florida. But they were lost to the history books for most of the last century.

In the early 1920s, Tulsa, Oklahoma, was a boisterous postwar boom town, getting rich quick on oil that had recently been discovered there. It was a place where the postwar Ku Klux Klan recruiters found fertile grounds. The isolationist mood, or the America First movement also called nativism, was also flourishing. In the popular mood of the country, America was white and Christian, and it was going to stay that way. In 1921, when a black shoe shiner was arrested for assaulting a white girl in an elevator, the publisher of the local paper—eager to win a local circulation war—published a front-page headline screaming, "To Lynch Negro Tonight."

It was a familiar story in the Deep South of that era—a black man accused of sexually assaulting a white woman. Soon after the paper hit the streets on June 21, 1921, whites began to gather outside the courthouse where the accused shoe shiner, Dick Rowland, was being held. (Rowland was eventually released when the woman did not press charges.) Blacks from the Tulsa neighborhood of Greenwood, some of them recently discharged war veterans, also began to descend on the courthouse to protect Rowland from being lynched. Shots were fired and soon the wholesale destruction of an entire community began in hellish force. A mob of more than 10,000 whites, fully backed by the white police force, went wild. It was called a riot but in modern parlance there is a better term—"ethnic cleansing." The white folks of Tulsa seemed determined to wipe the town clean of blacks.

As historian Tim Madigan put it in his book on Tulsa, *The Burning*, "It soon became evident that whites would settle for nothing less than scorched earth. They would not be satisfied to kill negroes, or to arrest them. They would also try to destroy every vestige of black prosperity."

Soon white women were looting black homes, filling shopping bags. White men carrying gasoline set fire to the Greenwood neighborhood. When it was over, there were many dead blacks, some of them dumped into mass graves, and their neighborhood was in cinders, with more than 1,200 homes burned. Insurance companies later refused to pay fire claims, invoking a riot exemption. To add to the crime, the story disappeared from local history. Even local newspaper files were eventually cleaned out to remove evidence of the incident.

For decades, the riot and killings were hushed up, kept alive only by oral traditions of a few survivors. Only after nearly eighty years of silence did Tulsa and the Oklahoma legislature come to grips with the past. Historians looking into the city's deadly riot believe that close to 300 people died during the violence. In 2000, the Tulsa Race Riot Commission, a panel investigating the incident, recommended reparations be paid to the survivors of what is still considered the nation's bloodiest race riot.

Tulsa was the worst but it was far from unique. Starting in 1919, there were violent attacks on blacks in a number of cities, not limited to the Deep South, such as East St. Louis, Chicago, and Washington, D.C. These mass incidents, coupled with the wave of lynchings that spread throughout the South, continued for years. And usually, as with the Tulsa incident, they escaped the notice of most historians. That was the case with another notorious attack on blacks, in Rosewood, Florida, in 1923. A small mill town on the Gulf Coast, Rosewood had approximately 120 residents, mostly black. They attended church and worked at the local mills. For the most part, there was a sense of peaceful coexistence with whites in the neighboring town of Sumner. But another trumped-up charge of a black man assaulting a white woman again set off the tinderbox.

On January 2, 1923, after word of the supposed incident got out, white men from Sumner went on a rampage. During a week of shootings and house burnings, black families fled into the woods or to the protection of a few white families who offered shelter. During the Rosewood massacre, at least six blacks were killed; several of them had been lynched and mutilated. Two whites also died in the fighting. The entire small community of Rosewood was practically wiped out. And as in Tulsa, the history was soon erased from local memory in a conspiracy of silence, shame, and fear.

In 1982, a report in the *St. Petersburg Times* related the details of the incident, and the Florida state legislature was pressed to compensate the victims. In 1994, nine living victims received $150,000 in reparations. (The story was told in the 1997 film *Rosewood*.)

Must Read: *At the Hands of Persons Unknown: The Lynching of Black America* by Phillip Dray; *The Burning: Massacre, Destruction, and the Tulsa Race Riot of 1921* by Tim Madigan.

Why were Sacco and Vanzetti executed?

People might have loved Ruth—although maybe not in Boston—and they called him the Bambino. But apart from that nickname, things Italian were not held in high regard in America of the 1920s. Nicola Sacco and Bartolomeo Vanzetti had three strikes against them. They were Italian. They were immigrants. And they were anarchists. In 1920, those traits won no popularity contests in America.

When a payroll holdup at a shoe factory in Braintree, Massachusetts, left two men dead, an eyewitness said that two of the robbers "looked Italian." On the strength of that, Sacco and Vanzetti, known anarchists, were arrested. They were carrying guns at the time of their arrest. A few weeks earlier, another Italian anarchist had died when he "jumped" from the fourteenth floor of a building where he was in police custody. Sacco and Vanzetti were quickly tried by a judge whose mind was already made up about what he called "those anarchist bastards." The two men became darlings of the intellectual and leftist world. They eventually became martyrs. (Years later, FBI files and ballistics reports showed that Sacco was probably guilty and Vanzetti probably innocent.)

Guilty or not, the pair died because the country was in a frenzied, lynch mob mood created by President Wilson's attorney general, A. Mitchell Palmer (1872–1936). After a bomb exploded outside his home in 1919, Palmer unleashed a hysterical Red Scare that was the equal of the more infamous McCarthy era some thirty years later. A month earlier, bombs had been mailed to some of America's most prominent men, including John D. Rockefeller and J. P. Morgan. Although none of the intended targets was injured, the maid of one U.S. senator had her hands blown off by a letter bomb. Palmer was riding the nation's case of postwar jitters, a ride that he thought might take him all the way to the White House. To most Americans in 1919, the world had been turned upside down. The country went through a bout of economic dislocation of the sort that typically follows a high-powered wartime economy. Inflation was high and unemployment rose, bringing a new era of labor unrest. But it wasn't a good time for unions. During the war, the Wobblies (see p. 301) had been broken by the government. Wobbly leader Bill Haywood skipped bail and fled to revolutionary Russia, where he later died.

Progressivism and reform were one thing. Communism was another. The Communists had taken over in Russia. Anything faintly tainted by socialism was presumed dangerous. To many Americans, anything faintly *foreign* was dangerous. Anarchism had nothing to do with Communism, but both were lumped together in the press and in the popular mind. Most immigrants were neither Communists nor anarchists, but they were so *different*. Under Palmer, mass arrests and deportations followed. Although a small federal investigation agency, the Bureau of Investigation, had existed since early in the century, Congress had been leery of creating a national police force. The first special agents of the Bureau of Investigation had no arrest power and were not authorized to carry weapons. But in August 1919, Palmer created the Radical Division—later renamed the General Intelligence Division—and appointed a supercharged anti-Communist named J. Edgar Hoover (1895–1972) to lead it.

Born in Washington, D.C., Hoover was the youngest of four children. He attended law school, earning a law degree and master's degree in four years. During the time he worked as a clerk in the Library of Congress, he mastered the Dewey Decimal System—later applying the numbering system to the future FBI's files. During the war, his father suffered a breakdown, and Hoover was unable to enlist. Instead he joined the Justice Department and was placed in charge of the Enemy Alien Registration Unit. After the war and the bombings, Hoover was appointed to head the new division charged with rounding up and deporting radicals. With a propensity for orderliness and an early disregard for constitutional rights, Hoover began amassing files on so-called radicals on more than 45,000 index cards. As Ronald Kessler writes in *The Bureau*, "Hoover made no distinction between criminal conduct and beliefs. . . . Hoover recommended that a German who had 'engaged in a conversation with a Negro in which he indulged in pro-German utterances and in derogatory remarks regarding the United States government' be jailed. The man, who had been in the United States for thirty years, was imprisoned."

In 1920, based on Hoover's index cards, the bureau and local police conducted a dragnet, arresting thousands of alien residents. Known as the Palmer Raids, these arrests became notorious. Most of the mass arrests led to no charges or trials. But 556 people were deported, including the anarchists Emma Goldman and Alexander Berkman, who were sent to the Soviet Union.

Congress questioned the Palmer Raids, but J. Edgar Hoover established a pattern. Lawyers who testified against him or condemned the raids became the subjects of investigations. Files were opened on anyone Hoover viewed as a threat or enemy. It was a way of obtaining confidential information and using it to intimidate and exact revenge that Hoover followed throughout his long career as one of the most powerful men in America. As Kessler concludes, "After Hoover became director, he began to maintain a special Official and Confidential file in his office. The 'secret files,' as they became widely known, would guarantee that Hoover would remand director as long as he wished."

With official America on the warpath against "foreign influences," private America joined the hunt. The Ku Klux Klan revived once more, with a vengeance. The economic dislocation following the war gave the Klan its opening. New leadership gave it a respectability it had lacked before. But its violence was as deadly as ever. While blacks remained the chief targets of Klan venom, the new message of hate spread to include Jews, Catholics, and foreigners. By 1924, the "new"

Klan claimed between 4 million and 5 million members, not limited to the South. In 1923, Oklahoma's governor, J. C. Walton, declared martial law because he feared that the Klan was creating a state of insurrection. The largest Klan rally in American history was held in Chicago in 1919. The pace of lynchings, which had slackened during the war years, was revived with vicious frenzy.

Reflecting the great fear of people and things foreign, and the retreat from Europe's affairs, Congress put the brakes on immigration. In 1921, a tight quota system began to limit immigration sharply. In 1924, the quotas were further reduced, and by 1929, the total number of immigrants allowed to enter the United States was lowered to 150,000. Most of these were white Anglo-Saxons from Great Britain.

The "huddled masses yearning to breathe free" would have to hold their breath and huddle a little longer.

Must Read: *J. Edgar Hoover: The Man and the Secrets* by Curt Gentry.

Why was Prohibition one of the greatest social and political disasters in American history?

Nowadays, the night belongs to Michelob. Football stadiums ring with the chant "Less Filling! Tastes Great!" Budweiser comes wrapped in images of the workingman and the American flag. And attempts to limit beer sales at ball games are shot down as un-American. From the late-twentieth-century perspective, it is hard to imagine that this is the same country that once outlawed alcohol.

America has always had a love affair with simple solutions to complex problems. Indians on good land? Move 'em out. You want Texas? Start a war with Mexico. Crime problem? Bring back the death penalty. Prayer in schools will solve the moral lapse of the nation. Busing schoolchildren will end racial segregation. The solutions always seem so simple when politicians proclaim them, masses take up the cry and laws are passed with an outpouring of irresistible popular support. The problem is that these broad solutions rarely work the way they are supposed to.

America's grandest attempt at a simple solution was also its biggest failure. The constitutional amendment halting drinking in America was supposed to be an answer to social instability and moral decline at the beginning of the twentieth century. It should stand forever as a massive memorial to the fact that complex problems demand complex responses, and that Americans balk whenever somebody tries to legislate their private morality and personal habits.

Proposed by Congress during World War I, the Eighteenth Amendment to the Constitution prohibited "the manufacture, sale, or transportation of intoxicating liquors" within the United States. It also cut off the import and export of beer, wine, and hard liquor. In January 1919, the amendment became part of the Constitution when Nebraska voted in favor of ratification—only Rhode Island and Connecticut failed to ratify the amendment—and a year later it became the law of the land, when Congress passed the Volstead Act to enforce the law.

To President Herbert Hoover, it was "a great social and economic experiment, noble in motive and far-reaching in purpose." To Mark Twain, Prohibition drove "drunkenness behind doors and into dark places, and [did] not cure it or even diminish it."

Prohibition didn't just spring up as some wartime cure-all for the nation's social ills. The Prohibition spirit had been alive in America since colonial times, but was greatly revived in the nineteenth century, especially in the West, where drunkenness and immorality became inseparably linked. It was there that primarily women waged war on "demon rum" and, though they lacked the vote, first demonstrated the political clout they carried. The temperance movement was strongest in Midwestern and western states in the years after the Civil War. As the primary victims of social and economic ills spawned by alcoholism, women held prayer vigils in the streets outside the many saloons that had sprung up in the cattle era, then moved to grassroots organizing. In 1874, the Women's Christian Temperance Union (WCTU) came together to fight alcohol, becoming the first broad-based national women's organization in America.

By the turn of the century, the temperance gang lost its temper, led by the militancy of Carrie Nation (1846–1911). Striding into the saloons of Kansas with an ax and shouting, "Smash, women, smash!"

Nation and her followers reduced bars, bottles, glasses, mirrors, tables, and everything else in their path to splinters and shards of glass.

The sense of dislocation left after the war, the desire for "normalcy," the fear that emerged in Red Scares and Ku Klux Klan revivals, all helped pave the way for the Eighteenth Amendment. Prohibition was a notable example of the American predilection for living by one set of standards and publicly proclaiming another. In public, politicians wanted to be seen as upholding the Calvinist-Protestant ethic. Privately, most Americans consumed some alcohol before Prohibition and continued to do so afterward.

Once in place, Prohibition proved virtually unenforceable. "Bootlegger," "rum runner," and "moonshine" became part of the language. For the rich, there were "speakeasies," the ostensibly private clubs, requiring a codeword entry, that often operated under the watchful eye of the corner cop. For the poor, there was bathtub gin. Pharmacists wrote prescriptions for "medicinal" doses of alcohol, and more Catholics must have gone to Mass, because production of legal sacramental wine increased by hundreds of thousands of gallons.

Some social historians claim that Prohibition had some beneficial effects: the rate of alcoholism decreased and, with it, alcohol-related deaths. Others argue that wages weren't being spent on alcohol. This view overlooks the increased fatalities from the deadly use of rubbing alcohol in "bathtub gin." It also ignores the death toll and cost of the rise of organized crime, which may have existed before Prohibition but gained its stranglehold by controlling most of the smuggling and distribution of illicit liquor—this was the heyday of Al Capone (1898–1947) in Chicago.

Few who wanted to drink were prevented. As an attempt to restore morality, Prohibition probably produced the opposite effect. The willingness to break the law contributed to a wider decline in moral standards. Official corruption, its prevalence reduced since the earlier days of reformers and muckrakers, skyrocketed as organized crime spent millions in payoffs to government officials, from cops on the beat paid to keep a benevolent eye on the local speakeasy, to senators, judges, mayors, and governors on the criminal payroll.

While the "dry" West may have stayed sober and decent, the cities entered F. Scott Fitzgerald's Jazz Age under Prohibition. It was the Roaring Twenties, the era of the hip flask filled with smuggled gin, of the rumble seat and of the flapper—the "new woman" of the twenties. With her bobbed hair, short dresses, and exotic dances, the modern woman had two other things her mother lacked. The first was birth control, in the form of diaphragms introduced through the efforts of Margaret Sanger (1883–1966), who was arrested for "distributing obscene materials" from her New York clinic. Far from being widely available, the new method of contraception nonetheless brought the subject into the open for the first time in America.

The second was the vote.

AMERICAN VOICES
MARGARET SANGER in *The Woman Rebel,*
a monthly newspaper she published
to promote contraception (October 1914):

My work in the nursing field for the past fourteen years has convinced me that the workers desire the knowledge of prevention of conception. My work among women of the working class proved to me sufficiently that it is they who are suffering because of the law which forbids the imparting of information. To wait for this law to be repealed would be years and years hence. Thousands of unwanted children may be brought into the world in the meantime, thousands of women made miserable and unhappy.
Why should we wait?

Margaret Sanger, the greatest pioneer and proponent of the American birth control movement, was born in Corning, New York. She became a public health nurse and was convinced by the poverty she saw that contraception was a necessary step in social equality. In 1915, she was indicted for sending birth control information through the mail and then for operating a birth control clinic in Brooklyn, New York. After her first arrest, Sanger fled the country and returned when the case was dismissed. She was arrested a second time in 1916 and jailed for thirty days. She later became a founder of the Planned Parenthood Federation of America.

Who were the suffragists?

Women in America always endured plenty of suffering. What they lacked was "suffrage" (from the Latin *suffragium* for "vote").

American women as far back as Abigail Adams—who admonished her husband John to "Remember the Ladies" when he went off to declare independence—had consistently pressed for voting rights, but just as consistently had been shut out. It was not for lack of trying. But women were fighting against the enormous odds of church, Constitution, an all-male power structure that held fast to its reins, and many of their own who believed in a woman's divinely ordained, second-place role.

But in the nineteenth century, more women were pressed to work, and they showed the first signs of strength. In the 1860 Lynn, Massachusetts, shoe worker strike, many of the 10,000 workers who marched in protest were women. (At the time in Lynn, women made $1 per week against the $3 per week paid to men.) Women were also a strong force in the abolitionist movement, with Harriet Beecher Stowe attracting the most prominence. But even in a so-called freedom movement, women were accorded second-rate status.

To many male abolitionists, the "moral" imperative to free black men and give them the vote carried much greater weight than the somewhat blasphemous notion of equality of the sexes. In fact, it was the exclusion of women from an abolitionist gathering that sparked the first formal organization for women's rights. The birth of the women's movement in America dates to July 19, 1848, when Elizabeth Cady Stanton (1815–1902) and Lucretia Mott (1793–1880) called for a women's convention in Seneca Falls, New York, after they had been told to sit in the balcony at a London antislavery meeting. Of the major abolitionist figures, only William Lloyd Garrison supported equality for women. Even Frederick Douglass, while sympathetic to women's rights, clearly thought it secondary in importance to the end of slavery. The abolitionist movement did produce two of the most remarkable women of the era in Harriet Tubman (see p. 200), the escaped slave who became an Underground Railroad "conductor" and later a Union spy during the Civil War, and Sojourner Truth, a charismatic black spiritual leader and prominent spokeswoman for the rights of women.

With the Civil War's end, abolition lost its steam as a moral issue and women pressed to be included under the protection of the Fourteenth Amendment, which extended the vote to black males. But again women had to wait as politicians told them that the freed slaves took priority, a stand with which some women of the day agreed, creating a split in the feminist movement over goals and tactics. Hardliners followed Elizabeth Cady Stanton into the National Woman Suffrage Association (NWSA); moderates willing to wait for black male suffrage started the American Woman Suffrage Association (AWSA), leaving a rift that lasted twenty years. (The two wings of the women's movement reunited in 1890 in the National American Woman Suffrage Association, or NAWSA, with Stanton as its first president.)

Much of the political energy absorbed by abolition was shifted to the temperance movement after the war. Groups like the WCTU, whose greatest strength lay in the West, proved to women that they had organizational strength. Amelia Bloomer (1818–94) didn't invent the pantaloons that bore her name, but she popularized them in her newspaper, *The Lily*, a journal preaching temperance as well as equality.

Susan B. Anthony (1820–1906), called "the Napoleon of women's rights," came from the same Quaker-abolitionist-temperance background as Stanton, and the two women became friends and powerful allies, founding the NWSA together. A forceful and tireless organizer and lobbyist, she pushed for local reforms in her home state of New York while continuing to urge the vote for women at the national level. But by the turn of the century, Anthony's position fell from favor. Women shifted tactics, concentrating on winning the vote state by state, a strategy that succeeded in Idaho and Colorado, where grassroots organizations won the vote for women. After 1910, a few more western states relented, and the movement gained new momentum.

At about the same time, the suffragists took a new direction, borrowed from their British counterparts. The British "suffragettes" (as opposed to the commonly used American term "suffragist") had been using far more radical means to win the vote. Led by Emmeline Pankhurst, British suffragettes chained themselves to buildings, invaded Parliament, blew up mailboxes, and burned buildings. Imprisoned for these actions, the women called themselves "political prisoners" and went on hunger strikes that were met with force-feedings. The cruelty of this official response was significant in attracting public sympathy for the suffragette cause.

These militant tactics were brought back to America by women who had marched with the British. Alice Paul (1885–1977) was another Quaker-raised woman who studied in England and had joined the Pankhurst-led demonstrations in London. At the 1913 inauguration of Woodrow Wilson, who opposed the vote for women, Paul organized a demonstration of 10,000. Her strategy was to hold the party in power—the Democrats in this case—responsible for denying women the vote. By this time, several million women could vote in various states, and Republicans saw, as they had in winning the black vote in Grant's time, that there might be a political advantage in accepting universal suffrage.

President Wilson's views were also dictated by politics. He needed to hold on to the support of the Democratic South. That meant opposing women's voting. Southern Democrats were successfully keeping black men from voting; they certainly didn't want to worry about black women as well. Ironically, Wilson's wife, Edith Galt, proved how capable women could be at running things. During the period when Wilson was immobilized by a stroke in 1919, she literally took over the powers of the presidency, making presidential-level decisions for her invalid husband.

After Wilson's 1916 reelection, in which women in some states had voted against him two to one, the protest was taken to Wilson's doorstep as women began to picket around the clock outside the White House. Eventually imprisoned, Paul and others imitated the British tactic of hunger strikes. Again, sympathies turned in favor of the women. After their convictions were overturned, the militant suffragists returned to their White House protests.

In 1918, Paul's political tactics paid off as a Republican Congress was elected. Among them was Montana's Jeannette Rankin (1880–1973), the first woman elected to Congress. Rankin's first act was to introduce a constitutional suffrage amendment on the House floor. The amendment was approved by a one-vote margin. It took the Senate another eighteen months to pass it, and in June 1919, the Nineteenth Amendment was submitted to the states for ratification. Now fearful of the women's vote in the approaching presidential election, Wilson shifted to support of the measure. One year later, on August 26, 1920, Tennessee delivered the last needed vote, and the Nineteenth Amendment was added to the Constitution. It stated simply that "the right of citizens of the United States to vote shall not be denied by the United States or by any State on account of sex."

It took more than 130 years, but "We, the People" finally included the half of the country that had been kept out the longest.

AMERICAN VOICES
H. L. MENCKEN, famed writer for the *Baltimore Sun*, describing the scene in Dayton, Tennessee, during the Scopes Monkey Trial (July 14, 1925):

It was nearly eleven o'clock—an immensely late hour for those latitudes—but the whole town was still gathered in the courthouse yard, listening to the disputes of theologians. The Scopes trial had brought them in from all directions. There was a friar wearing a sandwich sign announcing that he was the Bible champion of the world. There was a Seventh Day Adventist arguing that [defense attorney] Clarence Darrow was the beast with seven heads described in Revelation XIII, and that the end of the world was at hand. There was an ancient who maintained that no Catholic could be a Christian. There was the eloquent Dr. T. T. Martin, of Blue Mountain, Miss., come to town with a truck load of torches and hymn-books to put Darwin in his place. There was a singing brother bellowing apocalyptic hymns. There was William Jennings Bryan, followed everywhere by a gaping crowd. Dayton was having a roaring time. It was better than the circus. The real religion was not present.

Mencken had been dispatched to cover what was then the "trial of the century." Schoolteacher John T. Scopes had been charged with illegally teaching the Darwinian theory of evolution. He was defended by Clarence Darrow, the most prominent defense attorney of the day. The prosecution was led by William Jennings Bryan, the Populist leader. Scopes was found guilty and paid a $100 fine. (The trial is the source of the play and later film *Inherit the Wind*.)

What was the scandal over Teapot Dome?

As one century ended and another began under a cloud of corporate scandals and questions about government regulation of business, one thing is for certain. Enron is as American as apple pie. There is nothing new under the sun, and cases of corporate corruption, with government officials receiving handsome payoffs, crop up like weeds in America's history. In the nineteenth century, there had been fixing of gold prices, scandals in the Grant administration, topped by the Crédit Mobilier scandal (see p. 267). In the 1920s, the corruption would flower again, threatening a genial Republican president who liked to leave his hands off business.

Tired of the war and eight years of Democrat Woodrow Wilson, a weary nation welcomed the noncontroversial Warren G. Harding, a small-town, self-made businessman with matinee-idol good looks. Opposed by James M. Cox—who ran with Wilson's young assistant secretary of the navy, Franklin D. Roosevelt—Harding and his running mate, Calvin Coolidge, the governor of Massachusetts, easily won in a low-turnout election. (Socialist Eugene V. Debs garnered 3.5 percent of the vote.) Harding was popular, but by many accounts, may have been the laziest man ever elected president.

Harding's was a classic Republican administration. Tax cuts. Help for big business. An America-first foreign policy that rejected Wilson's League of Nations and set up stiff tariffs to protect American industry.

But his administration would also soon be dogged by what came to be called the Harding scandals. The first of these involved the siphoning of millions of dollars allocated for Veterans Administration hospitals. In another seamy episode, Harding's attorney general Harry Daugherty was implicated in fraud related to the return of German assets seized during the war, and avoided conviction only by invoking the Fifth Amendment.

But the most famous of the Harding scandals involved a place called Teapot Dome. Two federal oil reserves—one in Elk Hills, California, and the other in Teapot Dome, Wyoming—were marked for the future use of the U.S. Navy. But the interior secretary, Albert B. Fall, contrived to have these lands turned over to his department. He then sold off drilling leases to private developers in return for hundreds of thousands of dollars in bribes and kickbacks in the form of cash, stock, and cattle. In August 1923, as this scandal was being uncovered by a Senate investigation, Harding suffered a fatal heart attack—misdiagnosed by an incompetent surgeon general as food poisoning—while in San Francisco on his way home from a trip to Alaska. Interior Secretary Fall was later convicted for accepting a bribe, thereby achieving the distinction of becoming the first cabinet officer in American history to go to jail.

Calvin Coolidge, untainted by the scandals, took Harding's place and handily won reelection in 1924.

Did Henry Ford invent the automobile?

Autos and airplanes. The prosperity of the twenties was due in large part to a shift from the nineteenth century's Industrial Revolution, symbolized by the railroads, to a twentieth-century revolution in technology. The invention and widespread commercial development of both the automobile and the airplane defined that shift. And during this period, both industries were defined by two American icons, Henry Ford and Charles A. Lindbergh. In their day, both men were revered. History has not been so kind.

Henry Ford (1864–1947) did not invent the automobile or the assembly line. But his perfected versions of them made him one of the richest and most powerful men in America. The son of an Irish immigrant farmer, Ford had a mechanical inclination. In 1890, he went to work for the Edison company in Detroit and built his first gasoline-driven car there. Europeans had taken the lead in the development of the automobile, and the Duryea brothers of Massachusetts were the American pioneers. Ford borrowed from their ideas, envisioning the auto as a cheap box on wheels with a simple engine, and brought out his first Model T in 1909. In a year he sold almost 11,000 of them.

But Ford envisioned a car for the masses. When Ford and his

engineers introduced the moving assembly line, an idea proposed in a 1911 book by Frederick W. Taylor, the mass-produced Model T revolutionized the auto industry. The efficiency of the assembly line cut the price tag on the Model T from $950 in 1908 to under $300. By 1914, Ford Motors turned out 248,000 Model Ts, almost half of all autos produced, at the rate of one every 24 seconds. Realizing enormous profits, Ford made headlines by paying his workers $5 per day, almost double the going rate. Ford himself was clearing up to $25,000 per day. Paying his workers more money was Ford's only way to keep them from quitting the monotonous, dehumanizing assembly line. He also realized that it was one way to enable his workers to buy Fords.

For Americans, it was love at first sight with the automobile. It is fair to say the Model T revolutionized American life. When Congress enacted highway fund legislation in 1916 and the country embarked on a massive road-building era, the American dream of freedom on the open road became a new reality. In a short time the auto industry became the keystone of the American economy, in good times and bad. New industries in roadside services—such as service stations, diners, and motels—sprang to life all over the country. The country cottage was no longer the exclusive preserve of the Vanderbilts and Morgans. The auto gave the working and middle classes a sense of accomplishment. The new, auto-induced sense of freedom, and the economic prosperity created by the automobile and related industries, helped to open up American society in the 1920s.

Henry Ford cared little for social improvements or the broad sweep of history. "History is more or less bunk," he said. Autocratic and conservative, he tyrannized his workers. He fired anyone caught driving a competitor's model. Gangster tactics were used to maintain discipline in plants, and unionizing efforts were met with strike-breaking goon squads. Unions were kept out of Ford plants until 1941. Ford's attitude was that workers were unreliable and shiftless. In the midst of the Depression, he blamed the workingman's laziness for the nation's economic problems. "The average worker," said Ford, "won't do a day's work unless he is caught and can't get out of it."

His conservatism spilled over into his political beliefs. An isolationist in foreign policy—although his plants won big defense jobs during both world wars—Ford was also an outspoken anti-Semite. Ford bought a newspaper, the *Independent,* that became an anti-Jewish mouthpiece. The paper was involved in the American publication of *The Protocols of the Elders of Zion,* an anti-Semitic propaganda tract that had first appeared in Russia in 1905 to castigate Jews. But Ford's conservative, stubborn streak cost him in the long run. Unwilling to adapt to changing styles, Ford Motors later slipped behind more aggressive competitors like General Motors. Yet at his death in 1947, Henry Ford remained an American folk hero for personifying the rags-to-riches American myth.

What was so lucky about Lucky Lindy?

Lucky Lindy was the other great hero of the era. Like Ford, Charles Lindbergh (1902–75) invented nothing. The Wright brothers had begun their famous experiments at Kitty Hawk, North Carolina, in 1903, and the Lockheed brothers built their early commercial planes in 1913. Strictly speaking, Lindbergh wasn't even the first to fly across the Atlantic. A pair of Englishmen had flown from Newfoundland to Ireland in 1919 (a route considerably shorter than Lindbergh's).

But the war in Europe had given a real boost to the commercial potential of the airplane. While the air industry was not as economically crucial to the twenties as Ford's automobile, it was symbolic of the venturesome spirit of the times. Lindbergh's design of his aircraft, which he called *The Spirit of St. Louis,* allowed him to become the first man to fly solo across the Atlantic. It was an act of enormous daring, skill, and flying ability. The 3,600-mile flight began on Long Island on May 20, 1927. Attempting to win a $25,000 purse promised to the first pilot to go from New York to Paris, Lindbergh carried only a few sandwiches, a quart of water, and letters of introduction. He wouldn't need those. When he landed in Paris thirty-three hours later, Lindbergh was smothered in the adulation of France and the rest of Europe. His hero's welcome would be repeated around the world as he became, like Ford, the symbol of do-anything American inventiveness and daring. A reclusive personality, Lindbergh became best known by his newspaper nickname, Lucky Lindy, and he was the world's most familiar celebrity.

That celebrity led to the great tragedy in his life. After his marriage to Anne Spencer Morrow, daughter of a U.S. senator and later a renowned writer, he lived in the glare of international publicity. In May 1932, their son, nineteen-month-old Charles Jr., was kidnapped, and a $50,000 ransom demand was met. But the child was found murdered. Like the Sacco and Vanzetti affair, the case of Bruno Hauptmann, the man electrocuted for the crime in 1936, has never quite gone away. More than sixty years after Hauptmann's execution, there were many who claimed that he was innocent, the victim of a frame-up. There is little question that the country's antiforeign frenzy at the time helped convict him, but the evidence in the case was always strong against him. The infamous kidnapping, which dominated newspapers in the midst of the Depression's worst year, prompted congressional passage of the so-called Lindbergh Law which made kidnapping a federal offense if the victim is taken across state lines or if the mail service is used for ransom demands, a measure making kidnapping across state lines a capital crime.

Ford and Lindbergh shared something besides their fame and success. By the late 1930s, both men were notorious for their conservative, isolationist, and anti-Semitic political views. Lindbergh made several trips to Germany to inspect the German air force (Luftwaffe) and, in 1938, was presented with a medal by Hermann Goering, first leader of Hitler's storm troopers, founder of the Gestapo, and Hitler's air minister. Ford also received a medal from Hitler himself in 1938. After pronouncing Germany's military superiority, Lindbergh returned to America to become an outspoken leader of the isolationist America First movement, funded with Ford money, that tried to keep the United States out of World War II. In one speech, Lindbergh nearly killed the movement when he warned Jews in America to "shut up" and borrowed the well-worn Nazi tactic of accusing "Jewish-owned media" of pushing America into the war. Although he was in the air corps reserve, Lindbergh's criticism of Roosevelt forced him to resign his commission. During the war, he served as a consultant to Ford and later flew combat missions in the Pacific. After the war, he was a consultant to the Defense Department. His heroics kept his reputation intact.

Must Read: *Lindbergh* by A. Scott Berg.

From HERBERT HOOVER'S "Rugged Individualism"
campaign speech (October 22, 1928):

When the war closed, the most vital of all issues both in
our own country and throughout the world was whether
Governments should continue their wartime ownership
and operation of many instrumentalities of production and
distribution. We are challenged with a peace-time choice
between the American system of rugged individualism
and a European philosophy of diametrically opposed doctrines—doctrines of paternalism and state socialism.

. . . Our American experiment in human welfare has
yielded a degree of well-being unparalleled in all the world.
It has come nearer to the abolition of poverty, to the abolition of fear of want than humanity has ever reached before.

Why did investors panic in 1929, leading to the Great Crash?

When Herbert Hoover made that speech, America did seem to be a
place of unlimited opportunity. Apart from a huge underclass of the
unemployed and poor farmers that Hoover overlooked and prosperity bypassed, the bulk of the country probably agreed with Hoover's
sentiment. The year 1927 was one more in the prosperous years of the
Roaring Twenties. Lindbergh's 1927 flight to Paris came in the midst
of the country's "Coolidge boom." An avatar of unlimited potential,
Lindbergh added another boost to American feelings of confidence,
invincibility, and Hoover's "rugged individualism."

With such good feelings in the air, Hoover was elected by a huge
margin in 1928. But another factor in his election was the religion
of his Democratic opponent, New York governor Al Smith, a Roman
Catholic. "A vote for Smith is a vote for the Pope," proclaimed campaign banners in 1928. Smith also favored repeal of Prohibition, and
another slogan said Smith would bring "Rum, Romanism, and Ruin"
to America. But more than anything else, the Hoover victory was made
possible by "general prosperity."

And nowhere was the prosperity more conspicuous than on Wall Street, home of the New York Stock Exchange. During the 1920s, new companies like General Motors had issued stock that was making many an investor, large and small, seemingly wealthy. An ambitious young man like Joseph P. Kennedy (1888–1969), unfettered by the restraints of any regulatory authority (the Securities and Exchange Commission was a later creation), could make a large fortune for himself with not always scrupulous means. In fact, a great number of the most success-ful men in those days were operating in shady territory. Working in "pools," crooked manipulators bought cheap shares of stock, drove up the prices among themselves, then lured outside investors into the pool. The pool operators then dumped their stocks at artificially in-flated prices, leaving the "sucker" holding a bag of overpriced stock.

The most notorious of the wealthy crooks of the day was the "Swed-ish match king," Ivar Krueger. Claiming to be an intimate of the crowned heads of Europe, Krueger built a huge financial empire on credit granted by some of the era's leading financial institutions. Fea-tured on the cover of *Time* as a giant of business, Krueger was a con man of the first order, whose empire was based on deception. He issued worthless securities and later counterfeited Italian government bonds. Equally notorious was Samuel Insull, a "self-made" millionaire who used millions put up by working-class investors—many of them public employees caught in the spell of Insull's magnificent wealth—to build a public utilities empire, all the while manipulating stock prices to his benefit. Before the crash, Insull controlled an empire of holding com-panies, and he personally held eighty-five directorships, sixty-five board chairmanships, and eleven company presidencies.

The paper wealth being acquired masked a rot in the American economy. American farmers continued to struggle following the post-war collapse of agricultural prices. Before the Great Depression, un-employment was already high as factories became mechanized and the worker at the bottom was let go. Housing starts fell in 1927, al-ways an ominous sign in the American economy. The problems were not only America's. International production intensified, but demand slackened and warehouses filled up. The wealth of the world was con-centrated in the hands of a small class at the top. The wealth trickling down from the top was not enough. The great bulk of the population simply couldn't create the demand needed to keep up with the increasing supply. The American consumer could not consume all goods that American manufacturers were producing.

Yet thousands of Americans were drawn to the lure of fortunes made in the market. Like moths to the flame, people pulled their life savings from banks and put them into stocks and securities, like Insull Utilities Investments. The easygoing rules of the day meant that investors had to put down only ten to twenty percent in cash to buy stock; the rest was available on cheap credit. The Federal Reserve fed the frenzy with artificially low interest rates set by old-line Republicans beholden only to their corporate pals. Banks loaned millions to feed speculative schemes. The American public was in enormous debt and their "wealth" was all on paper.

By late 1929, barely a year after Hoover had spoken about the abolition of poverty, the cracks in the foundation began to show. Steel and automobile production, two centerpieces of the American economy, were in decline. Yet still the stock market rose, reaching its peak in late September 1929. But the house of cards was about to tumble. Skittish European investors began to withdraw their investments in the United States. When brokers called customers to pay off the amounts owed on stocks bought with borrowed money, these investors had to sell off their stocks to raise cash. This created a wave of fear—the fear of losing everything—that quickly gained momentum. As stock prices fell, more brokers called on customers to put up more cash, and a vicious cycle was unleashed, sending prices on the stock exchange plunging. On October 24, Black Thursday, 13 million shares of stock were sold off. A combine of bankers led by John P. Morgan Jr. set up a pool of cash to prop up prices, as Morgan's father had done in 1907 during a similar panic in the market. This attempt to inspire confidence failed. By the following week, on October 29—Black Tuesday—more than 16 million shares were sold off as panic swept the stock exchange. (In today's world, hundreds of millions of shares change hands daily. But in 1929, the market was much smaller and there were no computers recording deals.) Within days, the "wealth" of a large part of the country, which had been concentrated in vastly inflated stock prices, simply vanished.

AMERICAN VOICES
FREDERICK LEWIS ALLEN, in his social history
of the period, *Since Yesterday*:

> The official statistics of the day gave the volume of trading
> as 16,410,030 shares, but no one knows how many sales
> went unrecorded in the yelling scramble to sell. There are
> those who believe that the true volume may have been
> twenty or even twenty-five million. Big and small, insiders
> and outsiders, the high-riders of the Big Bull Market
> were being cleaned out: the erstwhile millionaire and his
> chauffeur, the all-powerful pool operator and his suckers,
> the chairman of the board with his two-thousand-share
> holding and the assistant bookkeeper with his ten-share
> holding, the bank president and his stenographer. . . . The
> disaster which had taken place may be summed up in a single
> statistic. In a few short weeks it had blown into thin air
> *thirty billion dollars*—a sum almost as great as the entire
> cost of the United States participation in the [first] World
> War, and nearly twice as great as the entire national debt.

What was so "great" about the Great Depression?

Wall Street's Great Crash of 1929 did not "cause" the decade of the
Great Depression that followed, any more than the assassination of
Archduke Ferdinand had "caused" World War I. The crash was a
symptom of the economy's serious disease. It was the fatal heart attack
for a patient also suffering from terminal cancer. By the time the
market rallied a few years later in the Little Bull Market, it was too late.
The damage had been done. The crash had been the last tick of a time
bomb that, when it exploded, brought down the world economy.

America had suffered depressions before. But none of them had
been capitalized like the Depression of the 1930s. None had ever lasted
so long, and none had ever touched so many Americans so devastatingly.
After the crash, the economy was paralyzed. In one year, 1,300
banks failed. There was no such thing as Federal Deposit Insurance

guaranteeing the savings of working people. Hard-earned savings disappeared as 5,000 banks closed during the next three years, their assets tied up in the speculating that created wealth but disappeared in the crash, or in mortgages that the jobless could no longer pay. Without banks to extend credit and capital, businesses and factories closed, forcing more workers onto unemployment lines. In 1931, Henry Ford blamed the laziness of workers for the calamity. A short time later, he closed a plant and, with it, 75,000 jobs were lost.

The jolted American system got two more shocks when the empires of Ivar Krueger and Samuel Insull came tumbling down. Insull had built a pyramid of holding companies and used them to push up the value of his stock. By 1932, the artificial values had fallen to their true worth, declining in value by some 96 percent. Indicted by a Chicago grand jury, Insull fled to Greece, where he hoped to escape extradition. When Greece later signed an extradition treaty with the United States, Insull, who had once surrounded himself with three dozen bodyguards, disguised himself as a woman and sailed for Turkey. Eventually he was brought back to the United States and tried. But Insull escaped punishment. The holding companies he had used were outside regulation; all his manipulations were technically legal.

Ivar Krueger was less lucky. Living in a luxurious Paris apartment, he was also revealed as a swindler. Once an adviser to President Hoover, he had stolen more than $3 million from investors. Krueger didn't wait for an indictment. He shot himself in the spring of 1932, before the worst of his schemes was even brought into the open.

Before the Great Depression, America had absorbed periodic depressions because most people lived on farms and were able to produce what they needed to survive. But the American and world economy had been thoroughly revolutionized in the early twentieth century. This was an urbanized, mechanized America in which millions were suddenly unemployed, with no farms to go home to. Statistics are virtually meaningless when it comes to the magnitude of joblessness. Official numbers said 25 percent of the workforce was unemployed. Other historians have said the number was more like 40 to 50 percent.

Through his last three desperate years in office, Herbert Hoover continued to voice optimism. Like most economists of his day, Hoover believed that depressions were part of the business cycle. America had

suffered them before and had shaken them off after a period of dislocation. But this time was different. Hoover made a long, steady stream
of pronouncements about how the corner had been turned. Instead,
things turned bleaker. As millions were losing their homes, unable
to pay rent or mortgages, Hoover and other members of the wealthy
class made some incredible statements. When the International Apple
Shippers' Association, overstocked with apples, decided to sell its vast
surplus to unemployed men on credit so that they could resell them
on street corners for a nickel apiece, Hoover remarked, "Many people
have left their jobs for the more profitable one of selling apples." Henry
Ford, who put 75,000 men out of work and on the road as "hoboes" in
search of work, said of the hundreds of thousands of wandering men,
women, and children, "Why, it's the best education in the world for
those boys, that traveling around! They get more experience in a few
months than they would in years at school." J. P. Morgan believed that
there were 25 or 30 million families in the "leisure class"—that is, able
to employ a servant. He was startled to learn that there were fewer than
two million servants in the entire country.

Hoover clung to his optimistic line. "Business and industry have
turned the corner," he said in January 1930. "We have now passed
the worst," was the cheery word in May. Prosperity was always right
around the corner. But the country never seemed to reach that corner.
Hoover has come down in history as a do-nothing Nero who fiddled
while Rome burned. That portrait is not quite accurate. The problem
was that just about everything he tried either backfired or was too little,
too late. In 1930, he went along with a protectionist bill—the Hawley-
Smoot Tariff Bill—which threw up trade barriers around the United
States. This simply prompted the European countries to do the same
thing, worsening the crisis both in the United States and in Europe. By
1931, the Depression had spread throughout Europe, where the scars
of the war were still not healed and the crush of wartime debt contributed to the crisis. Austria, England, France, and, most ominously,
Germany were all sucked into a violent whirlpool of massive unemployment and staggering inflation.

Hoover was steadfast in his refusal to allow the government to help
the jobless, homeless, and starving through government relief programs he viewed as Socialist and Communist. He did, at least, ignore

the advice of one of the nation's wealthiest men, Treasury Secretary Andrew Mellon (1855–1937), whose tax policies in the 1920s had contributed to underlying flaws in the American economy. Mellon advised a complete laissez-faire response, proposing to "liquidate labor, liquidate stocks, liquidate the farmer, liquidate real estate." He thought that through this scorched-earth policy, "people will work harder, live a more moral life. Values will be adjusted and enterprising people will pick up the wrecks from less competent people." Hoover eased the aging Mellon out of the Treasury and made him ambassador to England.

Hoover set up a belated public works program that, by the time it started, was woefully inadequate, unable to replace all the local building projects that had been killed by the banking collapse. In 1932, bowing to the pressure of the time and going against his deep conservative grain, Hoover created the Reconstruction Finance Corporation, which loaned money to railroads and banks.

But even in this, Hoover was snakebit. To the millions of unemployed and starving, the RFC was a bitter symbol of Hoover's willingness to aid corporations while showing complete indifference to the poor. In spite of the growing misery, the lengthening bread lines, the "Hoovervilles" of cardboard shacks being thrown up in America's large cities, the utter despair of hundreds of thousands without homes or hope, Hoover staunchly refused to allow government to issue direct aid. By his lights, it was socialism to do so, and was completely contrary to his notion of "rugged individualism."

What was the Bonus Army?

In the midst of the Depression, buglers called President Hoover and the first lady to seven-course dinners served by a small army of white-gloved servants. President Hoover thought that keeping up regal trappings and spiffy appearances was good for national morale. Outside, Americans were fighting for scraps from garbage cans. But some "rugged individuals" were going to give Hoover an unpleasantly close look at life on the other side of the Depression fence.

In the summer of 1932, the Depression's worst year, 25,000 former "doughboys"—World War I infantrymen, many of whom were combat veterans—walked, hitchhiked, or "rode the rails" to Washington, D.C. Organizing themselves into a penniless, vagrant army, they squatted, with their families, in abandoned buildings along Pennsylvania Avenue and pitched an encampment of crude shacks and tents on the banks of the Anacostia River. They had come to ask Congress to pay them a "bonus" promised to veterans in 1924 and scheduled to be paid in 1945. Starving and desperate men, they had families going hungry, no jobs, and no prospects of finding one. They needed that bonus to survive. Calling themselves the Bonus Expeditionary Force (BEF), they were better known as the Bonus Army.

Their pleas for relief fell on deaf ears. To Hoover, Congress, lawmen, and the newspapers, these weren't veterans but "Red agitators." (Hoover's own Veterans Administration surveyed the Bonus Army and found that 95 percent of them were indeed veterans.) Instead of meeting the BEF's leaders, Hoover called out the troops, commanded by General Douglas MacArthur (1880–1964) with his young aide Dwight Eisenhower (1890–1969). The assault was led by the Third Cavalry, sabers ready, under the command of Major George Patton (1885–1945). Behind the horses, the U.S. Army rolled out to meet the ragged bunch of men, women, and children with tear gas, tanks, and bayonets.

Patton's cavalry first charged the Bonus Marchers, now mixed with curious civilians who were getting off from work on this hot July afternoon. Following the cavalry charge came the tear-gas attack, routing the Bonus Army from Pennsylvania Avenue and across the Eleventh Street Bridge. Disregarding orders—a common thread running through his career—MacArthur decided to finish the job by destroying the Bonus Army entirely. After nightfall, the tanks and cavalry leveled the jumbled camp of tents and packing-crate shacks. It was all put to the torch. There were more than one hundred casualties in the aftermath of the battle, including two babies suffocated by the gas attack.

Pushed out of the nation's capital, the Bonus Army dissipated, joining the other two million Americans "on the road." Some states, like California, posted guards to turn back the poor. The violence in Washington, D.C., was the largest but not the only demonstration of a growing anger and unrest in America. During 1931 and 1932, there had been a number of riots and protests, mostly by the unemployed and hungry, sometimes by children, that were put down with harsh police action.

The assault on the Bonus Marchers came as the 1932 presidential campaign was getting under way. A grim Herbert Hoover had been renominated in June by the Republicans on a platform that promised to balance the budget, keep tariffs high on foreign goods, and—in a reversal of its position four years before—repeal Prohibition, allowing the states to control alcohol.

Believing that only a major disaster could prevent them from re-capturing the White House, held by Republicans for twelve years, the Democrats met in Chicago. Three leading candidates emerged for the nomination: Al Smith, the 1928 standard-bearer who had been swamped by Hoover; the powerful Speaker of the House, John Nance Garner of Texas, who had the support of newspaper czar William Randolph Hearst, who in turn controlled the California delegation; and Al Smith's handpicked successor as governor of New York, Franklin D. Roosevelt (1882–1945). Roosevelt led after the first ballot, but lacked the votes to win the nomination. In a classic "smoke-filled room" deal, Garner was promised the vice-presidency in return for his support of Roosevelt. On the fourth ballot, with Hearst throwing California's delegates to Roosevelt, the popular governor won the nomination. Roosevelt immediately wanted to demonstrate that he was not going to be bound by any traditions. He flew to Chicago to accept the nomination, launching the tradition of the nominee's speech to the convention. Roosevelt also wanted to demonstrate to the country that although crippled by polio, he would not be stopped from going where he wanted.

Not everyone agreed that it was a great choice. Two of the leading newspapermen of the day were H. L. Mencken and Walter Lippmann (1899–1974). Mencken said the convention had nominated "the weakest candidate." Lippmann, perhaps the most influential columnist in the country at the time, was even more disparaging. He called FDR an "amiable boy scout" who lacked "any important qualifications for the office."

It didn't matter. The Democrats could have run an actual Boy Scout that year and won. The country might not have been sure about wanting FDR, who ran a conservative campaign but promised a "new deal" for the country and the repeal of Prohibition, establishment of public works, and aid to farmers. But they were sure they didn't want Herbert Hoover. "General Prosperity" led the way for Hoover in 1928. But "General Despair" knocked him out in 1932. Roosevelt won the election with 57 percent of the popular vote, carrying forty-two of forty-eight states. The Democrats also swept into majorities of both houses of Congress.

After Roosevelt's inauguration, the Bonus Army returned to Washington. Roosevelt asked his wife, Eleanor (1884–1962), to go and speak to the men, and let them have plenty of free coffee. The first lady mingled with the marchers and led them in songs. One of them later said, "Hoover sent the army. Roosevelt sent his wife."

Must Read: *The Great Depression: America, 1929–1941* by Robert S. McElvaine.

American Voices
From Franklin D. Roosevelt's
first inaugural address, March 4, 1933:

This is pre-eminently the time to speak the truth, the whole truth, frankly and boldly. Nor need we shrink from honestly facing conditions in our country today. This great nation will endure as it has endured, will revive and will prosper.

So first of all let me assert my firm belief that the only thing we have to fear is fear itself—nameless, unreasoning, unjustified terror which paralyzes needed efforts to convert retreat into advance.

Most of Roosevelt's campaign speeches had been written for him, but a handwritten first draft of the inaugural address shows this to be Roosevelt's own work. Yet the speech's most famous line was old wine in a new bottle. Similar sentiments about fear had been voiced before. The historian Richard Hofstadter notes that Roosevelt read Thoreau in the days before the inauguration and was probably inspired by the line "Nothing is so much to be feared as fear."

What were the New Deal and the Hundred Days?

When he took the Democratic nomination with a ringing acceptance speech, Roosevelt promised the people a "new deal." In his inaugural, he promised a special session of Congress to deal with the national economic emergency. He came through on both promises.

The legislative centerpiece of Roosevelt's response to the Great Depression, the New Deal was a revolution in the American way of life. A revolution was required because Roosevelt's election did not signal a turnaround for the depressed American economy. Between Election Day and the inauguration, the country scraped bottom. Bank closings continued as long lines of panicky depositors lined up to get at their savings. Governors around the country began to declare "bank holidays" in their states. On March 5, his first day in the White House, Roosevelt did the same thing, calling for a nationwide four-day bank holiday. That night he talked to Americans about how banking worked in the first of his "fireside chats"—radio addresses aimed at educating the public, soothing fears, and restoring the confidence and optimism of a nation that had little left.

Then he called Congress to a special emergency session. From March through June, the One Hundred Days, the U.S. Congress passed an extraordinary series of measures, sometimes without even reading them. Roosevelt's approach was, "Take a method and try it. If it fails, try another."

The result was the "alphabet soup" of new federal agencies, some of them successful, some not.

Like the other President Roosevelt of an earlier era, FDR looked to the nation's human resources and created the Civilian Conservation Corps (CCC), which provided jobs for young men from eighteen to twenty-five years old in works of reforestation and other conservation.

The Agricultural Adjustment Administration (AAA) was created to raise farm prices by paying farmers to take land out of production. This plan had two major drawbacks. The nation was outraged to see pigs slaughtered and corn plowed under by government decree to push up farm prices while there were so many people starving. And thousands of mostly black sharecroppers and tenant farmers, lowest on the economic pecking order, were thrown off the land when farmers took their land out of production.

The object of even greater controversy, the Tennessee Valley Authority (TVA), a federally run hydroelectric power program, was one of the most radical departures. Under the TVA Act, the federal government created a huge experiment in social planning. The TVA not only produced hydroelectric power, but built dams, produced and sold fertilizer, reforested the area, and developed recreational lands. (The TVA also created the Oak Ridge facility, which later provided much of the research and development of the atomic bomb.) It was an unprecedented involvement of government in what had once been the exclusive—even sacred—domain of private enterprise, and was wildly condemned as communistic.

The Hundred Days also saw creation of the Federal Deposit Insurance Corporation (FDIC), designed to protect savings; the Home Owners Loan Corporation, which refinanced mortgages and prevented foreclosures; and a Federal Securities Act to begin policing the activities of Wall Street. In 1934, the Securities and Exchange Commission (SEC) was created, and Roosevelt appointed Joseph Kennedy, a notorious speculator in his day, to be its first chief. The thinking was that Kennedy would know all the tricks that any crooked brokers might try to pull. In May 1933, the Federal Emergency Relief Administration (FERA) was created and given $500 million in federal relief funds for the most seriously destitute, the beginning of a federal welfare program.

One of the final acts of the Hundred Days was passage of the most controversial New Deal bill, the National Industrial Recovery Act, aimed at stimulating industrial production. This act was a huge attempt at government control of production, labor, and costs. To gain the acceptance of business and labor, it contained goodies for both. It allowed manufacturers to create "business codes," a legal form of price fixing that would have been forbidden under antitrust laws while giving workers minimum wages, maximum hours, and collective bargaining rights.

To its organizers, the act took on the trappings of a holy crusade. To oversee the law, the National Recovery Administration (NRA) was created, with its Blue Eagle symbol. Companies and merchants pledged to the NRA displayed the eagle and the motto "We Do Our Part," and consumers were advised to buy only from those places that displayed the NRA symbol. Massive marches and parades in support of the program took place across the country. A million people marched in an NRA parade in New York City.

But abuses by industry were widespread. Prices were fixed high, and production was limited in most cases, creating the opposite of the intended effect of increasing jobs and keeping prices low. The NRA did spur labor union recruitment, and the United Mine Workers under John L. Lewis (1880–1969) grew to half a million members. A barrel-chested dynamo, Lewis then joined with other unions to form the Committee for Industrial Organization (CIO), which splintered off from the conservative AFL in 1938 but soon was its rival in numbers and influence.

The first Hundred Days came to an end with passage of the NIRA bill, but the Great Depression was still far from over. Yet in this short time, Roosevelt had not just created a series of programs designed to prop up the economy. His New Deal marked a turning point in America as decisive as 1776 or 1860. It was nothing less than a revolutionary transformation of the federal government from a smallish body that had limited impact on the average American into a huge machinery that left few Americans untouched. For better or worse, Roosevelt had begun to inject the federal government into American life on an unprecedented scale, a previously unthinkable reliance on government to accomplish tasks that individuals and the private economy were unwilling or unable to do. From the vantage point of the twenty-first century, there is little in modern America that is unaffected by the decisions made in Washington. It is difficult to imagine a time when a president, creating the federal machinery designed to carry the country out of crisis, was viewed as a Communist leading America down the road to Moscow.

What was the WPA?

The New Dealers worked overtime, but the Depression went on. While production and consumption rose, they remained well below precrash levels. The unemployment figures never fell much below 10 percent, and they were much higher in some cities. The mid-thirties brought the droughts and winds that created the Dust Bowl of the plains states, sending thousands of farmers off the foreclosed farms and on the road. This was the woeful exodus immortalized by John Steinbeck in *The Grapes of Wrath*.

With the "try anything" approach, Roosevelt set up new programs. For each program that died or failed to do its job, he was ready to create a new one. When the Supreme Court unanimously killed the NRA as unconstitutional, Roosevelt tried the WPA. The Works Progress Administration, created in 1935 with Harry Hopkins (1890–1946) as its head, was set up for federal construction projects. (In 1939 its name was changed to the Work Projects Administration.) Critics immediately called the WPA a "make-work boondoggle," and it provoked the common image of the workman leaning on a shovel. But under Hopkins, the WPA was responsible for 10 percent of new roads in the United States, as well as new hospitals, city halls, courthouses, and schools. It built a port in Brownsville, Texas; roads and bridges connecting the Florida Keys with the mainland; and a string of local water supply systems. Its large-scale construction projects included the Lincoln Tunnel under the Hudson River connecting New York and New Jersey; the Triborough Bridge system linking Manhattan to Long Island; the Federal Trade Commission building in Washington, D.C.; the East River Drive (later renamed the FDR Drive) in Manhattan; the Fort Knox gold depository; and the Bonneville and Boulder dams. (Boulder Dam was renamed Hoover Dam by a Republican-controlled Congress in 1946.) Apart from building projects, the WPA set up artistic projects that employed thousands of musicians, writers, and artists.

But Roosevelt's greatest contribution may have been psychological rather than simply legislative. He possessed a singular, natural gift for restoring confidence, rebuilding optimism, and creating hope where all hope seemed to have been lost. Herbert Hoover had embarked on some of the same paths that FDR took toward recovery. But the stern, patrician Hoover, totally removed from the people, lacked any of the sense of the common person that FDR possessed naturally, despite being a child of wealth and privilege. His "fireside chats" over the radio gave listeners the distinct impression that Roosevelt was sitting in their parlors or living rooms speaking to them personally. While Roosevelt's name was unmentionable in conservative Republican households, where he was referred to as "that man," he was practically deified by the larger American public, including blacks, who began to desert the Republican Party, their home since Reconstruction days, for Roosevelt's Democrats.

Why did Franklin D. Roosevelt try to "pack" the Supreme Court?

The New Deal and the NRA in particular were bitter medicine to conservative Wall Streeters and corporate leaders, most of them Republicans. To them, they reeked of socialism and Communism. Even though things were getting better, obscene whispers and cruel jokes were common about the crippled Roosevelt and his wife, Eleanor: Eleanor had given FDR gonorrhea, which she had contracted from a Negro; she was going to Moscow to learn unspeakable sexual practices. Some of the rumors were tinged with anti-Semitism, like the one that Roosevelt was descended from Dutch Jews who had changed their names. Roosevelt was undaunted by the critics. He was interested only in results. And the larger public seemed to agree.

The first proof came in the 1934 midterm elections. Traditionally the party in power loses strength between presidential contests. Instead, the Democrats tightened their control of both the House and the Senate. In the presidential race of 1936, Roosevelt's popularity climbed to new heights. He told Raymond Moley, the Columbia professor who led Roosevelt's "brain trust" of academic advisers, that there was only one issue in the campaign of 1936: "It's myself," said Roosevelt. "The people must either be for me or against me." Opposed by Kansas Governor Alf Landon, a progressive Republican, FDR racked up an overwhelming reelection victory with more than 60 percent of the popular vote, carrying every state but Maine and Vermont. After the election, someone suggested FDR balance the budget by selling the two states to Canada.

Following his reelection, FDR seemed at the peak of his power and prestige. But he was about to be dealt the most crushing defeat of his political life. A year after it was created, the National Recovery

Administration was killed. In *Schechter v. United States* (May 1935), the Supreme Court, dominated by aging, conservative Republicans, ruled that the NRA was unconstitutional. This was followed by Court decisions that killed off the Agricultural Adjustment Administration, the Securities and Exchange Act, a coal act, and a bankruptcy act. In all, the conservative judges shot down eleven New Deal measures. Emboldened by his recent victory, Roosevelt went on the offensive against the Court. Reviving an old proposal that would allow the president to appoint an additional justice for each member reaching the age of seventy, Roosevelt wanted to "pack" the Supreme Court with judges who would be sympathetic to New Deal legislation.

It was, perhaps, the greatest misjudgment of his career. Even when one of the older judges retired and Roosevelt was able to appoint Hugo Black, a New Dealer, FDR remained committed to the bill. But he was almost alone. Alarmed by the measure's threat to the system and constitutional checks and balances, the Senate beat it back. It was Roosevelt's first loss in Congress in five years, and it opened a small floodgate of other defeats. In 1938, Roosevelt, looking to avenge his Court measure defeat, targeted a number of southern senators who had opposed his Supreme Court plan for defeat in the midterm elections. The strategy backfired, resulting in a costly Election Day defeat for Roosevelt's handpicked candidates. Roosevelt's once-invincible armor seemed to be cracking.

But even after the court-packing debacle and his 1938 political defeats, Roosevelt remained the most powerful man in the country and perhaps the world. Only one man might have rivaled FDR's power at the time. Ironically, he had come to office in March 1933, a few days before Roosevelt's first inauguration. Like Roosevelt, he had come to power largely because he offered a desperate nation a means of dealing with its economic crisis. He, too, would have the young men of his country go into the countryside in a uniformed group like Roosevelt's CCC. But these young men would be called Brownshirts. When the Reichstag (the German parliament building) burned to the ground in February 1933, Adolf Hitler (1889–1945) was only the chancellor of Germany, appointed to the post by an aging and weak German president Hindenburg. Blaming the Communists for the fire that destroyed the seat of Germany's parliament, Adolf Hitler's National Socialist

Party had the scapegoat it needed to unite the country behind its cause and its fuehrer.

Roosevelt may have lost the fight with the "nine old men" of the Supreme Court in 1937, but he was looking to Europe and what surely would be much bigger battles.

What happened to Amelia Earhart?

After Charles Lindbergh, the most famous flier of the day was Amelia Earhart (1897–1937). Born in Kansas, she graduated high school in Chicago in 1915 and became something of a wanderer, taking up flying along the way. In 1928, she flew across the Atlantic with two men, becoming overnight an outspoken American heroine and a model of "rugged feminism." When she married the publisher George Putnam in 1931, Earhart made it clear that she would continue her career. By 1932 she had set the record for a transatlantic flight and was going on to pile up an impressive list of achievements.

Her boldest plan came in 1937, when she planned to fly around the world with navigator Fred Noonan. Departing from Miami, Florida, in June, Earhart reached New Guinea and took off for Howland Island in the Pacific on July 1. Then her radio messages stopped and she disappeared. A naval search found no sign of the plane, and speculation about the flier's fate fed newspapers for months. The remains of her plane were never found. Many people believed that she was a great pilot—others, a lousy one—who had attempted the impossible. Perhaps she got lost over the Pacific, ran out of fuel, and crashed in the vast expanses, ending in a watery grave.

But another of those theories, strongly held by the historian William Manchester, indicates the temper of the times. The late 1930s was an era of increasing military buildup in answer to the economic crisis of the Depression, especially by Italy, Germany, and Japan, the three nations that would later join in the Axis. Looking to become predominant in its Asian sphere, Japan was arming heavily and building strong defenses on a string of Pacific islands it had been granted in 1919 under the Treaty of Versailles. Saipan, Guam, and Tinian were part of the Mariana Islands chain, unknown to most Americans at the time but soon to become a painful part of America's wartime vocabulary. Passing over the Marianas, Earhart caught a glimpse of the fortifications that the Japanese were building on the islands, Manchester contends in his book *The Glory and the Dream*. Under existing treaties, these fortifications were illegal and an indication of Japan's intentions. Manchester says, "She was almost certainly forced down and murdered."

The irony may be that given the country's isolationist temper at the time, even if Earhart had seen this buildup and lived to tell what the Japanese were doing, her warnings might have been ignored. In 1937, America was in no mood for joining anybody else's wars.

What was Lend-Lease?

"Suppose my neighbor's house catches fire," said FDR to a press conference on December 17, 1940. "If he can take my garden hose and connect it up with his hydrant, I may help him put out the fire. Now what do I do? I don't say to him, 'Neighbor, my garden hose cost me fifteen dollars; you have to pay me fifteen dollars for it.' What is the transaction that goes on? I don't want fifteen dollars—I want my garden hose back after the fire is over."

This was part of FDR's brilliance. What was complex, he made simple; the dangerous seemed innocuous. With this homey analogy, President Roosevelt was preparing to bring the country one step closer to a reality it had been avoiding for most of a decade. The neighbor's house was not only on fire—it was about to burn to the ground.

Even as Roosevelt spoke, the German Luftwaffe was throwing everything it had at England during the devastating Battle of Britain. In this sixteen-week air war, which cost Britain more than nine hundred planes and thousands of civilian lives, while Germany lost 1,700 aircraft, London and the industrial heart of England were being bombed into ruin. Down to only $2 billion in gold reserves, England was about to run out of the cash it needed to keep its defenses alive. Publicly pledged to neutrality, FDR was doing everything in his power—and even beyond his legal powers—to assist the British cause. But his hands were tied by the strong isolationist mood in the country and in Congress, and the president could only watch and wonder how to stop Hitler.

The answer came a few weeks after the "garden hose" press conference, as Roosevelt introduced the Lend-Lease bill. Under it, he was granted unprecedented powers to aid any country whose defense was deemed vital to the defense of the United States. America would "lend" tanks, warplanes, and ships that could be returned "in kind" after the war. Congress almost unanimously sided with Roosevelt, except for the hard-line isolationists like Senator Robert A. Taft, who compared the loan of war equipment not to a garden hose but to chewing gum—you wouldn't want it back.

The path to Lend-Lease had been a long and torturous one for Roosevelt. Preoccupied with the Depression crisis, Roosevelt was little concerned with events in Europe. Too many Americans had fresh memories of the horrors of 1918, and isolationist sentiment in the country was overwhelming. When a congressional investigation showed that munitions makers had garnered enormous profits during World War I, the desire to avoid Europe's problems gained greater strength.

Of even less concern than events in Europe was the changing scene in Asia. In 1931, while Herbert Hoover was still in office, the Japanese invaded China and established a puppet state called Manchukuo in Manchuria. Little was said or done by the United States or anyone else. A few months later, Japan bombarded Shanghai and extended its control over northern China. The League of Nations condemned Japan, which laughed and withdrew from the League. Adolf Hitler, who became Chancellor of Germany in 1933, a few days before Roosevelt was inaugurated, watched with interest as Japan's aggressive empire building went unpunished.

Who were the Fascists?

The word "fascist" gets thrown about quite a bit these days. In the 1960s, the police were called "fascist pigs." Anybody who doesn't like another government simply calls it fascist. Generally, fascism has come to mean a military dictatorship built on racist and powerfully nationalistic foundations, generally with the broad support of the business class (distinguishing it from the collectivism of Communism). But when Benito Mussolini adopted the term, he used it quite proudly.

The first of the modern dictators, Benito Mussolini (1883–1945), called Il Duce (which simply means "the leader"), was the son of a blacksmith, who came to power as prime minister in 1922. A preening bully of a man, he organized Italian World War I veterans into the anti-Communist and rabidly nationalistic "blackshirts," a paramilitary group that used gang tactics to suppress strikes and attack leftist trade unions. Riding the anti-Communist fervor in Italy, he was accepted by a people who wanted "order." His rise to power was accompanied by the beatings of opponents and the murder of a key Socialist Party leader.

In 1925, Mussolini installed himself as head of a single-party state he called *fascismo*. The word came from *fasces*, a Latin word referring to a bundle of rods bound around an ax, which had been a Roman symbol of authority and strength. While most of Europe disarmed, Mussolini rearmed Italy during the twenties. A failure at actual governing, Mussolini saw military adventurism as the means to keep the Italian people loyal, and Italy embarked on wars in Africa and in support of General Francisco Franco's Spanish rebels.

The rise to power of the three militaristic, totalitarian states that would form the wartime Axis—Germany, Japan, and Italy—as well as Fascist Spain under General Franco, can be laid to the aftershocks, both political and economic, of the First World War. It was rather easy, especially in the case of Germany and Italy, for demagogues to point to the smoldering ruins of their countries and the economic disaster of the worldwide depression and blame their woes on foreigners. Under the crushing weight of the war's costs, the people might be said to have lacked the will *not to believe.*

Mussolini blamed Italy's problems on foreigners, and promised to make the trains run on time. (Contrary to popular belief, he did not.) The next step was simply to crush opposition through the most ruthless form of police state. In Germany, Adolf Hitler (1889–1945) made scapegoats not only of the Communists and foreign powers who he claimed had stripped Germany of its land and military abilities at Versailles, but also of Jews, who he claimed were in control of the world's finances. The long history of anti-Semitism in Europe, going back for centuries, simply fed the easy acceptance of Hitler's argument.

Like Mussolini and his blackshirts, Hitler organized his followers into a strong-arm gang of Brownshirts, and later into an elite uniformed guard called the SS. In 1930, his National Socialist (Nazi) Party, with its platform of placing blame for Germany's economic misery on Jews, Marxists, and foreign powers, attracted the masses of unemployed and began to win increasing numbers of seats in Germany's parliament, the Reichstag, and Hitler was named chancellor by an aging President Hindenburg. When the Reichstag burned and Communists were blamed, Hitler had the incident he needed to grab dictatorial powers and concentrate them under a police state that simply crushed all opposition. Skilled in nationalistic theatrics, bankrolled by militant industrialists, supported by an increasingly powerful army and secret police, and able to captivate and enthrall his country with pomp and jingoism, Hitler was the essence of the fascist leader.

Hitler made no secret of his plans. From the start, he announced that he wanted to reunite the German-speaking people separated when the map of Europe was redrawn following the Treaty of Versailles. He also pledged to rearm Germany so that it would never be forced to accept terms as it had at Versailles in 1918. By 1935, Germany was committed to a massive program of militarization, modernizing its armaments and requiring universal military service. That same year, Mussolini invaded Ethiopia, which bordered Italian Somaliland in Africa. American attempts to avoid entanglement in these "European" problems led to passage of the Neutrality Act in 1935, which barred the sale of munitions to all belligerents. Facing strong isolationist sentiment, led by Henry Ford, Charles Lindbergh, and the vitriolic, anti-Semitic Catholic "radio priest," Father Charles Coughlin (1891–1979), Roosevelt had to swallow the unpleasant bill. Curiously unrestricted by the embargo were petroleum products. Oil and gasoline sales to Italy tripled as the modernized Italian army crushed the nearly primitive Ethiopian resistance.

In 1936, the Spanish Civil War broke out. The Fascist (Falangist) rebels under General Francisco Franco (1892–1975), with the military support of Germany and 50,000 Italian troops, sought to overthrow the left-leaning Spanish Republic, which in turn was receiving support from the Soviet Union. The Spanish Civil War was a proxy war in which German arms, weapons, and tactics were being battle-tested.

Again, America's official position remained neutral and isolationist, even as many Americans went to Spain to fight in the losing loyalist or Republican cause.

The pace of events became more rapid. In July 1937, Japan attacked China once more, this time conquering Peking. The following October, Roosevelt made a subtle shift from isolationism. Like Wilson before the First World War, Roosevelt always sympathized with England, and like Wilson, Roosevelt professed a desire to avoid American involvement in the war. Saying that "America actively engages in the search for peace," he recommended "quarantining" the aggressors, acknowledging without identifying them.

In March 1938, Germany absorbed Austria in the Anschluss (annexation), and in September, Hitler demanded the return of the German Sudetenland, which had been incorporated into Czechoslovakia after 1918. At a conference in Munich, the prime ministers of Great Britain and France accepted this demand and pressed the Czechs to turn over the land. That was simply Hitler's prelude to a more ambitious land grab.

Recognizing the paucity of resistance, Hitler simply took the rest of Czechoslovakia in early 1939. He next set his sights on Poland, demanding the city of Danzig (modern-day Gdansk). Hitler now had Roosevelt's full attention, but Roosevelt lacked the votes at the time even to overturn the Neutrality Act that prevented him from arming France and Great Britain for the war that everyone now knew was surely coming.

In August 1939, Germany and the Soviet Union signed a nonaggression pact, a prelude to a joint attack on Poland by Germany from the west and Russia from the East. France and England could stand by and appease Hitler no longer. Both countries declared war on Germany on September 3.

As the German military had planned in 1914, Germany went for a quick, decisive victory that would crush France and give it control of Europe. But unlike 1914, when the British and French held off the German assault, the Nazi plan was far more successful. The Nazi onslaught, the Blitzkrieg ("lightning war"), leveled resistance in Denmark, Norway, the Netherlands, Belgium, and France. By the summer of 1940, Hitler controlled most of western Europe, and the British and

French armies had been sent reeling from Dunkerque, on the Strait of Dover.

Roosevelt was able to force through a stopgap "cash and carry" bill that allowed the Allies to buy arms. After Italy joined Germany in the attack on France, Roosevelt froze the assets of the conquered nations still held in the United States, to prevent the Germans from using them. Without legal authority, FDR began to sell the English "surplus" American arms. After the fall of France, FDR came up with the idea of "trading" aging American destroyers to the British in exchange for bases, the deal that was the prelude to Lend-Lease.

What did FDR know about a Japanese attack, and when did he know it?

At 7 A.M., Hawaiian time, on Sunday, December 7, 1941, two U.S. Army privates saw something unusual on their mobile radar screens. More than 50 planes seemed to be appearing out of the northeast. When they called in the information, they were told it was probably just part of an expected delivery of new B-17s coming from the mainland United States. The men were told not to worry about it. What they saw was actually the first wave of 183 Japanese planes that had arrived at Hawaii on Japanese carriers and struck the American naval base with complete surprise.

At 0758 the Pearl Harbor command radioed its first message to the world. AIR RAID PEARL HARBOR. THIS IS NOT A DRILL. An hour later, a second wave of 167 more Japanese aircraft arrived. The two raids, which had lasted only minutes, accounted for eighteen ships, of them eight battleships, sunk, capsized, or damaged, and 292 aircraft, including 117 bombers, damaged or wrecked. And 2,403 Americans, military and civilian, had been killed, with another 1,178 wounded. The following afternoon, President Roosevelt requested and won a declaration of war against Japan. With that done, Germany declared war on America under its treaty terms with Japan. Soon America was at war with Germany and Italy as well.

No question has tantalized historians of the wartime period more than this one: Did President Roosevelt know the Japanese were going to attack Pearl Harbor, and did he deliberately allow the attack that took more than 2,000 American lives in order to draw America into the most deadly, destructive war in history?

There are two basic camps regarding FDR and America's entry into the war. The first holds that FDR was preoccupied with the war in Europe and didn't want war with Japan. American strategic thinking of the time, perhaps reflecting Anglo-Saxon racism about Japanese abilities, dismissed the Japanese military threat. War with Japan would sap American resources that should be directed toward the defeat of Germany. Supporting this camp is the large body of evidence of the American diplomatic attempts to forestall war with Japan.

The other camp holds that FDR viewed Japan—allied to the German-Italian Axis—as his entrée into the European war. This stand holds that FDR made a series of calculated provocations that pushed Japan into war with America. The ultimate conclusion to this view is that FDR knew of the imminent Japanese attack on Pearl Harbor and not only failed to prevent it, but welcomed it as the turning point that would end isolationist obstruction of his war plans.

Neither view is seamless, and the reality may lie in some combination of the two, with such factors as human frailty, overconfidence on both sides, and the tensions of a world already at war thrown in. You might also cast a vote for historical inevitability. A clash between Japan and the United States and other Western nations over control of the economy and resources of the Far East and Pacific was bound to happen. A small island nation with limited resources but great ambitions, Japan had to reach out to control its destiny. That put the highly militarized and industrialized empire on a collision course with the Western nations that had established a colonial presence in the Pacific and Asia, and had their own plans for exploiting that part of the world.

With that in mind, certain facts remain. Japanese-American relations were bad in the 1930s, and worsened when the Japanese sank an American warship, the *Panay*, on the Yangtze River late in 1937, a clear violation of all treaties and an outright act of war. But America was not ready to go to war over a single ship. Attempting to influence the outcome of China's struggle against Japan, Roosevelt loaned money to the Nationalists in China and began to ban exports to Japan of certain goods that eventually included gasoline, scrap iron, and oil.

Were these provocations to force Japan into war, or sensible reactions to Japanese aggression in China and elsewhere in Asia? The Japanese were intent on dominating the Asian world and proved themselves quite ruthless in achieving that goal. In Nanking, China, atrocities committed against the Chinese rank with the worst of human behavior. The people of Korea still bear historic grudges against the Japanese for the cruelty of their wartime rule, such as forced labor and the forced prostitution of thousands of Korean women as "comfort maidens" who were made to work in brothels servicing Japanese soldiers.

Historical opinion divides on this point. It is clear that moderation on either side might have prevailed. But in the United States, the secretary of state was demanding complete Japanese withdrawal from their territorial conquests. At the same time in Japan, hawkish militants led by General Hideki Tojo (1884–1948) had gained power. Moderation was tossed aside, and the two speeding engines continued on a runaway collision course.

By late in 1941, it was more than apparent that war was coming with Japan. American and foreign diplomats in Japan dispatched frequent warnings about the Japanese mood. Nearly a year before the Pearl Harbor attack, Joseph Grew, the U.S. ambassador in Tokyo, had wired a specific warning about rumors of an attack on Pearl Harbor. And more significantly, the Japanese diplomatic code had been broken by American intelligence. Almost all messages between Tokyo and its embassy in Washington were being intercepted and understood by Washington.

There is no longer any doubt that some Americans knew that "zero hour," as the Japanese ambassador to Washington called the planned attack, was scheduled for December 7. They even knew it would come at Pearl Harbor. According to John Toland's account of Pearl Harbor, *Infamy*, Americans had not only broken the Japanese code, but the Dutch had done so as well, and their warnings had been passed on to Washington. A British double agent code-named Tricycle had also sent explicit warnings to the United States.

Here is where human frailty and overconfidence, and even American racism, take over. Most American military planners expected a Japanese attack to come in the Philippines, America's major base in the Pacific; the American naval fortifications at Pearl Harbor were believed to be too strong to attack, as well as too far away for the Japanese.

The commanders there were more prepared for an attack by saboteurs, which explains why the battleships were packed together in the harbor, surrounded defensively by smaller vessels, and why planes were parked in neat rows in the middle of the airstrip at Hickam Field, ready to be blasted by Japanese bombing runs.

Many Americans, including Roosevelt, dismissed the Japanese as combat pilots because they were all presumed to be "nearsighted." The excellence of their eyes and flying abilities came as an expensive surprise to the American military. There was also a sense that any attack on Pearl Harbor would be easily repulsed. Supremely overconfident, the Navy commanders on Pearl Harbor had been warned about the possibility of attack, but little was done to secure the island. The general impression, even back in Washington in the Navy secretary's office, was that the Japanese would get a bad spanking, and America would still get the war it wanted in Europe.

In his history of espionage and presidential behavior, *For the President's Eyes Only*, Christopher Andrew makes this case: "The 'complete surprise' of both Roosevelt and Churchill reflected a failure of imagination as well as of intelligence. It did not occur to either the president or the prime minister that the 'little yellow men,' as Churchill sometimes spoke of them and Roosevelt thought of them, were capable of such a feat of arms. When General Douglas MacArthur first heard the news of the attack by carrier-borne aircraft on Pearl Harbor, he insisted that the pilots must have been mercenaries."

Regardless of whether or not the attack was invited and why specific warnings were ignored or disregarded, the complete devastation of the American forces at Pearl Harbor was totally unexpected. Even today, the tally of that attack is astonishing. Eighteen ships were sunk or seriously damaged, including eight battleships. Of these eight, six were later salvaged. Nearly two hundred airplanes were destroyed on the ground, and 2,403 people died that morning, nearly half of them aboard the battleship *Arizona*, which took a bomb down its smokestack and went to the bottom in minutes.

A day after the attack, Roosevelt delivered his war message to Congress. The long-running battle between isolationists and interventionists was over.

While the revisionists and conspiracy theorists persist, a convincing case for Roosevelt trying to avoid war with Japan has been made by many prominent historians. Among them are Joseph Persico, who wrote:

> The revisionist theory requires a certain path of logic. First, FDR had to know that Pearl Harbor was going to be bombed. His secretaries of State, War and Navy either did not know or, if they did, they all lied and conspired in the deaths of twenty-four hundred Americans and the near-fatal destruction of the Pacific Fleet. . . . For FDR to fail to alert the defenders of an attack that he knew was coming, we must premise that the president had enlisted men of the stature of Stimson, Hull, Knox and Marshall in a treasonous conspiracy, or that he had a unique source of information on Japanese fleet movements unknown to anyone else in the government.

The eminent British military historian John Keegan is equally dismissive of the conspiracy notion. "These charges defy logic," Keegan wrote in *The Second World War*. "Churchill certainly did not want war against Japan, which Britain was pitifully equipped to fight, but only American assistance in the fight against Hitler. . . . Roosevelt's foreknowledge can be demonstrated to have been narrowly circumscribed. Although the American cryptanalysts had broken both the Japanese diplomatic cipher Purple and the naval cipher . . . such instructions did not include details of war plans."

There is another issue, as Americans have learned since September 11, 2001, a new generation's day of infamy. Having intelligence and using it well are two very different things. The left hand does not always know what the right is doing, as the FBI and CIA demonstrated in revealing the pieces of the puzzle they had before the terrorist attacks of September 11. But that does not suggest that their failure to see the whole puzzle complete leads to a conspiracy theory in which America wanted to create a war against Islam. While understanding the past can sometimes help understand the present, this may be one case in which knowing the present can help reconcile the mysteries of the past.

Must Read: For an overview of the period leading up to Pearl Harbor and an account of the days surrounding the attack, *The Borrowed Years: 1938–1941, America on the Way to War* by

Richard M. Ketchum; for the "Roosevelt knew" side, *Day of Deceit: The Truth About FDR and Pearl Harbor* by Robert B. Stinnet, an exhaustive collection of the information American intelligence had collected about the impending attack. There are several excellent books that address the other side. Among them are *For the President's Eyes Only* by Christopher Andrew; *Roosevelt's Secret War: FDR and World War II Espionage* by Joseph E. Persico.

AMERICAN VOICES

From FRANKLIN D. ROOSEVELT'S war message to Congress (December 8, 1941):

Yesterday, December 7, 1941—a date which will live in infamy—the United States of America was suddenly and deliberately attacked by naval and air forces of the Empire of Japan.

The United States was at peace with that nation and, at the solicitation of Japan, was still in conversation with its government and its emperor, looking toward the maintenance of peace in the Pacific.

. . . The attack yesterday on the Hawaiian Islands has caused severe damage to American naval and military forces. I regret to tell you that very many American lives have been lost. . . .

Yesterday, the Japanese Government also launched an attack against Malaya.

Last night, Japanese forces attacked Hong Kong.

Last night, Japanese forces attacked Guam.

Last night, Japanese forces attacked the Philippine Islands.

Last night, the Japanese attacked Wake Island.

And this morning, the Japanese attacked Midway Island.

. . . No matter how long it may take us to overcome this premeditated invasion, the American people, in their righteous might, will win through to absolute victory.

MILESTONES IN WORLD WAR II
1938

March 13 The Anschluss (annexation of Austria). German troops march into Austria to "preserve order." Hitler declares Austria "reunited" with Germany.

September 30 The Munich Pact. The British and French allow Hitler to annex the Sudetenland, an area of Czechoslovakia with a largely German-speaking population. Through this policy of "appeasement," British prime minister Neville Chamberlain (1869–1940) believes that Germany will be satisfied and that there will be "peace in our time." Winston Churchill, later first lord of the admiralty, thinks otherwise. "Britain and France had to choose between war and dishonor," says the future prime minister. "They chose dishonor. They will have war."

October 3 Hitler triumphantly enters the Sudetenland.

1939

March 14 After taking the Sudetenland, Germany invades the rest of Czechoslovakia.

April 1 The three-year-old Spanish Civil War ends with German- and Italian-supported Fascist victory. The United States recognizes the new government of General Francisco Franco (1892–1975).

April 7 Italy invades Albania, its small neighbor across the Adriatic Sea.

July 14 Reacting to growing international tension over Germany's provocations in Europe, President Roosevelt asks Congress to repeal an arms embargo so that the United States can sell arms to England and other nonfascist countries.

September 1 Germany invades Poland. Claiming a Polish attack on German soldiers, Germany's modernized forces overrun the small, unprepared, and outdated Polish army.

September 3   After Hitler ignores their demand for German withdrawal from Poland, Great Britain and France formally declare war on Germany. Twenty-eight Americans die aboard a British ship torpedoed by a German submarine, but Roosevelt proclaims American neutrality in the war. Five days later he declares a limited national emergency, giving him broad powers to act. A few weeks later he announces that all U.S. offshore waters and ports are closed to the submarines of the warring nations.

September 28   Germany and Russia partition Poland, which Russia invaded from the east on September 17, two weeks after Germany entered Poland from the west. The United States refuses to recognize the partition, and maintains diplomatic relations with a Polish government-in-exile in Paris.

October 11   A letter written by Albert Einstein is delivered to Roosevelt by Alexander Sachs, a financier and adviser to the president. In it, Einstein discusses the implications of a nuclear chain reaction and the powerful bombs that may be constructed. He says, "A single bomb of this type, carried by boat and exploded in a port, might very well destroy the whole port, together with some of the surrounding territory." Roosevelt orders a plan to develop the atomic bomb, which becomes the Manhattan Project.

November 4   The Neutrality Act is signed. This measure will allow the United States to send arms and other aid to Britain and France.

1940

January   "The Battle of the Atlantic." German submarines begin torpedo attacks on Allied shipping, sinking nearly 4.5 million tons of ships in the first two months of the year.

March 18   Mussolini and Hitler announce Italy's formal alliance with Germany against England and France. Mussolini calls this the "Axis" on which Europe will revolve.

April 9   Norway and Denmark are overrun by Germany.

May 10 Luxembourg, Belgium, and the Netherlands are invaded by Germany. On the same day, Winston Churchill replaces the disgraced Neville Chamberlain as prime minister.

May 26–June 4 Dunkerque. Pressed to the coast of France, British and French troops converge on this small coastal town on the Dover Strait. The Royal Navy, assisted by hundreds of small fishing and merchant ships, evacuates more than 300,000 troops as the advancing Germans bomb and shell the fleeing troops. Churchill makes one of his memorable speeches: "We shall fight on the beaches, we shall fight on the landing grounds, we shall fight in the fields and the streets. . . . We shall never surrender."

June 5 Germany invades France. Ten days later, Paris falls. By June 22, France surrenders and a pro-German government is installed in the city of Vichy. In London, a Free French government headed by General Charles de Gaulle (1890–1970) vows to resist.

June 10 President Roosevelt announces a shift from neutrality to "non-belligerency," meaning more active support for the Allies against the Axis.

June 28 The Alien Registration Act (the Smith Act) is passed. It requires aliens to register and makes it illegal to advocate the violent overthrow of the U.S. government.

July 10 The Battle of Britain. The first aerial attack on England by the German air force begins the devastating air war over England. For four months, German bombers pound London and other strategic points. Taking heavy civilian and military losses, the staunch British air defense destroys 1,700 German planes. Failure to control the airspace over England is a key factor in the Nazi decision not to launch an invasion across the Channel.

July 20 Congress authorizes $4 billion for the construction of a two-ocean navy.

September 3 Roosevelt gives fifty American destroyers to England in exchange for the right to construct bases in British possessions in the Western Hemisphere. This trade inspires the Lend-Lease program.

September 16   The Selective Training and Service Act requires men from twenty-one to thirty-five years of age to register for military training.

September 26   President Roosevelt announces an embargo on shipments of scrap metal outside the Western Hemisphere, aimed at cutting off supplies to Japan.

November 5   Roosevelt wins reelection to an unprecedented third term, defeating Republican Wendell Willkie by 449 electoral votes to 82.

December 29   In a year-end "fireside chat," Roosevelt says that the United States will become the "arsenal of democracy." Many peacetime factories are converted to war production, and this shift to a wartime economy shakes off the last effects of the Great Depression. During the war, America will produce 297,000 planes, 86,000 tanks, 12,000 ships, and enormous quantities of other vehicles, arms, and munitions. As in the case of the North in the Civil War and the United States in World War I, the American industrial capacity to mass-produce war materials provides the margin of victory. America and its allies do not so much outfight Germany and Japan as outproduce them.

1941

March 11   The Lend-Lease Act is signed into law. It narrowly passes Congress as isolationist sentiment remains strong.

May 27   A limited state of emergency is declared by President Roosevelt after Greece and Yugoslavia fall to the Axis powers. An American merchant ship, *Robin Moor*, is sunk by a U-boat near Brazil.

June 14   German and Italian assets in the United States are frozen under President Roosevelt's emergency powers. Two days later, all

German consulates in the United States are ordered closed, and on June 20, all Italian consulates are also shut down.

June 22 Germany invades Russia, breaking the "nonaggression" pact signed in 1939. Two days later, President Roosevelt promises U.S. aid to Russia under Lend-Lease.

July 25 After the Japanese invade French Indochina, President Roosevelt freezes Japan's assets in the United States, halting trade between the countries and cutting off Japanese oil supplies. This move is later cited by the Japanese as a cause for attacking the United States.

August 14 After meeting secretly on warships stationed near Newfoundland, Roosevelt and Churchill announce the Atlantic Charter, a document that lays out eight goals for the world, including open trade, international economic cooperation, safe boundaries, freedom of the seas, and abandonment of the use of force. Its call for "self-determination" is aimed at freeing nations under Axis domination rather than the many Allied colonial interests in such places as India, Indochina, and the Philippines.

October 17 The U.S. destroyer *Kearney* is torpedoed by a U-boat, leaving eleven Americans dead. Two weeks later, the destroyer *Reuben James* is sunk by a U-boat, with 100 Americans lost. Hitler knows that war with the United States is now inevitable.

November 3 The U.S. ambassador to Japan, Joseph Grew, warns of a possible Japanese surprise attack. Roosevelt and the cabinet receive his message on November 7.

November 17 Japanese envoys in Washington propose removing restrictions on trade. American secretary of state Cordell Hull rejects the proposal, calling for Japanese withdrawal from China and Indochina.

December 7 One day after President Roosevelt appeals to Emperor Hirohito to use his influence to avert war, the Japanese attack Pearl Harbor, the major U.S. base in Hawaii, killing 2,403 American soldiers, sailors, and civilians. Eighteen ships and 292 aircraft are destroyed or damaged. Defying all American expectations of their military capabilities, the Japanese make simultaneous strikes on Guam, Midway, and British bases in Hong Kong and Singapore. Japan declares war on the United States.

December 8   Addressing a joint session of Congress, Roosevelt asks for a declaration of war on Japan. The Senate vote is unanimously in favor; the House approves 388–1, with pacifist Jeannette Rankin, the first woman elected to the House, the lone dissenter.

December 11   (Europe) Responding to the state of war between the United States and Japan, Germany and Italy declare war on the United States, giving President Roosevelt the fight with Hitler that he wanted.

December 17   (Pacific) Admiral Chester Nimitz (1885–1966) is given command of the Pacific fleet, replacing Admiral Kimmel, who was in charge of Pearl Harbor and is the scapegoat for the disaster. Nimitz will organize and direct the American counterattack in the Pacific.

December 23   (Pacific) The Japanese take Wake Island, an American possession in the middle of the North Pacific.

December 25   (Pacific) Hong Kong falls to Japan.

1942

January 2   (Pacific) Japan takes control of the Philippines as General MacArthur withdraws to Corregidor, an island fortress in Manila Bay.

January 14   (Home front) A presidential order requires all aliens to register with the government. This is the beginning of a plan to move Japanese-Americans into internment camps in the belief that they might aid the enemy.

January 26   (Europe) For the first time since the end of World War I, American troops arrive in Europe, landing in Northern Ireland.

February 20   (Home front) Roosevelt approves the plan to remove Japanese-Americans from their homes and send them to internment camps in Colorado, Utah, Arkansas, and other interior states. Eventually 100,000 Japanese-Americans will be moved, losing their homes and possessions. Many of the young men who are relocated join special U.S. Army units that perform with high honor.

February 23   (Home front) In one of the only assaults on the continental United States, an oil refinery in California is shelled by a Japanese submarine.

February 27–March 1   (Pacific) A Japanese fleet virtually destroys the American and British fleet in the Java Sea.

March 11   (Pacific) General MacArthur leaves the Philippines for Australia, vowing, "I shall return." General Jonathan Wainwright (1883–1953) is left in command of the American forces, who move to the Bataan Peninsula.

AMERICAN VOICES
GENERAL BENJAMIN O. DAVIS,
commander of the Tuskegee Airmen and the first
black general in the U.S. Air Force:

> All the blacks in the segregated forces operated like they had to prove they could fly an airplane when everyone believed they were too stupid.

Benjamin O. Davis (1912–2002) was the son of the Army's first black general, Benjamin O. Davis Sr. The first black cadet to graduate from West Point, he was one of the first black pilots in the military. His leadership of the famed Tuskegee Airmen, an all-black unit that was highly decorated during World War II, helped integrate the Air Force, and he became its first black general in 1954.

During his four years at West Point, no one would room with Davis. He later said, "Living as a prisoner in solitary confinement for four years had not destroyed my personality nor poisoned my attitude toward other people. When my father told me of the many people who were pulling for me, I said, 'It's a pity none of them were at West Point.'" At first rejected by the Air Corps, which did not accept blacks, Davis went to Tuskegee Army Air Field in 1941 when the Roosevelt administration told the War Department to create a black flying unit. Davis commanded the squad—the 99th Pursuit Squadron, better known as the Tuskegee Airmen.

In 1948, after the war, President Truman signed the order providing for the complete integration of America's armed forces.

April 9   (Pacific) Seventy-five thousand American and Philippine troops surrender to the Japanese after a stoic resistance to overwhelming Japanese numbers. The captives are marched over 100 miles in the infamous Bataan Death March, during which thousands of prisoners are executed or die of starvation and thirst before they reach Japanese prison camps. A few weeks later, General Wainwright is captured by the Japanese, surrendering all American forces in the Philippines. (A classic photograph later shows an emaciated Wainwright embracing MacArthur after the Japanese surrender.)

April 18   (Pacific) Led by Major General James Doolittle, U.S. bombers raid Tokyo and other Japanese cities. Although the raids have little military effect, carrying the war to Japan provides an important psychological boost to American morale and alters Japanese strategic thinking.

April 28   (Home front) Coastal "blackouts" go into effect along a fifteen-mile strip on the eastern seaboard. Following Pearl Harbor, there are real fears of bombing attacks by Germany as well as the more realistic threat of German U-boats operating in the Atlantic.

May 4–8   (Pacific) The Battle of the Coral Sea. In an early turning point off New Guinea, U.S. Navy planes severely damage a Japanese fleet, forestalling a Japanese invasion of Australia. For the first time in naval history, ships in battle do not engage each other directly; all the fighting is carried out by carrier-launched planes.

May 15   (Home front) Gasoline rationing goes into effect. A few days later, price ceilings on many retail products take effect.

June 3–6   (Pacific) The Battle of Midway. In a major naval confrontation off the small North Pacific island, the U.S. Navy wins another crucial battle in the Pacific war. Although the carrier *Yorktown* is damaged, the Japanese lose four carriers and many of their best-trained pilots, and the Japanese naval advantage is eliminated, ending the threat to Australia. By this time the Japanese control an enormous area extending westward to Burma, north to Manchuria, south to New Guinea, and including the small islands of the Pacific. The territory represents about 10 percent of the Earth's surface.

June 13   (Home front) Eight German saboteurs land in various spots on the East Coast from submarines. They are quickly captured and tried as spies, and six are executed.

   In Washington, two important new agencies are established. The Office of War Information (OWI) will become the government's wartime propaganda arm and home to numerous writers and filmmakers. The Office of Strategic Services (OSS), led by William Donovan (1883–1959), is the country's espionage agency and forerunner to the postwar CIA.

August 7   (Pacific) In the first U.S. offensive of the war, marines land on Guadalcanal in the Solomon Islands, northeast of Australia. It is the beginning of a two-pronged offensive aimed at dislodging the Japanese from islands that will provide stepping-stones for an eventual invasion of Japan. The war in the Pacific has been given a strategic backseat to the war in Europe, and American Pacific forces will often be poorly supported, lacking ammunition and other supplies. This is the case on Guadalcanal, the first in a series of bloody, savagely fought battles in the Pacific.

August 22   (Europe) The Battle of Stalingrad. The Germans begin an offensive against the city that they expect will complete their conquest of the Soviet Union. This is the beginning of an epic Russian stand that costs hundreds of thousands of lives on both sides, but is a turning point as Hitler's eastern offensive ends in a harsh failure.

October 25–26   (Pacific) Attempting to stop the American landing on Guadalcanal, the Japanese fleet is met by the U.S. Navy in the Battle of Santa Cruz. The Japanese again suffer heavy aircraft losses.

November 12–15   (Pacific) In the naval battle of Guadalcanal, the U.S. fleet under Admiral William Halsey (1882–1959) destroys a Japanese fleet, sinking twenty-eight warships and transports, rendering the Japanese unable to reinforce their troops on Guadalcanal.

November 18   (Home front) The draft age is lowered to eighteen years.

November 25   (Europe) The three-month siege of Stalingrad has turned against the German army, which is eventually surrounded. By the time the German army surrenders, in February 1943, its casualties will surpass 300,000. The Russian victory marks the end of the German offensive in Russia, and Germany begins its long retreat from the eastern front.

December 1   (Home front) Coffee and gasoline join the list of rationed items.

1943

January 14–24   (Europe) Meeting at the Casablanca Conference, Roosevelt and Churchill map out strategy for the eventual invasion of Europe.

February 7   (Home front) Shoe rationing is announced, limiting civilians to three pairs of leather shoes per year.

February 9   (Pacific) U.S. Marines take control of Guadalcanal after four months of savage combat in which they have been cut off from supplies and were reduced to eating roots.

February 14–25   (Europe) At the Kasserine Pass in Tunisia, the Afrika Korps of Field Marshal Erwin Rommel (1891–1944) defeats U.S. forces. But American troops regroup under the new command of George S. Patton (1885–1945) and stop Rommel's drive. They eventually link up with British forces under Field Marshal Bernard

Montgomery (1887–1976), who was chasing Rommel from Egypt. Probably Germany's best wartime field commander, Rommel is recalled to Germany and is later involved in a botched attempt to assassinate Hitler, which will lead to Rommel's suicide.

March 2–4 (Pacific) The U.S. Navy scores another major victory over a Japanese convoy in the Battle of the Bismarck Sea off New Guinea.

April 1 (Home front) Meats, fats, and cheese are now rationed. Attempting to stem inflation, President Roosevelt freezes wages, salaries, and prices.

May 7 (Europe) In a pincer action, Montgomery and Patton link their armies in Tunis, forcing the surrender of all German and Italian troops in North Africa. Ignoring the warnings of Rommel to withdraw these troops, Hitler and Mussolini have pressed more troops into North Africa in a drive aimed at gaining control of the Suez, through which England's oil supply moves. In a few weeks, more than 250,000 Axis soldiers lay down their weapons. Combined with combat casualties, more than 350,000 Axis troops are killed or captured in North Africa, against 18,500 American casualties.

May 16 (Europe) In Warsaw, Poland, the last fighters in the Jewish ghetto are overwhelmed after their stoic but doomed resistance against the Nazis. The survivors are shipped to death camps, and the ghetto is razed.

May 27 (Home front) President Roosevelt issues an executive order forbidding racial discrimination by government contractors. At about this time, anti-black riots in Detroit leave thirty-four people dead.

May 29 (Home front) An issue of the *Saturday Evening Post* is published with a cover illustration by Norman Rockwell that introduces an American icon known as Rosie the Riveter. The character is a sandwich-munching, brawny, yet innocent-looking woman in coveralls, cradling her rivet gun in her lap, goggles pushed up onto her forehead. Her feet rest on a copy of *Mein Kampf*. Rockwell borrowed the idea for Rosie from a figure in Michelangelo's Sistine Chapel frescoes. Rockwell's Rosie is an admiring tribute to the more than 6 million women who have entered the job force during the war, many of them taking up positions in what was considered "man's work," including the defense industries.

July 10   (Europe) The invasion of Sicily. Allied forces under General Dwight D. Eisenhower's command begin an assault that will capture the strategic island by August 17, giving the Allies control of Mediterranean shipping and a base from which to launch an invasion of mainland Italy. Allied casualties in the five weeks of fighting top 25,000, while more than 167,000 Germans and Italians are killed or wounded.

July 19   (Europe) Preceded by an air drop of millions of leaflets calling on Italians to surrender, the Allies begin to bomb targets in and around Rome. Within a week, Mussolini is forced to resign by King Victor Emmanuel, and the new prime minister, Pietro Badoglio, considers an Italian surrender. By September 3, when the Allies launch an invasion of the mainland from Sicily, Prime Minister Badoglio has signed a secret armistice ending Italian military resistance.

September 9   (Europe) The invasion of Salerno. More than 700 ships deliver an Allied invasion force that meets fierce resistance, as the Germans have prepared for this invasion by reinforcing Italy with their best troops. Every inch of the Allied advance is hard-fought, as the Germans are dug into well-defended mountain positions and the Italian winter is one of the harshest on record. By October 1, the port of Naples is in Allied hands, but the departing Germans put the torch to books and museums as retribution for Italy's "betrayal." Italy declares war on Germany.

November 20   (Pacific) The Battle of Tarawa. One of the equatorial Gilbert Islands, the Tarawa atoll possesses an airstrip, an important prize in the Pacific fighting. Using British guns captured at Singapore, the Japanese are well defended on the small island of Betio, about half the size of Central Park. Ignoring islanders' warnings of tricky tides, the landing's commanders send in waves of marines who are trapped before reaching the beaches. The marines' casualties total 3,381, although the airstrip is eventually taken.

November 28–December 1 (Europe) The Teheran Conference brings together Roosevelt, Churchill, and Joseph Stalin, the first time all three have met in person. They confer about the coming invasion of Europe.

1944

January 22 (Europe) The invasion of Anzio. Allied forces hit this coastal town near Rome in an attempt to encircle German forces in central Italy. But the Germans pin down the Americans on Anzio's beach. At the inland monastery town of Monte Cassino, fierce fighting takes a heavy toll on both sides.

January 31 (Pacific) After taking control of the airstrip at Tarawa, the U.S. amphibious invasion force under Admiral Nimitz continues its step-by-step sweep into the North Pacific with an invasion of the Marshall Islands.

February 20–27 (Europe) The U.S. Army Air Corps begins a massive bombing campaign against German aircraft production centers. A week later, on March 6, more than 600 U.S. bombers make their first raid on Berlin. While it is presumed that the strategic bombing has been costly to the German economy and morale, a survey initiated by President Roosevelt will later show that the bombing was devastating but did not work "conclusively." Just as the British economy has survived the German Blitz, the Germans are able to shift production around with no discernible fall-off.

May 3 (Home front) Meat rationing ends, except for certain select cuts.

May 18 (Europe) The German stronghold at Monte Cassino in central Italy finally falls. It has been under Allied siege for months, a costly campaign of dubious strategic value. A few weeks later, at Anzio, Americans trapped on the beaches for months break through as British troops mount an offensive from Italy's west. The Allies are driving toward Rome, and arrive in the city on June 4.

June 6 (Europe) D-Day. The Allied invasion of Europe, code-named Operation Overlord, commences just after midnight. The largest invasion force in history, it comprises 4,000 invasion ships, 600 warships, 10,000 planes, and more than 175,000 Allied troops. Although an invasion has been expected by the Germans, the secret of Overlord is well kept. The plan, at the mercy of the weather, includes a feint farther north near Calais, but the true objective is the Normandy coast between Cherbourg and Le Havre—beaches that have been given names like Juno and Sword, Omaha and Utah. It takes four days of fierce fighting and heavy casualties on both sides before the two main beachhead armies are joined. Despite heavy casualties, the Allies send the Germans backward toward Germany, and a million Allied troops are soon on the continent. But this is only the beginning of the end. It will take almost a full year of fierce combat before the German surrender.

June 13   (Europe) Germany launches the world's first guided missiles, the ramjet-powered V-1 "buzz bombs," across the English Channel at London; only one reaches its target, but by the end of summer, they kill some 6,000 people. These "vengeance weapons" are the creation of a team of rocket scientists led by Dr. Wernher von Braun, who will become an American citizen in 1955 and boost the American space program.

June 15   (Pacific) B-29 Superfortress bombers, based in China, begin to raid Japan. At the same time, U.S. troops begin an offensive on the Marianas—Saipan, Guam, and Tinian. The first target, Saipan, is supposed to be captured in three days. But these islands have been held by the Japanese for twenty-five years, and their defenses are strong. The battle for Saipan is a monthlong fight that claims 3,400 American lives and more than 27,000 Japanese. A grisly aftermath of the fighting is the mass suicide of civilians who jump from a cliff because Japanese propaganda has warned them of American sadism.

June 22   (Home front) President Roosevelt signs the Servicemen's Readjustment Act that will provide funds for housing and education after the war. It is better known as the GI Bill.

June 27   (Europe) The French port of Cherbourg is captured by the Allies, although it has been badly sabotaged and booby-trapped by the departing Germans.

July 9–25 (Europe) After the British take Caen, and St.-Lô falls, Patton's tank troops of the Third Army break through a German line, isolating German troops in Brittany.

July 20 (Europe) With defeat becoming more certain, a group of German officers plot to kill Hitler and take control of the government. The coup fails when Hitler escapes injury from a bomb planted in a suitcase at his headquarters. The leaders of the plot are discovered and executed, and thousands of possible conspirators are killed.

August 10 (Pacific) Guam falls to U.S. forces after three weeks of intense fighting. The Japanese losses are put at 17,000; some 1,200 Americans die and another 6,000 are wounded. The completed conquest of the Marianas will give the United States an airbase from which to begin a large-scale bombardment of Japan. Napalm is used for the first time in these bombings, and the island of Tinian is the base from which the *Enola Gay* will make its fateful flight a year later.

August 14 (Home front) With war production requirements easing, production of vacuum cleaners and other domestic products is allowed to resume.

August 15 (Europe) A second invasion front is opened in southern France as Allied troops sweep up the Rhone River valley, meeting little resistance.

August 25 (Europe) French troops led by General LeClerc retake Paris. On the following day, General de Gaulle, leader of the Free French, enters Paris in a ceremonial parade. On August 27, Eisenhower and other Allied leaders enter Paris. Relatively untouched by the war, Paris has flourished under German occupation, and the great fashion houses have prospered. Frenchwomen who are suspected of having slept with Germans are led into the streets to have their heads shaved.

September 12 (Europe) The second wave of von Braun's missiles, the V-2s, which are the first modern rockets, are launched across the Channel. Five hundred hit London. These are more accurate, but they are too few, too late to make any impact on the war's outcome.

October 20   (Pacific) General Douglas MacArthur, in the now-famous photograph, wades ashore at Leyte Island, the Philippines, fulfilling his promise to return. Three days later, the Battle of Leyte Gulf results in a major Japanese naval defeat. The Japanese now begin to resort to the infamous kamikaze suicide attacks, in which Japanese pilots attempt to crash their explosive-laden planes into American ships. Kamikaze attacks will result in the loss of some 400 ships and nearly 10,000 American seamen.

November 7   (Home front) President Roosevelt wins his unprecedented and unequaled fourth term by defeating New York governor Thomas Dewey.

December 16   (Europe) The Battle of the Bulge. In the last major German counteroffensive, Allied troops are pushed back in Belgium's Ardennes Forest. (As Allied lines fall back, a "bulge" is created in the center of the line, giving the battle its familiar name.) Two weeks of intense fighting in brutal winter weather follow before the German offensive is stopped. One of the most famous moments in the long battle comes when the American 101st Airborne Division is encircled by Germans in Bastogne. When the German general demands surrender, General Anthony McAuliffe reportedly replies, "Nuts." The 101st is relieved a few days later as Patton sends in his tanks. This last-gasp German gamble is followed by rapid defeat for Germany.

1945

February 1   (Europe) One thousand American bombers raid Berlin.

February 4–11   (Europe) The Yalta Conference. Meeting in the Crimea, Churchill, Stalin, and an ailing Roosevelt discuss plans for the final assault on Germany, and agree to create a peace organization that will meet in San Francisco on April 25 and will become the United Nations. More significantly, the meeting also produces the groundwork for the postwar division of Europe among the Allies.

February   (Pacific) A monthlong siege in the Philippines ends with U.S. troops retaking Manila.

February 13   Dresden, the capital of the German state of Saxony, is firebombed by 1,400 Allied planes as part of an all-out air assault on Germany. With no strategic value and undefended, Dresden was also near a POW camp holding more than 25,000 Allied prisoners. Some 650,000 incendiary bombs were dropped on Dresden, killing more than 100,000 Germans.

March 7   (Europe) American forces cross the Rhine River at Remagen, and by the end of the month, all German forces have been pushed back into Germany.

March 9   As U.S. planes begin to bombard Japan more heavily, Tokyo is attacked by a massive firebombing. Two thousand tons of gasoline-gel and oil-gel incendiary bombs are dropped on the city, beginning a firestorm, fanned by winds, that the U.S. Strategic Bombing Survey called a "conflagration." The water in Tokyo's shallow canals actually boiled. The U.S. Strategic Bombing Survey estimates that "probably more persons lost their lives by fire in Tokyo in a six-hour period than at any time in the history of man." More than 100,000 men, women, and children die in Tokyo on this night, and another million are injured; a million lose their homes. In the next few days, the cities of Nagoya, Osaka, and Kobe are also firebombed until the U.S. Air Force literally runs out of bombs. In ten days, the firebombings kill at least 150,000 people and burn out the centers of Japan's four largest cities.

March 16   (Pacific) Iwo Jima. A monthlong struggle for this rocky, eight-square-mile piece of volcanic island comes to an end. Possessing Japan's last line of radar defense to warn against American air attacks, Iwo Jima is a strategically significant prelude to the invasion of Okinawa. The combined naval and ground attack begins one of the most terrible and hard-fought battles of the war.

The U.S. military considers the use of poison gas shells before sending in troops but decides against it, probably because of the outcry against poison gas in World War I. The famous image of the six marines—three of whom will die on Iwo Jima—raising the flag atop Mount Suribachi becomes an American icon of the day. Losses on both sides are horrifying, with the U.S. Marines suffering 6,821 killed and more than 21,000 wounded; the 50 percent casualty rate was the highest in Marine Corps history. More than 20,000 Japanese defenders died while only 1,083 were taken prisoner.

April 1   (Pacific) In the next stepping-stone, U.S. troops invade Okinawa on Easter Sunday, or, as the soldiers note ironically, April Fool's Day. The Japanese allow the troops to land, and then systematically attempt to destroy their naval support, beginning a fight that will last almost three months, the bloodiest battle of the Pacific, which will eventually cost 80,000 American casualties.

April 11   U.S. troops reach the Elbe River. They halt there and meet advancing Russian troops on April 25.

April 12   (Home front) After suffering a massive cerebral hemorrhage, President Roosevelt dies at his retreat in Warm Springs, Georgia. Vice President Harry S Truman (1884–1972) is sworn in as president.

April 14   President Truman, aware of the existence of the Manhattan Project but not its purpose, is told about the atomic bomb. Truman is initially reluctant to use the weapon, and orders a search for alternatives. He is also confronted with the idea that the secret of the bomb should be shared with America's allies, including Stalin's Russia. Development continues, and a search for potential Japanese targets of an atomic bomb is proposed.

April 30   With Russian shells falling on Berlin, Hitler marries his mistress, Eva Braun, in his bombproof Berlin bunker. He then poisons her and kills himself. His remains are never recovered.

May 7   (Europe) The Germans formally surrender to General Eisenhower at Rheims, France, and to the Soviets in Berlin. President Truman pronounces the following day V-E Day.

June 5 (Europe) The United States, Russia, England, and France agree to split occupied Germany into eastern and western halves, and to divide Berlin, which is within the eastern, Russian-occupied half of Germany.

June 21 (Pacific) Okinawa falls. The Japanese have lost 160,000 men in fighting on the island; more than 12,500 Americans die on Okinawa.

July 5 (Pacific) General MacArthur completes the recapture of the Philippines; 12,000 Americans have died in the ten-month fight for the islands. With the reconquest of the Philippines and the securing of Okinawa as a base, the United States begins to plan for an invasion of Japan.

July 16 (Home front) The first atomic bomb is successfully detonated in a secret test at Alamogordo, New Mexico, the fruits of the top-secret Manhattan Project begun in 1942 by President Roosevelt and continued under Truman.

August 6 (Pacific) Hiroshima. The U.S. B-29 Superfortress *Enola Gay* drops the atomic bomb on this industrial city. The destructive capacity of this now-primitive weapon levels the city, killing some 80,000 immediately, seriously injuring another 100,000 (out of a total population of 344,000), and leveling 98 percent of the city's buildings. The bomb's force astounds even its makers, who have not truly understood its destructive potential or the effects of radiation. Three days later, on August 9, a second bomb is dropped on Japan, this one on the city of Nagasaki, and Stalin declares war on Japan, launching an invasion of Manchuria.

August 14 (Pacific) Fighting ends in the Far East. Three days later the Allies divide Korea along the 38th parallel, with Soviet troops occupying the northern half and U.S. troops holding the south.

September 2 (Pacific) General MacArthur, named Supreme Commander of Allied Powers in Japan, accepts the formal, unconditional surrender of Japan aboard the USS *Missouri* in Tokyo Bay. In December, MacArthur is appointed by Truman to attempt to negotiate a settlement between the Nationalist Chinese under Chiang Kai-shek and the Communists under Mao Zedong.

What was the cost of World War II?

While there is no "official" casualty count for the Second World War, it was clearly the greatest and deadliest war in history, costing more than 50 million lives. The estimates of battle losses are numbing: 7.5 million Russians; 3.5 million Germans; 1.2 million Japanese; 2.2 million Chinese. Great Britain and France each lost hundreds of thousands of men. The civilian toll was even higher. Probably 22 million Russians died during the war years. The German "final solution," or extermination of the Jews, took the lives of at least 6 million Jews, most of these dying in the concentration camps. Millions more Slavs, Eastern Europeans, Gypsies, and homosexuals were similarly engulfed by the Holocaust. For the United States, combat casualties were close to 300,000 dead and nearly 700,000 wounded.

The wartime cooperation between the Soviets and the West, the creation of the United Nations, and the frightful power of the atomic bomb raised hopes that this truly would be the war to end all wars. But just three months into the new year, former prime minister Winston Churchill, turned out of office in the 1945 elections, addressed a college audience at Fulton, Missouri. He told the gathering and the world, "An Iron Curtain has descended across the continent, allowing 'police governments' to rule Eastern Europe."

One war was over. The next—the Cold War—was under way.

What was the Yalta Conference?

In February 1945, the war in Europe was moving toward its final days. Soviet armies were already in Hungary and Poland and approaching Berlin. On the western front, Allied forces pushed back Hitler's personally planned counteroffensive in the Ardennes Forest in the brutal Battle of the Bulge. American and Soviet troops were moving toward their meeting on the Elbe River. But the Pacific war was still going strong. Japan was far from defeated, although plainly in retreat.

Against this background the Allied Big Three—Winston Churchill, Franklin D. Roosevelt, and Joseph Stalin (1879–1953), the men who conducted the war against Germany—met together in Yalta, in a former czarist palace on the Black Sea. This was to be a "mopping-up" meeting. The major wartime decisions had been made earlier at meetings between Roosevelt and Churchill at Casablanca, and at a summit of the Big Three in Teheran.

Recently inaugurated for a fourth term, but greatly aged by twelve years of governing a fractious nation through the Depression and the war, Roosevelt was in poor health. He came to Yalta with three goals: to establish a meaningful United Nations; to persuade the Russians to declare war on Japan and thereby to hasten the end of that part of the war; and to decide the fate of Poland, that sizable chunk of territory that had been at the heart of the war since Germany and Russia both invaded it.

Of these three issues, Russian commitment to the war against Japan was uppermost in Roosevelt's mind. Work on a secret weapon to be used against Japan was still going on, but even the few who knew of the existence of the Manhattan Project held no great hopes for the atomic bomb's usefulness. Roosevelt had to consider the advice of his generals, like MacArthur, who conservatively estimated that a million American casualties would result from the eventual invasion of Japan. To Roosevelt and Churchill, obtaining Stalin's commitment to join the fight against Japan was crucial. To Roosevelt's generals, it was worth any price.

Stalin knew that.

Roosevelt and Churchill, who had held most of the cards during the war, found themselves in the dangerous position of dealing with the master of the Soviet Union from a position of weakness. Stalin finally agreed to enter an anti-Japanese alliance, but the price was substantial: the Soviets would control Manchuria and Mongolia, and would be ceded half of Sakhalin Island and the Kurile Islands, off northern Japan; a Soviet occupation zone would be created in Korea; and in the United Nations, a veto power would be given to the major nations, of which the Soviet Union was one, along with the United States, Great

Britain, France, and China (still under the wavering control of Chiang Kai-shek's American-supported Nationalists).

Later it would be said that Roosevelt, the "sick man" of the Yalta Conference, had given away Poland (and the rest of Eastern Europe). In fact, he couldn't give away what wasn't his to give. The Red Army and Communist partisan forces in Eastern Europe held control of almost all this territory. In private, Churchill urged Eisenhower to continue pushing his armies as far east of the Elbe River as possible, a position with which U.S. General George Patton was in complete agreement. But Ike disagreed. Patton had to pull back, and the Russians "liberated" Czechoslovakia, eastern Germany, and Berlin.

At Yalta, the Polish issue was "solved" by redrawing its borders and, in a replay of Versailles, adding lands that had been Germany's. In the spirit of Allied unity, Stalin agreed to guarantee all Eastern European countries the right to choose their governments and leaders in free elections. Roosevelt believed that a United Nations, with American commitment (which the League of Nations lacked), could solve problems related to these issues as they arose. Perhaps more tragically, Roosevelt saw his personal role as the conciliator as a key to lasting peace.

As the historian James McGregor Burns wrote in *The Crosswinds of Freedom*, "Holding only weak hands in the great poker game of Yalta, Roosevelt believed he had won the foundations of future peace. It was with hope and even exultation that he and his party left Yalta for the long journey home. Above all he left with confidence that, whatever the problems ahead, he could solve them through his personal intervention."

How did FDR die?

Any hopes Roosevelt had of maintaining peace through his personality went to his grave with him. On April 12, 1945, Roosevelt suffered a cerebral hemorrhage while resting at his retreat in Warm Springs, Georgia, where he was staying with his longtime mistress, Lucy Rutherford. His death left the nation and much of the world dizzy and disoriented. Even the Japanese issued a sympathetic message. He was still vilified by many, but to most Americans, FDR had been an immutable force, a Gibraltar-like presence on the American scene. He had guided America as it licked the Great Depression and the Nazis. To younger Americans, including many of those in uniform, he was the only president they had known.

Practically beatified by a generation of Americans, Franklin D. Roosevelt appears, more than fifty-five years after his death—like Washington, Lincoln, and other "great men" of American history—less a saint than a man flawed by his humanity. He was foremost a politician, perhaps the greatest ever in America, and like all politicians, he made bargains. There are large questions left by his legacy. For instance, although he was greatly admired and overwhelmingly voted for by blacks, FDR's approach to the question of blacks in America was confused. His wife, Eleanor, consistently pushed for greater social equality for blacks and all minority groups. But American life and the Army remained segregated, although blacks slowly reached higher ranks, and war contractors were forbidden to practice segregation.

Another lingering question has concerned his response to the Holocaust. Prior to the American entry into the war, the Nazi treatment of Jews evoked little more than weak diplomatic condemnation. It is clear that Roosevelt knew about the treatment of Jews in Germany and elsewhere in Europe, and about the methodical, systematic destruction of the Jews during the Holocaust. Clearly, saving the Jews and other groups that Hitler was destroying en masse was not a critical issue for American war planners.

The Pearl Harbor issue also refuses to go away. Few historians are willing to go so far as to condemn Roosevelt for sentencing 2,000 Americans to die when they might have been saved. Instead, the consensus is that his military advisers underestimated the abilities of the Japanese to reach Hawaii, and exaggerated the U.S. military's ability to defend itself against such an attack. The internment of Japanese Americans during the war is an everlasting stain on Roosevelt and the entire nation.

In a private light, FDR was later shown to have carried on a long-term relationship with Lucy Rutherford. If revealed, this secret might have brought him down. But in contrast to what has befallen politicians in more recent times, no stories about FDR and Rutherford ever appeared, much less film or photographs. He was protected by the press and the Secret Service, just as John F. Kennedy would be for sexual behavior far more indiscreet and dangerous than Roosevelt's love affair had been.

Yet FDR's legacy remains. Just as Washington was "the indispensable man" of his time, so was FDR in the era of Depression and war. If history does come down to the question of personality, was there another man in America who could have accomplished what Roosevelt did? Despite flaws and contradictions, he knew that a failure to improve the nation's economic and psychological health might produce a victory for the forces of racism and militarism that produced different leaders in other countries. Few presidents—none since Lincoln during the Civil War—held the near-dictatorial powers Roosevelt commanded during the Depression and the war. Yet, if he was a quasi-dictator at the height of his political power, FDR's overall record is certainly benign. The same economic shock waves that brought Roosevelt to power produced Mussolini and Hitler, demagogic madmen with visions of world conquest, who ruled brutal, racist police states. Like many another canonized American hero, Roosevelt was far from sainthood. Yet consider the alternative.

Must Read: *No Ordinary Times: Franklin and Eleanor Roosevelt: The Home Front in World War II* by Doris Kearns Goodwin.

AMERICAN VOICES
HARRY TRUMAN, from his diaries (as quoted in
The Making of the Atomic Bomb by Richard Rhodes):

We have discovered the most terrible bomb in the history of the world. It may be the fire destruction prophesied in the Euphrates valley Ersa, after Noah and his fabulous Ark.

Anyway we "think" we have found a way to cause a disintegration of the atom. An experiment in the New Mexican desert was startling—to put it mildly. . . .

This weapon is to be used against Japan between now and August 10th. I have told the Sec. of War, Mr. Stimson, to use it so that military objectives and soldiers and sailors are the target and not women and children. Even if the

Japs are savages, ruthless, merciless and fanatic, we as the leaders of the world for the common welfare cannot drop this terrible bomb on the old Capital or the new.

He & I are in accord. The target will be a purely military one and we will issue a warning statement asking the Japs to surrender and save lives. I'm sure they will not do that, but we will give them the chance. It is certainly a good thing for the world that Hitler's crowd or Stalin's did not discover this atomic bomb. It seems to be the most terrible thing ever discovered, but it can be made to be the most useful.

Did the United States have to drop atomic bombs on Hiroshima and Nagasaki?

Okay, Mr. President. Here's the situation. You're about to invade Japan's main islands. Your best generals say hitting these beaches will mean half a million American casualties. Other estimates go as high as a million. General MacArthur tells you that the Japanese will continue guerrilla-style resistance for ten years. Based on horrific battle experience—from Guadalcanal to Okinawa—you believe the Japanese will fight to the death. They have 6 million battle-hardened troops who have shown complete willingness to fight to the death for their homeland—a samurai tradition of complete devotion to the divine emperor that is incomprehensible to Americans. Japanese civilians have jumped off cliffs to prevent capture by Americans, and there are reports that mainland Japanese civilians are being armed with sharpened bamboo spears. But you also remember Pearl Harbor and the Bataan Death March and other wartime atrocities committed by Japanese. Vengeance, in the midst of a cruel war, is not incomprehensible.

Now you have a bomb with the destructive power of 20,000 tons of TNT. It worked in a test, but it may not work when you drop it out of a plane. Why not give a demonstration to show its power? Your advisers tell you that if the show-detonation is a dud, the Japanese resistance will harden.

Modern history has presented this pair of options—the Big Invasion versus the Bomb—as "Truman's choice." It was a choice Truman inherited with the Oval Office. President Roosevelt had responded to Albert Einstein's 1939 warning—a warning Einstein later regretted—of the potential of an atomic bomb by ordering research that became the Manhattan Project in 1942. Known to only a handful of men, Truman not among them, the project was a $2 billion (in pre-inflation 1940s dollars) effort to construct an atomic weapon. Working at Los Alamos, New Mexico, under the direction of J. Robert Oppenheimer (1904–67), atomic scientists, many of them refugees from Hitler's Europe, thought they were racing against Germans developing a "Nazi bomb." That effort was later proved to be far short of success. The first atomic bomb was exploded at Alamogordo, New Mexico, on July 16, 1945. Truman was alerted to the success of the test at a meeting with Churchill and Stalin at Potsdam, a city in defeated Germany.

Before the test detonation, there were already deep misgivings among both the scientific and military communities about the morality of the bomb's destructive power. Many of its creators did not want it to be used, and lobbied to share its secrets with the rest of the world to prevent its use. Truman ignored that advice. With Churchill and China's Chiang Kai-shek, he issued the Potsdam Declaration, warning Japan to accept a complete and unconditional surrender or risk "prompt and utter destruction." Although specific mention of the bomb's nature was considered, this vague warning was the only one issued.

When the Japanese first failed to respond to, and then rejected, his ultimatum, Truman ordered the fateful go-ahead. It was a self-perpetuating order that took on a life of its own. After Hiroshima, nobody said, "Don't drop another one," so the men proceeded under the orders they had been given.

Almost since the day the first bomb was dropped on Hiroshima, critics have second-guessed Truman's decision and motives. A generation of historians has defended or repudiated the need for unleashing the atomic weapon. The historical justification was that a full-scale invasion of Japan would have cost frightful numbers of American and Japanese lives.

Many critics have dismissed those estimates as implausibly high, and say that the Japanese were already nearing their decision to submit when the bombs were dropped. A study made after the war by a U.S. government survey team reached that very conclusion. But coming as it did a year after the war was over, that judgment didn't help Truman make his decision.

Other historians who support the Hiroshima drop dispute that criticism. Instead, they point to the fact that some of the strongest militarists in Japan were planning a coup to topple a pro-surrender government. Even after the Japanese surrender, Japanese officers were planning kamikaze strikes at the battleship on which the surrender documents would be signed. The view that accepts "atomic necessity" offers as evidence the actual Pacific fighting as it moved closer to Japan. And it is a convincing exhibit. Each successive island that the Americans invaded was defended fanatically, at immense cost on both sides. The Japanese military code, centuries old and steeped in the samurai tradition, showed no tolerance for surrender. Indeed, even in Hiroshima itself, there was anger that the emperor had capitulated.

But were the bomb and an invasion the only options? Or was there another reality? A top-secret study made during the period and revealed in the late 1980s says there was, and destroys much of the accepted justification for the Hiroshima bombing. According to these Army studies, the crucial factor in the Japanese decision to surrender was not the dropping of the bombs but the entry of the Soviet Union into the war against Japan. These documents and other recently revealed evidence suggest that Truman knew at Potsdam that Stalin would declare war against Japan early in August. Nearly two months before Hiroshima, Army Chief of Staff George C. Marshall had advised the president that the Soviet declaration of war would force Japan to surrender, making the need for an American invasion unnecessary. It was a fact with which Truman seemed to agree.

So if the estimates of an invasion's costs and ending the war quickly were not the only considerations, why did the United States use these terrible weapons?

What history has confirmed is that the men who made the bomb really didn't understand how horrifying its capabilities were. Of course they understood the destructive power of the bomb, but radiation's dangers were far less understood. As author Peter Wyden tells it in *Day One*, his compelling account of the making and dropping of the bomb, scientists involved in creating what they called "the gadget" believed that anyone who might be killed by radiation would die from falling bricks first.

But apart from this scientific shortfall, was there another strategic element to the decision? Many modern historians unhesitatingly answer yes. By late 1945 it was clear to Truman and other American leaders that victory over Germany and Japan would not mean peace. Stalin's intention to create a buffer of Socialist states surrounding the Soviet Union and under the control of the Red Army was already apparent. Atomic muscle-flexing may have been the overriding consideration in Truman's decision.

The age of nuclear saber rattling did not begin with the dropping of the bomb on Hiroshima, but with the Potsdam meeting, where Stalin and Truman began the deadly dance around the issue of atomic weaponry. Truman was unaware that Stalin, through the efforts of scientist-spy Klaus Fuchs, who was working at Los Alamos and passing secrets to the Soviets, knew as much about the atomic bomb as the president himself—if not more.

Some historians have pointed to the second attack on Nagasaki as further proof of this atomic "big stick" theory. Having demonstrated the thirteen-kiloton bomb at Hiroshima, Truman still wanted to show off a large bomb used against Nagasaki to send a clear message to the Soviets: We have it and we're not afraid to use it.

If Truman viewed these bombs as a message to the Soviets, that message, and the frightful nuclear buildup on both sides in the postwar years, dictated American and Soviet policies in the coming decades of Cold War confrontation.

Must Read: *The Making of the Atomic Bomb* by Richard Rhodes; *Truman* by David McCullough.

CHAPTER SEVEN

COMMIES, CONTAINMENT, AND COLD WAR

America in the Fifties

What was the Truman Doctrine?

What were the Pumpkin Papers?

Why were the Rosenbergs executed for espionage?

What was McCarthyism?

Who fought in the Korean War?

Milestones in the Korean War

What were the results of the Korean War?

What was Teddy Roosevelt's grandson doing in Iran?

What was *Brown v. Board of Education*?

Why did the arrest of a woman named Rosa Parks change American life?

Why did President Eisenhower send the Army into Little Rock, Arkansas?

What was Sputnik?

How did a doll in stiletto heels and a Chicago publisher change America?

What we think of as the fifties really began in 1945. The war was over. The boys came home. America was triumphant, now first among nations. "The American Century" proclaimed earlier by *Time* magazine's publisher Henry Luce, seemed to be fully under way.

It was time to enjoy Uncle Miltie, Lucy, and daring novels like *Forever Amber* and *Peyton Place*. Most people fondly recall the postwar era as a respite of prosperity and social normality, a comfortable time. For eight of those years, Dwight D. Eisenhower (1890–1969), the gentle-faced golfer whom America called Ike, held office, a comforting president. His campaign buttons simply read "I Like Ike," and that said it all. With his wife, Mamie, as first lady, it was like having everyone's favorite aunt and uncle sitting in the White House.

America started to watch television—more than 4 million sets were sold in 1950—and listen to the comfortable sound of Perry Como. There was no hip-swiveling jailhouse rocker on the scene. Yet.

America moved to the comfortable suburbs; 13 million new homes went up between 1948 and 1958, many of them in the cookie-cutter fashion pioneered by developer William J. Levitt's phenomenally successful Levittown, Long Island. (In Levittown, there were no separate drinking fountains for blacks as there were in southern states. But they weren't necessary. In Levittown, no blacks needed apply. The houses were for whites only from the beginning.) Coming back from the Big War and later the Korean conflict, former GIs wasted no time, and America's maternity wards were overflowing—76.4 million "baby boomers" were born between 1946 and 1964. The country was reading Dr. Spock's *Baby and Child Care* and Norman Vincent Peale's *The Power of Positive Thinking*.

But not everything was rosy—even though America saw Red wherever it looked. There were Commies everywhere. In Eastern Europe and Asia. In the State Department and the Army. They seemed to be under every rock. Even in Hollywood!

There was also a generation of young writers looking at the underside of this dream, straining against the new American dream and its conformist constraints. In his first novel, *The Naked and the Dead* (1948),

Norman Mailer (1923–2007) presented a different and uncomfortable picture of the American GI in combat. A short-story writer named J. D. Salinger (1919–2010) would capture the alienation of youth forever in his novel *The Catcher in the Rye* (1951). In several novels of the period, including *The Adventures of Augie March* (1953), Saul Bellow (1915–2005) would also express the angst of a generation. By 1955 with *On the Road*, Jack Kerouac (1922–69) would help lead a generation of "beats" who broke the era's social restraints, becoming self-proclaimed outcasts from a nation that prized stability and "normality" above all. Books like David Riesman's *The Lonely Crowd* (1950) and William Whyte's *The Organization Man* (1956) also examined this peculiar American need to conform, an American characteristic that Tocqueville had perceptively brought to light more than a hundred years earlier.

What was the Truman Doctrine?

Any dreams for an era of postwar cooperation between the two new giants of the world, the United States and the Soviet Union, quickly evaporated. The map of Europe had been redrawn, and in Churchill's ominous phrase, an Iron Curtain had descended across Eastern Europe as the Soviets under Stalin established a ring of Socialist states around its flanks. The future would bring a string of flare-ups as the two nations contended for power and influence.

In 1947, when it appeared that Greece and Turkey were the next targets for Communist takeovers, and the British informed President Truman that they would be unable to defend the existing governments, Truman asked Congress for aid to both countries. In what became known as the Truman Doctrine, the president told Congress, "I believe that it must be the policy of the United States to support free peoples who are resisting subjugation by armed minorities or by outside pressures."

With $400 million worth of American advisers and military aid, the Greek and Turkish governments prevailed. But instead of installing representative government in the so-called cradle of democracy, Athens came under the rule of an oppressive, right-wing military regime, as did Turkey. But that was less important to political leaders of the United States at the time than that both countries remain aligned with the United States.

The philosophy behind the Truman Doctrine came from a State Department official named George F. Kennan. Writing under the pseudonym X in the influential journal *Foreign Affairs*, Kennan introduced the pivotal concept of "containment," which essentially meant using American power to counter Soviet pressure wherever it developed. Containment of the Communist threat would color every foreign policy decision in America for decades to come, as well as help bring about the great domestic fear of Communism that swept the country during the 1950s. In addition to the Truman Doctrine, containment also led to the establishment of the North Atlantic Treaty Organization (NATO) in 1949 to defend Western Europe against Soviet bloc attack, and the Marshall Plan to address the serious economic crisis in postwar Europe.

Must Read: *Truman* by David McCullough.

AMERICAN VOICES
SECRETARY OF STATE GEORGE C. MARSHALL'S
Harvard commencement address justifying
the European Recovery Program,
known as the Marshall Plan (June 5, 1947):

The truth of the matter is that Europe's requirements for the next three or four years of foreign food and other essential products—principally from America—are so much greater than her present ability to pay that she must have substantial additional help, or face economic, social and political deterioration of a very grave character.

. . . Aside from the demoralizing effect on the world at large and the possibilities of disturbances arising as a result of the desperation of the people concerned, the consequences to the economy of the United States should be apparent to all. It is logical that the United States should do whatever it is able to do to assist in the return of normal

> economic health in the world, without which there can be
> no political stability and no assured peace. Our policy is
> directed not against any country or doctrine but against
> hunger, poverty, desperation, and chaos.

Conceived by Undersecretary of State Will Clayton and first proposed by Secretary of State Dean Acheson (1893–1971), the Marshall Plan, also known as the European Recovery Program, pumped more than $12 billion into selected war-torn European countries during the next four years. (The countries participating were Austria, Belgium, Denmark, France, West Germany, Great Britain, Greece, Iceland, Italy, Luxembourg, the Netherlands, Norway, Sweden, Switzerland, and Turkey.) It provided the economic side of Truman's policy of containment by removing the economic dislocation that might have fostered Communism in Western Europe. It also set up a Displaced Persons Plan under which some 300,000 Europeans, many of them Jewish survivors of the Holocaust, were granted American citizenship. By most accounts, the Marshall Plan was the most successful undertaking of the United States in the postwar era and is often cited as the most compelling argument in favor of foreign aid.

To some contemporary critics on the left, the Marshall Plan was not simply pure American altruism—the goodhearted generosity of America's best intentions. To them, it was an extension of a capitalist plan for American economic domination, a calculated Cold War ploy to rebuild European capitalism. Or, to put it simply, if there were no Europe to sell to, who would buy all those products the American industrial machine was turning out?

By any measure, the Marshall Plan must be considered an enormously successful undertaking that helped return a devastated Europe to health, allowing free market democracies to flourish while Eastern Europe, hunkered down under repressive Soviet-controlled regimes, stagnated socially and economically.

AMERICAN VOICES
JACKIE ROBINSON to his wife, in 1947:

If you come down to Ebbets Field today, you won't have any trouble recognizing me. My number's forty-two.

When Jackie Robinson (1919–72) said that to his wife, it was on the day he became the first black man to play modern major league baseball. Robinson joined the Brooklyn Dodgers that year and was named Rookie of the Year. In 1949, he won the National League's Most Valuable Player award.

Although he started as a first baseman, Robinson gained his greatest fame playing second base. An outstanding hitter, Robinson finished with a .311 lifetime batting average and was also a superior runner and base stealer. He played all ten years of his major league career with the Dodgers and was elected to the National Baseball Hall of Fame in 1962.

But the simple numbers of sports statistics and achievements do not tell his story. Born in Cairo, Georgia, Jack Roosevelt Robinson starred in four sports at the University of California at Los Angeles. Robinson served during World War II, and in 1945 joined the Kansas City Monarchs of the Negro American League. In 1946, he played minor league baseball for the Montreal Royals. And then Branch Rickey of the Dodgers made the decision to bring Robinson to the big leagues.

When Jackie Robinson broke baseball's color line, it was one more crack in the foundation of American racism and segregation. Jackie Robinson helped America take one more crucial step in breaking down the racial barriers that had divided America. And he would pay a heavy price for his bold move. For much of his career, he regularly received death threats and heard poisonous insults. And not just from the stands in some Deep South backwater, but from the opposing dugout in places like Philadelphia, the City of Brotherly Love and birthplace of America's freedom. Robinson later recounted hearing the opposing Phillies players scream at him:

"Hey, nigger, why don't you go back to the cotton field, where you belong?"

"They're waiting for you in the jungles, black boy!"

"We don't want you here, nigger."*

What were the Pumpkin Papers?

To many Americans in the days and years following the war, Communism was on the march around the world. Roosevelt and his "eastern establishment" liberal coterie had "given away" Eastern Europe, surrendering it to Stalin at Yalta. In one of the first tests of U.S. resolve, the Soviets had tried to close off Berlin, forcing the United States to conduct a massive airlift in 1948 that finally cracked the Russian hold on the city. In China, the Nationalists were crushed by Mao's Communist forces in 1949. At about the same time, it was revealed that the Soviets had the atomic bomb. The world seemed to be in the grasp of a Communist conspiracy of international domination, and the president had responded with the Truman Doctrine, with the complete support of a bipartisan Congress.

The obsessive fear of Communism in America was nothing new. Americans had been battling the Red Menace for years, and the first wave of Red hysteria had followed World War I (see Chapter 6). But it seemed as if the fears were much more real now, heightened by the terror of the mushroom cloud. Communism was the cutting issue on which people voted. To be "soft" on Communism was political suicide, and ambitious young men, like Representative Richard M. Nixon (1913–94) of California, could see that Communist bashing was the ticket to the future.

Responding to this anti-Red pressure, Truman had set up loyalty boards in 1947 to check on reports of Communist sympathizers in the

---

*In case you think it only happened a long time ago in a very different America, Randall Kennedy's fascinating book, *Nigger: The Strange Career of a Troublesome Word*, recounts how Michael Jordan and Tiger Woods heard the same words growing up. Worse still was the mail routinely received by slugger Hank Aaron as he pursued Babe Ruth's legendary career home run record in 1973. Typical of his mail was a letter that read, "Dear Nigger Henry, You are not going to break this record established by the great Babe Ruth if you can help it. . . . Whites are far more superior than jungle bunnies. . . . My gun is watching your every move."

federal government. Thousands were investigated, but there was no meaningful trace of subversion, even though careers were destroyed as suspicion replaced evidence. These were the first of the anti-Communist "witch hunts" in which the burden of proof was on the accused, who couldn't face or know his unnamed accusers. Hearsay testimony from unreliable witnesses became Holy Writ.

The fear got front-page headlines in 1949, when Whittaker Chambers (1901–61), a repentant, "reformed" Communist Party member and later a senior editor at *Time* magazine, charged that Alger Hiss was a member of the Communist Party and part of a high-reaching Soviet spy ring. To those who knew Hiss, this was nonsense that took the anti-Soviet paranoia too far. A Roosevelt New Dealer, Hiss (1904–96) was born and bred to the eastern establishment, with impeccable credentials as a progressive and a long, distinguished career in public service, beginning as a law clerk under Supreme Court Justice Oliver Wendell Holmes. But to conservatives, Hiss was blemished because he had been with Roosevelt at Yalta and was secretary general of the United Nations organizing conference in 1945–46. Both Yalta and the UN were increasingly viewed as parts of the Communist scheme for weakening America and achieving world domination. In 1947, Hiss was serving as president of the prestigious Carnegie Endowment for International Peace, a foundation devoted to furthering the wealthy steel magnate's commitment to a worldwide peace process, with the blessing of diplomat John Foster Dulles (later Eisenhower's secretary of state) — and his brother Allen Dulles (legendary founder of the CIA). With his many such friends, Hiss's integrity and loyalty were unquestioned at the highest levels of government.

Disheveled, overweight, and a somewhat ill-bred character, Chambers claimed that in the 1930s, Hiss had been a Communist who had given Chambers classified documents to be passed on to Moscow. Pressed by Congressman Richard Nixon in a 1948 hearing before the House Un-American Activities Committee (HUAC) investigating alleged Communist subversion in government, Hiss denied the allegations. Everything in Hiss's demeanor and bearing seemed to demolish the allegations made by the unseemly Chambers, who was also the subject of a whisper campaign that he was mentally unstable, an alcoholic, and a homosexual. But there were also some damaging revelations that left nagging suspicions. The most sensational of these came to light when Chambers produced microfilm copies of stolen State Department documents that Chambers said Hiss had given him to pass on to the Soviets. Chambers had hidden them inside a hollowed-out pumpkin in his garden. Overnight, these became the Pumpkin Papers.

In Hiss's undoing was Richard Nixon's moment. As Sam Tanenhaus wrote in his monumental biography of Chambers, "Nixon was motivated by more than dislike of Hiss. He also saw a political opportunity. No stranger to the Communists in government issue, Nixon had ridden it to an upset victory over a popular incumbent, Jerry Voorhis, in 1946 and since his arrival in Washington had been diligently throwing out lines to its dense network of Red hunters. . . . With brilliant clarity, Nixon grasped that the emerging Chambers-Hiss mystery could yield great political dividends for the man who solved it. And so he pitched himself into the case with methodical intensity few in Washington — or anywhere — could match."

His reputation damaged by the evidence that Chambers had provided to support his charges, Hiss sued Chambers for libel, and the evidence against this paragon of American progressive liberalism turned out to be strong. In the courtroom, Chambers showed that he knew intimate details of Hiss's life, and even produced papers showing that Hiss had once given him an old car. In the wake of the failed libel suit, Hiss was indicted for perjury for lying to a congressional committee. While the statute of limitations protected Hiss from espionage charges, a federal grand jury indicted him in 1948. Tried and convicted in January 1950, Hiss was sentenced to five years in prison and served three years before his release in 1954. (His personal fortune gone after his conviction, Hiss was also disbarred and became a printing salesman in New York City. In 1975, at age seventy, he was readmitted to the bar in Massachusetts, and continued to work for vindication until his death in 1996.)

For most of the next half-century, people continued to argue this case with passion. More than twenty books have been written about the case, which, until fairly recently, remained one of the litmus tests of one's political views: liberals were certain of Hiss's innocence, conservatives of his guilt. But in the wake of the Cold War coming to an end, new evidence in the case has surfaced, and many uncertainties have been removed.

When selected Moscow archives were opened to researchers after the fall of the Soviet Union in 1991, the Hiss side was bolstered when old KGB files were searched and none indicated that Hiss had spied for the Soviets. But there was more damning evidence to follow. First a researcher discovered documents in 1993 that related to Noel Field, another prominent State Department official who had actually defected to the Communists in 1949. According to Field, Hiss had tried to recruit him into the Communist underground. Then in 1995, the highly secret American National Security Agency (NSA), the organization that intercepts and translates messages from around the world, released what are known as the "Venona traffic," thousands of cables sent from U.S.-based Soviet agents to their home office in Moscow. These cables implicate Hiss as part of a large espionage network centered in the federal government.

Must Read: *Perjury: The Hiss-Chambers Case* by Allen Weinstein; *Whittaker Chambers* by Sam Tanenhaus.

Why were the Rosenbergs executed for espionage?

The explosive Hiss story captured the headlines at about the same time that Americans learned that Klaus Fuchs, a respected German-born physicist who had worked on the Manhattan Project developing the atomic bomb at Columbia University and later at Los Alamos during the war, had been passing America's atomic secrets to the Russians. Harry Gold, an American associate of Fuchs who was a chemist, was caught at the same time as an American couple, David and Ruth Greenglass. Greenglass, a young American soldier who also worked at Los Alamos, testified that he had passed on crude drawings of atomic weapons to his brother-in-law and sister, Julius and Ethel Rosenberg. According to FBI documents released later, J. Edgar Hoover urged Ethel's arrest to force Julius to talk. They were arrested in 1950, along with another conspirator, Morton Sobell. They were tried in 1951 for conspiracy to commit espionage.

Claiming innocence at their trial, the Rosenbergs relied on the Fifth Amendment when asked if they were Communists. Greenglass gave detailed testimony about the information he had given to the

Rosenbergs and said Ethel transcribed notes for her husband. Gold, who had already been sentenced to thirty years, said Soviet officer Anatoli Yakovlev was Julius Rosenberg's contact in the KGB. Their day in court came in the midst of the Korean War, presided over by Judge Irving R. Kaufman, a judge who, by all appearances, seemed in league with the prosecution. Sobel was sentenced to thirty years in jail; the Rosenbergs were sentenced to death, even though J. Edgar Hoover opposed the death penalty for Ethel, fearing public reaction to the execution of the mother of two small children. The other conspirators were also given prison sentences, including Fuchs himself, because they all agreed to help the prosecution, which the Rosenbergs refused to do. And that was ultimately the reason they were sent to the electric chair on June 19, 1953.

The evidence against the Rosenbergs at the time, especially the testimony of Greenglass and Gold, was strong. But ever since, the Rosenbergs' defenders have passionately claimed that the Rosenbergs were framed, convicted, and executed in an atmosphere of anti-Semitic, anti-Communist frenzy. What has emerged, particularly since the release of Soviet documents in the 1990s, confirms what had largely been the consensus: that Julius Rosenberg was indeed a spy, but that the secrets he passed along were far less damaging than those Fuchs turned over. In 1997, a man who professed to be Rosenberg's Soviet "handler" said Rosenberg had passed military secrets but not atomic secrets. As for Ethel, the former Soviet spy said she knew what her husband, Julius, was doing but was not involved, an assessment confirmed by the Venona cables that also apparently confirmed Hiss's guilt. In addition, Greenglass eventually admitted to journalist Sam Roberts in his 2001 book, *The Brother*, that he had lied about his sister to save himself.

What was McCarthyism?

It was from this toxic cloud of hysteria that Senator Joseph McCarthy (1909–57) emerged, and was taken up by the right-wing press as a new Paul Revere. He was the freshman senator from Wisconsin, elected to the Senate in 1946 by lying about his wartime service record and smearing his primary and general election opponents. In a short time, this scruffy, mean-spirited alcoholic was lining his pockets with lobbyist money and was generally thought of as the worst senator in Washington. By 1950, he was looking for the issue that would keep his leaky political boat from sinking.

McCarthy found that issue when he was fed some obsolete documents relating to old investigations of Communists in government jobs. In February 1950, McCarthy told a women's club in Wheeling, West Virginia, that he held, "here in my hand," a list of 205 men in the State Department named as members of the Communist Party who were part of a spy ring. The numbers changed from day to day, and even McCarthy wasn't sure where he had gotten them. His bulging briefcase of "evidence" generally held only a bottle of bourbon. But this was the beginning of his "big lie," consisting of evidence and charges fabricated by a desperate man. In the following days, the emptiness of McCarthy's "evidence" should have ended his Senate career. But it didn't work out that way. In 1950, America was more than ready to believe what Senator McCarthy had to say.

Although a Senate committee investigated and then refuted everything McCarthy claimed, its findings were ignored. True or not, McCarthy's irresponsible accusations caught the public ear, made headlines, and sold newspapers. The Senate investigations dismissing his charges got buried on the back pages with the ship sailing notices.

Time has altered the meaning of McCarthyism. In 1950, it meant a brave, patriotic stand against Communism, with the broad support of the media and people. Now it has come to mean a smear campaign of groundless accusations from which the accused cannot escape, because professions of innocence become admissions of guilt, and only confessions are accepted. Many of those who came before McCarthy, as well as many who testified before the powerful House Un-American Activities Committee (HUAC), were willing to point fingers at others to save their own careers and reputations. To fight back was to be tarred with McCarthy's "Communist sympathizer" brush. For many, particularly in the entertainment industries of radio, motion pictures, and television, that meant "blacklisting" that ruined careers. In this cynical atmosphere, laws of evidence and constitutional guarantees didn't apply to "devious Communists." For four years, McCarthy was as powerful as any man in Washington. He could force the president to clear appointments through him, and McCarthy's rampage forced President Eisenhower to institute a new round of "loyalty" programs to prove that he, too, was "tough" on Communism.

But in 1954, McCarthy took up a battle that turned against him when he challenged the U.S. Army to purge supposed Communists from the Pentagon. With the resourceful assistance of Roy Cohn, a young attorney whom McCarthy had earlier dispatched overseas to eradicate "communistic books" from U.S. International Information Administration libraries, McCarthy had begun to attack certain Army officers as Communists. Once again he captivated the public imagination with his charges. But this time he overreached himself. The Army was Ike's turf. Eisenhower and the Army started to hit back, first by investigating David Schine, Roy Cohn's wealthy companion on his book-purge trip, who, having subsequently been drafted into the Army, had used McCarthy's influence to win soft military assignments.

The media also turned on him. CBS's legendary reporter Edward R. Murrow (1908–65), the man who had brought the Blitz of London live to America on radio during the war, took aim at McCarthy on his TV program *See It Now*, a predecessor to *60 Minutes*. By simply showing clips of McCarthy without editorializing, Murrow allowed the senator's bluster to undermine him, exposing McCarthy for the charlatan he was.

During the thirty-six days of the Army-McCarthy hearings, McCarthy finally came undone, his cudgel-like attacks, remorseless crudeness, and unfounded accusations being revealed in an unpleasant light. The daily televised hearings dissolved as Joseph Welch, the respected lawyer representing the Army, turned the tables on McCarthy and routed him in public. The hearings ended inconclusively, but the rest of the Senate smelled blood. By the end of 1954, McCarthy was condemned by his peers, and his public support eroded. His hold on the Senate and the public gone, McCarthy spiraled downward in a pathetic drunken tailspin. He died in May 1957 of health problems brought on by his alcoholism.

Must Read: *The Great Fear: The Anti-Communist Purge Under Truman and Eisenhower* by David Caute.

Who fought in the Korean War?

As if Hiss and the Rosenbergs, Mao's millions and McCarthyism, and the Soviet bomb weren't enough to strike fear into 1950s America, 90,000 North Koreans did the trick. In June 1950, after a large-scale artillery barrage, the sound of bugles signaled the massed charge of North Koreans who came down out of the mountains to roll over an American-sponsored government in South Korea. Armed and trained by the Soviets, this was the most efficient fighting force in Asia after the Soviet Red Army.

This was the onset of the Korean War, a "hot war" in the midst of the Cold War maneuvering, and one that cost more than 2 million Korean lives as well as 100,000 American casualties. As political strife in South Korea continues even today to move through successive phases of protests and militaristic repression, it is still not really over.

Most contemporary American perceptions of the Korean War come from the TV series *M*A*S*H*. The Korean conflict remains something of an ambiguity, unlike the "people's war" that preceded it or the unpopular war that followed it. For Americans at home in the 1950s, Korea wasn't the "good war." Korea was a far-off mystery, and fighting for containment lacked the moral urgency that had been behind the crusade against the Nazi scourge and the "murderers" of Pearl Harbor and Bataan. But American boys were being soundly whipped by the Korean invaders. President Truman and General MacArthur said we should fight, and in 1950, that was good enough for most Americans.

Americans still relied on radio and newsreels for their news, rather than the television that would bring Vietnam into the living room with such astonishing immediacy. But there are some clear parallels between Korea and America's tragedy in Vietnam. (Moreover, the first American involvement in Vietnam actually came during the Korean War, in the form of aid to the French anti-Communist effort in Indochina.) In both wars, an American-supported right-wing government was under attack by Communist insurgents supported by the Soviet Union and China. Both wars were fought to "contain" Asian Communism in nations split by postwar agreements with the Soviets. The Asian Communists were assumed in 1950 to be part of a worldwide Communist conspiracy that reached right into the heart of America's government—as Senator McCarthy was "proving."

While the rebels in both places were fighting a civil war for reunification under their control, the stakes were high in Washington and Moscow, which poured in the military support to keep the wars going. While the United States provided the bulk of the troops and funds in Korea and Vietnam, both wars were ostensibly fought by an alliance of nations. But although the United States actually fought in Korea under a United Nations flag, it held no such pretensions in Vietnam. There is one other significant difference. In Vietnam, the United States fought against a mainly Vietnamese force of both guerrillas and North Vietnamese regulars. In Korea, the fighting started out against the North Koreans, but it quickly escalated into a much deadlier and more dangerous war against the massive armies of Red China.

At home, both wars produced "hawks" who supported total commitment to the effort. In the Korean period, they were led by General MacArthur and the powerful "China lobby" of senators and media moguls like Henry Luce who wanted all-out war against Communism—including an assault on Mao's China. Although Korea never produced the broad social divisions that came later with Vietnam, the American people had little heart for the fighting in Korea.

As with Vietnam, the war in Korea helped end the presidency of a Democratic President—Harry S Truman, in this case—and opened the way for a Republican—Dwight D. Eisenhower. (The Twenty-second Amendment, ratified in 1947, limits a president to two terms or to a single elected term for a president who has served more than two years of his predecessor's term, as Truman had. Truman was exempt from these provisions, however, and could have run again in 1952, but chose not to.)

MILESTONES IN THE KOREAN WAR
1950

June 25 Trained and equipped by the Soviet Union, 90,000 North Korean troops pour over the 38th parallel border and invade the Republic of Korea. The following day, President Truman authorizes the U.S. Navy and Air Force to assist South Korean armies in defending against the invasion. Within three days, North Korean troops, encountering token resistance from what is essentially a South Korean military police force, capture the capital, Seoul, located only forty miles south of the border.

June 27 The United Nations Security Council first adopts a cease-fire resolution. The Soviet Union's envoy to the UN is not present, as he is boycotting the Security Council because it recognizes Nationalist China instead of Communist China. The resolution passes the Security Council, nine to zero. In a few weeks, a second resolution will commit a UN force to support the South Korean government.

June 30 General Douglas MacArthur visits the collapsing South Korean front lines and calls for U.S. troops. President Truman commits U.S. ground troops to South Korea, announces a naval blockade of the Korean coast, and extends the draft for another year. He also increases aid to the French fight against Communist rebels in Indochina.

July 8 A third UN resolution acknowledges American leadership of UN forces, and General Douglas MacArthur is placed in command of UN troops in South Korea. Although U.S. and South Korean troops will form the bulk of the UN forces, soldiers from sixteen nations, including Australia, Great Britain, and the Philippines, also see action. Initially, U.S. troops prove woefully unprepared for combat. Pulled from soft occupation duty in Japan, they lack training and are out of shape and ill armed. American military strength is at its lowest state of readiness since Pearl Harbor. In the first weeks of fighting, U.S. forces are pushed back to a defensive perimeter at Pusan. American air power, which controls the skies over Korea and harasses North Korean supply routes, is the only reason North Korea fails to overwhelm the South.

July 20   Three all-black units of the 25th Infantry Division recapture the town of Yechon with light casualties. It is the first sizable American ground victory in the Korean War. Poorly trained and equipped, the segregated 25th proved its ability to fight in the face of the continued widespread view within the military that "Negroes won't fight."

August 6   The North Korean offensive is finally stopped by the line around Pusan.

September 15   In what is usually considered the single most brilliant stroke in his long military career, General MacArthur leads an amphibious assault on the port city of Inchon, deep behind North Korean lines. The invasion force encounters light resistance and moves quickly toward Seoul. With dangerously overextended supply lines, the North Koreans are trapped between MacArthur's landing force and the defenders at Pusan. They begin an immediate retreat back across the border. Two weeks after the landing at Inchon, Seoul is recaptured by UN troops, who meet unexpectedly stiff resistance from remaining North Korean troops in the capital.

September 29   The UN forces reach the 38th parallel, marking the boundary separating North and South. Presumably, the aims of the war have been accomplished with the North driven back across its border. But Korean president Syngman Rhee announces his intention to continue the war by uniting Korea under his rule and punishing the North for its aggression. This plan is fully supported by MacArthur, a staunch anti-Communist, and the American military command in Washington, but any action against China is expressly ruled out.

October 7 Shifting from the containment policy to a goal of over-throwing a Communist government, MacArthur's UN forces invade North Korea. The move is denounced by the Communist government of China, which says it will not stand idly by. The Chinese threat is ignored as a bluff. The United States has no relations with China, and only recognizes the Nationalist government of Chiang Kai-shek on Taiwan (Formosa). Nearly one million Chinese troops had been massed in Manchuria.

October 15 President Truman and General MacArthur meet on Wake Island. Truman wants to rein in the headstrong soldier who has spent his career countering presidential orders. Truman leaves Wake thinking that MacArthur is resolved to abide by his general orders.

October 20 UN troops capture the North Korean capital of Pyong-yang and continue to advance north toward the Yalu River, the border with Manchuria.

November 1 Massing under the cover of smoke from huge forest fires, Chinese troops attack South Korean troops in the North, de-stroying one army.

November 2 General MacArthur announces that the Chinese constitute a serious threat. Under attack by the Chinese, the U.S. Eighth Army retreats south.

November 4 A massive Chinese counteroffensive begins. MacArthur reports that the Chinese are in Korea in such numbers that they threaten his command, and demands reinforcements.

November 6 Abandoning their concealment tactics, a million Chinese move into Korea. U.S. pilots watch a steady stream of Chinese troops cross the Yalu River separating Korea from Manchuria. MacArthur announces a plan to bomb the Yalu bridges, but it is overruled by Washington. MacArthur begins a political offensive in favor of all-out war against the Chinese that will not only reunite Korea but topple the Communist government in China, allowing Chiang Kai-shek to retake the mainland. In his worst strategic maneuver, MacArthur has split his armies, and the Chinese easily drive through the center of the UN forces.

December 5 In the face of enormous Chinese manpower willing to accept huge casualties, UN troops abandon Pyongyang and are eventually pushed out of the North. The Chinese continue their offensive, promising to drive the Americans into the sea. MacArthur reports to Truman, "We face an entirely new war."

December 8 President Truman announces an embargo on U.S. goods shipped to China.

December 16 President Truman declares a national emergency and calls for an army buildup to 3.5 million men. Three days later, Dwight Eisenhower, who is serving as president of Columbia University, is named supreme commander of Western European defense forces.

December 29 General MacArthur announces that the United States should attack China, and advocates atomic attacks on China and the use of half a million Nationalist Chinese troops to overthrow the Communist government in China.

1951

January 4 Chinese troops capture Seoul. MacArthur complains about being hampered by Truman's decision not to bomb Chinese supply dumps in China. UN troops eventually regroup and halt the Chinese offensive.

March 14 UN forces recapture Seoul and eventually push Chinese troops back across the border.

April 5 In the United States, Julius and Ethel Rosenberg are sentenced to death after being convicted of passing atomic secrets to the Soviet Union. The execution will be carried out in June 1953.

April 11 President Truman removes General MacArthur as commander in Korea after MacArthur openly defies Truman's plan to negotiate a Korean peace. In March, General Matthew B. Ridgway takes command of forces in Korea. Returning to the United States as a national hero and greeted by huge crowds (some reports put

New York crowds welcoming MacArthur in a ticker-tape parade at 7 million), MacArthur later addresses a joint session of Congress with a speech urging an expanded war against China. There is a huge popular outcry against Truman, and thousands of letters calling for his impeachment descend on the White House and Congress.

AMERICAN VOICES
PRESIDENT HARRY S TRUMAN on the firing of
General MacArthur, from Merle Miller's biography
of Truman, *Plain Speaking* (1973):

> **I fired him because he wouldn't respect the authority of the president. That's the answer to that. I didn't fire him because he was a dumb son of a bitch, although he was, but that's not against the law for generals. If it was, half to three-quarters of them would be in jail.**

July 10   While fighting continues, the United States joins peace talks between the UN and China. The U.S. goal is a negotiated truce confirming the status quo before the war—a return to the containment policy.

1952

January 24   Peace talks with the Chinese are declared stalled. The war continues, fought primarily in a seesaw battle in North Korea's cold, rugged mountain terrain. These battles, for Heartbreak Ridge, Bloody Ridge, the Punchbowl, and other hills, essentially end in a bloody stalemate, bringing to mind the trench warfare of World War I.

November 4   Dwight D. Eisenhower is elected president. Richard M. Nixon is his vice president. His opponent, Democrat Adlai Stevenson, has won only nine states.

December 5   President-elect Eisenhower visits troops in Korea and attempts to break the stalemate in truce talks.

1953

July 27 An armistice is signed at Panmunjon, halting the Korean fighting. The war ends where it started, at the 38th parallel.

What were the results of the Korean War?

The war cost America more than 54,000 dead and another 100,000 casualties. More than 2 million Koreans were killed in the fighting. After three years, the situation in Korea was almost exactly what it had been when the North first attacked the South. All the fighting and deaths had changed almost nothing, and it has remained that way to this day. At home, the war produced a massive call for militarization and a buildup of American conventional and nuclear forces — strengthening what President Eisenhower himself would later label "the military-industrial complex."

AMERICAN VOICES
From the "Checkers" speech by RICHARD NIXON
(September 1952):

I should say this—that Pat [Nixon's wife] doesn't have a mink coat. But she does have a respectable Republican cloth coat. And I always tell her that she would look good in anything.

One other thing I should probably tell you, because if I don't they'll be saying this about me, too. We did get something, a gift, after the nomination. A man down in Texas heard Pat on the radio mention the fact that our two youngsters would like to have a dog and, believe it or not, the day before we left on this campaign trip we got a message from Union Station in Baltimore, saying they had a package for us. . . . You know what it was?

It was a little cocker spaniel dog in a crate that he had sent all the way from Texas—black and white, spotted, and our little girl Tricia, the six-year-old, named it Checkers.

And you know the kids, like all kids, love that dog and I
just want to say this, right now, that regardless of what they
say about it, we're going to keep it.

Nixon's speech came in the midst of Eisenhower's campaign
against Adlai Stevenson. While the Republicans ran on a platform of
scourging Democratic corruption in Washington, Nixon was accused
of keeping a "secret slush fund" provided by "fat cat" contributors. It
certainly existed, but was legal. The appearance of the "war chest" was
terrible for the Republicans, however, and Nixon was on the verge of
resigning from the ticket. Instead, he took to the airwaves in a televised
speech that would be called maudlin and mawkish by the media. But
the speech won heartland votes, and it saved Nixon's career and the
Republican ticket's chances.

AMERICAN VOICES
CHARLES "ENGINE" WILSON,
an executive at General Motors who became
Eisenhower's secretary of defense,
to the Senate Armed Forces Committee (1952):

For years I thought that what was good for our country was
good for General Motors, and vice versa.
The difference did not exist.

Often quoted as, "What's good for General Motors is good for the
USA," these were in fact Wilson's exact words, though the sentiment
is much the same. The country's and the world's largest corporation,
General Motors was the first corporation to gross a billion dollars. In
1948, Wilson had signed a historic agreement with the United Auto
Workers (UAW), guaranteeing not only traditional wage increases but
also raises tied to a cost-of-living index. The contract, called the Treaty
of Detroit, brought GM labor peace for a generation.

What was Teddy Roosevelt's grandson doing in Iran?

Part of the Republican campaign during 1952 had been to blame Democrats for losing parts of the world to the Communists. Once in power in 1953, Eisenhower's administration wanted to make sure that it would not be accused of the same thing. But, as David Halberstam writes in his history *The Fifties*, "The Korean war proved there were certain domestic restraints on American military involvement in the third world. The Eisenhower administration quickly found a solution in the Central Intelligence Agency, which had developed a covert operations capability in addition to its mandated role of gathering intelligence. This willingness to use the CIA for paramilitary and other clandestine operations was a marked contrast from the policies of the Truman years."

The Republican administration's first opportunity would come in a struggle with the Soviet Union for control of oil in a place that for most Americans was more of a storybook land than a real place. Once known as Persia, Iran had been a battleground in the First World War when the Russians battled the Ottoman Turks (then allied with Germany) over the area's territory and oil. After the war, a cavalry officer named Reza Khan overthrew the government, named himself shah, and changed the family name to Pahlavi. During World War II, the shah tried to remain neutral, but British and Soviet forces—then allies against Nazi Germany—had forced Shah Reza from the throne and installed his son, Mohammad Reza Pahlavi, as the new shah. He agreed to a treaty with Britain and the Soviet Union, allowing them to use the Trans-Iranian railway to ship oil and to keep troops in Iran for the duration of the war.

The British treated Iran as a colony, taking the country's oil as if it were theirs. While the British were earning millions of pounds, the Iranians were given only a small share of the profits. The British also established segregated facilities for British oil workers in Iran, increasing tensions and resentments among the Iranian people. In 1951, a group of Iranian nationalists led by Mohammad Mossadegh demanded an end to British control of the oil industry. Mossadegh became Iran's Soviet-leaning prime minister, and the oil industry was placed under government ownership and control. The shah was reduced to a figurehead.

Then, at the request of the British, the CIA engineered a coup that would restore the shah—whose CIA code name was Boy Scout—to power. With the blessings of Secretary of State John Foster Dulles and his brother Allen Dulles, head of the CIA, the chief organizer of the coup was Kermit Roosevelt, grandson of President Theodore Roosevelt (and cousin of Franklin D. Roosevelt). A CIA desk chief who specialized in the Middle East, Roosevelt secretly drove from Baghdad to Teheran, where he convinced the young shah that London and Washington would back him if he seized control. Roosevelt organized massive public demonstrations in favor of the shah, and the cooperative Teheran police suppressed any counterdemonstrations. Although Roosevelt succeeded on this occasion, he was generally opposed to such CIA interventions. According to CIA historian James Srodes in his book *Allen Dulles*, a biography of the spy legend, Roosevelt later resigned from the CIA rather than participate in a plan to overthrow Egypt's Nasser.

The shah was in power. Mossadegh was toppled and arrested. The coup had accomplished all of America's immediate goals. And, as David Halberstam notes, "It had been done quickly, cleanly, and on the cheap." In the short term, this clandestine success encouraged the CIA. Covert intervention in Third World countries would increasingly become a part of America's Cold War containment policy, led by CIA planners. Even as the Iran venture was concluded, a new plan was hatched to supplant a leftist government in Guatemala that threatened the status of United Fruit, an American company that all but owned Guatemala.

But what about longer term? If history is about connecting the dots, fast forward a few years. During the early 1960s, the shah attempted a series of economic and social reforms, including a land reform program that redistributed the holdings of wealthy landlords among the peasants who worked the land. He also promoted education, improved social welfare services, and gave women the right to vote. At the same time, he exercised nearly absolute control over the government through a hated secret police force, called the SAVAK. Opposition began to grow, especially among students and conservative Muslims.

Barely a quarter of a century later, the ultimate unforeseen outcome of the CIA coup came about. In January 1979, mass demonstrations, strikes, and riots led to the shah's departure from Iran. The fundamentalist Islamic cleric Ayatollah Ruhollah Khomeini declared Iran an Islamic republic, and the ayatollah became the country's supreme leader. When President Carter allowed the shah to enter the United States for medical treatment and refused to hand him over for trial in Iran, Iranian revolutionaries seized the U.S. embassy in Teheran, taking a group of Americans as hostages. This was the beginning of a long history of the fundamentalist Islamic movement, whose anti-Americanism would ultimately lead to September 11, 2001.

AMERICAN VOICES
From *Invisible Man*, by RALPH ELLISON (1952):

I am an invisible man. No, I am not a spook like those who haunted Edgar Allan Poe; nor am I one of your Hollywood-movie ectoplasms. I am a man of substance, of flesh and bone, fiber and liquids—and I might even be said to possess a mind. I am invisible, understand, simply because people refuse to see me. Like the bodiless heads you sometimes see in circus sideshows, it is as though I have been surrounded by mirrors of hard, distorting glass. When they approach me they see only my surroundings, themselves, or figments of their imagination—indeed, everything and anything except me.

What was *Brown v. Board of Education*?

Every day, eight-year-old Linda Brown wondered why she had to ride five miles to school when her bus passed the perfectly lovely Sumner Elementary School, just four blocks from her home. When her father tried to enroll her in Sumner for fourth grade, the Topeka, Kansas, school authorities just said no. In 1951, Linda Brown was the wrong color for Sumner.

In July 1950, a year before Linda was turned away, segregated black troops from the 24th Infantry Regiment scored the first American victory of the Korean War when they recaptured Yechon. A few months after that, PFC William Thompson was awarded the Medal of Honor for heroism in Korea—the first black so honored since the Spanish-American War. (It's hard to win combat awards when the Army will only let you peel potatoes and dig slit trenches.) In September 1950, Gwendolyn Brooks (b. 1917) won the Pulitzer Prize for poetry for her book *Annie Allen*, the first black ever cited by the Pulitzer Committee. And that month, American diplomat Ralph J. Bunche (1904–71) was awarded the Nobel Peace Prize for his mediation of the Palestinian conflict, the first black to win that honor.

For most of the country's 15 million American blacks—in 1950, they were called Negroes—these accomplishments held little meaning. In the first place, a good many of those 15 million people couldn't read about these achievements. Illiteracy among America's largest racial minority (approximately 10 percent of the total population in 1950) was commonplace. Schools for blacks, where they existed, didn't offer much in the way of formal education. The law of the land remained "separate but equal," the policy dictated by the Supreme Court's 1896 *Plessy v. Ferguson* ruling (see pp. 282–83). "Separate but equal" kept Linda Brown out of the nearby Topeka schoolhouse and dictated that everything from maternity wards to morgues, from water fountains to swimming pools, from prisons to polling places, was either segregated or for whites only. Exactly how these "separate" facilities were "equal" remained a mystery to blacks: If everything was so equal, why didn't white people want to use them?

Nowhere was the disparity more complete and disgraceful than in the public schools, primarily but not exclusively in the heartland of the former Confederacy. Schools for whites were spanking new, well maintained, properly staffed, and amply supplied. Black schools were usually single-room shacks with no toilets, a single teacher, and a broken chalkboard. If black parents wanted their children to be warm in the winter, they had to buy their own coal. But a handful of courageous southern blacks—mostly common people like teachers and ministers and their families—began the struggle that turned back these laws.

Urged on by Thurgood Marshall (1908–93), the burly, barb-tongued attorney from Baltimore who led the NAACP's Legal Defense and Educational Fund, small-town folks in Kansas, South Carolina, Virginia, and Delaware balked at the injustice of "separate but equal" educational systems. The people who carried these fights were soon confronted by threats ranging from loss of their jobs to dried-up bank credit and ultimately to threats of violence and death. In 1951, one of these men was the Reverend Oliver Brown, the father of Linda Brown, who tried to enroll his daughter in the all-white Topeka school. Since Brown came first in the alphabet among the suits brought against four different states, it was his name that was attached to the case that Thurgood Marshall argued before the Supreme Court in 1953.

Marshall seemed to have momentum on his side. In 1950, the Supreme Court had already made three important decisions that chipped away at the *Plessy* ruling: the *Sweatt* decision said equality involved more than physical facilities; the *McLaurin* decision said black students in state universities could not be segregated after admission; and the *Henderson* case banned railroad dining-car segregation. But these were limited, circumscribed cases without broader interpretations.

There had also been a change in the makeup of the Court itself. After the arguments in *Brown v. Board of Education* were first heard, Chief Justice Fred M. Vinson, the Truman appointee who had ordered the other justices flown back to Washington to ensure that the Rosenberg execution would proceed on schedule, died of a heart attack. In 1953, with reargument of the case on the horizon, President Eisenhower appointed Earl Warren (1891–1974) chief justice of the United States. No legal giant, Warren was a good Republican soldier, a fairly moderate California governor, and the vice presidential candidate on the 1948 Dewey ticket. His past held only one black mark—at least in retrospect. As California's attorney general, he had pressed the cause of internment of Japanese Americans during World War II, a policy he had then helped carry out in his first term as California's governor. But in 1953, that seemed like evidence of good sense rather than the grievous smudge it would be today.

Certainly nobody at the time suspected that Warren would go on to lead the Court for sixteen of its most turbulent years, during which the justices took the lead in transforming America's approach to racial equality, criminal justice, and freedom of expression. President Eisenhower, the good general and hero of democracy who marched firmly in place when it came to civil rights, later said the appointment of Warren was "the biggest damfool mistake I ever made."

From the moment the justices began to confer on the case, Warren—as yet unconfirmed by the Senate—made it clear that he would vote to overturn *Plessy* because he believed that the law could no longer tolerate separating any race as inferior, which was the obvious result of "separate but equal" laws. But Warren was an adroit politician as well as a jurist. He knew that the case was so important and politically charged that it demanded unanimity. Achieving that unanimity was less simple than forming his own decision. But through gentle persuasion, Warren was able to shape the consensus he wanted—and what the case needed. All nine of the brethren not only voted to overturn *Plessy*, but allowed Warren's single opinion to speak for them. When Warren read the simple, brief ruling, it was the judicial equivalent of the shot heard 'round the world.

In *Simple Justice*, a monumental study of the case and the history of racism, cruelty, and discrimination that preceded it, Richard Kluger eloquently assessed the decision's impact:

> The opinion of the Court said that the United States stood for something more than material abundance, still moved to an inner spirit, however deeply it had been submerged by fear and envy and mindless hate. . . . The Court had restored to the American people a measure of the humanity that had been drained away in their climb to worldwide supremacy. The Court said, without using the words, that when you stepped on a black man, he hurt. The time had come to stop.

Of course, *Brown* did not cause the scales to fall from the eyes of white supremacists. The fury of the South was quick and sure. School systems around the country, South and North, had to be dragged kicking and screaming through the courts toward desegregation. The states fought the decision with endless appeals and other delaying tactics, the calling out of troops, and ultimately violence and a venomous outflow of racial hatred, targeted at schoolchildren who simply wanted to learn.

Must Read: *Simple Justice: The History of* Brown v. Board of Education *and Black America's Struggle for Equality* by Richard Kluger.

We come then to the question presented: Does segregation of children in public schools solely on the basis of race, even though the physical facilities and other "tangible" factors may be equal, deprive the children of the minority group of equal educational opportunities? We believe that it does. . . .

To separate them from others of similar age and qualifications solely because of their race generates a feeling of inferiority as to their status in the community that may affect their hearts and minds in a way unlikely ever to be undone. . . .

. . . We conclude that in the field of public education the doctrine of "separate but equal" has no place. Separate educational facilities are inherently unequal.

Why did the arrest of a woman named Rosa Parks change American life?

In its historic judgment, the Supreme Court gave the civil rights movement its Ten Commandments. What the movement lacked was its Moses. Rosa Parks may not have been Moses, but she certainly was a voice crying out from Egyptian bondage. In 1955, Egypt was Montgomery, Alabama.

A forty-three-year-old seamstress who worked in a downtown Montgomery department store, Rosa Parks was on her way home from work on a December day. Loaded down by bags filled with her Christmas shopping, Rosa Parks boarded a city bus and moved to the back—legally, traditionally, and, it seemed, eternally—the Negro section. Finding no seats there, she took one toward the middle of the bus. When the driver picked up more white passengers, he called out, "Niggers move back," an order to vacate the white seats even if it meant standing. Mrs. Parks refused. Active in the local chapter of the NAACP, Rosa Parks had already decided that she would make a stand if asked to give up her seat.

Unwilling to leave that seat, Rosa Parks was arrested for violating Montgomery's transportation laws. Mrs. Parks was ordered to court on the following Monday. But over the weekend, the blacks of Montgomery found their Moses. Meeting to protest Mrs. Parks's arrest and the reason for it, the black community of Montgomery selected the twenty-seven-year-old pastor of Mrs. Parks's church, the Dexter Avenue Baptist Church, as its leader. Calling for a peaceful form of resistance, the young minister urged his people to boycott the buses of Montgomery. His name was Martin Luther King Jr. (1929–68). In a short time the bus boycott and the movement it inspired in Montgomery would raise him to world fame and make him one of the nation's most admired and reviled men.

King was born in Atlanta, the son of one of that city's prominent black ministers and grandson of the man who had organized a protest that created Atlanta's first black high school, named for Booker T. Washington, which King himself attended. He went on to Atlanta's Morehead College, studied theology and philosophy at Crozier Theological Seminary and the University of Pennsylvania, and had completed his Ph.D. in systematic theology from Boston University in 1955 when he took the call at Dexter Avenue. Buttressed by the twin principles of nonviolence and civil disobedience inspired by Henry David Thoreau and India's Mahatma Gandhi, King planned to shape a civil rights movement using the fundamental moral teachings of Christianity—love, forgiveness, humility, faith, hope, community—as its bedrock. The Montgomery boycott, begun on December 5, 1955, presented him with the first opportunity to try this approach.

For more than a year, the boycott was hugely effective. Angry because they couldn't make these Negroes ride the buses, the whites of Montgomery looked for other ways to retaliate. Mrs. Parks was re-arrested for failing to pay her fine. King was arrested, first on a drunk-driving charge and later for conspiring to organize an illegal boycott. Insurance companies canceled the auto insurance on cars being used to circumvent the buses. When peaceful means failed, black homes were firebombed. A shotgun blast broke the windows of King's home. And of course the KKK appeared on the scene, to march through the streets of Montgomery.

The case wound its way back to Washington, where the Supreme Court, now armed with the *Brown* precedent, was beginning to roll back "separate but equal" statutes in all areas of life. The Court ordered an end to Montgomery's bus segregation in November 1956, and on the morning of December 21, 1956, the blacks of Montgomery went back to the buses. They had won a battle, but the war was just beginning. The peaceful boycott movement gathered momentum and was duplicated throughout the South. For the next ten years these peaceful protests led the civil rights movement until the painfully slow process finally boiled over in the urban racial violence of the mid-1960s.

Despite the success of the protest, the international notoriety Martin Luther King had gained created some dissension within the ranks, according to David J. Garrow's book *Bearing the Cross*. Mrs. Parks, who lost her job as a seamstress, later took a job at the Hampton Institute in Virginia, and remained a living symbol of the civil rights movement.

In 1957, King moved to Atlanta and organized the Southern Christian Leadership Conference (SCLC). Later that year he led the first civil rights march to Washington in a prayer pilgrimage. This time 50,000 blacks joined him. In the future he would return with hundreds of thousands.

In the meantime, the Supreme Court had issued a second ruling in May 1955, known as *Brown II*, which attempted to address some of the practical concerns of its desegregation order. Walking a dangerous tightrope without a safety net, the Court reasserted that the states in the suits must begin to make a prompt, reasonable start toward full compliance with the 1954 ruling. But Warren concluded with the now-famous phrase that this process should move with "all deliberate speed." The Court had told the country to go fast slowly. Of course, to the advocates of integration, the emphasis was on speed. To segregationists, "deliberate" meant sometime in the days of Buck Rogers.

AMERICAN VOICES
RELMAN MORIN, an Associated Press reporter, at
Little Rock, Arkansas (September 23, 1957):

They were carrying books. White bobby-sox, part of the
high school uniform, glinted on the girls' ankles. They
were all nicely dressed. The boys wore open-throat shirts
and the girls, ordinary frocks.

They weren't hurrying. They simply strolled across perhaps 15 yards from the sidewalk to the school steps. They
glanced at the people and the police as though none of this
concerned them.

You can never forget a scene like that.

Nor the one that followed.

Like a wave, the people who had run toward the four
negro men, now swept back toward the police and the barricades.

"Oh, God, they're in the school," a man yelled.

Morin won the Pulitzer Prize for his account of the arrival of nine
black students for the first day of classes in a Little Rock, Arkansas,
public high school.

Why did President Eisenhower send the Army into Little Rock, Arkansas?

Through all of these Supreme Court decisions and during the Montgomery boycott and other peaceful protests that followed, the Eisenhower White House stood as a vacuum of moral leadership on the
civil rights issue. While the Cold War general was making the world
"safe for democracy," his own vision of a free society seemed to have
no room for blacks.

Apparently fearful of alienating the powerful bloc of "Dixiecrats,"
the southern Democratic congressmen whose votes he needed, Eisenhower was ambiguous in his public comments. He promised to uphold

the laws of the land, but refrained from endorsing the Court's rulings. At the time, a word of leadership or outrage at Jim Crow conditions from this popular president might have given the civil rights movement additional vigor and force. Instead, Eisenhower was ultimately forced to act, with great reluctance, in a showdown that was more about presidential power than about the rights of black children.

In September 1957, the governor of Arkansas, Orville Faubus, posted 270 fully armed men from the Arkansas National Guard outside Little Rock Central High School. Their duty was to prevent nine black children from entering the previously all-white school. On American television and all over the world, people watched with revulsion as the children tried to enter school and were turned away by the guard as an angry, jeering mob spat and cursed at them, all under the watchful eyes of the guardsmen. A federal district court order forced Faubus to allow the children into the school, but the governor withdrew the Arkansas state guard, leaving the protection of the black children to a small contingent of resentful local policemen, some of whom refused to carry out the order.

Finally, Eisenhower, to defend the sovereignty of the federal court, had to order 1,100 paratroopers from the 101st Airborne to Little Rock and place the state national guard under his direct orders. For the first time since Reconstruction, U.S. troops were in the South to protect the rights of blacks. Eisenhower had not acted out of concern for the students' rights or safety, but because he believed that he couldn't allow the force of federal law to be ignored.

The troops remained in Little Rock Central High for the rest of the school year, and eight of the black students stayed through the year despite curses, harassment, and abuse. Whatever else it proved, Little Rock showed that the civil rights movement was going to need the full force of the federal government to enforce the laws that the Supreme Court had created.

AMERICAN VOICES

From "The Southern Manifesto" signed by ninety-six
congressmen from the South in response to the *Brown*
decision (March 12, 1956):

This unwarranted exercise of power by the court, contrary
to the Constitution, is creating chaos and confusion in the
states principally affected. It is destroying the *amicable relations between the white and Negro races that have been
created through ninety years of patient effort by the good
people of both races* [emphasis added]. It has planted hatred and suspicion where there has been heretofore friendship and understanding.

What was Sputnik?

On the educational Richter scale, *Brown* had been the equivalent of
the Great San Francisco Earthquake. It leveled everything. While
Brown's tremors sent shock waves across the country, America got an-
other tremendous jolt that shook the country to its foundations. On
October 4, 1957, the Soviet Union launched Sputnik I (whose name in
Russian meant "little companion"), man's first artificial satellite.

Weighing in at about 185 pounds, Sputnik was a little bigger than
a basketball and traveled 18,000 miles per hour some 560 miles above
the Earth, emitting a steady *beep-beep-beep* radio signal. The launch
was not only an unexpected technological achievement but a work of
propaganda genius. The Soviets had given Sputnik an orbit and trajec-
tory that sent the satellite over the earth's most populous areas and low
enough that it could be seen at times with the assistance of powerful
binoculars. Ham radio operators could pick up the distinctive message
it beamed back to Earth.

The Sputnik shock was redoubled in November when the Russians
lofted a second satellite, dubbed Sputnik II. Not only was this a substantially larger satellite, weighing more than 1,100 pounds, but it carried
a passenger. A small dog was strapped into the satellite, hooked up to
monitoring equipment that relayed information about the physical effects of space travel. The space pooch, a terrier named Laika ("barker"

in Russian), was also the first sacrifice to the space race. In the rush to get the dog into space, the Russians had not planned for reentry, and the dog was put to sleep with a radio-controlled injection.

These two events brought a wave of shock, fear, and panic in America. It was unthinkable, but the Soviets had beaten the United States into space. The paranoia that the twin Sputnik launchings induced was extraordinary, and it worked on two levels. In the early frosts of the Cold War, the Soviet achievement was more than a publicity coup. Sputnik was frightful evidence that the USSR might possess missiles powerful enough to reach America. More realistically, it meant that the Soviets had taken the lead in development of the intercontinental ballistic missile, thereby fundamentally altering the balance of power between the two competing powers. Sputnik obliterated the American assumption of its nuclear superiority. It was all the more reason to dig that fallout shelter in the backyard.

The fear of the bomb merged with the reality of man moving into space and the constant drumbeat of anti-Communist hysteria to produce a paranoid pop culture that blossomed in the science fiction books and films of the fifties. Before World War II, science fiction had been a respectable sort of fantasy, most popularly practiced by H. G. Wells or the pleasant utopian visions of Edward Bellamy's novel *Looking Backward*. Radio's Buck Rogers gave new life to notions of space travel and futuristic death rays, but that was mostly child's play. The specter of totalitarian police states in Germany and the Soviet Union, heightened by the threat of the bomb, had turned science fiction darker. The trend began with such classics as George Orwell's *1984* and Aldous Huxley's *Brave New World*, and was later reflected in such books as Ray Bradbury's *Fahrenheit 451*, the classic about a futuristic society in which all books are burned, which was written in the midst of Senator McCarthy's witch hunts and a movement to purge American libraries of "subversive" works. In the movies, the paranoia was reflected in films like *Invasion of the Body Snatchers*.

A more serious but equally hysterical fear rocked the American education system, reeling under the pressures of desegregation. Already struggling against the Soviets in an arms race, America now found itself left at the starting line in the new "space race." Worse than that, America didn't even have its sneakers on. To all the wise men in the land, the reason for America's sad technological performance while the Soviets had leaped into space was obvious: the American education system was falling down, while the Soviet system, which rigorously drilled its children in math and the sciences, was producing a super-race of mathematicians and scientists who would rapidly outdistance American children in their achievements.

The decline in American standards was blamed on that favorite of whipping boys, "progressive education." In the late 1950s, "back to basics" was the call to arms. It is a story that was replayed in the mid-1980s, when it was determined that America's schools were falling prey to a "rising tide of mediocrity." The eighties also produced a new archvillain who was out-educating America's children. Instead of the Soviets, the new bogeyman was the Japanese, and the media were filled with reports of the superiority of the Japanese educational system, an uncanny reprise of the debate in the late fifties. Once again, "back to basics" was the simplistic answer to the problems of the miserable American school systems.

The practical response to Sputnik was a total overhaul of American education, with a new commitment on the part of the federal government to aid public schools, along with an overhaul of research and development in the rocketry field, spearheaded by a compelling urgency to overtake the Soviets in the area of missile delivery systems. Sputnik had been the space equivalent of the Russian atomic bomb. In the years ahead, the United States would devote enormous resources to victory in the new space race.

The country responded with backyard bomb shelters and "duck and cover" fallout drills. But the government also unleashed a massive wave of federal funds to improve science and math education while launching a full-court press to surpass the Soviets in technology. Learning calculus was now an act of patriotism. The space race was off and running.

Success would be built on failures. And the first of these was nearly devastating. On December 6, 1957—uncomfortably close to the anniversary of Pearl Harbor in many minds—a Vanguard rocket that was to carry America's first satellite into space blew up on the launching pad. It was an inauspicious beginning to America's race for the moon. (Recently released Oval Office tapes of President Kennedy discussing the

Apollo program show that he was primarily interested in demonstrating America's superiority over the Soviets. And many military men from the early generation of the space program, which would continue to be dominated by military projects, thought that the Moon might provide a launching site for missiles that could be aimed at the Soviet Union.)

Someday—say 500 years from now—October 4 may become Sputnik Day and occupy the same place that Columbus Day does in modern times—a date that marked the opening of a dramatic new era in history, for better or for worse. The spirit of the ancient quest for the stars has always been about human curiosity, the desire to know the unknowable, to move out, to create. And if Sputnik and the space race era have a message, it may be that combining technical wizardry with sheer courage and determination can produce the best of the human spirit.

When Sputnik was launched, the idea that American astronauts and cosmonauts of the former Soviet Union would someday be living and working together on a space station would have been implausible. But that is the reality. Once enemies, now colleagues and friends. Beyond that, it is worth remembering that the shock of October 4, 1957, just like those of December 7, 1941, and November 22, 1963, eventually passed. The nation survived the knockdowns, stood up, and was strengthened.

AMERICAN VOICES
From DWIGHT D. EISENHOWER's farewell address
(January 17, 1961):

[The] conjunction of an immense military establishment and large arms industry is new in the American experience. The total influence—economic, political, even spiritual—is felt in every city, every state house, every office of the federal government. We recognize the imperative need for the development. Yet we must not fail to comprehend its grave implications. Our toil, resources, and livelihood are all involved; so is the very structure of our society.

In the councils of government, we must guard against the acquisition of unwarranted influence, whether sought or unsought, by the military-industrial complex. The potential for the disastrous rise of misplaced power exists and will persist.

As the leading proponent of Cold War containment, Eisenhower had presided over the rise of this "military-industrial complex," created to give the United States the military might it needed to carry out the containment policy, a policy that continued to dictate American decision making in the White House and Congress in the decades ahead.

How did a doll in stiletto heels and a Chicago publisher change America?

In 1959, wearing a zebra-striped swimsuit and tall stiletto heels, Barbie made her debut at the American Toy Fair in New York. Created by Ruth Handler, the youngest of ten children of Polish immigrants, Barbie became an instant icon of popular culture and one of the world's best-selling toys. Ruth Handler had founded Mattel in 1945 with her husband, Oscar, a specialist in plastic design. Inspired by their own daughter's fascination with paper dolls, the Handlers wanted to produce a doll that looked more like a real teenager. The doll Ruth Handler created was actually modeled on a German sex toy called Lilli, which Handler had seen on a European trip. Barbie was named after the Handlers' daughter, and her later male counterpart, Ken, was named after their son.

Needless to say, there aren't many teenagers who look like Barbie. In fact, it was later determined that if Barbie were five feet six, her measurements would be 39–21–33. But that did not matter. After battling prudish male executives at Mattel, Handler launched the doll into history. At the time, the doll business was dominated by baby dolls, from a far more innocent time. Barbie flew off the shelf in the postwar baby boom years. In a 1977 interview, Ruth Handler told the *New York Times,* "Every little girl needed a doll through which to project herself into her dream of her future. If she was going to do role playing of what she would be like when she was 16 or 17, it was a little stupid to play with a doll that had a flat chest. So I gave it beautiful breasts."

Although feminists would later object that Barbie gave young girls an unrealistic body image and others would criticize Barbie as overtly sexual, that didn't stop Barbie from becoming a phenomenon. A half-billion Barbies later—more than one billion counting sales of her side-kick dolls—and the statuesque young girl with platinum hair and blue eyes was still going strong by 2002.

Barbie's grand entrance came just a few years after another American icon arrived on the scene. In 1953, a twenty-seven-year-old man from Chicago, with some advertising experience, had pasted together a magazine on his kitchen table. He printed 70,000 copies, hoping to sell at least 30,000 of them at 50 cents an issue. The magazine included a nude calendar shot of America's hottest starlet, a young model who had taken the name Marilyn Monroe. Born Norma Jean Mortenson, Monroe had been discovered by a *Yank* magazine photographer doing a wartime shoot of women at work in munitions factories. He launched Monroe's modeling career, which led to a break in Hollywood in a crime film called *The Asphalt Jungle*. As her film career was about to take off, a man called her studio, Twentieth Century–Fox, asking for $10,000 or he would release a nude photo of Monroe. The studio wouldn't pay, but Monroe decided to let the story out herself. Hugh Hefner learned about the photo, paid $500 for the rights to publish it, and *Playboy* became an overnight American sensation.

Hefner originally titled his new magazine for men *Stag Party* until the publisher of a hunting magazine called *Stag* forced him to change it.

AMERICAN VOICES
HUGH HEFNER, in the first issue of *Playboy*:

We like our apartment. We enjoy mixing up cocktails and an hors d'oeuvre or two, putting a little mood music on the phonograph, and inviting in a female for a quiet discussion on Picasso, Nietzsche, jazz, sex.

Less than a year and a half after the first issue, circulation had climbed to 100,000, Hugh Hefner had money in the bank and was turning down offers from larger publishers to sell them the magazine. He had created a new American dream—and was living it out himself.

It was also about this time that a young singer from Mississippi was beginning to send female fans into a paroxysm. Parents shook their heads at the gyrating hips of Elvis Presley. But he, and a new kind of music, had clearly arrived.

Playboy. Barbie. Elvis.

As Ike got ready to leave office, he was turning the lights out on a very different America.

Must Read: *The Fifties* by David Halberstam.

CHAPTER EIGHT

THE TORCH IS PASSED

From Camelot to Hollywood on the Potomac

How did Richard Nixon's five o'clock shadow spoil his 1960 campaign for president?

What happened at the Bay of Pigs?

What was the Cuban Missile Crisis?

What was *The Feminine Mystique*?

Who was right? The Warren Commission or Oliver Stone?

Did *Mississippi Burning* really happen?

What was the Tonkin Resolution?

Milestones in the Vietnam War

What happened in Watts?

Who was Miranda?

What happened at My Lai?

How did a successful break-in in Pennsylvania change the FBI?

Why did Richard Nixon and Henry Kissinger try to stop the *New York Times* from publishing the Pentagon Papers?

Why did "Jane Roe" sue Wade?

How did a botched burglary become a crisis called Watergate and bring down a powerful president?

A Watergate Chronology

How did OPEC cripple America during the 1970s?

What was "voodoo economics"?

What happened to the space shuttle *Challenger*?

Why was Ronald Reagan called the "Teflon president"?

What was the "gay plague"?

What happened to the Evil Empire?

Camelot. The Age of Aquarius. "All You Need Is Love." Hippies and Haight-Ashbury. "Be Sure to Wear Some Flowers in Your Hair." "Tune In. Turn On. Drop Out." Free love. Men on the moon. Woodstock.

It has come down as "the sixties," a romantic fantasy set to a three-chord rock beat. But the era viewed so nostalgically as the days of peace, love, and rock and roll didn't start out with much peace and love. Unless you focus on the fact that Enovid, the first birth control pill, was approved by the Food and Drug Administration in 1960.

The flip side of the sixties was a much darker tune. Riots and long, hot summers. Assassinations. Rock-star obituaries etched in acid. A war that only a "military-industrial complex" could love. *Sympathy for the Devil.* Altamont Speedway.

The "bright shining moment" of the JFK years—the media-created myth of *Camelot* manufactured in the wake of Kennedy's death—began with the same Cold War paranoia that set the tone of the previous decade. The "liberal" Kennedy campaigned in 1960 as a hard-line anti-Communist, and used a fabricated "missile gap" between the United States and the Soviet Union as a campaign issue against Republican candidate Richard Nixon. What we call the sixties ended with the death throes of an unpopular, costly war in a quagmire called Vietnam.

But it was an extraordinary era in which all the accepted orthodoxies of government, church, and society were called into question. And, unlike the glum, alienated mood of the fifties, the new voices questioning authority had a lighter side. Joseph Heller (1923–99) was one of the first to capture the new mood of mordant humor in his first novel, *Catch-22* (1961), which was a forecast of the antimilitary mood that would form to oppose the war in Vietnam. But the new generation of poets was more likely to use an amplified guitar than a typewriter to voice its discontent. In the folk music of Peter, Paul, and Mary and Bob Dylan, and later in the rock-and-roll revolution, "counterculture" was blasting out of millions of radios and TVs. Of course, the record business found it a very profitable counterculture.

And it spilled into the mainstream as entertainers like the Smothers Brothers brought irreverence to prime time—which promptly showed them the door.

The seventies got under way with the downfall of a corrupt White House in a sinkhole called Watergate. Vietnam and Watergate seemed to signal a change in the American political landscape. The years that followed were characterized by a feeling of aimlessness. Under Gerald Ford (1913–2006), who replaced the disgraced Nixon, and Jimmy Carter (b. 1924), America suffered the indignity of seeing its massive power in a seeming decline. But this slide was not the result of a superpower confrontation with the archvillain Soviets. Instead, a series of smaller shocks undid the foundation: the forming of OPEC by major oil producing countries to place a stranglehold on the world's oil supplies; the acts of international terrorists, who struck with seeming impunity at the United States and other Western powers, culminating in the overthrow of the once mighty shah of Iran; and the imprisonment of American hostages in the American embassy in Teheran.

More than anything else, it was that apparent decline, reflected in America's economic doldrums, that brought forth a president who represented, to the majority of Americans, the cowboy in the white hat who they always believed would ride into town. After the doubt and turmoil produced by the seventies, Ronald Reagan (1911–2004) seemed to embody that old-fashioned American can-do spirit. For many critics, the question was who was going to do what, and to whom? A throwback to Teddy Roosevelt and his "big stick," Reagan also saw the White House as a bully pulpit. His sermons called back the "good old days"—which, of course, only appeared so good in hindsight.

Though it is still too soon to assess properly the long-term impact of his presidency, Ronald Reagan has already begun to be judged by history. To those who admire him, he was the man who restored American prestige and economic stability, and forced the Soviet Union into structural changes through a massive buildup of American defenses. To critics, he was the president who dozed through eight years in office while subordinates ran the show. In some cases, those underlings proved to be corrupt or simply cynical. In perhaps the most dangerous instance, a lieutenant colonel working in the White House was allowed to make his own foreign policy.

How did Richard Nixon's five o'clock shadow spoil his 1960 campaign for president?

"If you give me a week, I might think of one." That's what President Eisenhower told a reporter who asked what major decisions Vice President Richard Nixon (1913–94) had participated in during their eight years together. Although Ike later said he was being facetious, he never really answered the question, and the remark left Nixon with egg on his face and the Democrats giddy.

That was in August 1960, as Nixon and John F. Kennedy (1917–63) ran neck and neck in the polls. How many wavering Nixon votes did Ike's little joke torpedo? It would have taken only a shift of about a hundred thousand votes out of the record 68,832,818 cast to change the result and the course of contemporary events.

Most campaign historians cite Ike's cutting comment as a jab that drew blood, but that was not the knockout punch in this contest. Posterity points instead to the face-off between the contenders—the first televised debates in presidential campaign history—as the flurry of verbal and visual punches from which Nixon never recovered. In particular, the first of these four meetings is singled out as the blow that sent the vice president to the canvas. More than 70 million people watched the first of these face-to-face meetings. Or maybe "face-to–five o'clock shadow" is more accurate.

Recovering from an infection that had hospitalized him for two weeks, Nixon was underweight and haggard-looking for the debate. Makeup artists attempted to conceal his perpetual five o'clock shadow with something called Lazy Shave that only made him look more pasty faced and sinister. Jack Kennedy, on the other hand, was the picture of youth and athletic vigor. While radio listeners thought there was no clear winner in the debates, television viewers were magnetized by Kennedy. If FDR was the master of radio, Kennedy was the first "telegenic" candidate, custom-tailored for the instant image making of the television age.

Broadcast on September 26 from Chicago, the first debate focused on domestic affairs, an advantage for Kennedy because Nixon was acknowledged to be more experienced in international matters. It was Nixon, after all, who had stood face-to-face with Nikita Khrushchev in Moscow, angrily wagging a finger at the Soviet leader during their "kitchen debate" in 1959. But in the first TV debate, Kennedy had Nixon on the defensive by listing the shortcomings of the Eisenhower administration. With deft command of facts and figures, Kennedy impressed an audience that was skeptical because of his youth and inexperience. He stressed his campaign theme that the Republicans had America in "retreat," and he promised to get the country moving again.

The audience for the three subsequent debates fell off to around 50 million viewers. The impressions made by the first debate seemed to be most lasting. Kennedy got a boost in the polls and seemed to be pulling out in front, but the decision was still too close to call. Invisible through most of the contest, Eisenhower did some last-minute campaigning for Nixon, but it may have been too small an effort, too late.

Two events in October also had some impact. First, Nixon's running mate, Republican Henry Cabot Lodge, promised that there would be a Negro in the Nixon cabinet. Nixon had to disavow that pledge, and whatever white votes he won cost him any chance at black support. A second Kennedy boost among black voters came when Martin Luther King Jr. was arrested prior to the final debate. Kennedy called King's wife, Coretta, to express his concern, and Robert Kennedy helped secure King's release on bail. Nixon decided to stay out of the case. King's father, who had previously stated he wouldn't vote for a Catholic, announced a shift to Kennedy. "I've got a suitcase of votes," said Martin Luther King Sr., "and I'm going to take them to Mr. Kennedy and dump them in his lap." He did just that. When Kennedy heard of the senior King's earlier anti-Catholic remarks, he won points by humorously defusing the situation, commenting, "Imagine Martin Luther King having a bigot for a father. Well, we all have fathers, don't we?"

Kennedy certainly had a father. Joseph Kennedy Sr., FDR's first chairman of the Securities and Exchange Commission and later his ambassador to Great Britain, where his anti-Semitic and isolationist views won him no points, stayed in the background in the campaign. Bankrolling and string pulling, Joseph Kennedy had orchestrated his son's career from the outset with his extensive network of friends in the media, the mob, and the Catholic church. A few examples: Writer John Hersey's "Survival," the now deflated account of Kennedy's wartime heroics aboard PT-109, overlooked the fact that Kennedy and his crew were sleeping in a combat zone when a Japanese destroyer rammed them. Joe Kennedy made sure his son was decorated by a high-ranking Navy official. When JFK ran for the House, Joe arranged for the Hersey article to appear in *Reader's Digest* and then made sure every voter in Kennedy's district got a copy. Publication of JFK's first book, *Why England Slept*, was arranged by Kennedy pal journalist Arthur Krock, who then reviewed the book in the *New York Times*. Kennedy's second book, the best-selling and Pulitzer Prize–winning *Profiles in Courage*, was the output of a committee of scholars and Kennedy speechwriter Theodore Sorensen.

Other friends of Joe Kennedy, like Henry Luce and William Randolph Hearst, had added to building the Kennedy image. Through Frank Sinatra, another Joe Kennedy crony, funds of dubious origin were funneled into the Kennedy war chest. Also through Sinatra, JFK met a young woman named Judith Campbell, who would soon become a regular sexual partner. What Kennedy didn't know at the time was that Judith Campbell was also bedding Mafia chieftain Sam Giancana and a mob hit man named John Roselli. In a few months, they would all converge as Giancana and Roselli were given a "contract" to pull off the CIA-planned assassination of Fidel Castro.

The debate, his father's war chest, his appeal to women (the public appeal, not the private one, which remained a well-protected secret), the newly important black vote, and vice presidential candidate Lyndon B. Johnson's role in delivering Texas and the rest of the South all played a part in what was the closest presidential election in modern history (until the Bush-Gore race of 2000). Nixon actually won more states than Kennedy, but it was a Pyrrhic victory. Kennedy had sewn up the biggest electoral vote states. The margin of difference in the popular vote was less than two-thirds of a percentage point.

But, as the saying goes, "Close only counts in horseshoes and hand grenades." Despite some Republican protests of voting fraud in Illinois, Nixon went back to California, where he lost the race for governor to Pat Brown in 1962. After that, as if he were finally leaving the national stage, he would famously tell reporters, "You won't have Nixon to kick around anymore."

America got its youngest president, his beautiful young wife, its youngest attorney general in Jack's brother Robert F. Kennedy (1925–68), and a new royal family whose regal intrigues were masked by sun-flooded pictures of family games of touch football.

> Let the word go forth from this time and place, to friend and foe alike, that the torch has been passed to a new generation of Americans—born in this century, tempered by war, disciplined by a hard and bitter peace, proud of our ancient heritage—and unwilling to witness the slow undoing of those human rights to which this nation has always been committed, and to which we are committed today at home and around the world. . . .
>
> Now the trumpet summons us again—not as a call to bear arms, though arms we need—but a call to bear the burden of a long twilight struggle, year in and year out, "rejoicing in hope, patient in tribulation"—a struggle against the common enemies of man: tyranny, poverty, disease and war itself.
>
> . . . And so, my fellow Americans: ask not what your country can do for you—ask what you can do for your country.

What happened at the Bay of Pigs?

In March 1961, during his first hundred days in office, Kennedy announced a program that perfectly symbolized his inaugural appeal to "ask what you can do for your country." The Peace Corps would dispatch the energy of American youth and know-how to assist developing nations. Directed by another family courtier, Sargent Shriver, husband of John's sister Eunice, the Peace Corps was the new generation's answer to Communism, promoting democracy with education, technology, and idealism instead of the fifties rhetoric of containment. Linked with the Alliance for Progress, a sort of Marshall Plan aimed at Latin America, the Peace Corps was the visible symbol of the vigor that Kennedy wanted to breathe into a stale American system.

What the Peace Corps idealism masked was a continuing policy of obsessive anti-Communism that would lead to one of the great disasters in American foreign policy. This failure would bring America to its most dangerous moment since the war in Korea and, in the view of many historians, help create the mind-set that sucked America into the Vietnamese quicksand. It took its unlikely but historically fitting name from an obscure spot on the Cuban coast, Bahía de Cochinos. The Bay of Pigs.

If the operation had not been so costly and its failed results so dangerously important to future American policy, the Bay of Pigs fiasco might seem comical, a fictional creation of some satirist trying to create an implausible CIA invasion scenario.

The plan behind the Bay of Pigs sounded simple when put to the new president by Allen Dulles (1893–1961), the legendary CIA director and a holdover from the Eisenhower era, when his brother, John Foster Dulles (1888–1959), had been the influential secretary of state. It was Allen Dulles's CIA operatives who dreamed up the Cuban operation involving a force of highly trained and well-equipped anti-Castro Cuban exiles called La Brigada during the waning days of the Eisenhower administration, part of a larger CIA venture called the Cuba Project aimed at overthrowing and if necessary assassinating Fidel Castro. As James Srodes writes in *Dulles*, his admiring biography of the CIA director, "Some of the schemes the CIA discussed with President Eisenhower (and later with President Kennedy) bordered on the lunatic. There were suggestions that Castro could be sprayed with hallucinogens, or his cigars laced with botulism, or his shoes dusted with thallium powder in the hope that his beard would fall out."

Supported by CIA-planted insurgents in Cuba who would blow up bridges and knock out radio stations, the brigade would land on the beaches of Cuba and set off a popular revolt against Fidel Castro, eliminating the man who had become the greatest thorn in the paw of the American lion. The most secret aspect of the plan, as a Senate investigation revealed much later, was the CIA plot to assassinate

Castro using Mafia hit men Sam Giancana and John Roselli, who were also sleeping with Judith Campbell, the president's steady partner. The Mafia had its own reasons for wanting to rid Cuba of Castro. (Giancana and Roselli were both murdered mob style in 1975 and 1976, respectively. Giancana was assassinated before he could testify before the Senate Intelligence Committee; Roselli testified, but his decomposing body was later found floating in an oil drum off Florida.)

For most of the century, since Teddy Roosevelt and company had turned Cuba into an American fiefdom in the Caribbean after the Spanish-American War, the island's economy was in nearly total American control. Almost all the sugar, mining, cattle, and oil wealth of Cuba was in American hands. The Spanish-American War had also given the United States a huge naval base at Guantanamo. But American gangsters had a rich share, too. While American businessmen controlled the Cuban economy, the casinos and hotels of Havana, a hot spot in the Caribbean, were controlled by the Mafia from New Orleans and Las Vegas.

All that had come to an end in 1958, when Fidel Castro and Che Guevara marched out of the hills with a tiny army and sent dictator Fulgencio Batista into exile. At first, Castro got good press notices in the United States and made a goodwill visit to Washington, professing that he was no Communist. But that didn't last long.

Cuban Communism became a campaign issue in 1960 as Nixon and Kennedy tried to outdo each other on the Castro issue. As they campaigned, the plans for La Brigada's invasion were being hatched by the CIA, a plan that had the enthusiastic encouragement of Vice President Richard Nixon and the nominal approval of Eisenhower. When Kennedy arrived in office, the plans only awaited the presidential okay. Briefed by Dulles himself before his inauguration, Kennedy agreed that preparations should continue. After his inauguration, momentum took over.

The CIA planners cockily pointed to their successful 1954 Guatemala coup that had installed a pro-American regime there as proof of their abilities. Before that, in 1953, the CIA had overseen a coup in Iran that installed the shah of Iran, an immediate success with much longer-term disastrous effects. But Cuba, as they were sadly going to learn, was not Guatemala. From the Cuban plan's outset, the agency men in charge of the invasion (including a fanatical CIA operative named E. Howard Hunt, who also wrote third-rate spy novels and would later be involved in the Watergate debacle) bungled and blustered. Almost every step of the plan was misguided. The CIA overestimated themselves, underestimated Castro and the popular support he enjoyed, relied on sketchy or nonexistent information, made erroneous assumptions, and misrepresented the plot to the White House.

The secret invasion proved to be one of the worst-kept secrets in America. A number of journalists had uncovered most of the plan, and several editors, including those at the *New York Times*, were persuaded by the White House to withhold the information. When the curtain finally came down, it was on a tragedy.

On April 17, 1961, some 1,400 Cubans, poorly trained, underequipped, and uninformed of their destination, were set down on the beach at the Bay of Pigs. Aerial photos of the beaches were misinterpreted by CIA experts, and Cuban claims that there were dangerous coral reefs that would prevent boats from landing were ignored by invasion planners, who put American technology above the Cubans' firsthand knowledge. CIA information showing the target beaches to be unpopulated was years out of date. The bay happened to be Fidel's favorite fishing spot, and Castro had begun building a resort there, including a seaside cabin for himself.

The invasion actually began two days earlier with an air strike against Cuban airfields, meant to destroy Castro's airpower. It failed to do that, and instead put Castro on the alert. It also prompted a crackdown on many suspected anti-Castro Cubans who might have been part of the anticipated popular uprising on which the agency was counting. Assuming the success of the air strike without bothering to confirm it, the agency didn't know Castro had a number of planes still operable, including two jet trainers capable of destroying the lumbering old bombers the CIA had provided to the invaders. But these planes wouldn't have counted for much if the air "umbrella" that the CIA had promised to La Brigada had materialized. President Kennedy's decision to keep all American personnel out of the invasion squashed that, and Castro's fliers had a field day strafing and bombing the invasion "fleet." The CIA-leased "navy" that was to deliver the invasion force and its supplies turned out to be five leaky, listing ships, two of which were quickly sunk by Castro's small air force, with most of the invasion's supplies aboard.

Cuban air superiority was responsible for only part of the devastation. Castro was able to pour thousands of troops into the area. Even though many of them were untried cadets or untrained militia, they were highly motivated, well-equipped troops supported by tanks and heavy artillery. While the invasion force fought bravely, exacting heavy casualties on Castro's troops, they lacked ammunition and, most important, the air support promised by the CIA. Eventually they were pinned down on the beaches, while American Navy fliers, the numbers on their planes obscured, could only sit and wonder why they had to watch their Cuban allies being cut to pieces. U.S. ships, their identifying numbers also pointlessly obscured, lay near the invasion beach, also handcuffed. Frustrated naval commanders bitterly resented their orders not to fire. In Washington, Kennedy feared that any direct U.S. combat involvement might send the Russians into West Berlin, precipitating World War III.

The sad toll was 114 Cuban invaders and many more defenders killed in the fighting; 1,189 others from La Brigada were captured and held prisoner until they were ransomed from Cuba by Robert Kennedy for food and medical supplies. Four American fliers, members of the Alabama Air National Guard in CIA employ, also died in the invasion, but the American government never acknowledged their existence or their connection to the operation.

What was the Cuban Missile Crisis?

Those were the immediate losses. The long-term damage was more costly. American prestige and the goodwill Kennedy had fostered around the world dissipated overnight. Adlai Stevenson, the former presidential contender serving as the U.S. representative to the United Nations, was shamed by having to lie to the General Assembly about the operation because he was misled by the White House. In Moscow, Kennedy was perceived as a weakling. Soviet leader Nikita Khrushchev (1894–1971) immediately saw the Bay of Pigs defeat as the opening to start arming Cuba more heavily, precipitating the missile crisis of October 1962.

When American spy flights produced evidence of Soviet missile sites in Cuba, America and the Soviet Union were brought to the brink of war. For thirteen tense days (recently dramatized in a film of that title that conveys much of the drama of the situation, if not all the facts), the United States and the Soviet Union stood toe to toe as Kennedy, forced to prove himself after the Bay of Pigs, demanded that the missile sites be dismantled and removed from Cuba. To back up his ultimatum, Kennedy ordered a naval blockade to "quarantine" Cuba, and readied a full-scale American invasion of the island. With Soviet ships steaming toward the island, Soviet premier Khrushchev warned that his country would not accept the quarantine. People around the world nervously awaited a confrontation. Through back channels a secret deal was struck that the Soviets would dismantle the missiles in exchange for a promise not to invade Cuba. On Sunday, October 28, Radio Moscow announced that the arms would be crated and returned to Moscow. Nuclear disaster was averted, temporarily.

The damage done to U.S. credibility by the Bay of Pigs fiasco had seemingly been undone. But the lesson of the foolishness of committing American military support to anti-Communism hadn't really sunk in. Kennedy was still willing to make an anti-Communist stand in the world. The next scene would be as distant from America as Cuba was close, a small corner of Asia called Vietnam.

(Recently released documents also reveal that during the Missile Crisis and his entire presidency, JFK suffered from more ailments, was in much greater pain, and was taking many more medications than the press, public, or family members and close aides knew. Although his back problem was well known, Kennedy also suffered from Addison's disease, a life-threatening lack of adrenal function, along with digestive problems and other ailments. Taking as many as eight medications a day, Kennedy used painkillers such as codeine, Demerol, and methadone; anti-anxiety agents such as librium; Ritalin and other stimulants; sleeping pills; and hormones to keep him alive. For all his intense suffering, there is no suggestion that these ailments or the medications ever incapacitated President Kennedy. On the other hand, it seems unlikely that any presidential candidate who revealed this array of medical problems could be elected.)

AMERICAN VOICES
RACHEL CARSON (1907–64),
from *Silent Spring* (1962):

Over increasingly large areas of the United States, spring now comes unheralded by the return of the birds, and the early mornings are strangely silent where once they were filled with the beauty of bird song.

As crude a weapon as the cave man's club, the chemical barrage has been hurled against the fabric of life.

In *Silent Spring*, biologist-writer Rachel Louise Carson warned of the dangers of the indiscriminate and persistent use of pesticides such as DDT. The book helped launch the United States environmental protection movement.

What was *The Feminine Mystique*?

Every so often a book comes along that really rattles America's cage. *Uncle Tom's Cabin* in 1850. Upton Sinclair's *The Jungle* in 1906. In the 1940s and 1950s, John Hersey's *Hiroshima* and the Kinsey studies, *Sexual Behavior in the Human Male* and *Sexual Behavior in the Human Female*. *Silent Spring* in 1962. All these books delivered karate chops to the American perception of reality.

In 1963, it was a book that introduced America to what the author called "the problem without a name." Betty Friedan (1921–2006), a summa cum laude Smith graduate and freelance writer who was living out the fifties suburban dream of house, husband, and family, dubbed this malady "the feminine mystique."

The book reached millions of readers. Suddenly, in garden clubs, coffee klatches, and college sorority houses, talk turned away from man catching, mascara, and muffin recipes. Women were instead discussing the fact that society's institutions—government, mass media and advertising, medicine and psychiatry, education and organized religion—were systematically barring them from becoming anything more than housewives and mothers.

Friedan's book helped jump-start a stalled women's rights movement. Lacking a motivating central cause and aggressive leadership since passage of the Nineteenth Amendment after World War I (see p. 334), organized feminism in the United States was practically nonexistent. In spite of forces that brought millions of women into the workforce—like the wartime factory jobs that made Rosie the Riveter an American heroine—women were expected to return to the kitchens after the menfolk came home from defending democracy. Although individuals like Eleanor Roosevelt, Amelia Earhart, Margaret Sanger, and Frances Perkins—the first woman cabinet officer and a key player in FDR's New Deal—were proven achievers, most women were expected to docilely accept the task of managing house and family, or to hold a proper "woman's job" like teaching, secretarial work, or, for the poorer classes, factory labor. In all these jobs, women were invisible. Once married, of course, the "ideal woman" stopped working. The idea of career as fulfillment was dismissed as nonsense, and that minority of pioneer "career women" was viewed practically as a class of social deviants. Overnight, Friedan made women question those assumptions.

The Feminine Mystique had its shortcomings. It was essentially about a white, middle-class phenomenon. It failed to explore the problems of working-class, poor, and minority women, whose worries ran far deeper than personal discontent. It also ignored the fact that a substantial portion of American women were satisfied in the role that Friedan had indicted.

But the book was like shock treatment. It galvanized American women into action at the same moment that an increasingly aggressive civil rights movement was moving to the forefront of American consciousness. And it came just as the government was taking its first awkward steps toward addressing the issue of inequality of the sexes. In one of his first acts, President Kennedy had formed a Commission on the Status of Women, chaired by the extraordinary Eleanor Roosevelt, then in her seventies. In 1964, a more substantial boost came when women actually received federal protection from discrimination because the legislative tactics of one crusty conservative congressman backfired.

Howard W. Smith of Virginia, an eighty-one-year-old vestige of the Old South, was looking for ways to shoot down the 1964 Civil Rights Act with "killer amendments." To the laughter of his House colleagues, Smith added "sex" to the list of "race, color, religion or national origin," the categories that the bill had been designed to protect. Assuming that nobody would vote to protect equality of the sexes, Smith was twice struck by lightning. The bill not only passed, but now protected women as well as blacks. Women were soon bringing appeals to the Equal Employment Opportunities Commission, even though its director complained that the bill was "conceived out of wedlock" and wasn't meant to prevent sex discrimination. That complaint came too late. Women filed more discrimination complaints with the EEOC than did any other single group. It was the foot in the door, and a new generation of activist women was ready to push the door harder.

In 1966, some 300 charter members formed the National Organization for Women (NOW) with Friedan as its first president. In the years ahead, NOW spearheaded a movement that would splinter and change as younger women grew more angry and defiant, radicalized by the same forces that were altering the civil rights and antiwar movements. But it is safe to say that no movement so fundamentally altered America's social makeup as the feminist movement of the past three decades. The workplace. Marriage and family life. The way we have babies—or choose not to have them. Few corners of American life were left untouched by the basic shifts in attitude that feminism created.

Of course, the process is far from complete. The federal government, from the White House to Congress and the judiciary, is still largely male, middle-aged, white, and wealthy. The upper crust of American corporate management remains male-dominated. A considerable gap in salaries still exists between men and women. And it is still presumed impossible or at least unlikely for a woman to be elected president in this country, even though forceful leaders like Indira Gandhi, Golda Meir, Margaret Thatcher, and Corazón Aquino of the Philippines have shown they are capable of acting as effectively, and even as ruthlessly, as any man.

Forty years after Friedan gave a name to the problem, the greatest irony may be the new yearning created for a generation of younger women brought up to put careers first and families second. In a strange twist on the question plaguing Friedan's generation, several research-ers have written books that examine the deep dissatisfaction that many successful women in their thirties and forties feel as the new century begins. Both unmarried, childless women and career-bound mothers are looking at their designer business suits, corporate perks, and power offices with a new sense of unfulfilled promise. It is now their turn to wonder about that silent question, "Is this all?"

AMERICAN VOICES
From MARTIN LUTHER KING'S "I Have a Dream"
speech in Washington, D.C. (August 1963):

I say to you today, my friends, that in spite of the difficul-ties and frustrations of the moment I still have a dream. It is a dream deeply rooted in the American dream.

I have a dream that one day this nation will rise up and live out the true meaning of its creed: "We hold these truths to be self-evident, that all men are created equal."

I have a dream that one day on the red hills of Geor-gia the sons of former slaves and the sons of former slave-owners will be able to sit down together at the table of brotherhood.

I have a dream that one day even the state of Missis-sippi, a desert state sweltering with the heat of injustice and oppression, will be transformed into an oasis of free-dom and justice.

I have a dream that my four children will one day live in a nation where they will not be judged by the color of their skin but by the content of their character.

King's most memorable speech was the culmination of the massive march on Washington, D.C., that drew a quarter of a million blacks and whites to the capital. In his biography of King, *Bearing the Cross*, author David J. Garrow calls the speech the "clarion call that con-veyed the moral power of the movement's cause to the millions who had watched the live national network coverage. Now, more than ever before . . . white America was confronted with the undeniable justice of blacks' demands." The march was followed by passage of the Civil Rights Act, signed into law by Lyndon Johnson in June 1964, and the awarding of the Nobel Peace Prize to Dr. King in October 1964.

AMERICAN VOICES
MALCOLM X, following the March on Washington:

Not long ago, the black man in America was fed a dose of another form of the weakening, lulling, and deluding effects of so-called "integration."

It was that "Farce on Washington," I call it. . . .

Yes, I was there. I observed that circus. Who ever heard of angry revolutionists all harmonizing "We Shall Overcome . . . Someday . . ." while tripping and swaying along arm-in-arm with the very people they were supposed to be angrily revolting against? Who ever heard of angry revolutionists swinging their bare feet together with their oppressor in lily-pad park pools, with gospels and guitars and "I Have A Dream" speeches?

If Martin Luther King Jr. gave J. Edgar Hoover bad dreams, Malcolm X (1925–65) was his worst nightmare. Born Malcolm Little, in Omaha, Nebraska, Malcolm had escaped a fire set by white men when he was four years old. His father was a follower of Marcus Garvey, a black separatist leader who worked to establish close political and economic ties to Africa. In 1931, Malcolm's father was found dead after being run over by a streetcar. Malcolm believed white racists were responsible for his father's death. When Malcolm was twelve years old, his mother was committed to a mental hospital, and he spent the rest of his childhood in foster homes.

In 1941, Malcolm moved to Boston and fell into street crime. He was arrested for burglary and sent to prison in 1946. While in prison, he joined the Nation of Islam, commonly called the Black Muslims, and took the name Malcolm X, renouncing his "slave name." He quickly rose as a charismatic and forceful spokesman for the movement and became the Nation of Islam's most effective minister. But in 1964, Malcolm X broke with the Nation of Islam. Soon afterward, he made a pilgrimage to the holy city of Mecca and underwent a radical change. In the form of Islam he discovered in Mecca, Malcolm X had a new vision of racial harmony, as he made clear in a letter to his followers that appeared in *The Autobiography of Malcolm X* (written with Alex Haley). "You may be shocked by these words coming from me," he wrote. "But on the pilgrimage, what I have seen, and experienced, has forced me to *re-arrange* much of my thought-patterns previously held, and to *toss aside* some of my previous conclusions."

Adopting the Muslim name El-Hajj Malik El-Shabazz, he returned to the United States to form the Organization for Afro-American Unity, and was clearly tilting toward a more conciliatory racial message. On February 21, 1965, Malcolm X was fatally shot while giving a speech in Harlem's Audubon Ballroom. Three members of the Nation of Islam were convicted of the crime. But, as with other assassinations during that era, the truth behind Malcolm's death remained buried in suspicious circumstances.

Who was right? The Warren Commission or Oliver Stone?

Americans probe this question as if we are searching for a missing tooth. We keep running our tongue over the empty space.

This question has inspired a cottage industry of conspiracy theorists and literally thousands of books. In the view of an American majority, none of them has yet to answer the question to full and verifiable satisfaction. Some innate paranoia in the American makeup finds it far more appealing to believe that Kennedy's death was the result of some intricately constructed byzantine conspiracy. The list of possible suspects reads like an old-fashioned Chinese restaurant menu. Just choose one from Column A and one from Column B. The choices include a smorgasbord of unsavory characters with the motive and ability to kill Kennedy: teamsters and gangsters; Cubans, both pro- and anti-Castro; white supremacists; CIA renegades; KGB moles; and, of course, lone assassins. Then Oliver Stone's movie *JFK* (1991) created an entire new generation of doubters, who also grew up with *The X-Files*, a show that elevated antigovernment conspiracy paranoia to televised art. A younger generation, completely distrustful of the "official explanation," began to cite Stone's film as source material in their term papers.

The conspiracy theories linger because many of the basic facts of the assassination remain shrouded in controversy and mythology. What is true is that JFK went to Texas in the fall of 1963 to shore up southern political support for his upcoming 1964 reelection bid. The Texas trip began well in San Antonio and Houston, where the president and the first lady were met by enthusiastic crowds. Everyone agreed that Dallas would be the tough town politically, and several advisers told Kennedy not to go. A few months before, the good folks of Dallas had spat on Adlai Stevenson, JFK's UN ambassador. But even in Dallas on November 22, things went better than expected, and crowds cheered the passing motorcade. In the fateful limousine, Texas governor John Connally's wife leaned over and told the president, "Well, you can't say Dallas doesn't love you."

Then the car made its turn in front of the Texas School Book Depository, and three shots rang out. Kennedy and Governor Connally were hit. The limousine carrying them sped off to the hospital. The president died, and Lyndon B. Johnson (1908–73) took the oath of office aboard Air Force One as a shocked and bloodied Jackie Kennedy looked on. Within hours, following the murder of a Dallas policeman, Lee Harvey Oswald was in custody and under interrogation. But two days later, as Oswald was being moved to a safer jail, Jack Ruby, owner of a Dallas strip joint, jumped from the crowd of policemen and shot Oswald dead in full view of a disbelieving national television audience.

This is where controversy takes over. A grieving, stunned nation couldn't cope with these events. Rumors and speculation began to fly as the country learned of the strange life of Lee Harvey Oswald—that he was an ex-marine who had defected to Russia and come back with a Russian wife; that he was a Marxist and a Castro admirer; that he had recently been to the Cuban embassy in Mexico City.

Responding to these rumors, which were growing to include the suggestion that Lyndon Johnson himself was part of the conspiracy, LBJ decided to appoint a commission to investigate the assassination and to determine whether any conspiracy existed. After his first week in office, Johnson asked Chief Justice Earl Warren to head the investigation. Warren reluctantly accepted the job when Johnson said that he feared nuclear war might result if the Cubans or Soviets proved to be behind the assassination.

The commission was appointed on November 29, 1963. Besides Chief Justice Earl Warren, the other members were Senator Richard B. Russell, Democrat of Georgia; Senator John S. Cooper, Republican of Kentucky; Representative T. Hale Boggs, Democrat of Louisiana; Representative Gerald R. Ford, Republican of Michigan; Allen W. Dulles, former director of the CIA; and John J. McCloy, former adviser to President Kennedy. During ten months, the commission took testimony from 552 witnesses.

The Warren Report was a summary of events related to the assassination issued in September 1964. It concluded that Lee Harvey Oswald, acting alone, shot Kennedy from a window on the sixth floor of the Texas School Book Depository building. The report also said that Jack Ruby acted alone in killing Oswald on November 24, 1963. The report found no evidence of a conspiracy involving Oswald and Ruby. It criticized the U.S. Secret Service and Federal Bureau of Investigation (FBI), and it asked for better measures in the future to protect the president.

But almost immediately after the Warren Report was issued, other investigations criticized the report's findings. In the decades since the Warren Commission tried to calm a very skittish nation, those findings are still viewed skeptically by a majority of the American public. The commission's detective work left much to be desired, and in later years, major new revelations followed. During the late 1970s, a special committee of the U.S. House of Representatives reexamined the evidence. It concluded that Kennedy "was probably assassinated as a result of a conspiracy." In particular, shocking facts were produced by the investigations into the activities of the CIA and the FBI during the 1970s. Among other startling discoveries, these investigations by a presidential commission and Congress uncovered the CIA's plans for assassinating Fidel Castro and other foreign leaders; that Kennedy's mistress Judith Campbell was also involved with the two gangsters hired by the CIA to kill Castro; and that FBI director J. Edgar Hoover had ordered a cover-up of bureau failures in the Oswald investigation in an effort to protect the bureau's integrity and public image.

Were there only three shots fired by someone in the Texas School Book Depository? Was Oswald the gunman who fired them? Or were other shots fired from the grassy knoll overlooking the route of the motorcade? Was Jack Ruby, who was both connected to the Dallas underworld and a friend of Dallas policemen, simply acting, as he said, to spare Mrs. Kennedy the pain of returning to Dallas to testify at a murder trial? Who were the two "Latins" that a New Orleans prostitute said she encountered on their way to Dallas a few days before the murder? Did "hundreds of witnesses" to the incident and investigation die suspiciously, as several conspiracy theorists claim?

More than 2,000 books have been written about the case since JFK's death, from attorney Mark Lane's *Rush to Judgment* and Edward Jay Epstein's *Inquest* to David Lifton's *Best Evidence* and David Scheim's *Contract on America: The Mafia Murder of President John F. Kennedy*. All have relied on serious flaws in the Warren investigation as well as material the Warren Commission never saw to support a variety of possible conspiracies. All have been greeted by a public feeding frenzy.

Far less sensational is *Final Disclosure*, a 1989 book that refutes all these theories, written by David W. Belin, the counsel to the Warren Commission and executive director of the Rockefeller Commission investigating abuses by the CIA. Obviously Belin, as a key staff member of the Warren Commission, had a personal interest to protect. But his book is well reasoned and amply supported by evidence. Examining the Warren Commission's total evidence, the subsequent CIA and FBI revelations, and the analysis of a controversial audio tape that supposedly proved the existence of a fourth shot and a second gunman, Belin deflated the most serious charges brought by the conspiracists, often by showing they have made highly selective use of evidence and testimony.

Far more exhaustive and comprehensive, and more controversial, than Belin's book is *Case Closed* by Gerald Posner. Using new technological resources and sophisticated computer studies, Posner reached an unambiguous and rather unassailable conclusion: Lee Harvey Oswald indeed acted alone, as did Jack Ruby. Writes Posner, "There is more than enough evidence available on the record to draw conclusions about what happened in the JFK assassination. But apparently most Americans, despite the strength of the evidence, do not want to accept the notion that random acts of violence can change the course of history and that Lee Harvey Oswald could affect our lives in a way over which we have no control. It is unsettling to think that a socio-pathic twenty-four-year-old loser in life, armed with a $12 rifle and consumed by his own warped motivation, ended Camelot. But for readers willing to approach this subject with an open mind, it is the only rational judgment."

Even so, that missing-tooth feeling remains for many Americans. While the arguments are convincing that Oswald and then Ruby acted alone, it seems that few people were willing to accept that conclusion. Their skepticism was one more indication of the deep-seated mistrust and lack of faith Americans had come to have in their government and political leadership.

Must Read: *Case Closed: Lee Harvey Oswald and the Assassination of JFK* by Gerald Posner.

AMERICAN VOICES
From LYNDON JOHNSON'S
"Great Society" speech (May 1964):

The Great Society rests on abundance and liberty for all. It demands an end to poverty and racial injustice, to which we are totally committed in our time. But that is just the beginning.

The Great Society is a place where every child can find knowledge to enrich his mind and to enlarge his talents. It is a place where leisure is a welcome chance to build and reflect, not a feared cause of boredom and restlessness. It is a place where the city of man serves not only the needs of the body and the demands of commerce, but the desire for beauty and the hunger for community.

It is a place where man can renew contact with nature. It is a place which honors creation for its own sake and for what it adds to the understanding of the race. It is a place where men are more concerned with the quality of their goals than the quantity of their goods.

In this speech, delivered during his election campaign against Republican Barry Goldwater, Johnson laid out the foundation for the ambitious domestic social program he carried out after his landslide victory over the conservative senator from Arizona. Johnson proposed attacking racial injustice through economic and educational reforms and government programs aimed at ending the cycle of poverty. The legislative record he then compiled was impressive, although social historians argue over its ultimate effectiveness. The Office of Economic Opportunity was created. Kennedy's proposed civil rights bill was passed, followed by a Voting Rights Act and the establishments of Project Head Start, the Job Corps, and Medicaid and Medicare. But while Johnson was carrying out the most ambitious social revolution since FDR's New Deal, he was also leading the country deeper and deeper into Vietnam. And that futile and disastrous path, more than any of his domestic initiatives, would mark Johnson's place in history.

Did *Mississippi Burning* really happen?

If Hollywood gets its way, the civil rights movement was saved when Gene Hackman and Willem Dafoe rolled into town like two gunslinging Western marshals. In this revisionist cinematic version of history, two FBI men bring truth and vigilante justice to the nasty Ku Klux Klan while a bunch of bewildered Negroes meekly stand by, shuffling and avoiding trouble.

The 1989 film *Mississippi Burning* was an emotional roller coaster. It was difficult to watch without being moved, breaking into a sweat, and finally cheering when the forces of good terrorized the redneck Klansmen into telling where the bodies of three murdered civil rights workers were buried. The movie gave audiences the feeling of seeing history unfold. But in the grand tradition of American filmmaking, this version of events had as much to do with reality as did D. W. Griffith's racist "classic," *Birth of a Nation.*

The movie opens with the backroads murder of three young civil rights activists in the summer of 1964. That much is true. Working to register black voters, Andrew Goodman and Michael Schwerner, two whites from the North, and James Chaney, a black southerner, disappeared after leaving police custody in Philadelphia, Mississippi. In the film, two FBI agents arrive to investigate, but get nowhere as local rednecks stonewall the FBI and blacks are too fearful to act. The murderers are not exposed until Agent Anderson (Gene Hackman), a former southern sheriff who has joined the FBI, begins a campaign of illegal tactics to terrorize the locals into revealing where the bodies are buried and who is responsible.

It is a brilliantly made, plainly manipulative film that hits all the right emotional notes: white liberal guilt over the treatment of blacks; disgust at the white-trash racism of the locals; excitement at Hackman's Rambo-style tactics; and, finally, vindication in the murderers' convictions.

The problem is that besides the murders, few of the events depicted happened that way. Pressed by Attorney General Robert Kennedy, FBI director J. Edgar Hoover sent a large contingent of agents to Mississippi, but they learned nothing. The case was broken only when Klan informers were offered a $30,000 bribe and the bodies of the three men were found in a nearby dam site. Twenty-one men were named in the indictment, including the local police chief and his deputy. But local courts later dismissed the confessions of the two Klansmen as hearsay. The Justice Department persisted by bringing conspiracy charges against eighteen of the men. Tried before a judge who had once compared blacks to chimpanzees, seven of the accused were nonetheless convicted and sentenced to jail terms ranging from three to ten years.

Although J. Edgar Hoover put on a good public show of anti-Klan FBI work, it masked his real obsession at the time. To the director, protecting civil rights workers was a waste of his bureau's time. Although the film depicts a black agent, the only blacks employed by the bureau during Hoover's tenure as head were his chauffeurs. The FBI was far more interested in trying to prove that Martin Luther King was a Communist and that the civil rights movement was an organized Communist front. Part of this effort was the high-level attempt to eavesdrop on King's private life, an effort that did prove that the civil rights leader had his share of white female admirers willing to contribute more than just money to the cause. Hoover's hatred of King boiled over at one point when he called King "the most notorious liar" in the country.

Another part of this effort involved sending King a threatening note suggesting he commit suicide.

What was the Tonkin Resolution?

When is a war not a war? When the president decides it isn't, and Congress goes along.

America was already more than ten years into its Vietnam commitment when Lyndon Johnson and Kennedy's best and brightest holdovers decided to find a new version of Pearl Harbor. An incident was needed to pull American firepower into the war with at least a glimmer of legitimacy. It came in August 1964 with a brief encounter in the Gulf of Tonkin, the waters off the coast of North Vietnam.

In the civil war that was raging between North and South since the French withdrawal from Indochina and the partition of Vietnam in 1954, the United States had committed money, material, advice, and, by the end of 1963, some 15,000 military advisers in support of the anti-Communist Saigon government. The American CIA was also in the thick of things, having helped foster the coup that toppled Prime Minister Ngo Dinh Diem in 1963 and then acting surprised when Diem was executed by the army officers who overthrew him.

Among the other "advice" the United States provided to its South Vietnamese allies was to teach them commando tactics. In 1964, CIA-trained guerrillas from the South began to attack the North in covert acts of sabotage. Code named Plan 34-A, these commando raids failed to undermine North Vietnam's military strength, so the mode of attack was shifted to hit-and-run operations by small torpedo boats. To support these assaults, the U.S. Navy posted warships in the Gulf of Tonkin, loaded with electronic eavesdropping equipment enabling them to monitor North Vietnamese military operations and provide intelligence to the South Vietnamese commandos.

Coming as it did in the midst of LBJ's 1964 campaign against hawkish Republican Barry Goldwater, President Johnson felt the incident called for a tough response. Johnson had the Navy send the *Maddox* and a second destroyer, the *Turner Joy*, back into the Gulf of Tonkin. A radar man on the *Turner Joy* saw some blips, and that boat opened fire. On the *Maddox*, there were also reports of incoming torpedoes, and the *Maddox* began to fire. There was never any confirmation that either ship had actually been attacked. Later, the radar blips would be attributed to weather conditions and jittery nerves among the crew.

According to Stanley Karnow's *Vietnam: A History*, "Even Johnson privately expressed doubts only a few days after the second attack supposedly took place, confiding to an aide, 'Hell, those dumb stupid sailors were just shooting at flying fish.'"

But that didn't stop Lyndon Johnson. Without waiting for a review of the situation, he ordered an air strike against North Vietnam in "retaliation" for the "attacks" on the U.S. ships. American jets flew more than sixty sorties against targets in North Vietnam. One bitter result of these air raids was the capture of downed pilot Everett Alvarez Jr., the first American POW of the Vietnam War. He would remain in Hanoi prisons for eight years.

President Johnson followed up the air strike by calling for passage of the Gulf of Tonkin Resolution. This proposal gave the president the authority to "take all necessary measures" to repel attacks against U.S. forces and to "prevent further aggression." The resolution not only gave Johnson the powers he needed to increase American commitment to Vietnam, but allowed him to blunt Goldwater's accusations that Johnson was "timid before Communism." The Gulf of Tonkin Resolution passed the House unanimously after only forty minutes of debate. In the Senate, there were only two voices in opposition. What Congress did not know was that the resolution had been drafted several months before the Tonkin incident took place.

Congress, which alone possesses the constitutional authority to declare war, had handed that power over to a man who was not a bit reluctant to use it. One of the senators who voted against the Tonkin Resolution, Oregon's Wayne Morse, later said, "I believe that history will record that we have made a great mistake in subverting and circumventing the Constitution." After the vote, Walt Rostow, an adviser to Lyndon Johnson, remarked, "We don't know what happened, but it had the desired result."

MILESTONES IN THE VIETNAM WAR

While American involvement in Vietnam and much of Southeast Asia came after the Second World War, the roots of Western involvement in the region date to the nineteenth-century colonial era when France took control of parts of the Vietnamese Empire in 1862. During World War II, Japan fought the French in Indochina. It was during that time that Ho Chi Minh (born 1890 in central Vietnam) emerged to create the Vietminh to battle both France and Japan. In 1918, Ho had left Vietnam for the West, and had tried to influence President Wilson to allow Vietnam self-determination at the Versailles peace talks after World War I. When that failed, he joined the French Communist Party and went to Moscow, returning in secret to Vietnam in 1941. In 1945, the Japanese seized control of Indochina, allowing the emperor to declare his independence from France.

In the immediate aftermath of the war, Ho declared the country independent as the Democratic Republic of Vietnam, encompassing the whole country. He dissolved the Communist Party to form a coalition government with other nationalists, and in 1946, France recognized the DRV as a free state within the French Union. But later that year, the French and Vietnamese would begin to fight the French-Indochina War.

1950

While U.S. troops fight in Korea, President Truman grants military aid to France for its war against Communist rebels in Indochina. The United States will ultimately pay the lion's share—75 to 80 percent—of France's military costs in the war against the Ho Chi Minh–led Vietminh rebels.

1954

Although the use of an atomic bomb is actively considered, President Eisenhower decides against providing direct military support to the French in their stand at their base at Dienbienphu. Eisenhower instead favors continued aid for France in Indochina, and tells the press in April that Southeast Asia may otherwise fall to Communism. Says Eisenhower, if you "have a row of dominoes set up, you knock over the first one, and what will happen to the last one is the certainty that it will go over very quickly."

May The French stronghold at Dienbienphu is overrun by Vietnamese forces under General Giap. The French withdraw from Indochina, and Vietnam is partitioned at a conference in Geneva, creating the Democratic Republic of Vietnam in the North and the Republic of South Vietnam with its capital at Saigon. A political settlement to the country's division is left to a future election that will never take place. The United States continues its direct involvement in Vietnam by sending $100 million in aid to the anti-Communist Saigon government led by Prime Minister Ngo Dinh Diem.

1955

Direct aid and military training are provided to the Saigon government. Vietnam, Cambodia, and Laos receive more than $200 million in U.S. aid this year.

October The Republic of Vietnam is proclaimed by Prime Minister Diem following a rigged election organized by the United States. Diem had rejected a unification election with the North.

1959

July 8 Two American soldiers, Major Dale Buis and Master Sergeant Chester Ovnard, are killed by Vietcong at Bienhoa. They are the first Americans to die in Vietnam during this era. By year's end, there are some 760 U.S. military personnel in Vietnam.

1960

At the request of the Diem government, the number of the U.S. Military Assistance Advisory Group is increased to 685.

November A military coup against Diem is foiled. The U.S. government advises Diem to implement radical reforms to eliminate corruption.

December   In the North, the Hanoi government announces a plan calling for reunification and overthrow of the Diem government. The National Liberation Front of South Vietnam is formed, and its guerrillas will be known as the Vietcong.

1961

After touring Vietnam, President Kennedy's advisers, Walt Rostow and General Maxwell Taylor, recommend sending 8,000 U.S. combat troops there. Instead, President Kennedy chooses to send more equipment and advisers. By year's end, there are 3,205 U.S. military personnel in Vietnam.

1962

February 6   The American Military Assistance Command Vietnam (MACV) is formed, based in Saigon.

May   President Kennedy sends 5,000 marines and fifty jets to Thailand to counter Communist expansion in Laos. The number of American advisers is increased to nearly 12,000.

1963

January   The Army of the Republic of South Vietnam suffers a major defeat against a much smaller Vietcong force at the Battle of Ap Bac. The performance of the Vietnamese troops and commanders, under American guidance, is disastrous.

May–August   Antigovernment demonstrations by Buddhist monks provoke violent reprisals. In protest, numerous monks commit suicide by setting themselves afire.

November   General Duong Van Minh and other South Vietnamese officers stage a coup and overthrow the Diem government with U.S. knowledge and CIA assistance. Diem and his brother are murdered. Three weeks later, President Kennedy is assassinated.

December   By the end of the year, President Johnson has increased the number of American advisers to 16,300, and the United States has sent $500 million to South Vietnam in this year alone. The CIA begins training South Vietnamese guerrillas as part of an ambitious covert sabotage operation against the North, under American direction.

1964

January Lieutenant General William Westmoreland (1914–2005) is appointed deputy commander of Military Assistance Command Vietnam.

January 30 General Nguyen Khanh seizes power in Saigon; General Minh is retained as a figurehead chief of state.

June Westmoreland is promoted to commander of MACV.

August 2 While conducting electronic surveillance ten miles off North Vietnam, in the Gulf of Tonkin, the American destroyer *Maddox* is pursued by three North Vietnamese torpedo boats. As the patrol boats close in, the *Maddox* opens fire and the patrol boats respond with torpedoes, which miss. The destroyer calls for air support from the nearby carrier *Ticonderoga*, and three United States fighter planes attack the boats. The *Maddox* sinks one patrol boat, cripples the other two, and withdraws. Two days later, the *Maddox* and a second destroyer, the *Turner Joy*, are ordered back to Tonkin to "reassert freedom of international waters."

August 4 President Johnson reports to congressional leaders that a second attack has been made on the *Maddox*, although this attack was never confirmed and was later shown not to have taken place.

August 5 U.S. planes bomb North Vietnam in retaliation for the "attacks" on the U.S. ships. The American bombing mission is called "limited in scale," but more than sixty sorties are flown, destroying oil depots and patrol boats. Two American planes are shot down and Everett Alvarez is captured, the first American prisoner of war in Vietnam. He is held for more than eight years.

August 7 By a unanimous vote in the House, and with only two dissenting votes in the Senate, Congress passes the Gulf of Tonkin

Resolution, giving President Johnson powers to "take all necessary measures to repel any armed attack against the forces of the United States and to prevent further aggression." Johnson later says the resolution was "like grandma's nightshirt—it covered everything."

August 26   President Johnson is nominated at the Democratic National Convention and chooses Hubert Humphrey as his running mate. Pledging before the election to "seek no wider war," Johnson defeats Republican candidate Barry Goldwater in a landslide, with a plurality of 15.5 million votes.

September   UN Secretary General U Thant proposes mediating talks with North Vietnam to avert a war. Withholding some information from Johnson, American officials reject these negotiations.

October 30   In a Vietcong attack on the U.S. airbase at Bien Hoa, six B-57 bombers are destroyed and five Americans are killed.

December 31   The number of American military advisers rises to 23,300.

1965

February 7   Following a Vietcong attack on a U.S. base at Pleiku in which eight Americans are killed, President Johnson orders air raids against North Vietnam and the beginning of a new round of escalation in the war, in what is named Operation Flaming Dart. Communist guerrillas then attack another American base, and Flaming Dart II is ordered in retaliation.

February 19   A series of competing coups result in Nguyen Cao Ky, an air force general, taking control of South Vietnam.

March 2   The United States begins Operation Rolling Thunder, the sustained bombing of North Vietnam. It will continue until October 31, 1968.

March 8   Two battalions of American marines land and are assigned to protect the airbase at Danang. They are the first American combat troops in Vietnam.

April 7   President Johnson calls for talks with Hanoi to end the war. The plan is rejected by Hanoi, which says any settlement must be based on its Vietcong program.

April 15   Students for a Democratic Society (SDS) sponsors a large antiwar rally in Washington.

June 11   Fellow generals choose Nguyen Cao Ky, a flamboyant young officer, as prime minister of a South Vietnamese military regime.

November 14–17   In the first major conventional clash of the war, U.S. forces defeat North Vietnamese units in the Ia Drang Valley.

December 25   President Johnson suspends bombing in an attempt to get the North to negotiate. By year's end, American troop strength is nearly 200,000, combat losses total 636 Americans killed, and at home, draft quotas have been doubled.

AMERICAN VOICES
PRESIDENT LYNDON B. JOHNSON, to his secretary
of defense, Robert S. McNamara (June 1965), quoted in
*Reaching for Glory: Lyndon Johnson's Secret White
House Tapes, 1964–1965:*

It's going to be difficult for us to very long prosecute effectively a war that far away from home with the divisions we have here—and particularly the potential divisions. I'm very depressed about it. Because I see no program from either Defense or State that gives me much hope of doing anything, except just praying and gasping to hold on during monsoon and hope they'll quit. I don't believe they're ever going to quit. And I don't see . . . that we have any . . . plan for a victory—militarily or diplomatically.

1966

January 31 The bombing of the North is resumed after failure of the "peace offensive" that was designed to promote negotiations.

March 10 In Hue and Danang, Buddhist monks demonstrate against the Saigon regime. Both cities are taken over by government troops.

June 29 American planes bomb oil depots near Haiphong and Hanoi, in response to North Vietnamese infiltration into the South to aid the Vietcong.

September 23 The U.S. military command in Vietnam announces that it is using chemical defoliants, Agent Orange among them, to destroy Communist cover.

October 25 A conference between Johnson and heads of six allied nations involved in Vietnam (Australia, the Philippines, Thailand, New Zealand, South Korea, and South Vietnam) issues a peace plan calling for the end of North Vietnamese aggression. By year's end, American troop strength in Vietnam is nearly 400,000.

1967

January 5 American casualties in Vietnam for 1966 are announced: 5,008 killed and 30,093 wounded. (Totals since 1961 are 6,664 killed, 37,738 wounded.)

January 8 Thirty thousand combined American and South Vietnamese troops begin Operation Cedar Falls, an offensive against enemy positions in the Iron Triangle, an area twenty-five miles northwest of Saigon. (Among the U.S. battalion commanders in this operation is General Alexander Haig.)

January 28 The North Vietnamese announce that U.S. bombing must stop before there can be peace talks.

July 7 The Joint Economic Committee of Congress reports that the war effort created "havoc" in the U.S. economy during 1966.

August   Testifying before Congress, Defense Secretary Robert McNamara says bombing of North Vietnam is ineffective.

September   Major Communist offensives begin. General Westmoreland fortifies Khe Sanh.

October 21   Two days of antiwar protests take place in Washington, and are the subject of Norman Mailer's book *Armies of the Night.*

December 8   The wave of antiwar protests becomes more organized and active. In New York, 585 protesters are arrested, including Dr. Benjamin Spock and poet Allen Ginsberg. Spock and four other protesters issue a pamphlet, *A Call to Resist Illegitimate Authority*, later published as a book and used as the basis for Spock's prosecution by the government. In the following days of antidraft protests, arrests are made in New Haven, Connecticut; Cincinnati; Madison, Wisconsin; and Manchester, New Hampshire. At year's end, U.S. troop strength stands at nearly half a million.

1968

January 21   The Battle of Khe Sanh. A strategic hamlet that General Westmoreland had heavily fortified and stockpiled with ammunition as a future staging point for attacks on the Ho Chi Minh Trail, the Communist supply route from the North, Khe Sanh becomes the scene of one of the war's most controversial sieges. When Vietcong and North Vietnamese regulars begin the siege of American forces at Khe Sanh, it is seen by many Americans, including Westmoreland, President Johnson, and the media as a repeat of the 1954 attack on the French stronghold at Dienbienphu. Westmoreland and Johnson are committed to preventing such a disaster, and Johnson tells one of his senior aides, "I don't want any damn Dinbinphoo."

A military catastrophe such as the French suffered is averted as Khe Sanh is heavily reinforced and supported by massive B-52 bombings. But at home, Americans watch the siege unfold like a nightly TV serial. Fought in the midst of the Tet Offensive (see below), the battle for Khe Sanh seems to be one more example of the resolve of the Vietnamese, who ultimately lost some 10,000 to 15,000 men at

Khe Sanh against 205 Americans killed. The siege lasts until April. Ironically, the base at Khe Sanh will be abandoned one year later, when a planned strike at the Ho Chi Minh Trail in Laos is canceled.

January 23 The intelligence vessel USS *Pueblo* is captured by North Korea.

January 31 The Tet Offensive. Although a brief truce is set to celebrate the Vietnamese lunar New Year holiday, the Vietcong launch a major offensive throughout South Vietnam, and the American embassy in Saigon is attacked. Hanoi had hoped for a general uprising in the South, which does not happen.

   Although most of the attacks are eventually repulsed, Tet is seen in the United States as a defeat and a symbol of the Vietcong's ability to strike at will anywhere in the country. It also damages the optimistic views of the war's progress that General Westmoreland and other American military leaders have been bringing back to Congress and the American people.

February 25 After twenty-six days of fighting since the Tet Offensive began, the city of Hue is recaptured by American and South Vietnamese forces. Mass graves reveal that an enormous atrocity was committed by the retreating Vietcong and North Vietnamese, who killed thousands of civilians suspected of supporting the Saigon government.

February 29 Defense Secretary Robert McNamara resigns after concluding that the United States cannot win the war. He is replaced by Clark Clifford.

March 12 Senator Eugene McCarthy, an outspoken opponent of the war, nearly defeats President Johnson in the New Hampshire Democratic primary, a stunning setback for Johnson as the incumbent president.

March 16 Following McCarthy's near upset of Johnson, Senator Robert F. Kennedy announces that he will campaign for the Democratic presidential nomination.

   This is also the date of the massacre of villagers at My Lai (see p. 491).

March 31 In an extraordinary television address, President Johnson announces a partial bombing halt, offers peace talks, and then stuns the nation by saying he will not run again.

April 4 Martin Luther King Jr. is assassinated in Memphis, Tennessee.

April 23 At New York's Columbia University, members of Students for a Democratic Society (SDS) seize five buildings in protest of Columbia's involvement in war-related research.

May 10 Peace talks begin in Paris between the United States and North Vietnam.

June 6 Following his victory in the California primary, Robert F. Kennedy is assassinated by Sirhan B. Sirhan.

June 14 Dr. Benjamin Spock is convicted of conspiracy to aid draft evasion. (The conviction is later overturned.)

August 26 The Democratic National Convention opens in Chicago. In the midst of antiwar protests and violent police response, the Democrats nominate Hubert Humphrey.

October 31 President Johnson orders an end to bombing of the North, in an attempt to break the stalemate at Paris. Progress at Paris will presumably help the chances of the Democratic ticket of Hubert Humphrey and Edmund Muskie.

November 6 In one of the closest presidential elections, the Republican ticket of Richard Nixon and Spiro Agnew defeats Democrat Hubert Humphrey, with third-party candidate George Wallace drawing more than 9 million votes. At year's end, American troop strength is at 540,000.

1969

January 25 Paris peace talks are expanded to include the South Vietnamese and Vietcong.

March 18 President Nixon and National Security Adviser Henry Kissinger order the secret bombing of Communist bases in Cambodia.

May 14   President Nixon calls for the simultaneous withdrawal of American and North Vietnamese forces from the South.

June 8   Nixon announces the withdrawal of 25,000 American troops, the first step in a plan called Vietnamization, the aim of which is to turn the war over to the South Vietnamese.

September 2   Ho Chi Minh, leader of the North since the 1950s, dies in Hanoi at the age of seventy-nine.

September 25   Congressional opposition to the war grows as ten bills designed to remove all American troops from Vietnam are submitted.

October 15   The first of many large, nationwide protests against the war, the so-called Moratorium is designed to expand the peace movement off the campuses and into the cities, drawing broader popular support. Led by Coretta Scott King, widow of Dr. Martin Luther King Jr., 250,000 protesters march on Washington.

November 3   Attempting to defuse protest, Nixon makes his "silent majority" speech, claiming that most of the nation supports his efforts to end the war.

November 15   A second Moratorium march on Washington takes place.

November 16   A 1968 massacre of civilians at the Vietnamese hamlet of My Lai is revealed. U.S. Army Lieutenant William L. Calley is tried and convicted for his role in the massacre. The atrocity further discredits the war and adds momentum to the peace movement in America.

December 1   The first draft lottery of the Vietnam era is instituted in an effort to reduce criticism of the draft as unfair. It signals the end of student draft deferments. By the end of the year, American troop strength has been reduced to 475,200.

1970

February 18   Following a long, theatrical trial highlighted by the courtroom antics of defendants Abbie Hoffman, Jerry Rubin, and others, the Chicago Seven are acquitted on charges of conspiring to incite a riot. They are convicted on lesser charges of conspiracy, which are later overturned.

February 20   National Security Adviser Henry Kissinger begins secret Paris negotiations with North Vietnamese envoy Le Duc Tho.

April 20   Nixon promises to withdraw another 150,000 men from Vietnam by year's end. The withdrawals are decreasing American casualties.

April 30   Nixon announces that U.S. troops have attacked Communist sanctuaries in Cambodia, following the overthrow of Prince Sihanouk by U.S.-aided Lon Nol.

May 4   As part of the widening campus protests against the war and the decision to send troops to Cambodia, a demonstration is held at Kent State University in Ohio. When national guardsmen open fire on the demonstrators, four students are killed. Ten days later, two more students are killed, at predominantly black Jackson State College in Mississippi.

October 7   Nixon proposes a "standstill cease-fire," and reissues a proposal for mutual withdrawal the next day.

November 23   A raid into North Vietnam, in an attempt to rescue American POWs, comes up empty-handed. Heavy bombing of the North continues.

At year's end, U.S. troop strength has been reduced to 334,600.

1971

January–February   The South Vietnamese, with American support, begin attacks on Vietcong supply lines in Laos. The operation is easily defeated by Communist troops.

March 29   An army court-martial finds William Calley guilty of premeditated murder at the village of My Lai. After three days in the stockade, Calley is released to "house arrest" by President Nixon.

June 13   The *New York Times* begins publication of the Pentagon Papers, the top-secret history of American involvement in Vietnam, which has been turned over by Pentagon employee Daniel Ellsberg to *Times* reporter Neil Sheehan. Nixon tries to stop publication of the documents, which reveal much of the duplicity within the government surrounding Vietnam. But on June 30, the Supreme Court rules that the *Times* and the *Washington Post* may resume publication. On Nixon's orders to investigate Ellsberg, a group is set up known as the "plumbers," whose purpose is to try to stop "leaks." The "plumbers" soon expand their activities to a campaign aimed at a Nixon "enemies list." Also on their agenda is a break-in at the Democratic National Committee offices at the Watergate Office Building in Washington, D.C.

November 12   President Nixon announces the withdrawal of 45,000 more men, leaving an American force of 156,800 in Vietnam.

1972

January 13   President Nixon announces withdrawal of an additional 70,000 troops.

January 25   President Nixon reveals that Henry Kissinger has been in secret negotiations with the North Vietnamese, and makes public an eight-point peace proposal calling for a cease-fire and release of all U.S. POWs, in exchange for U.S. withdrawal from Vietnam.

February 21   Nixon and Kissinger arrive in China to meet with Mao Zedong and Zhou Enlai, the Chinese premier.

March 30   The North Vietnamese launch a massive offensive across the Demilitarized Zone into the South. In five weeks, Hanoi's troops have penetrated deep into the South.

April 15   President Nixon orders resumption of bombing in the North, suspended three years earlier.

May 1 The city of Quang Tri is captured by the North.

May 8 President Nixon announces the mining of Haiphong Harbor and stepped-up bombing raids against the North.

June 17 Five men are arrested at the Democratic National Committee offices at the Watergate Office Building. They work for the Committee to Reelect the President. Subsequently, two former intelligence operatives, G. Gordon Liddy and E. Howard Hunt, are arrested for their involvement in the break-in, and the ensuing cover-up by the White House begins to unravel as "Watergate."

October 8 Henry Kissinger and Le Duc Tho achieve a breakthrough in their Paris negotiations. Henry Kissinger returns to the United States to say that peace is "within reach." The announcement is made two weeks before the presidential election, in which Nixon is opposed by the Democratic senator from South Dakota, George McGovern, an outspoken opponent of the war.

November 7 Nixon is reelected in a landslide victory. Following the election, Kissinger's talks with Le Duc Tho break down.

December 18 The United States resumes bombing raids over North Vietnam, which continue for eleven days. Communists agree to resume talks when bombing stops.

By year's end, American troop strength has been reduced to 24,000.

1973

January Kissinger resumes talks with the North. A cease-fire agreement is signed and formally announced on January 27. Defense Secretary Melvin Laird announces the end of the draft as the army shifts to an all-volunteer force. During the Vietnam War, 2.2 million American men have been drafted.

March 29 The last American ground troops leave Vietnam.

April 1 All American POWs held in Hanoi are released.

April 30   President Nixon's aides H. R. Haldeman, John Ehrlichman, and John Dean resign amid charges that the White House has obstructed justice in the Watergate investigation. On June 25, Dean accuses Nixon of authorizing a cover-up, and another White House aide reveals the existence of a secret taping system that has recorded conversations in the Oval Office.

July 16   The Senate begins an investigation of the secret air war against Cambodia.

August 14   The U.S. officially halts bombing of Cambodia.

August 22   Henry Kissinger becomes secretary of state.

October 10   Vice President Spiro Agnew resigns after pleading "no contest" to charges of tax evasion. House minority leader Gerald Ford is nominated by Nixon to replace Agnew under the Twenty-fifth Amendment, which allows the president to fill a vacancy in the vice presidency.

October 23   Kissinger and North Vietnam's Le Duc Tho are awarded the Nobel Peace Prize, which Le Duc Tho rejects because fighting continues in Vietnam.

November 7   Over the president's veto, Congress passes the War Powers Act, which restricts the president's power to commit troops to foreign countries without congressional approval.

1974

January   South Vietnam's President Thieu announces that war has begun again. Communists proceed to build up troops and supplies in the South.

July 30   The House Judiciary Committee votes to recommend impeachment of President Nixon on three counts of "high crimes and misdemeanors."

August 9   Nixon resigns and is replaced by Gerald Ford.

September 8   Ford pardons Nixon for all crimes he "committed or may have committed."

1975

In an offensive that lasts six months, combined Vietcong and North Vietnamese forces overrun South Vietnam and Cambodia.

April 13   The United States evacuates its personnel from Cambodia.

April 17   Phnom Penh, the capital of Cambodia (renamed Kampuchea), falls to the Communist Khmer Rouge.

April 23   President Ford calls the war "finished."

April 25   High-ranking South Vietnamese officials evacuate Saigon.

April 29   The last Americans are evacuated from Saigon, on the same day that the last two American soldiers are killed in Vietnam. On the following day, Communist forces take Saigon.

1977

January 21   President Jimmy Carter unconditionally pardons most of the 10,000 men who evaded the draft during the war.

1982

November 11   The Vietnam Veterans Memorial is unveiled in Washington, D.C. It commemorates the 58,000 American lives lost in Vietnam between 1959 and 1975.

Must Read: *The Best and the Brightest* by David Halberstam; *Vietnam: A History* by Stanley Karnow; *Our Vietnam: The War, 1954–1975* by A. J. Langguth.

What happened in Watts?

In the tumultuous decade after Rosa Parks refused to give up her bus seat (see Chapter 7), the civil rights movement coalesced behind the leadership of Martin Luther King Jr., achieved some gains through the courts and legislation, and moved the question of racial equality to the front burner of American life. For most of those ten years, blacks seemed willing to accept King's nonviolent vision of overcoming the hurdles of racism and segregation. But sometimes the front burner gets very hot. Before long, the pot was boiling over.

By 1965 the rhetoric and the actions of the civil rights movement changed because the country had changed. The war in Vietnam was moving into full swing. The year 1963 brought the assassination of President Kennedy, and Mississippi NAACP leader Medgar Evers (1925–63) was gunned down in front of his home in Jackson. The nonviolent integration movement was being met by violence and death. A Birmingham church was bombed, with four little girls killed. Goodman, Schwerner, and Chaney (see p. 464) were murdered in Mississippi in the summer of 1964. In February 1965, it was Malcolm X who went down. A month later, after thousands of marchers led by Martin Luther King, with U.S. Army protection, walked from Selma to Montgomery, a white civil rights worker named Viola Liuzzo was murdered. In the car with the Klansmen who shot her was an FBI informer.

Once solidly anchored by King's Southern Christian Leadership Council and the NAACP, with their emphasis on peaceful, court-ordered remedies, the movement was coming under fire. The violence in the air was producing a new generation of activists who lacked King's patience. Men like Floyd McKissick of the Congress for Racial Equality (CORE) and Stokely Carmichael of the Student Nonviolent Coordinating Committee (SNCC) were no longer willing to march to Dr. King's moderate tune. They preferred the martial drumbeat of Malcolm X's aggressive rhetoric. Built on frustration and anger, this basic split in tactics splintered the movement. By the summer of 1965, only days after the Voting Rights Act was signed into law, strengthening protection of black voter registration, the anger no longer just simmered. It boiled over. The scene was a section of Los Angeles called Watts.

This was not the Los Angeles of Hollywood, Malibu, and Bel Air. Watts was a rundown district of shabby houses built near the highway approaching Los Angeles International Airport. Ninety-eight percent black, Watts was stewing in a California heat wave. In the stewpot were all the ingredients of black anger. Poverty. Overcrowding. High unemployment. Crime everywhere. Drugs widely available. The nearly all-white police force was seen as an occupation army.

On August 11, a policeman pulled over a young black man to check him for drunken driving. A common occurrence for blacks, it happened much less frequently to white drivers. When the young man was arrested, a crowd gathered, at first joking and taunting, then growing more restive. Rumors of police brutality started to waft through the summer heat. The crowd grew larger and angrier. Soon the lone policeman called for reinforcements, and when the police arrived, they were met by hurled stones, bottles, and chunks of concrete. Within a few hours, the crowds had grown to a mob, and the frustration was no longer simmering in the August heat. It had exploded.

Watts was sealed off, and for a while all was quiet. But the next day the anger returned. By nightfall the small, roving bands had grown to a mob of thousands, hostile, angry, and beyond control. The rocks and bottles were replaced by Molotov cocktails as the riot erupted into a full-blown street rebellion. Black storeowners posted signs that read, "We Own This One." The signs didn't always help. Among the most popular looted items were weapons, and when police and firefighters responded to the violence and fires, they were met with a hail of bullets and gasoline bombs. All of the pent-up rage and helplessness boiled over in white-hot fury. Reason lost out. When Dick Gregory, the well-known standup comic and activist, tried to calm the crowds, he was shot in the leg. Mob frenzy had taken over. Watts was in flames.

The battle—for that was what it had become—raged on for days as thousands of national guardsmen poured in to restore order. There was open fighting in the streets as guardsmen set up machine-gun emplacements. Vietnam had seemingly come to L.A. By the sixth day of rioting, Watts was rubble and ashes. One European journalist even commented, "It looks like Germany during the last months of World War II."

The toll from six days of mayhem was thirty-four killed, including rioters and guardsmen; more than 1,000 injured; 4,000 arrested; and total property damage of more than $35 million.

But the aftermath of Watts was more than just a body count, police blotters, and insurance estimates. Something fundamental had occurred. There had been race riots before in America. In Detroit, during World War II, as many people had died as were killed in Watts.

There had been smaller riots in other northern cities in previous years. But Watts seemed to signal a sea change in the civil rights movement. When Martin Luther King toured the neighborhood, he was heckled. Saddened by the death and destruction, he admonished a local man, who responded, "We won because we made the whole world pay attention to us." The time of King's "soul power" was passing. The new call was for "black power."

The Watts summer of 1965 was only the first in a string of long, hot summers that left the cities of the North and Midwest smoldering with racial unrest. In the summer of 1966, several cities saw rioting. But the worst came in 1967, particularly when Newark and Detroit were engulfed in more rebellions. The death toll due to urban violence that year rose to more than eighty.

In the wake of these rebellions, presidential commissions were appointed, studies made, and findings released. They all agreed that the problem was economic at its roots. As Martin Luther King had put it, "I worked to get these people the right to eat hamburgers, and now I've got to do something to help them get the money to buy them." One of these studies, conducted by the National Advisory Commission on Civil Disorders, warned forebodingly that America was "moving toward two societies, one black, one white—separate and unequal."

That was on February 29, 1968. About a month later, Martin Luther King was killed in Memphis. His death set off another wave of riots that left cities smoldering. James Earl Ray, who confessed to the killing, was imprisoned. But nagging doubts, just as with the death of JFK, remain about the guilt of Ray—who died in 1998—and the existence of a wider conspiracy.

AMERICAN VOICES
RALPH NADER, from *Unsafe at Any Speed* (1965):

> **For more than half a century, the automobile has brought death, injury, and the most inestimable sorrow and deprivation to millions of people.**

Few politicians of the twentieth century have changed life in America as fundamentally as this lawyer born in Winsted, Connecticut, the son of Lebanese immigrants. Ralph Nader graduated from Princeton University and Harvard Law School and was working for the Department of Labor to crusade for "consumer protection"—the defense of the rights of consumers to safe products and ethical behavior from companies. His landmark book, *Unsafe at Any Speed*, argued that the U.S. automobile industry emphasized profits and style over safety. The National Traffic and Motor Vehicle Safety Act of 1966, which established safety standards for new cars, resulted largely from his work.

In later years, his studies resulted in stricter controls of the meat and poultry industries, coal mines, and natural gas pipelines. He publicized what he felt were the dangers of pesticides, food additives, radiation from color TV sets, and excessive use of X-rays. In 1971, Nader founded Public Citizen, Inc., which specialized in energy problems, health care, tax reform, and other consumer issues. Nader and his staff conducted a major study of Congress in 1972, and their findings were published in *Who Runs Congress?* In 1982, another Nader group published a study of the Reagan administration called *Reagan's Ruling Class: Portraits of the President's Top One Hundred Officials.* Nader was a coauthor of *The Big Boys: Power and Position in American Business* (1986), which looked at the structure and control of corporate business in the United States. Nader won another battle in 1989, when General Motors announced it would make air bags standard equipment on many 1990 models. Nader had promoted the use of the safety feature for more than ten years.

The same year that *Unsafe at Any Speed* was published witnessed another landmark event. Congress established a national Clearinghouse for Smoking and Health and ordered every cigarette package to come with a new label: "Caution: Cigarette smoking may be hazardous to your health." It was the beginning of a long anticigarette campaign that would fundamentally transform American society as few other social movements ever have. Before the surgeon general's 1964 report that linked cigarette smoking to lung cancer, cigarettes were part of the American way of life. By the end of the century, antismoking legislation had converted smokers into near pariahs, changing eating patterns in restaurants and work routines as smokers were forced to grab a smoke during breaks while standing outside their office buildings.

Who was Miranda?

For anyone who grew up on a TV diet of Joe Friday and *Dragnet*, *Streets of San Francisco*, *NYPD Blue*, and a hundred other cop shows, "Read him his rights" is a familiar bit of requisite dialogue. That is, for any cop shows that came after 1966. To America's lawmen, that was the year that the world started to come unglued.

Ernesto Miranda was hardly the kind of guy who might be expected to change legal history. But he did, in his own savage way. A high school dropout with a criminal record dating from his teen years, Miranda abducted a teenage girl at a Phoenix moviehouse candy counter in 1963 and drove her into the desert, where he raped her. Having a criminal record, Miranda was soon picked up, and was identified by the victim in a police lineup. After making a written confession in which he stated that he had been informed of his rights, Miranda was convicted and sentenced to prison for forty to fifty-five years. But at the trial, Miranda's court-appointed attorney argued that his client had not been told of his right to legal counsel.

The American Civil Liberties Union took the case of *Miranda v. Arizona* all the way to the Supreme Court, where it was heard by the Warren Court in 1966. The issue was the Fifth Amendment's protection against self-incrimination. On June 13, 1966, the Court announced a five-to-four ruling in favor of Miranda that said a criminal suspect must be told of his right to silence, that his remarks may be used against him, and that he had a right to counsel during interrogation, even if he could not afford one.

Depending on your point of view, it was either a great milestone for civil liberties and the protection of the rights of both the innocent and the criminal, or the beginning of the end of civilization.

And the notorious Miranda? On the basis of new evidence, he was convicted again on the same charges of kidnapping and rape, and imprisoned. He was eventually paroled, and ten years after the Court inscribed his name in legal history, Ernesto Miranda died of a knife wound suffered during a bar fight.

AMERICAN VOICES
MUHAMMAD ALI, heavyweight boxing champion:

Float like a butterfly, sting like a bee.
That's why they call me Muhammad Ali.

Few athletes reflect, or actually change, history as Muhammad Ali did. Born Cassius Marcellus Clay in Louisville, Kentucky, Muhammad Ali (b. 1942) became a professional boxer after winning the light heavyweight gold medal at the 1960 Summer Olympics. In 1964, he won the world heavyweight championship by knocking out Sonny Liston in an upset. And there the controversy began, and it would soon extend far beyond the boxing ring, or even sports.

Profoundly influenced by Malcolm X, Cassius Clay joined the Black Muslims, or Nation of Islam, in 1967 and changed his name to Muhammad Ali, rejecting his birth name as a "slave name." (In fact, American slave holders had typically given their slaves the names of Roman nobility.) He said he even threw his Olympic gold medal into the Ohio River.

During the next few years, Ali became one of the most colorful and controversial boxing champions of all time, said to be the world's most recognizable man. Widely admired for his extraordinary grace, speed, and boxing skills, he was equally disdained for his boastfulness as he made up poems that mocked his opponents or predicted, in verse, the round in which he would score a knockout.

But if he was disliked for these attitudes before 1967, his name change and adoption of the Muslim faith further alienated much of white America, which in the 1960s still wanted its athletes to be seen — on the playing fields — but not heard. Especially if they were considered "loudmouthed and uppity," as Ali was widely viewed. But in an era when "Black is beautiful" became a new motto for young blacks and soul singer James Brown was beginning the chant of "Say it loud, I'm black and I'm proud," Muhammad Ali was the living embodiment of both phrases. As other black leaders, like Malcolm X and Martin Luther King, fell, Muhammad Ali was lionized by a younger generation that was no longer content with the status quo.

The stakes changed later in 1967, when Ali offered a different rhyme:

> *Keep asking me no matter how long—*
> *On the war in Vietnam I sing this song—*
> *I ain't got no quarrel with the Viet Cong.*

Saying that "No Viet Cong ever called me nigger," Ali refused induction into the United States Army, basing his decision on religious principles. He was convicted on charges of refusing induction and sentenced to prison, but appealed the decision and stayed out of jail. However, most boxing groups stripped Ali of his title and, after his conviction, Ali could not box for three and a half years. While out of the ring, Ali remained on the world stage, and his views on the war and a racist America profoundly influenced a younger generation that was rejecting both the war and racism. At the 1968 Olympics in Mexico City, American sprinters hung their heads and raised their fists in a clenched-fist "black power" salute during the medal ceremony. It was an audacious display that cost the sprinters their medals and indicated how divided the country had become.

In 1971, the Supreme Court of the United States reversed Ali's conviction and he began a remarkable comeback and second career with a series of legendary fights against Joe Frazier. He regained the heavyweight championship by knocking out George Foreman, the defending champion, in Africa in 1974. Early in 1978, Ali lost the title to Leon Spinks in one of the greatest upsets in boxing history, but regained the title for a fourth time when he defeated Spinks in a rematch. In 1979, Ali gave up his title and announced his retirement. But in 1980, he came out of retirement and fought Larry Holmes for the World Boxing Council version of the title. Holmes defeated Ali by a technical knockout.

A few years later, Ali was diagnosed with Parkinson's disease, which many doctors attributed to the many severe blows he had absorbed in his remarkable career.

What happened at My Lai?

On March 16, 1968, in a small Vietnamese village, "something dark and bloody" took place. With those words, a lone veteran of the war forced the U.S. Army to reluctantly examine a secret that was no secret. America was forced to look at itself in a manner once reserved for enemies who had committed war crimes. With those words, America found out about the massacre of civilians by U.S. soldiers at My Lai.

The GIs of Charlie Company called it Pinkville. That was how it was colored on their maps of Vietnam's Quang Ngai province, because the village was suspected of being a stronghold for the Vietcong. Under the command of Lieutenant William L. Calley, Charlie Company of the American Division's Eleventh Infantry had nebulous orders from its company commander, Captain Ernest Medina, to "clean the village out." In the previous three months, Charlie Company had taken about 100 casualties without even seeing action. Sniper fire and booby traps were to blame. Frustrated and angry at the hand they had been dealt in a war in which there were no uniforms to separate "good gooks" from "bad gooks," the men of Charlie Company were primed to wreak havoc on a phantom enemy they had never been able to confront in an open battle.

Dropped into the village by helicopter, the men of Charlie Company found only the old men, women, and children of My Lai. There were no Vietcong, and no signs of any. There were no stashed weapons, no rice caches, nothing to suggest that My Lai was a staging base for guerrilla attacks. But under Lieutenant Calley's direct orders, the villagers were forced into the center of the hamlet, where Calley issued the order to shoot them. The defenseless villagers were mowed down by automatic weapons fire. Then the villagers' huts were grenaded, some of them while still occupied. Finally, small groups of survivors—some of them women and girls who had been raped by the Americans—were rounded up and herded into a drainage ditch, where they, too, were mercilessly machine-gunned. A few of the soldiers of Charlie Company refused to follow the order; one of them later called it "point-blank murder."

AMERICAN VOICES

VARNADO SIMPSON, a member of Lt. Calley's unit,
describing My Lai on March 16, 1968 (quoted in *Four
Hours in My Lai* by Michael Bilton and Kevin Sim):

That day in My Lai, I was personally responsible for killing
about twenty-five people. Personally. Men, women. From
shooting them, to cutting their throats, scalping them, to
cutting off their hands and cutting out their tongues. I did
it. I just went. My mind just went. And I wasn't the only
one that did it. A lot of other people did it. I just killed. . . .
I didn't know I had it in me.

During the massacre, Hugh C. Thompson, a twenty-five-year-old
helicopter pilot, saw the bodies in the ditch and went down to investigate. Placing his helicopter between the GIs and a band of children,
the pilot ordered his crew to shoot any American who tried to stop him.
He managed to rescue a handful of children. But that was one of the
day's few heroic deeds. Another witness to the massacre was an army
photographer who was ordered to turn over his official camera, but
kept a second, secret, camera. With it, he had recorded the mayhem in
which more than 560 Vietnamese, mostly women and children, were
slaughtered. Those pictures, when they later surfaced, revealed the extent of the carnage at My Lai. But not right away. Although many in
the chain of command knew something "dark and bloody" had happened that day, there was no investigation. The mission was reported
as a success back at headquarters.

But Ronald Ridenhour, a veteran of Charlie Company who had
not been at My Lai, began to hear the rumors from buddies. Piecing
together what had happened, he detailed the events in a letter he sent
to President Nixon, to key members of Congress, and to officials in the
State Department and Pentagon. The dirty little secret of My Lai was
out. Then reporter Seymour Hersh also got wind of the story and broke
it to an incredulous America in November 1968. Within a few weeks,
the army opened an investigation, but it remained secret. More than
a year had passed since the day My Lai became a killing ground. It
would be another two years before anyone was tried in the case.

In the immediate aftermath of the investigation, several officers still on active duty were court-martialed for dereliction of duty for covering up the massacre, a word the Pentagon never used. At worst, they were reduced in rank or censured. Four officers—Calley, Medina, Captain Eugene Kotouc, and Lieutenant Thomas Willingham—were court-martialed. Medina was acquitted, but later confessed that he had lied under oath to Army investigators. The other two officers were also acquitted. Only Lieutenant Calley was found guilty of premeditated murder of twenty-two villagers at My Lai, on March 29, 1971. Two days later, he was sentenced to life imprisonment. But President Nixon then reduced his sentence to house arrest in response to an outpouring of public support for Calley, who was seen as a scapegoat. Calley was later paroled. A documentary about My Lai that was broadcast in 1989 showed Calley, a prosperous businessman, getting into an expensive foreign car and driving off. He refused to comment on the incident.

To the war's supporters on the right, the atrocity at My Lai was an aberration and Calley a victim of a "leftist" antiwar movement. To the war's opponents, Calley and My Lai epitomized the war's immorality and injustice. In a sense, My Lai was the outcome of forcing young Americans into an unwinnable war. It has now been well documented that this was not the only crime against civilians in Vietnam. It was not uncommon to see GIs use their Zippo lighters to torch an entire village. As one officer said early in the war, after torching a hamlet, "We had to destroy this village to save it." That Alice in Wonderland logic perfectly embodied the impossibility of the American position.

Even though the United States would drop 7 *million tons* of bombs—twice the total dropped on Europe and Asia during all of World War II—on an area about the size of Massachusetts, along with Agent Orange and other chemical defoliants, the United States was losing the war. The political and military leadership of this country failed to understand the Vietnamese character, traditions, culture, and history. That failure doomed America to its costly and tragic defeat in Vietnam. As A. J. Langguth wrote in his excellent history of the war, *Our Vietnam*, "North Vietnam's leaders had deserved to win. South Vietnam's leaders had deserved to lose. And America's leaders, for thirty years, had failed the people of the North, the people of the South, and the people of the United States."

Astronaut NEIL ARMSTRONG (b. 1930) on July 20,
1969, as he became the first man to walk on the Moon:

**That was one small step for [a] man, one giant leap for
mankind.**

Armstrong's words, and the images of him stepping onto the lunar
surface, were seen and heard by the entire world. The moment was the
culmination of the obsessive push for putting a man on the Moon, a
challenge that began with the humiliation of Sputnik (see Chapter 7).
Armstrong and fellow Moon walker Buzz Aldrin planted an American
flag on the lunar surface and left a plaque that read, "Here men from
the planet Earth first set foot upon the Moon July, 1969 A.D. We came
in peace for all mankind."

How did a successful break-in in Pennsylvania change the FBI?

On the night of March 8, 1971, burglars broke into the offices of the
FBI in Media, Pennsylvania, and stole more than a thousand documents. Within two weeks of the break-in, copies of the stolen material were being sent to members of Congress and the media by the
enterprising and crusading burglars, who were never caught. One of
the documents that appeared in the *Washington Post* used the word
COINTELPRO. An NBC newsman who was an attorney made a Freedom of Information Act request for all COINTELPRO documents.
After a series of legal maneuvers by the FBI, one of J. Edgar Hoover's
secrets was out: COINTELPRO, which stood for Counter Intelligence
Program, was a twenty-year-old FBI campaign of illegal and improper
activities aimed at harassing political targets. Begun under J. Edgar
Hoover in 1956 to target the Communist Party in America for investigation and disruption, already then dwindling, the program continued for the next two decades. Eventually, domestic targets such as the
Socialist Workers Party, the Black Panthers, and the Ku Klux Klan
were victims of the FBI's illicit and almost laughably foolish smear

campaigns and illegal wiretaps. In the early days of the program, Ronald Kessler writes in *The Bureau*, "Agents questioned party officials at their places of employment to intimidate their employers, . . . planted evidence so that local police would arrest party members, and left what appeared to be FBI informant reports on the cars of party officials so that the party would drop them as suspected snitches. . . . The bureau informed the parents of one woman that she was living with a Communist out of wedlock. . . . The tactics were no different than those used by the KGB in Russia."

These might seem like innocent pranks, amateurish at times — almost amusing, if they weren't so potentially and actually dangerous, as events would prove.

By the early 1970s, COINTELPRO had widened its focus to include the antiwar movement and elements of the civil rights movement. When some antiwar groups turned to violence, most notably the Weathermen — or Weather Underground — Hoover turned COINTELPRO loose on them. During a wiretap of a Black Panther group, the FBI learned that actress Jean Seberg was pregnant. An international star of such movies as the French classic *Breathless* and *Lilith*, Seberg had become an outspoken opponent of both the war and American racism, and financially supported the Panthers. According to FBI documents, J. Edgar Hoover ordered, "Jean Seberg . . . should be neutralized." In 1970, the FBI leaked the rumor that Seberg was carrying the child of a member of the Black Panthers to an accommodating media. She had apparently had affairs with some members of the group, but none of them was the father of her child. But her pregnancy became the focus of international attention, and the paternity of the unborn child was "smeared" in papers and magazines, including *Newsweek* and the *Los Angeles Times*. The child was born prematurely in 1970 and died two days later. The body was then displayed in an open coffin to prove that she was white. (Seberg and her estranged husband, Romain Gary, a French writer, sued *Newsweek* in France and the magazine was forced to pay damages for invasion of privacy.) Seberg became increasingly despondent over the years, turning to pills and alcohol, and finally committed suicide in 1979.

The Seberg rumors had been manufactured by COINTELPRO. When the COINTELPRO program was revealed in 1971, Hoover ordered it shut down. For years the most powerful man in Washington because of the secret files he maintained on almost every politician and celebrity in America, Hoover survived the calls for his resignation, serving as director of the FBI until his death in 1972. But America was going to soon learn that COINTELPRO wasn't the only instance of the FBI being put to political use.

Why did Richard Nixon and Henry Kissinger try to stop the *New York Times* from publishing the Pentagon Papers?

In the summer of 1971, President Richard Nixon learned that what you don't know *can* hurt you.

In June 1971, the *New York Times* ran a headline that hardly seemed sensational: "Vietnam Archive: Pentagon Study Traces 3 Decades of Growing U.S. Involvement." What the headline did not say was that the study also traced thirty years of deceit and ineptitude on the part of the United States government.

In page after numbingly detailed page, the *Times* reprinted thousands of documents, cables, position papers, and memos, all referring to the American effort in Vietnam. Officially titled *The History of the U.S. Decision Making Process in Vietnam*, the material quickly became known as the Pentagon Papers. Richard Nixon was not aware of its existence. But it would shake his administration and the military establishment in America to their toes.

Ordered by Robert McNamara, one of Kennedy's "best and brightest" prior to his resignation as defense secretary in 1968, this massive compilation had involved the work of large teams of scholars and analysts. The avalanche of paper ran to some 2 million words. Among the men who had helped put it together was Daniel Ellsberg, a Rand Corporation analyst and onetime hawk who, like McNamara himself, became disillusioned by the war. Working at MIT after his resignation from Rand, which was involved in collecting and analyzing the papers, Ellsberg decided to go public with the information. He turned a copy over to *Times* reporter Neil Sheehan.

When the story broke, the country soon learned how it had been duped. Going back to the Truman administration, the Pentagon

Papers revealed a history of deceptions, policy disagreements within several White House administrations, and outright lies. Among the most damaging revelations were cables from the American embassy in Saigon, dating from the weeks before Prime Minister Diem was ousted with CIA encouragement and then executed. There was the discovery that the Tonkin Resolution had been drafted months before the incident occurred from which it took its name. And there were memos showing Lyndon Johnson committing infantry to Vietnam at the same time he was telling the country that he had no long-range plans for a strategy in Vietnam.

The papers did not cover the Nixon years, and White House reaction was at first muted, even gleeful at the prospect of the embarrassment it would create for the Democrats. But Nixon and his national security adviser, Henry Kissinger (b. 1923), soon realized that if something this highly classified could be leaked, so could other secrets. Both men were already troubled by leaks within the administration. How could they carry on the business of national security if documents this sensitive could be photocopied and handed out to the nation's newspapers like press releases? There was a second concern. The revelations in the Pentagon Papers had fueled the antiwar sentiment that was growing louder and angrier and moving off the campuses and into the halls of Congress.

The administration first tried to bully the *Times* into halting publication. Attorney General John Mitchell threatened the paper with espionage charges. These were ignored. Nixon then tried the courts and received a temporary injunction blocking further publication. But the brushfire started by the *Times* was growing into a forest fire. The *Washington Post* and the *Boston Globe* were also running the documents. A federal court ordered the *Post* to halt publication, and the question went to the Supreme Court. On June 30, the Court ruled six to three in favor of the newspapers on First Amendment grounds.

Kissinger and Nixon went nuclear. Said Nixon, "I want to know who is behind this. . . . I want it done, whatever the costs."

When Ellsberg was revealed as the culprit, a new White House unit was formed to investigate him. Their job was to stop leaks, so they were jokingly called the "plumbers." White House assistant Egil Krogh,

Nixon special counsel Charles Colson, and others in the White House turned to former CIA man E. Howard Hunt and ex-FBI agent G. Gordon Liddy to bring their special clandestine talents to the operation. One of their first jobs was to conduct a break-in at the offices of Daniel Ellsberg's psychiatrist. As a burglary, it was only marginally more successful than the next break-in planned by the group, at an office complex called Watergate.

Apart from setting into motion some of the events that would mutate into the Watergate affair, the publication of the Pentagon Papers had other important repercussions. From the government's standpoint, American security credibility had been crippled, severely damaging intelligence operations around the world, for better or worse. On the other side, the antiwar movement gained new strength and respectability, increasing the pressure on Nixon to end the U.S. involvement in Vietnam. And the Supreme Court's action in protecting the newspapers from prior restraint established and strengthened First Amendment principles.

But the Pentagon Papers case also reinforced a "bunker mentality" that already existed within the White House "palace guard." There was an us-against-them defensiveness emanating from the Oval Office. Publication of the Pentagon Papers made the Nixon White House far more aggressive in its defense of "national security," an idea that was expanded to include the protection and reelection of Richard Nixon by any means and at any cost.

Why did "Jane Roe" sue Wade?

"To be or not to be." For Shakespeare and the Supreme Court, that was and is the question. There is no other issue more emotionally, politically, or legally divisive in modern America than the future of abortion rights.

Many Americans thought the question was settled on January 22, 1973. That was the day the Supreme Court decided, by a seven-to-two margin, that it was unconstitutional for states to prohibit voluntary abortions before the third month of pregnancy; the decision also limited prohibitions that states might set during the second three months.

The decision grew out of a Texas case involving a woman who, out of desire to protect her privacy, was called Jane Roe in court papers. "Roe" was Norma McCorvey, a single woman living in Texas who became pregnant. She desired an abortion, but was unable to obtain one legally in her home state of Texas, and so she gave birth to a child she put up for adoption. Nonetheless, she brought suit against Dallas County District Attorney Henry Wade in an attempt to overturn the restrictive Texas abortion codes. The case ultimately reached the Supreme Court, which made the decision in the case known as *Roe v. Wade*.

For sixteen years the *Roe* precedent influenced a series of rulings that liberalized abortion in America. To many Americans, the right to an abortion was a basic matter of private choice, a decision for the woman to make. But to millions of Americans, *Roe* was simply government-sanctioned murder.

The mostly conservative foes of legal abortion—who call their movement "pro-life"—gained strength in the 1980s, coalescing behind Ronald Reagan and contributing to his election. And it will ultimately be Reagan's legacy through his appointments to the Supreme Court who determine the future of *Roe v. Wade*. In the summer of 1989, the Supreme Court decided five to four, in the case of *Webster v. Reproductive Health Services*, to give states expanded authority to limit abortion rights. The Court also announced that it would hear a series of cases that would give it the opportunity to completely overturn the *Roe* decision. (In 1998, McCorvey announced a conversion to Christianity and a complete break with the pro-choice movement. Henry Wade, the Dallas prosecutor she had sued and who also prosecuted Jack Ruby, the man who killed Lee Harvey Oswald, died in 2001.)

AMERICAN VOICES
From JUSTICE HARRY A. BLACKMUN's majority
decision in *Roe v. Wade* (January 22, 1973):

The Constitution does not explicitly mention any right of privacy. In a line of decisions, however . . . the Court has recognized that a right of personal privacy, or a guarantee of certain areas or zones of privacy, does exist under the Constitution. . . . They also make it clear that the right has some extension to activities relating to marriage; procreation; contraception; family relationships; and child rearing and education.

The right of privacy . . . is broad enough to encompass a woman's decision whether or not to terminate her pregnancy. . . . We need not resolve the difficult question of when life begins. When those trained in the respective disciplines of medicine, philosophy, and theology are unable to arrive at any consensus, the judiciary, at this point in the development of man's knowledge, is not in a position to speculate as to the answer.

How did a botched burglary become a crisis called Watergate and bring down a powerful president?

Break-ins and buggings. Plumbers and perjury. Secret tapes, smoking guns, and slush funds.

We know now that Watergate wasn't what Nixon press secretary Ron Ziegler called it, "a third-rate burglary." This nationally televised soap opera of corruption, conspiracy, and criminality only began to unravel with a botched break-in at the Watergate office complex. That ludicrous larceny was only a tiny strand in the web of domestic spying, criminal acts, illegal campaign funds, enemies lists, and obstruction of justice that emerged from the darkness as "Watergate." But it ended up with Richard Nixon resigning from the presidency in disgrace and only a few steps ahead of the long arm of the law.

After the Civil War and Vietnam, few episodes in American history have generated as many written words as the Watergate affair. Just about everybody who participated in this extraordinary chapter ended up writing a book about his view of the events. They were joined by the dozens of historians, journalists, and other writers who turned out books. The notoriety of Watergate gave convicted felon E. Howard Hunt a renewed lease on a life as a writer of inferior spy novels, a

pursuit in which he was joined by John Ehrlichman and even Spiro
Agnew, another of the rats who went down with the sinking ship that
was Richard Nixon's second administration. Even the rabidly right-
wing former FBI agent G. Gordon Liddy was able to parlay his macho,
fanatical, "hand over a lighted candle" image into a lucrative career
including playing guest roles on the eighties television series *Miami
Vice*, founding a "survivalist" camp to teach commando techniques to
weekend warriors, and going on a lecture tour that pitted Liddy in the
role of mad-dog conservative against sixties relic Timothy Leary, the
onetime high priest of psychedelic drugs.

This ludicrous aftermath has been combined with some of the
comical aspects of the bungled break-in and Howard Hunt's notoriously bad CIA-provided disguises to soften the image of Watergate's
implications. It seems almost opéra bouffe, a lighthearted satire. But
that perspective overlooks the seriousness of the crimes committed in
the name of national security and Richard Nixon's reelection—two
objectives that a large number of high-placed fanatics equated with
each other.

AMERICAN VOICES
RICHARD NIXON, from the Oval Office tapes:

I don't give a shit what happens, I want you to stonewall it,
let them plead the Fifth Amendment, cover up or anything
else, if it'll save the plan.

A WATERGATE CHRONOLOGY
1972

June 17   At the Watergate Office Building in Washington, D.C., five
men are arrested during a pathetically bungled break-in at the offices of the Democratic National Committee (DNC). The men are
all carrying cash and documents that show them to be employed
by the Committee to Re-elect the President (later given the acronym CREEP), and the purpose of the burglary is to plant listening
devices in the phones of Democratic leaders and obtain political

documents regarding the Democrats' campaign strategy. The men arrested include a former FBI agent and four anti-Castro Cubans who have been told that they are looking for material linking Castro to the Democratic Party. Two former White House aides working for CREEP, G. Gordon Liddy and E. Howard Hunt, are also arrested. Hunt, it will be learned, was one of the CIA agents responsible for planning the Bay of Pigs invasion and some of the Cubans arrested also took part in the invasion. The seven men are indicted on September 15. Even though their relationship to the election committee is established, none of the seven men connects the committee or the White House to the break-in.

November 7   After an October Gallup poll shows that less than half of the American people have even heard of the break-in, President Nixon defeats his Democratic challenger Senator George McGovern in a landslide, capturing 60.8 percent of the popular vote and 520 of the 537 electoral votes. McGovern carries only Massachusetts and Washington, D.C.

December 8   The wife of E. Howard Hunt dies in a plane crash in Chicago. She is carrying $10,000 in $100 bills. The money is "hush money" she was ferrying to someone in Chicago.

1973

February 7   Amid swirling rumors of widespread wrongdoing, corrupt financing, and political dirty tricks committed by the Nixon reelection committee, the Senate establishes a Select Committee on Presidential Campaign Activities, chaired by North Carolina Senator Sam Ervin (1896–1985).

March 23   Former CIA agent James W. McCord, one of the seven men convicted in the attempted burglary, admits in a letter to Judge John Sirica that he and other defendants have been under pressure to remain silent about the case. McCord reveals that others were involved in the break-in, and he eventually names John Mitchell, the former attorney general who had become chairman of the Committee to Re-elect the President, as the "overall boss."

April 20 L. Patrick Gray, acting director of the FBI, resigns after admitting he destroyed evidence connected to Watergate, on the advice of Nixon aides in the White House.

April 30 Nixon's chief of staff, H. R. Haldeman, domestic affairs assistant John Ehrlichman, and presidential counsel John Dean III all resign. In a televised speech announcing the shake-up, President Nixon denies any knowledge of a cover-up of White House involvement in the Watergate break-in.

May 11 Charges against Daniel Ellsberg and Anthony J. Russo are dropped for their theft and release of the Pentagon Papers. The judge makes this decision following the revelation that Watergate conspirators E. Howard Hunt and G. Gordon Liddy had burglarized the office of Ellsberg's psychiatrist in an attempt to steal Ellsberg's medical records.

June 25 Testifying before Ervin's Senate committee, John Dean accuses President Nixon of involvement in the Watergate cover-up and says the president authorized payment of "hush money" to the seven men arrested in the break-in.

July 16 In testimony that rocks the nation, White House aide Alexander Butterfield tells the Ervin committee that President Nixon secretly recorded all Oval Office conversations. This startling revelation provides the committee with the means to substantiate testimony implicating the president in the cover-up of the Watergate burglary. It also sets off a constitutional crisis over the president's right to keep the tapes secret under the umbrella of "executive privilege."

October 10 In an unrelated development that further damages White House credibility, Vice President Spiro Agnew, the chief voice of "law and order" in the Nixon White House, resigns after pleading nolo contendere (no contest) to tax evasion charges dating from his days as governor of Maryland. Two days later, President Nixon nominates House Minority Leader Gerald Ford to succeed Agnew under the provisions of the Twenty-fifth Amendment, allowing the president to fill a vacancy in the vice presidency.

October 20   The Saturday Night Massacre. President Nixon orders Attorney General Elliot Richardson to fire Watergate Special Prosecutor Archibald Cox, who has refused to accept the president's compromise offer to release a "synopsis" of the tapes. Richardson and his assistant, William D. Ruckelshaus, refuse to follow this order and both resign. Solicitor General Robert Bork, third in the Justice Department chain of command, fires Cox. (The Democrats' revenge will come when Ronald Reagan nominates Bork to the Supreme Court in 1988. Bork's nomination will open an acrimonious debate over his legal views, and he will be rejected by the Senate.) The resignations and the firing of Cox raise a storm of protest in Congress, and the House actively begins to consider impeachment of the president.

October 23   The House Judiciary Committee, chaired by Representative Peter Rodino, announces an investigation into impeachment charges against the president. Leon Jaworski is appointed special prosecutor in the Watergate investigation after Archibald Cox's firing.

October 30   After Nixon reluctantly agrees to turn over the Oval Office tapes, investigators learn that two tapes are missing.

November 21   Investigators learn that one of the tapes contains a mysterious eighteen-and-a-half-minute gap. The White House claims that Rosemary Woods, Nixon's secretary, accidentally erased part of the tape while transcribing it, a feat that, owing to the way the recording apparatus was set up, would have required the skills of a contortionist. (In January 1974, analysis of the tape will show that the erasure was deliberate.)

November 9   Six of the Watergate defendants are sentenced for their roles in the break-in. E. Howard Hunt receives a sentence of two and a half to eight years and a $10,000 fine. The others are given lesser sentences. G. Gordon Liddy is sentenced to twenty years, in part because of his refusal to cooperate with investigators.

November 13   Representatives of two oil companies plead guilty to making illegal contributions to the Nixon campaign. The next day,

Commerce Secretary Maurice Stans, who was the Nixon campaign treasurer, admits that such contributions were expected from major corporations. Two days later, three more companies—Goodyear, Braniff Airlines, and American Airlines—report similar donations.

November 30 Egil Krogh Jr., who headed the White House "plumbers" unit, pleads guilty to charges stemming from the break-in at the offices of Daniel Ellsberg's psychiatrist.

December 6 Gerald Ford is sworn in as vice president. Besides having been a member of the Warren Commission investigating the death of President Kennedy, Ford is best known for what Lyndon Johnson once said about him: "Shucks, I don't think he can chew gum and walk at the same time. . . . He's a nice fellow, but he spent too much time playing football without a helmet."

1974

January 4 Claiming "executive privilege," President Nixon refuses to surrender 500 tapes and documents subpoenaed by the Senate Watergate Committee.

March 1 Seven former White House staff members, including Haldeman, Ehrlichman, and former attorney general John Mitchell, are indicted for conspiring to obstruct the investigation of the Watergate break-in.

April 3 Following months of investigation by a separate congressional committee, President Nixon agrees to pay more than $400,000 in back taxes. Using suspect deductions, the president had paid taxes equivalent to those levied on a salary of $15,000, despite the president's $200,000 salary and other income.

April 29 In another nationally televised address, President Nixon offers a 1,200-page edited transcript of the tapes subpoenaed by the House Judiciary Committee and Special Prosecutor Jaworski. Both Jaworski and the committee reject the transcripts.

May 16 Richard Kleindienst, John Mitchell's successor as attorney general, pleads guilty to a misdemeanor charge of failing to testify accurately before a Senate committee. Kleindienst is the first attorney general ever convicted of a crime.

July 24 The Supreme Court rules unanimously that Nixon must turn over the tapes requested by the special prosecutor. Eight hours later, the White House announces it will comply with the order.

July 27 The House Judiciary Committee approves two articles of impeachment against Nixon, charging him with obstructing justice and accusing him of repeatedly violating his oath of office. Three days later the committee will recommend a third charge of unconstitutional defiance of committee subpoenas.

August 5 In another televised address, Nixon releases transcripts of a conversation with chief of staff H. R. Haldeman. The transcript shows that, six days after the break-in, Nixon ordered a halt to the FBI investigation of the affair. Nixon concedes that he failed to include this information in earlier statements, what he calls "a serious omission." This is the "smoking gun" that everybody has been looking for. Following the speech, Nixon's remaining congressional support disappears.

August 8 President Nixon announces his resignation, effective noon the following day. The decision comes in the wake of his revelation three days earlier, after which key Republican congressmen told him he would probably be impeached and convicted.

August 9 President Nixon formally resigns and leaves for California. Vice President Gerald Ford is sworn in as president.

August 21 President Ford nominates Nelson Rockefeller, the wealthy governor of New York and a three-time candidate for the Republican presidential nomination, as his choice for vice president.

September 8 President Ford grants Richard Nixon a "full, free and absolute pardon . . . for all offenses against the United States which he . . . has committed or may have committed or taken part in while President."

1975

January 1 Four of the former White House staffers charged with obstruction are found guilty. They are H. R. Haldeman, John Ehrlichman, John Mitchell, and White House attorney Robert Mardian. A fifth, Nixon assistant Kenneth Parkinson, is acquitted. The Watergate charges against Charles Colson are dropped after he pleads guilty to crimes connected with the Ellsberg-psychiatrist break-in. A seventh defendant, Gordon Strachan, is tried separately.

1976

In the presidential election, Jimmy Carter narrowly defeats President Ford. Besides the economic problems facing the country, Carter's victory is widely attributed to the post-Watergate atmosphere of cynicism and a very specific rejection of Ford for his pardon of Nixon in September 1974.

The final accounting of the Watergate affair produced an impressive list of "high crimes and misdemeanors," as the Constitution labels impeachable offenses. Some of them seem laughably innocuous in retrospect. But others were offenses against the law, against individual citizens, and against the Constitution itself. The Watergate "rap sheet" breaks down into five general categories, as follows:

1. BREAKING AND ENTERING

In the wake of the publication of the Pentagon Papers, Daniel Ellsberg became the prime target of the "plumbers." One of the group's first missions was to break into the office of Ellsberg's psychiatrist and steal Ellsberg's confidential medical records. Although they got in, they were unable to find any incriminating or embarrassing material about Ellsberg.

Some of the same team members later planned the break-in at the Democratic National Committee offices to install listening devices. This job was ordered by White House officials and with the knowledge of some of the president's closest advisers.

2. ILLEGAL CONTRIBUTIONS

A secret slush fund, controlled by Attorney General John Mitchell, was set up to finance a campaign of "dirty tricks" against key Democratic Party figures. Some of this money was used to pay the Watergate burglars for the job and later to keep them silent.

The slush fund was built out of illegal campaign contributions solicited by Nixon officials from some of the country's largest corporations, who thought they were buying "access" to the president. Other contributions were made to derail criminal investigations or antitrust activities going on in the Justice Department.

3. DIRTY TRICKS

Like the "plumbers," the dirty tricks team was set up in the White House for the purpose of damaging and embarrassing key Democrats. In fact, the Democrats didn't need any help—they were doing just fine by themselves. The activities ranged from ordering pizzas delivered to Democratic campaign offices to forging letters that were used to discredit and embarrass Democratic leaders like Senators Edmund Muskie and Henry Jackson.

Using material he culled from the Pentagon Papers, E. Howard Hunt forged cables that implied that President John Kennedy ordered the toppling and assassination of Vietnam's prime minister Diem in 1963. Hunt then tried unsuccessfully to plant these cables with major news magazines.

An "enemies list" was created, an extensive collection of opposition politicians, entertainers, newsmen, and other prominent public figures deemed disloyal by the White House. The list was used to target the people that the White House wanted to "screw" through the use of selected federal agencies. The list included Jane Fonda, Bill Cosby, and CBS newsman Daniel Schorr.

4. COVER-UP/OBSTRUCTION OF JUSTICE

White House officials, from the president down to lower-echelon staffers, ordered the payment of hush money from the campaign slush fund to the Watergate conspirators. These men also orchestrated the cover-up of White House involvement in the conspiracy.

President Nixon secretly pledged clemency to the Watergate burglars in return for their silence.

L. Patrick Gray, acting head of the FBI and in line for appointment to the permanent job of director, turned over FBI files on Watergate to White House staffers.

Nixon ordered ranking CIA officers to dissuade the FBI from investigating Watergate.

Incriminating evidence in E. Howard Hunt's White House safe was removed and destroyed.

Two of the White House tapes subpoenaed by the special prosecutor were discovered to be missing. Another tape contained a crucial eighteen-minute gap, the result of a deliberate erasure.

5. MISCELLANEOUS OFFENSES AND REVELATIONS

Nixon had used more than $10 million in government funds for improvements on his private homes in Florida and California, ostensibly in the name of "security." (The House did not include this charge as an impeachable offense. It was deemed a personal offense rather than an act against the state.)

Nixon had taken illegal tax deductions on some papers donated to a presidential library.

The illegal secret war against Cambodia was revealed.

What was the real payback for these abuses? President Nixon resigned in disgrace. But he was quickly pardoned, guaranteeing that his pension checks would keep coming. Within a short time, Nixon was "rehabilitated" by his party and the press, gradually easing his way back into a new role as "elder statesman" and foreign policy expert. Nixon died in 1994 and was eulogized by Democratic president Bill Clinton, whose wife, Hillary, had once been an assistant on the House Judiciary Committee and was involved in researching impeachment history for the Committee. (She and her husband would, of course, learn much more about impeachment, along with the rest of the country, in 1998, when Clinton became the second president in American history to be impeached. See Chapter 9.)

Liddy and Hunt both went to prison. Liddy wrote a book called *Will*, which was turned into a television miniseries. He later became a nationally syndicated radio talk show host, appealing to an extremely conservative audience. Hunt continued to write spy novels. John Mitchell was jailed and disbarred. His book was rejected by its publisher. Mitchell died in 1988.

Haldeman and Ehrlichman, the two aides closest to Nixon, also served brief jail terms. Both wrote successful books. John Dean served four months, but wrote *Blind Ambition,* his memoir of the Watergate affair, a best-seller also turned into a television miniseries.

Many of the other minor characters in Watergate served brief prison terms. A spate of legislation addressing the issues of ethics in government, campaign financing, and presidential powers all followed in Watergate's wake. The ensuing years brought more investigations that further revealed the extent of the abuses committed by the FBI and the CIA in the name of national security. More laws were passed.

Watergate and those revelations cost the Republicans the White House in 1976, when Gerald Ford, the man who pardoned Nixon, was defeated by Jimmy Carter, who ran as an "outsider" pledged to rid Washington of its corruption. New campaign financing laws went into effect, in an attempt to limit the impact of illegal campaign funds. It was assumed that such abuses were now in check and that nobody in the White House could manage such an illegal undertaking again.

How did OPEC cripple America during the 1970s?

The international hot spots during the fifties and sixties were Cold War battles waged in Eastern Europe, Africa, and Asia. But in the late sixties and early seventies, the scene shifted. The Middle East emerged as the world's most significant flash point, a political and military battlefield in which superpower rivalries took a backseat to an enmity as old as the Bible. As Arabs and Jews struggled over the existence of Israel and the future of the Palestinian Arabs, the United States got caught between a rock and a hard place.

Almost from the moment Israel was born in 1948 out of their war of independence, Israel occupied a singular, untouchable position in American foreign policy. This unique status was based on a tight web of philosophical, religious, social, political, and strategic conditions.

After the horrors of the Holocaust, Americans endorsed a homeland for the Jews. Culturally, Americans felt a kinship with Israelis and viewed with admiration the remarkable agricultural, industrial, and economic island they had created in the desert. The Israeli determination to build a nation seemed to mirror the pioneer spirit Americans romantically viewed as their own. The Israelis—many of them transplanted Europeans, along with American Jews—sounded, looked, and acted like Americans.

The Arabs, on the other hand, rode camels, wore funny robes, and carried around mats for praying at odd hours of the day. The typical American view of Arabs as rather backward was seemingly confirmed in a series of brief wars in which Israel easily defeated larger combined Arab armies, expanding its territories with each conquest. While the idea of Israel was widely accepted, the displacement of Palestinians was disregarded.

On the simplistic American scale of good versus bad, Israel was democratic and pro-Western. Strategically, Israel was a reliable client state in the midst of unstable Arab lands. For years, while these Arab states had remained in the control of Western oil companies, the American position was comfortable.

But as time passed, that position was transformed from one of unequivocal alliance with Israel to a more slippery footing, greased by oil diplomacy. Beginning in the 1960s, the Arabs increasingly took control of their valuable resource, and the balance of power began to shift. The seesaw tilting toward the Israelis got its most violent bounce after the October 1973 Yom Kippur War. Again the Israeli army prevailed, but its cloak of invincibility had been torn. While Israel beat back the combined offensive of several Arab states, Egyptian armies crossed the Suez and retook territory in the Sinai held by Israel since the Six-Day War of 1967.

But that was only a small part of the shifting sands of Middle East power politics. In an effort to compel the Israelis to return the lands captured in 1967, the Arab nations cut off oil shipments to the United States, Japan, and Western Europe in a boycott that precipitated the first great "energy crisis" of the 1970s. This boycott was made possible by the enormous reserves of petroleum controlled by the Middle Eastern countries, especially the Saudis, who were members of a group called

OPEC (the Organization of Petroleum Exporting Countries). Formed in 1960 by the world's principal oil exporters, including Saudi Arabia, Kuwait, Iran, Iraq, and Venezuela, OPEC lacked economic clout until the 1973 Arab boycott demonstrated its power in a world guzzling oil and dependent on other petroleum-related products. (Besides the obvious gasoline and home heating oil, hundreds of other products, such as plastics, fertilizers, paint, and ink, are petroleum based.)

In the United States, the boycott caused mayhem. A series of energy-saving measures were instituted, from Sunday closings of gas stations to a rationing system based on license plate numbers (plates having even numbers could buy gas one day; odd-numbered plates could buy it the next). Speed limits were lowered; environmental standards were relaxed; a new generation of gasoline mileage targets were set for automakers. American car companies, which had ignored the market for inexpensive, fuel-efficient cars pioneered by the Europeans and Japanese, soon found their once imperturbable empire crumbling around their expensive, gas-guzzling showboats. Overnight, a generation unaccustomed to the kind of sacrifices made during the Depression and World War II reacted angrily to the idea that a bunch of Arabs could shackle that great American freedom—owning and driving a car. As gas lines lengthened, frustration boiled over into fistfights and even gas-pump homicides. A bit of the American fabric was unraveling.

After the Arab boycott was lifted in March 1974, the future was altered. Having tasted power through the boycott, the OPEC members realized the control they actually possessed. Preboycott oil prices of about $3 per barrel rose to nearly $12 in 1974. The end of the boycott did not bring a return to the old pricing system. Oil prices stayed high, controlled by Arabs who could make the oil flow in a gush or just a trickle. The non-Arab OPEC members, such as Venezuela and Nigeria, were quite content to allow the prices to go as high as the Arabs wanted. American oil companies eagerly seized on the perception and reality of higher costs to force their prices up as well, bringing new profits to the oil companies at the expense of the American economy.

The following years of oil shortages and altered economic realities produced by the OPEC domination created the highest rates of unemployment since the Depression and historically high inflation—a combination of low growth and rising prices termed "stagflation"—striking a severe blow to American prestige and confidence. Once built on a bedrock of cheap labor and cheap oil, the American economy no longer enjoyed either.

An inflationary cycle of double-digit dimensions had been set in motion, and it would take Americans through a dizzying decade that seemed beyond the control of the country's leadership. The crisis, begun in Nixon's final days, became Gerald Ford's problem. His inability to "WIN"—"Whip Inflation Now" was his administration's inept, empty economic rallying cry—played a large part, along with post-Watergate disillusionment, in the 1976 election of former Georgia governor Jimmy Carter.

While America agonizingly transformed itself into a more efficient energy user and adjusted to new economic realities, it also began the search for alternative sources of energy. Congress, under Carter, funded development of wind, solar, and synthetic fuels. The American nuclear industry got a new boost as well. But there were still shocks to come. In 1978, Muhammad Reza Shah Pahlavi (1919–80), the shah of Iran, a military dictator established in 1954 through a CIA-backed coup, was overthrown by a fundamentalist Islamic revolution led by Ayatollah Ruhollah Khomeini (1900–89). Iran cut off oil exports, setting off another mild oil shortage. A year later, America's energy future was darkened when there was a major accident in the core of a nuclear reactor at Three Mile Island in Pennsylvania, which severely curtailed the planned development of nuclear power in this country. To make matters worse, that year OPEC announced another drastic price increase.

But it was the situation in Iran that would move to the foreground of American life, overshadowing Carter's historic achievement in negotiating a peace treaty between Egypt and Israel in 1978. On November 4, 1979, some 500 Iranians stormed the American embassy in Teheran, capturing ninety American diplomats and beginning a hostage crisis that effectively ended Jimmy Carter's hopes for governing effectively and being reelected. Carter's inability to free the hostages, including a disastrous, abortive rescue mission that ended with eight Americans dead in the Iranian desert, seemed to symbolize American powerlessness.

In 1980, America turned to a man it thought represented old-style American ideals and strength. Ronald Reagan (1911–2004), former movie star and governor of California, soundly defeated Carter in 1980 by promising to restore American prestige, power, and economic health. At the moment of Reagan's inauguration, as a last insult to Jimmy Carter and an omen of the good fortune Reagan would enjoy, the hostages were freed by Iran.

AMERICAN VOICES
From JIMMY CARTER'S "Crisis of Confidence" speech
(July 15, 1979):

All the legislation in the world can't fix what's wrong with America. So I want to speak with you first tonight about a subject even more serious than energy or inflation. I want to talk to you right now about a fundamental threat to American democracy. . . .

The threat is nearly invisible in ordinary ways. It is a crisis of confidence. It is a crisis that strikes at the very heart and soul and spirit of our national will. We can see this crisis in the growing doubt about the meaning of our own lives and in the loss of a unity of purpose for our nation.

The erosion of our confidence in the future is threatening to destroy the social and the political fabric of America.

What was "voodoo economics"?

If there is one thing America does not want from its presidents, it's a sermon. America wants pep talks. America wants the coach to tell the country that it only has to fear "fear itself." America likes the trumpet sounding a summons. Americans want to be told they're the best. When America thumbed its nose at Jimmy Carter's "Crisis of Confidence" speech, he belatedly learned that lesson. But Ronald Reagan knew it instinctively. He also understood a basic American political precept: This country, since the pre-Revolutionary days of James Otis back in Boston (see p. 64), doesn't like taxes.

When Ronald Reagan campaigned in 1980, he promised to cut

taxes, reduce government deficits, reduce inflation, and rebuild America's defenses. One of his Republican primary opponents said it could only be done "with mirrors." Another Republican called Reagan's ideas "voodoo economics." He was George Bush, later to become Reagan's loyal vice president and then president himself. Bush got a laugh with that line in 1980.

But Ronald Reagan got the last laugh when he was resoundingly elected, bringing to power a new conservative coalition pledged to reverse what it saw as the damage done by decades of liberal Democratic control of American economic and social policy. The Reagan coalition featured the "neo-conservatives," political theorists who put a new face on old-line anti-Communism; the so-called Moral Majority, the religious right wing led by Reverend Jerry Falwell, whose solutions to America's problems included returning prayer to public schools, outlawing abortion, and reducing government's role in social policy; conservative southerners, who responded to Reagan's call for a strengthened American defense and lower taxes; and, perhaps most importantly but least visibly, a blue-collar majority who saw their paychecks disappearing in taxes and an endless inflationary spiral.

The theoretical underpinning of Reagan's plans was called "supply side economics." The basic premise was that if taxes were cut, people would produce more goods and spend more money, creating more jobs and broader prosperity, which would lead to higher government revenues. Coupled with deep cuts in "wasteful" government spending, these revenues would provide a balanced budget. Reagan supporters even pointed to the fact that Democratic hero John Kennedy had had a similar idea in 1963, when he promoted a tax cut by saying, "A rising tide lifts all boats."

There certainly was nothing new about this idea. President Carter had proposed tax cuts, smaller government, and tight credit to keep down inflation. Earlier in American history, another Republican administration had used a similar strategy. Herbert Hoover had tried the same things during the Depression; back then the name for supply side economics was "trickle down economics."

With strong popular support and the congressional backing of a bloc of southern Democrats known as "boll weevils," Reagan's economic package sailed through Congress in 1981. But there was certainly no immediate relief, and the American economy was soon in the midst of a full-blown and devastating recession.

Unemployment was high, inflation continued, bankruptcies and business failures skyrocketed, and family farms went on the auction block. Committed to purging inflation from the world economic system, the Federal Reserve Board, led under Carter and Reagan by Paul Volcker, had adopted a policy of high interest rates to put the brakes on the economy. Without easy credit, houses go unbuilt, cars unsold, and businesses and factories contract or fold.

Oil had been at the root of the inflationary pressure, and it was only the eventual tumble in oil prices that relieved that pressure. Brought on by the international recession, the oil shortage became an oil glut. Buffeted by new competition from non-OPEC oil producers like Mexico, Norway, and Great Britain, OPEC's chokehold on the Western economies began to loosen. Suddenly awash in their unsold oil, the OPEC members saw their clout crippled as they struggled to maintain artificially high prices through production quotas that were routinely broken by OPEC's members.

The beneficiary of this reversal was none other than Ronald Reagan. The slide in oil prices signaled the beginning of the recovery. With oil prices falling, the heart of the inflationary dragon was cut out, and Ronald Reagan looked like St. George. Other pro-business Reagan policies, such as deregulating industry and ignoring the antitrust laws, fueled the recovery. Employment started to grow, and inflation, which had been running at 12 percent, dropped to less than 5 percent. The tax cuts passed in 1981, to be phased in over three years, fueled a resurgence in the financial markets and would reap a bonanza for the nation's wealthiest, but the poor and the middle class would feel few of its rewards.

The shift in tax policy was accompanied by a new reality in government spending. A succession of Reagan budgets slashed domestic spending in those areas that most affected the poor—the legacy of LBJ's Great Society. Welfare, housing, job training, drug treatment, and mass transportation all fell under the rubric of wasteful government spending. Yet in spite of these cuts and the passage of the tax changes meant to stimulate government revenues, the federal deficits ballooned. Apart from the reductions made by the tax cuts, the chief culprit in the deficits was the expansion of the defense budget. Although pledged publicly to cutting the budget, Reagan was merely overseeing a massive transfer of funds from the domestic sector to the Pentagon. For years, conservatives had complained that liberal social programs had tried to solve problems by "throwing money at them." Now, under President Reagan, the conservatives were going to solve the "weakness" of America's defenses by doing the same thing.

AMERICAN VOICES
THOMAS K. JONES, Reagan administration defense official in an interview with *Los Angeles Times* reporter Robert Scheer:

Dig a hole, cover it with a couple of doors and then throw three feet of dirt on top. It's the dirt that does it. . . . Everybody's going to make it if there are enough shovels to go around.

According to Robert Scheer's 1982 book, *With Enough Shovels*, T. K. Jones was the man responsible for administering a multimillion-dollar civil defense program, the centerpiece of which seemed to be making sure that America had plenty of doors, dirt, and shovels with which to build fallout shelters. This was his plan for saving American lives and putting the country back on its feet within a few years of an all-out nuclear war with the Soviet Union.

What happened to the space shuttle *Challenger*?

The Manhattan Project that developed the atomic bombs that those shovels would guard against had been the greatest scientific achievement of the century. The space program that put an American on the moon was certainly a close second. The Apollo program represented the pinnacle of human achievement and the greatest moment for NASA.

Its lowest point was unquestionably the tragic event that took place on the cold morning of January 28, 1986. The tenth launch of the space shuttle *Challenger* was scheduled as the twenty-fifth space shuttle mission. Francis R. (Dick) Scobee was the mission commander. The five other regular crew members were Gregory B. Jarvis, Ronald E. McNair, Ellison S. Onizuka, Judith A. Resnik, and Michael J. Smith. But this mission was different; the crew included Christa McAuliffe, a high school teacher from Concord, New Hampshire, mother of two and winner of a contest to become the first "citizen passenger" in space. The choice of McAuliffe was part of NASA's usually unerring sense of perfect pitch for public relations. If only its understanding of the weather, engineering, and physics had been so flawless.

The space shuttle program, which once again had captured flagging American enthusiasm for space exploration, had become rather humdrum in public opinion. Sending shuttles up had become as predictable as airline flights. But like the commercial airlines, NASA could fall behind schedule. By 1986, it was way behind schedule, and way over budget. Congressional budget hawks were looking for targets and NASA and the space program, a bloated bureaucracy, had become a sitting duck. Ronald Reagan's budget director, David Stockman, had argued for an end to all manned NASA missions. Reagan resisted, believing that the public imagination was still captivated by the space program.

As had become annoyingly routine with shuttle flights, this *Challenger* mission had been set back by several launch delays. Despite warnings from representatives of the shuttle's builders, NASA officials overruled the concerns of engineers and ordered a liftoff at 11:38 A.M. with the Florida temperature at thirty-six degrees. Seventy-three seconds into flight, with the nation watching its first "mom and apple pie" shuttle astronaut, the *Challenger* disintegrated into a ball of fire at an altitude of 46,000 feet (14,020 meters). Among the stunned audience watching the launch had been McAuliffe's parents and sister. Television cameras grippingly caught their faces going from excitement to bewilderment to disbelief in a matter of seconds as it became apparent that something had gone terribly wrong. Around the country, millions of schoolchildren had also tuned in to see a teacher being sent into space.

The concept of "civilian astronauts" had emerged as the shuttle program progressed from its early experimental days. The shuttle's first orbital mission began on April 12, 1981. That day, the shuttle *Columbia* was launched, with astronauts John W. Young and Robert L. Crippen at the controls. The fifty-four-hour mission went perfectly. Seven months later, the vehicle made a second orbital flight, proving that a spacecraft could be reused.

The first four shuttle flights each carried only two pilots, but the crew size was soon expanded to four, and later to seven or eight. Besides the two pilots, shuttle crews grew to include "mission specialists," experts in the scientific research to be performed, and "payload specialists," a term that was supposed to mean experts in the operation of the shuttle but which grew increasingly ambiguous. Soon it was applied to include a variety of passengers like a U.S. senator and a Saudi prince whose presence on board was more ceremonial than scientific. They were among the first non-astronauts, a group NASA eventually hoped would include journalists and artists. New Hampshire schoolteacher Christa McAuliffe was the first true "citizen passenger," who would deliver classroom lessons from space in a carefully calculated measure of NASA's public relations blitz.

In the wake of the disaster, President Reagan appointed a special commission to determine the cause of the accident. Its fourteen members were led by former secretary of state William P. Rogers, who made it clear from the outset that NASA would emerge unscathed at least publicly, and included Apollo hero Neil Armstrong and America's first woman in space, Sally Ride. In June 1986, the commission reported that the accident was caused by a failure of an O-ring in the shuttle's right solid rocket booster.

An O-ring? Think of the rubber ring that seals the top of a Mason jar of preserves. More sophisticated versions of these rubber rings sealed the joint between the two lower segments of the booster. The dramatic high point of the hearings came when committee member Richard P. Feynman, a veteran of the Manhattan Project and one of the country's most prominent physicists, dipped a piece of O-ring into a glass of ice water and used a vise clamp that came from from a local hardware store to show that the cold rubber was brittle. Design flaws in the joint and unusually cold weather during launch caused these O-rings to fail, a possibility that was apparent in test reports from one of the shuttle's contractors.

The commission had hit upon the physical cause of the disaster but the ultimate cause was the decision to hurry a launch to justify the shuttle program, which was falling further and further behind schedule and costing more than it was ever predicted to cost. The fact that NASA wanted to keep Christa McAuliffe's classroom lesson plan intact also played a role in the decision to launch, as did President Reagan's schedule. He was supposed to deliver the State of the Union Address that same night and planned to refer to the shuttle and McAuliffe. Although no direct evidence of political involvement in the launch decision was produced during the commission's hearings, many critics of NASA believed that the space agency was responding to White House pressure to stick to the schedule.

Why was Ronald Reagan called the "Teflon president"?

Ronald Reagan had a neat trick. When reporters yelled questions at him from a roped-off distance, he would cup his ear and apologize that he couldn't hear. In fact, he had some hearing troubles. But when it came to many issues, he had perfect political pitch. Whether winning a crowd with a quip, relating an anecdote to win points in a speech, or leading the nation in mourning, as he did after the space shuttle disaster, Reagan was finely tuned in to an admiring public that genuinely liked him, as even his most begrudging critics acknowledged. But through his eight years in the White House and in the period since President Reagan left office, many views of the Reagan presidency have served up a different perspective. They depicted a detached, disinterested executive who asked no questions, ignored details, and allowed subordinates to run amok. Even the revelation that the first lady consulted an astrologer, Joan Quigley, whose advice was taken seriously, seemed to slide off Reagan's back. As Bob Woodward later wrote, "the secret practice of making scheduling decisions based on astrology was irritating and irrational. [White House Chief of Staff Donald] Regan believed it was the most closely guarded domestic secret in the Reagan White House." Almost every memoir by former administration figures—most notably those by David Stockman and Donald Regan—as well as a number of books about Reagan's administration by journalists, such as Hedrick Smith's *The Power Game* and *The Acting President* by Bob Schieffer and Gary Paul Gates, present a picture of Reagan as ill informed and disengaged, with a poor memory and little interest in details.

Yet, through most of it, Ronald Reagan held on to extraordinary public approval ratings, if national polls are to be trusted. Reagan's uncanny ability to keep the controversies and problems of his eight years in office from sticking to him prompted the gently derisive nickname of "Teflon president." Part of that "Teflon" image was simply a matter of Reagan's extraordinary good luck. The fact that the American embassy hostages held in Teheran were freed at the moment Reagan took office, and through no effort of his own, seemed to give the Reagan years the first blush of serendipity. This image got another boost when Reagan survived an assassination attempt on March 30, 1981, and the country reveled in press reports of how he joked with the emergency room staff. It was only after George Bush's election that Reagan's one-time White House physician stated that the Twenty-fifth Amendment should have been invoked to transfer presidential powers temporarily to Vice President Bush while Reagan was under general anesthesia and recovering from emergency surgery. (Bush did become the first "acting president" under the Twenty-fifth Amendment in 1985 while Reagan had cancer surgery.)

But he emerged from the shooting unbowed, sitting taller in the saddle than ever in the American estimation. The surge in his approval polls after the shooting helped him ramrod through Congress the tax cuts and Pentagon spending plans he called for. After a generation of failed and disgraced presidents, Washington observers were marveling at Reagan's considerable power. This gloss of invincibility and his personal affability carried Reagan through scandals at the highest levels of his administration, all of which he was able to shrug off with a chuckle, a wave, and a bemused shrug. Even the public embarrassment of his wife feeding him lines to shout to reporters didn't dent the armor. The revelations of gross corruption by a large number of administration officials—the so-called sleaze factor that bubbled beneath the surface for his eight years—continued after Reagan's departure. In the summer of 1989, a new scandal broke through in revelations of abuses in the Department of Housing and Urban Development (HUD), led by a cabinet secretary, Samuel Pierce, whom Reagan once failed to recognize at a Rose Garden party.

Even major policy disasters seemed to roll off his back. When a terrorist bombing of a U.S. Marine barracks in Beirut killed 239 marines assigned to an indefensible position with no real justification for their presence other than to assert American interests in the area, Reagan assumed "responsibility" without any damage to his image and popularity. An American air raid on the home of Libyan strongman Muammar Khaddafy left only two American pilots and some civilians dead, including one of the Libyan leader's children. Yet Reagan's popularity soared after what amounted to an attempted assassination.

But Reagan's armor got its most severe test with the series of events that came to be called Iran-Contra. Although the full story of these events may never be learned, President Reagan personally escaped that controversy unscathed, even if it did serve to cripple his administration's final days.

The "facts" in Iran-Contra are still shrouded in some mystery, obfuscated by denials and silence from some of the key participants, including Director of Central Intelligence William Casey, who died before the extent of his involvement was fully known to the press and the public. The situation went back to a problem that had bedeviled Jimmy Carter right up to Ronald Reagan's inauguration—American hostages held in the Middle East. Unlike the Carter hostage dilemma, in which American diplomatic personnel were held by a surrogate arm of the Iranian government and whose whereabouts were known, the hostage situation facing Reagan involved a number of separate hostages held in the chaotic anarchy of civil war–ridden Lebanon by mysterious parties, assumed to be linked to Iranian leadership. In addition, one of these hostages, William Buckley, was the CIA head of station in Beirut, a fact likely known to his kidnappers. Reagan was personally tormented by the plight of the hostages and their families, but publicly stuck to his guns that there would be no yielding to terrorist demands. Such a trade-off, it was stated, would only encourage further hostage taking.

In the summer of 1985, Reagan's national security adviser, Robert McFarlane, was approached by a group of Israelis with a plan for winning release of the hostages. That plan involved a rather dubious Iranian arms merchant who proposed that Teheran would use its influence to free the hostages in return for a few hundred U.S. antitank missiles, which Iran needed to carry on its long war of attrition with neighboring Iraq. To McFarlane, the deal presented an opportunity not only to free the hostages but to establish contact with so-called moderates within the Iranian government. After returning from surgery to remove a malignancy, President Reagan met with key staffers to discuss the arms-for-hostages deal. Secretary of State George Shultz and Defense Secretary Caspar Weinberger both voiced strong opposition. (The two later said George Bush was present; Bush claimed he was not present at any meeting at which Shultz and Weinberger objected to the deal and always professed he was "out of the loop" on Iran-Contra.) No decision was voiced at the meeting, and Shultz and Weinberger left thinking the idea was dead.

But in McFarlane's account, Reagan called him with a go-ahead. Reagan would say he had no recollection of such a call. No formal record of this major decision was ever made. The first shipment of arms went through, and one hostage was released. The Iranian arms dealer withheld the news that CIA man Buckley, the man McFarlane wanted out most, was already dead, tortured before being executed. A second arms shipment, now being handled by one of McFarlane's Security Council deputies, Marine lieutenant colonel Oliver North, went awry, and no hostages were released.

While *Let's Make a Deal* went on with Iran, the Reagan administration was in the thick of another foreign policy struggle—the ongoing support of a rebel army known as the Contras, committed to overthrowing the Marxist Sandinista regime in Nicaragua. The Democratic-controlled Congress had taken the upper hand in its power struggle with the White House over Contra aid by passing an amendment that cut off all U.S. funds for the rebel army. But inside the White House, plans were hatched to make an end run around Congress by soliciting foreign money for the Contras, and that was done, with large amounts of private cash donations coming from wealthy conservative Republicans and, later, the Saudis. With money in the till, the problem became one of its disbursement. Even though Reagan was advised that sending such funds might be considered an impeachable offense, the plan went ahead, and that job was turned over to the same man who was in charge of the Iranian situation—Oliver North.

The man Reagan was later to call "a national hero" even as he fired him was seen by some White House staff as a power-grabbing zealot, delusional and willing to lie about his contacts and closeness with the president to advance his cause. A battle veteran of Vietnam and a fire-breathing anti-Communist, North had been involved in planning the military strike on the Caribbean island of Grenada to overthrow a Marxist government there on the pretext of rescuing American medical students.

To help him run his secret war in Nicaragua, North recruited a number of characters with past connections to the CIA and the American military, chief among them former Air Force general Richard Secord. At about this time, someone—nobody wants to take credit—came up with the idea of using profits being made from the sale of arms to Iran to fund the Contras. Hence the title Iran-Contra. CIA chief Casey was an enthusiastic supporter of the idea and became North's chief White House patron, soon expanding the idea into what was called a permanent "off-the-shelf" covert enterprise that would circumvent congressional oversight of CIA secret operations.

One of the many ironies in this muddle was that the story was broken by an obscure Middle Eastern magazine, which revealed that McFarlane and North had been to Teheran, where McFarlane had tried to deliver a Bible and a birthday cake to the Ayatollah Khomeini as a goodwill gesture. Within days of this revelation, the strings began to unravel in the White House, and a seemingly befuddled Ronald Reagan issued a stream of conflicting statements and press conferences that were contradicted as soon as he made them. On November 13, 1986, Reagan had given a national address in which he said that the United States had sent Iran "a small amount of defensive weapons" and "We did not trade weapons or anything else for hostages." Both assertions were completely false.

The immediate outcome of the story was the formation of a presidential commission composed of Senator John Tower, a conservative Republican (later to be rejected by the Senate as George Bush's defense secretary, owing to reports of his drinking and womanizing); former senator Edmund Muskie, Jimmy Carter's secretary of state; and retired General Brent Scowcroft, a former subordinate of Henry Kissinger. The Tower Commission released its report early in 1987, and it was a scathing rebuke of Reagan.

In an introduction to one published version of the report, *New York Times* Washington correspondent R. W. Apple Jr. wrote of the findings:

> The board painted a picture of Ronald Reagan very different from what the world had become accustomed to in the last six years. No trace here of the lopsided smile, the easy wave, the confident mien that carried him through every past crisis; this portrait is of a man confused, distracted, so remote that he failed utterly to control the implementation of his vision of an initiative that would free American hostages and reestablish American influence in Iran, with all of its present and future strategic importance. At times, in fact, the report makes the president sound like the inhabitant of a never-never land of imaginary policies.

The Tower Commission was followed by a congressional investigation in which all the deceptions, lies to Congress and the public, and illegality attached to large amounts of money passing through various sticky fingers began to be revealed. Although never taken as seriously by the public as was Watergate, the abuses of Iran-Contra were dangerous: a president seemingly out of touch with reality and allowing very junior officers to control major foreign policy adventures without any oversight; a plan to set up a secret CIA operation to circumvent the Congress; an attempt to ignore a law by using a technicality, a maneuver that even the president's closest advisers said might be an impeachable offense. With images of Richard Nixon's resignation and departure in disgrace still vivid, the specter of another impeachment proceeding was not theoretical.

In the aftermath of Iran-Contra, Admiral Poindexter, Air Force general Richard Secord, Albert Hakim (an Iranian-born U.S. citizen and arms dealer), and Oliver North were charged by a federal grand jury with conspiring to illegally divert profits from the U.S.-Iran arms sales to the Nicaraguan Contras. In 1989, a federal court convicted North on three charges relating to the Iran-Contra affair, including altering and destroying evidence. With the judge in the case calling him a "fall guy," North was sentenced to a suspended sentence, 1,200 hours of community service in a drug program, and a $150,000 fine that he would presumably pay out of his substantial speaking engagement fees. Poindexter was convicted on five charges and received a six-month prison term. North had worked under national security advisers Robert C. McFarlane and John M. Poindexter. In 1989, McFarlane pleaded guilty to withholding information from Congress during its investigation. In 1990, Poindexter was convicted of conspiracy and of lying to and obstructing Congress.

But none of the convictions stuck. In 1987, North and Poindexter had testified about the Iran-Contra affair during the congressional hearings and had received immunity, or freedom from prosecution, on matters of their testimony. The courts overturned the convictions of both North and Poindexter on grounds that their 1987 testimony might have influenced the outcome of their later trials. Only one person, former CIA agent Thomas G. Clines, went to prison as a result of Iran-Contra. He was sentenced to 16 months in prison for evading taxes on income from the operations.

In 1992, Caspar W. Weinberger, Reagan's secretary of defense, was charged with lying to Congress and government investigators in connection with the Iran-Contra affair. But Weinberger, who was indicted by Special Prosecutor Lawrence Walsh, was given a presidential pardon by George Bush in 1992. Bush also issued pardons to a number of key participants. Elliott Abrams and Alan Fiers Jr. had pleaded guilty to withholding information from Congress. Duane Clarridge had been indicted on seven counts of perjury and was awaiting trial. Clair George had been convicted of two felony counts of perjury and false statements and was awaiting sentencing when pardoned.

Bush's own role in Iran-Contra remained murky. During the investigation, he stated famously that he was "out of the loop." After Bush lost his 1992 bid for reelection, entries from diaries that were belatedly given to Special Prosecutor Walsh showed that Bush had been informed about the progress of the arms-for-hostages deal in 1986. Bob Woodward reported later in *Shadow* that Bush had said, "Good things, such as the release of the hostages and contacts with moderates, will in the long run—in my view—offset this." In the end, writes Woodward, "the records showed that Bush had attended many meetings on the Iran arms sales, but Independent Counsel Walsh felt at that point that his role was not central. . . . Some of Reagan's key national security people, even Secretary of State Shultz, supported this view. They dismissed Bush as a decorative yes man, a heartbeat away from the presidency but miles away from heavyweight decision making."

On January 18, 1994, Special Prosecutor Lawrence E. Walsh issued the final report of the Iran-Contra affair. The report said the Iran-Contra operations "violated United States policy and law," and it criticized the Reagan and Bush administrations for involvement in a cover-up. However, Walsh acknowledged that there was no credible evidence that the president authorized or was aware of the diversion of the profits from the Iran arms sales to assist the Contras.

Iran-Contra was a potentially dangerous escapade that might have seemed like the work of some novelist forming a scenario for a takeover of the inner workings of American government. Only Oliver North wasn't fiction. It is exactly his brand of zealotry that created the need for the system of checks and balances that exists at every level of the system.

(Two key Iran-Contra figures, Elliott Abrams and John Poindexter, resurfaced in 2002 in the administration of the younger Bush. Pardoned by senior Bush, Abrams was named to be President Bush's director of Middle Eastern affairs at the White House. John M. Poindexter, a national security adviser to President Reagan whose convictions on five felony counts were later overturned, was named to direct a controversial Pentagon project that would assemble information on suspected terrorists in the aftermath of September 11.)

AMERICAN VOICES

RYAN WHITE, who contracted AIDS from an infected blood-clotting medicine he took to counter hemophilia, speaking to a presidential commission on AIDS (1988):

I came face-to-face with death at thirteen years old. I was diagnosed with AIDS: a killer. Doctors told me I'm not contagious. Given six months to live and being the fighter that I am, I set high goals for myself. It was my decision to live a normal life, go to school, be with my friends, and enjoy day-to-day activities.

The school I was going to said they had no guidelines for a person with AIDS. . . . We began a series of court battles for nine months, while I was attending classes by telephone. Eventually, I won the right to attend school, but the prejudice was still there. . . . Because of the lack of education on AIDS, discrimination, fear, panic and lies surrounded me. I became the target of Ryan White jokes.

Ryan White died in 1990 at age eighteen.

What was the "gay plague"?

Germs and what goes on behind bedroom doors have always taken a backseat to dates and battles and speeches in most history books, but they have often had much more to do with history than most politicians, kings, generals, or court decisions ever did. Squeamishness among teachers, academics, and publishers, along with America's resilient Puritan ethics, have long meant that sex, disease, and death are the unmentionable parts of history that the schoolbooks leave out. During the 1980s and 1990s, however, sex and disease were never a bigger part of American history, as a new and terrifying ailment completely altered the way the country behaved and thought about sex.

"Rare Cancer Seen in 41 Homosexuals." The headline appeared inside the *New York Times* on July 3, 1981. Written by Dr. Lawrence K. Altman, a physician who covered medical news for the *Times*, the article was about 900 words long. Altman's story described how doctors were reporting a small but frightening number of patients who were mysteriously dying from a rare and especially fatal form of cancer. "The cause of the outbreak is unknown," Altman wrote, "and there is as yet no evidence of contagion."

Little did Altman or anyone else know in 1981 that the appearance of this rare cancer was the visible, early phase of one of the most deadly epidemics in human history. It would not only kill millions but completely alter social behavior, sexual attitudes, and relationships. The medical mystery Altman described would eventually blossom into the full-blown international plague of AIDS. More than twenty years after Altman's article, the first of more than 900 he would write on the subject, AIDS/HIV had affected some 60 million people worldwide and more than 20 million were dead, according to the United Nations World Health Organization (WHO).*

It was only a few years before Altman's article appeared that the medical world had announced one of its greatest victories with the eradication of smallpox. The last known naturally occurring case of smallpox was in Somalia in 1977, and the last known case was due to a lab accident in England in 1978. (Two research stores of smallpox are still secured in labs in the U.S. and Russia.) This triumph for modern science, along with the great strides made against polio, yellow fever, and a host of other killing diseases, left the medical world fairly confident.

Then came the mystery ailment. At first, the disease that became known as AIDS was ignored by Americans when the symptoms began to appear in 1981. It seemed to be limited to a few "special cases" in the population—male homosexuals and intravenous drug users. It was first identified as a "new" disease in 1980 and 1981 by physicians in Los Angeles and New York City who recognized that all the patients were previously healthy, young homosexual men suffering from otherwise rare forms of cancer and pneumonia. Among the homosexual community, word of a "gay plague" was spreading. Among the most fearful rumors was that someone actually was targeting homosexuals with this new disease. Some doctors first called the ailment GRID (for gay-related immune deficiency) before the Centers for Disease Control settled on the name AIDS (the acronym stands for "acquired immune deficiency syndrome").

For a variety of reasons—which included shrinking federal medical research budgets, competition among doctors who wanted to be the

---

*Based on recent UNICEF and WHO figures, 70 percent of those with AIDS/HIV live in sub-Saharan Africa, where many of the infected do not even know of their status because of the poor state of medicine in Africa. AIDS had also produced a cumulative 13 million orphans, with the vast majority of those also living in sub-Saharan Africa.

first to publish, and miscommunication of basic facts to the public — the initial response to the growing epidemic was slow. Then AIDS began to show up among young hemophiliacs and female sex partners of infected men. The sense of alarm started to grow. When the enormity of the problem became more apparent, and people realized that the nation's blood supply might be tainted, a sense of national panic ensued. Even as the course of the cause and course of the disease became known, the country was gripped by fear. It took some time to learn that AIDS is the final, life-threatening stage of infection with human immunodeficiency virus (HIV). The name refers to the fact that the virus severely damages the body's most important defense against disease, the immune system. After the discovery of the AIDS virus by the Pasteur Institute in Paris in 1983, Dr. Robert Gallo's team at the National Cancer Institute in Bethesda, Maryland, developed a blood test to detect the virus in 1985. The tests to detect evidence of HIV have been used to screen all blood donated in the United States since 1985. These tests were also used to analyze stored tissues from several people who died going back to the late 1950s, and scientists concluded that some of these people had died from AIDS.

In the early days of AIDS, the prevalence of the disease among homosexuals and drug users marginalized the disease, along with stigmatizing those who were suffering. On the community level, small towns were divided over whether to allow students with AIDS to attend schools, an issue brought to life by the poignant story of a young boy named Ryan White. Schools were also debating what role they should play in educating students about AIDS prevention. Condom distribution and "clean needle" exchanges, which were attempts to get infected hypodermics out of the hands of intravenous drug users, were suddenly part of the debate.

The American religious community was split among those who denounced AIDS victims as "immoral," and other religious groups who responded with greater compassion. But many Americans, though fearful of this new disease that came shrouded in unpleasant realities, felt somewhat removed from AIDS until it started to claim some very visible victims, including film actor Rock Hudson in July 1985. A longtime symbol of American virility and "wholesome" entertainment, Hudson had costarred with Hollywood beauties like Elizabeth Taylor and

Jennifer Jones and become a 1960s icon with a series of fluffy romantic comedies with Doris Day. He had moved on to a highly successful television career with *McMillan and Wife*, a detective show that ran for six seasons. Before Hudson's death, the face of AIDS was a stranger. But America was shocked to see the former matinee idol's emaciated and sunken image. His death helped open up a new national discussion of the subject. Eventually, other figures from the world of Hollywood, the arts, and sports began to die or announce that they were infected. They included tennis champion Arthur Ashe, who died in 1993, infected during a transfusion while in surgery. Los Angeles Lakers basketball star Magic Johnson announced he was infected with HIV in 1991, quit playing, and then, remarkably, resumed his career temporarily, a testament to the progress made in treating the disease, as well as the change in attitudes.

There was no aspect of American public and private life that the AIDS/HIV epidemic did not touch during the last two decades of the twentieth century. The economy was impacted as enormous amounts of money began to be devoted to keep up with the ill and infected. Budgets of hospitals, medical insurers, the national medical research facilities, public health and private welfare agencies were all strained to the limits.

The AIDS epidemic fundamentally altered the American landscape. By 1992, both political parties' nominating conventions prominently featured spokespeople for the AIDS community in prime-time network television speeches. Condoms, safe sex, anal sex—words never before uttered in polite society—all became part of American common parlance. In many ways, the AIDS crisis also brought homosexuality out of the American closet. Once taboo or tittered at, homosexuality was now openly discussed, accompanied by a new political activism among gay Americans. The word "gay" itself became a new part of the American lexicon. Even the staid *New York Times* eventually accepted the word. The health care and scientific research became politicized and radicalized. Not simply content with increasing funding for AIDS research, the "gay rights" movement began to press for new legislation that would rid America of institutional discrimination against homosexuals. Of course, these demands were not uniformly accepted. Emboldened by the success of AIDS activists in obtaining funding for medical research, women also spoke out forcefully about the disparity of funds being devoted to breast cancer research. The walls of the entire system of medical research, long an almost exclusive domain of white males, were falling down.

The losses from AIDS can't be totaled in sheer numbers. Just as an entire generation of America's young men—its "best and brightest"— were wiped out during the Civil War, millions of people around the world fell to AIDS. Their deaths were not only tragic, but the loss of their industry, ingenuity, invention, and potential is the truly incalculable cost of this disease. Twenty years after its appearance, scientists were still not certain how, when, or where the AIDS virus evolved and first infected people. One widely held suspicion is that HIV evolved from viruses that originally infected monkeys in Africa and was somehow transmitted to people.

Must Read: *And the Band Played On* by Randy Shilts.

AMERICAN VOICES
EDMUND WHITE (b. 1940), American writer, in *States of Desire: Travels in Gay America* (afterword to 1986 edition):

The Aids epidemic has rolled back a big rotting log and revealed all of the squirming life underneath it, since it involves, all at once, the main themes of our existence: sex, death, power, money, love, hate, disease, and panic. No American phenomenon has been so compelling since the Vietnam war.

ANTHONY PERKINS (1932–92), American actor best known for his role as Norman Bates in *Psycho* (quoted posthumously in *Independent on Sunday*, September 20, 1992):

I have learned more about love, selflessness and human understanding in this great adventure in the world of AIDS than I ever did in the cut-throat, competitive world in which I spent my life.

What happened to the Evil Empire?

History's long-range judgment of the Reagan years must wait, but the wear and tear of more than a dozen years out of office have not dulled his "Teflon" finish. Suffering from Alzheimer's disease, which was first diagnosed in 1994, Ronald Reagan remained a much-loved president at the turn of the century. (A majority of Americans surveyed in a 1999 Gallup poll predicted that Reagan will rank higher than other modern presidents.) Historians were tougher critics. In one post–Reagan era poll, academic historians and political scientists ranked him twenty-second among the then forty U.S. presidents. However, a C-Span poll in 2009 placed Ronald Reagan, who died in 2004, as the tenth best president.

Of course, much of the judgment is partisan. To admirers, Reagan's successes in changing the American mood, reducing marginal tax rates from 70 percent, and altering the political terrain in America, place him in the pantheon of great presidents. His critics point to his failures, most notably the creation of an enormous national debt; the foreign policy misadventures, in particular Iran-Contra; and a shortsighted plan to assist the rebels fighting the Soviet Union in Afghanistan. The aid given to the Afghan Islamic mujahideen effectively weakened the Soviet Union. But the failure to remain engaged in Afghanistan allowed that country to slip into the chaos and power vacuum in which the Taliban and their allied terrorist group Al Qaeda flourished. A few years after Reagan left office, the tremendous burden of debt his administration's policies had created during eight years was seen as an anchor on the American economy. The economic boom of the 1990s, which eventually produced budget surpluses, if only temporarily, had erased the worst of that black mark.

But Reagan ultimately may well go down in history for his unique role in altering relations with the Soviet Union and spearheading the beginning of the end of Soviet bloc Communism in Europe. Although the finish would not come until 1991, when his successor George Bush was in office, by the end of Reagan's second term, the handwriting was on the wall. The Soviet Union had been spiraling downward for a long time. A fatally inefficient industrial system; official corruption; deep political and social problems; competitive pressures not only from the United States but from China, Japan, and other emerging Asian countries; independence movements—some of them Islamic—within the various Soviet republics; and a long, costly, debilitating war in Afghanistan were all factors that had weakened the Kremlin's control over its empire. The Soviet economy was so deeply flawed that it has to be examined as the first cause of the USSR's collapse. For years, the Soviet Union had devoted as much as 25 percent of its national output to unproductive military expenditures. (By comparison, the United States allocated in the range of 4 to 6 percent of its much larger gross domestic product to defense.) While the rest of the world was speeding toward the twenty-first century, with rapidly changing technologies and increasing trade, the Soviet Union was saddled with a Third World economy stuck in the 1950s and an agricultural system that still resembled one from the nineteenth century.

In spite of these deep internal structural problems, the military might of the Soviet Union, its sheer size, and its authoritarian control over the Eastern European bloc had dominated relations with the United States for more than forty years. There was almost no aspect of life or history in America after World War II that was not impacted in some way by the competition known as the Cold War.

Reagan's second term coincided with the emergence of Mikhail Gorbachev as the leader of the Soviet Union. The two men began a remarkable working relationship that ushered in a new era in Soviet-American cooperation. At a 1987 summit meeting in Iceland, they agreed to the first treaty in history to reduce the nuclear arsenals of the two superpowers. When Reagan left office in January 1989, the Berlin Wall, long a symbol of division between Germany and all of Europe, was still standing. Within a year, it had been torn down. Germany was unified in 1990, and the Soviet Empire fell apart. On Christmas Day 1991, Gorbachev stepped down. In an astonishingly brief and peaceful revolution, the Cold War was over and European Communism, enforced by years of brutal Soviet suppression, was finished. Gorbachev, who won the Nobel Prize in 1990, was clearly the man who had taken history into his own hands. Other key players in the demise of the Soviet system and the end of the Cold War were England's Margaret Thatcher, George Bush, Germany's Helmut Kohl, Polish labor leader

Lech Wałesa, and Pope John Paul II, the first pope from a Communist country, whose travels to Eastern Europe helped fuel the anti-Soviet mood in that part of the world.

As Lou Cannon wrote, "His legacy in foreign affairs . . . shines brighter with the benefit of hindsight. Reagan launched a military buildup premised on a belief that the Soviet Union was too economically vulnerable to compete in a celebrated arms race and would come to the bargaining table if pressured by the West. *The message of freedom that he believed could energize the people of Eastern Europe and penetrate within the Soviet Union itself.* Many members of the political establishment thought these views were at best naive. They also were alarmed by Reagan's provocative comments about communism, particularly his description of the Soviet Union as an 'evil empire.' But times changed."

Must Read: *President Reagan: The Role of a Lifetime* by Lou Cannon.

AMERICAN VOICES
NATIONAL SECURITY ADVISER COLIN POWELL
to Ronald Reagan on his last day in office:

The world is quiet today, Mr. President.

Colin Luther Powell (b. 1937) was born in New York City, the son of Jamaican immigrants. With assistance from an affirmative action program designed to increase minority college enrollment, he graduated from the City College of New York and earned an MBA degree from George Washington University. Commissioned a second lieutenant in the Army in 1958, he served in Vietnam with the 23rd Division in 1968–69, and later commanded forces in South Korea, West Germany, and the United States. In 1986, Powell became commanding general of the Fifth Corps in Frankfurt, Germany, and President Ronald Reagan named him national security adviser, the first black man to fill that position, in 1987. During the next decade, he would extend those achievements.

In the spring of 2002, Russia was invited to join NATO, which had been created to stem the tide of Soviet Russia's military strength. Although Russia joined the defense alliance as a nonvoting member, it was still a remarkable turnabout in the history of Europe, America, and the world.

CHAPTER NINE

FROM THE EVIL EMPIRE TO THE AXIS OF EVIL

9/11: What really happened?

War in Afghanistan: Who? What? When? Where? Why?

Milestones in the War in Afghanistan

Why was America in Iraq?

Milestones in the War in Iraq

Should same-sex marriage be legal for all Americans? And what does same-sex marriage have to do with interracial marriage?

How do you keep a "bubble" from bursting?

How did America elect its first black president?

To many Americans, the Reagan years had brought about a clean break with the long post-Vietnam, post-Watergate mood of the country. This was true despite the fact that budget deficits were ballooning toward nosebleed territory. Wall Street was tottering through another periodic scandal—this time it was over manipulating "junk bonds." A banking crisis was costing taxpayers billions. Crack cocaine had become epidemic, bringing with it a deadly wave of urban crime. And the specter of AIDS had completely reshaped the American landscape. Still, on the surface at least, the Reagan years seemed to have restored a semblance of confidence in the country. And the chief beneficiary of that confidence was Reagan's vice president, George Bush.

What was Operation Desert Storm?

George Bush looked like a sure two-termer early on.

In his first two years as president, Bush had witnessed the stunning unraveling of Communism in Europe. In a reverse of the domino theory, which held that Communism would win successive victories in such countries as Vietnam if the U.S. allowed, the Berlin Wall crumbled, East and West Germany united, once-captive nations embraced democracy, and, astonishingly, the Soviet Union, the longtime adversary that Ronald Reagan had called the Evil Empire, simply and bloodlessly disintegrated. Not with a bang but a whimper.

Soviet leader Mikhail Gorbachev (b. 1931) had attempted to restructure the Soviet economy (*perestroika*) and loosen political restraints (*glasnost*). But he had let the genie out of the bottle. The Cold War was over. George Bush was the president on hand to usher in, he thought, a New World Order.

But even as the Evil Empire unraveled and a half century of Cold War tension and conflict wound down, Bush's presidential high point was to come in a part of the world that has confounded every American president since Truman: the Middle East. In Bush's case, the crisis came from Iraqi dictator Saddam Hussein's August 1990 invasion of neighboring oil-rich Kuwait. Mobilizing the United Nations against Saddam Hussein, Bush first ordered Operation Desert Shield, a defensive move to protect the vast oil fields of Saudi Arabia. Although there was considerable rhetoric about protecting freedom and liberty, it was difficult to make a case that the U.S. was going to war to defend democracy when it came to either Kuwait or Saudi Arabia, monarchies in which political parties are illegal and women are still treated as property. A quick move by Iraq's army into the Saudi kingdom would have given Iraq control of more than 40 percent of the world's oil reserves, a frightening prospect given Saddam Hussein's proven willingness to measure up to his chief role model, Joseph Stalin.

Leading a coalition of thirty-nine other nations and with United Nations approval, the United States spearheaded Operation Desert Storm, a devastating air war, followed by a 100-hour ground offensive. It was to be George Bush's shining moment.

The fourteenth former vice president who became president, Bush was the first vice president elected in his own right since Martin Van Buren in 1836. When someone gave Bush a portrait of Van Buren on Inauguration Day, he may have politely failed to mention that Van Buren served only a single term. He was turned out of office because of the terrible shape of the American economy back then! So you think history doesn't repeat itself?

MILESTONES IN THE GULF WAR

August 2   The UN Security Council issues a resolution condemning Iraq's invasion.

August 6   The UN Security Council imposes an embargo that prohibits all trade with Iraq except for medical supplies and food in certain circumstances.

August 7   The United States announces that it is sending troops to the Persian Gulf to defend Saudi Arabia from possible attack by Iraq.

August 25   The UN Security Council authorizes the use of force to carry out the embargo against Iraq.

November 29 The council gives coalition members permission "to use all necessary means" to expel Iraq from Kuwait if Iraq does not withdraw by January 15, 1991. Iraq does not withdraw.

1991

January 17 The air war begins at 3 A.M. The coalition's goal is to destroy Iraq's ability to launch attacks; eliminate Iraq's biological, chemical, and nuclear weapons facilities; and reduce Iraq's ability to defend itself. By late February, the air war reduces the number of Iraqi troops in Kuwait and southern Iraq to about 183,000, mostly through casualties and desertions.

Iraq responds to the allied air assault by launching Scud missiles at populated areas in Israel and Saudi Arabia. Crude and inaccurate by modern Western military standards, the Soviet-built Scuds have enormous psychological value, striking fear in the targeted cities. Among the chief fears is the possibility that Saddam will arm these missiles with either chemical or biological weapons as he has done in suppressing a rebellion by the ethnic minority Kurds in Iraq. The attacks on Israel are designed to draw the Israelis into the war. However, Israel does not enter the war, thus making it much easier to keep the coalition together.

February 24 At about 4 A.M., coalition forces launch a major three-pronged ground attack. U.S. and French troops invade Iraq from Saudi Arabia, west of Iraqi fortifications in Kuwait. They move rapidly north into Iraq and toward the Euphrates River to cut off Iraqi supply lines and to prevent an Iraqi retreat. U.S. and British troops cross into Iraq from Saudi Arabia. They move north into Iraq and then sweep east to attack the Iraqi troops. Coalition troops, consisting of U.S. Marines and troops from Egypt, Kuwait, Saudi Arabia, and Syria, assault Iraqi forces at several points across southern Kuwait. The troops quickly break through Iraqi fortifications, and about 63,000 Iraqi soldiers surrender.

February 26 Saddam Hussein orders his troops to leave Kuwait. But by that time, the Iraqi forces have been surrounded.

February 28   The coalition ends all military operations at 8 A.M., about 100 hours after the ground attack began. American losses for the operation were 148 killed in action and 7 missing in action.

The Gulf War lasted forty-two days: thirty-eight days of intense air strikes and four days of ground fighting. The U.S.-led coalition routed Saddam's army, overran Kuwait and southern Iraq, and liberated Kuwait. By stopping the offensive against Iraq without assaulting Baghdad and possibly overthrowing Saddam Hussein, President Bush and his advisers had fulfilled the UN's terms of the action against Iraq. (Ten years later, the consequences of that decision would impact many of the same men. In the wake of the September 11 attacks on the United States and the ensuing war in Afghanistan, still in positions of power were Colin Powell, the chairman of the Joint Chiefs of Staff during the Gulf War, now secretary of state under George W. Bush, forty-third president and son of the forty-first. Dick Cheney, the secretary of defense during the Gulf War, was now Bush's vice president.)

The Persian Gulf War devastated Iraq. As many as 100,000 Iraqi soldiers were killed and a great number of civilians also died. Iraqi roads, bridges, factories, and oil industry facilities were demolished. Water purification and sewage treatment facilities could not operate without electric power. A continuing trade embargo caused serious economic problems. In March 1991, Kurdish and Shiite Muslim uprisings, with encouragement from President Bush, who had promised American support that never came, broke out. But by April, Iraqi troops put down most of the rebellions with brutal efficiency.

In April, Iraq accepted the terms of a formal cease-fire agreement and the UN Security Council officially declared an end to the war. In the cease-fire agreement, Iraq agreed to the destruction of all its biological and chemical weapons, its facilities for producing such weapons, and any facilities or materials it might have for producing nuclear weapons. After the formal cease-fire, the UN continued the embargo to pressure Iraq to carry out these terms.

AMERICAN VOICES

GEORGE BUSH, accepting the 1988 Republican
presidential nomination:

The Congress will push me to raise taxes, and I'll say no,
and they'll push, and I'll say no, and they'll push again. And
all I can say to them is, "Read My Lips: No New Taxes."

How do you "downsize" a president?

With this swift and relatively low-casualty victory over Iraq, Bush's ratings soared like a Patriot missile, a defensive weapon that had been
hailed during the war for stopping Iraq's Scud missiles. Before the Gulf
War, Bush had already notched one win after U.S. troops swept into
Panama and captured dictator Manuel Noriega, who had been indicted
in a U.S. court on drug charges. Coupled with the victory in Kuwait,
American prestige seemed unmatched in Bush's New World Order.

But every missile that goes up must come down. Just as the Patriot missile's reliability, accuracy, and performance were questioned
after the war, the glow of the Reagan–Bush foreign policy coups vanished, dulled by a dizzying slide from postwar euphoria. Unemployment surged as the Federal Reserve's high interest rates, designed to
wring inflation out of the American economy, mired the economy in
a recession. The new corporate policy of "downsizing"—in old words,
"layoffs"—was pushing unemployment higher. And it was a different
kind of unemployment. The downsized now included the white-collar
workers who thought they had bought into corporate security, as well
as the blue-collar factory workers more accustomed to the traditional
cycle of layoffs and rehirings. Bush was viewed as out of touch with
average Americans, and publicity stunts such as shopping for socks at a
local mall only made him seem more disconnected.

Americans were cranky, and George Bush wasn't the only target.
Congress faced intense scrutiny as a series of scandals rocked the
House. Speaker Jim Wright and Democratic Whip Tony Coelho resigned following ethics investigations, and a congressional post office
scandal involving cushy check-writing privileges sounded like fraud to

most Americans. The House clearly enraged the public. To the average American, Congress fiddled while America burned.

Early in his presidency, Bush had to deal with the worst crisis in the banking industry since the Great Depression of the 1930s. Between 1980 and 1990, more than 1,000 savings and loan institutions failed and hundreds more neared bankruptcy, a crisis resulting from defaults on loans, poor regulation, and fraud and mismanagement in the industry. Soon after entering office, Bush proposed legislation to rescue and restructure the industry. The savings and loan bailout eventually cost taxpayers more than $400 billion to maintain failing banks, one of which involved Bush's third son, Neil, a board member of Silverado Savings, a Colorado bank.

Mounting budget deficits and deep anxiety over health care magnified these problems. The grim national mood darkened with the bitter debate over legal abortion, which President Bush opposed in a reversal of his own earlier position. "Gender gap" tensions rose higher when law professor Anita Hill charged that Clarence Thomas, Bush's choice to succeed civil rights legend Thurgood Marshall (1908–93) on the Supreme Court, had sexually harassed her when she was his assistant. For two days in October 1991, the nation was once again transfixed by Senate hearings in which the two testified about the charges. Thomas denied Hill's account and charged that a "lynch mob" was out to get him. Thomas was approved by the Senate 52–48, but the ugly episode, in which both Thomas and Hill became the targets of vicious character attacks, had further darkened the mood of the country along party, gender, and racial lines.

The depth of that racial animosity boiled over in April 1992 rioting that swept Los Angeles after four policemen were acquitted in the vicious 1991 beating of Rodney King. In two days of the worst American riots in a generation, President Bush had to order Marines and Army troops to keep peace in the city. When the violence subsided, fifty-two people had been killed and more than 600 buildings set afire, many of them burned to the ground.

But for American voters, George Bush's gravest sin seemed to be his broken tax promise. When Bush agreed to new taxes to reduce the deficit in 1990, Desert Storm was worth so much desert sand. Since colonial days, Americans have hated taxes and often reserved a special hell for politicians who raise them, especially after pledging not to. With the recession millstone around his neck, George Bush plunged in the polls—his 90 percent approval ratings sharply downsized—as the 1992 election approached.

AMERICAN VOICES
Sign in BILL CLINTON'S campaign headquarters,
attributed to campaign director James Carville:

IT'S THE ECONOMY, STUPID.

Can a man called Bubba become president?

Although it won't go down as one of the great presidential pronouncements like, "Ask not what your country can do for you—ask what you can do for your country," when candidate Bill Clinton told America, "I tried it once, but I didn't inhale," it certainly was memorable.

During the primary battles of 1992, Bill Clinton was asked by reporters about smoking marijuana in his college days, and his reply left many Americans choking with laughter. A Rhodes scholar who attended Oxford, where he avoided the Vietnam-era draft, Arkansas governor Bill Clinton (b. 1946) dodged many uncomfortable questions during the 1992 campaign. But Americans were less interested in pot smoking, draft dodging, and womanizing than in solving America's problems. Running as an "agent of change" who promised reforms, Bubba Clinton and his vice presidential running mate, Senator Al Gore of Tennessee, became the first "baby boomers" to win the White House, following a raucous election most notable for the third-party candidacy of H. Ross Perot.

A man whose political fame would be built on assailing big government and excessive government spending, Ross Perot (b. 1930) had built his Electronic Data Systems into a billion-dollar firm with large and very profitable government contracts. With his deep pockets, the amply financed Perot ran as an independent with a campaign aimed at overhauling government. His folksy style and can-do approach appealed to millions of American voters who were completely disenchanted with the two major political parties, whose differences seemed marginal and who seemed most concerned with fund-raising and retaining control. But when he abruptly canceled his unorthodox campaign, Perot was dismissed as a wealthy kook. Then, only weeks before Election Day, Perot stunned the political world by rejoining the fray.

In a series of three-way televised debates, the most indelible image was that of President George Bush checking his wristwatch at the Richmond, Virginia, debate as if his limo was double-parked with the engine and the meter running. When advised to fire up his campaign, Bush turned to name calling, deriding Clinton and Gore as "bozos." Gore, an environmentalist and author of a book about the risks of global warming, was dismissed as "ozone man." Then a week before the election, the Iran-Contra special prosecutor announced a grand jury indictment of Caspar Weinberger, and questions about Bush's role in the Iran-Contra case were pushed back into the headlines.

Garnering nearly 20 million votes (19 percent), Perot drew disaffected voters from Bush and probably skewed the race, allowing the Clinton-Gore ticket to win with 43 percent to Bush's 37 percent. In later years, Bush would claim that the indictment of Weinberger and the failure of Federal Reserve Chairman Alan Greenspan (p. 557) to cut interest rates quickly enough doomed his presidency. But Ross Perot and the Reform Party, like several other successful third-party candidates in American history, had probably been the big difference, tipping the balance in a very closely divided and unhappy America.

Must Read: *Shadow: Five Presidents and the Legacy of Watergate* by Bob Woodward; *First in His Class: The Biography of Bill Clinton* by David Maraniss.

AMERICAN VOICES
Retired Arizona SENATOR BARRY GOLDWATER
(1909–98), a longtime leader of the conservative
movement in the Republican Party, on the question
of homosexuals in the military:

You don't need to be "straight" to fight and die for your country. You just need to shoot straight.

Who took out a Contract with America?

It may be called a "honeymoon," but Bill Clinton must have been wondering when the fun would start. Before he unzipped his suitcases in the White House, Clinton's brief "honeymoon" period was over. Having pledged to overturn the ban on homosexuals in the military, Clinton found himself walking into a Pentagon Chainsaw Massacre. Accepting a compromise "don't ask don't tell" policy, Clinton retreated from his promise, hinting at the policy and personnel reversals that would plague his first two years.

Two potential choices for attorney general were shot down in what was called Nanny-gate, the use of illegal aliens as childcare workers and nonpayment of taxes on those workers. Another Justice Department nominee, a widely respected black woman from the academic world named Lani Guinier, was attacked as a "quota queen." Clinton withdrew her name as head of the civil rights division rather than stand up to a Republican firestorm. The accuracy of the charges against Guinier was never challenged, but a new style of "scorched earth" attacks in the guise of congressional advice and consent had been unleashed. The rough-and-tumble horse trading and attacks on presidential appointees had long been a cloakroom matter in Washington, mostly out of public view. Appointments had traditionally been treated as a president's prerogative and, while there have been notable rejections of presidential appointees, most presidents get to make the appointments they want. But under the new rules, aided and abetted by twenty-four-hour news networks eager for blood in the water, the process had turned vicious. The personal tone of the assaults had been ratcheted up in the wake of the Bork and Thomas nominations. Republicans were looking for payback.

Each of these early setbacks to the Clinton agenda overshadowed a slowly recovering economy and, more surprisingly, the shrinking deficit. Risking that Americans wanted to be done with the excessive deficits, Clinton had gambled on a tax package that included tough deficit reduction restrictions in 1993. Passage of a free trade pact with Mexico and Canada (known as NAFTA) and a major anticrime package that included new handgun controls — known as the Brady Bill in honor of James Brady, the White House press secretary who had been severely wounded and permanently injured in the assassination attempt on Ronald Reagan—were also victories.

But Clinton's gaffes were eclipsing his successes. Some miscues were trivial, such as the criticism over a $200 haircut. Others cut deeper. A standoff with a religious cult led by David Koresh in Waco, Texas, turned disastrous when an FBI assault on the compound led to a deadly fire (see p. 578). Bedeviled by continuing reports of his womanizing, dismissed during the primary campaigns as "bimbo eruptions," Clinton was also being dogged by one woman's alleged sexual harassment suit based on events that took place when Clinton was governor of Arkansas. The suit attracted only passing attention when it first surfaced—dismissed as another "bimbo eruption." But these stories would eventually become connected to an ongoing investigation of the Clintons' Arkansas investments and real estate deals, known as Whitewater. When White House aide Vincent Foster, a longtime Clinton friend from Arkansas, committed suicide, his death was tied into Whitewater as well, and official Washington went into a full-blown scandal investigation mode.

The policy stumbles, personal embarrassments, and major missteps culminated in the 1993 defeat of Clinton's legislative keystone, the overhaul of the health-care system. Establishing a commission to examine American health-care policies, Clinton's first mistake may have been his choice of his wife, Hillary Rodham Clinton, to head the commission. A controversial figure in her own right, the first lady stepped on congressional toes on the way to proposing a far-reaching plan that would cover all Americans. But the Clintons saw their prize project wither, bucked by Congress and an intense lobbying effort by the health-insurance industry. This sharp rebuttal of Bill Clinton's policy centerpiece was an omen of 1994's midterm elections.

In a political earthquake, Republicans swept control of the House of Representatives for the first time in forty years. They were led by Georgia representative Newt Gingrich, who trumpeted a conservative list of promises called the Contract with America. This "contract" promised a laundry list of favorite Republican right-wing positions, including a balanced budget amendment, increased defense spending, term limits for congressional seats, an amendment to end legal abortion, and a reform of the welfare system. They were joined by a Republican majority in the Senate, setting the stage for a struggle between the White House and Congress as America moved toward the final presidential election of the twentieth century.

A brilliant politician with finely tuned skills in the new world of "talk show" politics, Clinton was able to co-opt some of the Contract with America as he deftly moved to the political center, guided more often by his influential consultant, pollster Dick Morris, than by his political advisers. In November 1995, Clinton regained the upper hand when he battled Gingrich and the Republican Congress over the budget, a stalemate that actually led to a shutdown of the United States government. For a few days, nonessential federal workers were sent home because there was no funding to pay them. Most Americans barely noticed that the government was out of business. Clinton also co-opted one of the centerpieces of the Contract with America by championing a major overhaul of the welfare system despite opposition from traditional Democratic Party allies.

It was also during that budget confrontation with Newt Gingrich and the Republican House in mid-November 1995 that President Clinton took notice of a White House intern named Monica Lewinsky.

Must Read: *All Too Human: A Political Education* by George Stephanopoulos.

American Voices
First Lady Hillary Rodham Clinton on the *Today* show (January 27, 1998):

This started out as an investigation of a failed land deal. I told everybody in 1992, "We lost money." . . . Well it was true. It's taken years but it was true. We get a politically motivated prosecutor who is allied with the right-wing opponents of my husband. . . . I do believe that this is a battle. I mean, look at the very people who are involved in this, they have popped up in other settings. . . . [T]his vast right-wing conspiracy that has been conspiring against my husband since the day he announced for president.

What is "is"?

In the media-driven world that American politics has become, when the "photo op" has become the chief means of communicating policy, presidents and their staffs have become increasingly sensitive to the "image." And for the public, it is those images—not always those of the president's choosing—that become fixed in history. Today, whenever we see an image of Richard Nixon, he is either toasting the Chinese leadership in the historic visit that marked the high point of his presidency, or flashing a V sign as he boarded the helicopter that took him from the White House in disgrace. Ronald Reagan is almost always smiling broadly as he rides a horse on his California ranch, or honoring the war dead at a D-Day memorial in Normandy. Jimmy Carter is immortalized in a cardigan sweater telling Americans to turn their thermostats down during an energy crisis.

Then there is the indelible image of Bill Clinton, wagging his finger as he indignantly told America on January 26, 1998, "I did not have sexual relations with that woman, Miss Lewinsky. I never told anybody to lie, not a single time, never. These allegations are false."

In fact, they were not false. At least not all of them. And on December 19, 1998, Bill Clinton became the second White House occupant in U.S. history to be impeached by the House of Representatives. (The first was Lincoln's successor, Andrew Johnson; see p. 249.) Four articles of impeachment were sent to the House by the Republican-controlled Judiciary Committee, but only two of them were adopted by the full House.

The long, tawdry history of the Clinton impeachment case dates to scandals during Clinton's years as attorney general and governor in Arkansas, and later as president. But they were also tied into the culture and history of Washington. The veneer of gentility in American politics had been erased, mostly since the 1970s Watergate era. The backroom political wrangling that had been kept behind closed doors changed into the no-holds-barred, pit-bull style of the eighties and nineties—with the full compliance of a new twenty-four-hour-a-day news media. In the new age of continuous cable and Internet news, the press no longer operated by the "old school" rules of the Washington press corps—rules under which FDR's wheelchair was never shown in photographs and reporters looked the other way when it came to JFK's numerous dalliances. The viciousness of the Robert Bork and Clarence Thomas hearings was all part of a new power game in which winning was the only thing.

Aided and abetted by his wife, Hillary, who sat by his side during a famous 60 *Minutes* television interview in which the couple confessed that they had marital problems, Clinton had been able to dodge stories of his womanizing during the 1992 campaign. But in 1994, a new story came along. An Arkansas woman named Paula Corbin Jones sued Clinton for sexually harassing her while he was governor in 1991. This story broke as the Clintons were being actively investigated by a special prosecutor, Independent Counsel Kenneth Starr, who was examining a tangle of Arkansas real estate deals known as Whitewater, as well as two separate cases involving misuse of FBI files by the White House and missing billing records from Hillary Clinton's Little Rock law firm. Starr's investigations were essentially going nowhere and Clinton's law team was successfully delaying the Jones suit until after the 1996 election—in which Clinton rather easily defeated veteran Republican senator Robert Dole, with Reform Party candidate Ross Perot playing a substantially diminished role.

In spite of these high-profile investigations, and in the midst of his reelection campaign, Clinton had become involved with Monica S. Lewinsky. She was, in 1995, a twenty-one-year-old White House intern. Between their first encounter and March 1997, when her internship ended, Lewinsky frequently and repeatedly engaged in what most people would call "sex" with Clinton in the Oval Office. As it turned out, Bill Clinton defined the word differently.

The Starr investigation and the Jones suit were proceeding when Jones's lawyers were informed of the Clinton-Lewinsky affair by Linda Tripp, a former White House staffer who worked in the Pentagon, where Lewinsky had been transferred. Tripp had surreptitiously taped the young woman discussing her involvement with the president. Clinton was then questioned about this relationship by the Jones law team under oath and denied the relationship. Starr received word of this denial and began an investigation into possible perjury and obstruction-of-justice charges against Clinton. In the course of videotaped testimony to prosecutors, Clinton was once asked, "Is that correct?"

Already notorious for his ability to wiggle around words, Clinton responded, "It depends on what the meaning of the word 'is' is."

In September 1998, just prior to the midterm congressional elections, Independent Counsel Starr released a report on his investigation to Congress. (He chose not to announce that the Clintons had been exonerated in the investigations of the FBI files and the law firm billing files.) Disgusted by the revelations in the Starr report of oral sex taking place during official calls to congressmen and media reports of Lewinsky's semen-stained dress, the American public seemed to be split three ways: those who hated Clinton, those who defended him, and a large middle ground that seemed to want the whole question to go away and the government to get on with its business. Pressing Clinton at every turn, the Republicans smelled blood in the water. But they apparently misread the American mood.

In a stunning reversal of American election tradition, the Democrats gained five seats in the House. (The party controlling the White House historically loses seats in the sixth year of a presidency.) Post-election analysis pointed to voters who were tired of the Republican obsession with the scandal. House Speaker Newt Gingrich, the leader of the conservative Republican "revolution," had gambled $10 million on last-minute advertising that attacked Clinton, and was largely blamed for the party's dismal showing. Within a week of the election, Gingrich announced his resignation from the House.

The essence of the case for impeachment of the president presented by Starr boiled down to a seamy affair about which the president had clearly lied while under oath and had possibly asked others to lie for him. These were the charges that the House took up on December 19, 1998, when they impeached the president for perjury and obstruction of justice.

In an almost farcical incident that captures the tenor of the times, Clinton's impeachment vote was nearly overshadowed when, on the same day, Louisiana congressman Robert Livingston, the speaker of the House designate, who was to have replaced Newt Gingrich, announced his retirement from the House. In dramatic fashion, he resigned after *Hustler* magazine publisher Larry Flynt had uncovered reports that Livingston had had at least four extramarital affairs. The revolution was eating its own.

Apart from the case of Richard Nixon, who certainly would have been impeached had he not resigned, Congress had dealt with fifteen impeachment proceedings since the first case in 1799. Twelve involved judges, one was a cabinet member, one a senator, and only one a president, Andrew Johnson. Of these fifteen impeachments, seven men had been removed from office (all of them federal judges); two cases were dismissed; and six ended in acquittal. Although these earlier impeachment cases provided a limited set of historical precedents, most of the questions regarding impeachment are fairly clear. During the Watergate hearings, a history of impeachment had been prepared for the House Judiciary Committee. One of the young lawyers who worked on it was a recent Yale Law graduate named Hillary Rodham.

During the framing of the Constitution in 1787, the rules regarding impeachment were vigorously debated by men who recognized the enormity of removing an official from office, especially an elective office. The working draft of the document called for removing the president only for bribery and for treason. After heated discussion over the question of how easy such a removal should be, Virginia's George Mason offered a compromise phrase that dated from old English law: "High Crimes and Misdemeanors." And it is that phrase that has caused the most controversy. To most people, the modern sense of the word "misdemeanor" means a petty crime. But many historians hold that when the Constitution was composed, "high misdemeanors" referred specifically to offenses against the state or community as opposed to a crime against people or property.

Alexander Hamilton, who would soon after be dragged publicly through a scandal owing to his own sexual misbehavior, explained this view in the *Federalist Papers*. To Hamilton, an impeachable offense had to be "of a nature which may with peculiar propriety be denominated POLITICAL, as they relate chiefly to injuries done immediately to the society itself." That was the reason that the 1974 Judiciary Committee rejected an article of impeachment against Richard Nixon for cheating on his personal income taxes. Even so, many impeachment proceedings, and certainly the one brought against Andrew Johnson, were politically motivated. As Gerald Ford said in 1970, as a member of the House, "An impeachable offense is whatever a majority of the House of Representatives considers it to be at a given moment in history."

On January 7, 1999, the Senate impeachment trial was formally opened by Chief Justice William H. Rehnquist. The Republican majority in the Senate meant that a strict party line vote would bring Clinton's conviction. Five days later, the Senate voted to acquit President Clinton on both articles of impeachment. On the first count of perjury, ten Republican senators joined the Democrats in a 55–45 vote of not guilty. On the second count of obstruction of justice, five Republicans joined the Democrats for an even 50–50 vote. Clinton was left to serve out his term. On Clinton's next-to-last day in office, his legal team cut a deal that spared Clinton from criminal charges. He admitted that he had made false statements under oath and surrendered his law license. He also agreed to a payment to Paula Jones, which, had it been agreed to earlier, would have probably prevented the whole Lewinsky affair from becoming public.

After Clinton left office, a final report by Independent Counsel Robert Ray, who succeeded Kenneth Starr, concluded in March 2002 that prosecutors had insufficient evidence to show that either the president or Hillary Rodham Clinton had committed any crimes. However, the report stated, "President Clinton's offenses had a significant adverse impact on the community, substantially affecting the public's view of the integrity of our legal systems." Clinton's defenders dismissed the report as they had dismissed most of the charges brought against him— the result of a partisan assault on a president deeply despised by many conservative Republicans. The report also marked an end of an era. Congress had allowed the law that created the role of the special prosecutor, a vestige of Watergate days, to lapse.

Did this long-running soap opera affect history? More to the point, did it affect policy? Many of Clinton's critics argued that the latter was certainly true. Twice during the Lewinsky scandal, Clinton had launched air strikes; once against Iraq, and once against suspected terrorist bases in Sudan and Afghanistan, thought to be the home of a then relatively obscure but very wealthy Saudi who was thought to be funding terrorist activity—Osama bin Laden. Republicans openly questioned these actions as a *Wag the Dog* scenario, so named for an eerily prescient film in which a war is fabricated to improve a president's fading political standing. After the second American missile attack, which was launched in response to the bombing of two separate American embassies, the Senate majority leader, Republican Trent Lott, stated openly, "Both the timing and the policy are open to question." Republican representative Gerald Solomon was even more critical. "Never underestimate a desperate president," he said in a press release. "What option is left for getting impeachment off the front page or maybe even postponed." (In retrospect, Clinton was later criticized for *not* having attacked bin Laden more aggressively.)

This suspicion about Clinton's motives carried over into the biggest military undertaking of his two terms, the leadership of a NATO alliance attack on Yugoslavia in March 1999 to stop the "ethnic cleansing" policies against ethnic Albanians in the province of Kosovo. In the wake of the breakup of the Soviet Union, former Eastern European Communist states like Yugoslavia had also come unglued. Some, like Poland and Czechoslovakia, had done so peacefully. But in Yugoslavia, that was not the case. Yugoslavia broke apart, and hostilities ensued among the republics along ethnic and religious lines. Croatia, Slovenia, and Macedonia declared independence in 1991, followed by Bosnia-Herzegovina in 1992. Serbia and Montenegro remained as the Republic of Yugoslavia.

Bitter fighting followed, especially in Bosnia, where Serbs reportedly engaged in "ethnic cleansing" of the Muslim population. A peace plan, the Dayton Accord, was brokered by the United States and signed by Bosnia, Serbia, and Croatia (in December 1995) with NATO responsible for policing its implementation. But in the spring of 1999, led by the United States, NATO conducted bombing strikes aimed at stopping Yugoslavia's campaign to drive ethnic Albanians out of the Kosovo region. Of this foreign policy decision, journalist Bob Woodward wrote, "When President Clinton led the NATO alliance to attack Yugoslavia to stop the ethnic cleansing in Kosovo, he voiced the right humanitarian motives. Yet there was a careless ad hoc quality to his decision making. The clearest lesson of Vietnam and the Gulf War seemed to have been ignored. When going to war, state clear political objectives and ensure that enough military force is committed to guarantee success. Yet . . . lingering in the background were the unavoidable suggestions that Clinton's actions were influenced by his need for personal atonement and his political desire to do something big and bold so historians would concentrate less on his impeachment."

Ultimately, the campaign against Yugoslavia in Kosovo proved largely a success, with American air power practically destroying Yugoslavia's ability to function. A peace accord was reached in June 1999 under which NATO peacekeeping troops entered Kosovo. President Slobodan Milosevic was ousted after the defeat. Later arrested, he was extradited in 2001 to the Hague, where a UN tribunal tried him for war crimes against humanity. In a landmark verdict, a UN tribunal had found Bosnian general Radislav Krstic guilty of genocide in August 2001 for his role in the mass killing of more than 5,000 Muslims in 1995.

Perhaps time and some future memoir will shed more light on the question of Clinton's legacy and the role his impeachment will play in it. Until then, journalist Jeffrey Toobin's assessment in *A Vast Conspiracy* seems appropriate. "To be sure he will be remembered as the target of an unwise and unfair impeachment proceeding. But just as certainly, history will haunt Clinton for his own role in this political apocalypse, and for that, despite his best efforts, this president can blame only himself."

Must Read: *A Vast Conspiracy: The Real Story of the Sex Scandal That Nearly Brought Down a President* by Jeffrey Toobin.

AMERICAN VOICES:
FEDERAL RESERVE CHAIRMAN ALAN GREENSPAN in testimony before the Senate Banking Committee (February 26, 1997):

Caution seems especially warranted with regard to the sharp rise in equity prices during the last two years. These gains have obviously raised questions of sustainability.

From the beginning of 1995 to the time Greenspan spoke, the Dow Jones Industrial Average had increased 80 percent.

What is "irrational exuberance"?

He saved the world at least three or four times. He cost George Bush I his reelection in 1992. He made everybody in America rich by causing the markets to soar. When he used the phrase "irrational exuberance" to describe a stock market that he feared might be too high in 1996, he sent tremors through the global economy. He caused a recession and crashed the market in 2001. He can jump tall buildings in a single bound. He is not a bird or a plane. He is the chairman of the Federal Reserve.

Who is Alan Greenspan, the "Fed chairman"? And how did he get to be the most powerful man in the world?

Until fairly recent times, few Americans ever heard of the Federal Reserve Board or cared who its chairman was. But in the person of Alan Greenspan, the Fed chairman became one of the most powerful people in the world. By the mid-1990s, his every pronouncement and television appearance was watched with the same reverence once given the Delphic oracle in ancient Greece. One financial news network even created a "briefcase index," a humorous attempt to determine if the thickness of the chairman's attaché case might provide some clue to the actions he was about to take—actions that could make or break fortunes and entire national economies with a word. While "Greenspan watching" became a national pastime during the 1990s, many people had a very basic question: Who was this man and what did he actually do?

The Federal Reserve Board, or the Fed, was created as the central bank of the United States in 1913 with passage of the Federal Reserve Act. An independent government regulatory agency, the Fed is supposed to preserve and protect a flexible but stable economy. To do that, it has power over the nation's currency and conducts the nation's monetary policy (simply put, the actions taken to influence how much money is theoretically in the economy at a given time, also known as the money supply). It also regulates banks. Since 1913, the act has been modified, and in 1978, the Full Employment and Balanced Growth Act instructed the Federal Reserve to seek stable prices—in other words, to fight inflation—and maximum sustainable growth for the economy, while also seeking to maximize employment.

And there's the rub, as they say. Economics (also known for good reason as "the dismal science") traditionally holds that growth is good, but too much growth is not good. An economy that is growing too fast will inevitably lead to inflation—which in its simplest terms is too much money chasing too few goods, or demand outstripping supply. Job growth is also good, but too much job growth is not; in theory, when too many people work, labor costs rise and lead to inflation. In the classic economic textbook view, a certain amount of unemployment is necessary, even desirable, because it limits rising labor costs and dampens consumer demand, helping to keep prices in check. Until the economic boom of the mid-1990s, economic orthodoxy said that the unemployment rate could not fall below 6 percent without provoking dangerous levels of inflation.

What, then, is "sustainable" growth? And what is "maximum employment"? These are two of the key questions that the Federal Reserve has to wrestle with in setting its policies—policies that can ultimately determine the cost of a home mortgage or car loan, the profits that support corporate survival and the stock market, or even, potentially, who is the next president.

Officially, the Federal Reserve system includes the board of governors in Washington, D.C., and the twelve district Federal Reserve banks and their outlying branches. The seven governors of the Federal Reserve system are nominated by the president and confirmed by the Senate to serve fourteen-year terms, nearly lifetime appointments that are supposed to guarantee that short-term political considerations will not enter into the Fed's deliberations and decision making. But like the Supreme Court, the Fed is keenly aware of which way the political winds are blowing. The chairman and the vice chairman of the board of governors are named by the president and confirmed by the Senate. They serve a term of four years, with no limit on the number of terms they may serve. (Greenspan was appointed to his fourth term in 2000. He retired in 2006 and was replaced by Ben Bernanke.)

There are twelve reserve banks, in Atlanta, Boston, Chicago, Cleveland, Dallas, Minneapolis, Kansas City, New York, Philadelphia, Richmond, St. Louis, and San Francisco. These banks oversee the banking industry, regulate the coin and paper currency in circulation, clear the majority of all banks' paper checks, and facilitate wire transfers of payments.

Why the Federal Reserve Matters:
A Glossary of Financial Terms and "Fedspeak"

Board of Governors: The board of governors of the Federal Reserve system is made up of seven governors, each appointed by the president and confirmed by the Senate, to fourteen-year terms. The chairman is a member of the board of governors, and his position as head of the Federal Reserve is based on a separate four-year appointment by the president. The board controls the discount rate (see p. 560), and each member of the board is a member of the Federal Open Market Committee (see p. 561).

Bonds, Bills, and Notes: A bond is a note or obligation requiring the borrower—usually a government or corporation—to pay the lender—an individual or institutional investor—the amount of the loan ("face value") at the end of a fixed period of time. It is one of the chief ways that governments and businesses raise cash to stay in business. Government and corporate bonds trade in an open bond market, and the prices of bonds move in the opposite direction of interest rates.

The United States Treasury issues several types of securities: *Treasury bonds* usually have maturities of between ten and thirty years, although thirty-year bonds were discontinued; *Treasury notes* are securities with a maturity of more than one year but less than ten years; and *Treasury bills* are securities with maturities ranging from thirteen weeks to one year. Together, these Treasury-issued securities are generally referred to as *bonds* and are considered safe investments with little or no risk to principal (the original investment). Corporations also issue bonds, which generally offer higher interest returns but higher degrees of risk. There are many types of corporate bonds, and they are rated in terms of their risk. The riskiest bonds, which usually offer the lowest credit quality but the highest potential returns, are also known as *junk bonds*.

Budget Deficit/Surplus: When the government budgets more spending annually than it takes in taxes, tariffs, and other fees it collects, the shortfall is a *deficit*. Accumulated deficits make up the *national* *debt.* Large deficits tend to lead to higher interest rates, as the government competes for capital with private business and consumers. But some economists hold that deficit spending is necessary, often to stimulate the economy and create jobs, or in a crisis such as a war. A *surplus* is created when the government takes in more than it spends. The surplus can then be saved against future budget expenses, used to reduce the debt, or returned to taxpayers in the form of tax cuts.

Central Bank: A national bank that operates to control and stabilize the currency and credit conditions in a country's economy, usually through the control of interest rates (*monetary policy*). The Federal Reserve is the central bank of the United States.

Consumer Price Index (CPI): A measure of the average change over time in the prices paid by consumers for certain goods and services. The CPI, announced on a monthly basis, is considered the broadest measure of the country's rate of *inflation* (see p. 561). Another statistical gauge, the Producer Price Index, or PPI, measures costs that producers—factories, manufacturers, farmers, etc.—pay to make and deliver their goods. Higher producer prices often lead to higher consumer prices as the business passes along its higher costs. During the 1990s, many economists argued that the CPI overstates the real inflation rate by as much as 1 percent because of difficulties in gauging prices on a national scale and out-of-date comparisons.

Discount Rate: The interest rate that the twelve Federal Reserve banks charge to private commercial banks, savings and loan associations, savings banks, and credit unions to borrow reserves from the Fed. This rate is controlled by the board of governors. In recent times, this rate has been the key means the Fed uses to set interest policy.

Easing or Tightening: To *ease,* or make credit more available, the Fed pumps money into the nation's banking system by buying U.S. Treasury bonds. This causes the *Fed funds rate* to go down, making it easier for consumers and businesses to borrow money. Normally used to fight a slow-growth economy or recession (negative growth), easing encourages the economy to grow as consumers and companies buy more "stuff."

To *tighten* credit, the Fed sells U.S. Treasury bonds, which withdraws money from the banking system. With the money supply decreased, banks become less willing to lend, making borrowing more difficult for businesses and consumers. When short-term interest rates rise, the economy's growth usually slows. Tightening credit is the Fed's main tool for fighting inflation.

Federal Open Market Committee (FOMC): A twelve-member committee that meets eight times a year (about every six weeks) to assess the state of the economy and set guidelines for the Federal Reserve regarding the sale and purchase of government securities in the open market. Chaired by the reserve chairman, the FOMC consists of the seven governors and the presidents of the twelve Federal Reserve banks, but only twelve people vote in the committee. They are the seven Fed governors, the president of the New York Federal Reserve Bank, and four of the other eleven Federal Reserve Bank presidents, who serve one-year voting terms on a rotating basis.

Fed Funds Rate: The average interest rate at which federal funds actually trade in a day. The Fed influences interest rates by *easing or tightening* through either the sale or the purchase of U.S. Treasury bonds, and this rate is controlled by the Federal Reserve's Federal Open Market Committee, or FOMC (see above). It is the rate that banks charge one another for overnight loans—a key "short-term" interest rate. The funds rate affects overall credit conditions in the country and is the Fed's main weapon against both inflation and a slow growth economy, or recession, a shrinking economy.

Fiscal Policy: The government's plan for spending and taxing. (It differs from monetary policy, which the Fed controls; see p. 562.)

Gross Domestic Product (GDP): Once known as the Gross National Product, this is the broadest measure of the output of a nation's economy—the total amount of all goods and services that a nation produces. Measuring the GDP determines whether the economy is growing or contracting and how fast it is moving in either direction.

Inflation: Simply put, too many dollars chasing too few goods, usually the result of demand outstripping supply. The result is rising prices, as measured by the *CPI* (see p. 560). While price increases are generally necessary to sustain business profits and wage growth, a rapid rise in prices of all goods and services is considered a danger to the economy. Fighting inflation and keeping a lid on sharp price rises are some of the key goals of the Fed.

Monetary Policy: The central bank's actions to influence interest rates and the supply of money available in the economy.

Productivity: Simply, the statistical measure of the average hourly output of workers. Ideally, productivity gains allow efficiencies that both reduce consumer costs and increase profits, which can then be shared with workers, increasing the standard of living. Productivity is viewed as a key to restraining inflation as the cost of goods falls because they are cheaper to produce.

During the 1990s, Alan Greenspan came to accept the theory that rapid and lasting gains in American productivity—the result of technological advances and a better educated and trained workforce, among many other factors—were the key to sustained economic expansion with little inflation.

Recession: A nationwide decline in overall business activity characterized by a drop in buying, selling, and production, and a rise in unemployment. Many economists consider a nation's economy in a recession if the output of goods and services falls for six consecutive months, or two quarters. When a recession grows worse and lasts longer, it becomes a *depression*.

Stocks: Certificates representing partial ownership in a corporation and a claim on the firm's earnings and assets. Stocks of profitable corporations normally yield payments of dividends, a portion of the corporate earnings distributed to shareholders. At its most basic, the value of stock often rises and falls as a company meets, or fails to meet, earnings expectations.

During Alan Greenspan's tenure at the Fed, which began in 1987, the American economy did some remarkable things. For ten years beginning in 1991, the economy grew steadily, sometimes rapidly, with relatively low inflation. Once upon a time, they called it the

"Goldilocks economy." Jobs were being created at a record clip, pushing unemployment ranks down to unprecedented peacetime levels. Inflation was tame. Corporations were making money. People had jobs and record numbers were investing in the stock market, primarily through their company's retirement plans. Everything seemed to be "just right," as Goldilocks would say.

New technologies, relative peace in the world with the end of the Cold War, the growth of global markets, and freer trade were all credited for powering this economic engine. But to many people, the guiding hand behind this remarkable economic turnaround was the sometimes inscrutable Alan Greenspan.

Chairman of the board since 1987, Alan Greenspan was appointed by President Reagan to replace Paul Volcker, a Democrat. An imposingly tall, cigar-smoking, powerful personality, Volcker had been responsible for setting interest rates extremely high in an attempt to battle the excessive inflation of the late 1970s. Volcker's chairmanship had lasted from 1979 to 1987, and his bitter anti-inflation remedy of high interest rates had worked over the long haul, reducing the inflation rate from 13.3 percent to just 1.1 percent. However, the policy was also responsible, in large measure, for Jimmy Carter's inability to get the economy moving, one of the chief reasons he was so handily trounced by Ronald Reagan in 1980. Reagan's political team was going to name a Fed chairman that they hoped wouldn't similarly cripple Reagan's presidency.

They thought they had found him in a Republican economist who had made a fortune in economic forecasting and was a free-market true believer. Born in 1926 in New York City, Alan Greenspan was a Depression-era child whose mother, a furniture store salesperson, and father, a self-educated stock market analyst, divorced when he was three. He attended George Washington High School in upper Manhattan where he was, coincidentally, three years behind future secretary of state Henry Kissinger. From there, he went on to study clarinet and piano at what later became the Juilliard School of Music, dropping out after two years to play in a big band. Always a lover of statistics and numbers, he enrolled at NYU while still in the band to study economics, graduating summa cum laude in 1948, and getting his master's degree in economics in 1950. In 1952, he married a painter who introduced him to the influential writer Ayn Rand, the Russian-born novelist whose best known works are *The Fountainhead* (1943) and *Atlas Shrugged* (1957). Devoutly anti-Socialist and anti-religious, Rand set forth a moral and economic philosophy, called Objectivism, based on individualism and self-interest. Greenspan was a committed disciple of Rand's philosophy, which eschewed government interference and celebrated the individual over the greater society.

During the 1950s, Greenspan and a partner formed an economic consulting team that forecast changes in the economy and made a considerable fortune during the postwar boom years. During the 1970s, he had served as an economic adviser to President Ford. He was also given high marks for chairing a bipartisan commission charged with shoring up the Social Security system. Following that, he was working in the private sector when the call came from Ronald Reagan.

Two months after he took office in August 1987, Greenspan faced a Wall Street crisis of near 1929 proportions. On one day in October, the stock market lost 508 points, more than 22 percent of its value, in the Crash of '87. The nation's largest financial institutions, which were facing huge investment losses along with the customers who owed them money, were in danger of cracking and crumbling. It was a potential repeat of the Great Crash of 1929, when the stock market collapse had begun a run on banks that led to the downfall of the American banking system. Nearly sixty years later, if one or more of the companies in the very elaborate network of banks and brokerage houses that made up the world's financial system had failed to make payments, or even delayed payments, a devastating domino effect might once again have been triggered. The next morning, Greenspan issued a terse announcement: "The Federal Reserve Bank, consistent with its responsibilities as the nation's central bank, affirmed today its readiness to serve as a source of liquidity to support the financial system."

The statement, meant to soothe roiled nerves on Wall Street, would have been meaningless without action behind it. Like two Dutch boys putting their fingers in the leaking dikes, Greenspan and the New York Fed Bank president worked the phones to executives of the nation's largest banks, getting them to extend credit to some of their insolvent debtors, and promising that the Fed would back them up. It was done behind the scenes. It broke some rules, but it was what the Fed had failed to do in 1929. And this time, the dikes held.

Greenspan's 1987 gambit made him a hero on Wall Street. Five weeks after the stock market crisis, a *Wall Street Journal* headline read: "Passing a Test: Fed's New Chairman Wins a Lot of Praise on Handling the Crash." And he parlayed his success into new power. Before the Greenspan era, the FOMC voted as a body on each change in interest rates. In the aftermath of the 1987 crash, Greenspan persuaded his colleagues to give him new powers by changing the process. While the committee would vote on an overall policy direction—either in the direction of raising or cutting interest rates—the timing and size of rate setting were left to the chairman. As Bob Woodward writes of this shift, the FOMC was "basically ceding operational control to Greenspan."

The powerful post of chairman became even more powerful. In other hands, this much power might have been dangerous. But the consensus is that Greenspan's swift, decisive actions and behind-the-scenes reassurances had prevented a greater meltdown. During the next few years, he headed off several other potential global financial catastrophes, including the huge banking losses of the 1990s, the collapse of the Mexican peso in 1994, the "Asian contagion" of 1998, when several newly important Asian economies basically failed, a collapse of the Russian ruble following the end of Soviet rule, and the failure of Long-Term Capital Management, an investment firm whose failure might have brought down a number of large banks, possibly setting off another domino effect with devastating consequences for the financial markets.

Greenspan did that by building consensus among his fellow central bankers, with a deft mastery of minute details of the working of the American economy. He established credibility as an inflation fighter, which reassured Wall Street. But he also began to realize that the old economic rules had changed. Perhaps most important, he rolled up his sleeves—literally—to work with statisticians and realized that the changes in technology and other efficiencies in productivity meant that the economy could grow and unemployment fall without appreciable inflation.

Ironically, the Republican banker–inflation fighter was viewed by some as one of the reasons behind a Republican president's defeat.

Republicans, including George Bush himself, later said that Greenspan had been responsible for his defeat in the 1992 election. Years later, Bush said in a 1998 *Wall Street Journal* interview, "I think that if interest rates had been lowered more dramatically that I would have been reelected President, because the recovery that we were in would have been more visible. I reappointed him, and he disappointed me." While some economists agree that Fed rate cuts came too late and too slowly during the recession of 1990–91, the causes for Bush's defeat were probably more complex than Greenspan's interest rate decisions and more likely hinged on the Perot candidacy. (See "Can a man called Bubba become president?" p. 545.)

The flip side of that irony lies in the other key to Greenspan's success—his alliance with President Bill Clinton in engineering what many economists believe was the underpinning of the financial boom of the 1990s. The two struck a bargain to keep interest rates low if the president would work with Congress to reduce the federal deficit. Greenspan's deal with Democrat Clinton, and Clinton's ability to broker that balanced budget plan with Congress to deliver on deficit reduction, may ultimately be considered Clinton's single most important accomplishment as president—perhaps removing some of the sting of being only the second president to be impeached in American history.

The other question economists and others argue about was whether Greenspan was right back in 1996. Was there "irrational exuberance"? And was that the cause of the massive meltdown that crippled Wall Street from 2000 forward? In a short space of time, the NASDAQ stock average, which had rocketed to 5,000 on the strength of a flood of money being invested in new technology companies, the Internet, and "dot.com" startups, fell back below 2,000. The Dow Jones Industrial Average, which topped out at more than 11,000 points in 2000, tumbled back below the 9,500 range—later moving down to 7,500—as America entered its first recession in a decade and people learned for the first time in a decade that stocks can move up and down. Technology hysteria, "bubble" mentality, crowd psychology, stock analysts and brokers who touted everything as a "buy," thereby inflating stock prices, as well as revelations of an increasing number of possible frauds committed against shareholders by corporations and accountants who were disguising their profits by "cooking the books" all served to overheat the financial markets.

In many ways, the 2000 stock market meltdown was comparable to the great losses of 1929, except this crash affected selected industries and did not take the entire banking community down with it as thoroughly. Decades of federal regulation governing stock markets and banking, and a more diverse economy that was in far better fundamental shape than the 1929 economy had been, served to prevent a global financial catastrophe on the order of the Great Crash of 1929.

Must read: *Maestro: Greenspan's Fed and the American Boom* by Bob Woodward.

Is that chad dimpled, pregnant, or hanging?

"Those who cast the votes decide nothing. Those who count the votes decide everything."

Joseph Stalin, to whom that quote is attributed, may well be smiling in the Socialist Paradise, if there is one. The Soviet dictator would have certainly appreciated the American presidential race of 2000 and the strange goings-on in the state of Florida. A smile might also cross the face of William "Boss" Tweed, the notorious nineteenth-century "fixer" of all things political in New York City. On Election Day in 1871, Tweed said, "As long as I count the votes, what are you going to do about it?"

If it hadn't been so important, it would have been completely comical. Citizens of the richest, most powerful, most technologically advanced country in the world—on the verge of launching the International Space Station into orbit 300 miles above Earth—were reduced to holding paper ballot cards up to the light to see if a hole had been punched through the paper or not. As the world watched the state of Florida in electoral disarray, America was learning a whole new vocabulary of "chads"—the small bits of paper produced when a hole is poked through a punch card. For all of America's fears of going into the year 2000 with the much-dreaded possibility of a Y2K computer bug that would crash the world's entire information and technology apparatus, it was the simple act of pushing a sharp stick through a piece of paper that actually wreaked the most havoc.

It had been a very long time since America had seen a presidential election so close: the Nixon-Kennedy race of 1960, to be exact. It had been even longer since Americans had seen an election in which the candidate with the most popular votes lost. That dates back to the controversial race of 1888, when Grover Cleveland won the popular vote and Benjamin Harrison won the Electoral College vote and became president. But these are the strange but true vagaries of American presidential politics.

Election Day 2000 pitted the sitting vice president against the son of the man who had been defeated eight years earlier in the election of 1992. On the face of it, the incumbent vice president, enjoying the fruits of the longest and most successful era in American economic history, had the cards in his favor. The economy, though flagging, was still strong, with employment high and inflation low. Prosperity is usually good for an incumbent. There was relative peace in the world. The American effort in Bosnia had been a success, with little cost in American lives. To be sure, there were problems, but Al Gore thought that his biggest problem was embracing everything good about the Clinton years while distancing himself from the scandals that had nearly destroyed Bill Clinton's presidency.

On the other side was the two-term governor of Texas, George W. Bush. Dismissed as an intellectual lightweight, he campaigned as a "compassionate conservative" who would restore honor and dignity to a White House besmirched by Clinton's reprehensible behavior. Both men had survived bruising primary battles. Gore had fought off an insurgency from former New Jersey senator Bill Bradley, a Rhodes scholar and former professional basketball player for the New York Knicks who appealed to the more liberal wing of the Democratic Party. Bush had confronted a strong popular campaign waged by Arizona senator John McCain, a conservative Republican who was a much admired war hero, survivor of years of captivity in a North Vietnamese prison in Hanoi. The primary campaigns had left both candidates battered, and in a fairly unmemorable campaign, neither distinguished himself. Interestingly, one of the most historic aspects of the campaign—the first

Jewish nominee for vice president in the person of Connecticut senator Joseph Lieberman—barely made a ripple.

There were also two significant independent candidates adding intrigue to the race. Consumer advocate Ralph Nader represented the liberal environmentalist Green Party. Patrick Buchanan, the fiery archconservative former Republican candidate, had wrested control of Ross Perot's once crucial Reform Party. But neither of these two men was included in any of the debates between the two main party candidates, and it seemed that they would have little impact on the national vote. But as Tip O'Neill, the famed Massachusetts congressman and speaker of the house, once said, "All politics is local." And Nader and Buchanan would prove to have an impact on a few important local races.

On the eve of the election, surveys had the race too close to call. America seemed to be split in two. And for once the polls were right. As the voting booths closed across the country on election night, the closeness of the election was apparent, but Gore seemed to have a slim edge. Late on election night, network television projections declared Al Gore the victor in the state of Florida, giving him the electoral votes needed to win the presidency. The balloons of victory were soon floating in the air. But they were about to burst. In a stunning turnaround, the network projections were retracted. Florida was proving too close to call.

In Florida, earlier on Election Day, state Democratic officials had already begun to receive reports of confused voters in several election districts who believed that they may have miscast their votes. Many of them were Jewish senior citizens, traditionally Democratic Party loyalists, who feared that they might have cast votes for Reform Party candidate Patrick Buchanan, considered by many Jews to be an anti-Semite, largely because of remarks he had once made about Hitler. Others thought that they had pushed out two holes in the paper punch cards. Would their votes still count? At the same time, Ralph Nader, on the Green Party ticket, was drawing about 100,000 votes in Florida. It was not a huge number, but his votes were presumably drawn from more liberal and reformist independent voters who might have been more likely to choose Gore if Nader had not been in the race.

In the early hours of the morning, television networks completed the turnabout and projected George Bush the winner of Florida's electoral votes, giving him the presidency. Gore telephoned Bush to concede. Told that the race in Florida was too close to call, Gore then retracted his concession and the projection of Bush as the winner was also retracted. Governed by Jeb Bush, the Republican candidate's brother, Florida had been considered a key state in the election. Nobody could have imagined just how key—and chaotic—it was going to be.

On the day after Election Day, Gore had a lead in the national popular vote and was ahead in electoral votes, with 255 to 246 for Bush; 270 electoral votes are needed to win the presidency. While two other states were also still undecided, the balance of the election hung on the outcome in Florida, with its 25 electoral votes.

Before the day was out, the first suits contesting ballots in some Florida counties, like the first scattered gunshots in a battle, were filed by both sides. While an incomplete count of Florida's votes gave Bush a statewide lead of 1,784 votes, prompting a mandatory statewide mechanical recount, voters in heavily Democratic Palm Beach County filed a suit challenging the results there. They were specifically challenging the "butterfly ballot," a paper ballot with candidates' names shown in two facing columns. Voters were expected to punch out a hole that corresponded to their candidate. But the ballot had confused many voters, especially the "early bird special" vote, Florida's large, politically active retiree community. Many voters worried that they had mistakenly voted for Buchanan; some, realizing they had made a mistake, punched a second hole instead of requesting a new ballot. Ballots with two votes cast would be invalidated as "overvotes."

Over the course of the next month, Florida became an armed camp of dueling lawyers and "spin doctors" all trying to sway the courts and public opinion. Battling through local, county, state, and federal courts, the two sides fought over which votes should be counted, who should count them, and whether it was too late to count them under Florida law. Finally, on December 1, the U.S. Supreme Court heard arguments on an appeal by the Republican candidate George Bush. On December 4, the U.S. Supreme Court vacated a Florida Supreme Court decision extending the deadline for certification of votes, and returned the case to the state court for clarification. When the Florida Supreme Court ordered a manual recount of all ballots in which a vote for president was not recorded by a machine and restored 383 votes from partial recounts in two Florida counties, the Bush legal team again appealed to the U.S. Supreme Court.

On December 9, in a five-to-four decision, the Supreme Court halted the manual recounts pending a hearing of Bush's appeal, and on December 11, the Court heard oral arguments from the two sides. Finally, in high drama at 10 P.M., on December 12, the U.S. Supreme Court issued two unsigned rulings that reversed the Florida Supreme Court's order to proceed with the recount. Technically speaking, the Court had sent the decision back to the Florida Supreme Court for review, while noting at the same time that there was no time for a recount because of constitutional deadlines.

On December 13, in a televised address, Al Gore again conceded to Bush. George W. Bush addressed the nation as president-elect. For the first time since John Quincy Adams was elected, America had another set of father-son presidents. More significantly, for the first time in American history, the Supreme Court had played a decisive role in the outcome of a presidential election.

The final official results showed that Gore had won the national popular vote 51,003,894 (48.41 percent of the popular vote) against Bush's 50,495,211 (47.89 percent of the popular vote), a difference of 508,683 votes, or approximately one half of one percent of the popular vote. Ralph Nader, the Green Party candidate, took 2,834,410 votes, less than 3 percent of the national vote. However, in Florida Nader garnered 97,488 votes. Many political analysts agreed that Nader had played the spoiler's role, drawing support from Gore in Florida, as well as a few other close states.

Patrick Buchanan, the archconservative Republican who turned controversial Reform Party candidate, polled only 446,743 votes, a mere 0.42 of the national presidential vote. In 1992, Ross Perot had won 19 percent of the popular vote under the Reform Party banner. Four years later, the Reform movement still managed to deliver Perot more than 8 million votes. But the controversial Buchanan, a former speechwriter for Richard Nixon, had splintered the Reform Party, rendering it insignificant. It was clear, however, that Buchanan's candidacy had hurt Al Gore because of the confusion over the ballot in Florida, where Buchanan tallied 17,484 votes.

While the debacle in Florida captured the world spotlight for thirty-six days, the election was not only about the Sunshine State. The spotlight of the post-election drama was deservedly on Florida and the dueling lawyers and press conferences. And much of the post-election analysis focused on how likely it was that Gore would have won the state without the Nader-Buchanan factor and the large number of disqualified ballots. But the official electoral tally showed Bush winning the electoral vote with 271 votes to Gore's 266. (Gore should have had 267, but one elector from Washington, D.C., abstained.)

Mostly overlooked was the fact that the sitting vice president, beneficiary of the greatest economic boom in modern times and with the country enjoying relative peace and prosperity, could have won the Oval Office simply by carrying one of a handful of other states that had voted for Clinton-Gore four years earlier:

Tennessee   Gore's home state, where he and his father had both been elected U.S. Senator, with its eleven electoral votes, a state carried by Bill Clinton in 1992 and 1996.

Arkansas   With six electoral votes, the home state of President Bill Clinton had also voted Democratic in 1992 and 1996. But it went to George Bush in 2000 by 50,000 votes.

West Virginia   Another state won easily by Bill Clinton in 1992 and 1996, West Virginia gave Bush five electoral votes by a margin of some 40,000 votes. One key to the Bush win there was the lavish campaign spending by the coal industry, one of the chief beneficiaries of President Bush's environmental policies. These included new rules that removed restrictions from "mountaintop removal," a form of coal mining in which entire tops of mountains were sheared off to mine coal. This technique, which created vast amounts of earth and rock, and had them dumped into rivers and streams, had been prohibited under previous Environmental Protection Agency rules.

Ohio   Of the states won by Clinton in 1992 and 1996 that Gore could not hold in 2000, the largest Electoral College vote lay here with twenty-one electoral votes. Once considered a solid Democratic stronghold with a powerful union vote, Ohio went to Bush.

(Although Nader took more than 100,000 votes in Ohio, his candidacy was a smaller factor there than elsewhere.)

New Hampshire The closest race of all was in this small New England state with its four electoral votes. Had they gone to Gore, he would have won the election. The only New England (and northeastern) state carried by George Bush, New Hampshire had been carried by Bill Clinton in both 1992 and 1996. But in 2000, Bush won the "Live Free or Die" state by 7,211 votes, out of some 600,000 presidential votes cast. Here the Green Party's Ralph Nader may have played the most crucial spoiler role in this independent-minded and often quirky state. Nader won more than 22,000 votes, presumably drawing from liberal and reform-minded voters who might have otherwise voted in the Democratic camp.

Much of the commentary in this extraordinary and bizarre election also focused on the unprecedented role of the Supreme Court. Had the Rehnquist Court, which often divided between five conservative justices (William Rehnquist, Sandra Day O'Connor, Antonin Scalia, Clarence Thomas, and Anthony Kennedy) and four more liberal justices (Stephen Breyer, David Souter, Ruth Bader Ginsburg, and John Paul Stevens), acted properly in its decision? Or had the Court overreached its legitimate bounds in essentially deciding the election? The answer to that question, predictably, seemed to depend on the political preference of the person who answered. At one end of the spectrum were those who found the Court's opinion perfectly acceptable, usually Republican Bush supporters. One constant in their view: the Supreme Court had to overturn a flawed and politically biased ruling made by the Democratic majority in the Florida State Supreme Court—even if that flew in the recent tradition of the Republican Party's devotion to states' rights. That was the view expressed by one Republican legal scholar who argued that the decision was poorly reasoned and badly written but, in the end, fundamentally the correct one.

In the highly partisan postdecision atmosphere, it was difficult to find a conservative voice that disagreed with the Supreme Court. But, writing in the *Weekly Standard* (December 25, 2000), John J. DiIulio

Jr. was one of the few who did: "To any conservative who truly respects federalism, the majority's opinion is hard to respect. . . . The arguments that ended the battle and 'gave' Bush the presidency are constitutionally disingenuous at best. They will come back to haunt conservatives and confuse, if they do not cripple, the principled conservative case for limited government, legislative supremacy, and universal civic deference to legitimate, duly constituted state and local public authority." He concluded, "There was a time when conservatives would rather have lost a close, hotly contested presidential election, even against a person and a party from whom many feared the worst, than advance judicial imperialism, diminish respect for federalism, or pander to mass misunderstanding and mistrust of duly elected legislative officials. . . . Desirable result aside, it is bad constitutional law."

On the other end of the spectrum were those—generally Democrats and Gore supporters—who thought the decision a judicial outrage. Harvard's Alan Dershowitz called it the "single most corrupt decision in Supreme Court history." It was difficult to find a Gore supporter who thought that the Court had done the right thing. Perhaps the most outraged was famed attorney Vincent Bugliosi, who argued, in a bestselling book called *The Betrayal of America*, that the majority was not only mistaken, but actually criminal. "Considering the criminal intention behind the decision, legal scholars and historians should place this ruling above the Dred Scott case (*Scott v. Sandford*) and *Plessy v. Ferguson* in egregious sins of the Court. The right of every American to have his or her vote counted, and for Americans (not five unelected Justices) to choose their President was callously and I say criminally jettisoned by the Court's majority to further its own political ideology."

Bugliosi's sense of outrage seemed not to be shared by most Americans—and it should be noted that close to half of all eligible Americans did not vote to begin with—who were apparently relieved that the Supreme Court had put the country out of its electoral misery. The prevailing attitude seemed to be any decision was better than no decision and the endless bickering between lawyers in Florida.

For weeks and months after the election, the close votes, the political stratagems of the two candidates, and the Supreme Court's behavior were debated and deliberated. But the real scandal of the election came in discovering how many votes routinely don't count in American elections because of voting machine problems and other Election Day irregularities. In most elections, these uncounted votes rarely affected the outcome, so the media did not pay much attention to uncounted votes and "double counted" or "overvotes" that were rejected in the official tally. But in 2000, when every vote truly became precious, Americans learned how disposable their votes actually could be. And it should come as no surprise to learn that most of the votes that never get counted come largely from the poorest districts, often with large minority populations, where the least money is traditionally spent to modernize election machines and ensure that every vote, supposedly considered an American's most precious birthright, is counted.

This disintegration of millions of votes, coupled with the fact that the popular vote had been upstaged by the Electoral College—that nineteenth-century vestige of a fear of too much democracy—at least briefly rekindled the call to be rid of the Electoral College once and for all. If it ever had its usefulness as a means of guaranteeing that a president had to be elected by a diverse geographical population and not just those in a few large states, that rationale no longer existed for many commentators.

The intense public interest in the close election of 2000, the debate over the Supreme Court's remarkable intrusion into presidential politics, and the push for election reform, including the end of the Electoral College, were big stories in America—for a very short time. As the nation busied itself with "business as usual," complacency about the election seemed to set in—except perhaps among a handful of Democratic true believers convinced that their man was the "real" president.

But in a broader historical sweep, the strange election of 2000 was more or less forgotten a year later, eclipsed by the events of September 11, 2001.

Must Read: *Too Close to Call: The Thirty-Six-Day Battle to Decide the 2000 Election* by Jeffrey Toobin; *Bush v. Gore: The Court Cases and the Commentary* edited by E. J. Dionne Jr. and William Kristol.

Where is Fox Mulder when we need him?

Remember the child's rhyme about the little girl with the curl right in the middle of her forehead? "When she was good, she was very, very good. When she was bad she was horrid."

That sort of summarizes the history of the FBI during the past twenty years. It was, to put it another way, the best of times and the worst of times for the G-men.

To an older generation of television-watching Americans, the FBI was always perfect. Every week, an FBI agent played by Efrem Zimbalist Jr. solved a crime, supposedly taken from FBI case files, within an hour. But by the time *The X-Files* appeared, a new disillusioned generation, fed on tales of cover-ups, conspiracy, and questionable competence, saw the FBI as a bureau of disinformation campaigns and malevolent leadership. The Truth may be "out there," as Agent Fox Mulder of *The X-Files* told us each week, but it probably lies somewhere between these television views of the FBI.

The recent history of the FBI—and related intelligence and law enforcement agencies like the Immigration and Naturalization Service (INS), the Drug Enforcement Agency (DEA), the Bureau of Alcohol, Tobacco, and Firearms (BATF), and the CIA—is a record of stunning successes combined with embarrassing and dismal failures.

- **Ruby Ridge:** The confrontation between federal agents and the Weaver family in Ruby Ridge, Idaho, became one of the most controversial and widely discussed examples of abuse of federal power, feeding a whole subculture of Americans who distrust their government. Ruby Ridge began with an abortive arrest by U.S. marshals of a self-proclaimed Christian white separatist named Randall Weaver. The Weaver family lived in a remote mountain cabin near Ruby Ridge in northern Idaho. Their racist and anti-Semitic views would be anathema to the vast majority of Americans. Randall Weaver had failed to appear for a hearing on a charge of selling unregistered firearms—two sawed-off shotguns—to an BATF undercover agent in 1989. This failure was due to a typographical error in the letter advising Weaver of the date for his court appearance. The court nonetheless issued a bench warrant for his arrest. (A jury later determined Weaver had been entrapped although the Justice Department investigation of the case found that there was no illegal entrapment.)

On August 21, 1992, during a check of Weaver's property—which, it was later determined, constituted an illegal search by the marshals—one of Weaver's dogs began to bark and was shot by a federal agent. It was later revealed that one of the marshals had thrown stones at the dogs to see what it would take to agitate them. A gun battle ensued, and Weaver's fourteen-year-old son, Sammy, was shot in the back while running away. In the gunfire that followed, a marshal was also shot and killed.

The next day, when Randy Weaver stepped out of his cabin to retrieve his son's body, an FBI sniper shot him. As Weaver and two companions tried to get back in the cabin, Weaver's wife, Vicki, stood in the cabin doorway holding an infant. The sniper fired again, killing Mrs. Weaver instantly. According to FBI guidelines, deadly force is allowed only when necessary to protect someone against immediate danger. These limits are implicit in the Constitution and have been established through Supreme Court rulings.

At a subsequent trial, the government claimed that Weaver and another man were shot because they had threatened to shoot at an FBI helicopter. The judge threw out that charge for insufficient evidence. An Idaho jury found Weaver and a companion innocent on most of the serious charges against them. Weaver's attorney, Gerry Spence, said afterward, "A jury today has said that you can't kill somebody just because you wear badges, and then cover up those homicides by prosecuting the innocent."

A later investigation of the fiasco by the Justice Department, one of the most intensive internal reviews of an FBI investigation ever, concluded in a 1994 report that the FBI's hostage rescue team overreacted to the threat of violence and instituted a shoot-on-sight policy that violated bureau guidelines and Fourth Amendment restrictions on police power. The FBI disciplined twelve agents and employees, including Larry Potts—the head of the criminal division at the time who was later promoted.

All these investigations and recommendations came long after the fact. Too long after to be of any help when the FBI confronted its next deadly siege, near a Texas town called Waco.

Must Read: *From Freedom to Slavery: The Rebirth of Tyranny in America* by Gerry Spence.

- **Waco:** On February 28, 1993, the Treasury Department's Bureau of Alcohol, Tobacco, and Firearms staged a disastrous raid on a ramshackle compound in Mount Carmel, Texas, ten miles east of Waco. More than 100 agents were serving arrest warrants for gun violations on members of the Branch Davidian religious sect and its leader, David Koresh. A high school dropout, Koresh, like many cult leaders, was a charismatic type whose rambling discourses on the Bible and the coming apocalypse enthralled his followers. And like other cult leaders, Koresh had begun to use his religious leadership as a sexual tool. He preached that women members of the group had to have sex with him to become true disciples, and he had allegedly fathered as many as a dozen children by different "wives," some of them girls as young as twelve years old.

  He allegedly used traditional mind-manipulation techniques on his followers. A spartan environment, surrender of possessions, and slavish loyalty were used to create a world in which the sect members were utterly dependent on him. Discipline was central to Koresh's methods, and often inhumane. Children were routinely paddled to the point of bleeding. Adults were forced to stand in sewage pits. Nonetheless, while their practices were considered bizarre, immoral, or even illegal, many sect members held jobs outside the compound.

  But Koresh had also embarked on an ambitious plan to acquire weapons. It was for these weapons, including assault rifles, hundreds of thousands of rounds of ammunition, and parts for making machine guns, that the BATF staged its raid. In the ill-planned BATF raid, the question of who fired first was never clearly answered. Survivors said that they did not shoot until they were fired upon by the federal agents. Four BATF agents were killed and several Branch Davidians lay dead.

  That same day President Clinton ordered the FBI to take over the case. The initial FBI strategy was to make life hellish for the Branch

Davidians by gradually shrinking the perimeter around the compound, shining searchlights at the house for twenty-four hours a day, and then playing ear-splitting noises. Koresh only used these ploys to strengthen his apocalyptic predictions and make himself more messianic to his followers. After negotiations in a fifty-one-day standoff went nowhere, and believing that the children inside the compound were at risk, Attorney General Janet Reno approved a plan to end the siege with an assault, and President Clinton endorsed the plan on April 18. The FBI planned to step up pressure by using CS gas, a type of gas deemed more effective than tear gas. The decision was made despite the fact that, as James Bovard noted in his book *Lost Rights*, "A few months earlier, the U.S. government had signed an international treaty banning the use of CS in warfare, effectively recognizing that its effects were so harsh that its use on enemy soldiers was immoral. But the international treaty did not prohibit the U.S. government from using CS against American citizens."

Despite fears of a mass suicide, as had happened in Guyana when 900 followers of cult leader Jim Jones had taken their lives, the FBI launched its raid at about 6 A.M. A modified tank began battering holes near the compound entrance and spraying a mist of CS gas. The Branch Davidians began firing at the tanks. By 9 A.M., a tank had smashed in the front door of the compound and the FBI thought the standoff was over. The FBI planned to continue the pressure of gas and tanks closing in until the cult members surrendered. But at around noon, wisps of smoke appeared, and the building was soon in flames, whipped by high winds blowing off the Texas prairie. Agents entering the building to try to rescue cult members found children in a concrete pit filled with water, rats, and excrement. There were no fire trucks on the scene, as the FBI thought that they would be endangered if a gunfight broke out.

When the conflagration was over, eighty Davidians, including twenty-seven children, were identified as having died in the fire. Seven, including Koresh, had gunshot wounds in their heads. Almost immediately, claims began to be circulated that the FBI had deliberately set the fire.

Later investigations, bolstered by evidence from listening devices that had been secretly sent into the compound in which

Davidians were heard saying "Spread the fuel," indicated that internal fires had been set by the Davidians. Kerosene and gasoline were detected on the clothes of some of the surviving cult members, but there remained a possibility that some of the fires may have started in the assault itself. In the aftermath, two BATF members were fired but later reinstated at a lower rank. No FBI officials were disciplined. Eight of the surviving Branch Davidians were convicted on charges ranging from weapons violations to voluntary manslaughter.

The country had always been supportive of the FBI and its handling of the case, but the two cases combined had a powerful impact on the public perception of the FBI and other agencies. According to Ronald Kessler's *The Bureau*, "By 1999, a majority of the public believed that the FBI had murdered innocent people at Waco . . . and Ruby Ridge."

- **Oklahoma City:** Waco would have aftershocks. On April 19, 1995, the second anniversary of the Waco fire, a truck bomb exploded in front of the Alfred P. Murrah Federal Building in downtown Oklahoma City, blowing out the entire front of the high-rise office building and killing 168 people, 19 of them children. Suspicion was cast immediately on Arab terrorists in the wake of the World Trade Center bombing that had taken place in 1993. But within a few hours, the FBI had a piece of the truck used in the bombing and had traced it to a Kansas truck rental shop.

  Within days, Timothy McVeigh was identified as the key suspect in the bombing. A decorated Gulf War veteran, McVeigh was already in jail awaiting a hearing. He had been arrested by an Oklahoma state trooper on the day of the bombing for driving without license plates and for carrying a concealed weapon. A fellow conspirator, Terry Nichols, had also been identified and captured and agreed to testify against his partner. McVeigh was convicted and then scheduled for execution. But even when the FBI had done things right, things now went wrong. Just days before McVeigh's scheduled execution in May 2001, the FBI revealed to the convicted bomber's attorneys that it had failed to turn over 3,000 pages of documents relating to the case. McVeigh's scheduled execution was delayed by the new attorney general, John Ashcroft, while the condemned man's attorneys reviewed the documents. The papers had no impact, other than to delay the execution and give the bureau another black eye. McVeigh was executed in June 2001, the first federal execution in America since 1963.

- **The Unabomber:** Between 1978 and 1998, the United States was plagued by a wave of mail bombings. Most of the bombs, which consisted of hundreds of nails, cut-up razor blades, and metal fragments, were made to look like ordinary parcels, which exploded when their victims opened them. Because the earliest of these bombs targeted professors of science and engineering as well as airline executives, the FBI dubbed the perpetrator the Unabomber (UNA = "Universities and Airlines"). The Unabomber struck sixteen times, killing three people, injuring twenty-three others, and causing millions to live in fear.

  In 1995, the media were sent a 35,000-word manifesto written by the Unabomber describing his targets as modern industry and technology. According to this document, he believed that the only way to restore humanity's self-esteem was to destroy the institutions that fostered technology and innovation. The FBI ultimately spent the next seventeen years and $50 million tracking down the Unabomber in the longest, most expensive manhunt in history.

  The case broke only when the Unabomber's own brother recognized the political rhetoric in the manifesto. A genius-level former professor, Ted Kaczynski, now identified as the Unabomber, had taken to living in the mountains of Montana in a shack without electricity or plumbing. Assisted by the brother, who received a reward that he then distributed to the families of victims, the FBI arrested Kaczynski on April 3, 1996. He pleaded guilty to the bombings and expressed no remorse for his actions. In 1998, he was sentenced to four consecutive life terms in a Colorado penitentiary.

- **Olympic Park:** When a pipe bomb exploded on July 26 in the midst of the 1996 Atlanta Olympics, FBI agents were immediately suspicious of a security guard who had alerted police to an abandoned mysterious backpack twenty-three minutes before the bomb exploded. The guard, Richard Jewell, had helped evacuate the area after the bombing, which killed two people. Three days later, a local newspaper reported that Jewell was the innocent victim of a bungled investigation and an irresponsible media feeding frenzy that essentially presumed his guilt. The FBI eventually focused its investigation on Eric Robert Rudolph, a fugitive charged with an abortion clinic bombing in Birmingham, Alabama, and Atlanta. (The subject of an intensive manhunt, Rudolph was captured in 2003.)

- **Los Alamos:** Bombs of another sort figured in still another FBI fiasco, the pursuit of a spy supposedly selling atomic bomb secrets to the Chinese. When a Chinese defector to Taiwan gave up bundles of classified documents, suspicion fell immediately on Wen Ho Lee, a Chinese-American scientist at the Los Alamos nuclear laboratory since 1978. The Department of Energy initially investigated the matter but turned the case over to the FBI. In fact, no one was even certain that the secrets had ever been stolen. But in 1999, an indictment was brought against Wen Ho Lee, charging him with copying atomic bomb secrets. Denied bail and shackled in extremely harsh conditions as he awaited trial, Wen Ho Lee professed innocence. The case against him eventually fell apart. In the end, the government settled for a guilty plea to the lesser charge of making copies and mishandling national security information, and Lee was sentenced to time already served. Whether Wen Ho Lee—or anyone, for that matter—had sold documents to the Chinese was never a certainty. But the FBI had again bungled a high-profile investigation. A federal prosecutor who investigated the case said, "This was a paradigm of how not to manage and work an important counterintelligence case." (In late 2002, Wen Ho Lee reported that he was unable to find employment either at a university or in a laboratory.)

- **Walker/Ames/Hanssen:** The Wen Ho Lee case was one in a string of highly visible espionage cases that left the FBI's counterspying abilities open to serious question. One was the Walker case. Without detection for seventeen years, Navy communications specialist John Walker and his son Michael had spied for the Soviets, selling them important U.S. Navy secrets. Walker began spying in 1968, undetected by FBI surveillance of the Soviet embassy in Washington, and brought his son into the operation in 1983. He also brought his brother Arthur Walker, a retired Navy commander who was working for a defense contractor, into the ring. John Walker was caught only when his marriage failed and his embittered ex-wife alerted the FBI about his activities. Walker was arrested in May 1985, along with his son, brother, and a fourth accomplice. After cooperating with the government, John Walker got a life term, his son a twenty-five-year term, Arthur Walker received three concurrent life sentences and was fined $250,000, and the fourth accomplice was sentenced to a 365-year term and a fine of $410,000.

The second major counterintelligence failure of the period was a CIA-centered fiasco that spilled over to the FBI. Aldrich Ames, the son of a CIA operative, joined the CIA in 1962. By the mid-1980s, he was spying for the Soviets, but it took years for the CIA or FBI to catch on to him, despite the fact that Ames was living way above his means. With a government salary of about $70,000, Ames drove a Jaguar and lived in a house worth half a million dollars. Over the years, the FBI had observed Ames meeting with the Soviets, but were stonewalled by the CIA, who never pressed the investigation when asked. As it turned out, Ames had received $2.5 million from the Soviets since 1985 and had betrayed more than a hundred CIA operations. In 1994, he was eventually caught, pleaded guilty, and was sentenced to life without parole.

The Walker and Ames cases were thought to be massive intelligence failures. But they paled against the damage done by Robert Hanssen, an FBI agent who worked for the Soviets and had access to the most sensitive government secrets. A former Chicago policeman, Hanssen joined the FBI in 1976. Just three years later, he began selling classified documents to the Soviets. His wife discovered his spying and made him confess to a Roman Catholic priest who told him to give his spying profits to Mother Teresa, but Hanssen continued his damaging betrayal. Through the 1980s and 1990s, Hanssen sold secrets to the Soviet KGB, exposing double agents who were working for the United States.

In January 2001, Hanssen was arrested and charged with spying for the Russians. He pleaded guilty to selling 6,000 pages of documents along with computer disks to the Soviet Union and later the Russians over a period of twenty-one years. Ames's spying had led directly to more deaths, but Hanssen had turned over far more

damaging information. The FBI and CIA needed Hanssen's cooperation, so he was given life in prison without possibility of parole.

In summarizing the Hanssen case, Ronald Kessler writes in
The Bureau, "Hanssen felt confident that the FBI would not catch
him—not even if he broke into an FBI official's computer . . . [that]
he could put erotic stories on the Internet using his real name and
heavily mortgage his house without raising any suspicion. So complacent was the FBI that, when a computer repair technician found
hacker software on Hanssen's computer, no one asked about it. Nor
were five-year background checks done on a regular basis, as is required for agents with Hanssen's level of clearances.

All of these failures—which must also be measured against the FBI's
noteworthy but usually overlooked successes in counterintelligence—
would be embarrassing to the agencies, disturbing to American taxpayers, and perhaps even shocking—if not for the events of September 11,
2001. Less than a year after the September 11 terror attacks, reports
of the significant information that various FBI field agents had begun
to collect about Islamic terrorists who were actively plotting an attack
using airplanes started to surface. These revelations came after administration officials and the head of the FBI had pointedly told Americans
that there had been no warning of the attacks.

Clearly, many FBI agents were on to the possibility of a terror strike.
A memo written by one FBI field agent in Phoenix warned about
Middle Eastern men with possible connections to terror groups enroll-
ing in flight schools. His memo went to New York and Washington
FBI offices, but no further action was taken. Even when a man was
arrested in August before the terror attacks because of his suspicious
behavior at a flight training school, their reports were apparently not
taken seriously up the chain of command. Documents relating back
to the 1993 World Trade Center bombing also had never been translated from Arabic. Similar hints of potential hijackings had come to
the CIA, but the two agencies have always been known for their fierce
turf protection. Congressional requirements that the CIA not be involved in domestic spying—spawned after CIA abuses were revealed in
the 1970s—also created a roadblock to intelligence sharing that might
have proven valuable. The level of the FBI's awareness as well as its

inability to piece together important clues to the impending terror attacks is still unclear. In June 2002, President Bush ordered a massive reorganization of America's intelligence gathering and domestic security branches into a new cabinet-level department, which was created late in 2002.

AMERICAN VOICES

GERRY SPENCE, attorney for Randy Weaver,
in *From Freedom to Slavery* (1995):

> These are dangerous times. When we are afraid, we want to be protected, and since we cannot protect ourselves against such horrors as mass murder by bombers, we are tempted to run to the government, a government that is always willing to trade the promise of protection for our freedom, which left, as always, the question: How much freedom are we willing to relinquish for such a bald promise?

Written in the aftermath of the Oklahoma City bombing in 1995, Spence's words were eerily prescient. Seven years later, in the wake of the September 11 terrorist attacks, the scenario Spence described in discussing the Oklahoma City bombing would also be the Bush administration's reaction to the new terrorist threat.

America in 2000: A Statistical Snapshot

The U.S. Constitution requires a census to be taken every ten years for the purpose of apportioning seats in Congress. The first U.S. census was taken in 1790, shortly after Washington became president. It took eighteen months to complete and counted 3.9 million people.

As the nation grew, so did the scope of the census. Questions about the economy—factories, agriculture, mining, and fisheries—were added over the decades. In 1850, census takers asked the first questions about social issues. In 1940, the Census Bureau began using statistical sampling techniques. Computers came along in 1950.

Census 2000 showed that the resident population of the United States on April 1, 2000, was 281,421,906, an increase of 13.2 percent over 1990. Women held a slight advantage over men (143,368,000 women to 138,054,000 men). This increase of 32.7 million people was the largest total census-to-census population increase in U.S. history, exceeding even the "baby boom" jump of 28 million between 1950 and 1960. The fastest-growing region in the U.S. was the West; the fastest-growing states were Nevada, Arizona, Colorado, and Idaho. The largest state, California, recorded the largest numeric increase, with 4.1 million people added to the state's population. Reflecting the movements west and south, the nation's population center, a statistical measurement of where the "middle" of the country is, moved 12.1 miles south and 32.5 miles west, to a point near Edgar Springs, Missouri.

The Census Bureau also keeps a running estimate of the U.S. population. Taking the 2000 census as a starting point, the clock assumed one birth every 8 seconds; one death every 14 seconds; a net gain of one international immigrant every 34 seconds and one returning U.S. citizen every 3,202 seconds. That results in an overall net gain of *one person every 11 seconds.*

In political terms, the 2000 census meant changes in the makeup of Congress as 12 of the 435 House seats were reallocated to account for the population shifts, with most of the new House seats moving to the South and West from the North and Midwest.

Winners (State and number of new House seats): Arizona 2; California 1; Colorado 1; Florida 2; Georgia 2; Nevada 1; North Carolina 1; Texas 2.

Losers: Connecticut 1; Illinois 1; Indiana 1; Michigan 1; Mississippi 1; New York 2; Ohio 1; Oklahoma 1; Pennsylvania 2; Wisconsin 1.

Since the Electoral College is based on the number of seats in Congress, these changes would also affect the 2004 presidential race.

The American dream had also changed. The well-packaged and expertly marketed 1950s vision of Dad, Mom, two kids, dog, house, and two-car garage was a thing of the past—a romantic notion that barely ever existed in America. The new American household was smaller. Married-couple households declined to just a little over half of all households. People living alone, the second most common living arrangement, rose to more than a quarter of all households.

Single-mother households remained at 12 percent of all households while unmarried men increased to 4 percent. And 5 percent of all households were unmarried-partner households. *Leave It to Beaver* was on its way to becoming an endangered species in America.

The nation was also getting older. The median age in the U.S. in 2000 was 35.3 years, the highest it has ever been. That increase reflected the aging of the baby boom generation, those born between 1946 and 1964.

Although people thought of the 1990s as the decade of economic prosperity, eleven states experienced increased poverty. In terms of weekly wages, census data showed that most gains were made by those already earning the most, with the lower wage earners making much smaller gains. In other words, the rising tide lifted all the boats, but some boats were lifted a little higher. Or as one of the pigs in George Orwell's *Animal Farm*, put it, "All animals are equal but some animals are more equal than others."

Most shocking of all was the fact that child poverty remains one of America's most stunning failures. Overall, the nation's official child poverty rate fell to 16 percent, which is still above the lows of the late 1960s and 1970s when it was around 14 percent. Even with reduced childhood poverty, the United States lags behind most other wealthy nations. America's poorest children have a lower standard of living than those in the bottom 10 percent of any other nation except Britain.

And in a country whose political leadership routinely says, "No child will be left behind," American infant mortality rates ranked 33rd in the world, only slightly better than Cuba's. Eighteen percent of women in America received no prenatal care. Fourteen percent of children had no medical care. The vaunted Welfare Reform Act of 1996, which promised to move people from "welfare to work," succeeded largely in putting people in jobs that left them officially poor or close to the poverty line. And just to be clear on what the government considers poverty, in 1999, the threshold for a family of four was $16,954, approximately what an average Wal-Mart employee receives annually for a forty-hour workweek.

The 2000 census depicted a more racially diverse America. For the first time, respondents were allowed to select one or more race categories, and nearly 7 million people (2.4 percent) took advantage of the opportunity. Of the other 275 million who reported only one race,

75.1 percent reported white; 12.3 percent black or African American; 0.9 percent American Indian or Alaska native; 3.6 percent Asian. A separate question collected information on Hispanic or Latino origins. Hispanics, who may be of any race, totaled 35.3 million, or about 13 percent of the total population.

Yet widespread patterns of segregation of whites and minorities continue in America, in spite of the improvements in income and education for minority Americans. And home ownership remained a sore point with minorities, who are much less likely to own their homes— generally considered the golden ticket to the American dream.

Was there any good news for America? Well, the 2000 census showed that Americans who relied on outhouses and bathtubs in the kitchen had fallen below the one million mark for the first time in American history.

More significantly, ten years after the Los Angeles rioting that followed the acquittal of four white policemen in the savage beating of a black man named Rodney King—resulting in one of the worst racially motivated riots in American history—the progress is worth noting. Under the George W. Bush administration, the two highest-ranking members of the American foreign policy team were black. Perhaps even more astonishing, they were black Republicans! One of them, National Security Adviser Condoleezza Rice, is a black woman. The other, Colin Powell, is the child of Jamaican immigrants who, having benefited from affirmative action policies, as he is quick to point out, rose through the ranks of the American military to become the highest-ranking officer in the Pentagon under George Bush and then the first black secretary of state. There is no doubt that Colin Powell would have been a credible presidential candidate had he chosen—or if he ever chooses—to run. The institution that cultivated Colin Powell, the American military, is generally credited with being the most successfully integrated institution in American society.

Also among the growing number of black corporate leaders, the heads of American Express and AOL Time Warner, the world's largest media company, are black men. The daughter of sharecroppers was named to head Brown University, one of the most prestigious jobs in the academic world. The most powerful, influential, and widely admired woman in American media—and perhaps in all America—is

Oprah Winfrey. At the 2002 Academy Awards, history was made when two black performers, Denzel Washington and Halle Berry, received Oscars. Two more of the most widely admired Americans are athletes who need only be mentioned as Tiger and Michael. In other words, America has moved beyond tokenism in some very visible and meaningful ways.

Of course, social mobility, corporate power, sports and entertainment achievements, and political office are only part of the story. Much of America still resides in very separate black and white worlds. Poverty and unemployment still affect minorities in much greater numbers than in white America. The question of how those disparities can be addressed is still a troubling one for America. Affirmative action policies, which have been used to address the inequities of the past, have come under increasing fire for being unfair "quotas" that solve past discrimination by discriminating against deserving whites, in either college admissions or business practices. At another end of the spectrum, there are serious black scholars who feel that the United States should still pay "reparations" to the descendants of American slaves, just as Japanese Americans imprisoned during World War II by the government were reimbursed, and families of Holocaust victims have received reparation payments.

Native Americans also lay claim to deserving more from the government for the treatment their people received over the centuries.

AMERICAN VOICES

Bin Laden Preparing to Hijack U.S. Aircraft and Other Attacks.
> —Presidential daily briefing provided to President Clinton in 1998.

Bin Laden Determined to Strike in U.S.
> —Headline of a presidential daily briefing provided to George W. Bush on August 6, 2001.

At 8:46 on the morning of September 11, 2001, the United States became a nation transformed.
> —"Executive Summary," *The 9/11 Report* (June 2004).

9/11: What really happened?

In the spring of 2010, Iran's president Mahmoud Ahmadinejad, the former mayor of Teheran, who was elected president of Iran in 2005 and whose animosity toward America and the Western world in general has been well documented, announced on Iranian state television that "September 11 was a big lie and a pretext for the war on terror and a prelude to invading Afghanistan." Over the years, President Ahmadinejad had also called the Holocaust a "lie," and many of his Iranian compatriots as well as other Muslims believed him.

But in the case of 9/11, there are a surprising number of Americans who agreed with the Iranian leader. As the ninth anniversary of the terror strikes aimed against the United States approached, many Americans continued to believe that they didn't *really* know what took place on 9/11.

Almost since the day they happened, the events of 9/11 have spawned a wide range of conspiracy theories, spread through books and on the Internet. Some of the most extreme conspiracy theorists suggested that the United States government, perhaps in collusion with the owner of the "Twin Towers" of the World Trade Center, staged the 9/11 attacks. For a variety of suggested reasons, they contend Americans were behind the awful destruction of September 11, 2001, one of the most significant events in recent American history, a disaster that directly led America into two wars and into an era of fighting global terrorism that profoundly affected life and politics in America as well as the rest of the world.

A national commission, established by Congress only after intense pressure from the families of September 11 victims, attempted to answer many of the questions that Americans had about the attacks: about Al Qaeda, the organization that had planned and carried them out; about the response of the government and especially the intelligence community to the threat of terror; and, finally, about the aftermath of the most deadly attack on American soil since Pearl Harbor.

The coordinated attacks came on the morning of September 11, 2001, when a group of nineteen hijackers, all of them Arab men, seized four commercial airliners and crashed two of them into the World Trade Center in lower Manhattan (site of an earlier Islamic terrorist bombing in 1993), and a third into the Pentagon in Arlington, Virginia. The fourth plane was presumed to be heading toward another target in Washington, D.C., possibly the White House, when the passengers and crew attempted to retake the plane and it crashed into a field near Shanksville, in rural Pennsylvania, killing all on board. The total number of victims in the attacks is officially listed as 2,973, with others claiming that a number of rescue workers at the World Trade Center site have died from ailments that came as a result of their work at the site—in essence, "collateral damage" from the hijackings.

Within minutes of the hijackings and crashes, the FBI opened what would become the largest criminal investigation in American history. Within seventy-two hours, the identities of the hijackers were known. All were from Arab nations: Saudi Arabia (eleven of the men were Saudis), United Arab Emirates, Lebanon, and Egypt. The specific planning of the attacks was attributed to a man well known to American intelligence, Khalid Sheikh Mohammed (KSM), who grew up in Kuwait, attended college in the United States—where he had earned a degree in mechanical engineering in 1986—and eventually entered the anti-Soviet jihad ("holy war") in Afghanistan. (KSM was captured in Pakistan, transferred to the controversial "detainee" American prison built in Guantánamo, Cuba, and at this writing was awaiting trial. He has, according to official accounts, confessed to planning the 9/11 attacks along with a number of terrorist acts that were either foiled or carried out.)

Thomas Kean, the former Republican governor of New Jersey, and the former Democratic representative Lee Hamilton led the work of the 9/11 Commission. In reconstructing the long series of events leading up to 9/11, as well as the United States government's response to the attacks, the commission won high praise, for both its depth and the clarity with which its final report was written. The commission report laid out the trail of Islamic terror threats and activities against the United States and its interests: the February 1993 bombing of the World Trade Center that killed six; a plot to blow up the Holland Tunnel, connecting lower Manhattan to New Jersey; the October 1993 downing of an American helicopter in Mogadishu, Somalia—the event depicted in the book and film *Black Hawk Down*—that was accomplished with the help of Al Qaeda; a series of murderous bombings in Saudi Arabia in 1995 and 1996; the August 1998 attacks on the U.S. embassies in Kenya and Tanzania that killed 244 people; and, in October 2000, just a few weeks before the presidential election, the assault on the USS *Cole*, a U.S. Navy destroyer, in Yemen, killing seventeen American sailors.

At the center of these acts was a man known to the American intelligence community as "Usama Bin Ladin" (as the Commission Report called him) or, more widely, Osama bin Laden. The wealthy son of a Saudi family, he had moved from financing terror to forming and leading the group that became known as Al Qaeda, Arabic for "the base," in the late 1980s. Its stated mission was to rid Muslim countries of Western influence and replace their governments with fundamentalist Islamic regimes. Al Qaeda, according to Jayshree Bajoria and Greg Bruno of the Council on Foreign Relations, grew out of a group that was fighting the Russians who had invaded Afghanistan in 1979. "In the 1980s, the Services Office—run by bin Laden and the Palestinian religious scholar Abdullah Azzam—recruited, trained, and financed thousands of foreign mujahadeen, or holy warriors, from more than fifty countries. Bin Laden wanted these fighters to continue the 'holy war' beyond Afghanistan. He formed al-Qaeda around 1988."

Ten years later, in February 1998, bin Laden issued a fatwa, or holy decree, declaring that it was the will of God that every Muslim should kill Americans because of America's "occupation" of Islam's holy places in Saudi Arabia (particularly since American combat troops were stationed in the kingdom during the first Gulf War against Iraq) and for aggression against Muslims, especially in supporting Israel.

At various times during the Clinton administration, numerous attempts were made to kill or capture bin Laden and other senior al Qaeda leaders with both air strikes and cruise missiles.

When the 9/11 Commission released its sobering report in July 2004, it was only after tremendous resistance from the Bush White House and the intelligence community. A member of the commission, John Farmer, a former federal prosecutor, attorney general of New Jersey, and dean of Rutgers Law School, would later write in his 2009 book *The Ground Truth*, "The Bush administration . . . demonstrated that leadership is undermined by dissembling. The false and misleading account the administration peddled about its response to the 9/11 attacks may have worked for a time. . . . At the end of the day, however, the Administration's story raised more questions than it answered, and led directly to the formation of the 9/11 Commission."

One of the commission's first conclusions was that the attacks "were a shock but they should not have come as a surprise." The nineteen-month investigation laid bare the failures of the Central Intelligence Agency (CIA), the Federal Bureau of Investigation (FBI), the Pentagon, the National Security Council (NSC), and virtually every other government agency responsible for defending the nation.

Apart from the unsuccessful attempts to kill bin Laden, the 9/11 Committee laid out a series of grievous intelligence failings, which kept different arms of the American intelligence community from sharing information that could have led to the capture of the hijackers. Some of these were turf battles between agencies, others simple human error. In the end, the results were disastrous. "Across the government, there were failures of imagination, policy capabilities and management. . . . Terrorism was not the overriding national security concern for the U.S. Government under either the Clinton or the pre 9/11 Bush administrations," the report said in a damning assessment.

In public, the Bush administration maintained that it was not time for "finger-pointing," and balked at any independent investigation of the run-up to the 9/11 catastrophes and the nation's response to the emergency.

The official foot-dragging at the White House, in particular, only seemed to heighten the belief that a conspiracy to conceal the truth was at work. The editors of the magazine *Popular Mechanics* would write in March 2005, in a comprehensive article examining the "conspiracy theories":

The collapse of both World Trade Center towers—and the smaller WTC 7 a few hours later—initially surprised even some experts. But subsequent studies have shown that the WTC's structural integrity was destroyed by intense fire as well as the severe damage inflicted by the planes. That explanation hasn't swayed conspiracy theorists.

Responding to the compelling questions that surrounded the 9/11 tragedies, the notably apolitical *Popular Mechanics* had set out to investigate some of the claims made by the advocates of conspiracy theories. The editors wrote:

Healthy skepticism, it seems, has curdled into paranoia. Wild conspiracy tales are peddled daily on the Internet, talk radio and in other media. Blurry photos, quotes taken out of context and sketchy eyewitness accounts have inspired a slew of elaborate theories. . . . In the end we were able to debunk each of these assertions [made by conspiracy theorists] with hard evidence and a healthy dose of common sense. We learned that a few theories are based on something as innocent as a reporting error on that chaotic day. Only by confronting such poisonous claims with irrefutable facts can we understand what really happened on a day that is forever seared into world history.

The article in *Popular Mechanics* specifically addressed and rebutted many of the major questions and controversies raised about 9/11 and the destruction of the World Trade Center in particular. Offering extensive support for their statement, the magazine's editors concluded that "The widely accepted account that hijackers commandeered and crashed the four 9/11 planes is supported by reams of evidence, from the cockpit recordings to forensics."

Among the chief claims of the conspiracy theorists was the contention that the impact of the planes could not have caused the towers to fall and that the buildings had also been wired with explosives. *Popular Mechanics* instead offered a plausible scientific explanation; summarizing, it said that the plane debris had "sliced through the utility shafts at the North Tower's core, creating a conduit for burning jet fuel—and fiery destruction throughout the building." The burning fuel was not hot enough to melt steel but was hot enough to weaken the structural strength of the building's steel frames. The fuel ignited other combustible materials, including furniture, rugs, curtains, and paper. As Forman Williams, a professor of engineering at the University of California, told *Popular Mechanics*, "The jet fuel was the ignition source. It burned for maybe 10 minutes, and the towers were still standing in 10 minutes. It was the rest of the stuff burning afterward that was responsible for the heat transfer that eventually brought them down."

The *Popular Mechanics* article and multiple investigations of the catastrophic events of 9/11 by government agencies and by writers—such as Lawrence Wright in his award-winning account of Al Qaeda, *The Looming Tower,* and James Bamford in *Body of Secrets,* his analysis of the role of the National Security Agency (NSA) in failing to prevent the attacks—have all confirmed the voluminous facts that the 9/11 Commission reported. These conclusions are supported by thousands of phone intercepts made by the NSA, the precise record of communications between the planes and ground control, and the heart-wrenching records of telephone calls made by those who died on board the planes and those who were able to communicate before the towers crashed.

However, in his book *The Ground Truth,* the 9/11 Commission member John Farmer also noted that as of June 2009, there was still no plan to have "interoperability" of emergency communications, one of the key recommendations of the commission. While some cities have acted to improve emergency communications, which failed disastrously at the World Trade Center (and would also contribute to the fatally inadequate response to Hurricane Katrina in the summer of 2005), Farmer noted, "National interoperable communications will not be achieved . . . for the foreseeable future."

Must Reads: *The 9/11 Report; The Ground Truth* by John Farmer; *102 Minutes* by Jim Dwyer and Kevin Flynn; *The Looming Tower: Al Qaeda and the Road to 9/11* by Lawrence Wright; *Body of Secrets: Anatomy of the Ultra-Secret National Security Agency* by James Bamford.

War in Afghanistan: Who? What? When? Where? Why?

To most Americans, Afghanistan is another of those countries that are as obscure and remote as the dark side of the moon. Slightly smaller than Texas, with 29 million people (2010 est.), Afghanistan is a land-locked country, a landscape of stark mountains and harsh desert in central Asia. Its name typically suggests either a crocheted blanket or a breed of dog.

The nation of Afghanistan piqued some Americans' curiosity when the Soviet Union invaded it in 1978. However, that was mostly because the invasion meant an American-led boycott of the 1980 summer Olympics in Moscow. With the assistance of the CIA, Afghan rebels kept up a protracted war against the Soviet Union and the Afghan regime it had installed. This region was, as many Americans noted with some relish, "the Soviets' Vietnam."

In 1988, a UN-mediated agreement paved the way for the Soviet Union's withdrawal, leading to a civil war for control of the country. Eventually, the Taliban, a radical fundamentalist Islamic insurgent group, seized power in 1996. They immediately began to enforce a rigid Islamic code in the country. The Taliban were in control of Afghanistan at the time of the attacks on 9/11 and had turned parts of the country into a training ground for terrorist groups, including bin Laden's Al Qaeda. Initially the Taliban were a mixture of mujahideen, or Islamic "holy warriors," who fought against the Soviet invasion of the 1980s, with the backing of the United States' CIA, and a group of Pashtun tribesmen who spent time in Pakistani religious schools, or madrassas, and received assistance from Pakistan.

According to the Council on Foreign Relations:

The Taliban practiced Wahhabism, an orthodox form of Sunni Islam similar to that practiced in Saudi Arabia. With the help of government defections, the Taliban emerged as a force in Afghan politics in 1994 in the midst of a civil war between forces in northern and southern Afghanistan. They gained an initial territorial foothold in the southern city of Kandahar, and over the next two years expanded their influence through a mixture of force, negotiation, and payoffs. In 1996, the Taliban captured Kabul, the Afghan capital, and took control of the national government.

Taliban rule was characterized by a strict form of Islamic law, requiring women to wear head-to-toe veils, banning television, and jailing men whose beards were deemed too short. One act in particular, the destruction of the giant Buddha statues in

Bamiyan, seemed to symbolize the intolerance of the regime. The feared Ministry for the Promotion of Virtue and Prevention of Vice authorized the use of force to uphold bans on un-Islamic activities.

The Taliban had also allowed Osama bin Laden, who had fought by their side against the Soviets, to freely use Afghan territory to train Al Qaeda recruits. On August 20, 1998, U.S. cruise missiles struck bin Laden's training camps north of Kabul. In 1999, the United Nations imposed sanctions on the Taliban for their refusal to turn bin Laden over to the United States for prosecution. Throughout this period, the CIA maintained its support of an Afghan opposition group, the Northern Alliance, which it hoped would overthrow the Taliban regime.

MILESTONES IN THE WAR IN AFGHANISTAN

2001

September 9   Ahmed Shah Massoud, a leader of the anti-Taliban Northern Alliance, is assassinated in a bombing.

September 11   Following the 9/11 attacks, President George W. Bush demands that the Taliban turn over Al Qaeda leaders or face destruction.

September 18   President Bush signs a joint resolution authorizing the use of force against those responsible for the 9/11 attacks.

October 7   The United States, with British support, commences the bombing of Afghanistan, beginning Operation Enduring Freedom. Canada, France, Australia, and Germany pledge future support to the war effort.

October 26   The USA PATRIOT (Providing Appropriate Tools Required to Intercept and Obstruct Terrorism) Act is signed into law. The law increases the ability of law enforcement agencies to search telephone, e-mail communications, medical, financial, and other records. It also eases restrictions on foreign intelligence gathering within the United States; expands the authority of the Treasury

Department to regulate financial transactions, and broadens the power of law enforcement to detain and deport immigrants suspected of activities related to terrorism. The act was supported by wide margins in both houses of Congress.

November 9   The Northern Alliance, with CIA support, breaks through Taliban positions at Mazar-e-Sharif. Coalition forces take the Afghan capital, Kabul.

November 14   The UN Security Council calls for a "central role" for the UN in establishing a transitional government in Afghanistan.

December 3–17   The battle of Tora Bora leaves an estimated 200 Al Qaeda fighters dead, but Osama bin Laden is nowhere to be found.

December 9   Taliban forces collapse, and the Taliban leaders, along with Al Qaeda leaders, escape into the mountainous area between Afghanistan and Pakistan.

Hamid Karzai is sworn in as head of an interim power-sharing government.

2002

February   The new Afghan national army begins training with assistance from U.S. forces.

March   Operation Anaconda, the first major ground assault by combined U.S. and Afghan forces, takes place. But U.S. military planners are increasingly focusing on a potential invasion of Iraq.

July   Hamid Karzai, head of the transitional government, escapes an assassination attempt in his hometown, Kandahar.

November   The U.S. Congress passes legislation calling for $2.3 billion in reconstruction funds and an additional $1 billion to expand the NATO-led International Security Force.

2003

February   Afghanistan remains the world's largest producer of the opium poppy, according to the United Nations.

March 20   The United States begins the invasion of Iraq (see "Milestones in the War in Iraq," p. 605).

April   The North Atlantic Treaty Organization (NATO) agrees to take over command of security forces in Afghanistan; it is NATO's first operational commitment outside Europe in its history, as it was initially formed to defend Western Europe against the Soviet threat.

May 1   Secretary of Defense Donald Rumsfeld declares an end to "major combat" in Afghanistan. The announcement coincides with President George Bush's "mission accomplished"—a declaration that fighting in Iraq has come to an end (see "Milestones in the War in Iraq," p. 605).

2004

January   An assembly agrees on a constitution for Afghanistan.

April 22   Pat Tillman, a former star player for the Arizona Cardinals in the National Football League, who left the pros to join the army, is killed in Afghanistan. The army initially characterizes his death as the result of a firefight with hostile forces, and promotes it as an act of battlefield heroism. However, his death will later be ruled a result of a "friendly-fire" incident in which he was killed by three shots to the head.

AMERICAN VOICES
JON KRAKAUER, *Where Men Win Glory:
The Odyssey of Pat Tillman*:

Although it wasn't Tillman's intention, when he left the Cardinals to join the Army he was transformed overnight into an icon of post 9/11 patriotism. Seizing the opportunity to capitalize on his celebrity, the Bush Administration endeavored to use his name and image to promote what it had christened the Global War on Terror. Tillman abhorred this role. As soon as he decided to enlist, he stopped talking to the press altogether, although his silence did nothing to squelch America's fascination with the football star who had traded the bright lights and riches of the NFL for boot camp and a bad haircut. . . . Unencumbered by biographical insight, people felt emboldened to invent all manner of personae for Tillman after his passing.

October 9   Hamid Karzai becomes the first democratically elected leader of Afghanistan.

October 29   Osama bin Laden releases a videotape three weeks after Afghanistan's election and just a few days before the U.S. presidential election in which George Bush wins reelection.

2005

September   The first Afghan parliamentary and provincial elections in more than three decades are held.

2006

Summer   In a resurgence of violence, Taliban forces step up attacks and suicide bombings. NATO troops take over military operations in the south. There is severe fighting in the region as the Taliban presence remains strong.

2007

May   The Taliban's most senior military commander, Mullah Dadullah, is killed during fighting with U.S. and Afghan forces.

November   Taliban forces kill six Americans, bringing the U.S. death toll in Afghanistan for 2007 to 100, the highest for any year since the beginning of the war.

2008

June Taliban fighters free 1,200 prisoners, including 400 Taliban prisoners of war, in an assault on a Kandahar jail.

July A bomb attack on the Indian embassy in Kabul kills more than forty people; days later insurgents kill nine American soldiers in a single attack.

2009

January When President Bush leaves office, there are approximately 60,000 international troops—roughly half of them from the United States—on the ground in Afghanistan.

February 17 President Obama orders 17,000 additional troops sent to Afghanistan.

November President Karzai wins another term following a disputed election with widespread claims of election fraud.

December 1 Replicating the strategy that had apparently succeeded in pacifying Iraq's most violent areas, President Obama announces an "Afghan surge"; another 30,000 American troops would deploy in 2010. Saying that the deployment is not an open-ended commitment, Obama declares that a troop withdrawal would begin in July 2011.

2010

July 26 The U.S. commander in Afghanistan, General Stanley A. McChrystal, is relieved of command. He and some of his subordinates had been quoted making disdainful remarks about top Obama administration officials to a reporter from *Rolling Stone* magazine. President Obama names General David Petraeus, the architect of the "Iraq surge" strategy, to replace McChrystal.

July A six-year archive of classified military documents about the war in Afghanistan is released online by WikiLeaks, an organization dedicated to whistle-blowing and exposing corruption by governments and corporations. The documents, released to major newspapers around the world, show that American forces are struggling against a revived Taliban insurgency in Afghanistan and fuel growing skepticism in Congress and among Americans about the war effort.

October 7   On the ninth anniversary of the invasion of Afghanistan, American casualties in the war there had reached 1,321 military fatalities. In addition, 811 members of NATO and other coalition forces had been killed in Afghanistan. As the war entered its tenth year, public support for the war was slipping in both the United States and Western Europe. The Netherlands had withdrawn its troops and the Canadians would follow. President Obama confirmed that his troop withdrawal would still begin in July 2011.

2011

May 1   President Obama announces that Osama bin Laden had been killed by a team of U.S. Navy SEALs in a compound in Pakistan.

AMERICAN VOICES
PRESIDENT GEORGE W. BUSH, from the State of
the Union address, January 2002:

Our . . . goal is to prevent regimes that sponsor terror from threatening America or our friends and allies with weapons of mass destruction. Some of these regimes have been pretty quiet since September 11. But we know their true nature. North Korea is a regime arming with missiles and weapons of mass destruction, while starving its citizens. Iran aggressively pursues these weapons and exports terror, while an unelected few repress the Iranian people's hope for freedom. Iraq continues to flaunt its hostility toward America and to support terror. . . . States like these, and their terrorist allies, constitute an axis of evil, aiming to threaten the peace of the world.

This address, given a few months after the 9/11 terrorist attacks took place and the war against Afghanistan began, may go down as Bush's signature speech. The phrase "axis of evil," meant to conjure up the image of the Axis in World War II—Germany, Japan, and Italy—was more symbolic than an actual alliance among the countries Bush mentioned. Iraq and Iran were uneasy neighbors who had fought a devastating war against each other a decade earlier. North Korea was an economic shambles. But the Bush administration viewed all three as sources of funding, training, and support for terrorists.

Why was America in Iraq?

Following George W. Bush's election in 2000, the United States and the United Kingdom continued to bomb Iraqi air defense systems as part of the "no-fly zones" established by the United Nations after the 1991 Gulf War. In that war, Bush's father, the first President Bush, had led a multinational coalition against Saddam Hussein's Iraq following its invasion of neighboring Kuwait (see "What was Operation Desert Storm?," pp. 539–40). Although there were also UN-mandated sanctions against Iraq, these were widely disregarded.

Then, according to National Security Council adviser Richard Clarke, in the wake of 9/11 and the invasion of Afghanistan, Secretary of Defense Donald Rumsfeld and other Bush administration officials expressed an immediate interest in attacking Iraq. In a controversial book, *Against All Enemies*, Clarke contended that the Bush administration was obsessed with Saddam Hussein and became distracted from the war in Afghanistan and the hunt for Osama bin Laden. Clarke's account was later corroborated by several high-ranking members of the military and was borne out by a CBS News report. The high-powered obsession of the Bush administration with Saddam Hussein's Iraq was also documented by the filmmaker Charles Ferguson, who recorded in *No End in Sight*, "One day after the September 11 attacks, senior Pentagon officials including Defense Secretary Donald Rumsfeld and Undersecretary Douglas Feith spoke to senior military officers about Iraq and the need to remove Saddam. Eighteen months later, they got their wish."

One year after the 9/11 attacks, President Bush spoke at the United Nations and demanded that Iraq eliminate its weapons of mass destruction (WMD), refrain from supporting terrorism, and end the repression of its people. These three reasons became the ostensible justification for America's going to war in Iraq—in the first preemptive war in American history—to achieve "regime change," that is, to eliminate Saddam Hussein as Iraq's leader. But unlike his father, who had mustered a large coalition of nations in 1991, President Bush decided to go to war despite the objections of most of America's Western allies. The principal exception was Great Britain, although Spain and Italy also joined in the U.S. invasion of Iraq.

With National Security Adviser Condoleezza Rice raising fears of "a mushroom cloud" and by constantly connecting Iraq to Al Qaeda and the 9/11 attacks—in spite of substantial evidence to the contrary—the United States went to war, unprovoked, against Iraq in March 2003.

In *Fiasco* (2006), a widely praised, stinging assessment of that war three years after it began, the *Washington Post*'s senior correspondent Thomas E. Ricks wrote, even as the war dragged on:

> President George W. Bush's decision to invade Iraq in 2003 ultimately may come to be seen as one of the most profligate actions in the history of American foreign policy. The consequences of his choices won't be clear for decades, but it is already abundantly apparent in mid-2006 that the U.S. government went to war in Iraq with scant solid international support and on the basis of incorrect information—about weapons of mass destruction and a supposed nexus between Saddam Hussein and al Qaeda's terrorism—and then occupied the country negligently. Thousands of U.S. troops and an untold number of Iraqis have died. Hundreds of billions of dollars have been spent, many of them squandered. Democracy may yet come to Iraq and the region, but so too may civil war or a regional conflagration, which in turn could lead to a spiraling of oil prices and a global economic shock. . . . Spooked by its own false conclusions about the threat, the Bush administration hurried its diplomacy, short-circuited its war planning, and assembled an agonizingly incompetent occupation.

MILESTONES IN THE WAR IN IRAQ

2001

October   The State Department begins planning a post–Saddam Hussein transition in Iraq, including discussions with Iraqi expatriates.

November   In the aftermath of 9/11, a small group of senior U.S. military planners is instructed to begin planning for a possible invasion of Iraq.

2002

July 23   The "Downing Street memo"—prepared by a senior British intelligence official and subsequently leaked—states, "Bush wanted to remove Saddam, through military action, justified by the conjunction of terrorism and WMD [weapons of mass destruction]. But the intelligence and the facts were being fixed around the policy." (*The Sunday Times* of London publishes the leaked memo in May 2005.)

September 8   In a speech, National Security Adviser Condoleezza Rice describes the threat posed by Iraq: "The problem here is that there will always be some uncertainty about how quickly [Iraq] can acquire nuclear weapons. But we don't want the smoking gun to be a mushroom cloud."

November 27   After the UN Security Council declares Iraq in breach of a disarmament resolution, Iraq allows weapons inspectors to return to the country in search of banned weapons.

2003

January 28   In his State of the Union Address, President Bush declares, "The British government has learned that Saddam Hussein recently sought significant quantities of uranium from Africa."

February   The army general Eric Shinseki testifies to a Senate committee that "something in the order of several hundred thousand soldiers" would be required to stabilize Iraq. Shinseki is publicly rebuked by both Secretary of Defense Rumsfeld and one of Bush's security officials, Paul Wolfowitz.

February 6   Secretary of State Colin Powell addresses the UN Security Council to present the American case for war. The Security Council rejects an explicit authorization for the use of force.

March 18   United Nations weapons inspectors leave Iraq.

March 19   Operation Iraqi Freedom commences with air strikes. Most Iraqi forces melt into the civilian population; Iraqi forces, including the feared Republican Guard, are quickly overwhelmed, but there is no evidence of any chemical or biological weapon used by Iraqi forces.

April 9   U.S. Marines topple a statue of Saddam Hussein in a major square in Baghdad.

April   Order in Iraq begins to break down amid widespread looting. The national archives and museum and all government ministries, except the ministry of oil, are looted. Asked at a press conference about the looting, Secretary of Defense Donald Rumsfeld says, "Stuff happens" and "Freedom is untidy."

April 1   Special Forces rescue Private First Class Jessica Lynch, who had been captured by Iraqi forces on March 23. The Pentagon, desperate for positive news, inflates her story into heroic proportions. Lynch is given an honorable medical discharge later in April. Along with the media, she will eventually accuse the government of embellishing her story as part of a propaganda effort by the Pentagon.

May 2   Aboard the USS *Abraham Lincoln*, under a banner reading "Mission Accomplished," President Bush delivers an address in which he declares the "end of major combat operations" in Iraq.

May 6   L. Paul Bremer is appointed to supervise the occupation of Iraq, replacing General Jay Garner, as chaos sweeps Iraq. On May 9, Bremer disbands the entire Iraqi military and intelligence services. He also announces that some 50,000 members of Saddam Hussein's Baath Party are prohibited from any government work.

July 6 Former ambassador Joseph Wilson publishes an article on the *New York Times* op-ed page in which he states that Saddam Hussein could not obtain uranium from sources in Africa, contradicting the claim made by President Bush in the State of the Union Address a few months earlier, in January. At this time, Wilson's wife, Valerie Plame, is a CIA operative; her classified identity will soon (July 14) be revealed to the press. The leak of her name and identity will eventually be traced to Lewis "Scooter" Libby, chief of staff to Vice President Dick Cheney. Libby will be convicted (in March 2007) of four counts of obstruction of justice, perjury, and making false statements to investigators and sentenced to thirty months in prison; but President Bush will commute his sentence in July 2007.

August 19 A bombing attack on UN headquarters in Baghdad kills more than twenty people, including the UN special representative, Sergio Vieira de Mello. The UN closes its Iraq mission.

December 13 Saddam Hussein is captured in his hometown, Tikrit.

2004

January 4 The Bush administration concedes that its prewar arguments about extensive stockpiles of WMD appear to have been mistaken.

March 31 Four American employees of a private security contractor, Blackwater, are killed in the city of Fallujah and their bodies are hung from a bridge. The incident leads to a bloody siege of the city, which has become the center of an insurgency by Sunni Iraqis, many of them former loyalists of Saddam Hussein.

April 30 Photographs of prisoners at Abu Ghraib prison abused by U.S. soldiers are first published. Seven soldiers are later convicted of torturing and humiliating Iraqi prisoners, but no senior officers are charged or punished.

May 8   An interim constitution for Iraq is ratified.

November   President Bush is reelected for a second term, defeating Senator John Kerry of Massachusetts.

2005

January 30   Iraqi national elections are held but are largely boycotted by Sunni political parties.

March   A presidential commission concludes that "not one bit" of prewar intelligence about chemical, biological, and other weapons in Iraq was accurate.

August 6   In neighboring Iran, the hard-line Islamist mayor of Teheran, Mahmoud Ahmadinejad, is elected president.

2006

February 22   A mosque in Samarra, one of the holiest sites for Shiite Muslims, is bombed. The attack leads to a dramatic escalation of sectarian violence, with Shiites attacking Sunnis in large-scale killings.

May 20   Nouri al-Maliki takes over as prime minister of Iraq.

November 7   In U.S. midterm elections, the Republicans lose control of the House of Representatives, largely as a result of growing opposition to the war. Secretary of Defense Donald Rumsfeld steps down and is replaced by Robert Gates, a moderate who had been privately critical of the war.

December 6   The Iraq Study Group, formed earlier to analyze the situation in Iraq, concludes that it "is grave and deteriorating" and "U.S. forces seem to be caught in a mission that has no foreseeable end."

December 30   Following separate trials for "crimes against humanity" and genocide, Saddam Hussein is hanged.

2007

January 10 The presidential campaign to replace George Bush begins; President Bush announces a "surge" of additional troops to Iraq. General David Petraeus is assigned to implement the new strategy.

2008

November 4 Barack Obama, a critic of the Iraq war who has voted against it in the Senate and campaigned to end it, is elected president. Obama asks Secretary of Defense Gates to remain in the post.

November 27 Iraq's government approves an agreement calling for the withdrawal of U.S. forces by December 31, 2011. By September 2009, the U.S. troop presence in Iraq will decline to 130,000. (There will still be tens of thousands of private American contractors doing Defense Department work in Iraq at that time.)

2009

June 30 American troops begin to withdraw from Baghdad and other Iraqi cities as part of the drawdown.

2010

March Iraqi parliamentary elections are held, and despite bombings, there is 62 percent turnout.

August 31 President Obama declares an end to the seven-year combat mission in Iraq. However, some 50,000 American forces remain in the country to provide security and training for Iraqi forces. More than 4,400 American soldiers and more than 70,000 Iraqis lost their lives in the conflict, according to figures cited by the *New York Times*.

October 1 After months of political haggling since the March elections, Prime Minister Nouri Kamal al-Maliki was reelected. The party of anti-American cleric Moktada al-Sadr, the exiled religious leader whose forces had once battled American and coalition forces in several cities, backed Maliki. The deadline for withdrawing the rest of the American forces remained December 2011.

(**Sources:** *No End in Sight: Iraq's Descent into Chaos*, Council on Foreign Relations; *The World Almanac and Book of Facts 2010*.)

AMERICAN VOICES
CHARLES H. FERGUSON, documentary filmmaker, *No End in Sight: Iraq's Descent into Chaos* (2008):

Yet never in my wildest nightmares did I imagine that the occupation of Iraq would be conducted with such arrogance, stupidity, and incompetence as it was. Despite all my training and experience, which included lessons in skepticism, I would have laughed if someone had told me before the war, look, it's going to be like this: They won't start any planning for the occupation at all until two months before the war, and then they'll start completely from scratch. They'll exclude the State Department and CIA people who know the most about the country. They won't have any telephones or e-mail for months after they arrive in Iraq. Our troops will stand by as nearly every major building in the country is looted, destroyed, and burned. They will spend the first month preparing to install an Iraqi government, restart the administration of the country, and recall the Iraqi army for use in security and reconstruction. And then, with no consultation or warning, in a one-week period, a newly appointed head of the U.S. occupation will reverse all those decisions, crippling the administration of the country and throwing half a million men into the street, destitute. As an insurgency builds, they will deny its existence and refuse to negotiate, even when the leaders of the insurgency signal a desire for compromise. They will airlift $12 billion in hundred-dollar bills into the country, with no accounting controls, and three-quarters of it will remain permanently unaccounted for.

Must Read: *The Assassin's Gate* by George Packer; *Cobra II* by Michael R. Gordon and General Bernard E. Trainor; *Fiasco: The American Military Adventure in Iraq* by Thomas E. Ricks; *The Dark Side* by Jane Mayer; *Chain of Command: The Road from 9/11 to Abu Ghraib* by Seymour M. Hersh; *The Forever War* by Dexter Filkins.

AMERICAN VOICES
MILDRED LOVING, June 2007:

Surrounded as I am now by wonderful children and grandchildren, not a day goes by that I don't think of Richard and our love, our right to marry, and how much it meant to me to have that freedom to marry the person precious to me, even if others thought he was the "wrong kind of person" for me to marry. I believe all Americans, no matter their race, no matter their sex, no matter their sexual orientation, should have that same freedom to marry. Government has no business imposing some people's religious beliefs over others. I am still not a political person, but I am proud that Richard's and my name is on a court case that can help reinforce the love, the commitment, the fairness, and the family that so many people, black or white, young or old, gay or straight seek in life. I support the freedom to marry for all. That's what Loving, and loving, are all about.

Mildred Loving issued this statement on the fortieth anniversary of the Supreme Court ruling in the case of *Loving v. Virginia*, the decision that made it unconstitutional for states to prohibit interracial marriages.

Should same-sex marriage be legal for all Americans? And what does same-sex marriage have to do with interracial marriage?

It surprises most people to learn that when Barack Obama was born—yes, in Hawaii in 1960—his white mother and black father could not have been married in the state of Virginia, home state of eight American presidents. Interracial marriage did not gain full constitutional protection until June 12, 1967, when the Supreme Court issued its ruling in the case of *Loving v. Virginia*, striking down all state laws prohibiting "miscegenation," or interracial marriage, in America.

Mildred and Richard Loving brought the case. He was white and she was black and they had married legally in Washington, D.C., in June 1958. But when the couple traveled to Virginia, Richard Loving was arrested for the crime of being married to a black woman. The Lovings pleaded guilty to the charge and were sentenced to one year in jail. The trial judge suspended the sentence for a period of twenty-five years if the couple agreed to leave the state and not return for twenty-five years. At the time, the trial judge wrote in his opinion:

> Almighty God created the races white, black, yellow, malay and red, and he placed them on separate continents. And, that but for the interference with his arrangement, there would be no cause for such marriage. The fact he separated the races shows that he did not intend for the races to mix.

The Lovings returned to Washington, D.C., but later filed a motion of appeal in the case. They lost the early rounds, but their case eventually wound its way to the Supreme Court.

On June 12, 1967, the Supreme Court ruled that anti-miscegenation laws, such as those in Virginia, violated the Fifth Amendment's "due process" clause ("No person shall be . . . deprived of life, liberty, or property, without due process of law") and the "equal protection" clause of the Fourteenth Amendment ("No state shall . . . deny to any person within its jurisdiction the equal protection of the laws").

In declaring the unanimous opinion, Chief Justice Earl Warren wrote: "Marriage is one of the 'basic civil rights of man,' fundamental to our very existence and survival."

With the passage of time, fewer and fewer Americans ever heard of the Loving case, and interracial marriage no longer seemed controversial. But interest in the case was reawakened in light of the controversy that accompanied a spate of court decisions and legislation legalizing civil unions and marriages between same-sex partners. The question of same-sex unions and same-sex partners obtaining basic legal protections surged to the forefront of American society in the 1990s as some states were moving to permit some form of same-sex union. While not a major national political issue in 1996, the question was significant enough to spur Congress to pass the Defense of Marriage Act, signed into law by President Clinton, in September of that year. The law essentially defined marriage as a legal union between one man and one woman and said that no state, or the federal government, needed to treat a relationship between persons of the same sex as a marriage, even if that relationship was recognized as a marriage in another state.

The controversy over "gay marriage" accelerated in 2000, when Vermont became the first state to permit civil unions, on April 26. In 2004, the issue came to greater prominence during the presidential race between George Bush and his Democratic opponent, Senator John Kerry of Massachusetts. It had been elevated to the national stage in 2003, when the Massachusetts supreme judicial court extended the right to marry to same-sex couples, a decision that took effect in May 2004. Although Bush and Kerry agreed in defining marriage as a union between a man and a woman, conservatives used the issue to assault "liberal" judges who were "legislating from the bench."

By 2008, the controversy had grown as a court in California, the nation's most populous state, also issued a decision that effectively legalized same-sex marriage there. A rush of same-sex marriages occurred in California at the same time that a constitutional amendment known as Proposition 8 was put on the ballot. The initiative was designed to restore the definition of marriage as opposite-sex only. On Election Day 2008, Proposition 8 passed, but at the same time, the courts recognized the 18,000 same-sex marriages that had already taken place in the state, creating two classes of "marriage."

Since 2008, same-sex marriage has also become legal in Connecticut by legislation (2008), in Iowa by court decision (2009), in Vermont by legislation (2009), and in New Hampshire by legislation (2010).

Maine briefly legalized same-sex marriage, only to have it defeated in a public referendum in November 2009. In addition, New Jersey created a same-sex legal union, and at least ten other states offer some form of legal unions providing some of the rights of legal marriage to same-sex and otherwise unmarried couples. In March 2010, Washington, D.C., legalized same-sex marriages by an act of the city council. And in June 2011, New York's state legislature legalized same-sex marriage. In a related development, the policy of "Don't Ask, Don't Tell" was declared unconstitutional and homosexuals could freely serve in the American military.

Under the Defense of Marriage Act, the federal government does not recognize these marriages or unions. This is significant in regard to federally guaranteed benefits extended to spouses, such as disability or Social Security. However, some states that do not offer same-sex marriage do recognize these out-of-state marriages, leading to a crazy quilt of differing protections. All this means the question of "equal protection under the law," the constitutional guarantee affirmed in Loving v. Virginia, may ultimately leave this issue in the hands of the United States Supreme Court.

On August 4, 2010, a federal judge ruled that California's Proposition 8, which overturned the state's same-sex marriage law, was unconstitutional. In his decision, Judge Vaughn R. Walker said that the ban discriminated against gay men and women. "Excluding same-sex couples from marriage is simply not rationally related to a legitimate state interest," Judge Walker wrote.

The argument for overturning Proposition 8 was based in part on the precedent of the Loving case. More surprisingly, a team that included the attorneys David Boies and Ted Olson argued the suit for the plaintiffs. (The state of California did not participate in the case.) These two men were best known as the opposing lawyers in Bush v. Gore, the arguments over the election of 2000 that culminated in the historic Supreme Court decision that made George Bush president. Boies had represented Vice President Al Gore, and Olson had represented George W. Bush and then, following Bush's victory, served as solicitor general under him.

A staunch conservative Republican whose wife—the attorney and Fox News commentator Barbara Olson—had died aboard the plane that crashed into the Pentagon on 9/11, Ted Olson once said, "Creating a second class of citizens is discrimination, plain and simple." He also told the *New York Times* that "his support of same-sex marriage stemmed from longstanding personal and legal conviction. He sees nothing inconsistent with that stance and his devotion to conservative legal causes: the same antipathy toward 'government discrimination.' "

The decision in the California case seemed destined for the Supreme Court.

American Voices
President George W. Bush, commenting on the relief efforts in the wake of Hurricane Katrina, led by the director of the Federal Emergency Management Agency (FEMA), Michael Brown, Mobile, Alabama, September 2, 2005:

Brownie, you're doing a heckuva job. The FEMA Director's working 24 hours a day.

The most costly storm in American history made its first landfall in southeast Florida on August 25, 2005, as a Category 1 hurricane. After weakening slightly, Katrina moved over the Gulf of Mexico and began to strengthen over the Gulf's warm, shallow waters, eventually being upgraded to a Category 5 hurricane on August 28. That day, Mayor Ray Nagin of New Orleans ordered a mandatory evacuation of the city. Thousands of residents either chose to stay or were unable to leave because of inadequate preparations for transporting so many people. Responding to a request for 700 buses by the Louisiana National Guard, FEMA sent 100. More than 30,000 people took refuge in the city's football stadium, the Superdome. They had roughly thirty-six hours' worth of food.

Katrina was at Category 3 strength when it made landfall again on Monday, August 29, in Louisiana. Despite weakening, Katrina caused massive storm surges, measuring up to twenty-five to twenty-eight feet, throughout southeast Louisiana, Mississippi, and Alabama. Combined with strong winds and heavy rainfall, the storm surges contributed to the failure of the New Orleans levee system on August 30. The levees, a system of canals that ringed New Orleans, a city that mostly lies below sea level, were topped, as predicted by two federal agencies—the National Weather Service and the National Hurricane Center—and entire neighborhoods were inundated. This scenario had actually been forecast by a FEMA exercise thirteen months before Katrina struck, according to MSNBC.

By Wednesday, August 31, New Orleans had fallen into chaos and thousands of residents, mostly poor and African American, were trapped in the Superdome, where people were dying. Lacking sufficient supplies and sanitary facilities, the evacuation center at the Superdome soon became a hellish scene of crime and horror. When asked where FEMA's director, Mike Brown, was as the situation unraveled, his secretary told reporters that Brown was pressed for time, since they were caught in traffic and Brown had a lunchtime restaurant reservation he did not want to miss.

While many communities along the Gulf Coast were severely damaged by the storm, New Orleans was the center of the calamity. About 80 percent of the city was eventually flooded, displacing more than 1 million people from their homes. An exact death count was never established, but the fatalities from Katrina were estimated at more than 1,833, with property damage in excess of $125 billion.

The reaction of the government to the Katrina disaster was considered grossly disorganized and inefficient, at every level from Ray Nagin, the mayor of New Orleans, and Louisiana's first female governor, Kathleen Blanco, to the entire federal response. But President Bush and the performance of FEMA and its director Michael Brown in particular came in for the most criticism. President Bush was criticized for failing to take the situation seriously and then for making what was considered only a cursory flyover of the area a few days after the hurricane struck. Then after claiming that nobody had predicted the failure of the levees, the president was contradicted by videotapes, which showed him being given specific warnings of the impending disaster at a briefing before Katrina made its devastating landfall. Michael Brown, however, paid the price. He was recalled to Washington and resigned ten days after the infamous press conference in which the president had praised him.

One year after the Katrina disaster, Brown stated on MSNBC that at the insistence of the White House, he had lied about what had happened. "The lie was that we were working as a team and that everything was working smoothly. And how we would go out, and I beat myself up daily for allowing this to have happened, to sit there and go on television and talk about how things are working well, when you know they are not behind the scenes, is just wrong. . . . That's exactly why I think that's the biggest mistake that I made, was not leveling with the American people, and saying, you know what, this is a catastrophic event, and it's not working at the state, local, or the federal level."

AMERICAN VOICES
HENRY PAULSON, then Secretary of the Treasury in
the Bush administration, in *On the Brink*:

It was Thursday morning, September 4, 2008, and we were in the Oval Office of the White House discussing the fate of Fannie Mae and Freddie Mac, the troubled housing finance giants. For the good of the country, I had proposed that we seize control of the companies, fire their bosses, and prepare to provide up to $100 billion of capital support for each. If we did not act immediately, Fannie and Freddie would, I feared, take down the financial system, and the global economy, with them.

AMERICAN VOICES
Excerpt from an exchange between Representative
HENRY WAXMAN (Democrat, California) and
the former chairman of the Federal Reserve,
ALAN GREENSPAN, during congressional testimony
over the collapse of the financial system, October 2008:

REP. HENRY WAXMAN: You found a flaw in the reality . . .

ALAN GREENSPAN: Flaw in the model that I perceived in the critical functioning structure that defines how the world works, so to speak.

REP. HENRY WAXMAN: In other words, you found that your view of the world, your ideology, was not right, it was not working?

ALAN GREENSPAN: That is—precisely. No, that's precisely
the reason I was shocked, because I had been going for
forty years or more with very considerable evidence that
it was working exceptionally well.

How do you keep a "bubble" from bursting?

The catastrophic flooding of New Orleans and much of the Gulf Coast
after Hurricane Katrina gave the word "underwater" a deadly realism
and terrifying finality. Images of people clinging to rooftops as flood-
waters surged around them made certain of that. But the word "underwater" acquired a whole new meaning to Americans when a financial
perfect storm threatened to inundate the American economy, and with
it the rest of the world's financial systems.

In the language of economics, real estate, and banking, "underwater" describes a house that is worth less than the amount it is mortgaged
for. During an incredible boom time in America, such an idea was far
removed from the minds of most people, including many of the world's
economists and central bankers, such as Alan Greenspan. For more
than a decade, skyrocketing housing values continued to propel the
American economy, aided by increasingly elaborate mortgage products that promised to put millions of Americans in reach of a "McMan-
sion" of their own. Housing, for obvious reasons, is a major driver of the
economy and for a time in America, there was only one way for house
prices to go—up.

But if mortgage debt was rain, and the banks that held those mortgages and the investment houses that bought and sold mortgage-backed
securities were the canals holding in the water, the levees were about to
break. Soon, millions of Americans found themselves with houses that
were "underwater"—and banks began to foreclose on those houses in an
effort to avoid their own bankruptcies. The vastly inflated "bubble" in
housing prices had been pricked. And as the bubble deflated, it threatened to bring America back to the hopeless days of the Great Depression.

The "subprime" crisis. The credit crisis. The Great Recession. It was
an economic downturn unlike anything most living Americans had ever
seen. And for a while, the nation teetered on the edge of another Great
Depression. Would the financial system, now intricately linked across

borders, actually hold? Would the financial levees hold? Or would a financial flood of debt come washing over the country, inundating homes and businesses just as the waters had drowned New Orleans in 2005?

As the nation prepared to elect a new president in 2008, the deluge certainly seemed to be coming. For months, the country had teetered at the edge of economic disaster. Slumping housing sales. Plummeting retail sales. Personal and corporate bankruptcy filings on the rise. Employers slashing payrolls at the fastest pace in decades. One of the most visible of American retailers, Circuit City—home of the electronic playthings that had become as American as two cars in the garage and a chicken in every pot—shut its doors.

The immediate crisis had begun in early 2007 with the deepening troubles of a number of Wall Street investment firms whose risky bets in mortgage-backed securities—a financial invention of the previous decades that had proved extremely profitable while housing prices were going up—came crashing down as a recession burst the bubble in American housing prices.

Many of those mortgages were underwritten and held by two agencies, known widely as Fannie Mae (the Federal National Mortgage Association) and Freddie Mac (the Federal Home Loan Mortgage Association). Fannie Mae was created in the Depression era to purchase mortgages, allowing lenders to free up money to make more mortgages. In 1968, Fannie Mae was converted into a private, shareholder-owned corporation. At the same time, Freddie Mac was created to compete with Fannie Mae in order to create an efficient secondary mortgage market. In the 1980s, Fannie Mae created the mortgage-backed security. Over the years, the two corporations had also been politically pressured to ease loan requirements to low-income and middle-income earners. This meant greater risks for corporations that were responsible to their shareholders to make a profit yet still were exposed to political pressure. By 1999, Steven Holmes of the *New York Times* warned, "Fannie Mae is taking on significantly more risk, which may not pose any difficulties during flush economic times. But the government-subsidized corporation may run into trouble in an economic downturn, prompting a government rescue similar to that of the savings and loan industry in the 1980s." A series of accounting scandals then hit Fannie Mae as well, and the troubled agency was taking water.

By 2007, Holmes's prediction came true. As more subprime loans went into default, the two mortgage giants teetered. Although they were not legally backed by the federal government, most investors believed that the government would not let them fail. In 2008, the two companies were placed in "conservatorship" inside another federal agency. Shareholders, many of whom believed that Fannie and Freddie were "guaranteed" by the federal government, now held nearly worthless shares in the two mortgage giants, which together held more than half of all U.S. mortgages in 2008.

The Bush administration, already badly damaged by the political fallout from the failing war in Iraq and the president's response to Hurricane Katrina, suddenly had to deal with a new levee about to burst—the entire American banking system seemed unable to hold back the floodtide, largely begun by underwater mortgages and the inability of a growing number of Americans to meet their monthly mortgage payments, especially in the case of adjustable-rate mortgages, which increased as interest rates climbed. By the time Barack Obama was elected president, the insurance giant AIG announced that it had lost $24.5 billion in the summer of 2008, and the Bush administration announced a plan to save it. In November, the ailing financial giant Citigroup, once the standard-setter for global bankers, reached a rescue agreement with the Treasury, the Federal Reserve, and the Federal Deposit Insurance Corporation (FDIC). It would mean that the government was about to become a major shareholder in the bank. Also in November, Bush's secretary of the treasury, Henry Paulson, announced that the $700 billion bank bailout plan known as the Troubled Asset Relief Program (TARP) would be used to stabilize and stimulate credit markets.

Then two of Detroit's "big three" automakers—General Motors and Chrysler, the backbone of American manufacturing for a century—asked Congress for a taxpayer-financed rescue.

It was a series of extraordinary events, a cataclysm of failing financial dominoes that had not been seen in America since the time of the Great Depression—and the fear of another Great Depression was not exaggerated. In his book *The Big Short*, the financial writer Michael Lewis wrote, "Every major firm on Wall Street was either bankrupt or fatally intertwined with a bankrupt system."

In *Too Big to Fail*, his exhaustive history of the crisis, the financial columnist Andrew Ross Sorkin described it this way:

> In the span of a few months, the shape of Wall Street and the global financial system changed almost beyond recognition. Each of the former Big Five investment banks failed, was sold, or was converted into a bank holding company. Two mortgage-lending giants and the world's largest insurer were placed under government control. And in early October [2008], with a stroke of the president's pen, the Treasury—and by extension, American taxpayers—became part-owners in what were once the nation's proudest financial institutions, a rescue that would have seemed unthinkable only months earlier.

Once in place in January 2009, the Obama administration basically had to continue a jerry-rigged rescue plan begun by the Treasury Department and Federal Reserve under the outgoing Bush administration while also trying to battle a long, deep recession that was pushing unemployment higher. The job losses were adding to the crisis, as the unemployed were unable to pay their mortgages and consumer spending ground to a near-halt. In February 2009, the American Recovery and Investment Act (the "stimulus") was passed, intended to boost the nation's struggling economy, with a combination of tax cuts and spending. (No Republicans in the House and only three Republican senators supported the legislation.)

A year later, the levees seemed to have held, but at enormous cost to taxpayers. The notion that Americans were bailing out wealthy bankers and investment firms while millions of average Americans lost their homes and their jobs helped fuel rage against Washington and Wall Street. Some of this rage emerged in the Tea Party movement, which attracted Americans angry over the size of government and its intrusion into the free market. And as Andrew Ross Sorkin put it:

> That of course raises a more pointed question. Once the crisis was unavoidable, did the government's response mitigate it or make it worse? To be sure, if the government had stood aside and done nothing as a parade of financial giants filed for bankruptcy,

the rest would have been a market cataclysm far worse than the one that actually took place. On the other hand, it cannot be denied that federal officials—including Paulson, Bernanke and Geithner—contributed to the market turmoil through a series of inconsistent decisions. They offered a safety net to Bear Stearns and backstopped Fannie Mae and Freddie Mac but allowed Lehman to fall into Chapter 11, only to rescue AIG soon after. What was the pattern? What were the rules? There didn't appear to be any, and when investors grew confused—wondering whether a given firm might be saved, allowed to fail, or even nationalized—they not surprisingly began to panic.

AMERICAN VOICES

CONGRESSMAN BARNEY FRANK, discussing the financial crisis on *60 Minutes*, December 11, 2008:

The problem in politics is this: You don't get any credit for disaster averted. Going to the voters and saying, "Boy, things really suck, but you know what? If it wasn't for me, they would suck worse." That is not a platform on which anybody has ever gotten elected in the history of the world.

How did America elect its first black president?

In mid-October 2008, a few weeks before the presidential election pitting the one-term Democratic senator Barack Obama of Illinois against Arizona's veteran Republican senator, the Vietnam War hero John McCain, NBC News and the *Wall Street Journal* released a poll taken among registered voters. Of the respondents, 2 percent said race made them more likely to vote for Barack Obama, 4 percent said it made them less likely to vote for Barack Obama, 2 percent said they were not sure how it swayed them, and 92 percent said race was not a major factor.

Those numbers may reflect people saying what they thought the pollsters wanted to hear. But even so, the fact that more than nine out of ten people would claim that race was not a factor was still extraordinary. In a country where racial politics, racial relations, the history of slavery, and the civil rights movement have been such an emotionally scarring part of the national debate for such a long time, the idea that a very large majority said race was not a factor in their vote was nothing short of a shock.

What surprised a good many veteran political observers just as much was that this young, little-known senator from Illinois had burst onto the scene and defeated the Democratic powerhouse Hillary Clinton in a primary race that the senator from New York and former first lady thought was her prize—a step to becoming America's first female president.

Just as they would be in the presidential campaign, the policies of the outgoing president George W. Bush and Americans' desire for change were key issues throughout the primary campaign. Bush was unpopular. Polls consistently showed that only 20 to 30 percent of the American public approved of his job performance.

On that count, Barack Obama held a distinct advantage. As the war in Iraq became increasingly unpopular, it was Obama who could campaign as the Democrat who had opposed the war. As a senator, he had voted against the measure authorizing the war; Hillary Clinton had voted for it. Apart from that crucial difference, there were few serious policy disagreements between the two Democrats. (Days after his election, Obama offered the post of secretary of state to Senator Clinton, his bitter primary rival, who accepted the job.)

Obama's primary victory was fueled largely by that discontent, along with a desire for "change."

During the general election campaign, the major party candidates ran on a platform of change and reform in Washington. Domestic policy and the economy eventually emerged as the main themes in the last few months of the election campaign after the onset of the 2008 economic crisis.

But the unpopular war in Iraq was a key issue during the campaign before the economic crisis. When John McCain said the United States could be in Iraq for as long as the next 50 to 100 years, his remark proved costly. Running against George Bush as much as against John McCain, Obama linked McCain, a stalwart supporter of the war in Iraq, to the unpopular President Bush; this was not difficult, since McCain himself said he supported Bush 90 percent of the time that the president was in office.

McCain attempted to depict Obama as inexperienced, but the

desire for "change" seemed more important to Americans than "experience." It seemed there was an awful lot of experience behind the Bush team, and many Americans thought that this team had made a mess of things. Of what value was experience?

McCain also undercut his own argument for experience with the historic selection of the first woman to run for vice president on the Republican ticket, Governor Sarah Palin of Alaska, who quickly became a lightning rod of controversy in the election. Palin had been governor only since 2006, and before that had been a council member and mayor of the small Alaskan town of Wasilla. When several media interviews suggested that Palin lacked basic knowledge on certain key issues, serious doubts were raised about her qualifications to be vice president or president.

But the war and experience—Obama's or Palin's—soon took a backseat to the economic crisis engulfing the country. The campaign played out against the recession and the credit crisis. McCain's prospects suffered as he made some costly misjudgments about the economy and was once again linked to the Republican administration that was being blamed for the crisis. It didn't help when he told an interviewer that he didn't know how many houses he and his wife owned. (The answer was seven.) His out-of-touch image took another hit when, on September 15, the day of the Lehman Brothers bankruptcy, McCain declared that "the fundamentals of our economy are strong."

The first African-American to be elected president of the United States, Barack Obama won the election with 52.93 percent of the popular vote to McCain's 45.65 percent. No third-party candidate had a serious impact on the race this time, unlike in 2000, when Ralph Nader was widely thought to be a "spoiler" who hurt Al Gore's prospects. In the electoral vote, Obama won 365 votes to McCain's 173, a fairly convincing if not sweeping victory.

"He had secured a victory," wrote John Heilemann and Mark Halperin in their book *Game Change*:

> that was as dazzling as it was historic. His 53 percent of the popular vote was the largest majority secured by a Democrat since Lyndon Johnson. He swept the blue [traditionally Democratic] states, captured the battlegrounds of Pennsylvania, Ohio and

Florida, and picked up red [traditionally Republican] states across the country: Colorado, Indiana, North Carolina, Virginia. He dominated among black voters (95–4), Hispanic voters (66–32), and young voters (66–32). His share of the white vote, 43 percent, was higher than what Gore or Kerry had attained—and among whites age eighteen to twenty-nine, he trounced McCain, 68–31.

In both the primary campaign against Hillary Clinton and the general election, Obama had effectively used the Internet, especially in raising campaign contributions and appealing to younger voters, a generation much less influenced by political traditions of race, geography, or gender. And in that sense, his election was transforming.

Markos Moulitsas Zuniga, founder of an influential Internet site called Daily Kos, a liberal-progressive blog, saw Obama's win as representing "the future of our nation—young and multicultural. And the exit polling suggests that Republicans are headed for some rough waters ahead if they don't recognize this. . . . The white vote kept McCain peripherally competitive. But Republicans are tentatively holding onto a shrinking portion of the electorate, while Democrats enjoy massive advantages with the fastest growing demographics."

American Voices
President-Elect Barack Obama, speaking at Chicago's Grant Park following his victory, on election night, November 4, 2008:

If there is anyone out there who still doubts that America is a place where all things are possible; who still wonders if the dream of our founders is alive in our time; who still questions the power of our democracy, tonight is your answer.

President Obama arrived in the White House to be greeted by two wars and a financial crisis unequaled since the Great Depression. The severe economic downturn began officially in December 2007, a fact not declared until much later, and ended in June 2009. This crisis, which some have called the Great Recession, played out while the

Obama administration also pledged to tackle major reforms in the financial industry, salvage a teetering American automobile industry confronting the once unthinkable idea of the demise of General Motors, close the notorious and controversial prison facility maintained by the U.S. military at a base in Guantánamo, Cuba—and overhaul the nation's health-care policies.

In a little over a year, the Obama administration—usually in the face of united Republican opposition—had completed what the financial journalist David Leonhardt of the *New York Times* called "16 months of activity that rival any other since the New Deal in scope or ambition. Like the Reagan Revolution or Lyndon Johnson's Great Society, the new progressive period has the makings of a generational shift in how Washington operates."

In fairly rapid succession, the Obama administration crafted an economic stimulus bill that also set out to reform and remake the nation's educational system. In May 2009, Obama nominated Sonia Sotomayor to replace the retiring Supreme Court justice David Souter. Born in the Bronx, New York, of Puerto Rican descent, she had been appointed to the federal court by George H. W. Bush and elevated by Bill Clinton. After being nominated by Obama, Sotomayor was confirmed by the Senate in August 2009, becoming the first Hispanic justice (and the third woman) in the history of the Supreme Court. In August 2010, Obama made a second appointment to the Supreme Court when his solicitor general, Elena Kagan, the former dean of Harvard Law School, was confirmed by the Senate. When Kagan took her seal in October 2010, it marked the first time that three women had served on the Supreme Court concurrently. As both women replaced so-called liberal members of the Supreme Court, they were not expected to change the balance of what had become one of the most "conservative" Courts in recent history.

After months of contentious and brutal debate, Obama also signed a health-care reform bill—a few weeks after the death of its greatest champion in the Senate, Edward Kennedy of Massachusetts—that created the largest expansion of the nation's social safety net in half a century. The bill was intended to expand insurance coverage largely for middle-class and poor families and paid for some of it by taxing households making more than $250,000 a year. Obama then set out to revise the nation's financial rules, in a way to specifically address the excesses that led to both the dot-com crash and the meltdown that in turn led to the Great Recession.

The crucial midterm elections of 2010 arrived with the nation still mired in a sluggish economy, with few new jobs being created, the wars in Iraq and Afghanistan continuing, and a disgruntled electorate unhappy with both Congress and President Obama. As popular discontent grew over taxes, the role of the government, and uncertainty about the health-care reform that had been passed, there was a significant power shift in Washington. Winning sixty-three seats in the House, in what the president himself called a "shellacking," the Republicans regained control of the lower chamber of Congress. The Republicans also gained six Senate seats, and while the Democrats retained their majority there, the Obama administration would be moving into its second half with his abilities to shape the country's agenda sharply curtailed.

AMERICAN VOICES
JUDGE LEWIS A. KAPLAN, of the United States District Court in Manhattan, October 6, 2010:

The court has not reached this conclusion lightly. It is acutely aware of the perilous nature of the world in which we live. But the Constitution is the rock upon which our nation rests. We must follow it not when it is convenient, but when fear and danger beckon in a different direction.

Judge Kaplan wrote this as part of a decision that barred prosecutors from using a crucial witness in the trial of a former Guantánamo detainee. The witness excluded by the judge had been identified and located after the accused man had been interrogated in a secret overseas jail run by the CIA. The accused terrorist's lawyers said he had been tortured there.

To the American Nazi party, *Hustler* magazine, and other odious figures in Supreme Court history, add the Rev. Fred Phelps Sr. and the members of the Westboro Baptist Church in Topeka, Kan. Their antigay protests at the funeral of a soldier slain in Iraq were deeply repugnant but protected by the First Amendment. . . . One friend of the court brief called the protestors' message "uncommonly contemptible." True, but it is in the interest of the nation that strong language about large issues be protected, even when it is hard to do so.

— *New York Times* editorial, October 7, 2010

In a case that was being heard by the United States Supreme Court, the *New York Times* and other press organizations filed a brief in support of a Kansas church group that held protests at the funerals of fallen American soldiers to express their opposition to homosexuality. The Kansas church members believed that "God hates homosexuality and hates and punishes America for its tolerance of homosexuality, particularly in the United States military," according to the *Times* editorial. The Court had to decide if the First Amendment protected these protests.

Both of these cases—an accused terrorist being protected by the U.S. Constitution's guarantees of a fair trial and the church group that intruded on the grief of soldiers' families and claimed the protection of free speech—are part of the messy ripples of history.

The great historian Edward Gibbon once called history "little more than the register of the crimes, follies, and misfortunes of mankind." Voltaire called it a trick played by the living upon the dead. According to Thomas Carlyle, history is "a distillation of rumor." And Henry Ford said history is "more or less bunk."

This American history is a little bit of these and then some. But one thing history is *not* is boring. History is alive and human—and changing all the time. We need to rewrite it. And we need to learn from it. America has survived a lot. Revolution. A civil war. Two world wars. Depressions and recessions. Presidents and politicians, bad and good. A cold war that took the world to the brink of mass destruction on more than one occasion. And then a terrorist attack that shook the very foundations of the country's security and sense of trust.

As the country has taken its first uncertain steps into the new century, remembering America's history becomes all the more important. What's past, after all, *is* prologue.

APPENDIX 1

The Bill of Rights and Other Constitutional Amendments

Meeting in New York City on September 25, 1789, the first Congress submitted twelve proposed changes to the Constitution—called articles or amendments—for ratification by the states. (See p. 131 for more on the Bill of Rights.) These amendments dealt with certain individual and states' rights not specifically named in the Constitution. Ten of these articles, which were originally proposed as Amendments Three through Twelve, were declared ratified in 1791 and are now known as Amendments One through Ten, or the Bill of Rights. The other two amendments from the original list of twelve proposed were not ratified by the necessary number of states at the time. The first related to the apportionment of representatives; the second, relating to the pay of Congress, was finally ratified in 1992 and became Amendment Twenty-seven.

Since 1791, another seventeen changes have been made to the

Constitution, a process that begins when Congress proposes an amendment, which must clear both the House and the Senate by a two-thirds majority. Although state conventions can propose amendments, all the existing amendments have been proposed by the Congress. The proposed amendment is sent to the states for ratification. Three quarters of the states are needed to ratify, and that is usually done by state legislatures (although there has been one exception; see Amendment Twenty-one).

Amendment One

Prohibits the establishment of religion. Guarantees freedom of religion, of speech, of the press, the right to assemble, and the right to petition.

> *Congress shall make no law respecting an establishment of religion, or prohibiting the free exercise thereof, or abridging the freedom of speech, or of the press; or the right of the people peaceably to assemble, and to petition the Government for a redress of grievances.*

Amendment Two

Guarantees the limited right to keep and bear arms.

> *A well regulated Militia, being necessary to the security of a free State, the right of the people to keep and bear Arms, shall not be infringed.*

Among the most controversial and ambiguous of the amendments, the Second Amendment was intended to provide for the effectiveness of the militia, which would presumably protect the citizenry against Indians, foreign powers, or the power of the federal government, at a time when there was little or no standing army.

Under current court interpretations, it does not provide for unlimited gun ownership, but merely prevents the federal government from disarming the members of the National Guard. In decisions dating further back, the Supreme Court has consistently ruled that the

Second Amendment does not bind the states, so that state and local governments are free to enact gun control laws if they desire. In the case of federal laws, since a 1939 case involving sawed-off shotguns, *United States v. Miller*, the courts have consistently held that the Second Amendment only confers a *collective* right to keep and bear arms, which must have a "reasonable relationship to the preservation or efficiency of a well regulated militia." Congress has placed many restrictions on the manufacture, sale, transfer, and possession of weapons, and these statutes have all been upheld as constitutional.

Not everyone agrees with that interpretation, even though it has stood for more than sixty years. As constitutional scholar Leonard W. Levy writes, "The Second Amendment is as vague as it is ambiguous. Some think it upholds the collective right of state militias to bear arms, while others, probably more accurate in so far as original intent is concerned, argue that it protects the right of individuals to keep arms."

Until 2002, no administration had challenged the so-called collective right established by *Miller* in 1939. But in 2002, Attorney General John Ashcroft announced that the Justice Department would seek to challenge the collective view in favor of the individual rights view, a stance vigorously supported by the National Rifle Association. In footnotes in two filings with the Supreme Court in May, the government said that the Second Amendment protected the rights of individuals "to possess and bear their own firearms, subject to reasonable restrictions designed to prevent possession by unfit persons or to restrict the possession of types of firearms that are particularly suited to criminal misuse."

In June 2008, the Supreme Court, led by George W. Bush appointee Chief Justice John Roberts (appointed in 2005, following the death of Chief Justice William Rehnquist), went beyond the Bush administration's arguments. In *District of Columbia v. Heller*, the Court struck down a thirty-two-year-old Washington, D.C., ban on handguns as incompatible with the Second Amendment. The majority opinion in the five-to-four ruling stated that an individual right to bear arms is supported by "the historical narrative" both before and after the Second Amendment was adopted, wrote Justice Antonin Scalia. The Constitution does not permit "the absolute prohibition of handguns held and used for self-defense in the home."

Amendment Three

Sets conditions for quartering of soldiers.

No Soldier shall, in time of peace, be quartered in any house, without the consent of the Owner, nor in time of war, but in a manner prescribed by law.

A reaction to the enforced quartering of British troops in colonial America before independence was achieved, this amendment has never been the basis for a Supreme Court decision since its adoption. It does mean, however, that the Army can't just move into your house if it decides it needs a barracks for some troops. The only significant case that invoked the Third Amendment involved striking corrections officers who lived in housing owned by New York State. While the officers were on strike, the State of New York moved National Guard troops into their homes, but the courts found that the amendment did not apply.

Amendment Four

Protects from unreasonable search and seizure.

The right of the people to be secure in their persons, houses, papers and effects, against unreasonable searches and seizures, shall not be violated, and no Warrants shall issue, but upon probable cause, supported by Oath or affirmation and particularly describing the place to be searched, and the persons or things to be seized.

At the heart of the debate over "criminals' rights," this amendment was intended to protect privacy and personal security as essential to liberty. This means that no one can be arrested without a warrant naming a specific individual with a specified crime. Arrests without warrants may be made in the case of a felony when the police arrest someone suspected of a crime. After such an arrest, a judge must determine if there is probable cause to hold that person. A police officer can also arrest someone who commits a minor infraction, or misdemeanor, in the presence of the arresting officer.

The amendment also permits only "reasonable" searches and covers evidence that is uncovered during a search that relates to a separate crime. All of these issues depend on the court hearing them. No warrant is necessary for police to look for something outside a building or private yard or property.

Amendment Five

Guarantees provisions for prosecution and due process of law. Double jeopardy restriction. Private property not to be taken without compensation.

> *No person shall be held to answer for a capital, or otherwise infamous crime, unless on a presentment or indictment of a Grand Jury, except in cases arising in the land or naval forces, or in the Militia, when in actual service in time of War or public danger; nor shall any person be subject for the same offence to be twice put in jeopardy of life or limb; nor shall be compelled in any criminal case to be a witness against himself; nor be deprived of life, liberty, or property, without due process of law; nor shall private property be taken for public use, without just compensation.*

"Pleading the Fifth" has acquired the connotation of "He must be hiding something" for many people. If you have nothing to hide, they reason, you would tell the truth. But the idea behind protection from self-incrimination is part of a tradition of reasoning that begins with the presumption of innocence and was designed to check the power of the government. Written by men who knew the unlimited power of a monarch or church to compel evidence, the Bill of Rights placed the interest of the individual above that of the state. Under this amendment, the Constitution requires the state to establish guilt by independent evidence, protecting everyone from a potentially abusive government.

Amendment Six

Guarantees the right to a speedy trial, witnesses, counsel.

> *In all criminal prosecutions, the accused shall enjoy the right to a speedy and public trial, by an impartial jury of the State and district wherein the crime shall have been committed, which district*

shall have been previously ascertained by law, and to be informed of the nature and cause of the accusation; to be confronted with the witnesses against him; to have compulsory process for obtaining Witnesses in his favor, and to have the Assistance of Counsel for his defence.

This amendment also protects the individual's rights in criminal proceedings. Having seen people taken to jail under a monarchy, never to be seen again, the authors of the Bill of Rights wrote specific protections against that possibility. Speedy trials, public trials instead of secret inquisitions, jury trials in the district where the crime is committed, the right to confront accusers, and the guarantee of legal representation are all bedrock rights in the American system of justice.

Amendment Seven

Guarantees the right of trial by jury in federal civil cases.

In suits at common law, where the value in controversy shall exceed twenty dollars, the right of trial by jury shall be preserved, and no fact tried by a jury shall be otherwise re-examined in any Court of the United States, than according to the rules of the common law.

This amendment gives a right to a trial by jury for monetary damages in federal court. The Constitution does not require a jury in civil cases in state courts.

Amendment Eight

Protects from excessive bail or fines; cruel and unusual punishment.

Excessive bail shall not be required, nor excessive fines imposed, nor cruel and unusual punishments inflicted.

Another of the amendments that protect the rights of the accused, it allows the accused to post bail, a guarantee that he will return for trial, in order to be free from detention to prepare his defense. A judge can determine that factors such as the gravity of the offense and previous record weigh against bail.

More controversial is the "cruel and unusual punishment" line, which has been used to argue against the death penalty. Under current Court rulings, the death penalty is not considered cruel and unusual, although the United States is one of the few industrialized nations that permits the death penalty.

Deterrent Argument: One widely accepted argument has been that the death penalty acts as a deterrent, preventing further murders. Statistically speaking, there is no evidence to support that idea. In fact, some statistics suggest that the opposite is true. Over the last twenty years, the homicide rates in states with the death penalty have been 50 to 100 percent higher than the rates in states without it, a 2000 *New York Times* study found. Twelve states do not have the death penalty, and the homicide rates in ten of them are below the national average. Of the seven states with the lowest homicide rates, five do not have the death penalty. The lowest homicide rate in the country belongs to Iowa, which abolished the death penalty in 1965. On the other end, of the twenty-seven states with the highest homicide rates, all but two have the death penalty.

The fact is that homicide rates are often determined by many other factors, including demographics, unemployment, and poverty. However, states without the death penalty often have noticeably different homicide rates than states that are similar in other ways. North Dakota, a no-death-penalty state, has a lower homicide rate than South Dakota or Wyoming. Massachusetts, which has not executed anyone since 1947, has a lower homicide rate than Connecticut. The homicide rate in West Virginia, which does not have the death penalty, is 30 percent lower than that of neighboring Virginia, which has one of the highest execution rates in the country.

Cost Argument: Those who favor the death penalty often cite the high cost of maintaining criminals in prison.

Opponents of the death penalty point out that the cost of the litigation involved in most executions that go through lengthy appeals processes is much higher than the cost of imprisonment.

Racial Injustice Argument: Critics of the death penalty cite the widespread disparity in capital crime convictions of minority defendants.

The Innocent with the Guilty Argument: DNA, false evidence, faulty evidence, police misbehavior, and prosecutorial misconduct have all been shown to be factors in overturning convictions in recent years.

Obviously once an execution is carried out, there is no do-over. Opponents of the death penalty argue that the execution of an innocent person by the state is not worth all the potentially positive values of capital punishment.

Punitive Argument: Those who favor the death penalty, in spite of all the arguments against it, often argue as a last resort that it is the only punishment that truly fits the crime. In addition, they point to the large numbers of murders committed by prison inmates against guards and fellow prisoners.

Opponents argue that life in prison, with no chance of parole, can be considered a far worse fate than a quick and painless death by lethal injection.

The execution of convicted terrorist bomber Timothy McVeigh in 2001 came at a time when the country was reexamining its attitudes about the death penalty. The governor of Illinois, a conservative Republican who previously supported capital punishment, and the governor of Maryland, a Democrat, both announced a moratorium on executions when a significant number of death row convictions were overturned in their states. In some of these cases, new DNA evidence proved a convicted person's innocence; other convictions had been found to be based on tainted evidence or misconduct by police investigators, technicians, or prosecutors.

In 2002, the Supreme Court issued two rulings that also reflected changing attitudes toward the death penalty. In the first case, the Court ruled that the execution of the mentally retarded qualified as cruel and unusual punishment. In another case, the Court held that juries rather than judges must determine if the death penalty is to be used.

Amendment Nine

Establishes the rule of the construction of the Constitution.

The enumeration in the Constitution of certain rights, shall not be construed to deny or disparage others retained by the people.

This amendment is at the heart of the Constitution, and it is based on the idea that all human beings have certain fundamental rights. Some of these rights are specifically mentioned ("enumerated") in the Constitution, but others are not. Alexander Hamilton believed that the Bill of Rights was flawed because it listed certain rights that gave specific protections, but left the government free to act on any that had not been specifically set down. To protect those rights, including those that were expressed in the Declaration of Independence as "life, liberty and the pursuit of happiness," this amendment covers fundamental rights not set forth in the Constitution.

The Ninth Amendment is at the heart of the debate over the right of privacy. That concept, never specifically mentioned in the Constitution, was first established in 1965 by the Supreme Court in a case involving contraceptive devices, and added to in several later cases. But most people know it as the underpinning of what is still the most controversial and divisive ruling in recent history, *Roe v. Wade* (1973), which legalized abortion. The Court also recognized that a woman's right to choose contraception or abortion is "central to personal dignity and autonomy." (For more on this issue, see "Why Did 'Jane Roe' sue Wade?" p. 498.)

Amendment Ten

Lays out the rights of states under the Constitution.

The powers not delegated to the United States by the Constitution, nor prohibited by it to the States, are reserved to the States respectively, or to the people.

This amendment was a sort of additional "fail safe" designed to allay fears that a central national government might someday exceed its proper powers. It has been the cornerstone of the states' rights philosophy, but does not diminish or add to the authority of the federal government.

Amendment Eleven

Establishes rules for suing states.
[Proposed by Congress in 1794; declared ratified in 1798, although it was later discovered that ratification had actually come in 1795.]

The Judicial power of the United States shall not be construed to extend to any suit in law or equity, commenced or prosecuted against one of the United States by Citizens of another State, or by Citizens or Subjects of any Foreign State.

The amendment prohibits anyone from suing a state in federal court without the state's consent. It amended Section 2 of Article II, which seemed to provide that a state could be sued in federal court by citizens of its own state or citizens of a different state. The amendment applies only to suits brought by individuals. It does not affect the right of the federal government to sue a state or one state to sue another. The immunity from suit in federal court also does not apply to subdivisions of the state, so a citizen may sue a city, county, school board, or other municipal entity.

Amendment Twelve

Sets the manner of choosing the president and vice president.
[Proposed in 1803; ratified in 1804.]

The Electors shall meet in their respective states and vote by ballot for president and vice president, one of whom, at least, shall not be an inhabitant of the same state with themselves; they shall name in their ballots the person voted for as president, and in distinct ballots the person voted for as Vice President, and they shall make distinct lists of all persons voted for as president, and of all persons voted for as Vice President, and of the number of votes for each, which lists they shall sign and certify, and transmit sealed to the seat of the government of the United States, directed to the president of the Senate;—The president of the Senate shall, in presence of the Senate and House of Representatives, open all the certificates and the votes shall then be counted;—The person hav-

ing the greatest number of votes for president, shall be the presi-
dent, if such number be a majority of the whole number of Elec-
tors appointed; and if no person have such majority, then from the
persons having the highest numbers not exceeding three on the list
of those voted for as president, the House of Representatives shall
choose immediately, by ballot, the president. But in choosing the
president, the vote shall be taken by states, the representation from
each state having one vote; a quorum for this purpose shall con-
sist of a member or members from two thirds of the states, and a
majority of all the states shall be necessary to a choice. [And if the
House of representatives shall not chose a President whenever the
right of choice shall devolve upon them, before the fourth day of
March next following, then the Vice President, shall act as presi-
dent, as in the case of the death or other constitutional disability
of the president.] The person having the greatest number of votes
as Vice President, shall be the Vice President, if such number be
a majority of the whole number of Electors appointed, and if no
person have a majority, then from the two highest numbers on the
list, the Senate shall choose the Vice President; a quorum for the
purpose shall consist of two thirds of the whole number of Sena-
tors, and a majority of the whole number shall be necessary to a
choice. But no person constitutionally ineligible to the office of
President shall be eligible to that of Vice President of the United
States. [Bracketed portion was superseded by Section 3 of Amend-
ment Twenty in 1933.]

In American presidential elections, a voter does not actually vote for the candidate, but casts his ballot for a group of presidential electors, known as a "slate," selected by the various political parties in the state, who are pledged to that party's candidate. (For more, see Appendix 2, "Is the Electoral College a Party School?") The number of electors in each state is equal to the combined total of senators and representatives in the House from that state. In the winner-take-all system of American presidential elections, the state's electors go to the winner of the popular vote in the state, no matter how close the vote. This is what makes it possible, as in the 2000 election of George Bush, for the president to be elected by a minority of the popular vote. This has happened twice before in American history. The first time, in 1876, Rutherford B. Hayes won over Samuel J. Tilden with a minority vote (see p. 661). And in 1888, William Harrison beat Grover Cleveland with a minority of the popular vote.

(*Amendments Thirteen, Fourteen, and Fifteen are known as the Reconstruction Amendments. See p. 246, "What was Reconstruction?"*)

Amendment Thirteen

Abolishes slavery.
[Proposed by Congress in January 1865; ratified in December 1865.]

> *Neither slavery nor involuntary servitude, except as punishment for crime whereof the party shall have been duly convicted, shall exist within the United States, or any place subject to their jurisdiction.*
>
> *Congress shall have the power to enforce this article by appropriate legislation.*

This amendment outlawed slavery in America. In recent times, the amendment has been raised in other contexts, such as "peonage," in which a debtor is held to work off a debt. However, the military draft is not considered involuntary servitude, nor is requiring welfare recipients to work. Some students who object to compulsory community service have raised this amendment as an argument, but all courts have so far rejected that claim.

Amendment Fourteen

Extends citizenship to former slaves.
[Proposed by Congress in June 1866; ratified in July 1868.]

Section 1
1. All persons born or naturalized in the United States, and subject to the jurisdiction thereof, are citizens of the United States and of the State wherein they reside.

2. *No state shall make or enforce any law which shall abridge the privileges or immunities of citizens of the United States;*

3. *nor shall any States deprive any person of life, liberty, or property, without due process of law;*

4. *nor deny to any person within its jurisdiction the equal protections of the laws.*

[Sections 2, 3, and 4 of this amendment, which dealt with issues relating to the Civil War, are now obsolete.]

Section 5

The Congress shall have the power to enforce, by appropriate legislation, the provisions of this article.

First, and most important, this amendment declared that Negroes were citizens and created national citizenship independent of state citizenship. This was a repudiation of the famed *Dred Scott* decision of 1857 (see p. 210). All children born in the United States are citizens except those of enemy aliens in wartime and children of foreign diplomats. (Children born to American citizens abroad are also American citizens by birth, under a law passed in 1934.)

Clause 2, the "privileges and immunities" clause, means that rights that come with U.S. citizenship may not be abridged by the states.

Clause 3, the "due process" clause, means that the law must not be arbitrary and must be conducted with fairness. It has been the subject of more Supreme Court cases than any other.

Clause 4 is mostly concerned with discriminatory laws of a state against any group and was originally designed to eliminate discrimination because of race or color. This clause was the basis for much of the decision in *Brown v. Board of Education* (1954), which ruled that segregation deprives people of equal opportunities (see p. 424).

Section 5 provided the constitutional authority under which the Civil Rights Acts of the 1960s were passed. These laws outlawed racial discrimination in a wide variety of areas including employment, schools, public facilities, housing, and real estate.

Amendment Fifteen

Gives black males the vote.

[Proposed by Congress in February 1869; ratified in February 1870.]

Section 1

The right of citizens of the United States to vote shall not be denied or abridged by the United States or by any States on account of race, color, or previous condition of servitude.

Section 2

The Congress shall have the power to enforce this article by appropriate legislation.

Often called the most important right of all, the right to vote is the citizen's voice in electing people who will ensure his other rights. This amendment outlawed the denial of the right to vote based on race or color. The right applied to all state, local, and party primary elections. (Of course, sex was another question that would not be solved until the Nineteenth Amendment was ratified in 1920.)

Amendment Sixteen

Authorizes income taxes.

[Proposed by Congress in July 1909; ratified in February 1913.]

The Congress shall have power to lay and collect taxes on incomes, from whatever source derived, without apportionment among the several States, and without regard to any census or enumeration.

It is safe to say that this is everybody's least favorite amendment, but it made one of life's two proverbial certainties—the other being death, of course—fully constitutional. The first income tax was imposed during the Civil War. In 1895, the Supreme Court ruled that income taxes were unconstitutional. This amendment was adopted to overcome that ruling and permits Congress to place direct taxes on income from all sources.

Amendment Seventeen

Provides for direct election of senators.

[Proposed by Congress in May 1912; ratified in April 1913.]

The Senate of the United States shall be composed of two Senators from each State, elected by the people thereof, for six years; and each Senator shall have one vote. The electors in each State shall have the qualifications requisite for electors of the most numerous branch of the State legislatures.

When vacancies happen in the representation of any State in the Senate, the executive authority of such State shall issue writs of election to fill such vacancies: Provided, That the legislature of any State may empower the executive thereof to make temporary appointments until the people fill the vacancies by election as the legislature may direct. This amendment shall not be so construed as to affect the election or term of any Senator chosen before it becomes valid as part of the Constitution.

Prior to ratification of this amendment, U.S. senators were chosen by state legislatures under Article I, Section 3 of the Constitution. The amendment also provides for appointments by the governor of a state in which a vacancy occurs because of death or resignation.

Amendment Eighteen

Prohibits liquor.

[Proposed by Congress in December 1917; ratified in January 1919.]

1. After one year from the ratification of this article the manufacture, sale, or transportation of intoxicating liquors within, the importation thereof into, or the exportation thereof from the United States and all territory subject to the jurisdiction thereof for beverage purposes is hereby prohibited.

2. The Congress and the several States shall have concurrent power to enforce this article by appropriate legislation.

3. This article shall be inoperative unless it shall have been ratified as an amendment to the Constitution by the legislatures of the several States, as provided in the Constitution, within seven years from the date of the submission to the States by the Congress.

The historic ban on liquor that began the period in American history known as Prohibition was overwhelmingly approved in the state legislatures. It was adopted by all the states except Connecticut and Rhode Island.

The Eighteenth Amendment and Prohibition were then repealed by ratification of Amendment Twenty-one in 1933.

Amendment Nineteen

Establishes nationwide vote for women.

[Proposed by Congress in June 1919; ratified in August 1920.]

The right of citizens of the United States to vote shall not be denied or abridged by the United States or by any State on account of sex.

Congress shall have the power to enforce this article by appropriate legislation.

Although ratified, this amendment was rejected by the following states: Alabama, Georgia, Louisiana, Maryland, Mississippi, South Carolina, and Virginia. While it guaranteed the vote to women, states could enact their own voting requirements. The amendment also did not require states to allow women to serve on juries or be eligible for public office. All states have since permitted women to serve on juries and serve in public office.

Amendment Twenty

Establishes terms of assuming office for president, vice president, and Congress.

[Proposed by Congress in March 1932; ratified in January 1933.]

1. The terms of the President and Vice President shall end at noon on the 20th day of January, and the terms of Senators and Representatives at noon on the 3d day of January, of the years in which such terms would have ended if this article had not been ratified; and the terms of their successors shall then begin.

2. The Congress shall assemble at least once in every year, and such meeting shall begin at noon on the 3d of January, unless they shall by law appoint a different day.

3. If, at the time fixed for the beginning of the term of the President, the President elect shall have died, the Vice President elect shall become President. If a President shall not have been chosen before the time fixed for the beginning of his term, or if the President elect shall have failed to qualify, then the Vice President elect shall act as President until a President shall have qualified; and the Congress may by law provide for the case wherein neither a President elect nor a Vice President elect shall have qualified, declaring who shall then act as President, or the manner in which one who is to act shall be selected, and such person shall act accordingly until a President or Vice President shall have qualified.

4. The Congress may by law provide for the case of the death of any of the persons from whom the House of Representatives may choose a President whenever the right of choice shall have devolved upon them, and for the case of the death of any of the persons from whom the Senate may choose a Vice President whenever the right of choice shall have devolved upon them.

5. Sections 1 and 2 shall take effect on the 15th day of October following the ratification of this article [October 1933].

6. This article shall be inoperative unless it shall have been ratified as an amendment to the Constitution by the legislatures of three fourths of the several States within seven years from the date of its submission.

Before this amendment was ratified, the newly elected president and Congress did not assume their offices until March following the November elections. This was a holdover from the eighteenth century when travel and communications were much slower and the pace of the government very different. However, it meant that the Congress that convened in December possibly included defeated officials to carry out the legislative and executive business of government in what was known as a "lame duck" session. Of course, the sitting president remains in power until the president-elect is inaugurated in January. While Congress is not in session, the "lame duck" president still functions, and controversial decisions and appointments are often made during this period.

Now, the old session of Congress adjourns before the elections and the new session begins in January with newly elected congressmen taking their seats at once.

Section 3 addressed a problem caused by the Twelfth Amendment. Under that amendment, the three top vote getters in a presidential race were sent to the House of Representatives in case there was no winner in the Electoral College. It was possible that none of the three could get a majority of the votes in the House, where each state is given a single vote. This section says that the vice president elect would serve until the House elected someone by a majority, or if there was no vice president elect, the House could declare who should act as president.

Amendment Twenty-one

Repeals Prohibition.

[Proposed by Congress in February 1933; ratified in December 1933. It was rejected by South Carolina.]

1. The eighteenth article of amendment to the Constitution of the United States is hereby repealed.

2. The transportation or importation into any State, territory, or possession of the United States for delivery or use therein of intoxicating liquors, in violation of the laws thereof, is hereby prohibited.

3. This article shall be inoperative unless it shall have been ratified as an amendment to the Constitution by conventions in the several States, as provided in the Constitution, within seven years from the date of the submission hereof to the States by the Congress.

While overturning the federal prohibition on liquor, the amendment gave the states full power to pass their own laws regarding sale of liquor within their boundaries. A number of state, county, and municipal governments continued Prohibition. However, by 1966, no state-wide Prohibition existed.

This is the only amendment that has ever been ratified by conventions instead of by the state legislatures.

Amendment Twenty-two

Sets presidential term limits.
[Proposed by Congress in March 1947; ratified in February 1951.]

No persons shall be elected to the office of the President more than twice, and no person who has held the office of President, or acted as president, for more than two years of a term to which some other person was elected President shall be elected to the office of President more than once. But this article shall not apply to any person holding the office of president when this Article was proposed by the Congress.

This article shall be inoperative unless it shall have been ratified as an amendment to the Constitution by the legislatures of three fourths of the several states within seven years from the date of its submission to the States by the Congress.

This amendment was proposed and ratified following the unprecedented and unequaled four terms of Franklin D. Roosevelt, who died during his fourth term in office. It limits a president to two terms, except in the case of a vice president who has succeeded to the presidency but serves two years or less of his predecessor's term. Harry Truman, having served more than three years of FDR's fourth term and been elected to a term of his own, could have run for a third term under the special provision of the amendment. Lyndon B. Johnson served only one year of President Kennedy's first term. He was then reelected in 1964 and was eligible to run again in 1968, but declined to run. Had he run and won, he would have served a total of nine years.

Amendment Twenty-three

Gives voters in the District of Columbia the presidential vote.
[Proposed by Congress in June 1960; ratified in March 1961.]

1. *The District constituting the seat of Government of the United States shall appoint in such manner as the Congress may direct:*

A number of electors of president and vice president equal to the whole number of Senators and Representatives in Congress to which the District would be entitled if it were a State, but in no event more than the least populous state; they shall be in addition to those appointed by the States, but they shall be considered, for the purpose of the election of the President and Vice President, to be electors appointed by a State; and they shall meet in the District and perform such duties as provided by the twelfth article of amendment.

2. *The Congress shall have power to enforce this article by appropriate legislation.*

Prior to this amendment, voters in the District of Columbia could not vote for president. The amendment guarantees that the District will always have at least three electoral votes, since the smallest state has two senators and at least one representative. In 1970, Congress approved a single delegate to the House of Representatives. This member cannot vote on the floor but can vote in committee and participate. The District has no representation in the Senate. If the District of Columbia were counted as the fifty-first state, it would rank fiftieth in population, behind Vermont but ahead of Wyoming, according to the 2000 census.

Amendment Twenty-four

Outlaws poll taxes in federal elections.

[Proposed by Congress in August 1962; ratified in January 1964.]

1. *The right of citizens of the United States to vote in any primary or other election for President or Vice President, of electors for President or Vice President, or for Senator or Representative in Congress, shall not be denied or abridged by the United States or any State by reason of failure to pay any poll tax or other tax.*

2. *The Congress shall have power to enforce this article by appropriate legislation.*

While some states had imposed some sort of poll tax—an income requirement in order to vote—following the Civil War Reconstruction era, many southern states had imposed taxes as a specific means to limit black voter participation. Passed during the period of civil rights legislation that included the Voting Rights Act of 1964, this amendment was aimed at eliminating one more hurdle to voting rights for all Americans.

Amendment Twenty-five

Sets rules in the event of presidential disability and succession.
[Proposed by Congress in July 1965; ratified in February 1967.]

1. In case of the removal of the President from office or of his death or resignation, the Vice President shall become President.

2. Whenever there is a vacancy in the office of the Vice President, the President shall nominate a Vice President who shall take office upon confirmation by a majority vote of both Houses of Congress.

3. Whenever the President transmits to the President pro tempore of the Senate and the Speaker of the House of Representatives his written declaration that he is unable to discharge the powers and duties of his office, and until he transmits to them a written declaration to the contrary, such power and duties shall be discharged by the Vice President as Acting President.

4. Whenever the Vice President and a majority of either the principal officers of the executive departments or of such other body as Congress may by law provide, transmit to the President pro tempore of the Senate and the Speaker of the House of Representatives their written declaration that the President is unable to discharge the power and duties of his office, the Vice President shall immediately assume the powers and duties of the office as Acting President.

Thereafter, when the President transmits to the President pro tempore of the Senate and the Speaker of the House of Representatives his written declaration that no inability exists, he shall resume the powers and duties of his office unless the Vice Presi-

dent and a majority of either the principal officers of the executive department or of such other body as Congress may by law provide, transmit within four days to the President pro tempore of the Senate and the Speaker of the House of Representatives their written declaration that the President is unable to discharge the powers and duties of his office. Thereupon Congress shall decide the issue, assembling within forty-eight hours for that purpose if not in session. If the Congress, within twenty-one days after receipt of the latter written declaration, or if Congress is not in session, within twenty-one days after Congress is required to assemble, determines by two thirds vote of both Houses that the President is unable to discharge the powers and duties of his office, the Vice President shall continue to discharge the same as Acting President; otherwise, the President shall resume the powers and duties of his office.

This amendment provides clear rules for the succession in the presidency, in cases of death, removal, resignation, or disability. It covers temporary as well as permanent succession by the vice president. The amendment fills the gap in constitutional law if the president is ill and provides for a situation in which the president might be severely disabled. The first time this amendment was invoked came during President Reagan's 1985 cancer surgery when Vice President Bush became the first "acting president." In 2002, Vice President Cheney became acting president while President George W. Bush underwent a colonoscopy and was sedated. Some observers, including physicians, think that the amendment should have been invoked after the 1981 assassination attempt on President Reagan, while he was undergoing surgery.

Amendment Twenty-six

Gives voting rights to eighteen-year-olds.
[Proposed by Congress in March 1971; ratified in June 1971.]

1. The right of citizens of the United States, who are eighteen years of age or older, to vote shall not be denied or abridged by the United States or by any State on account of age.

2. The Congress shall have the power to enforce this article by appropriate legislation.

Proposed during the Vietnam War era, while many eighteen-year-olds were being drafted to fight but couldn't vote and many others were vocally protesting the war, this amendment was ratified faster than any other in American history. At the time, most states' drinking age was also eighteen, but since then almost every state has raised the minimum drinking age to twenty-one years. The only notable Court case involving this amendment was the successful suit brought by college students who wanted to register to vote in the towns where they attended school. The Court found that the students do have that right.

Amendment Twenty-seven

Limits congressional pay raises.
[Ratified in 1992.]

No law, varying the compensation for the services of the Senators and Representatives, shall take effect, until an election of Representatives shall have intervened.

If the twenty-sixth was fastest, this was slowest. What a surprise! Congress took about 200 years to limit its ability to give itself a raise. To be fair, it was actually the states that dallied on this one.

This amendment, which delays any increase in congressional pay until a new Congress is elected, was written by James Madison as part of the original Bill of Rights and proposed by Congress in 1789. But it was not ratified until 1992, in the wake of outrage over congressional gridlock, the power of an incumbent Congress, budget deficits, and several pay raises that took effect immediately after their enactment. Those states that had originally ratified the amendment in the late 1700s did not have to ratify it again. While it theoretically denies a member of Congress from voting himself a raise, the overwhelming number of incumbents who successfully run for reelection means that they usually have to wait just a few months for the raise to come through.

APPENDIX 2

Is the Electoral College a Party School?
A Presidential Election Primer

Final figures from the presidential election of 2000 showed that 51.2 percent of Americans of voting age participated in this chance to choose a leader. Plenty of emerging democracies with no voting tradition do better than that. With 50,459,211 votes, George W. Bush was elected with a little more than 47.87 percent of the popular vote. (Al Gore's 50,992,335 votes equaled 48.38 percent of the popular vote.)

Although the 2000 turnout represented a slight uptick from the 49 percent who voted in the Clinton-Dole-Perot race in 1996, the fact remains that about half of the American voting-age population doesn't bother to vote. For years, people have been troubled by this continuing American trend toward anemic presidential election turnouts. Many critics of modern American politics point a finger at the numbing banality of presidential campaigns that are all gloss and television image making but little substance. The public perception of a taint in 2000 left many voters embittered to learn that their ballots were not being counted.

Without doubt, there is tremendous apathy in this country when Election Day rolls around—the sense that it doesn't really matter who gets elected, because nothing changes. This is obviously a dangerous attitude that might produce an unpleasant result somewhere down the line.

Another reason some people don't bother to vote for president is that it is an insufferably long, drawn-out, and confusing process. This brief introduction to presidential politics is meant to take some of the mystery out of the presidential election system.

What is the Electoral College?

No aspect of the American system is less understood and more bewildering than the Electoral College. Grown men turn weak and stammer when asked who makes up the Electoral College. The subject of a once-every-four-years debate over its existence, the institution plods on, an enigma to those average Americans who think the voters decide who will be president.

Like almost every other creation of the American political system, the Electoral College was the result of a compromise. When the Founding Fathers sat down to write the Constitution and figure out the rules for electing the president, there was only one certainty: George Washington would be the first president. As Ben Franklin told the delegates, "The first man at the helm will be a good one. Nobody knows what sort may come afterwards."

The obvious answer would have seemed to be direct election by the people. But this was opposed by those among the Founding Fathers who feared that too much democracy was a dangerous thing. To maintain control over the presidential process, they came up with the idea of the Electoral College, which gave each state presidential "electors" equal to the number of its senators and representatives in Congress. These "electors," chosen by whatever means the separate states decided, would vote for two men. The candidate with a majority of electoral votes became president and the second-place finisher became vice president.

But the real safety valve built into this plan was the agreement that if the electoral vote failed to produce a clear winner, the election would be sent to the House of Representatives, where each state would get a single vote. In an era in which no political parties existed, the common wisdom was that after George Washington, no man could win the votes needed for election, and the real decisions would be made by the enlightened men in the Congress.

Within a short time after Washington, two presidential elections failed to produce a victor and were sent to the House of Representatives. In 1800, Thomas Jefferson and Aaron Burr, from the same party, received seventy-three electoral votes each. The election went to the House, which put Jefferson in the White House. Following this election, the voting for president and vice president was separated under the Twelfth Amendment. Then, in 1824, Andrew Jackson led in the popular vote but failed to win a majority of electoral votes. In this case, the House of Representatives bypassed Jackson in favor of John Quincy Adams.

It has happened two more times in American political history. In 1876, Samuel J. Tilden beat Rutherford B. Hayes in the popular vote. But in some scandalous post-election politicking, Hayes collected enough tainted electoral votes to steal the victory. Then again in 1888, Grover Cleveland won the popular vote but lost to Benjamin Harrison in the Electoral College.

In 2000, the Electoral College was equal to the 435 members of the House and 100 members of the Senate, plus three electoral votes for the District of Columbia. And who are the mysterious electors? These people, who cannot be members of Congress, are mostly loyalists, or party hacks, appointed by their state political parties to fulfill the largely ceremonial task of casting the electoral votes that were decided on Election Day. However, there is no law stating that these electors must vote for their party's popularly elected candidate. That antique loophole mostly leads to symbolic protest votes, such as the elector from West Virginia who, in 1988, voted for Lloyd Bentsen for president instead of Michael Dukakis. Tradition and party loyalty have dictated that the Electoral College has upheld the people's choice on Election Day.

It is difficult to justify the existence of the Electoral College, but it lives on chiefly because most people believed in that old adage, "If it ain't broke, don't fix it." The Electoral College system had basically affirmed the popular vote for more than 100 years. Until the 2000 election. Promises of reform or a constitutional amendment to do away with the Electoral College have floundered in the aftermath of September 11.

But the Electoral College serves another purpose—intended or not—that is either good or bad, depending on your point of view: the Electoral College makes it almost impossible for a third-party candidate to mount a serious challenge to the major party candidates, providing a built-in constitutional shield for the two major parties. Third-party candidates are then left to either make only symbolic campaigns or, in some cases, affect the outcome by drawing off support from either of the two main party candidates.

An attempt to amend the Constitution so as to abolish the Electoral College and replace it with simple direct election of the president was killed in the Senate in 1979. But the issue raises its head every four years, when people look around and wonder why America needs this antiquated contraption that was only created in the first place to deprive the electorate of its power.

What is a caucus?

Presumed to be derived from the Algonquian word *caucauasu* ("one who advises"), the earliest political caucuses were meetings of party leaders to choose candidates and discuss other party business. These caucuses were the first "smoke-filled rooms" in which powerful party bosses determined who the presidential candidates would be.

In modern political parlance, the word "caucus" is inseparably linked with Iowa, scene of the first state caucus of the presidential campaign season. In the Iowa caucuses, party members in small towns meet to stand up and declare for a candidate. The process is not binding and doesn't select any actual delegates to the national nominating convention, but it has become an early test of a candidate's strength, and leads to major media visibility. Ever since an obscure Georgia governor named Jimmy Carter won the Iowa caucuses in 1976 and went from

"Jimmy who?" to front-runner, the significance of this small group of Iowans has been inflated all out of proportion to its real weight. In the 1988 race, the significance of Iowa dropped a few notches when Representative Richard Gephardt won the Democratic Iowa caucus and then proceeded to disappear from the presidential radar screen. Iowa is really only as significant today as the media make it.

What is a primary?

Unlike a caucus, which is a public meeting, a primary election is essentially a statewide secret nominating ballot in which candidates vie for a share of their party's delegates to the national convention from that state. The first direct primary was held in Minnesota in 1900, and was soon widely adopted by other states.

The traditional first primary state is New Hampshire, which has made the state a significant testing ground for candidates. Perhaps the most famous New Hampshire primary in recent history occurred in 1968, when Senator Eugene McCarthy lost to President Lyndon B. Johnson, but ran so close a contest that it helped bring about Johnson's decision not to run and brought Senator Robert Kennedy into the race.

But, as with the caucus in Iowa, New Hampshire's significance is entirely out of proportion to its population and the number of delegates it actually produces for the winning candidate.

In a series of recent party reforms by both Democrats and Republicans, primary elections have gathered far more weight than they once had in determining candidates. Unlike the old days, when nominees were selected by party insiders who controlled large blocs of delegates, primaries now provide the majority of delegates, allowing a candidate to lock up the nomination well in advance of the nominating convention.

What is a delegate count?

All the caucuses and primaries are aimed at one goal: to accumulate enough delegates to the nominating convention to win the party's bid to run for president. Before the reforms of the late 1960s and 1970s, most of these delegates were merely political hirelings controlled by party regulars, kingmakers who had the most say in picking a candidate. In recent years the shift to direct selection of delegates to the nominating convention through presidential preference primaries has diluted the strength of power brokers and put far more power into the hands of the electorate.

The delegate count is simply the tally of delegates to the nominating convention committed to a candidate. The candidate with the majority of votes wins the nomination. In past years, few candidates were assured of the party bid before the nominating convention. The drama, suspense, and back room dealing that accompanied dozens of roll call votes at the conventions has been replaced by highly choreographed pageants that basically only affirm the candidate who has gathered sufficient delegates to take the nomination during the primary season. Although party rules are flexible and are constantly changing to suit political moods, the ascendancy of the primaries over the old system of political bosses means the days of the deadlocked nominating convention are probably over.

APPENDIX 3

U.S. Presidents and Their Administrations

Year* President (Party)	Opponent
1. 1789 George Washington VP: John Adams	—

Only ten states actually took part in the first presidential election. The New York legislature did not choose electors; North Carolina and Rhode Island had not yet ratified the Constitution.

1792 George Washington VP: John Adams	—
2. 1796 John Adams (Federalist) VP: Thomas Jefferson	Thomas Jefferson (Dem.-Rep.)

---

*The year refers to the calendar year in which the president was elected, in which case his term begins in January of the following year. In the case of vice presidents who took office following the death or resignation of the president, the date refers to the year in which they took office.

3. 1800 Thomas Jefferson   John Adams, Aaron Burr
        (Dem.-Rep.)
        VP: Aaron Burr

Prior to the evolution of a clear two-party system and separate election of the president and vice president, there were often three or four contenders for the presidency, often from the same party. The most famous instance of this came in 1800. Jefferson, who was unofficially his party's candidate for president, and Burr, both Democratic-Republicans, tied with seventy-three electoral votes. The two opposing Federalist candidates, John Adams and Charles C. Pinckney, trailed with sixty-five and sixty-four, respectively. The election was decided in the House of Representatives in the so-called Revolution of 1800 (see Chapter 3).

3. 1804 Thomas Jefferson   Charles Pinckney
        (Dem.-Rep.)   (Federalist)
        VP: George Clinton

This was the first election in which electors voted for president and vice president on separate ballots.

4. 1808 James Madison (Dem.-Rep.) Charles Pinckney
                                  (Federalist)
        VP: George Clinton
    1812 James Madison (Dem.-Rep.) DeWitt Clinton (Federalist)
        VP: Elbridge Gerry
5. 1816 James Monroe (Dem.-Rep.) Rufus King (Federalist)
        VP: Daniel D. Tompkins
    1820 James Monroe (Dem.-Rep.) John Quincy Adams
                                  (no party)
        VP: Daniel D. Tompkins
6. 1824 John Quincy Adams   Andrew Jackson
        (Dem.-Rep.)   (Dem.)
        VP: John C. Calhoun

In the 1824 election, there were four legitimate candidates for the presidency: John Quincy Adams, Andrew Jackson, Henry Clay, and William H. Crawford. Jackson won the most popular and electoral votes, but lacked the majority of electoral votes needed. The election was thrown to the House of Representatives, which went for John Quincy Adams when Clay, a powerful House leader, threw his support to the New Englander in the so-called corrupt bargain.

7. 1828 Andrew Jackson (Dem.)   John Quincy Adams
                                        (Dem.-Rep.)
          VP: John C. Calhoun
   1832 Andrew Jackson (Dem.)   Henry Clay
          VP: Martin Van Buren

On September 26, 1831, the Antimasonic Party, one of the first serious "third parties," chose William Wirt as its candidate in America's first nominating convention. Wirt finished fourth in the race, with two electoral votes.

8. 1836 Martin Van Buren (Dem.)   William H. Harrison (Whig)
          VP: Richard M. Johnson
9. 1840 William Henry Harrison   Martin Van Buren (Dem.)
          (Whig)
          VP: John Tyler
10. 1841 John Tyler (Whig)

On Harrison's death, of pneumonia on April 4 after one month in office, Tyler became the first vice president to succeed to the office owing to the death of a sitting president, on April 6, 1841. Tyler retained Harrison's cabinet, and named no new vice president. There was no constitutional provision for replacing a vice president until ratification of the Twenty-fifth Amendment in 1967.

11. 1844 James K. Polk (Dem.)   Henry Clay (Whig)
          VP: George M. Dallas
12. 1848 Zachary Taylor (Whig)   Lewis Cass (Democrat)
          VP: Millard Fillmore
13. 1850 Millard Fillmore (Whig)
          (Succeeded Taylor on his death in July 1850.)
14. 1852 Franklin Pierce (Dem.)   Winfield Scott (Whig)
          VP: William R. King
15. 1856 James Buchanan (Dem.)   John C. Frémont (Rep.)
          VP: John C. Breckinridge

16. 1860 Abraham Lincoln (Rep.)   John C. Breckinridge (Dem.),
                                      John Bell (Constitutional
                                        Union),
                                      Stephen A. Douglas (Dem.)
    VP: Hannibal Hamlin
    1864 Abraham Lincoln (Union)   George McClellan (Dem.)
    VP: Andrew Johnson (Dem.)
17. 1865 Andrew Johnson
    (Succeeded Lincoln following his assassination on April
        15, 1865.)
18. 1868 Ulysses S. Grant (Rep.)   Horatio Seymour (Dem.)
    VP: Schuyler Colfax
    1872 Ulysses S. Grant (Rep.)   Horace Greeley
                                    (Liberal Republican)
    VP: Henry Wilson

The candidates of the Liberal Republicans and the Northern Democrats in 1872 were Greeley and B. Gratz Brown. Greeley died on November 29, 1872, before his 66 electors voted. In the electoral balloting for president, 63 of Greeley's votes were scattered among four other men, including Brown.

19. 1876 Rutherford B. Hayes (Rep.)   Samuel J. Tilden (Dem.)
    VP: William A. Wheeler

Tilden won a small majority in the popular vote and led in the Electoral College, but was one short of the required number of electoral votes. Twenty-two electoral votes were in dispute because Florida, Louisiana, South Carolina, and Oregon each sent in two sets of election returns. To win, Tilden needed just one of these; Hayes needed all twenty-two. The chairman of the Republican Party claimed Hayes had won all twenty-two votes, and the dispute lasted until March 1877. The vote was accompanied by widespread fraud, especially in the South. Congress was left to decide the issue, and an electoral commission was established to settle the question. Splitting on straight partisan lines, the commission gave the election to Hayes, who had promised the South that he would bring an end to Reconstruction and withdraw federal troops from their states.

20. 1880   James A. Garfield (Rep.)   Winfield S. Hancock (Dem.)
            VP: Chester A. Arthur
21. 1881   Chester A. Arthur (Rep.)
            (Succeeded Garfield following his assassination in
                September 1881.)
22. 1884   Grover Cleveland (Dem.)   James G. Blaine (Rep.)
            VP: Thomas A. Hendricks
23. 1888   Benjamin Harrison (Rep.)   Grover Cleveland (Dem.)
            VP: Levi P. Morton

In the election of 1888, Cleveland won the popular vote with 48.6 percent of the votes cast, but lost the election in the Electoral College, where Harrison won 233–168.

24. 1892   Grover Cleveland (Dem.)   Benjamin Harrison (Dem.)
            VP: Adlai E. Stevenson
25. 1896   William McKinley (Rep.)   William J. Bryan (Dem.)
            VP: Garret Hobart
     1900 William McKinley (Rep.)   William J. Bryan (Dem.)
            VP: Theodore Roosevelt
26. 1901   Theodore Roosevelt (Rep.)
            (Succeeded McKinley following his assassination on
                September 14, 1901.)
     1904 Theodore Roosevelt (Rep.)   Alton B. Parker (Dem.),
                                             Eugene V. Debs (Socialist)
            VP: Charles Warren Fairbanks
27. 1908   William H. Taft (Rep.)   William J. Bryan (Dem.),
                                             Eugene V. Debs (Socialist)
            VP: James S. Sherman
28. 1912   Woodrow Wilson (Dem.)   Theodore Roosevelt
                                                (Progressive),
                                             William Taft (Rep.)
            VP: Thomas R. Marshall
     1916 Woodrow Wilson (Dem.)   Charles E. Hughes (Rep.)
            VP: Thomas R. Marshall
29. 1920   Warren G. Harding (Rep.)   James M. Cox (Dem.)
            VP: Calvin Coolidge

30. 1923 Calvin Coolidge (Rep.) (Succeeded Harding, who died of
           a heart attack on August 2, 1923.)

   1924 Calvin Coolidge (Rep.)   John W. Davis (Dem.)
           VP: Charles G. Dawes

31. 1928 Herbert C. Hoover (Rep.)   Alfred E. Smith (Dem.)
           VP: Charles Curtis

32. 1932 Franklin D. Roosevelt (Dem.) Herbert Hoover (Rep.)
           VP: John Nance Garner

   1936 Franklin D. Roosevelt (Dem.) Alfred M. Landon (Rep.)
           VP: John Nance Garner

   1940 Franklin D. Roosevelt (Dem.) Wendell Willkie (Rep.)
           VP: Henry A. Wallace

   1944 Franklin D. Roosevelt (Dem.) Thomas E. Dewey (Rep.)
           VP: Harry S Truman

33. 1945 Harry S Truman (Dem.)
           (Succeeded Roosevelt at his death on April 12, 1945.)

   1948 Harry S Truman (Dem.)   Thomas E. Dewey (Rep.)
           VP: Alben W. Barkley

34. 1952 Dwight D. Eisenhower (Rep.) Adlai Stevenson (Dem.)
           VP: Richard M. Nixon

   1956 Dwight D. Eisenhower (Rep.) Adlai Stevenson (Dem.)
           VP: Richard M. Nixon

35. 1960 John F. Kennedy (Dem.)   Richard M. Nixon (Rep.)
           VP: Lyndon B. Johnson (Dem.)

36. 1963 Lyndon B. Johnson
           (Succeeded Kennedy following his assassination on
             November 22, 1963.)

   1964 Lyndon B. Johnson (Dem.)   Barry Goldwater (Rep.)
           VP: Hubert H. Humphrey

37. 1968 Richard M. Nixon (Rep.)   Hubert H. Humphrey (Dem.)
           VP: Spiro T. Agnew

   1972 Richard M. Nixon (Rep.)   George McGovern (Dem.)
           VP: Spiro T. Agnew
           VP: Gerald Ford

Nixon's running mate, Agnew, the former governor of Maryland, was
accused of tax fraud and having taken bribes while a county executive.

He later pleaded no contest to the tax evasion charge and resigned as vice president. Under the Twenty-fifth Amendment, enacted in 1967 to ensure orderly succession in the event of a president's death or resignation, Nixon appointed Representative Gerald Ford as vice president, and Congress confirmed him.

38. 1974 Gerald Ford (Rep.)

Ford succeeded Nixon following his resignation on August 9, 1974, in the wake of the Watergate scandal. Ford, under the Twenty-fifth Amendment, appointed Governor Nelson Rockefeller of New York as vice president.

39. 1976	Jimmy Carter (Dem.) VP: Walter Mondale	Gerald Ford (Rep.)
40. 1980	Ronald Reagan (Rep.) VP: George Bush	Jimmy Carter (Dem.)
1984	Ronald Reagan (Rep.) VP: George Bush	Walter Mondale (Dem.)
41. 1988	George Bush (Rep.) VP: J. Danforth Quayle	Michael Dukakis (Dem.)
42. 1992	William Jefferson Clinton (Dem.) VP: Albert Gore Jr.	George Bush (Rep.), H. Ross Perot (Ind.)
1996	William Jefferson Clinton (Dem.) VP: Albert Gore Jr.	Robert Dole (Rep.), H. Ross Perot (Ind.)
43. 2000	George W. Bush (Rep.) VP: Richard Cheney	Albert Gore Jr. (Dem.)
2004	George W. Bush (Rep.) VP: Richard Cheney	John Kerry (Dem.)
44. 2008	Barack H. Obama (Dem.) VP: Joseph Biden	John McCain (Rep.)

SELECTED READINGS

The following selection of readings and references begins with general books and histories that cover broad themes and large sections of American history. This guide to general readings is then followed by a listing of books keyed by chapter to the present work.

The great breadth and number of sources used in documenting this history would have made standard footnoting cumbersome. For the sake of readability, I have chosen to attribute any direct citations in the text; all other sources used are included in the following annotated listings.

I have attempted to use only those sources that are either standard works still in print or generally available through public libraries, and recently published works that include the most up-to-date scholarship.

Andrew, Christopher. *For the President's Eyes Only: Secret Intelligence and the American Presidency from Washington to Bush.* New York: Harper-Collins, 1995. Exhaustive history of America's spies and their influence on American presidents.

Bamford, James. *Body of Secrets: Anatomy of the Ultra-Secret National Security Agency.* New York: Doubleday, 2001. An in-depth history of the National Security Agency, the world's most powerful, farthest-reaching espionage organization, with new material describing the lapses that preceded the 9/11 attacks.

Bennett, Lerone, Jr. *Before the Mayflower: A History of Black America* (5th ed.). Chicago: Johnson, 1982. A standard work that assesses the impact of blacks in America and the course of black American history.

Beschloss, Michael. *Presidential Courage: Brave Leaders and How They Changed America.* New York: Simon and Schuster, 2007. Good overview of how several presidents—from Jackson and Lincoln to Kennedy and Reagan—dealt with crisis through their personal courage.

Bettmann, Otto L. *The Good Old Days—They Were Terrible!* New York: Random House, 1974. An amusing corrective to the widely accepted notion that things used to be much better, on a variety of subjects including education, pollution, and work.

Boller, Paul F., Jr. *Presidential Campaigns.* London: Oxford University Press, 1984. A refreshingly humorous look at the history of America's curious process of selecting presidents. Anecdotal and entertaining, as well as fascinating history.

———. *Presidential Wives: An Anecdotal History.* New York: Oxford University Press, 1988. Like his earlier books in a series about the presidents, this offers a unique snapshot view of presidential spouses, with fascinating and revealing stories of their role.

Brandon, William. *The American Heritage Book of Indians.* New York: American Heritage, 1963. A lavishly illustrated history with much fascinating detail about Indian life and history.

Buckley, Gail. *American Patriots: The Story of Blacks in the Military from the Revolution to Desert Storm.* New York: Random House, 2001. The largely untold story of the role of blacks in America's military history.

Burns, James McGregor. *The American Experiment: The Vineyard of Liberty.* New York: Knopf, 1982.

———. *The American Experiment: The Workshop of Democracy.* New York: Knopf, 1985.

———. *The American Experiment: The Crosswinds of Freedom.* New York: Knopf, 1989. A political scientist and mainly a middle-of-the-roader in terms of interpretation, Burns is always lucid and entertaining. These three volumes cover the period from the making of the Constitution through the Reagan years.

Carroll, Andrew, ed. *Letters from a Nation.* New York: Kodansha, 1997. Collection of personal letters, by both the celebrated and the obscure, spanning 350 years of American history. A wonderful personal view of history.

Colbert, David, ed. *Eyewitness to America: 500 Years of American History in the Words of Those Who Saw It Happen.* New York: Pantheon, 1997. Documentary narratives and eyewitness accounts that create a fascinating and human montage of actual events, both famous and less familiar. Like the letters above, it brings a vividly personal side to the historical record.

Cook, Chris, with Whitney Walker. *The Facts on File World Political Almanac: From 1945 to Present* (4th ed.). New York: Checkmark, 2001. Valuable reference to contemporary events in international politics, including treaties, elections, and political terms.

Cowan, Tom, and Jack Maguire. *Timelines of African-American History: 500 Years of Black Achievement.* New York: Roundtable/Perigee, 1994. Useful reference presenting year-by-year landmarks in black history in America.

Cunliffe, Marcus. *The Presidency.* New York: American Heritage, 1968. A thematic approach rather than a simple chronology, this is the work of a historian who analyzes the men who shaped the office.

Eskin, Blake, and the editors of *George* magazine. *The Book of Political Lists.* New York: Villard, 1998. An irreverent and entertaining reference guide, dealing with everything from presidents with royal blood to openly gay politicians.

Davis, Kenneth C. *America's Hidden History: Untold Tales of the First Pilgrims, Fighting Women, and Forgotten Founders Who Shaped a Nation.* New York: Smithsonian/HarperCollins, 2008. Explores six little-known stories, from the European arrival through the Revolution.

———. *A Nation Rising: Untold Tales of Flawed Founders, Fallen Heroes, and Forgotten Fighters from America's Hidden History.* New York: HarperCollins, 2010. The first fifty years of the nineteenth century through six dramatic tales that most textbooks leave out.

Evans, Sara M. *Born for Liberty: A History of Women in America.* New York: Free Press, 1989. A good overview of women's roles in the making of the country.

Fitzgerald, Frances. *America Revised: History Schoolbooks in the Twentieth Century.* Boston: Little, Brown, 1979. A revealing study of the textbooks that shaped American impressions of our history.

Friedman, Lawrence M. *Crime and Punishment in American History.* New York: Basic Books, 1993. A panoramic overview of crime and punishment from colonial days to modern times.

Greenberg, Ellen. *The House and Senate Explained: The People's Guide to Congress.* New York: Norton, 1996. A simple reference guide to the procedures and practices of Congress.

———. *The Supreme Court Explained.* New York: Norton, 1997. A simple guide to the mysteries of how the nation's highest court gets, hears, and decides cases.

Grun, Bernard. *The Timetables of History: A Horizontal Linkage of People and Events.* New York: Simon and Schuster, 1975. A chronology of world history, tracing developments in politics, culture, science, and other fields. Useful for seeing American history in the larger context of world events.

Heffner, Richard D. *A Documentary History of the United States*. New York: New American Library, 1985. American history through major speeches, writings, court decisions, and other written documents.

Hirsch, E. D., Jr. *Cultural Literacy: What Every American Needs to Know*. Boston: Houghton Mifflin, 1987. What we don't know and why.

Hirsch, E. D., Jr., Joseph F. Kett, and James Trefil. *The Dictionary of Cultural Literacy*. Boston: Houghton Mifflin, 1988. What we need to know, in bite-size portions.

Hofstadter, Richard, and Clarence L. Ver Steeg. *Great Issues in American History: From Settlement to Revolution, 1584–1776*. New York: Vintage, 1958. This and the succeeding volumes in the series are a presentation of history through major writings, speeches, and court decisions, with interpretive essays.

———. *Great Issues in American History: From the Revolution to the Civil War, 1765–1865*. New York: Vintage, 1958.

———. *Great Issues in American History: From Reconstruction to the Present Day, 1864–1981*. New York: Vintage, 1982.

Hoxie, Frederick E., ed. *Encyclopedia of North American Indians*. Boston: Houghton Mifflin, 1996. Excellent reference with entries covering all aspects of Indian life in North America, from prehistoric to modern times.

Hoyt, Edwin P. *America's Wars and Military Excursions*. New York: McGraw-Hill, 1987. An encyclopedic but entertaining overview of America's battles, large and small, naughty and nice.

Hymowitz, Carol, and Michele Weissman. *A History of Women in America*. New York: Bantam, 1978. A useful overview of women's achievements and their role in American history and society.

Irons, Peter. *A People's History of the Supreme Court*. New York: Viking Penguin, 1999. History of the Court from a contrarian perspective.

Josephy, Alvin M., Jr. *500 Nations: An Illustrated History of North American Indians*. New York: Knopf, 1994. A lavishly illustrated companion book to a television documentary recounting American history from the Native American point of view.

Kennedy, Randall. *Nigger: The Strange Career of a Troublesome Word*. New York: Pantheon, 2002. A fascinating small book that traces the origins and use of this controversial word.

Kohn, George Childs, ed. *The New Encyclopedia of American Scandal*. New York: Facts on File, 2001. From Abscam to the Zenger case, and everything in between, including the Lewinsky scandal and the O. J. Simpson case.

Lavender, David. *The American Heritage History of the West*. New York: American Heritage, 1965. Glossy pictorial history with much useful information, though somewhat dated now.

Lipsky, Seth. *The Citizen's Constitution: An Annotated Guide*. New York:

Basic Books, 2009. Handy guide to the meaning behind the words of America's rule of law.

McEvedy, Colin. *The Penguin Atlas of North American History to 1870.* New York: Penguin, 1988. Using a progressively changing map of North America, the author traces the course of American history from prehistory to the Civil War.

McPherson, James M., general ed. *"To the Best of My Ability": The American Presidents.* New York: Dorling Kindersley, 2000.

Miller, Nathan. *Star-Spangled Men: America's Ten Worst Presidents.* New York: Scribner, 1998. Can you guess who the ten worst are? An entertaining, no-holds-barred, and very subjective list that includes Carter, Taft, Coolidge, Grant, and Nixon. Kennedy and Jefferson don't make the list, but get special treatment as "overrated."

Morison, Samuel Eliot. *The Oxford History of the American People.* London: Oxford University Press, 1965. This is history pretty much the way you may have learned it in school, a highly traditional approach that tends to skim over the unsavory moments in American history and celebrates the nobility of American progress.

Ravitch, Diane, and Chester Finn. *What Do Our Seventeen-Year-Olds Know?* New York: Harper and Row, 1987. This is the controversial study, funded by the National Endowment for the Humanities, that created a furor when its findings were released showing an astonishing lack of fundamental knowledge of American history and literature among high school juniors.

Schlesinger, Arthur M., general ed. *The Almanac of American History* (rev. and updated ed.). New York: Barnes and Noble, 1993. From 986 to 1982, a day-by-day compendium of events, with introductory essays and brief entries on major people and events in American history. A valuable general reference book.

Shenkman, Richard. *Presidential Ambition: How the Presidents Gained Power, Kept Power, and Got Things Done.* New York: HarperCollins, 1999. Interesting behind-the-scenes look at power in the White House.

Spitzer, Robert J., ed. *The Politics of Gun Control* (2nd ed.). New York: Seven Bridges, 1998. A collection of scholarly and journalistic articles relating to the history and meaning of the Second Amendment.

Wade, Wyn Craig. *The Fiery Cross: The Ku Klux Klan in America.* New York: Simon and Schuster, 1987. Traces the development of the Klan from post–Civil War days to modern times.

Waldman, Carl. *Atlas of the North American Indian* (rev. ed.). New York: Facts on File, 2000.

Weiner, Tim. *Legacy of Ashes: The History of the CIA.* New York: Random House, 2008. National Book Award winner, a grim history of the gross failures of the agency, including those in the run-up to 9/11 and the Iraq War.

Whitney, David C. *The American Presidents.* Garden City, N.Y.: Doubleday,

1985. A very basic reference to the American presidents through Reagan, with biographical sketches and a brief overview of events during each administration.

Williams, T. Harry. *The History of American Wars: From 1745 to 1918.* New York: Knopf, 1985. Unfinished at the time of the author's death, this book presents a solid historical interpretation of events in America's wars.

World Almanac. *The Little Red, White, and Blue Book.* New York: Pharos, 1987. A brief chronology of American history from Columbus on.

Zinn, Howard. *A People's History of the United States.* New York: Harper and Row, 1980. Looking at American history from the view of the "losers" (Indians, women, blacks, the poor, etc.), this is revisionist history at its best, and serves as a useful and necessary corrective to such traditional views as those of Morison and other standard American historians.

CHAPTER 1. BRAVE NEW WORLD

Bailyn, Bernard. *The Peopling of British North America.* New York: Knopf, 1986.

―――. *Voyagers to the West: A Passage in the Peopling of America on the Eve of the Revolution.* New York: Knopf, 1986.

Boorstin, Daniel J. *The Americans: The Colonial Experience.* New York: Random House, 1958.

Desowitz, Robert S. *Who Gave Pinta to the Santa Maria? Torrid Diseases in a Temperate World.* New York: Norton, 1997. A history of disease in the Americas, including the exchange of diseases with Europe after Columbus's arrival.

Diamond, Jared. *Guns, Germs, and Steel: The Fates of Human Societies.* New York: Norton, 1998. Pulitzer Prize–winning examination of the origins of cultures and societies that provides a convincing explanation for the differences in development in different places. Excellent discussion of the peopling of the Americas and the clash between European and Native American civilizations.

Granzotto, Gianni. *Christopher Columbus.* Garden City, N.Y.: Doubleday, 1985. By an Italian historian, a comprehensive and realistic portrait of America's European discoverer.

Jennings, Francis. *The Invasion of America: Indians, Colonialism, and the Cant of Conquest.* Chapel Hill: University of North Carolina Press, 1975. As the title implies, this book departs from the traditional view of a European "discovery" of America, calling it instead an "invasion."

Klein, Herbert S. *The Middle Passage: Comparative Studies in the Atlantic Slave Trade.* Princeton, N.J.: Princeton University Press, 1978. A standard history of the slave trade.

Kurlansky, Mark. *Cod: A Biography of the Fish That Changed the World.* New

York: Walker, 1997. Why Europeans really sailed across the Atlantic, and what fed them along the way. A fascinating account of how dependent the settlement of North America was on the pursuit of this fish.

Lauber, Patricia. *Who Discovered America?* New York: Random House, 1970. A young-adult book that provides a very adequate introduction to the pre-Columbian history of the Americas.

Magnusson, Magnus, and Hermann Palsson. *The Vinland Sagas: The Norse Discovery of America*. New York: Penguin, 1965.

McNeill, William H. *Plagues and Peoples*. New York: Anchor, 1977. How disease has affected and altered the course of history.

Morison, Samuel Eliot. *The European Discovery of America: The Northern Voyages*. London: Oxford University Press, 1971.

———. *The European Discovery of America: The Southern Voyages*. London: Oxford University Press, 1974. These two volumes have been abridged and combined by Morison in *The Great Explorers*. New York: Oxford University Press, 1978.

———. *Christopher Columbus, Mariner*. New York: New American Library, 1985. Originally written in the 1940s, a rather admiring, and now dated, view of the explorer by a renowned naval historian.

Nash, Gary B. *Red, White and Black: The Peoples of Early America*. Englewood Cliffs, N.J.: Prentice-Hall, 1974. A harsh revisionist view of the European arrival.

Parkman, Francis. *France and England in America* (2 vols.). New York: Library of America, 1983. Writing for the general public during the mid-nineteenth century, Parkman was one of America's first great historian writers.

Philbrick, Nathaniel. *Mayflower: A Story of Courage, Community, and War*. New York: Viking, 2006. A wonderful revision of the Pilgrim and Puritan founding myth, from the arrival through the Indian wars.

Quinn, David Beers. *England and the Discovery of America: 1481–1620*. New York: Knopf, 1974.

———. *Set Fair for Roanoke: Voyages and Colonies, 1584–1606*. Chapel Hill: University of North Carolina Press, 1985.

Shorto, Russell. *The Island at the Center of the World: The Epic Story of Dutch Manhattan and the Forgotten Colony That Shaped America*. New York: Doubleday, 2004. Brilliant narrative of the Dutch arrival in the future New York City.

Smith, John. *Captain John Smith's History of Virginia*. New York: Bobbs-Merrill, 1970. The legendary explorer-adventurer's highly colorful and suspect account of his life and times.

Snell, Tee Loftin. *The Wild Shores: America's Beginnings*. Washington, D.C.: National Geographic Society, 1974.

Stannard, David E. *American Holocaust: The Conquest of the New World*.

New York: Oxford University Press, 1992. An unvarnished account of the mass destruction of entire societies and millions of people following the arrival of Europeans in the Americas.

CHAPTER 2. SAY YOU WANT A REVOLUTION

Alden, John R. *George Washington: A Biography*. Baton Rouge: Louisiana State University Press, 1970. A sound and readable one-volume biography.

Boatner, Mark M., III. *Encyclopedia of the American Revolution*. New York: McKay, 1996. A complete, authoritative, one-volume reference to the names, places, and events of the Revolution.

Brands, H. W. *The First American: The Life and Times of Benjamin Franklin*. New York: Doubleday, 2000. A thorough and lively account of America's first international celebrity and probably the most interesting man of the eighteenth century.

Brookhiser, Richard. *Founding Father: Rediscovering George Washington*. New York: Free Press, 1996. A laudatory "moral biography" that underscores Washington's essential role in the creation of the country.

Butterfield, L. H., Marc Friedlander, and Mary-Jo Kline, eds. *The Book of Abigail and John: Selected Letters of the Adams Family*. Boston: Harvard University Press, 1975.

Cohen, I. Bernard. *Science and the Founding Fathers: Science in the Political Thought of Thomas Jefferson, Benjamin Franklin, John Adams, and James Madison*. New York: Norton, 1995. Intriguing look at the significance of the scientific knowledge of these four founding fathers and its impact on their politics, a subject overlooked in most histories.

Commager, Henry Steele. *The Empire of Reason: How Europe Imagined and America Realized the Enlightenment*. Garden City, N.Y.: Doubleday/ Anchor, 1977. A dean of American history contrasts the European experience of the Enlightenment with America's more practical political experiment.

Cunliffe, Marcus. *George Washington: Man and Monument* (rev. ed.). Boston: Little, Brown, 1984. How Washington was viewed in his time versus his true biography.

Demos, John. *Entertaining Satan: Witchcraft and the Culture of Early New England*. London: Oxford University Press, 1982.

————. *The Unredeemed Captive: A Family Story from Early America*. New York: Knopf, 1994. A prizewinning account of life in colonial New England, this narrative focuses on the capture of a young girl who chose to remain with her Indian captors.

Draper, Theodore. *A Struggle for Power: The American Revolution*. New York: Times Books, 1996. A thorough and fascinating perspective on the years leading up to the Revolution.

Edgar, Walter. *Partisans and Redcoats: The Southern Conflict That Turned the Tide of the American Revolution*. New York: Morrow, 2001. A valuable history of the overlooked campaign in the Carolinas that ultimately led to the British surrender.

Ellis, Joseph J. *Founding Brothers: The Revolutionary Generation.* New York: Knopf, 2001. A best-selling group portrait of the key founders—John Adams, Aaron Burr, Benjamin Franklin, Alexander Hamilton, Thomas Jefferson, James Madison, and George Washington—focusing on the crucial decade of the 1790s.

Fenn, Elizabeth A. *Pox Americana: The Great Smallpox Epidemic of 1775–1782.* New York: Farrar, Straus and Giroux, 2001. A fascinating book exploring the overlooked role of disease in history—in this case a near-plague during the American Revolution that killed far more Americans than the war did.

Ferling, John. *Setting the World Ablaze: Washington, Adams, Jefferson, and the American Revolution.* New York: Oxford University Press, 2000. A lively group biography that examines this trio: the "pen" (Jefferson), the "tongue" (Adams), and the "sword" (Washington) who ushered the United States into existence.

Fleming, Thomas. *Liberty! The American Revolution.* New York: Viking, 1997. Excellent companion book to a public television series tracing the American struggle for independence.

Flexner, James Thomas. *Washington: The Indispensable Man.* Boston: Little, Brown, 1969. This single volume reduces the material found in Flexner's four-volume study, another standard among biographies of Washington.

Franklin, Benjamin. *The Autobiography and Other Writings.* New York: Signet, 1961.

Freeman, Douglas S. *George Washington: A Biography.* New York: Scribner, 1985. An abridgment of the seven volumes that constitute Freeman's biography, considered the standard history of Washington.

Hawke, David Freeman. *Everyday Life in Early America.* New York: Harper and Row, 1988. One in a series of books looking at the daily lives of Americans during different eras.

Hill, Frances. *A Delusion of Satan: The Full Story of the Salem Witch Trials.* New York: Doubleday, 1995. A fascinating account of the notorious 1691 witch hunts.

Hofstadter, Richard. *America at 1750: A Social Portrait.* New York: Knopf, 1971. A snapshot of everyday life in colonial America.

Isaacson, Walter. *Benjamin Franklin: An American Life.* New York: Simon and Schuster, 2003. Entertaining biography of America's first international celebrity and one of the key Founders.

Jennings, Francis. *The Creation of America: Through Revolution to Empire.* New York: Cambridge University Press, 2000. An alternative history showing the colonists as conquerors and the Revolution as a rebellion over control of the conquered America.

Kerber, Linda K. *Women of the Republic: Intellect and Ideology in Revolutionary America.* Chapel Hill: University of North Carolina Press, 1980. A groundbreaking view of the Revolution through women's eyes.

Ketchum, Richard M. *The Winter Soldiers.* Garden City, N.Y.: Doubleday, 1973. Military history of the months between the Declaration of Independence and the crucial Christmas victory at Trenton and later Princeton.

————. *Saratoga: Turning Point of America's Revolutionary War.* New York: Henry Holt, 1997. A stirring account of one of the most important battles in American history, the 1777 battle in upstate New York that prevented the British from controlling the Hudson River.

Kitman, Marvin. *George Washington's Expense Account.* New York: Simon and Schuster, 1970. A funny and revealing book that gives a line-by-line examination of the account the commander submitted to Congress after the war.

Langguth, A. J. *Patriots: The Men Who Started the American Revolution.* New York: Simon and Schuster, 1989. A vividly readable history of the Revolution and the personalities behind it.

Levin, Phyllis Lee. *Abigail Adams: A Biography.* New York: St. Martin's, 1987. A thorough biography of one of America's most intriguing personalities. (See also McCullough, *John Adams.*)

Maier, Pauline. *American Scripture: Making the Declaration of Independence.* New York: Knopf, 1997. An excellent account of the "real story" of the creation of the Declaration by the Second Continental Congress.

McCullough, David. *John Adams.* New York: Simon and Schuster, 2001. Pulitzer Prize–winning assessment of one of the chief architects of the Revolution, the second president, and the founding member of an American dynasty.

Meacham, Jon. *American Gospel: God, the Founding Fathers, and the Making of a Nation.* New York: Random House, 2006. Excellent overview of the spiritual beliefs of key Founders and their struggle for a secular republic.

Nash, Gary B. *The Urban Crucible: Northern Seaports and the Origins of the American Revolution.* Cambridge, Mass.: Harvard University Press, 1986. The role of the working class in the quest for independence.

Norton, Mary Beth. *Liberty's Daughters: The Revolutionary Experience of American Women.* Boston: Little, Brown, 1980. Explores a vastly overlooked segment of American history, the role of women during the War for Independence.

Paine, Thomas. *Common Sense, The Rights of Man, and Other Essential Writings.* New York: Meridian, 1984. (Many other editions of Paine's writings are available.)

Peterson, Marshall D., ed. *The Portable Thomas Jefferson.* New York: Viking, 1975.

Quarles, Benjamin. *The Negro in the American Revolution.* Chapel Hill: University of North Carolina Press, 1961. An important and overlooked chapter in American history.

Rossiter, Clinton. *The First American Revolution*. New York: Harcourt Brace and World, 1956. This paperback standard contains part 1 of Rossiter's book *Seedtime of the Republic*.

———, ed. *The Federalist Papers: Hamilton, Madison and Jay*. New York: Mentor, 1961. A definitive collection of the essays that argued for ratification of the Constitution.

Smith, Jean Edward. *John Marshall: Definer of a Nation*. New York: Henry Holt, 1996. Definitive biography of the most influential chief justice in American history.

Tuchman, Barbara W. *The First Salute: A View of the American Revolution*. New York: Knopf, 1988. The two-time Pulitzer Prize–winner examines key points in the American Revolution, focusing on the intervention of France and the Netherlands and the war's decisive campaign culminating in the victory at Yorktown.

Wilkins, Roger. *Jefferson's Pillow: The Founding Fathers and the Dilemma of Black Patriotism*. Boston: Beacon, 2001. Examines the choice faced by those fighting for freedom who kept slaves.

Wills, Garry. *Inventing America: Jefferson's Declaration of Independence*. Garden City, N.Y.: Doubleday, 1978. An in-depth examination of the composition of the Declaration.

Zall, Paul M., ed. *The Wit and Wisdom of the Founding Fathers*. Hopewell, N.J.: Ecco, 1996. Quotations and aphorisms showing the lighter side — usually not seen — of Washington, Adams, Franklin, and Jefferson.

CHAPTER 3. GROWTH OF A NATION

Adams, Henry. *History of the U.S.A. During the Administration of Thomas Jefferson, 1801–1805*. New York: Library of America, 1986.

———. *History of the U.S.A. During the Administration of James Madison, 1809–1817*. New York: Library of America, 1986.

Adler, Mortimer J. *We Hold These Truths: Understanding the Ideas and Ideals of the Constitution*. New York: Macmillan, 1987. A readable primer on constitutional rights.

Alderman, Ellen. *In Our Defense: The Bill of Rights in Action*. New York: Morrow, 1991. An excellent discussion for the legal layperson of the dilemmas posed by the Bill of Rights when conflicting "rights" bump into each other, with fascinating examples drawn from actual cases.

Amar, Akhil Reed. *America's Constitution: A Biography*. New York: Random House, 2005. A lively and readable history of the Constitution from its beginnings.

Ambrose, Stephen. *Undaunted Courage: Meriwether Lewis, Thomas Jefferson, and the Opening of the American West*. New York: Simon and Schuster,

1996. An exciting account of one of the great adventures in American history, the expedition through uncharted America following the Louisiana Purchase.

Bergon, Frank, ed. *The Journals of Lewis and Clark*. New York: Viking Penguin, 1989.

Boorstin, Daniel J. *The Americans: The National Experience*. New York: Random House, 1965. A sequel to *The Colonial Experience*, carrying the American story from the Revolution to the Civil War.

Brodie, Fawn. *Thomas Jefferson: An Intimate History*. New York: Norton, 1974. The controversial "psychobiography" that restarted the issue of Jefferson's relationship with his slave Sally Hemings.

Chernow, Ron. *Alexander Hamilton*. New York: Penguin, 2004. Pulitzer Prize–winning biography of the controversial first secretary of the treasury.

Daniels, Jonathan. *Ordeal of Ambition: Jefferson, Hamilton and Burr*. Garden City, N.Y.: Doubleday, 1970. The stormy relationship of three men at the center of American politics at the beginning of the nineteenth century.

Davis, William C. *Three Roads to the Alamo: The Lives and Fortunes of David Crockett, James Bowie, and William Barret Travis*. New York: Harper-Collins, 1998. A daunting 800-page account of one of the most mythologized events in American history, the siege of the Alamo in Texas's war for independence from Mexico.

Ehle, John. *Trail of Tears: The Rise and Fall of the Cherokee Nation*. Garden City, N.Y.: Doubleday, 1988. Excellent popular history of the Cherokee nation's deadly forced march after being ousted from their tribal lands.

Fleming, Thomas. *Duel: Alexander Hamilton, Aaron Burr, and the Future of America*. New York: Basic Books, 1999. Fascinating retelling of the fateful duel and the extraordinary intersection of personality and politics at the beginning of the nineteenth century.

Gordon-Reed, Annette. *Thomas Jefferson and Sally Hemings: An American Controversy*. Charlottesville: University Press of Virginia, 1997. Arguing in scholarly and lawyerly fashion, the author dispassionately presents the evidence for both sides of the case, which weighs in favor of the likelihood of the notorious relationship.

———. *The Hemingses of Monticello: An American Family*. New York: Norton, 2008. The eminent scholar looks at the family of Thomas Jefferson's supposed lover, down to 1826.

Gutman, Herbert G. *The Black Family in Slavery and Freedom*. New York: Random House, 1976. An important scholarly work.

Hendrickson, Robert A. *The Rise and Fall of Alexander Hamilton*. New York: Van Nostrand Reinhold, 1981. An abridgment of the author's *Hamilton I* and *Hamilton II*.

Jahoda, Gloria. *The Trail of Tears: The Story of the American Indian Removal, 1813–1855*. New York: Holt, Rinehart and Winston, 1975.

Ketcham, Ralph, ed. *The Anti-Federalist Paper and the Constitutional Convention Debates.* New York: Mentor, 1986. (Other editions are available.) The text of essays published in opposition to the Constitution. (See also Rossiter, *The Federalist Papers.*)

Kitman, Marvin. *The Making of the President, 1789.* New York: Harper and Row, 1989. Amusing look at the first presidential "campaign."

Larkin, Jack. *The Reshaping of Everyday Life: 1790–1840.* New York: Harper-Collins, 1988. One in a series of books looking at the daily lives of Americans.

Lavender, David. *The Way to the Western Sea: Lewis and Clark Across the Continent.* New York: Harper and Row, 1989. An exciting narrative account of the epic expedition undertaken after the Louisiana Purchase.

Lester, Julius. *To Be a Slave.* New York: Dial, 1968. An excellent book aimed at young adults, recapturing the life of a slave.

Levy, Leonard W. *Original Intent and the Framers' Constitution.* New York: Macmillan, 1988. Rejecting the arguments of both right and left, this is an insightful reconstruction of what the framers had in mind—and why they didn't think it mattered what they thought.

Malone, Dumas. *Jefferson and His Times* (6 vols.). Boston: Little, Brown, 1948–1981. This is the standard scholarly biography of Jefferson, but many alternative views of Jefferson now exist.

Meacham, Jon. *American Lion: Andrew Jackson in the White House.* New York: Random House, 2008. Pulitzer Prize–winning account of one of the most influential presidents in U.S. history.

Morris, Richard. *Witnesses at the Creation: Hamilton, Madison, Jay and the Constitution.* New York: Holt, Rinehart and Winston, 1985. Examines the impact of these three men on the writing and ratification of the Constitution.

————. *The Forging of the Union: 1781–1789.* New York: Harper and Row, 1987. A basic recounting of the creation of the Constitution.

Padover, Saul K. *Jefferson.* New York: Harcourt Brace and World, 1942. A sound one-volume biography, now somewhat dated by new discoveries.

Rogin, Michael P. *Fathers and Children: Andrew Jackson and the Destruction of the American Indian.* New York: Knopf, 1975. An unsparing look at Jackson's record in matters pertaining to the Indians.

Rossiter, Clinton, ed. *The Federalist Papers.* New York: Mentor, 1999. (Many other editions are available.) A collection of the series of essays written by Alexander Hamilton, James Madison, and John Jay in defense of the Constitution as it was being debated before ratification by the states.

Chapter 4. Apocalypse Then

Bernstein, Iver. *The New York City Draft Riots.* New York: Oxford University Press, 1990. Scholarly, in-depth treatment of the 1863 rioting that followed the Conscription Act and left hundreds dead in New York.

Brands, H. W. *The Age of Gold: The California Gold Rush and the New American Dream*. New York: Random House, 2002.

Catton, Bruce. *A Stillness at Appomattox*. Garden City, N.Y.: Doubleday, 1953.

———. *This Hallowed Ground*. Garden City, N.Y.: Doubleday, 1956.

———. *The American Heritage Picture History of the Civil War*. New York: American Heritage, 1960.

———. *The Coming Fury*. Garden City, N.Y.: Doubleday, 1961.

———. *Terrible Swift Sword*. Garden City, N.Y.: Doubleday, 1963.

———. *Never Call Retreat*. Garden City, N.Y.: Doubleday, 1965.

———. *Gettysburg, the Final Fury*. Garden City, N.Y.: Doubleday, 1968. Classic military histories, although Catton is now somewhat dated by more recent works.

Davis, Burke. *Sherman's March*. New York: Random House, 1980. Excellent account of the infamous march to the sea.

———. *The Long Surrender*. New York: Random House, 1985. Excellent account of the closing days of the war.

Douglass, Frederick. *Narrative of the Life of Frederick Douglass*. New York: Signet, 1968. (Other editions are available.) Originally written and published in 1845, this autobiography by a self-taught slave is an American classic, perhaps the most eloquent indictment of slavery ever written.

Eisenhower, John S. D. *So Far from God: The U.S. War with Mexico, 1846–1848*. New York: Random House, 1989. A narrative account of the war with Mexico by the son of the president.

Foner, Eric. *Reconstruction: America's Unfinished Revolution*. New York: Harper and Row, 1988. A massive book that examines the social, political, and economic aspects of this controversial period.

Foote, Shelby. *The Civil War: A Narrative* (3 vols.). New York: Random House, 1958–74. A narrative account sometimes called "America's Odyssey."

Goodwin, Doris Kearns. *Team of Rivals: The Political Genius of Abraham Lincoln*. New York: Simon and Schuster, 2005. The men who surrounded Lincoln in his cabinet.

Kaplan, Justin. *Walt Whitman: A Life*. New York: Simon and Schuster, 1980. One of the best portraits of the poet and his times.

Kolchin, Peter. *American Slavery: 1619–1877*. New York: Hill and Wang, 1993. Scholarly but very useful and carefully researched history of slavery in the United States.

Kunhardt, Philip B., Jr., Philip B. Kunhardt III, and Peter W. Kunhardt. *Lincoln: An Illustrated Biography*. New York: Knopf, 1992. A wonderfully illustrated photobiography, companion to a public television series.

Litwack, Leon F. *Been in the Storm So Long: The Aftermath of Slavery*. New York: Knopf, 1979. A standard work on postwar life for former slaves.

Lowery, Thomas P. *The Story the Soldiers Wouldn't Tell: Sex in the Civil War*. Mechanicsburg, Pa.: Stackpole, 1994. Fascinating look at the true underside of the war—from brothels and venereal diseases to nineteenth-century homosexuality.

McFeely, William S. *Grant: A Biography*. New York: Norton, 1981. A strong single-volume life of the soldier and president.

———. *Frederick Douglass*. New York: Norton, 1991. Excellent account of the former slave turned abolitionist leader.

McPherson, James M. *Battle Cry of Freedom: The Civil War Era*. London: Oxford University Press, 1988. This prizewinning book is an indispensable single-volume history of the war and the events leading up to it.

Mellon, James. *Bullwhip Days: The Slaves Remember*. New York: Weidenfeld and Nicolson, 1988. Compiled during the Depression, this volume brings together reminiscences of life by the last surviving slaves.

Mitchell, Lt. Col. Joseph B. *Decisive Battles of the Civil War*. New York: Putnam's, 1955.

Oates, Stephen B. *To Purge This Land with Blood: A Biography of John Brown*. New York: Harper and Row, 1970. Excellent account of the controversial abolitionist.

———. *Fires of Jubilee: Nat Turner's Fierce Rebellion*. New York: Harper and Row, 1975. A dramatic account of the most famous American slave uprising and its controversial and charismatic leader.

———. *With Malice Toward None: The Life of Abraham Lincoln*. New York: Harper and Row, 1977. This biography of Lincoln is one of the best and most balanced single-volume histories of Lincoln's life and times.

Rosengarten, Theodore. *Tombee: Portrait of a Cotton Planter*. New York: Morrow, 1986. Using diaries, the author re-creates a vivid portrait of southern plantation life in this prizewinning best seller.

Sears, Stephen W. *The Landscape Turned Red: The Battle of Antietam*. New York: Ticknor and Fields, 1983. A compelling account of one of the bloodiest battles in American history.

Stampp, Kenneth M. *The Peculiar Institution: Slavery in the Ante-Bellum South*. New York: Knopf, 1956. Groundbreaking study of the "peculiar institution" by one of the deans of Civil War scholarship.

———, ed. *The Causes of the Civil War*. New York: Spectrum/Prentice-Hall, 1974. A collection of scholarly essays discussing the full range of social, economic, political, and moral causes of the war.

Swanson, James L. *Manhunt: The 12-Day Chase for Lincoln's Killer*. New York: Morrow, 2006. Thrilling account of the days following Lincoln's assassination.

Ward, Geoffrey C., with Ric Burns and Ken Burns. *The Civil War*. New York: Knopf, 1990. Companion to the award-winning PBS television series.

Winik, Jay. *April 1865: The Month That Saved America*. New York: Harper-

Collins, 2001. A best-selling narrative portrait of the crucial last month of the Civil War.

CHAPTER 5. WHEN MONOPOLY WASN'T A GAME

Adams, Henry. *The Education of Henry Adams: An Autobiography*. Boston: Houghton Mifflin, 1988.

Addams, Jane. *Twenty Years at Hull-House*. New York: Macmillan, 1910. The personal account of the remarkable reformer who started one of the nation's first settlement houses in Chicago.

Anbinder, Tyler. *Five Points: The Nineteenth-Century New York City Neighborhood That Invented Tap Dance, Stole Elections, and Became the World's Most Notorious Slum*. New York: Free Press, 2001. Portrait of New York's underside.

Brady, Kathleen. *Ida Tarbell: Portrait of a Muckraker*. New York: Putnam, 1984. Life of the crusading journalist.

Brown, Dee. *Bury My Heart at Wounded Knee: An American Indian History of the American West*. New York: Holt, Rinehart and Winston, 1970. A modern classic, retelling American history from the Indian perspective.

Chernow, Ron. *The House of Morgan: An American Banking Dynasty and the Rise of Modern American Finance*. New York: Grove, 1990. Winner of the National Book Award, a biography of the first family of American finance.

——. *Titan: The Life of John D. Rockefeller*. New York: Random House, 1998. A great biography of a man who has been called the Jekyll and Hyde of American capitalism—a rapacious robber baron who was one of America's great philanthropists as well.

Collier, Peter, and David Horowitz. *The Rockefellers: An American Dynasty*. New York: New American Library, 1977. A popular history of the family by a pair of modern "muckraking" journalists, this book covers the rise of John D. Rockefeller.

Connell, Evan S. *Son of the Morning Star: Custer and the Little Bighorn*. Berkeley, Calif.: North Point, 1984. A novelist recounts the most famous battle of the Plains Indian wars with a compelling character study of the controversial soldier.

Dray, Philip. *At the Hands of Persons Unknown: The Lynching of Black America*. New York: Random House, 2002. A compelling social and cultural account of the history of thousands of black Americans lynched between the 1880s and World War II.

Ferguson, Niall. *The Pity of War*. New York: Basic Books, 1999. Monumental reassessment of World War I and its aftermath.

Fussell, Paul. *The Great War and Modern Memory*. London: Oxford University Press, 1975. An award-winning book about the British experience of trench warfare from 1914 to 1918, emphasizing the literature that this experience produced.

Hofstadter, Richard. *The Age of Reform: From Bryan to F.D.R., 1890–1940.* New York: Knopf, 1955. Pulitzer Prize–winning landmark history of the populist and progressive movements at the beginning of the twentieth century.

Josephson, Matthew. *The Robber Barons.* New York: Harcourt Brace, 1934. An American classic recounting the corrupt growth of some of America's greatest fortunes.

———. *The Politicos.* New York: Harcourt Brace, 1963. A 1938 sequel to the muckraking *The Robber Barons* chronicles America's Gilded Age.

Kaplan, Justin. *Mr. Clemens and Mark Twain.* New York: Simon and Schuster, 1966.

———. *Lincoln Steffens: A Biography.* New York: Simon and Schuster, 1974. A life of one of the most prominent muckrakers.

Karnow, Stanley. *In Our Image: America's Experience in the Philippines.* New York: Random House, 1989. A fascinating study of America's long entanglement in the Philippines, dating from the time of the Spanish-American War and the insurrection, and carrying through to events following the overthrow of the Marcos dictatorship by Corazon Aquino.

Keegan, John. *The First World War.* New York: Knopf, 1999. A narrative history by one of America's preeminent military historians.

Lewis, David Levering. *W. E. B. DuBois: A Biography of a Race, 1868–1919.* New York: Henry Holt, 1993. Winner of the 1994 Pulitzer Prize, a definitive biography of the premier architect of the civil rights movement in America.

Manchester, William. *The Arms of Krupp: 1587–1968.* Boston: Little, Brown, 1964. This history of the German munitions and armament family provides a fascinating account of the rise of militarism in Germany that played prominently in both world wars.

Marshall, S. L. A. *World War I.* New York: American Heritage, 1964. A military historian, the author concentrates on the armed confrontations, with far less emphasis on the causes and effects of the war or its long-term consequences.

McCullough, David. *The Great Bridge.* New York: Simon and Schuster, 1972. The fascinating story of the construction of the Brooklyn Bridge.

———. *The Path Between the Seas: The Creation of the Panama Canal, 1870–1914.* New York: Simon and Schuster, 1977. The epic story of the creation of the canal.

———. *Mornings on Horseback.* New York: Simon and Schuster, 1981. An excellent biography of the young Teddy Roosevelt.

Menand, Louis. *The Metaphysical Club: A Story of Ideas in America.* New York: Farrar, Straus and Giroux, 2001. Winner of the Pulitzer Prize in history, this fascinating "intellectual history" examines the impact of four people, including Oliver Wendell Holmes and William James, who changed the way Americans thought about education, democracy, and other philosophical notions.

Morris, Edmund. *The Rise of Theodore Roosevelt*. New York: Coward, Mc-Cann and Geohegan, 1979. An admiring yet balanced and excellent account of Roosevelt's life, to his first inauguration.

———. *Theodore Rex*. New York: Random House, 2001. Excellent account of Theodore Roosevelt's presidential years, a sequel to *The Rise of Theodore Roosevelt*.

Painter, Nell Irvin. *Standing at Armageddon: The United States, 1877–1919*. New York: Norton, 1987. A fascinating portrait of the country during this period of transition from minor power to empire.

Tuchman, Barbara W. *The Guns of August*. New York: Macmillan, 1962. The Pulitzer Prize–winning account of European events leading to World War I and the first fighting at the Battle of the Marne.

———. *The Zimmerman Telegram*. New York: Macmillan, 1966. An account of the diplomatic turmoil and conspiracy between Germany and Mexico that helped push America into World War I.

Williams, John Hoyt. *A Great and Shining Road: The Epic Story of the Transcontinental Railroad*. New York: Times Books, 1988.

Woodward, C. Vann. *The Strange Career of Jim Crow* (3rd rev. ed.). London: Oxford University Press, 1974.

CHAPTER 6. BOOM TO BUST TO BIG BOOM

Ahamed, Liaquat. *Lords of Finance: The Bankers Who Broke the World*. New York: Penguin, 2009. Pulitzer Prize–winning history of the Great Depression, focusing on the small group of central bankers who were behind the meltdown in 1929. Great economic history with new relevance.

Allen, Frederick Lewis. *The Big Change: America Transforms Itself: 1900–1950*. New York: Harper and Row, 1952. A classic by one of the great journalist-historians of the first half of the twentieth century.

———. *Only Yesterday: An Informal History of the 1920s*. New York: Harper and Row, 1931.

———. *Since Yesterday: The 1930s in America*. New York: Harper and Row, 1939. A social and cultural history of life in the Depression years.

Armor, John, and Peter Wright. *Manzanar: Photographs by Ansel Adams; Commentary by John Hersey*. New York: Times Books, 1988. A detailed chronicle of the Japanese-American internment camp, illustrated by Ansel Adams's photo documentary of the camp.

Badger, Anthony J. *FDR: The First Hundred Days*. New York: Hill and Wang, 2008. A brief, very readable, balanced overview of the intense period of New Deal legislation introduced as Roosevelt battled the Great Depression.

Berg, A. Scott. *Lindbergh*. New York: Putnam, 1998. Winner of the Pulitzer Prize, a definitive account of the dramatic life of the heroic, tragic, and later controversial aviator.

Blum, John Morton. *V Was for Victory: Politics and American Culture During World War II*. New York: Harcourt Brace Jovanovich, 1976. Excellent social history of life on the home front during World War II.

Brooks, John. *Once in Golconda: A True Drama of Wall Street, 1920–1938*. New York: Norton, 1969. Magazine journalist's classic telling of Wall Street's Great Crash and its aftermath; his story of easy credit, inflated egos, and greed has been repeated often.

Chang, Iris. *The Rape of Nanking: The Forgotten Holocaust of World War II*. New York: Basic Books, 1997. A gripping account of one of the worst atrocities of World War II, the assault on the civilian population of Nanking, China, by the Japanese in 1937.

Collier, Peter, and David Horowitz. *The Fords: An American Epic*. New York: Summit, 1987. Well-told overview of the man who transformed America's auto industry and with it the country, and his heirs.

Davis, Kenneth S. *FDR: The New York Years, 1928–1933*. New York: Random House, 1985.

———. *FDR: The New Deal Years, 1933–1937*. New York: Random House, 1986.

———. *FDR: The War President, 1940–1943*. New York: Random House, 2000. These three volumes (part of five total by the late historian [no relation to present author]) form a comprehensive overview of FDR's rise to the presidency.

Egan, Timothy. *The Worst Hard Time: The Untold Story of Those Who Survived the Great American Dust Bowl*. New York: Houghton Mifflin, 2006. Excellent account of the toll taken on average Americans on the Great Plains by the great dust storms and drought that crushed the nation's agricultural heart in the 1930s.

Flood, Charles Bracelen. *Hitler: The Path to Power*. Boston: Houghton Mifflin, 1989. A biography that documents Hitler's rise to unquestioned power in the aftermath of World War I and the Depression.

Fussell, Paul. *Wartime: Understanding and Behavior in the Second World War*. London: Oxford University Press, 1989. Intriguing social history by a World War II veteran and leading writer of military history.

Gentry, Curt. *J. Edgar Hoover: The Man and the Secrets*. New York: Norton, 1991. Detailed biography of America's "top cop," who held virtually unchecked public power for fifty years.

Galbraith, John Kenneth. *The Great Crash 1929*. Boston: Houghton Mifflin, 1955. The famous economist explains, in layman's language, the speculative bubble that led to the crash (updated introduction added in 1997).

———. *A Life in Our Times: Memoirs*. Boston: Houghton Mifflin, 1981. An autobiography by the economist, diplomat, and historian, especially interesting for Galbraith's experiences as a member of the bombing survey team that toured both Germany and Japan after the war and concluded that American saturation bombing was inconclusive in both instances.

Goodwin, Doris Kearns. *No Ordinary Time — Franklin and Eleanor Roosevelt: The Home Front in World War II.* New York: Simon and Schuster, 1994. Everything a biography should be: the characters of history come to life vividly in this brilliantly written history of life inside the White House during World War II.

Hersey, John. *Hiroshima.* New York: Knopf, 1946. The classic account of the aftermath of the bombing of Hiroshima.

Kazin, Alfred. *On Native Grounds.* New York: Harcourt Brace and World, 1942. A fascinating and very readable collection of literary criticism, focusing on major American writers of the 1930s and 1940s.

Keegan, John. *The Second World War.* New York: Viking, 1989. With extensive illustrations and maps, a comprehensive account of the "largest single event in human history," as the author calls it.

Ketchum, Richard M. *The Borrowed Years: 1938–1941, America on the Way to War.* New York: Random House, 1989. An excellent history of America as it waited to enter the war in Europe, concluding with a convincing re-creation of the days that led up to Pearl Harbor.

Kurzman, Dan. *Fatal Voyage: The Sinking of the USS Indianapolis.* New York: Atheneum, 1990. The harrowing story of the fate of the Navy cruiser that carried the vital parts of the atomic bomb and was then torpedoed, with tremendous loss of American life.

Lash, Joseph P. *Eleanor and Franklin.* New York: Norton, 1971. Sympathetic, fascinating portrait by a family intimate.

Leckie, Robert. *Delivered from Evil: The Saga of World War II.* New York: Harper and Row, 1987. A massive updated single-volume history of the war.

Madigan, Tim. *The Burning: Massacre, Destruction, and the Tulsa Race Riot of 1921.* New York: St. Martin's, 2001. A harrowing case study of the deadliest urban riot in American history.

Manchester, William. *The Glory and the Dream: A Narrative History of America, 1932–1972.* Boston: Little, Brown, 1974. Brilliant narrative panorama of America from the Depression to the Watergate era.

———. *American Caesar: Douglas MacArthur, 1880–1964.* Boston: Little, Brown, 1978. This splendid biography of MacArthur is admiring but not blind to the general's shortcomings. MacArthur's life as a soldier — as well as his father's before him — covers almost every facet of American military involvement from the Spanish-American War to the Korean War.

———. *Goodbye, Darkness: A Memoir of the Pacific.* Boston: Little, Brown, 1979. The historian's re-creation of the Pacific fighting in which he was a participant as a U.S. Marine.

McCullough, David. *Truman*. New York: Simon and Schuster, 1992. Pulitzer Prize–winning biography of the man who had to replace FDR and who dropped the first atomic bombs.

McElvaine, Robert S. *The Great Depression: America, 1929–1941*. New York: Times Books, 1993. A sweeping history of the era.

Mencken, H. L. *A Choice of Days*. New York: Vintage, 1980. This is a collection of pieces from three autobiographical works by the American journalist and social critic.

Morgan, Ted. *FDR: A Biography*. New York: Simon and Schuster, 1985. A sound and accessible one-volume biography.

Persico, Joseph E. *Roosevelt's Secret War: FDR and World War II Espionage*. New York: Random House, 2001. Richly detailed history of FDR's use of spies; addresses many intriguing questions and convincingly argues that FDR did not "allow" Pearl Harbor.

Powers, Richard Gid. *Secrecy and Power: The Life of J. Edgar Hoover*. New York: Free Press, 1987. A solid and unbiased account of the life of one of America's most powerful men, the director of the FBI.

Rhodes, Richard. *The Making of the Atomic Bomb*. New York: Simon and Schuster, 1986. Winner of the Pulitzer Prize, an epic account of the politics and people behind the creation of the first atomic bombs and the dropping of those bombs on Japan.

Shlaes, Amity. *The Forgotten Man: A New History of the Great Depression*. New York: HarperCollins, 2008. A conservative economics writer's skeptical view of why the intervention of the New Deal did not "tame" the Great Depression.

Stinnett, Robert. *Day of Deceit: The Truth About FDR and Pearl Harbor*. New York: Simon and Schuster, 2000. Using newly declassified documents, the author argues that the Japanese attack plans were known and that America's leaders deliberately wished to push Japan into war, at the cost of thousands of American lives.

Taylor, A. J. P. *The War Lords*. New York: Penguin, 1976. A collection of lectures given by a prominent British historian, this book offers neat capsule biographies of the five men who conducted World War II: Mussolini, Hitler, Churchill, Stalin, and Roosevelt.

Terkel, Studs. *Hard Times: An Oral History of the Great Depression*. New York: Pantheon, 1970. Life in the worst years of the Depression, as told to the journalist.

———. *"The Good War": An Oral History of World War II*. New York: Pantheon, 1984.

Toland, John. *Rising Sun: The Decline and Fall of the Japanese Empire*. New York: Random House, 1970. Monumental Pulitzer Prize–winning account of Japan's rise and the Pacific War, from the invasion of Manchuria to the atomic bombings that ended the war.

————. *Adolf Hitler*. Garden City, N.Y.: Doubleday, 1976. A best-selling life of Hitler by a popular historian.

————. *Infamy: Pearl Harbor and Its Aftermath*. Garden City, N.Y.: Doubleday, 1982. Widely admired and well-documented account of the controversial attack.

Watt, Donald Cameron. *How War Came: The Immediate Origins of the Second World War*. New York: Pantheon, 1989.

Wyden, Peter. *Day One: Before Hiroshima and After*. New York: Simon and Schuster, 1984.

CHAPTER 7. COMMIES, CONTAINMENT, AND COLD WAR

Blair, Clay. *The Forgotten War: America in Korea, 1950–1953*. New York: Times Books, 1987.

Brady, James. *The Coldest War: A Memoir of Korea*. New York: Crown, 1990. A well-known journalist's vivid memoir of the Korean War, the often overlooked conflict in which as many American soldiers died in a little more than three years as in all of the Vietnam era.

Caute, David. *The Great Fear: The Anti-Communist Purge Under Truman and Eisenhower*. New York: Simon and Schuster, 1978. Excellent history of the anticommunist fears.

Garrow, David J. *Bearing the Cross: Martin Luther King, Jr., and the Southern Christian Leadership Conference*. New York: Morrow, 1986. A balanced and honest award-winning biography of the civil rights leader and the movement he led.

Halberstam, David. *The Fifties*. New York: Villard, 1993. A deft assessment of the social and historical currents in postwar America.

————. *The Children*. New York: Random House, 1998. A social history of the civil rights movement, focusing on many of the lesser-known heroes of the era.

————. *The Coldest War: America and the Korean War*. New York: Hyperion, 2007. A masterful narrative history of the "hidden war" in recent American history.

Kluger, Richard. *Simple Justice: The History of* Brown v. Board of Education *and Black America's Struggle for Equality*. New York: Knopf, 1976. Standard scholarly work on this subject.

Miller, Merle. *Plain Speaking*. New York: Putnam, 1974. This "oral history" of Harry S Truman presents a vivid picture of the president, who has grown in stature as time has passed.

Newhouse, John. *War and Peace in the Nuclear Age*. New York: Knopf, 1988. A companion to the PBS television series detailing the history of nuclear arms and superpower rivalries.

Oakley, J. Ronald. *God's Country: America in the Fifties*. New York: Dembner

Books, 1986. Nice social history of the decade, presenting a view that not all was well in this "happier, simpler time."

Tanenhaus, Sam. *Whittaker Chambers*. New York: Random House, 1997. The definitive biography of the key figure in one of the most controversial and divisive cases in American history—the charges of communist espionage brought against Alger Hiss by Whittaker Chambers, who became one of the Americans most hated (by his enemies) and revered (by his allies).

Weinstein, Allen. *Perjury: The Hiss-Chambers Case*. New York: Random House, 1997. An updated version of a complete, detailed history of the sensational spy case, with material drawn from files of the former Soviet spy agencies, the KGB and the GRU (military intelligence).

CHAPTER 8. THE TORCH IS PASSED

Barrett, Lawrence I. *Gambling with History: Reagan in the White House*. Garden City, N.Y.: Doubleday, 1983. Written by one of *Time* magazine's correspondents, this was among the first books to assess the Reagan years negatively, and it provides a useful history of his earliest days in office.

Belin, David. *Final Disclosure: The Full Truth About the Assassination of President Kennedy*. New York: Scribners, 1988. Unlike more sensational accounts, this book about the assassination by an investigator who worked for the Warren Commission convincingly negates most of the conspiracy theories surrounding JFK's murder.

Bernstein, Carl, and Bob Woodward. *All the President's Men*. New York: Simon and Schuster, 1974. Two journalists' account of the uncovering of the Watergate cover-up.

Beschloss, Michael R., ed. *Reaching for Glory: Lyndon Johnson's Secret Tapes, 1964–1965*. New York: Simon and Schuster, 2001. Tapes recorded in the Oval Office during the crucial decision-making period when the Vietnam war was escalated.

Bilton, Michael, and Kevin Sim. *Four Hours in My Lai*. New York: Viking, 1992. In-depth account of the atrocity in Vietnam by two television producers who interviewed soldiers involved in this massacre of civilians.

Cannon, Lou. *President Reagan: The Role of a Lifetime*. New York: Public Affairs, 2000. By a California reporter who covered Reagan for more than twenty-five years, an excellent single volume on Reagan's White House years.

Caro, Robert. *The Years of Lyndon Johnson: Master of the Senate*. New York: Knopf, 2002. The third volume in a prizewinning series about Johnson. This volume covers the twelve years that Johnson served in the Senate until his selection as Kennedy's vice president.

Carroll, Peter N. *It Seemed Like Nothing Happened: The Tragedy and Promise of America in the 1970s*. New York: Holt, Rinehart and Winston, 1982. A broad historical and cultural overview of the "me decade."

Caute, David. *The Year of the Barricades: A Journey Through 1968.* New York: Harper and Row, 1988. Portrait of the year that changed America.

Collier, Peter, and David Horowitz. *The Kennedys: An American Drama.* New York: Summit, 1984. Although it takes a tabloid approach, this book presents a damning and documented account of the rise of this powerful American regal family. Particularly interesting for its discussion of the family patriarch, Joseph P. Kennedy Sr.

Davis, John H. *The Kennedys: Dynasty and Disaster.* New York: McGraw-Hill, 1984. Another gossipy look, by a relative of Jacqueline Kennedy Onassis. Includes a lot of rumor and speculation, buttressed by documented revelations.

Dickstein, Morris. *Gates of Eden: American Culture in the Sixties.* New York: Basic Books, 1977. An examination of American politics in the period, through the literature and culture of the era.

Eichenwald, Kurt. *The Informant.* New York: Broadway, 2000. An exhaustive account of price fixing, influence peddling, and corporate corruption during the 1980s at the Archer Daniels Midland Company.

Epstein, Edward Jay. *Inquest: The Warren Commission and the Establishment of Truth.* New York: Viking, 1966. One of the first and most influential assaults on the Warren Commission's findings.

FitzGerald, Frances. *Fire in the Lake: The Vietnamese and the Americans in Vietnam.* Boston: Atlantic–Little, Brown, 1972. A now classic book on understanding the roots of the United States' involvement and failure in Vietnam.

Friedan, Betty. *The Feminine Mystique.* New York: Norton, 1963. The classic document on which the modern American feminist movement was built.

Gitlin, Todd. *The Sixties: Years of Hope, Days of Rage.* New York: Bantam, 1987. Written by an organizer of Students for a Democratic Society (SDS), a thoughtful and comprehensive analysis of an era that has been victimized by clichés.

Hackworth, Col. David H., and Julie Sherman. *About Face: The Odyssey of an American Warrior.* New York: Simon and Schuster, 1989. A fascinating best-selling account of a soldier who fought in both Korea and Vietnam and became something of a renegade in Southeast Asia.

Haing Ngor. *A Cambodian Odyssey.* New York: Macmillan, 1987. A riveting first-person account of the aftermath of the fall of Cambodia to communists, by the doctor turned actor who portrayed the character of Dith Pran in the film *The Killing Fields.*

Halberstam, David. *The Best and the Brightest.* New York: Random House, 1972. The classic account of the intellectuals and academics surrounding Kennedy who pushed America into Vietnam.

Hersh, Seymour M. *My Lai 4: A Report on the Massacre and Its Aftermath.*

New York: Random House, 1970. The journalist who broke the story and won the Pulitzer Prize recounts the entire episode.

———. *The Price of Power: Kissinger in the Nixon White House.* New York: Summit, 1983. A harshly critical account of the president and his powerful adviser and their approach to the wars in Southeast Asia.

Karnow, Stanley. *Vietnam: A History.* New York: Viking Penguin, 1983. An indispensable one-volume overview of the war in Vietnam.

Langguth, A. J. *Our Vietnam: The War, 1954–1975.* New York: Simon and Schuster, 2000. An excellent narrative history of the whole war by a former *New York Times* war correspondent.

Lukas, J. Anthony. *Nightmare: The Underside of the Nixon Years.* New York: Viking, 1976. A full and comprehensive account of the Watergate years, and the definitive work on the fall of Nixon.

Malcolm X, with Alex Haley. *The Autobiography of Malcolm X.* New York: Grove, 1964. A contemporary American classic: the story of a young man who rose from crime to become one of the most influential Americans in a generation.

Miller, Merle. *Lyndon: An Oral Biography.* New York: Putnam, 1980. The president's own words on his life and administration.

Posner, Gerald. *Case Closed: Lee Harvey Oswald and the Assassination of JFK.* New York: Random House, 1993. Unambiguously and convincingly argues the case for Oswald's being the lone assassin in the killing of JFK.

Safire, William. *Before the Fall: An Inside View of the Pre-Watergate White House.* Garden City, N.Y.: Doubleday, 1975. Safire, who was a speechwriter for Nixon and later a columnist for the *New York Times*, presents a vivid view of Nixon in power before the fallout from Watergate.

Scheer, Robert. *With Enough Shovels: Reagan, Bush, and Nuclear War.* New York: Random House, 1982. A disturbing examination of Reagan's stance regarding arms and the "winnability" of a nuclear war.

Schieffer, Bob, and Gary Paul Gates. *The Acting President.* New York: Dutton, 1989. A television newsman's overview of eight years of Reagan that provides a useful capsule of the period, including the Iran-contra situation.

Schlesinger, Arthur M. *A Thousand Days: JFK in the White House.* Boston: Houghton Mifflin, 1965. A partisan insider, the famous historian writes a fascinating view of Kennedy's presidency.

Shilts, Randy. *And the Band Played On: Politics, People, and the AIDS Epidemic.* New York: St. Martin's, 1999. One of the first books to examine the history of AIDS; highly critical of the medical and political response to the crisis.

Smith, Hedrick. *The Power Game: How Washington Works.* New York: Random House, 1988. A fascinating portrait of the real reins of power in Washington and how they are manipulated; especially useful in assessing the failures and successes of the Reagan administration.

Srodes, James. *Allen Dulles: Master of Spies*. Washington, D.C.: Regnery, 1999. Massive biography of the man who essentially created the CIA and, with his brother, Secretary of State John Foster Dulles, guided American foreign policy during the cold war.

Sumners, Harry G. *Vietnam War Almanac*. New York: Facts on File, 1985. An encyclopedic reference guide to the war, complete with maps, historical introduction, and a detailed chronology.

The Tower Commission Report: The Full Text of the President's Special Review Board: Introduction by R. W. Apple, Jr. New York: Bantam, 1987. The damning examination of Reagan's failures in allowing the Iran-contra scandal to occur.

White, Theodore. *America in Search of Itself: The Making of the President, 1956–1980*. New York: Harper and Row, 1982. A compilation of the author's "Making of" series, assessing the presidents of the past thirty-five years.

Wyden, Peter. *Bay of Pigs: The Untold Story*. New York: Simon and Schuster, 1979. This compelling narrative account tells the complete story of the disastrous invasion of Castro's Cuba.

CHAPTER 9. FROM THE EVIL EMPIRE TO THE AXIS OF EVIL

Bennett, William J. *Why We Fight: Moral Clarity and Terrorism*. New York: Doubleday, 2002. A defense of the post–September 11 war against terror in Afghanistan and elsewhere in the world.

Beschloss, Michael R., and Strobe Talbott. *At the Highest Levels: The Inside Story of the End of the Cold War*. Boston: Little, Brown, 1993. An exhaustive account of what may have been the biggest story of the twentieth century, the collapse of the Soviet Union.

Bovard, James. *Lost Rights: The Destruction of American Liberty*. New York: St. Martin's/Palgrave, 2000. A provocative indictment of the abuses of citizens by government agencies.

Bobbitt, Philip. *The Shield of Achilles: War, Peace, and the Course of History*. New York: Knopf, 2002.

———. *Terror and Consent: The Wars of the Twenty-First Century*. New York: Knopf, 2008.

Bugliosi, Vincent. *The Betrayal of America: How the Supreme Court Undermined the Constitution and Chose the President*. New York: Thunder's Mouth/Nation, 2001. A highly partisan view of the role of the Supreme Court in deciding the 2000 election.

Cassidy, John. *How Markets Fail: The Logic of Economic Calamities*. New York: Farrar, Straus and Giroux, 2009. An economist explains the severe downturns in recent American history.

Clarke, Richard A. *Against All Enemies: Inside America's War on Terror*. New York: Free Press, 2004. The controversial account by a member of the security team under Clinton and Bush of the failures preceding the 9/11 attacks.

Cullen, Dave. *Columbine*. New York: Twelve/Grand Central, 2009. An in-depth look at the Columbine massacre that debunks many of the commonly held notions about the two high school boys who were responsible.

Dionne, E. J., Jr., and William Kristol, eds. *Bush v. Gore: The Court Cases and the Commentary*. Washington, D.C.: Brookings Institution, 2001. A collection of the court decisions and editorial commentary by prominent journalists and scholars on both sides of the legal divide.

Drew, Elizabeth. *The Corruption of American Politics: What Went Wrong and Why*. Woodstock, N.Y.: Overlook, 2000. A veteran Washington correspondent's revealing look at the role of campaign financing in American politics.

Dwyer, Jim, and Kevin Flynn. *102 Minutes: The Untold Story of the Fight to Survive Inside the Twin Towers*. Times Books/Henry Holt, 2005. Often heart-wrenching journalistic account of the destruction of the World Trade Center on 9/11.

Ehrenreich, Barbara. *Nickel and Dimed: On (Not) Getting By in America*. New York: Henry Holt, 2001. Brilliantly examining the underside of the "new economy," a reporter works in America's world of minimum-wage jobs.

Eichenwald, Kurt. *Conspiracy of Fools: A True Story*. New York: Broadway Books, 2005. The Enron story, by an award-winning financial reporter.

Farmer, John. *The Ground Truth: The Untold Story of America Under Attack on 9/11*. New York: Riverhead/Penguin, 2009. Written by a member of the Presidential Commission in the aftermath of revelations that the commission did not get full information during its investigations.

Ferguson, Charles H. *No End in Sight: Iraq's Descent into Chaos*. New York: Public Affairs, 2008. Based on a documentary film showing the mismanagement of the invasion and ensuing occupation of Iraq.

Filkins, Dexter. *The Forever War*. New York: Knopf, 2008. The *New York Times* correspondent's coverage of the first chaotic years of the Iraq War.

Fox, Justin. *The Myth of the Rational Market: A History of Risk, Reward, and Delusion on Wall Street*. New York: HarperCollins, 2009.

Frazier, Ian. *On the Rez*. New York: Farrar, Straus and Giroux, 2000. A reporter's unsparing look at contemporary Indian life on the Pine Ridge Reservation in South Dakota.

Friedman, Thomas L. *From Beirut to Jerusalem*. New York: Farrar, Straus and Giroux, 1989 (updated 1995). A Pulitzer Prize–winning journalist's account of Middle East politics; excellent background on the history of the region and America's involvement in regional politics.

Gitlin, Todd. *Media Unlimited: How the Torrent of Images and Sounds Overwhelms Our Lives*. New York: Metropolitan, 2001.

Gordon, Michael R., and General Bernard E. Trainor. *Cobra II: The Inside Story of the Invasion and Occupation of Iraq.* New York: Pantheon, 2006. Excellent overview by the Pentagon correspondent (Gordon) and military columnist (Trainor) of the *New York Times.*

Halberstam, David. *War in a Time of Peace: Bush, Clinton, and the Generals.* New York: Scribner, 2001. Masterful account by the late journalist of two presidents, their relationships with the military, and their wars, in post-Vietnam America.

Heilemann, John, and Mark Halperin. *Game Change: Obama and the Clintons, McCain and Palin, and the Race of a Lifetime.* New York: Harper-Collins, 2010. Two journalists' inside account of the 2008 presidential campaign.

Hersh, Seymour M. *Chain of Command: The Road from 9/11 to Abu Ghraib.* New York: HarperCollins, 2004. The award-winning investigative journalist's account of the abuses inside an Iraqi prison under U.S. Army control.

Kean, Thomas H., and Lee Hamilton. *The 9/11 Report: The National Commission on Terrorist Attacks upon the United States with Reporting and Analysis by the New York Times.* New York: St. Martin's, 2004. Must-read account of the official investigation into 9/11.

Kessler, Ronald. *The Bureau: The Secret History of the FBI.* New York: St. Martin's, 2002. Covers the FBI's history from its inception to the September 11 attacks; insightful history by an investigative reporter formerly with the *Washington Post* and the *Wall Street Journal.*

Krakauer, Jon. *Where Men Win Glory: The Odyssey of Pat Tillman.* New York: Doubleday, 2009. The tragic death in Afghanistan of a former NFL player, by friendly fire, and the cover-up of the incident.

Lewis, Charles, and the Center for Public Integrity. *The Buying of the President 2004: Who's Really Bankrolling Bush and His Democratic Challengers—and What They Expect in Return.* New York: HarperPerennial, 2004. Nonpartisan, nonprofit Center for Public Integrity investigates the money behind the campaigns.

Lewis, Michael. *Liar's Poker.* New York: Norton, 1989. Excellent account of the changes in policy that led to the financial excesses and, later, the crash of 1987.

————. *The Big Short: Inside the Doomsday Machine.* New York: Norton, 2010. Behind the scenes at the 2008 market meltdown.

Mann, James. *Rise of the Vulcans: The History of the Bush War Cabinet.* New York: Viking, 2004. Account of the men who influenced the decision to go to war in Iraq.

Maraniss, David. *First in His Class: The Biography of Bill Clinton.* New York: Simon and Schuster, 1995. A political biography that ends on the night when Bill Clinton declared his candidacy for the presidency.

Mayer, Jane. *The Dark Side: The Inside Story of How the War on Terror Turned into a War on American Ideals.* New York: Doubleday, 2008. Hard-hitting exposé of the Bush war on terror policy decisions that led to waterboarding and other dubious and possibly illegal techniques.

Mitchell, Greg. *So Wrong for So Long: How the Press, the Pundits—and the President—Failed on Iraq.* New York: Union Square Press, 2008.

———. *Why Obama Won: The Making of a President 2008.* New York: Sinclair, 2009.

Obama, Barack. *Dreams from My Father: A Story of Race and Inheritance.* New York: Three Rivers, 2004.

O'Rourke, P. J. *Parliament of Whores: A Lone Humorist Tries to Explain the Entire U.S. Government.* New York: Atlantic Monthly Press, 1991. A cuttingly funny humorist takes on pork-barrel politics as a practice in modern America.

Packer, George. *The Assassins' Gate: America in Iraq.* New York: Farrar, Straus and Giroux, 2005. A veteran *New Yorker* writer, and a self-described "pro-war liberal," Packer details the history of infighting that led to the disastrous decision making in the Iraq war.

Palast, Greg. *The Best Democracy Money Can Buy: An Investigative Reporter Exposes the Truth About Globalization, Corporate Cons, and High Finance Fraudsters.* London: Pluto, 2002. The generally overlooked downside of the rise in the world economy and powerful institutions like the World Bank by a "muckraking" investigative reporter.

Paulson, Henry M. *On the Brink: Inside the Race to Stop the Collapse of the Global Financial System.* New York: Grand Central, 2010.

Phillips, Kevin. *Wealth and Democracy: A Political History of the American Rich.* New York: Broadway, 2002. A conservative historian assesses the impact of wealth on democracy in America, which has rarely served the common man.

Pollack, Kenneth M. *The Threatening Storm: The Case for Invading Iraq.* New York: Random House, 2002.

Remnick, David. *Lenin's Tomb: The Last Days of the Soviet Empire.* New York: Random House, 1993. A prizewinning journalist's acclaimed history of the collapse of the Soviet Union.

Ricks, Thomas E. *Fiasco: The American Military Adventure in Iraq.* New York: Penguin, 2006. By a *Washington Post* Pentagon correspondent, the title says it all.

Sorkin, Andrew Ross. *Too Big to Fail: The Inside Story of How Wall Street and Washington Fought to Save the Financial System from Crisis—and Themselves.* New York: Viking, 2009.

Spence, Gerry. *From Freedom to Slavery: The Rebirth of Tyranny in America.* New York: St. Martin's, 1995. An attack of the forces of government and corporate "tyranny" by the renowned criminal defense attorney who defended Randy Weaver.

Stephanopoulos, George. *All Too Human: A Political Education*. Boston: Little, Brown, 1999. A fascinating insider's view of the Clinton campaign and White House by a former "true believer."

Toobin, Jeffrey. *A Vast Conspiracy: The Real Story of the Sex Scandal That Nearly Brought Down a President*. New York: Simon and Schuster, 1999. Widely regarded as a balanced and definitive account of the Clinton-Lewinsky sex scandal that culminated in only the second presidential impeachment trial in history.

————. *Too Close to Call: The Thirty-Six-Day Battle to Decide the 2000 Election*. New York: Random House, 2001. The Bush-Gore controversy over Florida, a journalistic account.

Wills, Garry. *A Necessary Evil: A History of American Distrust of Government*. New York: Simon and Schuster, 1999. Instructive essay looking at tradition of anti-government attitudes in America and how the mood has grown more violent.

————. *Under God: Religion and American Politics*. New York: Simon and Schuster, 1990. Original look at religion and politics, especially since the 1988 election and the rise of the evangelical right.

Woodward, Bob. *The Commanders*. New York: Simon and Schuster, 1991. An account of the decision making that led to the Persian Gulf War, by the famous Watergate journalist, who is managing editor of the *Washington Post*.

————. *Shadow: Five Presidencies and the Legacy of Watergate*. New York: Simon and Schuster, 1999. An exploration of how changes that followed the Watergate scandal affected the administrations of Ford, Carter, Reagan, Bush, and Clinton.

————. *Maestro: Greenspan's Fed and the American Boom*. New York: Simon and Schuster, 2000. A lucid, brief, and revealing—if mostly laudatory—examination of the way the Federal Reserve works and how its chairman Alan Greenspan amassed, and used, his extraordinary power.

Wright, Lawrence. *The Looming Tower: Al-Qaeda and the Road to 9/11*. New York: Knopf, 2006. Excellent history of the terrorist organization and western intelligence failures that led to 9/11.

ACKNOWLEDGMENTS

Over the years since this book was first published, a great many people have assisted me with ideas and inspiration. The Don't Know Much About® series has grown because of the support, friendship, commitment, and hard work of a great many people, and I would like to honor them all. I would first like to thank my parents for those many trips to Fort Ticonderoga, Gettysburg, Freedomland, and all the other places that gave me a taste for the human side of history. From a very early age, when my father first tossed me into Lake Champlain to teach me to swim in the same waters that Ethan Allen and Benedict Arnold had crossed in 1775, I understood that history doesn't just happen in books. It happens to real people who do real things in real places. If we could only get that across to our kids in the classroom, history wouldn't be seen universally as "boring."

For their advice, hard work, and friendship, I would like to thank all my friends at the David Black Literary Agency: David Black, Leigh Ann Eliseo, Antonella Iannarino, Dave Larabell, Gary Morris, Susan Raihofer, and Joy Tutela.

This new edition was achieved only with the support and enthusiasm of many friends and colleagues at my publisher, and I am very grateful for all of the many people at HarperCollins, past and present, who made this book possible. For their support and assistance I thank Cathy Hemming, Susan Weinberg, Carie Freimuth, Christine

Caruso, Laurie Rippon, Roberto de Vicq de Cumptich, David Koral, Elliott Beard, Camillo LoGiudice, Leslie Cohen, Gail Winston, and Christine Walsh. I would also like to sing praises to the steadfast support of Harper's Carrie Kania, Jennifer Hart, and my editor Michael Signorelli, along with Erica Barmash, Mitchell Berg, Kate Blum, Diane Burrowes, Hope Innelli, Cal Morgan, Nicole Reardon, Andrea Rosen, Alberto Rojas, Robert Spizer, and Virginia Stanley. A special word of thanks to publicist Laura Reynolds.

Among those who helped me realize the original edition of this book, I would like to thank my original editor, Mark Gompertz, who gave me my first encouragement, and his friendship is still of great value to me. I would also like to thank Mark Levine and Steve Boldt for their insights and comments on the original manuscript. I am also grateful to the late Michael Dorris, who shared his special insights into the American Indian. I also thank Marga Enoch for her friendship and for the support and encouragement she has given to my career.

Over the years, many readers, teachers, parents, and students have shared their enthusiasm for history with me, and I wish to thank all who have corresponded with me. Their reactions and encouragement have meant a great deal to me.

One of the greatest pleasures of my life during the past thirteen years has been traveling the country and meeting the booksellers of America who have been so crucial to the success of this book and this series. As a former bookseller, I offer three cheers to the people who take books out of the shipping boxes, put them out on the shelves, and then sell them with honest and sincere appreciation for the importance of the written word.

Finally, my greatest thanks to my family. To my children, Jenny and Colin, for their patience, humor, support, and love. And to my wife, Joann, who had the wisdom a long time ago to tell me to write about the things I love, I give my eternal gratitude.

INDEX